ELEMENTS

OF

CRITICISM.

BY

HENRY HOME OF KAMES,

ONE OF THE LORDS COMMISSIONERS OF JUSTICIARY IN SCOTLAND.

REVISED, WITH OMISSIONS, ADDITIONS, AND A NEW ANALYSIS.

EDITED BY

PROF. JAMES R. BOYD, D.D.,

AUTHOR OF ELEMENTS OF RHETORIC, ECLECTIC MORAL PHILOSOPHY, EDITOR OF ENGLISH POETS WITH NOTES, ETC.

A. S. BARNES & COMPANY,
NEW YORK AND CHICAGO.

PREFACE,

BY THE AMERICAN EDITOR.

The work of Lord Kames, on Criticism, was first published in 1761, and dedicated to George III., then King of Great Britain. The royal patronage was solicited in its behalf, on the ground that it treats of the Fine Arts, which exert a beneficial influence in society, and that it attempts to form a standard of taste, by unfolding those principles that ought to govern the taste of every individual.

In showing the importance of such an attempt, he says. "It is rare to find one born with such delicacy of feeling, as not to need instruction: it is equally rare to find one so low in feeling, as not to be capable of instruction. And yet, to refine our taste with respect to beauties of art or of nature, is scarce endeavored in any seminary of learning: a lamentable defect, considering how early in life taste is susceptible of culture, and how difficult to reform it if unhappily perverted. To furnish materials for supplying that defect, was an additional motive for the present undertaking."

To Lord Kames we are greatly indebted for calling public attention to this subject, and for preparing a work that has long occupied a place in the colleges and academies of our own land. There seems to be no other work, even at this date, that is fitted to supply its place, nor, without great disadvantage to the cause of education, can it be laid aside; and yet, neither in its original form, nor with such additions as have been made, in this country, to the original work, is it free from some grave objections, that have served, in many instances, to prevent its adoption as a text-book, especially in female seminaries.

Hence some retrenchment becomes necessary to the highest usefulness of the work: and it will not be doubted that it may receive great improvement, by additions which may be made from the works of distinguished authors, who have written with great power and exquisite taste upon many of the topics treated by our author nearly a hundred years ago.

These views, upon inquiry, having been found to agree with those of not a few enlightened and experienced teachers, the Editor has been prompted to expend a large amount of labor, for the improvement of the work of Lord Kames, that its usefulness may be increased and perpetuated in colleges and other seminaries of learning, as well as in public and private libraries.

The chief points of superiority claimed for the present edition, are the following:

1. The matter heretofore contained in an Appendix has been brought forward; and constitutes, as it should, the first part of the Introduction, being needed as a preparation for an easy study of the volume, and likely to be overlooked as an appendix.

2. Frequent omissions have been made in the text and notes, where the matter was found to be either obsolete, of no utility, or objectionable on account of its indelicacy.

3. Many of the poetical quotations (particularly some of those in foreign languages), that seemed to be an incumbrance rather than an advantage to the work for purposes of education, have been abbreviated or omitted.

4. Space has thus been gained for a large amount of valuable matter, which has been carefully selected from modern authors who have treated certain topics more philosophically and accurately than Lord Kames, whose work was written nearly a century ago. These additions

both in the text and notes, that they may readily be distinguished from the original matter, have been inclosed in brackets. The most important of these are derived from Cousin on the Beautiful; from Lectures of Barron, Hazlitt, and President Hopkins; from Lord Jeffrey's celebrated dissertation on *Beauty* (in his Review of Alison on Taste); and from an elaborate essay on the *Philosophy of Style*, contained in a somewhat recent number of the Westminster Review. By these, and numerous other additions, where they seemed to be most needed, great value has been added to the original work; and in scarcely a less degree, by striking from it a large amount of matter that greatly impairs its excellence and usefulness.

5. It may also be stated, as a part of the Editor's labor, that he has prepared a *new Analysis* of the work, which, for the convenience both of teacher and student, has been distributed at the bottom of each page, with references to the paragraphs in which the topics are discussed.

It will be seen, therefore, that the present volume is not an abridgment of Kames, but it embraces the entire work, with the exception only of those portions which every instructor and intelligent reader must regard as blemishes, or consider useless, while large additions have been made, from recent and valuable sources, to render more complete and satisfactory the incomparable treatise (as here presented) of this highly talented, and justly distinguished and popular author. J. R. B.

GENEVA, N. Y., *Feb.* 2, 1855.

Oxford. 21 colleges and 9 halls.

CONTENTS.

INTRODUCTION

TERMS DEFINED OR EXPLAINED.

1. Every thing we perceive or are conscious of, whether a being or a quality, a passion or an action, is with respect to the percipient termed an *object*. Some objects appear to be *internal*, or within the mind; passion, for example, thinking, volition: some *external;* such as every object of sight, of hearing, of smell, of touch, of taste.

2. That act of the mind which makes known to me an external object, is termed *perception*. That act of the mind which makes known to me an internal object, is termed *consciousness*. The power or faculty from which consciousness proceeds, is termed an *internal sense*. The power or faculty from which perception proceeds, is termed an *external sense*. This distinction refers to the objects of our knowledge; for the senses, whether external or internal, are all of them powers or faculties of the mind.

3. But as self is an object that cannot be termed either external or internal, the faculty by which I have knowledge of myself, is a sense that cannot properly be termed either internal or external.

4. By the eye we perceive figure, color, motion, &c.: by the ear we perceive the different qualities of sound, high, low, loud, soft: by touch we perceive rough, smooth, hot, cold, &c.: by taste we perceive sweet, sour, bitter, &c.: by smell we perceive fragrant, fetid, &c. These qualities partake the common nature of all qualities, that they are not capable of an independent existence, but must belong to some being of which they are properties or attributes. A being with respect to its properties or attributes is termed a *subject* or *substratum*. Every substratum of visible qualities, is termed *substance;* and of tangible qualities, *body*.

5. Substance and sound are perceived as existing at a distance from the organ; often at a considerable distance. But smell, touch, and taste are perceived as existing at the organ of sense.

6. The objects of external sense are various. Substances are perceived by the eye; bodies by the touch. Sounds, tastes, and smells, passing commonly under the name of secondary qualities, require more explanation than there is room for here. All the objects of internal sense are attributes: witness deliberation, reason-

ing, resolution, willing, consenting, which are internal actions Passions and emotions, which are internal agitations, are also attributes. With regard to the former, I am conscious of being active; with regard to the latter, I am conscious of being passive.

7. Again, we are conscious of internal action as in the head: of passions and emotions as in the heart.

8. Many actions may be exerted internally, and many effects produced of which we are unconscious: when we investigate the ultimate cause of the motion of the blood, and of other internal motions upon which life depends, it is the most probable opinion that some internal power is the cause: and if so, we are unconscious of the operations of that power. But consciousness being implied in the very meaning of deliberating, reasoning, resolving, willing, consenting, such operations cannot escape our knowledge. The same is the case of passions and emotions; for no internal agitation is denominated a passion or emotion, but what we are conscious of.

9. The mind is not always the same; by turns it is cheerful, melancholy, calm, peevish, &c. These differences may not improperly be denominated *tones*.

10. Perception and sensation are commonly reckoned synonymous terms, signifying that internal act by which external objects are made known to us. But they ought to be distinguished. *Perceiving* is a general term for hearing, seeing, tasting, touching, smelling; and therefore *perception* signifies every internal act by which we are made acquainted with external objects; thus we are said to perceive a certain animal, a certain color, sound, taste, smell, &c. *Sensation* properly signifies that internal act by which we are made conscious of pleasure or pain felt at the organ of sense: thus we have a sensation of the pleasure arising from warmth, from a fragrant smell, from a sweet taste: and of the pain arising from a wound, from a fetid smell, from a disagreeable taste. In perception, my attention is directed to the external object: in sensation, it is directed to the pleasure or pain I feel.

The terms *perception* and *sensation* are sometimes employed to signify the objects of perception and sensation. Perception in that sense is a general term for every external thing we perceive; and sensation a general term for every pleasure and pain felt at the organ of sense.

11. Conception is different from perception. The latter includes a conviction of the reality of its object; the former does not; for I can conceive the most extravagant stories told in a romance, without having any conviction of their reality. *Conception differs also from imagination.* By the power of fancy I can imagine a golden mountain, or an ebony ship with sails and ropes of silk. When I describe a picture of that kind to another, the idea he forms of it is termed a *conception*. Imagination is active, conception is passive

12. Feeling, besides denoting one of the external senses, is a general term, signifying that internal act by which we are made conscious of our pleasures and our pains; for it is not limited, as sensation is, to any one sort. Thus feeling being the genus of which sensation is a species, their meaning is the same when applied to pleasure and pain felt at the organ of sense: and accordingly we say indifferently, "I feel pleasure from heat, and pain from cold," or, "I have a sensation of pleasure from heat, and of pain from cold." But the meaning of feeling, as is said, is much more extensive. It is proper to say, I feel pleasure in a sumptuous building, in love, in friendship; and pain in losing a child, in revenge, in envy: sensation is not properly applied to any of these.

The term *feeling* is frequently *used in a less proper sense*, to signify what we feel or are conscious of: and in that sense it is a general term for all our passions and emotions, and for all our other pleasures and pains.

13. That we cannot perceive an external object till an impression is made upon our body, is probable from reason, and is ascertained by experience. But it is not necessary that we be made sensible of the impression: in touching, in tasting, and in smelling, we are sensible of the impression; but not in seeing and hearing. We know indeed from experiments, that before we perceive a visible object, its image is spread upon the *retina tunica;* and that before we perceive a sound, an impression is made upon the drum of the ear: but we are not conscious either of the organic image or of the organic impression; nor are we conscious of any other operation preparatory to the act of perception; all we can say is, that we see that river, or hear that trumpet.*

14. Objects once perceived may be recalled to the mind by the power of *memory.* When I recall an object of sight in that manner, it appears to me precisely the same as in the original survey, only less distinct. For example, having seen yesterday a spreading oak growing on the brink of a river, I endeavor to recall these objects to my mind. How is this operation performed? Do I endeavor to form in my mind a picture of them, or a representative image? Not so. I transport myself ideally to the place where I saw the tree and river yesterday: upon which I have a perception of these objects similar in all respects to the perception I had when I viewed them with my eyes, only less distinct. And in this recollection, I am not conscious of a picture or representative image, more than in the original survey; the perception is of the tree and

* Yet a singular opinion that impressions are the only objects of perception, has been espoused by some philosophers of no mean rank; not attending to the foregoing peculiarity in the senses of seeing and hearing, that we perceive objects without being conscious of an organic impression, or of any impression [except in cases where the object of sight is very brilliant, or the sound excessively loud and grating].

river themselves, as at first. I confirm this by another experiment. After attentively surveying a fine statue, I close my eyes. What follows? The same object continues, without any difference but that it is less distinct than formerly.* This indistinct secondary perception of an object, is termed an *idea*. And therefore the precise

---

* This experiment, which every one may reiterate till entire satisfaction be obtained, is of greater importance than at first view may appear; for it strikes at the root of a celebrated doctrine, which for more than two thousand years has misled many philosophers. This doctrine, as delivered by Aristotle, is in substance, "That of every object of thought there must be in the mind some form, phantasm, or species; that things sensible are perceived and remembered by means of sensible phantasms, and things intelligible by intelligible phantasms; and that these phantasms have the form of the object without the matter, as the impression of a seal upon wax has the form of a seal without its matter." The followers of Aristotle add, "That the sensible and intelligible forms of things, are sent forth from the things themselves, and make impressions upon the passive intellect, which impressions are perceived by the active intellect." This notion differs very little from that of Epicurus, which is, "That all things send forth constantly and in every direction, slender ghosts or films of themselves (*tenuia simulacra*, as expressed by his commentator Lucretius); which striking upon the mind, are the means of perception, dreaming," &c. Des Cartes, bent to oppose Aristotle, rejects the doctrine of sensible and intelligible phantasms; maintaining, however, the same doctrine in effect, namely, That we perceive nothing external but by means of some image either in the brain or in the mind: and these images he terms *ideas* According to these philosophers, we perceive nothing immediately but phantasms or ideas; and from these we infer, by reasoning, the existence of external objects. Locke, adopting this doctrine, employs almost the whole of his book about ideas. He holds, that we cannot perceive, remember, nor imagine any thing, but by having an idea or image of it in the mind. He agrees with Des Cartes, that we can have no knowledge of things external, but what we acquire by reasoning upon their ideas or images in the mind; taking it for granted, that we are conscious of these ideas or images, and of nothing else. Those who talk the most intelligibly explain the doctrine thus. When I see in a mirror a man standing behind me, the immediate object of my sight is his image, without which I could not see him: in like manner, when I see a tree or a house, there must be an image of these objects in my brain or in my mind: which image is the immediate object of my perception; and by means of that image I perceive the external object.

One would not readily suspect any harm in this ideal system, other than the leading us into a labyrinth of metaphysical errors, in order to account for our knowledge of external objects, which is more truly and more simply accounted for by direct perception. And yet some late writers have been able to extract from it death and destruction to the whole world, levelling all down to a mere chaos of ideas. Dr. Berkeley, upon authority of the philosophers named, taking for granted that we cannot perceive any object but what is in the mind, discovered that the reasoning employed by Des Cartes and Locke to infer the existence of external objects, is inconclusive; and upon that discovery ventured, against common sense, to annihilate totally the material world. And a later writer, discovering that Berkeley's arguments might with equal success be applied against immaterial beings, ventures still more boldly to reject by the lump the immaterial world as well as the material; leaving nothing in nature but images or ideas floating *in vacuo*, without affording them a single mind for shelter or support.

When such wild and extravagant consequences can be drawn from the ideal system, it might have been expected, that no man who is not crazy would have ventured to erect such a superstructure, till he should first be certain beyond all doubt of a solid foundation. And yet upon inquiry, we find the foundation of this terrible doctrine to be no better than a shallow metaphysical argument. *namely*, "That no being can act but where it is: and consequently, that and accurate definition of an idea, in contradistinction to an original perception, is, "That perception of a real object which is raised in the mind by the power of memory." Every thing we have any knowledge of, whether internal or external, passions, emotions, thinking, resolving, willing, heat, cold, &c., as well as external objects, may be recalled as above by the power of memory.*

---

it cannot act upon any subject at a distance." This argument possesses indeed one eminent advantage, that its obscurity, like that of an oracle, is apt to impose upon the reader, who is willing to consider it as a demonstration, because he does not clearly see the fallacy. The best way to give it a fair trial, is to draw it out of its obscurity, and to state it in a clear light, as follows: "No subject can be perceived unless it act upon the mind, but no distant subject can act upon the mind, because no being can act but where it is: and, therefore, the immediate object of perception must be something united to the mind so as to be able to act upon it." Here the argument is completed in all its parts; and from it is derived the supposed necessity of phantasms or ideas united to the mind, as the only objects of perception. It is singularly unlucky, that this argument concludes directly against the very system of which it is the only foundation; for how can phantasms or ideas be raised in the mind by things at a distance, if things at a distance cannot act upon the mind? I say more, that it assumes a proposition as true, without evidence, *namely*, That no distant subject can act upon the mind. This proposition undoubtedly requires evidence, for it is not intuitively certain. And, therefore, till the proposition be demonstrated, every man without scruple may rely upon the conviction of his senses, that he hears and sees things at a distance.

But I venture a bolder step, which is, to show that the proposition is false. Admitting that no being can act but where it is, is there any thing more simple or more common, than the acting upon subjects at a distance by intermediate means? This holds in fact with respect both to seeing and hearing. When I see a tree, for example, rays of light are reflected from the tree to my eye, forming a picture upon the *retina tunica;* but the object perceived is the tree itself, not the rays of light, nor the picture. In this manner distant objects are perceived, without any action of the object upon the mind, or of the mind upon the object. Hearing is in a similar case; the air, put in motion by thunder, makes an impression upon the drum of the ear; but this impression is not what I hear, it is the thunder itself by means of that impression.

With respect to vision in particular, we are profoundly ignorant by what means and in what manner the picture on the *retina tunica* contributes to produce a sight of the object. One thing only is clear, that as we have no knowledge of that picture, it is as natural to conceive that it should be made the instrument of discovering the external object, and not itself, as of discovering itself only, and not the external object.

Upon the chimerical consequences drawn from the ideal system, I shall make but a single reflection. Nature determines us necessarily to rely on the veracity of our senses; and upon their evidence the existence of external objects is to us a matter of intuitive knowledge and absolute certainty. Vain therefore is the attempt of Dr. Berkeley and of his followers to deceive us, by a metaphysical subtilty, into a disbelief of what we cannot entertain even the slightest doubt. [See also Beattie's Moral Science, 104–106.]

* From this definition of an idea, the following proposition must be evident, That there can be no such thing as an innate idea. If the original perception of an object be not innate, which is obvious; it is not less obvious, that the idea or secondary perception of that object cannot be innate. And yet, to prove this self-evident proposition, Locke has bestowed a whole book of his treatise upon Human Understanding. So necessary it is to give accurate definitions, and so preventive of dispute are definitions when accurate. Dr. Berkeley has taken great pains to prove another proposition equally evident, That there can be no such thing as a general idea: all our original perceptions are of particular objects, and our secondary perceptions or ideas must be equally so.

15. *External objects* are distinguishable into *simple and complex.* Certain sounds are so simple as not to be resolvable into parts; and so are certain tastes and smells. Objects of touch are for the most part complex: they are not only hard or soft, but also smooth or rough, hot or cold. Of all external objects, visible objects are commonly the most complex: a tree is composed of a trunk, branches, leaves: it has color, figure, size. But as an action is not resolvable into parts, a perception, being an act of sense, is always simple. The color, figure, umbrage of a spreading oak, raise not different perceptions: the perception is one, that of a tree, colored, figured, &c. A quality is never perceived separately from the subject; nor a part from the whole. There is a mental power of abstraction, of which afterward; but the eye never abstracts, nor any other external sense.

16. Many particulars besides those mentioned enter into the perception of visible objects, *motion*, *rest*, *place*, *space*, *time*, *number*, &c. These, all of them, denote simple ideas, and for that reason admit not of a definition. All that can be done is to point out how they are acquired. The ideas of motion and of rest are familiar even to a child, from seeing its nurse sometimes walking, sometimes sitting: the former it is taught to call *motion;* the latter, *rest.* Place enters into every perception of a visible object: the object is perceived to exist, and to exist somewhere, on the right hand or on the left, and where it exists is termed *place.* Ask a child where its mother is, or in what place: it will answer readily, she is in the garden. Space is connected with size or bulk: every piece of matter occupies *room* or *space* in proportion to its bulk. A child perceives that when its little box is filled with playthings, there is no room or space for more. Space is also applied to signify the distance of visible objects from each other; and such space accordingly can be measured. Dinner comes after breakfast, and supper after dinner: a child perceives an interval, and that interval it learns to call *time.* A child sometimes is alone with its nurse; its mother is sometimes in the room; and sometimes also its brothers and sisters It perceives a difference between many and few; and that difference it is taught to call *number.*

17. The *primary perception of a visible object* is more complete, lively, and distinct than that of any other object. And for that reason, an idea, or secondary perception of a visible object, is also more complete, lively, and distinct than that of any other object. A fine passage in music may for a moment be recalled to the mind with tolerable accuracy: but after the shortest interval, it becomes no less obscure than the ideas of the other objects mentioned.

18. As the range of an individual is commonly within a narrow space, it rarely happens that every thing necessary to be known comes under our own perceptions. *Language* is an admirable con-

trivance for supplying that deficiency; for by language every man's perceptions may be communicated to all: and the same may be done by painting and other imitative arts. The facility of communication depends on the liveliness of the ideas; especially in language, which hitherto has not arrived at greater perfection than to express clear ideas: hence it is, that poets and orators, who are extremely successful in describing objects of sight, find objects of the other senses too faint and obscure for language. An idea thus acquired of an object at second-hand, ought to be distinguished from an idea of memory, though their resemblance has occasioned the same term *idea* to be applied to both; which is to be regretted, because ambiguity in the signification of words is a great obstruction to accuracy of conception. Thus Nature hath furnished the means of multiplying ideas without end, and of providing every individual with a sufficient stock to answer, not only the necessities, but even the elegancies of life.

19. Further, man is endued with a sort of creative power: he can fabricate images of things that have no existence. The materials employed in this operation are ideas of sight, which he can take to pieces and combine into new forms at pleasure: their complexity and vivacity make them fit materials. But a man hath no such power over any of his other ideas, whether of the external or internal senses: he cannot, after the utmost effort, combine these into new forms, being too obscure for that operation. An image thus fabricated cannot be called a secondary perception, not being derived from an original perception: the poverty of language, however, as in the case immediately above mentioned, has occasioned the same term *idea* to be applied to all. This singular power of fabricating images without any foundation in reality, is distinguished by the name *imagination.**

20. As ideas are the chief materials employed in reasoning and reflecting, it is of consequence that their nature and differences be understood. It appears now that *ideas may be distinguished into three kinds:* first, Ideas derived from original perceptions, properly termed ideas of memory; second, Ideas communicated by language or other signs; and third, Ideas of imagination. These ideas differ from each other in many respects; but chiefly in respect of their proceeding from different causes: The first kind is derived from real

* ["Memory is double:—not only do I remember that I have been in the presence of a certain object, but I represent to myself this absent object as it was, as I have seen, felt, and judged it:—the remembrance is then an image. In this last case, memory has been called by some philosophers imaginative memory. Such is the foundation of imagination; but imagination is something more still.

"The mind, applying itself to the images furnished by memory decomposes them, chooses between their different traits, and forms of them new images. Without this new power imagination would be captive in the circle of memory".—*Cousin's Lect. on the Beautiful*, p. 135.

existences that have been objects of our senses: language is the cause of the second, or any other sign that has the same power with language; and a man's imagination is to himself the cause of the third. It is scarce necessary to add, that an idea, originally of imagination, being conveyed to others by language or any other vehicle, becomes in their mind an idea of the second kind; and again, that an idea of this kind, being afterwards recalled to the mind, becomes in that circumstance an idea of memory.

21. We are not so constituted as to perceive objects with indifference: these with very few exceptions appear agreeable or disagreeable; and at the same time raise in us pleasant or painful emotions. With respect to external objects in particular, we distinguish those which produce organic impressions, from those which affect us from a distance. When we touch a soft and smooth body, we have a pleasant feeling as at the place of contact; which feeling we distinguish not, at least not accurately, from the agreeableness of the body itself; and the same holds in general with regard to all organic impressions. It is otherwise in hearing and seeing: a sound is perceived as in itself agreeable, and raises in the hearer a pleasant emotion; an object of sight appears in itself agreeable, and raises in the spectator a pleasant emotion. These are accurately distinguished: the pleasant emotion is felt as within the mind; the agreeableness of the object is placed upon the object, and is perceived as one of its qualities or properties. The agreeable appearance of an object of sight is termed *beauty;* and the disagreeable appearance of such an object is termed *ugliness.*

22. But though beauty and ugliness, in their proper and genuine signification, are confined to objects of sight, yet in a more lax and figurative signification, they are applied to objects of the other senses: they are sometimes applied even to abstract terms; for it is not unusual to say, *a beautiful theorem, a beautiful constitution of government.*

23. A *line* composed by a single rule [or prescribed mode], is perceived and said to be *regular:* a straight line, a parabola, an hyperbola, the circumference of a circle, and of an ellipse, are all of them regular lines. A *figure* composed by a single rule, is perceived and said to be regular: a circle, a square, a hexagon, an equilateral triangle, are regular figures, being composed by a single rule, that determines the form of each. When the form of a line or of a figure is ascertained by a single rule that leaves nothing arbitrary, the line and the figure are said to be perfectly regular; which is the case of the figures now mentioned, and the case of a straight line and of the circumference of a circle. A figure and a line that require more than one rule for their construction, or that have any of their parts left arbitrary, are not perfectly regular: a parallelogram and a rhomb are less regular than a square; the parallelogram being subjected to no rule as to the length of sides, other than that

the opposite sides be equal; the rhomb being subjected to no rule as to its angles, other than that the opposite angles be equal: for the same reason, the circumference of an ellipse, the form of which is susceptible of much variety, is less regular than that of a circle.

24. *Regularity*, properly speaking, belongs, like beauty, to objects of sight; and, like beauty, it is also applied figuratively to other objects: thus we say, *a regular government*, *a regular composition of music*, and, *regular discipline*.

25. When two figures are composed of similar parts, they are said to be uniform. Perfect *uniformity* is where the constituent parts of two figures are equal: thus two cubes of the same dimensions are perfectly uniform in all their parts. Uniformity less perfect is, where the parts mutually correspond, but without being equal: the uniformity is imperfect between two squares or cubes of unequal dimensions; and still more so between a square and a parallelogram.

26. Uniformity is also applicable to the constituent parts of the same figure. The constituent parts of a square are perfectly uniform; its sides are equal and its angles are equal. Wherein then differs regularity from uniformity? for a figure composed of uniform parts must undoubtedly be regular. *Regularity* is predicated of a figure considered as a whole composed of uniform parts: *uniformity* is predicated of these parts as related to each other by resemblance: we say, a square is a regular, not a uniform figure; but with respect to the constituent parts of a square, we say not, that they are regular, but that they are uniform.

27. In things destined for the same use, as legs, arms, eyes, windows, spoons, we expect *uniformity*. *Proportion* ought to govern parts intended for different uses: we require a certain proportion between a leg and an arm; in the base, the shaft, the capital of a pillar; and in the length, the breadth, the height of a room: some proportion is also required in different things intimately connected, as between a dwelling-house, the garden, and the stables; but we require no proportion among things slightly connected, as between the table a man writes on and the dog that follows him. Proportion and uniformity never coincide; things equal are uniform; but proportion is never applied to them: the four sides and angles of a square are equal and perfectly uniform; but we say not that they are proportional. Thus, proportion always implies inequality or difference; but then it implies it to a certain degree only: the most agreeable proportion resembles a *maximum* in mathematics; a greater or less inequality or difference is less agreeable.

28. *Order* regards various particulars. *First*, in tracing or surveying objects, we are directed by a sense of order: we perceive it to be more orderly, that we should pass from a principle to its accessories, and from a whole to its parts, than in the contrary direction *Next*, with respect to the position of things, a sense of

order directs us to place together things intimately connected. *Thirdly*, in placing things that have no natural connection, that order appears the most perfect, where the particulars are made to bear the strongest relation to each other that position can give them. Thus parallelism is the strongest relation that position can bestow upon straight lines: if they be so placed as by production to intersect, the relation is less perfect. A large body in the middle, and two equal bodies of less size, one on each side, is an order that produces the strongest relation the bodies are susceptible of by position: the relation between the two equal bodies would be stronger by juxtaposition; but they would not both have the same relation to the third.

29. *The beauty* or agreeableness *of a visible object, is perceived as one of its qualities;* which holds, not only in the primary perception, but also in the secondary perception or idea: and hence the pleasure that arises from the idea of a beautiful object. An *idea of imagination* is also pleasant, though in a lower degree than an idea of memory, where the objects are of the same kind; for an evident reason, that the former is more distinct and lively than the latter. But this inferiority in ideas of imagination, is more than compensated by their greatness and variety, which are boundless; for by the imagination, exerted without control, we can fabricate ideas of finer visible objects, of more noble and heroic actions, of greater wickedness, of more surprising events, than ever in fact existed: and in communicating such ideas by words, painting, sculpture, &c., the influence of the imagination is no less extensive than great.

30. In the nature of every man, there is somewhat original, which distinguishes him from others, which tends to form his character, and to make him meek or fiery, candid or deceitful, resolute or timorous, cheerful or morose. This original bent, termed *disposition*, must be distinguished from a *principle:* the latter signifying a law of human nature, makes part of the common nature of man; the former makes part of the nature of this or that man. *Propensity* is a name common to both; for it signifies a principle as well as a disposition.

31. *Affection*, signifying a settled bent of mind towards a particular being or thing, *occupies a middle place between disposition on the one hand, and passion on the other.* It is clearly distinguishable from disposition, which, being a branch of one's nature originally, must exist before there can be an opportunity to exert it upon any particular object; whereas affection can never be original, because, having a special relation to a particular object, it cannot exist till the object have once at least been presented. It is no less clearly distinguishable from passion, which, depending on the real or ideal presence of its object, vanishes with its object: whereas affection is a lasting connection; and like other connections, subsists even when

we do not think of the person. A familiar example will clear the whole. I have from nature a disposition to gratitude, which, through want of an object, happens never to be exerted; and which therefore is unknown even to myself. Another who has the same disposition, meets with a kindly office which makes him grateful to his benefactor; an intimate connection is formed between them, termed *affection;* which, like other connections, has a permanent existence, though not always in view. The affection, for the most part, lies dormant, till an opportunity offer for exerting it: in that circumstance, it is converted into the passion of gratitude; and the opportunity is greedily seized of testifying gratitude in the warmest manner.

32. *Aversion*, I think, is opposed to affection; not to desire, as it commonly is. We have an affection to one person: we have an aversion to another: the former disposes us to do good to its object, the latter to do ill.

33. What is a *sentiment?* It is not a perception; for a perception signifies the act by which we become conscious of external objects. It is not consciousness of an internal action, such as thinking, suspending thought, inclining, resolving, willing, &c. Neither is it the conception of a relation among objects; a conception of that kind being termed *opinion.* The term *sentiment* is appropriated to such thoughts as are prompted by passion.

34. *Attention* is that state of mind which prepares one to receive impressions. According to the degree of attention, objects make a strong or weak impression. Attention is requisite even to the simple act of seeing; the eye can take in a considerable field at one look; but no object in the field is seen distinctly, but that singly which fixes the attention: in a profound reverie that totally occupies the attention, we scarce see what is directly before us. In a train of perceptions, the attention being divided among various objects, no particular object makes such a figure as it would do single and apart. Hence, the stillness of night contributes to terror, there being nothing to divert the attention:

Horror ubique animos, simul ipsa silentia terrent.—*Æneid*, ii.

Zara. Silence and solitude are everywhere
Through all the gloomy ways and iron doors
That hither lead, nor human face nor voice
Is seen or heard. A dreadful din was wont
To grate the sense, which enter'd here from groans
And howls of slaves condemn'd, from clink of chains,
And crash of rusty bars and creaking hinges;
And ever and anon the sight was dash'd
With frightful faces and the meager looks
Of grim and ghastly executioners.
Yet more this stillness terrifies my soul
Than did that scene of complicated horrors.

Mourning Pride, Act V. Sc. 8.

And hence it is, that an object seen at the termination of a confined view, is more agreeable than when seen in a group with the surrounding objects:

The crow doth sing as sweetly as the lark
When neither is attended; and I think,
The nightingale, if she should sing by day,
When every goose is cackling, would be thought
No better a musician than the wren.—*Merchant of Venice.*

35. *In matters of slight importance, attention is mostly directed by will;* and for that reason, it is our own fault if trifling objects make any deep impression. Had we power equally to withhold our attention from matters of importance, we might be proof against any deep impression. But our power fails us here: *an interesting object seizes and fixes the attention beyond the possibility of control;* and while our attention is thus forcibly attached to one object, others may solicit for admittance: but in vain, for they will not be regarded. Thus a small misfortune is scarce felt in presence of a greater:

Lear. Thou think'st 'tis much, that this contentious storm
Invades us to the skin: so 'tis to thee;
But where the greater malady is fix'd,
The lesser is scarce felt. Thou'dst shun a bear;
But if thy flight lay toward the roaring sea,
Thou'dst meet the bear i' th' mouth. When the mind's free,
The body's delicate: the tempest in my mind
Doth from my senses take all feeling else,
Save what beats there. *King Lear*, Act III. Sc. 5.

36. *Genus*, *species*, *modification*, are terms invented to distinguish beings from each other. Individuals are distinguished by their qualities: a number of individuals considered with respect to qualities that distinguish them from others, is termed a *species:* a plurality of *species* considered with respect to their distinguishing qualities, is termed a *genus*. That quality which distinguisheth one genus, one species, or even one individual, from another, is termed a *modification:* thus the same particular that is termed a *property* or *quality*, when considered as belonging to an individual, or a class of individuals, is termed a *modification* when considered as distinguishing the individual or the class from another: a black skin and soft curled hair, are properties of a Negro: the same circumstances considered as marks that distinguish a Negro from a man of a different species, are denominated *modifications*.

37. *Objects of sight*, being complex, are *distinguishable into the several particulars that enter into the composition:* these objects are all of them colored; and they all have length, breadth, and thickness. When I behold a spreading oak, I distinguish in that object, size, figure, color, and sometimes motion: in a flowing river, I distinguish color, figure, and constant motion; a dye has color, black spots, six plain surfaces, all equal and uniform. *Objects of touch* have all of them extension: some of them are felt rough, some smooth: some of them are hard, some soft. *With respect to the other senses, some of their objects are simple, some complex:* a sound, a taste, a smell may be so simple as not to be distinguish-

able into parts: others are perceived to be compounded of different sounds, different tastes, and different smells.

38. The eye at one look can grasp a number of objects, as of trees in a field, or men in a crowd: these objects having each a separate and independent existence, are distinguishable in the mind, as well as in reality; and there is nothing more easy than to abstract from some and to confine our contemplation to others. A large oak with its spreading branches fixes our attention upon itself, and abstracts us from the shrubs that surround it. In the same manner, with respect to compound sounds, tastes, or smells, we can fix our thoughts upon any of the component parts, abstracting our attention from the rest. The *power of abstraction* is not confined to objects that are separable in reality as well as mentally; but also takes place where there can be no real separation: the size, the figure, the color of a tree, are inseparably connected, and have no independent existence; the same of length, breadth, and thickness: and yet we can mentally confine our observations to one of these, abstracting from the rest. Here abstraction takes place where there cannot be a real separation.

39. *Space and time* have occasioned much metaphysical jargon; but after the power of abstraction is explained as above, there remains no difficulty about them. It is mentioned above, that space as well as place enter into the perception of every visible object: a tree is perceived as existing in a certain place, and as occupying a certain space. Now, by the power of abstraction, *space* may be considered abstractedly from the body that occupies it; and hence the abstract term space. In the same manner, *existence* may be considered abstractedly from any particular thing that exists; and *place* may be considered abstractedly from any particular thing that may be in it. Every series or succession of things suggests the *idea of time;* and time may be considered abstractedly from any series of succession. In the same manner, we acquire the abstract term motion, rest, number, and a thousand other abstract terms; an excellent contrivance for improving speech, as without it speech would be wofully imperfect. Brute animals may have some obscure notion of these circumstances, as connected with particular objects: an ox probably perceives that he takes longer time to go round a long ridge in the plough, than a short one; and he probably perceives when he is one of four in the yoke, or only one of two. But the power of abstraction is not bestowed on brute animals; because to them it would be altogether useless, as they are incapable of speech.

40. *This power of abstraction is of great utility.* A carpenter considers a log of wood with regard to hardness, firmness, color, and texture: a philosopher, neglecting these properties, makes the log undergo a chemical analysis; and examines its taste, its smell, and its component principles: the geometrician confines his reason-

ing to the figure, the length, breadth, and thickness. In general, every artist abstracting from all other properties, confines his observations to those which have a more immediate connection with his profession.

41. It is observed above [14, note], that there can be no such thing as a general idea; that all our perceptions are of particular objects, and that our secondary perceptions or ideas must be equally so. Precisely, for the same reason, there can be *no such thing as an abstract idea.* We cannot form an idea of a part without taking in the whole; or of motion, color, figure, independent of a body. No man will say that he can form any idea of beauty, till he think of a person endued with that quality; nor that he can form an idea of weight, till he takes under consideration a body that is weighty. And when he takes under consideration a body endued with one or other of the properties mentioned, the idea he forms is not an abstract or general idea, but the idea of a particular body with its properties. But though a part and the whole, a subject and its attributes, an effect and its cause, are so intimately connected, as that an idea cannot be formed of the one independent of the other, yet we can reason upon the one abstracting from the other.

This is done by words signifying the thing to which the reasoning is confined; and such words are denominated *abstract terms.* The meaning and use of an abstract term are well understood, though of itself, unless other particulars be taken in, it raises no image nor idea in the mind. In language it serves an excellent purpose; by it different figures, different colors, can be compared, without the trouble of conceiving them as belonging to any particular subject; and they contribute with words significant to raise images or ideas in the mind.

42. The power of abstraction is bestowed on man for the purpose solely of reasoning. It tends greatly to the facility as well as clearness of any process of reasoning, that laying aside every other circumstance, we can confine our attention to the single property we desire to investigate.

43. *Abstract terms may be separated into three different kinds,* all equally subservient to the reasoning faculty. Individuals appear to have no end; and did we not possess the faculty of distributing them into classes, the mind would be lost in an endless maze, and no progress be made in knowledge. It is by the faculty of abstraction that we distribute beings into *genera* and *species*: finding a number of individuals connected by certain qualities common to all, we give a name to these individuals considered as thus connected, which name, by gathering them together into one class, serves to express the whole of these individuals as distinct from others. Thus the word animal serves to denote every being that can move voluntarily; and the words *man, horse, lion,* &c., answer

similar purposes. This is the first and most common sort of abstraction; and it is of the most extensive use, by enabling us to comprehend in our reasoning whole kinds and sorts, instead of individuals without end. The next sort of abstract terms comprehends a number of individual objects, considered as connected by some occasional relation. A great number of persons collected in one place, without any other relation but merely that of contiguity, are denominated *a crowd:* in forming this term we abstract from sex, from age, from condition, from dress, &c. A number of persons connected by the same laws and by the same government, are termed *a nation;* and a number of men under the same military command, are termed *an army.* A third sort of abstraction is, where a single property or part, which may be common to many individuals, is selected to be the subject of our contemplation; for example, whiteness, heat, beauty, length, roundness, head, arm.

44. *Abstract terms are a happy invention:* it is by their means, chiefly, that the particulars which make the subject of our reasoning, are brought into close union, and separated from all others however naturally connected. Without the aid of such terms, the mind could never be kept steady to its proper subject, but be perpetually in hazard of assuming foreign circumstances, or neglecting what are essential. We can, without the aid of language, compare real objects by intuition, when these objects are present; and when absent, we can compare them in idea. But when we advance farther, and attempt to make inferences and draw conclusions, we always employ abstract terms, even in thinking: it would be as difficult to reason without them, as to perform operations in algebra without signs; for there is scarce any reasoning without some degree of abstraction, and we cannot easily abstract without using abstract terms. Hence it follows, that without language man would scarce be a rational being.*

45. The same thing, in different respects, has different names. With respect to certain qualities, it is termed a *substance;* with respect to other qualities, a *body;* and with respect to qualities of all sorts, a *subject.* It is termed a *passive subject* with respect to an action exerted upon it; an *object* with respect to a percipient; a *cause* with respect to the effect it produces; and an *effect* with respect to its cause.

* [Compare Barron's Lectures, vol. ii. 377–86.]

THE NATURE, DESIGN, AND UTILITY OF THE PRESENT WORK

46. THAT nothing external is perceived till first it makes an impression upon the organ of sense, is an observation that holds equally in every one of the external senses. But there is a difference as to our knowledge of that impression: in touching, tasting, and smelling, we are sensible of the impression; that, for example, which is made upon the hand by a stone, upon the palate by an apricot, and upon the nostrils by a rose. It is otherwise in seeing and hearing; for I am not sensible of the impression made upon my eye when I behold a tree; nor of the impression made upon my ear, when I listen to a song (13). That difference in the manner of perceiving external objects, distinguisheth remarkably hearing and seeing from the other senses; and I am ready to show, that it distinguisheth still more remarkably the feelings of the former from that of the latter; every feeling, pleasant or painful, must be in the mind; and yet, because in tasting, touching, and smelling, we are sensible of the impression made upon the organ, we are led to place there also the pleasant or painful feeling caused by that impression;* but, with respect to seeing and hearing, being insensible of the organic impression, we are not misled to assign a wrong place to the pleasant or painful feelings caused by that impression; and therefore we naturally place them in the mind, where they really are: upon that account, they are conceived to be more refined and spiritual, than what are derived from tasting, touching, and smelling; for the latter feelings, seeming to exist externally at the organ of sense, are conceived to be merely corporeal.

The pleasures of the eye and the ear, being thus elevated above those of the other external senses, acquire so much dignity as to become a laudable entertainment. They are not, however, set on a level with the purely intellectual; being no less inferior in dignity to intellectual pleasures, than superior to the organic or corporeal: they indeed resemble the latter, being, like them, produced by external objects; but they also resemble the former, being, like

* After the utmost efforts, we find it beyond our power to conceive the flavor of a rose to exist in the mind: we are necessarily led to conceive that pleasure as existing in the nostrils along with the impression made by the rose upon that organ. And the same will be the result of experiments with respect to every feeling of taste, touch, and smell. Touch affords the most satisfactory experiments. Were it not that the delusion is detected by philosophy, no person would hesitate to pronounce, that the pleasure arising from touching a smooth, soft, and velvet surface, has its existence at the ends of the fingers, without once dreaming of its existing anywhere else.

them, produced without any sensible organic impression. Their mixed nature and middle place between organic and intellectual pleasures, qualify them to associate with both.

The pleasures of the eye and the ear have other valuable properties besides those of dignity and elevation: being sweet and moderately exhilarating, they are in their tone equally distant from the turbulence of passion, and the languor of indolence: and by that tone are perfectly well qualified, not only to revive the spirits when sunk by sensual gratification, but also to relax them when overstrained in any violent pursuit. Here is a remedy provided for many distresses; and, to be convinced of its salutary effects, it will be sufficient to run over the following particulars. Organic pleasures have naturally a short duration; when prolonged, they lose their relish; when indulged to excess, they beget satiety and disgust; and, to restore a proper tone of mind, nothing can be more happily contrived than the exhilarating pleasures of the eye and ear.* On the other hand, any intense exercise of intellectual powers becomes painful by overstraining the mind: cessation from such exercise gives not instant relief; it is necessary that the void be filled with some amusement, gently relaxing the spirits.

47. The transition is sweet and easy, from corporeal pleasures to the more refined pleasures of sense; and no less so, from these to the exalted pleasures of morality and religion. We stand therefore engaged in honor, as well as interest, to second the purposes of nature, by cultivating the pleasures of the eye and ear, those especially that require extraordinary culture,† such as arise from poetry, painting, sculpture, music, gardening, and architecture. This especially is the duty of the opulent, who have leisure to improve their minds and their feelings. The fine arts are contrived to give pleasure to the

* ["Now this" (says Dr. Mark Hopkins) "is precisely the use, and all the use that many make of the fine arts, and I may add, to some extent of the beauties of nature too. How many wealthy sensualists are there in our cities who give an appearance of elevation and refinement to their low and selfish mode of life, by collecting about them specimens of the arts! These men may be best compared to that amphibious animal, the frog. They come up occasionally from that lower element in which they live, into a region of light and beauty; but no sooner are they a little refreshed, than they plunge again into the mud of sensual gratification. It is men like these, who, when their capacity for the lower pleasures is exhausted, drive in their carriages about the cities of the Old World (perhaps we are not yet sufficiently corrupt), and set up to be *virtuosi*. It is easy to see how such a taste must bear upon morals."]

† A taste for natural objects is born with us in perfection; for relishing a fine countenance, a rich landscape, or a vivid color, culture is necessary. The observation holds equally in natural sounds, such as the singing of birds, or the murmuring of a brook. Nature here, the artificer of the object as well as of the percipient, hath accurately suited them to each other. But of a poem, a cantata, a picture, or other artificial production, a true relish is not commonly attained, without some study and much practice.

46. What precedes the perception of an external object.—The difference noticed with regard to the various senses.—The location of pleasant or painful feelings.—The rank to be assigned to the pleasures of the eye and ear. Their salutary influence.—Comparison with organic or corporeal pleasures.—The use that profligate men often make of the fine arts.

eye and the ear, disregarding the inferior senses. A taste for these arts is a plant that grows naturally in many soils; but, without culture, scarce to perfection in any soil: it is susceptible of much refinement; and is, by proper care, greatly improved. In this respect, a taste in the fine arts goes hand in hand with the moral sense, to which indeed it is nearly allied: both of them discover what is right and what is wrong; fashion, temper and education have an influence to vitiate both, or to preserve them pure and untainted: neither of them is arbitrary or local: being rooted in human nature, and governed by principles common to all men.* The design of the present undertaking, which aspires not to morality, is, to examine the sensitive branch of human nature, to trace the objects that are naturally agreeable, as well as those that are naturally disagreeable; and by these means to discover, if we can, what are the genuine principles of the fine arts. The man who aspires to be a critic in these arts, must pierce still deeper: he must acquire a clear perception of what objects are lofty, what low, what proper or improper, what manly, and what mean or trivial. Hence a foundation for reasoning upon the taste of any individual, and for passing sentence upon it: where it is conformable to principles, we can pronounce with certainty that it is correct; otherwise, that it is incorrect, and perhaps whimsical. Thus the fine arts, like morals, become a rational science; and, like morals, may be cultivated to a high degree of refinement.†

---

* [The following observations of Dr. Mark Hopkins are appropriate and important: "The fine arts may be made to pander directly to vice. From the middle rank, which the pleasures derived from them hold, they readily associate, as has been said, both with the higher and the lower. Thus music may quicken the devotions of a seraph, and lend its strains to cheer the carousals of the bacchanal; and poetry, painting, and sculpture, while they have power to elevate, and charm, and purify the mind, may be made direct stimulants to the vilest and lowest passions. It is indeed from this quarter that we are to look for danger from the prevalence of these arts. It was thus that they corrupted the ancient cities; and those who have seen the abominable statuary of Herculaneum and Pompeii, do not wonder that they were buried under a sea of fire. The same process of corruption through these arts, has gone to a fearful extent on the eastern continent, and has commenced in this country. Clothed in this garment of light, vice finds access where it otherwise could not. Under the pretence of promoting the fine arts, modesty is cast aside, and indecent pictures are exhibited, and respectable people go to see them. If I might utter a word of warning to the young, it would be to beware of vice dressed in the garments of taste. The beauties of nature are capable of no such perversion All the associations connected with them tend to elevate and to purify the mind. No case can be adduced in which a taste for gardening or for natural objects has corrupted a people. While, therefore, I believe that the cultivation of the arts, in their genuine spirit of beauty and of purity, has a tendency to improve the character, it would appear that they are greatly liable to abuse, and that they have been extensively abused."]

† [Upon the subject of *Taste* and *Genius*, Cousin thus remarks: "Three

---

47. The easy transition from corporeal pleasures to those of a higher order.—The arts which it is our interest to cultivate—Value of the fine arts. A taste for these allied to what?—The great liability of the fine arts to perversion and abuse.—Design of the present volume.—Cousin's account of Taste and Genius.

48. Manifold are *the advantages of criticism*, when thus studied as a rational science. In the first place, a thorough acquaintance with the principles of the fine arts redoubles the pleasure we derive from them. To the man who resigns himself to feeling without interposing any judgment, poetry, music, painting are mere pastime. In the prime of life, indeed, they are delightful, being supported by the force of novelty, and the heat of imagination: but in time they lose their relish; and are generally neglected in the maturity of life, which disposes to more serious and more important occupations. To those who deal in criticism as a regular science, governed by just principles, and giving scope to judgment as well as to fancy, the fine arts are a favorite entertainment; and in old age maintain that relish which they produce in the morning of life.

In the next place (2), a philosophic inquiry into the principles of the fine arts inures the reflecting mind to the most enticing sort of logic: the practice of reasoning upon subjects so agreeable, tends to a habit; and a habit, strengthening the reasoning faculties, prepares the mind for entering into subjects more intricate and abstract. To have, in that respect, a just conception of the importance of criticism, we need but reflect upon the ordinary method of education; which, after some years spent in acquiring languages, hurries us, without the least preparatory discipline, into the most profound philosophy. A more effectual method to alienate the tender mind from abstract science, is beyond the reach of invention; and accordingly, with respect to such speculations, our youth generally contract a sort of hobgoblin terror, seldom if ever subdued. Those who apply to the arts, are trained in a very different manner: they are led, step by step, from the easier parts of the operation, to what are more difficult; and are not permitted to make a new motion, till they are perfected in those which go before. Thus the science of criticism may be considered as a middle link, connecting the different parts of education into a regular chain. This science furnisheth an inviting opportunity to exercise the judgment: we delight to reason upon subjects that are equally pleasant and familiar; we proceed grad-

---

faculties enter into that complex faculty that is called taste:—imagination, sentiment, reason. Besides imagination and reason, the man of taste ought to possess an enlightened but ardent love of beauty: he must take delight in meeting it, must search for it, must summon it. To comprehend and demonstrate that a thing is not beautiful, is an ordinary pleasure—an ungrateful task; but to discern a beautiful thing, to make it evident, and make others participate in our sentiment, is an exquisite joy, a generous task. . . . .

"After having spoken of taste which appreciates beauty, shall we say nothing of genius which makes it live again? Genius is nothing else than taste in action, that is to say, the three powers of taste carried to their culmination, and armed with a new and mysterious power, the power of execution. What essentially distinguishes genius from taste, is the attribute of creative power. Taste feels, judges, discusses, analyzes, but does not invent. Genius is, before all, inventive and creative. The man of genius is not the master of the power that is in him: it is by the ardent, irresistible need of expressing what he feels, that he is a man of genius."—Lect. vii., Appleton's Ed.]

ually from the simple to the more involved cases; and in a due course of discipline, custom, which improves all our faculties, bestows acuteness on that of reason, sufficient to unravel all the intricacies of philosophy.*

Nor (3) ought it to be overlooked, that the reasonings employed on the fine arts are of the same kind with those which regulate our conduct. Mathematical and metaphysical reasonings have no tendency to improve our knowledge of man; nor are they applicable to the common affairs of life: but a just taste of the fine arts, derived from rational principles, furnishes elegant subjects for conversation, and prepares us for acting in the social state with dignity and propriety.

The science of rational criticism (4) tends to improve the heart no less than the understanding. It tends, in the first place, to moderate the selfish affections: by sweetening and harmonizing the temper, it is a strong antidote to the turbulence of passion, and violence of pursuit; it procures to a man so much mental enjoyment, that in order to be occupied, he is not tempted to deliver up his youth to hunting, gaming, drinking; nor his middle age to ambition; nor his old age to avarice. Pride and envy, two disgustful passions, find in the constitution no enemy more formidable than a delicate and discerning taste: the man upon whom nature and culture have bestowed this blessing, delights in the virtuous dispositions and actions of others: he loves to cherish them, and to publish them to the world: faults and failings, it is true, are to him no less obvious; but these he avoids, or removes out of sight, because they give him pain. On the other hand, a man void of taste, upon whom even striking beauties make but a faint impression, indulges pride or envy without control, and loves to brood over errors and blemishes.

In the next place, (5) delicacy of taste tends no less to invigorate the social affections, than to moderate those that are selfish. To be convinced of that tendency, we need only reflect, that delicacy of taste necessarily heightens our feeling of pain and pleasure; and of course our sympathy, which is the capital branch of every social passion. Sympathy invites a communication of joys and sorrows, hopes and fears: such exercise, soothing and satisfactory in itself, is necessarily productive of mutual good-will and affection.

One other advantage of rational criticism is reserved to the last (6) place, being of all the most important; which is, that it is a great support to morality. I insist on it with entire satisfaction, that no occupation attaches a man more to his duty, than that of cultivating a taste in the fine arts: a just relish of what is beautiful,

* [The rules of criticism are no more than the deductions of sound logic concerning beauty and deformity, from the permanent principles and feelings of human nature; and without a knowledge of these rules it is not to be expected that any performance will be so successful as to obtain any great or lasting portion of the public approbation.—Barron's Lect. vol. i. p 16.]

proper, elegant, and ornamental, in writing or painting, in architecture or gardening, is a fine preparation for the same just relish of these qualities in character and behavior. To the man who has acquired a taste so acute and accomplished, every action wrong or improper must be highly disgustful; if, in any instance, the overbearing power of passion sway him from his duty, he returns to it with redoubled resolution never to be swayed a second time: he has now an additional motive to virtue, a conviction derived from experience, that happiness depends on regularity and order, and that disregard to justice or propriety never fails to be punished with shame and remorse.*

49. Rude ages exhibit the triumph of authority over reason. Philosophers anciently were divided into sects, being Epicureans, Platonists, Stoics, Pythagoreans, or Skeptics: the speculative relied no farther on their own judgment but to choose a leader, whom they implicitly followed. In later times, happily, reason hath obtained the ascendant: men now assert their native privilege of thinking for themselves, and disdain to be ranked in any sect, whatever be the science. I am forced to except criticism, which, by what fatality I know not, continues to be no less slavish in its principles, nor less submissive to authority, than it was originally. Bossuet, a celebrated French critic, gives many rules; but can discover no better foundation for any of them, than the practice merely of Homer and Virgil, supported by the authority of Aristotle. Strange! that in so long a work, he should never once have stumbled upon the question, Whether, and how far, do these rules agree with human nature. It could not surely be his opinion, that these poets, however eminent for genius, were entitled to give law to mankind; and that nothing now remains, but blind obedience to their arbitrary will. If in writing they followed no rule, why should they be imitated? If they studied nature, and were obsequious to rational principles, why should these be concealed from us?

50. With respect to the present undertaking, it is not the author's intention to compose a regular treatise upon each of the fine arts; but only, in general, to exhibit their fundamental principles, drawn from human nature, the true source of criticism. The fine arts are intended to entertain us, by making pleasant impressions; and, by that circumstance, are distinguished from the useful arts; but, in

* Genius is allied to a warm and inflammable constitution; delicacy of taste to calmness and sedateness. Hence it is common to find genius in one who is a prey to every passion; but seldom delicacy of taste. Upon a man possessed of that blessing, the moral duties, no less than the fine arts, make a deep impression, and counterbalance every irregular desire; at the same time, a temper calm and sedate is not easily moved, even by a strong temptation.

---

48. Six advantages of a thorough acquaintance with the principles of the fine arts.
49. Whence the rules of criticism should be derived.—A comparison of former ages with the present on this point.

order to make pleasant impressions, we ought, as above hinted, to know what objects are naturally agreeable, and what naturally disagreeable. That subject is here attempted, as far as necessary for unfolding the genuine principles of the fine arts; and the author assumes no merit from his performance, but that of evincing, perhaps more distinctly than hitherto has been done, that these principles, as well as every just rule of criticism, are founded upon the sensitive part of our nature. What the author hath discovered or collected upon that subject, he chooses to impart in the gay and agreeable form of criticism; imagining that this form will be more relished, and perhaps be no less instructive, than a regular and labored disquisition. His plan is, to ascend gradually to principles, from facts and experiments; instead of beginning with the former, handled abstractedly, and descending to the latter. But, though criticism is thus his only declared aim, he will not disown, that all along it has been his view, to explain the Nature of Man, considered as a sensitive being capable of pleasure and pain: and, though he flatters himself with having made some progress in that important science, he is, however, too sensible of its extent and difficulty, to undertake it professedly, or to avow it as the chief purpose of the present work.

51. To censure works, not men, is the just prerogative of criticism, and accordingly all personal censure is here avoided, unless where necessary to illustrate some general proposition. No praise is claimed on that account; because censuring with a view merely to find fault, cannot be entertaining to any person of humanity. Writers, one should imagine, ought, above all others, to be reserved on that article, when they lie so open to retaliation. The author of this treatise, far from being confident of meriting no censure, entertains not even the slightest hope of such perfection. Amusement was at first the sole aim of his inquiries: proceeding from one particular to another, the subject grew under his hand; and he was far advanced before the thought struck him, that his private meditations might be publicly useful.

N. B. The Elements of Criticism, meaning the whole, is a title too assuming for this work. A number of these elements or principles are here unfolded: but, as the author is far from imagining that he has completed the list, a more humble title is proper, such as may express any number of parts less than the whole. This he thinks is signified by the title he has chosen, viz. Elements of Criticism.

---

50. More particular account of the plan of the present work.—Design of the fine arts: how distinguished from the useful.—The peculiar merit which this work claims to possess What, besides criticism, it aims at

51. The title of the work

ELEMENTS OF CRITICISM.

CHAPTER I.

PERCEPTIONS AND IDEAS IN A TRAIN.

52. A MAN, while awake, is conscious of a continued train of perceptions and ideas passing in his mind. It requires no activity on his part to carry on the train.* At the same time, we learn from daily experience, that the train of our thoughts is not regulated by chance: and if it depend not upon will, nor upon chance, by what law is it governed? The question is of importance in the science of human nature; and I promise beforehand, that it will be found of great importance in the fine arts.

53. It appears, that the relations by which things are linked together, have a great influence in directing the train of thought. Taking a view of external objects, their inherent properties are not more remarkable than the various relations that connect them together. Cause and effect, contiguity in time or in place, high and low, prior and posterior, resemblance, contrast, and a thousand other relations, connect things together without end. Not a single thing appears solitary and altogether devoid of connection; the only difference is, that some are intimately connected, some more slightly; some near, some at a distance.

54. Experience will satisfy us of what reason makes probable, that the train of our thoughts is in a great measure regulated by the foregoing relations: an external object is no sooner presented to us in idea, than it suggests to the mind other objects to which it is related; and in that manner is a train of thoughts composed. Such is the law of succession; which must be natural, because it

* For how should this be done? what idea is it that we are to add? If we can specify the idea, that idea is already in the mind, and there is no occasion for any act of the will. If we cannot specify any idea, I next demand, how can a person will, or to what purpose, if there be nothing in view? We cannot form a conception of such a thing. If this argument need confirmation, I urge experience: whoever makes a trial will find, that ideas are linked together in the mind, forming a connected chain; and that we have not the command of any idea independent of the chain.

52. State of the mind.——53. What directs the train of thought?

governs all human beings. The law, however, seems not to be inviolable: it sometimes happens that an idea arises in the mind without any perceived connection; as, for example, after a profound sleep.

55. But, though we cannot add to the train an unconnected idea, yet in a measure we can attend to some ideas, and dismiss others. There are few things but what are connected with many others; and when a thing thus connected becomes a subject of thought, it commonly suggests many of its connections: among these a choice is afforded; we can insist upon one, rejecting others; and sometimes we insist on what is commonly held the slighter connection. Where ideas are left to their natural course, they are continued through the strictest connections: the mind extends its view to a son more readily than to a servant; and more readily to a neighbor than to one living at a distance. This order, as observed, may be varied by will, but still within the limits of related objects; for though we can vary the order of a natural train, we cannot dissolve the train altogether, by carrying on our thoughts in a loose manner without any connection. So far doth our power extend; and that power is sufficient for all useful purposes: to have more power, would probably be hurtful, instead of being salutary.

56. *Will* is not the only cause that prevents a train of thought from being continued through the strictest connections: much depends on the present tone of mind: for a subject that accords with that tone is always welcome. Thus, in good spirits, a cheerful subject will be introduced by the slightest connection; and one that is melancholy, no less readily in low spirits: an interesting subject is recalled, from time to time, by any connection indifferently, strong or weak; which is finely touched by Shakspeare, with relation to a rich cargo at sea:

My wind, cooling my broth,
Would blow me to an ague, when I thought
What harm a wind too great might do at sea.
I should not see the sandy-hour glass run,
But I should think of shallows and of flats;
And see my wealthy Andrew dock'd in sand,
Vailing her high top lower than her ribs,
To kiss her burial. Should I go to church,
And see the holy edifice of stone,
And not bethink me straight of dangerous rocks?
Which touching but my gentle vessel's side,
Would scatter all her spices on the stream,
Enrobe the roaring waters with my silks;
And, in a word, but even now worth this,
And now worth nothing. *Merchant of Venice*, Act I. Sc. 1.

57. Another cause clearly distinguishable from that now mentioned, hath also a considerable influence to vary the natural train of

---

54. Illustrate how the train of thought is regulated by relations.
55. The power we have over our trains of thoughts. The natural course of ideas
56. Train of thought affected by the present tone of mind Cargo at sea

ideas; which is, that, in the minds of some persons, thoughts and circumstances crowd upon each other by the slightest connections. I ascribe this to a bluntness in the discerning faculty; for a person who cannot accurately distinguish between a slight connection and one that is more intimate, is equally affected by each: such a person must necessarily have a great flow of ideas, because they are introduced by any relation indifferently; and the slighter relations, being without number, furnish ideas without end. This doctrine is, in a lively manner, illustrated by Shakspeare.

Falstaff. What is the gross sum that I owe thee?

Hostess. Marry, if thou wert an honest man, thyself and thy money too. Thou didst swear to me on a parcel gilt-goblet, sitting in my Dolphin-chamber, at the round table, by a sea-coal fire, on Wednesday in Whitsun-week, when the Prince broke thy head for likening him to a singing man of Windsor; thou didst swear to me then, as I was washing thy wound, to marry me, and make me my Lady thy wife. Canst thou deny it? Did not Goodwife Keech, the butcher's wife, come in then, and call me Gossip Quickly? coming in to borrow a mess of vinegar; telling us she had a good dish of prawns; whereby thou didst desire to eat some; whereby I told thee they were ill for a green wound. And didst not thou, when she was gone down stairs, desire me to be no more so familiarity with such poor people, saying, that ere long they should call me Madame? And didst thou not kiss me, and bid me fetch thee thirty shillings? I put thee now to thy book-oath, deny it if thou canst?

Second Part, Henry IV. Act II. Sc. 2.

58. On the other hand, a man of accurate judgment cannot have a great flow of ideas; because the slighter relations, making no figure in his mind, have no power to introduce ideas. And hence it is, that accurate judgment is not friendly to declamation or copious eloquence. This reasoning is confirmed by experience; for it is a noted observation, That a great or comprehensive memory is seldom connected with a good judgment.

59. As an additional confirmation, I appeal to another noted observation, That wit and judgment are seldom united. Wit consists chiefly in joining things by distant and fanciful relations, which surprise because they are unexpected; such relations, being of the slightest kind, readily occur to those only who make every relation equally welcome. Wit, upon that account, is in a good measure incompatible with solid judgment; which, neglecting trivial relations, adheres to what are substantial and permanent. Thus memory and wit are often conjoined: solid judgment seldom with either.

60. Every man who attends to his own ideas, will discover order as well as connection in their succession. There is implanted in the breast of every man a principle of order, which governs the arrangement of his perceptions, of his ideas, and of his actions. With regard to perceptions, I observe that, in things of equal rank, such as sheep in a fold, or trees in a wood, it must be indifferent in what order they be surveyed. But, in things of unequal rank, our ten-

---

57. Order of ideas, in some minds, varied by the slightest connections. **Explain and illustrate.**

58. Accuracy of judgment not favorable to a flow of ideas.

59. Wit and judgment, why so seldom united.

dency is, to view the principal subject before we descend to its accessories or ornaments, and the superior before the inferior or dependent; we are equally averse to enter into a minute consideration of constituent parts, till the thing be first surveyed as a whole. It need scarce be added, that our ideas are governed by the same principle; and that, in thinking or reflecting upon a number of objects, we naturally follow the same order as when we actually survey them.

61. The principle of order is conspicuous with respect to natural operations; for it always directs our ideas in the order of nature: thinking upon a body in motion, we follow its natural course; the mind falls with a heavy body, descends with a river, and ascends with flame and smoke: in tracing out a family, we incline to begin at the founder, and to descend gradually to his latest posterity; on the contrary, musing on a lofty oak, we begin at the trunk, and mount from it to the branches: as to historical facts, we love to proceed in the order of time; or, which comes to the same, to proceed along the chain of causes and effects.

62. But though in following out an historical chain, our bent is to proceed orderly from causes to their effects, we find not the same bent in matters of science: there we seem rather disposed to proceed from effects to their causes, and from particular propositions to those which are more general. Why this difference in matters that appear so nearly related? I answer, The cases are similar in appearance only, not in reality. In an historical chain, every event is particular, the effect of some former event, and the cause of others that follow: in such a chain, there is nothing to bias the mind from the order of nature. Widely different is science, when we endeavor to trace out causes and their effects: many experiments are commonly reduced under one cause; and again, many of these causes under one still more general and comprehensive: in our progress from particular effects to general causes, and from particular propositions to the more comprehensive, we feel a gradual dilatation or expansion of mind, like what is felt in an ascending series which is extremely pleasing: the pleasure here exceeds what arises from following the course of nature; and it is that pleasure which regulates our train of thought in the case now mentioned, and in others that are similar. These observations, by the way, furnish materials for instituting a comparison between the synthetic and analytic methods of reasoning: the synthetic method, descending regularly from principles to their consequences, is more agreeable to the strictness of order; but in following the opposite course in the analytic method we have a sensible pleasure, like mounting upward, which is not felt in the other: the analytic method is more agreeable to the

---

60. The principle of order governing perceptions and ideas.—Things of equal and of unequal rank.

61. Instances of ideas following in the order of nature.

imagination; the other method will be preferred by those only who with rigidity adhere to order, and give no indulgence to natural emotions.

63. It now appears that we are framed by nature to relish order and connection. When an object is introduced by a proper connection, we are conscious of a certain pleasure arising from that circumstance. Among objects of equal rank, the pleasure is proportioned to the degree of connection: but among unequal objects where we require a certain order, the pleasure arises chiefly from an orderly arrangement; of which one is sensible in tracing objects contrary to the course of nature, or contrary to our sense of order: the mind proceeds with alacrity down a flowing river, and with the same alacrity from a whole to its parts, or from a principal to its accessories; but in the contrary direction, it is sensible of a sort of retrograde motion, which is unpleasant. And here may be remarked the great influence of order upon the mind of man; grandeur, which makes a deep impression inclines us, in running over any series, to proceed from small to great, rather than from great to small; but order prevails over that tendency, and affords pleasure as well as facility in passing from a whole to its parts, and from a subject to its ornaments, which are not felt in the opposite course. Elevation touches the mind no less than grandeur doth; and in raising the mind to elevated objects, there is a sensible pleasure: the course of nature, however, hath still a greater influence than elevation; and therefore, the pleasure of falling with rain, and descending gradually with a river, prevails over that of mounting upward. But where the course of nature is joined with elevation, the effect must be delightful; and hence the singular beauty of smoke ascending in a calm morning.

64. Every work of art that is conformable to the natural course of our ideas, is so far agreeable; and every work of art that reverses that course, is so far disagreeable. Hence it is required in every such work, that, like an organic system, its parts be orderly arranged and mutually connected, bearing each of them a relation to the whole, some more intimate, some less, according to their destination: when due regard is had to these particulars, we have a sense of just composition, and so far are pleased with the performance. Homer is defective in order and connection; and Pindar more remarkably. Regularity, order, and connection are painful restraints on a bold and fertile imagination; and are not patiently submitted to, but after much culture and discipline. In Horace there is no fault more eminent than want of connection: instances are without number. Of Virgil's Georgics, though esteemed the most complete work of that author, the parts are ill connected, and the transitions far from

---

62. Why, in matters of science, we reverse the order of nature in our arrangement.—The analytic and synthetic modes of reasoning.

63. The relish of the mind for order and connection. Instances.

being sweet and easy. The two prefaces of Sallust look as if by some blunder they had been prefixed to his two histories; they will suit any other history as well, or any subject as well as history. Even members of these prefaces are but loosely connected: they look more like a number of maxims, or observations, than a connected discourse.

65. An episode in a narrative poem, being in effect an accessory, demands not that strict union with the principal subject, which is requisite between a whole and its constituent parts: it demands, however, a degree of union, such as ought to subsist between a principal and accessory; and therefore will not be graceful if it be loosely connected with the principal subject. I give for an example the descent of Æneas into hell, which employs the sixth book of the Æneid: the reader is not prepared for that important event: no cause is assigned that can make it appear necessary, or even natural, to suspend for so long a time the principal action in its most interesting period: the poet can find no pretext for an adventure so extraordinary, but the hero's longing to visit the ghost of his father, recently dead: in the mean time the story is interrupted, and the reader loses his ardor. Pity it is that an episode so extremely beautiful, were not more happily introduced. I must observe, at the same time, that full justice is done to this incident, by considering it to be an episode; for if it be a constituent part of the principal action, the connection ought to be still more intimate.

66. In a natural landscape, we every day perceive a multitude of objects connected by contiguity solely; which is not unpleasant, because objects of sight make an impression so lively, as that a relation even of the slightest kind is relished. This, however, ought not to be imitated in description: words are so far short of the eye in liveliness of impression, that in a description connection ought to be carefully studied; for new objects introduced in description are made more or less welcome in proportion to the degree of their connection with the principal subject. In the following passage, different things are brought together without the slightest connection, if it be not what may be called verbal, *i. e.* taking the same word in different meanings.

> Surgamus: solet esse gravis cantantibus umbra.
> Juniperi gravis umbra: nocent et frugibus umbræ.
> Ite domum saturæ, venit Hesperus, ite capellæ.
>
> *Virg. Buc.* x. 75.

67. The relations among objects have a considerable influence in the gratification of our passions, and even in their production. But that subject is reserved to be treated in the chapter of emotions and passions. (Chap. ii. part i. sect. 4.)

---

64. The requisites, accordingly, in every work of art.—Remarks upon Homer, Pindar, Horace, Virgil, and Sallust.
65. Episodes. Example from the Æneid.
66. Rule for description.

There is not, perhaps, another instance of a building so great erected upon a foundation so slight in appearance, as the relations of objects and their arrangement. Relations make no capital figure in the mind, the bulk of them being transitory, and some extremely trivial: they are, however, the links that, by uniting our perceptions into one connected chain, produce connection of action, because perception and action have an intimate correspondence. But it is not sufficient for the conduct of life, that our actions be linked together, however intimately: it is besides necessary that they proceed in a certain order; and this is also provided for by an original propensity. Thus order and connection, while they admit sufficient variety, introduce a method in the management of affairs: without them our conduct would be fluctuating and desultory; and we should be hurried from thought to thought, and from action to action, entirely at the mercy of chance.

CHAPTER II.

EMOTIONS AND PASSIONS.

68. Of all the feelings raised in us by external objects, those only of the eye and the ear are honored with the name of *passion* or *emotion;* the most pleasing feelings of taste, or touch, or smell, aspire not to that honor. From this observation appears the connection of emotions and passions with the fine arts, which, as observed in the introduction, are all of them calculated to give pleasure to the eye or the ear; never once condescending to gratify any of the inferior senses. The design accordingly of this chapter is to delineate that connection, with the view chiefly to ascertain what power the fine arts have to raise emotions and passions. To those who would excel in the fine arts, that branch of knowledge is indispensable; for without it the critic, as well as the undertaker, ignorant of any rule, has nothing left but to abandon himself to chance. Destitute of that branch of knowledge, in vain will either pretend to foretell what effect his work will have upon the heart.

69. Human nature is a complicated machine, and is unavoidably so in order to answer its various purposes. The public indeed have been entertained with many systems of human nature that flatter the mind by their simplicity: according to some writers, man is entirely a selfish being; according to others, universal benevolence

---

67 The relations among objects affect our conduct.

68 Feelings that are distinguished by the name of passions. Their connection with the fine arts.—Object of the chapter.

is his duty: one founds morality upon sympathy solely, and one upon utility. If any of these systems were copied from nature, the present subject might be soon discussed. But the variety of nature is not so easily reached, and for confuting such Utopian systems without the fatigue of reasoning, it appears the best method to take a survey of human nature, and to set before the eye, plainly and candidly, facts as they really exist.

PART I.

CAUSES UNFOLDED OF THE EMOTIONS AND PASSIONS.

SECTION I.

Difference between Emotion and Passion.—Causes that are the most common and the most general.—Passion considered as productive of action.

70. It is a fact universally admitted, that no emotion or passion ever starts up in the mind without a cause: if I love a person, it is for good qualities or good offices: if I have resentment against a man, it must be for some injury he has done me: and I cannot pity any one who is under no distress of body nor of mind.

71. The circumstances now mentioned, if they raise an emotion or passion, cannot be entirely indifferent; for if so, they could not make any impression. And we find, upon examination, that they are not indifferent: looking back upon the foregoing examples, the good qualities or good offices that attract my love, are antecedently agreeable: if an injury did not give uneasiness, it would not occasion resentment against the author: nor would the passion of pity be raised by an object in distress, if that object did not give pain.

72. What is now said about the production of emotion or passion, resolves itself into a very simple proposition, That we love what is agreeable, and hate what is disagreeable. And indeed it is evident, that a thing must be agreeable or disagreeable, before it can be the object either of love or of hatred.

73. This short hint about the causes of passion and emotion, leads to a more extensive view of the subject. Such is our nature, that upon perceiving certain external objects, we are instantaneously

---

69. Theories of human nature.
70. Emotions or passions are not without cause. Examples.
71. Remarks on foregoing examples.
72. What we love—what we hate.

conscious of pleasure or pain: a gently-flowing river, a smooth extended plain, a spreading oak, a towering hill, are objects of sight that raise pleasant emotions: a barren heath, a dirty marsh, a rotten carcass, raise painful emotions. Of the emotions thus produced we inquire for no other cause but merely the presence of the object.

74. The things now mentioned raise emotions by means of their properties and qualities: to the emotion raised by a large river, its size, its force, and its fluency, contribute each a share: the regularity, propriety, and convenience of a fine building, contribute each to the emotion raised by the building.

75. If external properties be agreeable, we have reason to expect the same from those which are internal; and, accordingly, power, discernment, wit, mildness, sympathy, courage, benevolence, are agreeable in a high degree: upon perceiving these qualities in others, we instantaneously feel pleasant emotions, without the slightest act of reflection, or of attention to consequences. It is almost unnecessary to add, that certain qualities opposite to the former, such as dullness, peevishness, inhumanity, cowardice, occasion in the same manner painful emotions.

76. Sensible beings affect us remarkably by their actions. Some actions raise pleasant emotions in the spectator, without the least reflection; such as graceful motion, and genteel behavior. But as *intention*, a capital circumstance in human actions, is not visible, it requires reflection to discover their true character. I see one delivering a purse of money to another, but I can make nothing of that action, till I learn with what intention the money is given: if it be given to discharge a debt, the action pleases me in a slight degree if it be a grateful return, I feel a stronger emotion; and the pleasant emotion rises to a great height, when it is the intention of the giver to relieve a virtuous family from want. Thus actions are qualified by intention; but they are not qualified by the event; for an action well intended gives pleasure, whatever the event be. Further, human actions are perceived to be *right* or *wrong*; and that perception qualifies the pleasure or pain that results from them.

Emotions are raised in us, not only by the qualities and actions of others, but also by their feelings: I cannot behold a man in distress, without partaking of his pain; nor in joy, without partaking of his pleasure.

77. The beings or things above described occasion emotions in us, not only in the original survey, but also when recalled to the memory in idea: a field laid out with taste is pleasant in the recollection, as well as when under our eye: a generous action described

---

73. Emotions on perceiving certain external objects. The cause of such emotions.
74. How the external objects mentioned raise emotions.
75. Internal or mental causes of pleasant and painful emotions.
76. How we are affected by the actions of rational beings—Actions qualified by intention, not by event; distinguished as right or wrong.—Feelings of others, a cause of emotion

in words or colors occasions a sensible emotion, as well as when we see it performed; and when we reflect upon the distress of any person, our pain is of the same kind with what we felt when eye-witnesses. In a word, an agreeable or disagreeable object recalled to the mind in idea, is the occasion of a pleasant or painful emotion, of the same kind with that produced when the object was present: the only difference is, that an idea being fainter than an original perception, the pleasure or pain produced by the former is proportionably fainter than that produced by the latter.

78. Having explained the nature of an emotion, and mentioned several causes by which it is produced, we proceed to an observation of considerable importance in the science of human nature, which is, That desire follows some emotions, and not others. The emotions raised by a beautiful garden, a magnificent building, or a number of fine faces in a crowded assembly, is seldom accompanied with desire. Other emotions are accompanied with desire; emotions, for example, raised by human actions and qualities: a virtuous action raiseth in every spectator a pleasant emotion, which is commonly attended with desire to reward the author of the action: a vicious action, on the contrary, produceth a painful emotion, attended with desire to punish the delinquent. Even things inanimate often raise emotions accompanied with desire: witness the goods of fortune, which are objects of desire almost universally: and the desire, when immoderate, obtains the name of *avarice.* The pleasant emotion produced in a spectator by a capital picture in the possession of a prince, is seldom accompanied with desire; but if such a picture be exposed to sale, desire of having or possessing is the natural consequence of a strong emotion.

79. It is a truth verified by induction, that every passion is accompanied with desire; and if an emotion be sometimes accompanied with desire, sometimes not, it comes to be a material inquiry, in what respect a passion differs from an emotion. Is passion in its nature or feeling distinguishable from emotion? An internal motion or agitation of the mind, when it passeth away without desire, is denominated *an emotion:* when desire follows, the motion or agitation is denominated *a passion.* A fine face, for example, raiseth in me a pleasant feeling: if that feeling vanish without producing any effect, it is in proper language an emotion; but if the feeling, by reiterated views of the object, become sufficiently strong to occasion desire, it loses its names of emotion, and acquires that of passion. The same holds in all the other passions: the painful feeling raised in a spectator by a slight injury done to a stranger, being accompanied with no desire of revenge, is termed an emotion: but that injury raiseth in a stranger a stronger emotion, which, being accompanied with desire of revenge, is a passion: external ex-

77. Emotions of memory. How they differ from those of original perception.
78. Some emotions accompanied with desire; others not. Examples.

pressions of distress produce in the spectator a painful feeling, which being sometimes so slight as to pass away without any effect, is an emotion; but if the feeling be so strong as to prompt desire of affording relief, it is a passion, and is termed *pity*: envy is emulation in excess; if the exaltation of a competitor be barely disagreeable, the painful feeling is an emotion; if it produce desire to depress him, it is a passion.

80. To prevent mistakes, it must be observed, that desire here is taken in its proper sense, namely, that internal act, which, by influencing the will, makes us proceed to action. Desire in a lax sense respects also actions and events that depend not on us, as when I desire that my friend may have a son to represent him, or that my country may flourish in arts and sciences: but such internal act is more properly termed a *wish* than a *desire*.

81. Having distinguished passion from emotion, we proceed to consider passion more at large, with respect especially to its power of producing action.

We have daily and constant experience for our authority, that no man ever proceeds to action but by means of some antecedent desire or impulse. So well established is this observation, and so deeply rooted in the mind, that we can scarce imagine a different system of action: even a child will say familiarly, What should make me do this or that, when I have no desire to do it? Taking it then for granted, that the existence of action depends on antecedent desire, it follows that where there is no desire, there can be no action. This opens another shining distinction between emotions and passions. The former, being without desire, are in their nature quiescent: the desire included in the latter, prompts one to act in order to fulfil that desire, or, in other words, to gratify the passion.

82. The cause of a passion is sufficiently explained above: it is that being or thing, which, by raising desire, converts an emotion into a passion. When we consider a passion with respect to its power of prompting action, that same being or thing is termed its *object*: a fine woman, for example, raises the passion of love, which is directed to her as its object: a man, by injuring me, raises my resentment, and becomes thereby the object of my resentment. Thus the cause of a passion and its object are the same in different respects. An emotion, on the other hand, being in its nature quiescent, and merely a passive feeling, must have a cause; but cannot be said, properly speaking, to have an object.*

* [The *cause* of a passion is that which raises it; the *object* is that towards which it prompts us to act, or on which it inclines us to fix our attention. The

79. Distinction between passion and emotion.—How some emotions get the name of *passions*. Illustrations.
80. Definition of Desire.
81. Passion as producing action.—Another distinction between emotions and passions.
82. Whether the *cause* of a passion is identical with its *object*.—Is the same true of the cause of an *emotion*?—Beattie's remarks

83. The objects of our passions may be distinguished into two kinds, general and particular. A man, a house, a garden, is a particular object: fame, esteem, opulence, honor, are general objects, because each of them comprehends many particulars. The passions directed to general objects are commonly termed *appetites*, in contradistinction to passions directed to particular objects, which retain their proper name: thus we say an appetite for fame, for glory, for conquest, for riches; but we say the passion of friendship, of love, of gratitude, of envy, of resentment. And there is a material difference between appetites and passions, which makes it proper to distinguish them by different names: the latter have no existence till a proper object be presented; whereas the former exist first, and then are directed to an object: a passion comes after its object; an appetite goes before it, which is obvious in the appetites of hunger, thirst, and animal love, and is the same in the other appetites above mentioned.

84. By an object so powerful as to make a deep impression, the mind is inflamed, and hurried to action with a strong impulse. Where the object is less powerful, so as not to inflame the mind, nothing is felt but desire without any sensible perturbation. The principle of duty affords one instance: the desire generated by an object of duty, being commonly moderate, moves us to act calmly, without any violent impulse; but if the mind happen to be inflamed with the importance of the object, in that case desire of doing our duty becomes a warm passion.

85. The actions of brute creatures are generally directed by instinct, meaning blind impulse or desire, without any view to consequences. Man is framed to be governed by reason; he commonly acts with deliberation, in order to bring about some desirable end; and in that case his actions are means employed to bring about the end desired: thus I give charity in order to relieve a person from want; I perform a grateful action as a duty incumbent on me; and I fight for my country in order to repel its enemies. At the same time, there are human actions that are not governed by reason, nor are done with any view to consequences. Infants, like brutes, are mostly governed by instinct, without the least view to any end, good or ill. And even adult persons act sometimes instinctively: thus one in extreme hunger snatches at food, without the slightest consideration whether it be salutary: avarice prompts to accumulate

cause and the object of a passion are often, but not always, one and the same thing. Thus present good is both the cause and the object of *joy;* we rejoice *in* it, and we rejoice *on account* of it. But of *love* or *esteem*, the cause is some agreeable quality, and the object is some person supposed to possess that agreeable quality; of *resentment*, in like manner, injury is the cause, and the injurious person the object.—*Beattie.*]

83. **Objects of passion, particular and general. Instances.—How appetite differs from passion. Instances.**
84. **Influence of an object of duty.**

wealth, without the least view of use; and thereby absurdly converts means into an end: and animal love often hurries to fruition, without a thought even of gratification.

86. A passion when it flames so high as to impel us to act blindly without any view to consequences, good or ill, may in that state be termed *instinctive;* and when it is so moderate as to admit reason, and to prompt actions with a view to an end, it may in that state be termed *deliberative.*

87. With respect to actions exerted as means to an end, desire to bring about the end is what determines one to exert the action; and desire considered in that view is termed a *motive:* thus the same mental act that is termed *desire* with respect to an end in view, is termed a *motive* with respect to its power of determining one to act. Instinctive actions have a cause, namely, the impulse of the passion; but they cannot be said to have a motive, because they are not done with any view to consequences.

We learn from experience, that the gratification of desire is pleasant; and the foresight of that pleasure becomes often an additional motive for acting. Thus a child eats by the mere impulse of hunger: a young man thinks of the pleasure of gratification, which being a motive for him to eat, fortifies the original impulse: and a man farther advanced in life, hath the additional motive that it will contribute to his health.

88. From these premises, it is easy to determine with accuracy, what passions and actions are selfish, what social. It is the end in view that ascertains the class to which they belong: where the end in view is my own good, they are selfish; where the end in view is the good of another, they are social. Hence it follows, that instinctive actions, where we act blindly and merely by impulse, cannot be reckoned either social or selfish: thus eating, when prompted by an impulse merely of nature, is neither social nor selfish; but add a motive, that it will contribute to my pleasure or my health, and it becomes in a measure selfish. On the other hand, when affection moves me to exert an action to the end solely of advancing my friend's happiness, without regard to my own gratification, the action is justly denominated *social;* and so is also the affection that is its cause: if another motive be added, that gratifying the affection will also contribute to my own happiness, the action becomes partly selfish. If charity be given with the single view of relieving a person from distress, the action is purely social; but if it be partly in view to enjoy the pleasure of a virtuous act, the action is so far selfish.*

* A selfish motive proceeding from a social principle, such as that mentioned, is the most respectable of all selfish motives. To enjoy the pleasure

85. Actions prompted by instinct and by reason.—Actions of brutes, of infants, of adults
86 Instinctive passions.—Deliberative passions.
87. The same mental act termed a desire and a motive.—The foresight of the gratification of desire, a motive.

A just action, when prompted by the principle of duty solely, is neither social nor selfish. When I perform an act of justice with a view to the pleasure of gratification, the action is selfish: I pay a debt for my own sake, not with a view to benefit my creditor. But suppose the money has been advanced by a friend without interest, purely to oblige me: in that case, together with the motive of gratification, there arises a motive of gratitude, which respects the creditor solely, and prompts me to act in order to do him good; and the action is partly social, partly selfish. Suppose again I meet with a surprising and unexpected act of generosity, that inspires me with love to my benefactor, and the utmost gratitude. I burn to do him good: he is the sole object of my desire; and my own pleasure in gratifying the desire, vanisheth out of sight: in this case, the action I perform is purely social. Thus it happens, that when a social motive becomes strong, the action is exerted with a view singly to the object of the passion, and self never comes in view.

89. When this analysis of human nature is considered, not one article of which can with truth be controverted, there is reason to be surprised at the blindness of some philosophers, who, by dark and confused notions, are led to deny all motives to action but what arise from self-love. Man, for aught appears, might possibly have been so framed, as to be susceptible of no passions but what have self for their object: but man thus framed, would be ill fitted for society: his constitution, partly selfish, partly social, fits him much better for his present situation.*

90 Of self, every one hath a direct perception; of other things we have no knowledge but by means of their attributes: and hence it is, that of self the perception is more lively than of any other thing. Self is an agreeable object; and for the reason now given, must be more agreeable than any other object. Is this sufficient to account for the prevalence of self-love?†

91. In the foregoing part of this chapter it is suggested, that some circumstances make beings or things fit objects for desire, others

of a virtuous action, one must be virtuous; and to enjoy the pleasure of a charitable action, one must think charity laudable at least, if not a duty. It is otherwise where a man gives charity merely for the sake of ostentation; for this he may do without having any pity or benevolence in his temper.

* As the benevolence of many human actions is beyond the possibility of doubt, the argument commonly insisted on for reconciling such actions to the selfish system, is, that the only motive I can have to perform a benevolent action, or an action of any kind, is the pleasure that it affords me. So much then is yielded, that we are pleased when we do good to others; which is a fair admission of the principle of benevolence; for without that principle, what pleasure could one have in doing good to others? And admitting a principle of benevolence, why may it not be a motive to action, as well as selfishness is, or any other principle?

† [Consult Beattie's Moral Science, 286–9.]

88. Passions and actions that are selfish; social; neither. Illustrations.—Remarks on charity; on an act of justice; on meeting with an act of generosity.
89. The error of referring all actions to self-love. Its refutation
90. The predominance of self-love accounted for.

not. This hint ought to be pursued. It is a truth ascertained by universal experience, that a thing which in our apprehension is beyond reach, never is the object of desire; no man in his right senses desires to walk on the clouds, or to descend to the centre of the earth: we may amuse ourselves in a reverie, with building castles in the air, and wishing for what can never happen; but such things never move desire. And indeed a desire to do what we are sensible is beyond our power, would be altogether absurd. In the next place, though the difficulty of attainment with respect to things within reach often inflames desire, yet where the prospect of attainment is faint, and the event extremely uncertain, the object, however agreeable, seldom raiseth any strong desire: thus beauty, or any other good quality, in a woman of rank, seldom raises love in a man greatly her inferior. In the third place, different objects, equally within reach, raise emotions in different degrees; and when desire accompanies any of these emotions, its strength, as is natural, is proportioned to that of its cause. Hence the remarkable difference among desires directed to beings inanimate, animate, and rational: the emotion caused by a rational being is out of measure stronger than any caused by an animal without reason; and an emotion raised by such an animal, is stronger than what is caused by any thing inanimate. There is a separate reason why desire of which a rational being is the object, should be the strongest: our desires swell by partial gratification; and the means we have of gratifying desire, by benefiting or harming a rational being, are without end: desire directed to an inanimate being, susceptible neither of pleasure nor pain, is not capable of a higher gratification than that of acquiring the property. Hence it is, that though every emotion accompanied with desire, is, strictly speaking, a passion; yet, commonly, none of these are denominated passions, but where a sensible being, capable of pleasure and pain, is the object.

SECTION II.

Power of Sounds to raise Emotions and Passions.

92. Upon a review, I find the foregoing section almost wholly employed upon emotions and passions raised by objects of sight, though they are also raised by objects of hearing. As this happened without intention, merely because such objects are familiar above others, I find it proper to add a short section upon the power of sounds to raise emotions and passions.

I begin with comparing sounds and visible objects with respect to their influence upon the mind. It has already been observed, that

---

91. What is said of things beyond our reach; of things difficult to attain; of different objects equally within reach? Desires directed to beings inanimate, animate; rational.

of all external objects, rational beings, especially of our own species, have the most powerful influence in raising emotions and passions; and, as speech is the most powerful of all the means by which one human being can display itself to another, the objects of the eye must so far yield preference to those of the ear. With respect to inanimate objects of sight, sounds may be so contrived as to raise both terror and mirth beyond what can be done by any such object. Music has a commanding influence over the mind, especially in conjunction with words. Objects of sight may indeed contribute to the same end, but more faintly; as where a love poem is rehearsed in a shady grove, or on the bank of a purling stream. But sounds, which are vastly more ductile and various, readily accompany all the social affections expressed in a poem, especially emotions of love and pity.

93. Music, having at command a great variety of emotions, may, like many objects of sight, be made to promote luxury and effeminacy; of which we have instances without number, especially in vocal music. But, with respect to its pure and refined pleasures, music goes hand in hand with gardening and architecture, her sister arts, in humanizing and polishing the mind; of which none can doubt who have felt the charms of music. But, if authority be required, the following passage from a grave historian, eminent for solidity of judgment, must have the greatest weight. Polybius, speaking of the people of Cynætha, an Arcadian tribe, has the following train of reflections: "As the Arcadians have always been celebrated for their piety, humanity, and hospitality, we are naturally led to inquire, how it has happened that the Cynætheans are distinguished from the other Arcadians, by savage manners, wickedness, and cruelty. I can attribute this difference to no other cause, but a total neglect among the people of Cynætha, of an institution established among the ancient Arcadians with a nice regard to their manners and their climate: I mean the discipline and exercise of that genuine and perfect music, which is useful in every state, but necessary to the Arcadians; whose manners, originally rigid and austere, made it of the greatest importance to incorporate this art into the very essence of their government."

No one will be surprised to hear such influence attributed to music, when, with respect to another of the fine arts, he finds a living instance of an influence no less powerful. It is unhappily indeed the reverse of the former: for it has done more mischief by corrupting British manners, than music ever did good in purifying those of Arcadia.

94. The licentious court of Charles II., among its many disorders, engendered a pest, the virulence of which subsists to this day. The

---

92. Comparative influence of sounds and of visible objects to raise emotions and passions —Influence of rational beings; of speech; of music.

93. Music and her sister arts.—Polybius' account of the ancient Arcadians.

English comedy, copying the manners of the court, became abominably licentious; and continues so (1763) with very little softening. It is there an established rule, to deck out the chief characters with every vice in fashion, however gross. But, as such characters viewed in a true light would be disgustful, care is taken to disguise their deformity under the embellishments of wit, sprightliness, and good humor, which in mixed company makes a capital figure. It requires not much thought to discover the poisonous influence of such plays. A young man of figure, emancipated at last from the severity and restraint of a college education, repairs to the capital disposed to every sort of excess. The playhouse becomes his favorite amusement; and he is enchanted with the gayety and splendor of the chief personages. The disgust which vice gives him at first, soon wears off, to make way for new notions, more liberal in his opinion; by which a sovereign contempt for religion, and a declared war upon the chastity of wives, maids, and widows, are converted from being infamous vices to be fashionable virtues. The infection spreads gradually through all ranks, and becomes universal. How gladly would I listen to any one who should undertake to prove, that what I have been describing is chimerical! But the dissoluteness of our young men of birth will not suffer me to doubt of its reality. Sir Harry Wildair has completed many a rake; and in the *Suspicious Husband*, Ranger, the humble imitator of Sir Harry, has had no slight influence in spreading that character. What woman, tinctured with the playhouse morals, would not be the sprightly, the witty, though dissolute Lady Townly, rather than the cold, the sober, though virtuous Lady Grace? How odious ought writers to be who thus employ the talents they have from their Maker most traitorously against himself, by endeavoring to corrupt and disfigure his creatures! If the comedies of Congreve did not rack him with remorse in his last moments, he must have been lost to all sense of virtue. Nor will it afford any excuse to such writers, that their comedies are entertaining: unless it could be maintained, that wit and sprightliness are better suited to a vicious than a virtuous character. It would grieve me to think so; and the direct contrary is exemplified in the *Merry Wives of Windsor*, where we are highly entertained with the conduct of two ladies not more remarkable for mirth and spirit than for the strictest purity of manners.

SECTION III.

Causes of the Emotion of Joy and Sorrow.

95. THIS subject was purposely reserved for a separate section, because it could not, with perspicuity, be handled under the general

94. The corrupting influence of English comedy. How shown

head. An emotion accompanied with desire is termed *a passion;* and when the desire is fulfilled, the passion is said to be gratified. Now, the gratification of every passion must be pleasant; for nothing can be more natural, than that the accomplishment of any wish or desire should affect us with joy: I know of no exception but when a man stung with remorse desires to chastise and punish himself. The joy of gratification is properly called *an emotion;* because it makes us happy in our present situation, and is ultimate in its nature, not having a tendency to any thing beyond. On the other hand, sorrow must be the result of an event contrary to what we desire; for if the accomplishment of desire produce joy, it is equally natural that disappointment should produce sorrow.

An event, fortunate or unfortunate, that falls out by accident, without being foreseen or thought of, and which therefore could not be the object of desire, raiseth an emotion of the same kind with that now mentioned; but the cause must be different; for there can be no gratification where there is no desire. We have not, however, far to seek for a cause: it is involved in the nature of man, that he cannot be indifferent to an event that concerns him or any of his connections; if it be fortunate, it gives him joy; if unfortunate, it gives him sorrow.

96. In no situation doth joy rise to a greater height, than upon the removal of any violent distress of mind or body; and in no situation doth sorrow rise to a greater height, than upon the removal of what makes us happy. The sensibility of our nature serves in part to account for these effects. Other causes concur. One is, that violent distress always raises an anxious desire to be free from it; and therefore its removal is a high gratification: nor can we be possessed of any thing that makes us happy, without wishing its continuance; and therefore its removal, by crossing our wishes, must create sorrow. The principle of contrast is another cause: an emotion of joy arising upon the removal of pain, is increased by contrast when we reflect upon our former distress: an emotion of sorrow, upon being deprived of any good, is increased by contrast when we reflect upon our former happiness:

> *Jaffier.* There's not a wretch that lives on common charity,
> But's happier than me. For I have known
> The luscious sweets of plenty: every night
> Have slept with soft content about my head,
> And never wak'd but to a joyful morning.
> Yet now must fall like a full ear of corn,
> Whose blossom 'scap'd, yet's wither'd in the ripening.
>
> *Venice Preserved*, Act 1. Sc. 1.

It hath always been reckoned difficult to account for the extreme pleasure that follows a cessation of bodily pain; as when one is re-

---

95. When an emotion is called a passion.—Why gratified passion is pleasant. Exception.—Why the joy of gratification is termed an emotion.—The emotion raised by an accidental event, whether fortunate or unfortunate.

lieved from the rack, or from a violent fit of the stone. What is said explains this difficulty, in the easiest and simplest manner: cessation of bodily pain is not of itself a pleasure, for a *non-ens* or a negative can neither give pleasure nor pain; but man is so framed by nature as to rejoice when he is eased of pain, as well as to be sorrowful when deprived of any enjoyment. This branch of our constitution is chiefly the cause of the pleasure. The gratification of desire comes in as an accessory cause; and contrast joins its force, by increasing the sense of our present happiness. In the case of an acute pain, a peculiar circumstance contributes its part: the brisk circulation of the animal spirits occasioned by acute pain continues after the pain is gone, and produceth a very pleasant emotion. Sickness hath not that effect, because it is always attended with a depression of spirits.

97. Hence it is, that the gradual diminution of acute pain, occasions a mixed emotion, partly pleasant, partly painful: the partial diminution produceth joy in proportion; but the remaining pain balanceth the joy. This mixed emotion, however, hath no long endurance; for the joy that ariseth upon the diminution of pain soon vanisheth, and leaveth in the undisturbed possession that degree of pain which remains.

What is above observed about bodily pain, is equally applicable to the distresses of the mind; and accordingly it is a common artifice, to prepare us for the reception of good news by alarming our fears.

SECTION IV.

Sympathetic Emotion of Virtue, and its cause.

98. One feeling there is that merits a deliberate view, for its singularity as well as utility. Whether to call it an emotion or a passion, seems uncertain: the former it can scarce be, because it involves desire; the latter it can scarce be, because it has no object. But this feeling, and its nature, will be best understood from examples. A signal act of gratitude produceth in the spectator or reader, not only love or esteem for the author, but also a separate feeling, being a vague feeling of gratitude without an object; a feeling, however, that disposes the spectator or reader to acts of gratitude, more than upon an ordinary occasion. This feeling is overlooked by writers upon ethics; but a man may be convinced of its reality, by attentively watching his own heart when he thinks

96. In what cases do joy and sorrow rise to the greatest height? The causes assigned. Quotation from *Venice Preserved.*—Account for the pleasure that follows a cessation of bodily pain.

97. Emotion produced by the gradual diminution of acute pain. Distresses of the mind.

warmly of any signal act of gratitude: he will be conscious of the feeling, as distinct from the esteem or admiration he has for the grateful person. The feeling is singular in the following respect, that it is accompanied with a desire to perform acts of gratitude, without having any object; though in that state, the mind, wonderfully bent on an object, neglects no opportunity to vent itself: any act of kindness or good-will, that would pass unregarded upon another occasion, is greedily seized; and the vague feeling is converted into a real passion of gratitude: in such a state, favors are returned double.

99. In like manner, a courageous action produceth in a spectator the passion of admiration directed to the author: and besides this well-known passion, a separate feeling is raised in the spectator, which may be called *an emotion of courage;* because, while under its influence, he is conscious of a boldness and intrepidity beyond what is usual, and longs for proper objects upon which to exert this emotion:

> Spumantemque dari, pecora inter inertia, votis
> Optat aprum, aut fulvum descendere monte leonem.
>
> *Æneid*, iv. 158.

> Non altramente ill tauro, ove l'irriti
> Geloso amor con stimoli pungenti,
> Horribilmente mugge, e co'muggiti
> Gli spirti in se risveglia, e l'ire ardenti:
> E'l corno aguzza ai tronchi, a par ch' inviti
> Con vani colpi a'la battaglia i venti.
>
> *Tasso*, Canto vii. st. 55.

> So full of valor that they smote the air
> For breathing in their faces.
>
> *Tempest*, Act IV. Sc. 4.

The emotions raised by music, independent of words, must be all of this nature: courage roused by martial music performed upon instruments without a voice, cannot be directed to any object; nor can grief or pity raised by melancholy music of the same kind have an object.

100. For another example, let us figure some grand and heroic action, highly agreeable to the spectator: besides veneration for the author, the spectator feels in himself an unusual dignity of character, which disposeth him to great and noble actions; and herein chiefly consists the extreme delight every one hath in the histories of conquerors and heroes.

This singular feeling, which may be termed *the sympathetic emotion of virtue*, resembles, in one respect, the well-known appetites that lead to the propagation and preservation of the species. The appetites of hunger, thirst, and animal love, arise in the mind before they are directed to any object; and in no case whatever is the

98. Feelings produced by contemplating a signal act of gratitude. In what does their singularity consist?

99. The effect of contemplating a courageous action.—The effect of martial and of melancholy music.

mind more solicitous for a proper object, than when under the influence of any of these appetites.

The feeling I have endeavored to unfold, may well be termed *the sympathetic emotion of virtue;* for it is raised in the spectator, or in a reader, by virtuous actions of every kind, and by no other sort. When we contemplate a virtuous action, which fails not to prompt our love for the author, our propensity at the same time to such actions is so much enlivened, as to become for a time an actual emotion. But no man hath a propensity to vice as such: on the contrary, a wicked deed disgusts him, and makes him abhor the author; and this abhorrence is a strong antidote against vice, as long as any impression remains of the wicked action.

101. In a rough road, a halt to view a fine country is refreshing; and here a delightful prospect opens upon us. It is indeed wonderful to observe what incitements there are to virtue in the human frame: justice is perceived to be our duty, and it is guarded by natural punishments, from which the guilty never escape; to perform noble and generous actions, a warm sense of their dignity and superior excellence is a most efficacious incitement. And to leave virtue in no quarter unsupported, here is unfolded an admirable contrivance, by which good example commands the heart, and adds to virtue the force of habit. We approve every virtuous action, and bestow our affection on the author; but if virtuous actions produced no other effect upon us, good example would not have great influence: the sympathetic emotion under consideration bestows upon good example the utmost influence, by prompting us to imitate what we admire. This singular emotion will readily find an object to exert itself upon: and at any rate, it never exists without producing some effect; because virtuous emotions of that sort, are in some degree an exercise of virtue: they are a mental exercise at least, if they appear not externally. And every exercise of virtue, internal and external, leads to habit; for a disposition or propensity of the mind, like a limb of the body, becomes stronger by exercise. Proper means, at the same time, being ever at hand to raise this sympathetic emotion, its frequent reiteration may, in a good measure, supply the want of a more complete exercise. Thus, by proper discipline, every person may acquire a settled habit of virtue: intercourse with men of worth, histories of generous and disinterested actions, and frequent meditation upon them, keep the sympathetic emotion in constant exercise, which by degrees introduceth a habit, and confirms the authority of virtue: with respect to education in particular, what a spacious and commodious avenue to the heart of a young person is here opened!

---

100. Whence the delight taken in reading the history of heroes and conquerors.—Remarks upon the sympathetic emotion of virtue —Has man a propensity to vice *as such?*
101. Incitements to virtue in the human frame.—The effect of every exercise of virtue.—How habits of virtue may be acquired.

SECTION V.

In many instances one Emotion is productive of another. The same of Passions.

102. In the first chapter it is observed, that the relations by which things are connected, have a remarkable influence on the train of our ideas. I here add, that they have an influence, no less remarkable, in the production of emotions and passions. Beginning with the former, an agreeable object makes every thing connected with it appear agreeable; for the mind gliding sweetly and easily through related objects, carries along the agreeable properties it meets with in its passage, and bestows them on the present object, which thereby appears more agreeable than when considered apart. No relation is more intimate than that between a being and its qualities: and accordingly, every quality in a hero, even the slightest, makes a greater figure than more substantial qualities in others. The propensity of carrying along agreeable properties from one object to another, is sometimes so vigorous as to convert defects into properties: the wry neck of Alexander was imitated by his courtiers as a real beauty, without intention to flatter: Lady Percy, speaking of her husband Hotspur,

> ——————— By his light
> Did all the chivalry of England move,
> To do brave acts. He was indeed the glass,
> Wherein the noble youths did dress themselves.
> He had no legs that practised not his gait:
> And speaking thick, which Nature made his blemish,
> Became the accents of the valiant:
> For those who could speak slow and tardily,
> Would turn their own perfection to abuse,
> To seem like him.
>
> *Second Part, Henry IV.* Act II. Sc. 6.

103. The same communication of passion obtains in the relation of principal and accessory. Pride, of which self is the object, expands itself upon a house, a garden, servants, equipage, and every accessory. A lover addresseth his fair one's glove in the following terms:

> Sweet ornament that decks a thing divine.

Veneration for relics has the same natural foundation; and that foundation, with the superstructure of superstition, has occasioned much blind devotion to the most ridiculous objects—to the supposed milk, for example, of the Virgin Mary, or the supposed blood of St.

---

102. Influence of the relations of things in producing emotions and passions.—The influence of an agreeable object on connected objects.—The relation of a being and its qualities.—The propensity of carrying along agreeable properties from one object to another.—The wry neck of Alexander.—The speech of Lady Percy concerning Hotspur.

Januarius.* A temple is in a proper sense an accessory of the deity to which it is dedicated: Diana is chaste, and not only her temple, but the very icicle which hangs on it, must partake of that property:

> The noble sister of Poplicola,
> The moon of Rome; chaste as the icicle
> That's curdled by the frost from purest snow,
> And hangs on Dian's temple.
> *Coriolanus*, Act V. Sc. 3.

Thus it is, that the respect and esteem which the great, the powerful, the opulent naturally command, are in some measure communicated to their dress, to their manners, and to all their connections: and it is this communication of properties, which, prevailing even over the natural taste of beauty, helps to give currency to what is called *the fashion.*

104. By means of the same easiness of communication, every bad quality in an enemy is spread upon all his connections. The sentence pronounced against Ravaillac for the assassination of Henry IV. of France ordains that the house in which he was born should be razed to the ground, and that no other building should ever be erected on that spot. Enmity will extend passion to objects still less connected. The Swiss suffer no peacocks to live, because the Duke of Austria, their ancient enemy, wears a peacock's tail in his crest. A relation more slight and transitory than that of enmity, may have the same effect: thus the bearer of bad tidings becomes an object of aversion:

> Fellow, begone; I cannot brook thy sight;
> This news hath made thee a most ugly man.
> *King John*, Act III. Sc. 1.

> Yet the first bringer of unwelcome news
> Hath but a losing office: and his tongue
> Sounds ever after, as a sullen bell
> Remember'd tolling a departed friend.
> *Second Part, Henry IV.* Act I. Sc. 3.

In borrowing thus properties from one object to bestow them on another, it is not any object indifferently that will answer. The object from which properties are borrowed, must be such as to warm the mind and enliven the imagination. Thus the beauty of a woman, which inflames the imagination, is readily communicated to a glove, as above mentioned; but the greatest beauty a glove is susceptible

* But why worship the cross which is supposed to be that upon which our Saviour suffered? That cross ought to be the object of hatred, not of veneration. If it be urged, that as an instrument of Christ's suffering it was salutary to mankind, I answer, Why is not also Pontius Pilate reverenced, Caiaphas the high-priest, and Judas Iscariot?

103. The communication of passion in the relation of principal and accessory.—Pride.—Love.—Veneration for relics.—A temple.—Diana.—The fashion.

of, touches the mind so little, as to be entirely dropped in passing from it to the owner. In general, it may be observed, that any dress upon a fine woman is becoming; but that ornaments upon one who is homely, must be elegant indeed to have any remarkable effect in mending her appearance.*

105. The emotions produced as above may properly be termed *secondary*, being occasioned either by antecedent emotions or antecedent passions, which in that respect may be termed *primary*. And to complete the present theory, I must add, that a secondary emotion may readily swell into a passion for the accessory object, provided the accessory be a proper object for desire. Thus it happens that one passion is often productive of another: examples are without number; the sole difficulty is a proper choice. I begin with self-love, and the power it hath to generate love to children. Every man, besides making part of a greater system, like a comet, a planet, or satellite only, hath a less system of his own, in the centre of which he represents the sun darting his fire and heat all around; especially upon his nearest connections: the connection between a man and his children, fundamentally that of cause and effect, becomes, by the addition of other circumstances, the completest that can be among individuals; and therefore self-love, the most vigorous of all passions, is readily expanded upon children. The secondary emotion they produce by means of their connection, is sufficiently strong to move desire even from the beginning; and the new passion swells by degrees, till it rivals in some measure self-love, the primary passion. To demonstrate the truth of this theory, I urge the following argument. Remorse for betraying a friend, or murdering an enemy in cold blood, makes a man even hate himself: in that state, he is not conscious of affection to his children, but rather of disgust or ill-will. What cause can be assigned for that change, other than the hatred he has to himself, which is expanded upon his children. And if so, may we not with equal reason derive from self-love, some part at least of the affection a man generally has to them?

106. The affection a man bears to his blood relations, depends

---

* A house and gardens surrounded with pleasant fields, all in good order, bestow greater lustre upon the owner than at first will be imagined. The beauties of the former are, by intimacy of connection, readily communicated to the latter; and if it have been done at the expense of the owner himself, we naturally transfer to him whatever of design, art, or taste appears in the performance. Should not this be a strong motive with proprietors to embellish and improve their fields?

---

104. Bad qualities in an enemy diffused.—Sentence against Ravaillac.—The Swiss against peacocks.—The bearer of bad tidings. Illustrations from Shakspeare.—In borrowing properties from one object to bestow them on another, not every object will answer. Illustrate.

105. Distinction between secondary and primary emotions.—One passion productive of another.—Self-love produces love to childern.—Man compared to the solar system.—Self-hatred, arising from a base act, is extended to his children.

partly on the same principle: self-love is also expanded upon them; and the communicated passion is more or less vigorous in proportion to the degree of connection. Nor doth self-love rest here: it is, by the force of connection, communicated even to things inanimate: and hence the affection a man bears to his property, and to every thing he calls his own.

Friendship, less vigorous than self-love, is, for that reason, less apt to communicate itself to the friend's children, or other relations. Instances, however, are not wanting of such communicated passion, arising from friendship when it is strong. Friendship may go higher in the matrimonial state than in any other condition; and Otway, in *Venice Preserved*, takes advantage of that circumstance: in the scene where Belvidera sues to her father for pardon, she is represented as pleading her mother's merits, and the resemblance she bore to her mother:

> *Priuli.* My daughter!
> *Belvidera.* Yes, your daughter, by a mother
> Virtuous and noble, faithful to your honor,
> Obedient to your will, kind to your wishes,
> Dear to your arms. By all the joys she gave you
> When in her blooming years she was your treasure,
> Look kindly on me; in my face behold
> The lineaments of hers y' have kissed so often,
> Pleading the cause of your poor cast-off child.

And again,

> *Belvidera.* Lay me, I beg you, lay me
> By the dear ashes of my tender mother:
> She would have pitied me, had fate yet spard'd her.
> Act V. Sc. 1.

This explains why any meritorious action, or any illustrious qualification, in my son or my friend, is apt to make me over-value myself: if I value my friend's wife or son upon account of their connection with him, it is still more natural that I should value myself upon account of my connection with him.

107. Friendship, or any other social affection, may, by changing the object, produce opposite effects.

Pity, by interesting us strongly for the person in distress, must of consequence inflame our resentment against the author of the distress: for, in general, the affection we have for any man, generates in us good-will to his friends, and ill-will to his enemies. Shakspeare shows great art in the funeral oration pronounced by Antony over the body of Cæsar. He first endeavors to excite grief in the hearers, by dwelling upon the deplorable loss of so great a man: this passion, interesting them strongly in Cæsar's fate, could not fail to produce a lively sense of the treachery and cruelty of the con-

---

106. The affection a man bears to blood relations, and even to things inanimate, depends on what?—Communicated passion arising from friendship; especially in the matrimonial state. Instance from *Venice Preserved*.—The effect upon us of any meritorious qualification in a son or friend.

spirators; an infallible method to inflame the resentment of the people beyond all bounds:

> *Antony.* If you have tears, prepare to shed them now
> You all do know this mantle. I remember
> The first time ever Cæsar put it on;
> 'Twas on a summer's evening, in his tent,
> That day he overcame the Nervii—
> Look! in this place ran Cassius' dagger through;—
> See what a rent the envious Casca made.
> Through this the well-beloved Brutus stabb'd;
> And, as he pluck'd his cursed steel away,
> Mark how the blood of Cæsar follow'd it!
> As rushing out of doors, to be resolved,
> If Brutus so unkindly knock'd or no:
> For Brutus, as you know, was Cæsar's angel.
> Judge, oh you Gods! how dearly Cæsar loved him!
> This, this, was the unkindest cut of all;
> For when the noble Cæsar saw him stab,
> Ingratitude, more strong than traitor's arms,
> Quite vanquish'd him; then burst his mighty heart;
> And, in his mantle muffling up his face,
> Which all the while ran blood, great Cæsar fell,
> Even at the base of Pompey's statue.
> O what a fall was there, my countrymen!
> Then I, and you, and all of us, fell down,
> Whilst bloody treason flourish'd over us.
> O, now you weep; and I perceive you feel
> The dint of pity: these are gracious drops.
> Kind souls! what! weep you when you but behold
> Our Cæsar's vesture wounded? look you here!
> Here is himself, marr'd as you see, by traitors.
>
> *Julius Cæsar*, Act III. Sc. 6.

Had Antony endeavored to excite his audience to vengeance, without paving the way by raising their grief, his speech would not have made the same impression.

108. Hatred, and other dissocial passions, produce effects directly opposite to those above mentioned. If I hate a man, his children, his relations, nay his property, become to me objects of aversion: his enemies, on the other hand, I am disposed to esteem.

The more slight and transitory relations are not favorable to the communication of passion. Anger, when sudden and violent, is one exception; for, if the person who did the injury be removed out of reach, that passion will vent itself against any related object, however slight the relation be. Another exception makes a greater figure: a group of beings or things becomes often the object of a communicated passion, even where the relation of the individuals to the percipient is but slight. Thus, though I put no value upon a single man for living in the same town with myself; my townsmen, however, considered in a body, are preferred before others. This is still more remarkable with respect to my countrymen in general: the grandeur of the complex objects swells the passion of self-love

---

107. Any social affection, by changing the object, produces opposite effects.—Pity leads to resentment.—The funeral oration of Antony over the dead body of Cæsar. How adapted to excite to vengeance.

by the relation I have to my native country; and every passion, when it swells beyond its ordinary bounds, hath a peculiar tendency to expand itself along related objects. In fact, instances are not rare, of persons, who upon all occasions are willing to sacrifice their lives and fortunes for their country. Such influence upon the mind of man hath a complex object, or, more properly speaking, a general term.

109. The sense of order hath influence in the communication of passion. It is a common observation, that a man's affection to his parents is less vigorous than to his children: the order of nature in descending to children, aids the transition of the affection: the ascent to a parent, contrary to that order, makes the transition more difficult. Gratitude to a benefactor is readily extended to his children; but not so readily to his parents. The difference, however, between the natural and inverted order, is not so considerable, but that it may be balanced by other circumstances. Pliny gives an account of a woman of rank condemned to die for a crime; and, to avoid public shame, detained in prison to die of hunger: her life being prolonged beyond expectation, it was discovered that she was nourished by sucking milk from the breasts of her daughter. This instance of filial piety, which aided the transition, and made ascent no less easy than descent is commonly, procured a pardon to the mother, and a pension to both. The story of Androcles and the lion may be accounted for in the same manner: the admiration, of which the lion was the object for his kindness and gratitude to Androcles, produced good-will to Androcles, and a pardon of his crime.

And this leads to other observations upon communicated passions. I love my daughter less after she is married, and my mother less after a second marriage: the marriage of my son or of my father diminishes not my affection so remarkably. The same observation holds with respect to friendship, gratitude, and other passions: the love I bear my friend, is but faintly extended to his married daughter: the resentment I have against a man is readily extended against children who make part of his family; not so readily against children who are foris-familiated,* especially by marriage. This difference is also more remarkable in daughters than in sons. These are curious facts; and, in order to discover the cause, we must examine minutely that operation of the mind by which a passion is extended to a related object. In considering two things as related, the mind is not stationary, but passeth and repasseth from the one to the other, viewing the relation from each of them

[* *Foris-familiated;*—persons, who having received a portion of the paternal estate, give up all title to a further share.]

108. Operation of hatred and other dissocial affections.—Transitory relations, not favorable to the communication of passion. Two exceptions.

perhaps oftener than once; which holds more especially in considering a relation between things of unequal rank, as between the cause and the effect, or between a principal and an accessory: in contemplating, for example, the relation between a building and its ornaments, the mind is not satisfied with a single transition from the former to the latter; it must also view the relation, beginning at the latter, and passing from it to the former. This vibration of the mind in passing and repassing between things related, explains the facts above mentioned: the mind passeth easily from the father to the daughter; but where the daughter is married, this new relation attracts the mind, and obstructs, in some measure, the return from the daughter to the father; and any circumstance that obstructs the mind in passing and repassing between its objects, occasions a like obstruction in the communication of passion. The marriage of a male obstructs less the easiness of transition, because a male is less sunk by the relation of marriage than a female.

110. The foregoing instances are of passion communicated from one object to another. But one passion may be generated by another, without change of object. It in general is observable, that a passion paves the way to others similar in their tone, whether directed to the same or to a different object; for the mind, heated by any passion, is, in that state, more susceptible of a new impression in a similar tone, than when cool and quiescent. It is a common observation, that pity generally produceth friendship for a person in distress. One reason is, that pity interests us in its object, and recommends all its virtuous qualities: female beauty accordingly shows best in distress; being more apt to inspire love than upon an ordinary occasion. But the chief reason is, that pity, warming and melting the spectator, prepares him for the reception of other tender affections; and pity is readily improved into love or friendship, by a certain tenderness and concern for the object, which is the tone of both passions. The aptitude of pity to produce love, is beautifully illustrated by Shakspeare:

> *Othello.* Her father loved me; oft invited me
> Still question'd me the story of my life,
> From year to year; the battles, sieges, fortunes,
> That I had past.
> I ran it through, even from my boyish days,
> To th' very moment that he bade me tell it:
> Wherein I spoke of most disastrous chances,
> Of moving accidents by flood and field;
> Of hair-breadth 'scapes in th' imminent deadly breach
> Of being taken by the insolent foe,
> And sold to slavery; of my redemption thence,

---

109. Communication of passion modified by the sense of order.—Affection to parents and to children compared.—Gratitude to the children rather than parents of a benefactor.—Pliny's account of an instance of filial piety and its effects.—Story of Androcles and the lion.—Love to a daughter before and after marriage; and to a mother after a second marriage. Love to a friend and to his married daughter—The operation of mind examined by which a passion is extended to a related object. Its vibratory nature—Effect, when any circumstance obstructs the mind in passing and repassing between its objects.

And with it all my travel's history.
——— ——— ———All these to hear
Would Desdemona seriously incline;
But still the house-affairs would draw her thence,
Which ever as she could with haste dispatch,
She'd come again, and, with a greedy ear,
Devour up my discourse: which I observing,
Took once a pliant hour, and found good means
To draw from her a prayer of earnest heart,
That I would all my pilgrimage dilate,
Whereof by parcels she had something heard,
But not distinctively. I did consent,
And often did beguile her of her tears,
When I did speak of some distressful stroke
That my youth suffer'd. My story being done,
She gave me for my pains a world of sighs:
She swore, in faith, 'twas strange, 'twas passing strange—
'Twas pitiful, 'twas wondrous pitiful—
She wish'd she had not heard it:—yet she wish'd
That heaven had made her such a man:—she thank'd me,
And bade me, if I had a friend that loved her,
I should but teach him how to tell my story,
And that would woo her. On this hint I spake;
She loved me for the dangers I had past,
And I loved her, that she did pity them:
This only is the witchcraft I have used.
Othello, Act I. Sc. 8.

In this instance it will be observed that admiration concurred with pity to produce love.

SECTION VI.

Causes of the Passions of Fear and Anger.

111. Fear and anger, to answer the purposes of nature, are happily so contrived as to operate sometimes instinctively, sometimes deliberately, according to circumstances. As far as deliberate, they fall in with the general system, and require no particular explanation: if any object have a threatening appearance, reason suggests means to avoid the danger: if a man be injured, the first thing he thinks of, is what revenge he shall take, and what means he shall employ. These particulars are no less obvious than natural. But, as the passions of fear and anger, in their instinctive state, are less familiar to us, it may be acceptable to the reader to have them accurately delineated. He may also possibly be glad of an opportunity to have the nature of instinctive passions more fully explained than there was formerly opportunity to do. I begin with fear.

112. Self-preservation is a matter of too great importance to be left entirely to the conduct of reason. Nature hath acted here with her usual foresight. Fear and anger are passions that move us to

---

110. One passion generated by another without change of object.—Pity gives rise to what?—When female beauty shows to best advantage. Why?—Quotation from *Othello*.
111. Fear and anger operating instinctively and deliberately.

act, sometimes deliberately, sometimes instinctively, according to circumstances; and by operating in the latter manner, they frequently afford security when the slower operations of deliberate reason would be too late: we take nourishment commonly, not by the direction of reason, but by the impulse of hunger and thirst; and, in the same manner, we avoid danger by the impulse of fear, which often, before there is time for reflection, placeth us in safety. Here we have an illustrious instance of wisdom in the formation of man; for it is not within the reach of fancy to conceive any thing more artfully contrived to answer its purpose, than the instinctive passion of fear, which, upon the first surmise of danger, operates instantaneously. So little doth the passion, in such instances, depend on reason, that it frequently operates in contradiction to it: a man who is not upon his guard, cannot avoid shrinking at a blow, though he knows it to be aimed in sport; nor avoid closing his eyes at the approach of what may hurt him, though conscious that he is in no danger. And it also operates by impelling us to act even where we are conscious that our interposition can be of no service: if a passage-boat, in a brisk gale, bear much to one side, I cannot avoid applying the whole force of my shoulders to set it upright: and, if my horse stumble, my hands and knees are instantly at work to prevent him from falling.

113. Fear provides for self-preservation by flying from harm; anger, by repelling it. Nothing, indeed, can be better contrived to repel or prevent injury, than anger or resentment: destitute of that passion, men, like defenceless lambs, would lie constantly open to mischief.* Deliberate anger caused by a voluntary injury, is too well known to require any explanation: if my desire be to resent an affront, I must use means; and these means must be discovered by reflection: deliberation is here requisite; and in that case the passion seldom exceeds just bounds. But, where anger impels one suddenly to return a blow, even without thinking of doing mischief, the passion is instinctive: and it is chiefly in such a case that it is rash and ungovernable, because it operates blindly, without affording time for deliberation or foresight.

Instinctive anger is frequently raised by bodily pain, by a stroke, for example, on a tender part, which, ruffling the temper and unhinging the mind, is in its tone similar to anger: and when a man is thus beforehand disposed to anger, he is not nice nor scrupulous about an object; the person who gave the stroke, however accidentally, is by an inflammable temper held a proper object, merely for having occasioned the pain. It is still more remarkable, that a

* Brasidas being bit by a mouse he had caught, let it slip out of his fingers: "No creature," says he, "is contemptible, but what may provide for its own safety, if it have courage."—*Plutarch*, *Apothegmata*.

112. The advantages of the instinctive action of fear.—Wisdom of implanting in man the principle of fear.

stock or a stone by which I am hurt, becomes an object of my resentment: I am violently excited to crush it to atoms. The passion, indeed, in that case, can be but a single flash; for being entirely irrational, it must vanish with the first reflection. Nor is that irrational effect confined to bodily pain: internal distress, when excessive, may be the occasion of effects equally irrational: perturbation of mind, occasioned by the apprehension of having lost a dear friend, will, in a fiery temper, produce momentary sparks of anger against that very friend, however innocent: thus Shakspeare, in the *Tempest*,

> *Alonzo.* ———— Sit down and rest.
> Even here I will put off my hope, and keep it
> No longer for my flatterer; he is drown'd
> Whom thus we stray to find, and the sea mocks
> Our frustrate search on land. Well, let him go.
>
> Act III. Sc. 3.

The final words, *Well, let him go*, are an expression of impatience and anger at Ferdinand, whose absence greatly distressed his father, dreading that he was lost in the storm. This nice operation of the human mind, is by Shakspeare exhibited upon another occasion, and finely painted in the tragedy of *Othello:* Iago, by dark hints and suspicious circumstances, had roused Othello's jealousy; which, however, appeared too slightly founded to be vented upon Desdemona, its proper object. The perturbation and distress of mind thereby occasioned, produced a momentary resentment against Iago, considered as occasioning the jealousy, though innocent:

> *Othello.* Villain, be sure thou prove my love a whore;
> Be sure of it; give me the ocular proof,
> Or by the wrath of man's eternal soul,
> Thou hadst been better have been born a dog,
> Than answer my waked wrath.
> *Iago.* Is't come to this?
> *Othello.* Make me see't; or, at the least, so prove it,
> That the probation bear no hinge or loop
> To hang a doubt on: or woe upon thy life!
> *Iago.* My noble lord——
> *Othello.* If thou dost slander her, and torture me,
> Never pray more; abandon all remorse;
> On horror's head horrors accumulate;
> Do deeds to make heaven weep, all earth amazed;
> For nothing canst thou to damnation add
> Greater than that.
>
> *Othello*, Act II. Sc. 8.

114. This blind and absurd effect of anger is more gayly illustrated by Addison, in a story, the *dramatis personæ* of which are, a cardinal, and a spy retained in pay for intelligence. The cardinal is represented as minuting down the particulars. The spy begins with a low voice, "Such an one the advocate whispered to one of his friends within my hearing, that your Eminence was a very great

113. How do fear and anger, respectively, provide for the self-preservation of man?—Operations of deliberate anger; also, of instinctive anger. Not particular or always rational about its objects.—Effects of mental perturbation, illustrated in the *Tempest* and in *Othello*.

poltroon;" and after having given his patron time to take it down adds, That another called him "a mercenary rascal in a public conversation." The cardinal replies, "Very well," and bids him go on. The spy proceeds, and loads him with reports of the same nature, till the cardinal rises in a fury, calls him an impudent scoundrel, and kicks him out of the room.—*Spectator*, No. 439.

We meet with instances every day of resentment raised by loss at play, and wreaked on the cards or dice. But anger, a furious passion, is satisfied with a connection still slighter than that of cause and effect; of which Congreve, in the *Mourning Bride*, gives one beautiful example:

> *Gonsalez.* Have comfort.
> *Almeria.* Cursed be that tongue that bids me be of comfort,
> Cursed my own tongue that could not move his pity,
> Cursed these weak hands that could not hold him here,
> For he is gone to doom Alphonso's death.
>
> Act IV. Sc. 8.

115. I have chosen to exhibit anger in its more rare appearances, for in these we can best trace its nature and extent. In the examples above given, it appears to be an absurd passion, and altogether irrational. But we ought to consider, that it is not the intention of nature to subject this passion, in every instance, to reason and reflection: it was given us to prevent or to repel injuries; and, like fear, it often operates blindly and instinctively, without the least view to consequences: the very first apprehension of harm, sets it in motion to repel injury by punishment. Were it more cool and deliberate, it would lose its threatening appearance, and be insufficient to guard us against violence. When such is and ought to be the nature of the passion, it is not wonderful to find it exerted irregularly and capriciously, as it sometimes is where the mischief is sudden and unforeseen. All the harm that can be done by the passion in that state is instantaneous; for the shortest delay sets all to rights; and circumstances are seldom so unlucky as to put it in the power of a passionate man to do much harm in an instant.

Social passions, like the selfish, sometimes drop their character and become instinctive. It is not unusual to find anger and fear respecting others so excessive, as to operate blindly and impetuously, precisely as where they are selfish.

SECTION VII.

Emotions caused by Fiction.

116. THE attentive reader will observe, that hitherto no fiction hath been assigned as the cause of any passion or emotion: whether

114. The blind and absurd effect of anger illustrated by Addison.—Resentment on losing by play.
115. The useful purpose of the principle of instinctive anger.—Social passions sometimes become instinctive.

it be a being, action, or quality, that moveth us, it is supposed to be really existing. This observation shows that we have not yet completed our task; because passions, as all the world know, are moved by fiction as well as by truth. In judging beforehand of man, so remarkably addicted to truth and reality, one should little dream that fiction can have any effect upon him; but man's intellectual faculties are not sufficiently perfect to dive far even into his own nature. I shall take occasion afterwards to show, that the power of fiction to generate passion is an admirable contrivance, subservient to excellent purposes: in the mean time, we must try to unfold the means that give fiction such influence over the mind.

That the objects of our external senses really exist in the way and manner we perceive, is a branch of intuitive knowledge: when I see a man walking, a tree growing, or cattle grazing, I cannot doubt but that these objects are really what they appear to be: if I be a spectator of any transaction or event, I have a conviction of the real existence of the persons engaged, of their words, and of their actions. Nature determines us to rely on the veracity of our senses; for otherwise they could not in any degree answer their end, that of laying open things existing and passing around us.

By the power of memory, a thing formerly seen may be recalled to the mind with different degrees of accuracy. We commonly are satisfied with a slight recollection of the capital circumstances; and, in such recollection, the thing is not figured as in our view, nor any image formed: we retain the consciousness of our present situation, and barely remember that formerly we saw that thing. But with respect to an interesting object or event that made a strong impression, I am not satisfied with a cursory review, but must dwell upon every circumstance. I am imperceptibly converted into a spectator, and perceive every particular passing in my presence, as when I was in reality a spectator. For example, I saw yesterday a beautiful woman in tears for the loss of an only child, and was greatly moved with her distress: not satisfied with a slight recollection or bare remembrance, I ponder upon the melancholy scene: conceiving myself to be in the place where I was an eye-witness, every circumstance appears to me as at first: I think I see the woman in tears, and hear her moans. Hence it may be justly said, that in a complete idea of memory there is no past nor future: a thing recalled to the mind with the accuracy I have been describing, is perceived as in our view, and consequently as existing at present. Past time makes part of an incomplete idea only: I remember or reflect, that some years ago I was at Oxford, and saw the first stone laid of the Ratcliff library; and I remember that, at a still greater distance of time, I heard a debate in the House of Commons about a standing army.

---

116. Passions moved by fiction.—To what fiction owes its power to affect us.—How we know that external objects exist in the way and manner we perceive.—Things formerly

117. Lamentable is the imperfection of language, almost in every particular that falls not under external sense. I am talking of a matter exceedingly clear in the perception: and yet I find no small difficulty to express it clearly in words; for it is not accurate to talk of incidents long past as passing in our sight, nor of hearing at present what we really heard yesterday, or at a more distant time. And yet the want of proper words to describe ideal presence, and to distinguish it from real presence, makes this inaccuracy unavoidable. When I recall any thing to my mind in a manner so distinct as to form an idea or image of it as present, I have not words to describe that act, but that I perceive the thing as a spectator, and as existing in my presence; which means not that I am really a spectator, but only that I conceive myself to be a spectator, and have a perception of the object similar to what a real spectator hath.

As many rules of criticism depend on *ideal presence*, the reader, it is hoped, will take some pains to form an exact notion of it, as distinguished on the one hand from real presence, and on the other from a superficial or reflective remembrance. In contradistinction to real presence, ideal presence may properly be termed *a waking dream;* because, like a dream, it vanisheth the moment we reflect upon our present situation: real presence, on the contrary, vouched by eyesight, commands our belief, not only during the direct perception, but in reflecting afterwards on the object. To distinguish ideal presence from reflective remembrance, I give the following illustration. When I think of an event as past, without forming any image, it is barely reflecting or remembering that I was an eyewitness; but when I recall the event so distinctly as to form a complete image of it, I perceive it as passing in my presence; and this perception is an act of intuition, into which reflection enters not, more than into an act of sight.

Though ideal presence is thus distinguished from real presence on the one side, and from reflective remembrance on the other, it is however variable without any precise limits; rising sometimes towards the former, and often sinking towards the latter. In a vigorous exertion of memory, ideal presence is extremely distinct: thus, when a man, entirely occupied with some event that made a deep impression, forgets himself, he perceives every thing as passing before him, and hath a consciousness of presence similar to that of a spectator; with no difference but that in the former the perception of presence is less firm and clear than in the latter. But such vigorous exertion of memory is rare: ideal presence is oftener faint, and the image so obscure as not to differ widely from reflective remembrance.

---

seen, recalled by memory with various degrees of exactness. Whether past or future is thought of in a very vivid memory of such objects.

117. Explain *ideal presence* as distinguished from real presence, and also from a superficial or reflective remembrance. Ideal presence sometimes verges towards the one or the other of these

118. Hitherto of an idea of memory. I proceed to consider the idea of a thing I never saw, raised in me by speech, by writing, or by painting. That idea, with respect to the present subject, is of the same nature with an idea of memory, being either complete or incomplete. A lively and accurate description of an important event, raises in me ideas no less distinct than if I had been originally an eye-witness: I am insensibly transformed into a spectator, and have an impression that every incident is passing in my presence. On the other hand, a slight or superficial narrative produceth but a faint and incomplete idea, of which ideal presence makes no part. Past time is a circumstance that enters into this idea, as it doth into an incomplete idea of memory: I believe that Scipio existed about 2000 years ago, and that he overcame Hannibal in the famous battle of Zama. When I reflect so slightly upon that memorable event, I consider it as long past. But let it be spread out in a lively and beautiful description, I am insensibly transformed into a spectator: I perceive these two heroes in act to engage: I perceive them brandishing their swords, and cheering their troops; and in that manner I attend them through the battle, every incident of which appears to be passing in my sight.

I have had occasion to observe (Part I. sect. i. of the present chapter) that ideas, both of memory and of speech, produce emotions of the same kind with what are produced by an immediate view of the object; only fainter, in proportion as an idea is fainter than an original perception. The insight we have now got unfolds that mystery: ideal presence supplies the want of real presence; and in idea we perceive persons acting and suffering, precisely as in an original survey: if our sympathy be engaged by the latter, it must also in some degree be engaged by the former, especially if the distinctness of ideal presence approach to that of real presence. Hence the pleasure of a reverie, where a man, forgetting himself, is totally occupied with the ideas passing in his mind, the objects of which he conceives to be really existing in his presence. The power of language to raise emotions, depends entirely on the raising such lively and distinct images as are here described: the reader's passions are never sensibly moved, till he be thrown into a kind of reverie; in which state, forgetting that he is reading, he conceives every incident as passing in his presence, precisely as if he were an eye witness. A general or reflective remembrance cannot warm us into any emotion: it may be agreeable in some slight degree; but its ideas are too faint and obscure to raise any thing like an emotion: and were they ever so lively, they pass with too much precipitation to have that effect. Our emotions are never instantaneous; even such as come the soonest to their height, have different periods of birth and increment; and to give opportunity for these different periods, it is necessary that the cause of every emotion be present to the mind a due time; for an emotion is not carried to its height but by reiterated impressions. We know that to be the case of emotions arising from objects of sight; a quick succession, even of the most beautiful objects, scarce making any impression; and if this hold in the succession of original perceptions, how much more in the succession of ideas!

119. Though all this while I have been only describing what passeth in the mind of every one, and what every one must be conscious of, it was necessary to enlarge upon the subject; because, however clear in the internal conception, it is far from being so when described in words. Ideal presence, though of general importance, hath scarce ever been touched by any writer; and however difficult the explication, it could not be avoided in accounting for the effects produced by fiction. Upon that point, the reader I guess has prevented me: it already must have occurred to him, that if, in reading, ideal presence be the means by which our passions are moved, it makes no difference whether the subject be a fable or a true history: when ideal presence is complete, we perceive every object as in our sight; and the mind, totally occupied with an interesting event, finds no leisure for reflection. This reasoning is confirmed by constant and universal experience. Let us take under consideration the meeting of Hector and Andromache, in the sixth book of the Iliad, or some of the passionate scenes in King Lear: these pictures of human life, when we are sufficiently engaged, give an impression of reality not less distinct than that given by Tacitus describing the death of Otho: we never once reflect whether the story be true or feigned; reflection comes afterwards, when we have the scene no longer before our eyes. This reasoning will appear in a still clearer light, by opposing ideal presence to ideas raised by a cursory narrative; which ideas being faint, obscure, and imperfect, leave a vacuity in the mind, which solicits reflection. And accordingly, a curt narrative of feigned incidents is never relished: any slight pleasure it affords is more than counterbalanced by the disgust it inspires for want of truth.

To support the foregoing theory, I add what I reckon a decisive argument; which is, that even genuine history has no command over our passions but by ideal presence only; and consequently, that in this respect it stands upon the same footing with fable. To me it appears clear, that in neither can our sympathy hold firm against reflection; for if the reflection that a story is a pure fiction prevent our sympathy, so will equally the reflection that the persons described are no longer existing. What effect, for example, can the belief of the story of Lucretia have to raise our sympathy, when she died above 2000 years ago, and hath at present no painful feeling

---

118. The idea of a thing I never saw, raised by speech, writing, or painting.—Effect of a lively and accurate description; also of a superficial narrative.—The battle of Zama.—Ideal presence awakes sympathy.—Pleasure of reverie.—On what depends the power of language to raise emotions?—Influence of a general or reflective remembrance to excite emotion.—Are emotions instantaneous?

of the injury done her? The effect of history, in point of instruction, depends in some measure upon its veracity. But history cannot reach the heart, while we indulge any reflection upon the facts: such reflection, if it engage our belief, never fails at the same time to poison our pleasure, by convincing us that our sympathy for those who are dead and gone is absurd. And if reflection be laid aside, history stands upon the same footing with fable: what effect either may have to raise our sympathy, depends on the vivacity of the ideas they raise; and, with respect to that circumstance, fable is generally more successful than history.

120. Of all the means for making an impression of ideal presence, theatrical representation is the most powerful. That words, independent of action, have the same power in a less degree, every one of sensibility must have felt: a good tragedy will extort tears in private, though not so forcibly as upon the stage. That power belongs also to painting: a good historical picture makes a deeper impression than words can, though not equal to that of theatrical action. Painting seems to possess a middle place between reading and acting: in making an impression of ideal presence, it is not less superior to the former than inferior to the latter.

It must not, however, be thought that our passions can be raised by painting to such a height as by words: a picture is confined to a single instant of time, and cannot take in a succession of incidents: its impression indeed is the deepest that can be made instantaneously; but seldom is a passion raised to any height in an instant, or by a single impression. It was observed above, that our passions, those especially of the sympathetic kind, require a succession of impressions; and for that reason, reading and acting have greatly the advantage, by reiterating impressions without end.

Upon the whole, it is by means of ideal presence that our passions are excited; and till words produce that charm, they avail nothing: even real events entitled to our belief, must be conceived present and passing in our sight, before they can move us. And this theory serves to explain several phenomena otherwise unaccountable. A misfortune happening to a stranger, makes a less impression than one happening to a man we know, even where we are no way interested in him: our acquaintance with this man, however slight, aids the conception of his suffering in our presence. For the same reason, we are little moved by any distant event; because we have more difficulty to conceive it present, than an event that happened in our neighborhood.

---

119. How does the doctrine of ideal presence account for the equal impressiveness of fiction and true history? Reference to the Iliad, and King Lear.—Ideal presence contrasted with ideas raised by a cursory narrative.—When only does even real history exert a command over our passions?—What destroys the emotive power of history?

120. The most powerful means of making an impression of ideal presence. The next most powerful.—Comparative influence of painting, reading, and acting, in awakening strong feeling.—What is required even for real events, entitled to belief, to move us?—Misfortunes happening to strangers or to acquaintances.—Events distant or near

121. Every one is sensible, that describing a past event as present, has a fine effect in language: for what other reason than that it aids the conception of ideal presence? Take the following example:

> And now with shouts the shocking armies closed,
> To lances lances, shields to shields opposed;
> Host against host the shadowy legions drew,
> The sounding darts, an iron tempest, flew;
> Victors and vanquish'd join promiscuous cries,
> Triumphing shouts and dying groans arise,
> With streaming blood the slippery field is dyed,
> And slaughter'd heroes swell the dreadful tide.

In this passage we may observe how the writer, inflamed with the subject, insensibly advances from the past time to the present; led to that form ot narration by conceiving every circumstance as passing in his own sight: which at the same time has a fine effect upon the reader, by presenting things to him as a spectator. But change from the past to the present requires some preparation, and is not sweet where there is no stop in the sense: witness the following passage:

> Thy fate was next, O Phæstus! doom'd to feel
> The great Idomeneus' protended steel;
> Whom Borus sent (his son and only joy)
> From fruitful Tarne to the fields of Troy.
> The Cretan jav'lin reach'd him from afar,
> And pierced his shoulder as he *mounts* his car.—*Iliad*, v. 57.

It is still worse to fall back to the past in the same period; for that is an anticlimax in description:

> Through breaking ranks his furious course he bends,
> And at the goddess his broad lance extends:
> Through her bright veil the daring weapon drove,
> Th' ambrosial veil, which all the graces wove:
> Her snowy hand the razing steel profaned,
> And the transparent skin with crimson stain'd.—*Iliad*, v. 415.

Again, describing the shield of Jupiter:

> Here all the Terrors of grim war appear,
> Here rages Force, here tremble Flight and Fear,
> Here storm'd Contention, and here Fury frown'd,
> And the dire orb portentous Gorgon crown'd.—*Iliad*, v. 914.

Nor is it pleasant to be carried backward and forward alternately in a rapid succession:

> Then died Scamandrius, expert in the chace,
> In woods and wilds to wound the savage race;
> Diana taught him all her sylvan arts,
> To bend the bow and aim unerring darts:
> But vainly here Diana's arts he tries,
> The fatal lance arrests him as he flies;
> From Menelaus' arm the weapon sent,
> Through his broad back and heaving bosom went:
> Down sinks the warrior with a thund'ring sound,
> His brazen armor rings against the ground.—*Iliad*, v. 65.

---

121. The effect, in language, of describing a past event as present. Example.—Caution in changing from the past to the present. Example from the Iliad.—The effect of falling back again to the past in the same period. Examples from the Iliad.—The effect of being carried backward and forward alternately in rapid succession

122. It is wonderful to observe, upon what slight foundations Nature erects some of her most solid and magnificent works. In appearance at least, what can be more slight than ideal presence? And yet from it is derived that extensive influence which language hath over the heart; an influence which, more than any other means, strengthens the bond of society, and attracts individuals from their private system to perform acts of generosity and benevolence. Matters of fact, it is true, and truth in general, may be inculcated without taking advantage of ideal presence; but without it, the finest speaker or writer would in vain attempt to move any passion: our sympathy would be confined to objects that are really present; and language would lose entirely its signal power of making us sympathize with beings removed at the greatest distance of time as well as of place. Nor is the influence of language, by means of ideal presence, confined to the heart: it reacheth also the understanding, and contributes to belief. For when events are related in a lively manner, and every circumstance appears as passing before us, we suffer not patiently the truth of the facts to be questioned. An historian, accordingly, who hath a genius for narration, seldom fails to engage our belief. The same facts related in a manner cold and indistinct, are not suffered to pass without examination: a thing ill described is like an object seen at a distance, or through a mist; we doubt whether it be a reality or a fiction. Cicero says, that to relate the manner in which an event passed, not only enlivens the story, but makes it appear more credible. For that reason, a poet who can warm and animate his reader, may employ bolder fictions than ought to be ventured by an inferior genius: the reader once thoroughly engaged, is susceptible of the strongest impressions. A masterly painting has the same effect: Le Brun is no small support to Quintus Curtius; and among the vulgar in Italy, the belief of scripture history is, perhaps, founded as much upon the authority of Raphael, Michael Angelo, and other celebrated painters, as upon that of the sacred writers.

123. From the foregoing theory are derived many useful rules in criticism, which shall be mentioned in their proper places. One specimen shall be our present entertainment. Events that surprise by being unexpected, and yet are natural, enliven greatly an epic poem: but in such a poem, if it pretend to copy human manners and actions, no improbable incident ought to be admitted; that is, no incident contrary to the order and course of nature. A chain of imagined incidents linked together according to the order of nature, finds easy admittance into the mind; and a lively narrative of such incidents occasions complete images, or in other words, ideal presence: but our judgment revolts against an improbable incident;

---

122. The advantages to a speaker or writer in making use of ideal presence. Its influence not only on the heart, but on the understanding.—The support which animated poetry lends to fiction, and which a masterly painting lends to history.

and, if we once begin to doubt of its reality, farewell relish and concern—an unhappy effect; for it will require more than an ordinary effort to restore the waking dream, and to make the reader conceive even the more probable incidents as passing in his presence.

I never was an admirer of machinery in an epic poem, and I now find my taste justified by reason; the foregoing argument concluding still more strongly against imaginary beings, than against improbable facts: fictions of that nature may amuse by their novelty and singularity; but they never move the sympathetic passions, because they cannot impose on the mind any perception of reality. I appeal to the discerning reader, whether that observation be not applicable to the machinery of Tasso and of Voltaire: such machinery is not only in itself cold and uninteresting, but gives an air of fiction to the whole composition. A burlesque poem, such as the Lutrin or the Dispensary, may employ machinery with success; for these poems, though they assume the air of history, give entertainment chiefly by their pleasant and ludicrous pictures, to which machinery contributes: it is not the aim of such a poem to raise our sympathy; and for that reason a strict imitation of nature is not required. A poem professedly ludicrous, may employ machinery to great advantage; and the more extravagant the better.

124. Having assigned the means by which fiction commands our passions, what only remains for accomplishing our present task is to assign the final cause. I have already mentioned, that fiction, by means of language, has the command of our sympathy for the good of others. By the same means, our sympathy may also be raised for our own good. In the fourth section of the present chapter, it is observed, that examples both of virtue and of vice raise virtuous emotions; which becoming stronger by exercise, tend to make us virtuous by habit, as well as by principle. I now further observe, that examples confined to real events are not so frequent as without other means to produce a habit of virtue: if they be, they are not recorded by historians. It therefore shows great wisdom to form us in such a manner as to be susceptible of the same improvement from fable that we receive from genuine history. By that contrivance, examples to improve us in virtue may be multiplied without end: no other sort of discipline contributes more to make virtue habitual, and no other sort is so agreeable in the application. I add another final cause with thorough satisfaction; because it shows that the Author of our nature is not less kindly provident for the happiness of his creatures, than for the regularity of their conduct. The power that fiction hath over the mind affords an endless variety of refined amusements always at hand to employ a vacant hour.

---

123. One useful rule in criticism upon epic poetry, derived from the foregoing theory; —as to the incidents to be introduced.—Objections to the use of machinery in an epic poem. What is meant here by machinery.—What sort of poem may employ machinery to advantage.

such amusements are a fine resource in solitude; and, by cheering and sweetening the mind, contribute mightily to social happiness.

[To the above remarks of Lord Kames, it seems important to add, that they give but a partial, and what might prove a hurtful, view of an important subject. He gives no intimation that a large proportion of novels is adapted to corrupt the sentiments of the mind and the affections of the heart: he writes as if all novels were unexceptionable in their moral tendency; but since his day, nearly a century ago, it is painful to reflect what polluting streams of fiction have flowed from the press. Hence Lord Kames' remarks must be taken as true only within certain limits—on the supposition that the works of fiction are of good moral tendency.

It is (says Dr. Beattie in his Moral Science) the duty of poets, and other writers of fiction, to cherish, by means of sympathy, in those who read them, those affections only which invigorate the mind and are favorable to virtue, as patriotism, valor, benevolence, piety, and the conjugal, parental, and filial charities. Scenes of exquisite distress, too long continued, enervate and overwhelm the soul; and those representations are still more blamable, which kindle licentious passion, or promote indolence, affectation, or sensuality. Of the multitude of novels now published, it is astonishing and most provoking to consider how few are not chargeable with one or other of these faults, or with them all in conjunction.

In another place he remarks further:—To contract a habit of reading romances is extremely dangerous. They who do so lose all relish for history, philosophy, and other useful knowledge; acquire a superficial and frivolous way of thinking, and never fail to form false notions of life, which come to be very hurtful to young people when they go out into the world. I speak not rashly, but with too much evidence, when I affirm, that many young persons of both sexes have, by reading romances, been ruined; and that many of the follies, and not a few of the crimes, now prevalent, may be traced to the same source.]

PART II.

EMOTIONS AND PASSIONS, AS PLEASANT AND PAINFUL, AGREEABLE AND DISAGREEABLE.—MODIFICATIONS OF THESE QUALITIES

125. GREAT obscurity may be observed among writers with regard to the present point: particularly no care is taken to distinguish

---

124. The final cause (or design) of our being so constituted as to have our passions moved by fiction.—The good effects that may be secured by fiction.—Strictures upon Lord Kames' remarks.—Dr. Beattie's observations.

agreeable from pleasant, disagreeable from painful; or rather these terms are deemed synonymous. This is an error not at all venial in the science of ethics; as instances can and shall be given, of painful passions that are agreeable, and of pleasant passions that are disagreeable. These terms, it is true, are used indifferently in familiar conversation, and in compositions for amusement; but greater accuracy is required from those who profess to explain the passions.

I shall endeavor to explain these terms by familiar examples. Viewing a fine garden, I perceive it to be beautiful or agreeable; and I consider the beauty or agreeableness as belonging to the object, or as one of its qualities. When I turn my attention from the garden to what passes in my mind, I am conscious of a pleasant emotion, of which the garden is the cause: the pleasure here is felt, as a quality, not of the garden, but of the emotion produced by it. I give an opposite example. A rotten carcass is disagreeable, and raises in the spectator a painful emotion: the disagreeableness is a quality of the object; the pain is a quality of the emotion produced by it. In a word, agreeable and disagreeable are qualities of the objects we *perceive;* pleasant and painful are qualities of the emotions we *feel:* the former qualities are perceived as adhering to objects; the latter are felt as existing within us.

126. But a passion or emotion, besides being felt, is frequently made an object of thought or reflection: we examine it; we inquire into its nature, its cause, and its effects. In that view, like other objects, it is either agreeable or disagreeable. Hence clearly appear the different significations of the terms under consideration, as applied to passion; when a passion is termed *pleasant* or *painful*, we refer to the actual feeling; when termed *agreeable* or *disagreeable*, we refer to it as an object of thought or reflection; a passion is pleasant or painful to the person in whom it exists; it is agreeable or disagreeable to the person who makes it a subject of contemplation.

In the description of emotions and passions, these terms do not always coincide: to make which evident, we must endeavor to ascertain, first, what passions and emotions are pleasant, what painful; and next, what are agreeable, what disagreeable. With respect to both, there are general rules, which, if I can trust to induction, admit not a single exception. The nature of an emotion or passion, as pleasant or painful, depends entirely on its cause: the emotion produced by an agreeable object is invariably pleasant; and the emotion produced by a disagreeable object is invariably painful. (See Part vii. of this chapter.) Thus a lofty oak, a generous action, a valuable discovery in art or science, are agreeable objects that invariably produce pleasant emotions. A stinking puddle, a

---

125 **What distinction writers have failed to make.—The meaning of agreeable and disagreeable, pleasant and painful, illustrated by the instance of a fine garden and of a rotten carcass.**

treacherous action, an irregular, ill-contrived edifice, being disagreeable objects, produce painful emotions. Selfish passions are pleasant, for they arise from self, an agreeable object or cause. A social passion directed upon an agreeable object is always pleasant; directed upon an object in distress, it is painful. (See Part vii. of this chapter.) Lastly, all dissocial passions, such as envy, resentment, malice, being caused by disagreeable objects, cannot fail to be painful.

127. A general rule for the agreeableness or disagreeableness of emotions and passions is a more difficult enterprise: it must be attempted, however. We have a sense of a common nature in every species of animals, particularly in our own; and we have a conviction that this common nature is *right*, or *perfect*, and that individuals *ought* to be made conformable to it. To every faculty, to every passion, and to every bodily member, is assigned a proper office and a due proportion: if one limb be longer than the other, or be disproportioned to the whole, it is wrong and disagreeable: if a passion deviate from the common nature, by being too strong or too weak, it is also wrong and disagreeable: but as far as comformable to common nature, every emotion and every passion is perceived by us to be right, and as it ought to be; and upon that account it must appear agreeable. That this holds true in pleasant emotions and passions, will readily be admitted: but the painful are no less natural than the other; and therefore ought not to be an exception Thus the painful emotion raised by a monstrous birth or brutal action, is no less agreeable upon reflection, than the pleasant emotion raised by a flowing river or a lofty dome; and the painful passions of grief and pity are agreeable, and applauded by all the world.

128. Another rule more simple and direct for ascertaining the agreeableness or disagreeableness of a passion as opposed to an emotion, is derived from the desire that accompanies it. If the desire be to perform a right action in order to produce a good effect, the passion is agreeable: if the desire be to do a wrong action in order to produce an ill effect, the passion is disagreeable. Thus, passions as well as actions are governed by the moral sense. These rules by the wisdom of Providence coincide: a passion that is conformable to our common nature must tend to good; and a passion that deviates from our common nature must tend to ill.

This deduction may be carried a great way farther; but to avoid intricacy and obscurity, I make but one other step. A passion which, as aforesaid, becomes an object of thought to a spectator, may have the effect to produce a passion or emotion in him; for it is natural that a social being should be affected with the passions

---

126. Passions and emotions as objects of thought or reflection.—When a passion is termed pleasant or painful, and when agreeable or disagreeable.—On what the nature of an emotion as pleasant or painful depends. Illustrations.—Selfish passions.—Social passions.—Dissocial passions.

127. Rule for determining the agreeableness or disagreeableness of emotions and passions.—Based on the sense of a common nature which we deem perfect or right.

of others. Passions or emotions thus generated, submit, in common with others, to the general law above mentioned, namely, that an agreeable object produces a pleasant emotion, and a disagreeable object a painful emotion. Thus the passion of gratitude, being to a spectator an agreeable object, produceth in him the pleasant passion of love to the grateful person; and malice being to a spectator a disagreeable object, produceth in him the painful passion of hatred to the malicious person.

129. We are now prepared for examples of pleasant passions that are disagreeable, and of painful passions that are agreeable. Self-love, as long as confined within just bounds, is a passion both pleasant and agreeable: in excess it is disagreeable, though it continues to be still pleasant. Our appetites are precisely in the same condition. Resentment, on the other hand, is, in every stage of the passion, painful; but it is not disagreeable unless in excess. Pity is always painful, yet always agreeable. Vanity, on the contrary, is always pleasant, yet always disagreeable. But however distinct these qualities are, they coincide, I acknowledge, in one class of passions: all vicious passions tending to the hurt of others, are equally painful and disagreeable.

The foregoing qualities of pleasant and painful, may be sufficient for ordinary subjects; but with respect to the science of criticism, it is necessary that we also be made acquainted with the several modifications of these qualities, with the modifications at least that make the greatest figure. Even at first view one is sensible, that the pleasure or pain of one passion differs from that of another: how distant the pleasure of revenge gratified from that of love!—so distant, as that we cannot without reluctance admit them to be any way related. That the same quality of pleasure should be so differently modified in different passions, will not be surprising, when we reflect on the boundless variety of agreeable sounds, tastes, and smells daily perceived. Our discernment reaches differences still more minute, in objects even of the same sense: we have no difficulty to distinguish different sweets, different sours, and different bitters: honey is sweet, so is sugar, and yet the one never is mistaken for the other; our sense of smelling is sufficiently acute, to distinguish varieties in sweet-smelling flowers without end. With respect to passions and emotions, their differences as to pleasant and painful have no limits; though we want acuteness of feeling for the more delicate modifications. There is here an analogy between our internal and external senses: the latter are sufficiently acute for all the useful purposes of life, and so are the former. Some persons indeed, Nature's favorites, have a wonderful acuteness of sense, which to them unfolds many a delightful scene totally hid from vulgar

---

128. Another rule for ascertaining the agreeableness or disagreeableness of a passion.—Rule for passions or emotions, generated by thinking of the passions or emotions in others.—Instances of gratitude and malice

eyes. But if such refined pleasure be confined to a small number it is however wisely ordered that others are not sensible of the defect; nor detracts it from their happiness that others secretly are more happy. With relation to the fine arts only, that qualification seems essential; and there it is termed *delicacy of taste.*

Should an author of such a taste attempt to describe all those varieties in pleasant and painful emotions which he himself feels, he would soon meet an invincible obstacle in the poverty of language: a people must be thoroughly refined, before they invent words for expressing the more delicate feelings; and for that reason, no known tongue hitherto has reached that perfection. We must therefore rest satisfied with an explanation of the more obvious modifications.

130. In forming a comparison between pleasant passions of different kinds, we conceive some of them to be *gross*, some refined. Those pleasures of external sense that are felt as at the organ of sense, are conceived to be corporeal or gross (see the Introduction): the pleasures of the eye and the ear are felt to be internal, and for that reason are conceived to be more pure and refined.

The social affections are conceived by all to be more refined than the selfish. Sympathy and humanity are universally esteemed the finest temper of mind; and for that reason, the prevalence of the social affections in the progress of society is held to be a refinement in our nature. A savage knows little of social affection, and therefore is not qualified to compare selfish and social pleasure; but a man, after acquiring a high relish for the latter, loses not thereby a taste for the former: he is qualified to judge, and he will give preference to social pleasures as more sweet and refined. In fact they maintain that character, not only in the direct feeling, but also when we make them the subject of reflection: the social passions are far more agreeable than the selfish, and rise much higher in our esteem.

131. There are differences not less remarkable among the painful passions. Some are voluntary, some involuntary: the pain of the gout is an example of the latter; grief of the former, which in some cases is so voluntary as to reject all consolation. One pain softens the temper; pity is an instance: one tends to render us savage and cruel, which is the case of revenge. I value myself upon sympathy: I hate and despise myself for envy.

Social affections have an advantage over the selfish, not only with respect to pleasure, as above explained, but also with respect to pain. The pain of an affront, the pain of want, the pain of disappointment, and a thousand other selfish pains, are cruciating and tormenting,

---

129. Examples of pleasant passions that are disagreeable, and of painful passions that are agreeable.—Self-love; appetites; resentment; pity; vanity;—all vicious passions.—Modifications of the qualities already considered.—Why should the quality of pleasure be so differently modified in different passions?—Minute differences in objects even of the same sense. Analogy here between our external and internal senses.—What is meant by delicacy of taste?

130. Pleasant passions, as gross or refined.—Pleasures of external sense.—The social affections.

and tend to a habit of peevishness and discontent. Social pains have a very different tendency: the pain of sympathy, for example, is not only voluntary, but softens my temper, and raises me in my own esteem.

Refined manners and polite behavior must not be deemed altogether artificial: men who, inured to the sweets of society, cultivate humanity, find an elegant pleasure in preferring others, and making them happy, of which the proud, the selfish, scarce have a conception.

Ridicule, which chiefly arises from pride, a selfish passion, is at best but a gross pleasure: a people, it is true, must have emerged out of barbarity before they can have a taste for ridicule; but it is too rough an entertainment for the polished and refined. Cicero discovers in Plautus a happy talent for ridicule, and a peculiar delicacy of wit; but Horace, who made a figure in the court of Augustus, where taste was considerably purified, declares against the lowness and roughness of that author's raillery. Ridicule is banished France, and is losing ground in England.

Other modifications of pleasant passions will be occasionally mentioned hereafter. Particularly the modifications of *high* and *low* are to be handled in the chapter of grandeur and sublimity; and the modifications of *dignified* and *mean*, in the chapter of dignity and grace.

PART III.

INTERRUPTED EXISTENCE OF EMOTIONS AND PASSIONS.—THEIR GROWTH AND DECAY.

132. WERE it the nature of an emotion to continue, like color and figure, in its present state till varied by some operating cause, the condition of man would be deplorable: it is ordered wisely, that emotions should more resemble another attribute of matter, namely, motion, which requires the constant exertion of an operating cause, and ceases when the cause is withdrawn. An emotion may subsist while its cause is present; and when its cause is removed, may subsist by means of an idea, though in a fainter manner; but the moment another thought breaks in and engrosses the mind, the emotion is gone, and is no longer felt: if it return with its cause, or an idea of its cause, it again vanisheth with them when other

---

131. Painful passions, as voluntary or involuntary.—Advantage of social affections over the selfish.—Refined manners.—Ridicule.

thoughts crowd in. The reason is, that an emotion or passion is connected with the perception or idea of its cause so intimately as not to have any independent existence: a strong passion, it is true, hath a mighty influence to detain its cause in the mind; but not so as to detain it forever, because a succession of perceptions or ideas is unavoidable. Further, even while a passion subsists, it seldom continues long in the same tone, but is successively vigorous and faint: the vigor of a passion depends on the impression made by its cause; and a cause makes its deepest impression when, happening to be the single interesting object, it attracts our whole attention: its impression is slighter when our attention is divided between it and other objects; and at that time the passion is fainter in proportion.

133. The growth and decay of passions and emotions, traced through all their mazes, is a subject too extensive for an undertaking like the present: I pretend only to give a cursory view of it, such as may be necessary for the purposes of criticism. Some emotions are produced in their utmost perfection, and have a very short endurance, which is the case of surprise, of wonder, and sometimes of terror. Emotions raised by inanimate objects, trees, rivers, buildings, pictures, arrive at perfection almost instantaneously; and they have a long endurance, a second view producing nearly the same pleasure with the first. Love, hatred, and some other passions, swell gradually to a certain pitch, after which they decay gradually. Envy, malice, pride, scarce ever decay. Some passions, such as gratitude and revenge, are often exhausted by a single act of gratification: other passions, such as pride, malice, envy, love, hatred, are not so exhausted, but having a long continuance, demand frequent gratification. And with respect to emotions which are quiescent because not productive of desire, their growth and decay are easily explained: an emotion caused by an inanimate object cannot naturally take longer time to arrive at maturity, than is necessary for a leisurely survey: such emotion also must continue long stationary, without any sensible decay, a second or third view of the object being nearly as agreeable as the first: this is the case of an emotion produced by a fine prospect, an impetuous river, or a towering hill: while a man remains the same, such objects ought to have the same effect upon him. Familiarity, however, hath an influence here, as it hath everywhere: frequency of view, after short intervals especially, weans the mind gradually from the object, which at last loses all relish: the noblest object in the material world, a clear and serene sky, is quite disregarded, unless perhaps after a course of bad weather. An emotion raised by human virtues, qualities, or actions, may, by reiterated views of the object, swell imperceptibly, till it become so

---

132. Emotions require the presence of an operating cause.—The same passion varies in strength at different times. Why?

vigorous as to generate desire: in that condition it must be handled as a passion.

134. As to passion, I observe, first, that when nature requires a passion to be sudden, it is commonly produced in perfection; which is the case of fear and of anger. Wonder and surprise are always produced in perfection: reiterated impressions made by their cause exhaust these passions instead of inflaming them. This will be explained in chap. vi.

In the next place, when a passion hath for its foundation an original propensity peculiar to some men, it generally comes soon to maturity: the propensity, upon presenting a proper object, is immediately enlivened into a passion; which is the case of pride, of envy, and of malice.

In the third place, the growth of love and of hatred is slow or quick according to circumstances; the good qualities of a person raise in me a pleasant emotion, which, by reiterated views, is swelled into a passion involving desire of that person's happiness: this desire, being freely indulged, works gradually a change internally, and at last produceth in me a settled habit of affection for that person now my friend. Affection thus produced operates precisely like an original propensity; for to enliven it into a passion, no more is required but the real or ideal presence of the object. The habit of aversion or of hatred is brought on in the same manner. And here I must observe, by the way, that love and hatred signify commonly affection and aversion, not passion. The bulk of our passions are indeed affection or aversion inflamed into a passion by different circumstances: the affection I bear to my son is inflamed into the passion of fear when he is in danger; becomes hope when he hath a prospect of good fortune; becomes admiration when he performs a laudable action; and shame when he commits any wrong: aversion becomes fear when there is a prospect of good fortune to my enemy; becomes hope when he is in danger; becomes joy when he is in distress; and sorrow when a laudable action is performed by him.

Fourthly, passions generally have a tendency to excess, occasioned by the following means. The mind affected by any passion is not in a proper state for distinct perception, nor for cool reflection: it hath always a strong bias to the object of an agreeable passion, and a bias no less strong against the object of a disagreeable passion. The object of love, for example, however indifferent to others, is to the lover's conviction a paragon; and of hatred, is vice itself without alloy. What less can such delusion operate, than to swell the passion beyond what it was at first? for if the seeing or conversing with

133. Growth and decay of various emotions and passions.—Emotions raised by inanimate objects. Love, hatred, &c.—Further remarks concerning emotions caused by inanimate objects.—Effect of familiarity with them.—Emotions raised by reiterated views of human virtues.

a fine woman has had the effect to carry me from indifference to love, how much stronger must her influence be, when now to my conviction she is an angel! and hatred as well as other passions must run the same course. Thus between a passion and its object there is a natural operation, resembling action and reaction in physics: a passion acting upon its object, magnifies it greatly in appearance; and this magnified object reacting upon the passion, swells and inflames it mightily.

Fifthly, the growth of some passions depends often on occasional circumstances: obstacles to gratification, for example, never fail to augment and inflame a passion, because a constant endeavor to remove an obstacle preserves the object of the passion ever in view, which swells the passion by impressions frequently reiterated. Thus the restraint of conscience, when an obstacle to love, agitates the mind and inflames the passion:

> Quod licet, ingratum est: quod non licet, acrius urit.
> Si nunquam Danaën habuisset ahenea turris,
> Non esset Danaë de Jove facta parens.
>
> *Ovid*, *Amor*. l. 2.

At the same time, the mind, distressed with the obstacles, becomes impatient for gratification, and consequently more desirous of it. Shakspeare expresses this observation finely:

> All impediments in fancy's course,
> Are motives of more fancy.

We need no better example than a lover who hath many rivals. Even the caprices of the one beloved have the effect to inflame love; these occasioning uncertainty of success, tend naturally to make the anxious lover overvalue the happiness of fruition.

135. So much upon the growth of passions: their continuance and decay come next under consideration. And, first, it is a general law of nature, That things sudden in their growth are equally sudden in their decay. This is commonly the case of anger. And with respect to wonder and surprise, which also suddenly decay another reason concurs that their causes are of short duration: novelty soon degenerates into familiarity; and the unexpectedness of an object is soon sunk in the pleasure that the object affords. Fear, which is a passion of greater importance as tending to self-preservation, is often instantaneous; and yet is of equal duration with its cause: nay, it frequently subsists after the cause is removed.

In the next place, a passion founded on a peculiar propensity, subsists generally forever; which is the case of pride, envy, and

---

134. (1.) What is said of any passion which nature requires to be sudden? (2.) What of passions founded on an original propensity peculiar to some persons? (3.) What of the growth of love and hatred? Other passions to which these, by a change of circumstances give rise; fear, hope, &c. (4.) Whence the tendency of passions to excess is occasioned.—The action and reaction between a passion and its object. (5.) Growth of passion promoted by obstructions to gratification Illustrations given.

malice: objects are never wanting to inflame the propensity into a passion.

Thirdly, it may be laid down as a general law of nature, That every passion ceases upon attaining its ultimate end. To explain that law, we must distinguish between a particular and a general end. I call a particular end what may be accomplished by a single act: a general end, on the contrary, admits acts without number; because it cannot be said, that a general end is ever fully accomplished, while the object of the passion subsists. Gratitude and revenge are examples of the first kind: the ends they aim at may be accomplished by a single act; and, when that act is performed, the passions are necessarily at an end. Love and hatred are examples of the other kind; desire of doing good or doing mischief to an individual, is a general end which admits acts without number, and which seldom is fully accomplished: therefore these passions have frequently the same duration with their objects.

Lastly, it will afford us another general view, to consider the difference between an original propensity, and affection or aversion produced by custom. The former adheres too close to the constitution ever to be eradicated; and, for that reason, the passions to which it gives birth continue during life with no remarkable diminution. The latter, which owe their birth and increment to time, owe their decay to the same cause: affection and aversion decay gradually as they grow; and accordingly hatred as well as love are extinguished by long absence. Affection decays more gradually between persons, who, living together, have daily occasion to testify mutually their good-will and kindness: and, when affection is decayed, habit supplies its place; for it makes these persons necessary to each other, by the pain of separation. (See Chapter xiv.) Affection to children hath a long endurance, longer perhaps than any other affection: its growth keeps pace with that of its objects: they display new beauties and qualifications daily, to feed and augment the affection. But whenever the affection becomes stationary, it must begin to decay; with a slow pace, indeed, in proportion to its increment. In short, man with respect to this life is a temporary being: he grows, becomes stationary, decays; and so must all his powers and passions.

---

135. The continuance and decay of passions. (1.) Law concerning those of sudden growth; anger, &c. (2.) Concerning those founded on a peculiar propensity. (3.) The cessation of a passion on attaining its ultimate end. Distinguish between particular and general end. Examples of each kind. (4.) Difference between an original propensity and an affection or aversion produced by custom.—Effect of absence.—Affection between persons living together.—Affection to children.

PART IV

COEXISTENT EMOTIONS AND PASSIONS

136. FOR a thorough knowledge of the human passions and emotions, it is not sufficient that they be examined singly and separately: as a plurality of them are sometimes felt at the same instant, the manner of their coexistence, and the effects thereby produced, ought also to be examined. This subject is extensive; and it will be difficult to trace all the laws that govern its endless variety of cases: if such an undertaking can be brought to perfection, it must be by degrees. The following hints may suffice for a first attempt.

We begin with emotions raised by different sounds, as the simplest case. Two sounds that mix, and, as it were, incorporate before they reach the ear, are said to be concordant. That each of the two sounds, even after their union, produceth an emotion of its own, must be admitted; but these emotions, like the sounds that produce them, mix so intimately as to be rather one complex emotion than two emotions in conjunction. Two sounds that refuse incorporation or mixture, are said to be discordant; and when heard at the same instant, the emotions produced by them are unpleasant in conjunction, however pleasant separately.

Similar to the emotion raised by mixed sounds is the emotion raised by an object of sight with its several qualities: a tree, for example, with its qualities of color, figure, size, &c., is perceived to be one object; and the emotion it produceth is rather one complex emotion than different emotions combined.

With respect to coexistent emotions produced by different objects of sight, it must be observed that however intimately connected such objects may be, there cannot be a concordance among them like what is perceived in some sounds. Different objects of sight, meaning objects that can exist each of them independent of the others, never mix or incorporate in the act of vision: each object is perceived as its exists separately from others; and each raiseth an emotion different from that raised by the other. And the same holds in all the causes of emotion or passion that can exist independent of each other, sounds only excepted.

137. To explain the manner in which such emotions exist, similar emotions must be distinguished from those that are dissimilar. Two emotions are said to be similar, when they tend each of them to produce the same tone of mind: cheerful emotions, however different

136. Concordant and discordant sounds, and the emotions they raise.—Emotion raised by an object of sight, with its several qualities.—Coexistent emotions produced by different objects of sight.

their causes may be, are similar; and so are those which are melancholy. Dissimilar emotions are easily explained by their opposition to what are similar: pride and humility, gayety and gloominess, are dissimilar emotions.

Emotions perfectly similar, readily combine and unite,* so as in a manner to become one complex emotion: witness the emotions produced by a number of flowers in a parterre, or of trees in a wood. Emotions that are opposite or extremely dissimilar, never combine or unite: the mind cannot simultaneously take on opposite tones; it cannot at the same instant be both joyful and sad, angry and satisfied, proud and humble: dissimilar emotions may succeed each other with rapidity, but they cannot exist simultaneously.

Between these two extremes, emotions unite more or less in proportion to the degree of their resemblance, and the degree in which their causes are connected. Thus the emotions produced by a fine landscape and the singing of birds, being similar in a considerable degree, readily unite, though their causes are little connected. And the same happens where the causes are intimately connected, though the emotions themselves have little resemblance to each other; an example of which is a loved one in distress, whose beauty gives pleasure, and her distress pain: these two emotions, proceeding from different views of the object, have very little resemblance to each other; and yet so intimately connected are their causes, as to force them into a sort of complex emotion, partly pleasant, partly painful. This clearly explains some expressions common in poetry, *a sweet distress, a pleasant pain.*

138. It was necessary to describe with some accuracy in what manner similar and dissimilar emotions coexist in the mind, in order to explain their different effects, both internal and external. This subject, though obscure, is capable to be set in a clear light; and it merits attention, not only for its extensive use in criticism, but for the nobler purpose of deciphering many intricacies in the actions of men. Beginning with internal effects, I discover two, clearly distinguishable from each other, both of them produced by pleasant emotions that are similar; of which, the one may be represented by addition in numbers, the other by harmony in sounds. Two pleasant emotions that are similar, readily unite when they are coexistent; and the pleasure felt in the union is the sum of the two pleasures: the same emotions in succession, are far from making the same figure; because the mind, at no instant of the succession, is conscious

---

* It is easier to conceive the manner of coexistence of similar emotions than to describe it. They cannot be said to mix or incorporate, like concordant sounds: their union is rather of agreement or concord; and therefore I have chosen the words in the text, not as sufficient to express clearly the manner of their coexistence, but only as less liable to exception than any other I can find.

---

137. Similar emotions to be distinguished from dissimilar. Their respective tendencies. — In what proportion emotions unite, more or less.

of more than a single emotion. This doctrine may aptly be illustrated by a landscape comprehending hills, valleys, plains, rivers, trees, &c.: the emotions produced by these several objects, being similar in a high degree, as falling in easily and sweetly with the same tone of mind, are in conjunction extremely pleasant. This multiplied effect is felt from objects even of different senses, as where a landscape is conjoined with the music of birds and odor of flowers; and results partly from the resemblance of the emotions and partly from the connection of their causes: whence it follows, that the effect must be the greatest where the causes are intimately connected and the emotions perfectly similar. The same rule is obviously applicable to painful emotions that are similar and coexistent.

139. The other pleasure arising from pleasant emotions similar and coexistent, cannot be better explained than by the foregoing example of a landscape, where the sight, hearing, and smelling are employed: besides the accumulated pleasure above mentioned, of so many different similar emotions, a pleasure of a different kind is felt from the concord of these emotions. As that pleasure resembles greatly the pleasure of concordant sounds, it may be termed the *Harmony of Emotions*. This harmony is felt in the different emotions occasioned by the visible objects; but it is felt still more sensibly in the emotions occasioned by the objects of different senses, as where the emotions of the eye are combined with those of the ear. The former pleasure comes under the rule of addition: this comes under a different rule. It is directly in proportion to the degree of resemblance between the emotions, and inversely in proportion to the degree of connection between the causes: to feel this pleasure in perfection, the resemblance between the emotions cannot be too strong, nor the connection between their causes too slight. The former condition is self-evident; and the reason of the latter is, that the pleasure of harmony is felt from various similar emotions, distinct from each other, and yet sweetly combining in the mind; which excludes causes intimately connected, for the emotions produced by them are forced into one complex emotion. This pleasure of concord or harmony, which is the result of pleasing emotions, and cannot have place with respect to those that are painful, will be further illustrated, when the emotions produced by the sound of words and their meaning are taken under consideration. (Chap. xviii. sect. 3.)

The pleasure of concord from conjoined emotions, is felt even where the emotions are not perfectly similar. Though love be a

---

138. The effects of similar and dissimilar emotions.—Two *internal* effects produced by pleasant emotions that are similar. Illustrations.

139. Concord of similar emotions produced by objects in a landscape, especially by objects of the different senses. The pleasure of this harmony, proportional to what?—Why a slight connection between the causes of the emotions increases the pleasure felt.—The pleasure of concord from conjoined emotions, even when the emotions are not perfectly similar.

pleasant passion, yet by its softness and tenderness it resembles in a considerable degree the painful passion of pity or of grief; and for that reason, love accords better with these passions than with what are gay and sprightly.

140. Next as to the effects of dissimilar emotions, which we may guess will be opposite to what are above described. Dissimilar coexistent emotions, as said above, never fail to distress the mind by the difference of their tones; from which situation a feeling of harmony never can proceed; and this holds whether the causes be connected or not. But it holds more remarkably where the causes are connected; for in that case the dissimilar emotions being forced into an unnatural union, produce an actual feeling of discord. In the next place, if we would estimate the force of dissimilar emotions coexistent, we must distinguish between their causes as connected or unconnected: and in order to compute their force in the former case, subtraction must be used instead of addition; which will be evident from what follows. Dissimilar emotions forced into union by the connection of their causes, are felt obscurely and imperfectly; for each tends to vary the tone of mind that is suited to the other; and the mind thus distracted between two objects, is at no instant in a condition to receive a deep impression from either. Dissimilar emotions proceeding from unconnected causes, are in a very different condition; for as there is nothing to force them into union, they are never felt but in succession; by which means, each hath an opportunity to make a complete impression.

This curious theory requires to be illustrated by examples. In reading the description of the dismal waste, Book I. of *Paradise Lost*, we are sensible of a confused feeling, arising from dissimilar emotions forced into union, to wit, the beauty of the description, and the horror of the object described:

> Seest thou yon dreary plain, forlorn and wild,
> The seat of desolation, void of light,
> Save what the glimmering of these livid flames
> Casts pale and dreadful?

And with respect to this and many similar passages in *Paradise Lost*, we are sensible that the emotions, being obscured by each other, make neither of them that figure they would make separately. For the same reason, ascending smoke in a calm morning, which inspires stillness and tranquillity, is improper in a picture full of violent action. A parterre, partly ornamented, partly in disorder produces a mixed feeling of the same sort. Two great armies in act to engage, mix the dissimilar emotions of grandeur and of terror.

Suppose a virtuous man has drawn on himself a great misfortune by a fault incident to human nature, and somewhat venial: the remorse he feels aggravates his distress, and consequently raises our pity to a high pitch: we at the same time blame the man; and the indignation raised by the fault he has committed, is dissimilar to pity. These two passions, however, proceeding from the same object, are forced into a sort of union: but the indignation is so slight as scarce to be felt in the mixture with pity. Subjects of this kind are of all the fittest for tragedy; but of that afterwards. (Chapter xxii.)

141. Opposite emotions are so dissimilar as not to admit any sort of union, even where they proceed from causes the most intimately connected. A succession [to an estate] opens to me by the death of a worthy man, who was my friend as well as my kinsman: when I think of my friend, I am grieved; but the succession gives me joy. These two causes are intimately connected; for the succession is the direct consequence of my friend's death: the emotions, however, being opposite, do not mix; they prevail alternately, perhaps, for a course of time, till grief for my friend's death be banished by the pleasures of opulence. A virtuous man suffering unjustly, is an example of the same kind: I pity him, and have great indignation at the author of the wrong. These emotions proceed from causes nearly connected; but, being directed to different objects, they are not forced into union: their opposition preserves them distinct, and accordingly they are found to prevail alternately.

142. I proceed to examples of dissimilar emotions arising from unconnected causes. Good and bad news of equal importance arriving at the same instant from different quarters, produce opposite emotions, the discordance of which is not felt, because they are not forced into union: they govern alternately, commonly in a quick succession, till their force be spent:

Shylock. How now, Tubal, what news from Genoa? hast thou found my daughter?

Tubal. I often came where I did hear of her, but cannot find her.

Shy. Why, there, there, there, there! a diamond gone, cost me two thousand ducats in Frankfort! the curse never fell upon our nation till now; I never felt it till now: two thousand ducats in that, and other precious, precious jewels! I would my daughter were dead at my foot, and the jewels in her ear; O, would she were hears'd at my foot and the ducats in her coffin. No news of them; why, so! and I know not what's spent in the search; why, thou loss upon loss! the thief gone with so much, and so much to find the thief; and no satisfaction, no revenge, nor no ill luck stirring but what lights o' my shoulders; no sighs but o' my breathing, no tears but o' my shedding.

Tub. Yes, other men have ill luck too; Antonio, as I heard in Genoa——

Shy. What, what, what? ill luck, ill luck?

Tub. Hath an Argosie cast away, coming from Tripolis.

Shy. I thank God, I thank God; is it true? is it true?

Tub. I spoke with some of the sailors that escaped the wreck.

Shy. I thank thee, good Tubal; good news, good news, ha, ha: where, in Genoa?

Tub. Your daughter spent in Genoa, as I heard, one night, fourscore ducats.

Shy. Thou stick'st a dagger in me; I shall never see my gold again; fourscore ducats at a sitting, fourscore ducats!

---

140. The effects of dissimilar coexistent emotions, especially when the causes are connected. The comparative force of dissimilar coexistent emotions when proceeding from connected, and when from unconnected causes. Illustrated by the description of a disma waste, in *Paradise Lost*, &c.

141. Opposite emotions, though arising from causes closely connected, do not unite Examples.

Tub. There came divers of Antonio's creditors in my company to Venice that swear he cannot choose but break.

Shy. I am glad of it; I'll plague him, I'll torture him; I am glad of it.

Tub. One of them showed me a ring that he had of your daughter for a monkey.

Shy. Out upon her! thou torturest me. Tubal, it was my Turquoise; I had it of Leah when I was a bachelor; I would not have given it for a wilderness of monkeys.

Tub. But Antonio is certainly undone.

Shy. Nay, that's true, that's very true; go, fee me an officer, bespeak him a fortnight before. I will have the heart of him, if he forfeit; for were he out of Venice, I can make what merchandise I will. Go, go, Tubal, and meet me at our synagogue; go, good Tubal; at our synagogue, Tubal.

Merchant of Venice, Act III. Sc. 1.

In the same manner, good news arriving to a man laboring under distress, occasions a vibration in his mind from the one to the other. If the emotions be unequal in force, the stronger after a conflict will extinguish the weaker. Thus the loss of a house by fire, or of a sum of money by bankruptcy, will make no figure in opposition to the birth of a long-expected son, who is to inherit an opulent fortune, after some slight vibrations the mind settles in joy, and the loss is forgot.

143. The foregoing observations will be found of great use in the fine arts. Many practical rules are derived from them, which shall afterwards be mentioned; but for instant gratification in part the reader will accept the following specimen, being an application of these observations to music. It must be premised that no disagreeable combination of sounds is entitled to the name of music; for all music is resolvable into melody and harmony, which imply agreeableness in their very conception. Sounds may be so contrived as to produce horror and several other painful feelings, which, in a tragedy or in an opera, may be introduced with advantage to accompany the representation of a dissocial or disagreeable passion. But such sounds must in themselves be disagreeable, and upon that account cannot be dignified with the name of music. Secondly, the agreeableness of vocal music differs from that of instrumental; the former, being intended to accompany words, ought to be expressive of the sentiment that they convey; but the latter, having no connection with words, may be agreeable without relation to any sentiment: harmony, properly so called, though delightful when in perfection, hath no relation to sentiment; and we often find melody without the least tincture of it. It is beyond the power of music to raise a passion or a sentiment; but it is in the power of music to raise emotions similar to what are raised by sentiments expressed in words pronounced with propriety and grace; and such music may justly be termed *sentimental.* Thirdly, in vocal music, the intimate connection of sense and sound rejects dissimilar emotions, those especially that are opposite. Similar emotions produced by the

142. Examples of dissimilar emotions arising from unconnected causes.—Good and bad news, &c.—Case where the emotions are unequal in force.

sense and the sound, go naturally into union, and at the same time are concordant or harmonious; but dissimilar emotions, forced into union by these causes intimately connected, obscure each other, and are also unpleasant by discordance.

144. These premises make it easy to determine what sort of poetical compositions are fitted for music. In general, as music in all its various tones ought to be agreeable, it never can be concordant with any composition in language expressing a disagreeable passion, or describing a disagreeable object: for here the emotions raised by the sense and by the sound are not only dissimilar but opposite; and such emotions forced into union produce always an unpleasant mixture. Music accordingly is a very improper companion for sentiments of malice, cruelty, envy, peevishness, or of any other dissocial passion; witness among a thousand King John's speech in Shakspeare, soliciting Hubert to murder Prince Arthur, which, even in the most cursory view, will appear incompatible with any sort of music. Music is a companion no less improper for the description of any disagreeable object, such as that of Polyphemus in the third book of the Æneid, or that of Sin in the second book of Paradise Lost: the horror of the object described and the pleasure of the music would be highly discordant.

145. With regard to vocal music there is an additional reason against associating it with disagreeable passions. The external signs of such passions are painful—the looks and gestures to the eye, and the tone of pronunciation to the ear: such tones therefore can never be expressed musically, for music must be pleasant, or it is not music.

On the other hand, music associates finely with poems that tend to inspire pleasant emotions: music, for example, in a cheerful tone, is perfectly concordant with every emotion in the same tone; and hence our taste for airs expressive of mirth and jollity. Sympathetic joy associates finely with cheerful music; and sympathetic pain no less finely with music that is tender and melancholy. All the different emotions of love, namely, tenderness, concern, anxiety, pain of absence, hope, fear, accord delightfully with music; and accordingly a person in love, even when unkindly treated, is soothed by music; for the tenderness of love still prevailing accords with a melancholy strain. This is finely exemplified by Shakspeare in the fourth act of *Othello*, where Desdemona calls for a song expressive of her distress. Wonderful is the delicacy of that writer's taste, which fails him not even in the most refined emotions of human nature. Melancholy music is suited to slight grief, which requires or admits consolation; but deep grief, which refuses all consolation, rejects for that reason even melancholy music.

---

143. Foregoing observations applied to music.—Three things to be premised.
144. The sort of poetical compositions fitted for music.—In what sentiments is music an improper companion; for what objects also?

Where the same person is both the actor and the singer, as in an opera, there is a separate reason why music should not be associated with the sentiments of any disagreeable passion, nor the description of any disagreeable object; which is, that such association is altogether unnatural: the pain, for example, that a man feels who is agitated with malice or unjust revenge, disqualifies him for relishing music, or any thing that is pleasing; and therefore to represent such a man, contrary to nature, expressing his sentiments in a song, cannot be agreeable to any audience of taste.

146. For a different reason music is improper for accompanying pleasant emotions of the more important kind; because these totally engross the mind, and leave no place for music, nor for any sort of amusement. In a perilous enterprise to dethrone a tyrant, music would be impertinent even where hope prevails and the prospect of success is great: Alexander attacking the Indian town, and mounting the wall, had certainly no impulse to exert his prowess in a song.

It is true that not the least regard is paid to these rules either in the French or Italian opera; and the attachment we have to operas may at first be considered as an argument against the foregoing doctrine. But the general taste for operas is no argument: in these compositions the passions are so imperfectly expressed as to leave the mind free for relishing music of any sort indifferently; and it cannot be disguised that the pleasure of an opera is derived chiefly from the music, and scarce at all from the sentiments: a happy concordance of the emotions raised by the song and by the music is extremely rare; and I venture to affirm that there is no example of it, unless where the emotion raised by the former is agreeable as well as that raised by the latter.

147. Next in order, according to the method proposed, come external effects, which lead us to passions as the causes of external effects. Two coexistent passions that have the same tendency, must be similar; they accordingly readily unite, and in conjunction have double force. This is verified by experience; from which we learn that the mind receives not impulses alternately from such passions, but one strong impulse from the whole in conjunction; and indeed it is not easy to conceive what should bar the union of passions that have all of them the same tendency.

Two passions having opposite tendencies may proceed from the same cause considered in different views. Thus a female may at once be the cause both of love and of resentment; her beauty inflames the passion of love, her cruelty or inconstancy causes resent-

---

145. Additional reason in regard to vocal music against associating it with disagreeable passions.—With what sort of poems music well associates.—The various emotions that accord with music.—Desdemona.—Case of a person who is at the same time singer and actor, as in an opera.

146. Why music is improper for accompanying pleasant emotions of the more important kind.

ment. When two such passions coexist in the same breast, the opposition of their aim prevents any sort of union, and accordingly they are not felt otherwise than in succession; the consequence of which must be, either that the passions will balance each other and prevent external action, or that one of them will prevail and accomplish its end. Guarini, in his *Pastor Fido*, describes beautifully the struggle between love and resentment directed to the same object. (Act i. Sc. 3.)

Ovid paints in lively colors the vibration of mind between two opposite passions directed to the same object. Althea had two brothers much beloved, who were unjustly put to death by her son Meleager in a fit of passion: she was strongly impelled to revenge; but the criminal was her own son. This ought to have withheld her hand; but the story is more interesting, by the violence of the struggle between resentment and maternal love. (*Met.* lib. 8. l. 445.)

In cases of this kind, one circumstance always augments the fluctuation: after balancing between two actions, a resolution to prefer one of them is an inchoated gratification of the prevailing passion, which moderates it in some degree; and that circumstance tends to give a superiority to the opposite passion: another circumstance also concurs, that this opposite passion has, by restraint, acquired in the interim some additional force.

148. Love and jealousy connected by a common object, occupy the mind alternately: when the object is considered as beautiful, love prevails: when considered as possibly unfaithful, jealousy prevails. A situation of that kind affords great scope for fluctuation of passion; which is painted to the life by several masterly hands in words as well as in colors. Shakspeare handles the same subject, but in a manner uncommon, and peculiar to himself. In Othello's soliloquy, before putting his wife to death, love and jealousy are represented, each exerting its whole force, but without any struggle. Othello was naturally inflexible; and the tenderest love could not divert him from a purpose he approved as right, not even for a moment; but every thing consistent with such a character is done to reconcile the two opposite passions: he is resolved to put her to death, but he will not shed her blood, nor so much as ruffle her skin:

> *Othello.* It is the cause, it is the cause, my soul:—
> Let me not name it to you, you chaste stars!
> It is the cause.———Yet I'll not shed her blood,
> Nor scar that whiter skin of hers than snow,
> And smooth as monumental alabaster. [*Lays down the sword.*
> Yet she must die; else she'll betray more men.
> Put out the light, and then—Put out the light!—
> If I quench thee, thou flaming minister,
> I can again thy former light restore,
> Should I repent: but once put out *thy* light,
> Thou cunning'st pattern of excelling nature,

---

147. Coexistent passions as the causes of *external* effects.—Two coexistent passions having the same tendency.—Two passions of opposite tendencies proceeding from the same cause, considered in different views. Their effect upon action. Instance from Ovid

I know not where is that Promethean heat
That can thy light relumine.——[*Sets down the taper.*
When I have pluck'd thy rose,
I cannot give it vital growth again;
It needs must wither.—I'll smell thee on the tree: [*Kissing her*
O balmy breath, that dost almost persuade
Justice to break her sword!—One more; one more;
Be thus when thou art dead, and I will kill thee,
And love thee after.——One more, that's the last;
So sweet was ne'er so fatal! I must weep,
But they are cruel tears! this sorrow's heavenly;
It strikes where it doth love.—— Act V. Sc. 6.

PART V.

INFLUENCE OF PASSION WITH RESPECT TO OUR PERCEPTIONS, OPINIONS, AND BELIEF.

149. CONSIDERING how intimately our perceptions, passions, and actions are mutually connected, it would be wonderful if they should have no mutual influence. That our actions are too much influenced by passion, is a known truth; but it is not less certain, though not so well known, that passion hath also an influence upon our perceptions, opinions, and belief. For example, the opinions we form of men and things, are generally directed by affection: an advice given by a man of figure, hath great weight; the same advice from one in a low condition is despised or neglected; a man of courage underrates danger; and to the indolent the slightest obstacle appears insurmountable.

150. There is no truth more universally known, than that tranquillity and sedateness are the proper state of mind for accurate perception and cool deliberation; and for that reason, we never regard the opinion even of the wisest man, when we discover prejudice or passion behind the curtain. Passion hath such influence over us, as to give a false light to all its objects. Agreeable passions prepossess the mind in favor of their objects, and disagreeable passions, no less against their objects: a woman is all perfection in her lover's opinion, while in the eye of a rival beauty, she is awkward and disagreeable: when the passion of love is gone, beauty vanishes with it,—nothing left of that genteel motion, that sprightly conversation, those numberless graces, which formerly, in the lover's opinion, charmed all hearts. To a zealot every one of his own sect is a saint, while the most upright of a different sect are to him children of perdition: the talent of speaking in a friend is more regarded than

---

148. Love and jealousy in relation to the same object. *Othello.*
149. Influence of passion upon our perceptions, opinions, and belief. Examples.

prudent conduct in any other. Nor will this surprise one acquainted with the world: our opinions, the result frequently of various and complicated views, are commonly so slight and wavering, as readily to be susceptible of a bias from passion.

151. With that natural bias another circumstance concurs, to give passion an undue influence on our opinions and belief; and that is a strong tendency in our nature to justify our passions as well as our actions, not to others only, but even to ourselves. That tendency is peculiarly remarkable with respect to disagreeable passions: by its influence, objects are magnified or lessened, circumstances supplied or suppressed, every thing colored and disguised, to answer the end of justification. Hence the foundation of self-deceit, where a man imposes upon himself innocently, and even without suspicion of a bias.

There are subordinate means that contribute to pervert the judgment, and to make us form opinions contrary to truth; of which I shall mention two. First, it was formerly observed, that though ideas seldom start up in the mind without connection, yet that ideas suited to the present tone of mind are readily suggested by any slight connection: the arguments for a favorite opinion are always at hand, while we often search in vain for those that cross our inclination. Second, The mind taking delight in agreeable circumstances or arguments, is deeply impressed with them; while those that are disagreeable are hurried over so as scarce to make an impression: the same argument, by being relished or not relished, weighs so differently, as in truth to make conviction depend more on passion than on reasoning. This observation is fully justified by experience: to confine myself to a single instance; the numberless absurd religious tenets that at different times have pestered the world, would be altogether unaccountable but for that irregular bias of passion.

152. We proceed to a more pleasant task, which is, to illustrate the foregoing observations by proper examples. Gratitude, when warm, is often exerted upon the children of the benefactor; especially where he is removed out of reach by death or absence. (See part i. sect. i. of the present chapter.) The passion in this case being exerted for the sake of the benefactor, requires no peculiar excellence in his children: but the practice of doing good to these children produces affection for them, which never fails to advance them in our esteem. By such means, strong connections of affection are often formed among individuals, upon the slight foundation now mentioned.

Envy is a passion, which, being altogether unjustifiable, cannot be excused but by disguising it under some plausible name. At the

---

150. The proper state of mind for accurate perception and just deliberation.—How agreeable and disagreeable passions prepossess the mind. Instance of a lover; also of a zealot.

151. Tendency to justify our own passions. Influence of such a tendency.—Two subordinate means that serve to pervert our judgment.

same time, no passion is more eager than envy, to give its object a disagreeable appearance: it magnifies every bad quality and fixes on the most humbling circumstances:

> *Cassius.* I cannot tell what you and other men
> Think of this life; but for my single self,
> I had as lief not be, as live to be
> In awe of such a thing as I, myself.
> I was born free as Cæsar, so were you;
> We both have fed as well; and we can both
> Endure the winter's cold as well as he.
> For once, upon a raw and gusty day,
> The troubled Tyber chafing with his shores,
> Cæsar says to me, Dar'st thou, Cassius, now
> Leap in with me into this angry flood,
> And swim to yonder point?—Upon the word,
> Accoutred as I was, I plunged in,
> And bid him follow; so indeed he did.
> The torrent roar'd, and we did buffet it
> With lusty sinews; throwing it aside,
> And stemming it with hearts of controversy.
> But ere we could arrive the point proposed,
> Cæsar cried, Help me, Cassius, or I sink.
> I, as Æneas, our great ancestor,
> Did from the flames of Troy upon his shoulder
> The old Anchises bear; so from the waves of Tyber
> Did I the tired Cæsar; and this man
> Is now become a god, and Cassius is
> A wretched creature, and must bend his body
> If Cæsar carelessly but nod on him.
> He had a fever when he was in Spain,
> And when the fit was on him, I did mark
> How he did shake. 'Tis true this god did shake;
> His coward lips did from their color fly,
> And that same eye whose bend doth awe the world,
> Did lose its lustre; I did hear him groan;
> Aye, and that tongue of his, that bade the Romans
> Mark him, and write his speeches in their books,
> Alas! it cried——Give me some drink, Titinius,——
> As a sick girl. Ye gods, it doth amaze me,
> A man of such a feeble temper should
> So get a start of this majestic world,
> And bear the palm alone.—*Julius Cæsar*, Act I. Sc. 3.

Gloster, inflamed with resentment against his son Edgar, could even force himself into a momentary conviction that they were not related:

> O strange fasten'd villain!
> Would he deny his letter?—I never got him.
> *King Lear*, Act II. Sc. 3.

153. When by great sensibility of heart, or other means, grief becomes immoderate, the mind, in order to justify itself, is prone to magnify the cause: and if the real cause admit not of being magnified, the mind seeks a cause for its grief in imagined future events:

> *Busby.* Madam, your Majesty is much too sad;
> You promised when you parted with the King,
> To lay aside self-harming heaviness,
> And entertain a cheerful disposition.

---

152. Operation of gratitude: often productive of affection.—Envy, how excused. Its action towards its objects.—Speech of *Cassius.*

Queen. To please the King, I did; to please myself,
I cannot do it. Yet I know no cause
Why I should welcome such a guest as grief;
Save bidding farewell to so sweet a guest
As my sweet Richard: yet again, methinks,
Some unborn sorrow, ripe in Fortune's womb,
Is coming tow'rd me; and my inward soul
With something trembles, yet at nothing grieves,
More than with parting from my lord the king.
Richard II. Act II. Sc. 5.

Resentment at first is vented on the relations of the offender, in order to punish him: but as resentment, when so outrageous, is contrary to conscience, the mind, to justify its passion, is disposed to paint these relations in the blackest colors; and it comes at last to be convinced, that they ought to be punished for their own demerits.

Anger raised by an accidental stroke upon a tender part of the body is sometimes vented upon the undesigning cause. But as the passion in that case is absurd, and as there can be no solid gratification in punishing the innocent, the mind, prone to justify as well as to gratify its passion, deludes itself into a conviction of the action's being voluntary. The conviction, however, is but momentary: the first reflection shows it to be erroneous; and the passion vanisheth almost instantaneously with the conviction. But anger, the most violent of all passions, has still greater influence: it sometimes forces the mind to personify a stock or a stone, if it happen to occasion bodily pain, and even to believe it a voluntary agent, in order to be a proper object of resentment. And that we have really a momentary conviction of its being a voluntary agent, must be evident from considering, that, without such conviction, the passion can neither be justified nor gratified: the imagination can give no aid; for a stock or a stone imagined sensible, cannot be an object of punishment, if the mind be conscious that it is an imagination merely without any reality. Of such personification, involving a conviction of reality, there is one illustrious instance. When the first bridge of boats over the Hellespont was destroyed by a storm, Xerxes fell into a transport of rage, so excessive, that he commanded the sea to be punished with 300 stripes, and a pair of fetters to be thrown into it, enjoining the following words to be pronounced: "O thou salt and bitter water! thy master hath condemned thee to this punishment for offending him without cause; and is resolved to pass over thee in despite of thy insolence: with reason all men neglect to sacrifice to thee, because thou art both disagreeable and treacherous." (Herodotus, Book vii.)

154. Shakspeare exhibits beautiful examples of the irregular influence of passion in making us believe things to be otherwise than

---

153. Immoderate grief justifies itself, how?—When entertained towards the relatives of an offender, how resentment justifies itself.—Anger, raised by an accidental stroke, how attempted to be justified?—Xerxes and the Hellespont.

they are. King Lear, in his distress, personifies the rain, wind, and thunder; and in order to justify his resentment, believes them to be taking part with his daughters:

> *Lear.* Rumble thy bellyfull, spit fire, spout rain!
> Nor rain, wind, thunder, fire, are my daughters.
> I tax not you, you elements, with unkindness;
> I never gave you kingdoms, call'd you children;
> You owe me no subscription. Then let fall
> Your horrible pleasure.——Here I stand, your slave;
> A poor, infirm, weak, and despised old man!
> But yet I call you servile ministers,
> That have with two pernicious daughters join'd
> Your high-engender'd battles, 'gainst a head
> So old and white as this. Oh! oh! 'tis foul!
> Act III. Sc. 2.

King Richard, full of indignation against his favorite horse for carrying Bolingbroke, is led into the conviction of his being rational:

> *Groom.* O, how it yearn'd my heart, when I beheld
> In London streets that coronation day,
> When Bolingbroke rode on Roan Barbary,
> That horse that thou so often hast bestrid,
> That horse that I so carefully have dress'd.
> *K. Rich.* Rode he on Barbary! tell me, gentle friend,
> How went he under him?
> *Groom.* So proudly as he had disdain'd the ground.
> *K. Rich.* So proud that Bolingbroke was on his back!
> That jade had eat bread from my royal hand.
> This hand hath made him proud with clapping him.
> Would he not stumble? would he not fall down
> (Since pride must have a fall), and break the neck
> Of that proud man that did usurp his back?
> *Richard II.* Act V. Sc. 11.

Hamlet, swelled with indignation at his mother's second marriage, was strongly inclined to lessen the time of her widowhood, the shortness of the time being a violent circumstance against her; and he deludes himself by degrees into the opinion of an interval shorter than the real one:

> *Hamlet.* ———— That it should come to this!
> But two months dead! nay, not so much; not two;—
> So excellent a king, that was to this,
> Hyperion to a satyr: so loving to my mother,
> That he permitted not the winds of heaven
> Visit her face too roughly. Heaven and earth!
> Must I remember—why, she would hang on him,
> As if increase of appetite had grown
> By what it fed on; yet, within a month,—
> Let me not think—Frailty, thy name is *Woman!*
> A little month! or ere these shoes were old,
> With which she follow'd my poor father's body,
> Like Niobe, all tears——Why she, e'en she——
> (O heav'n! a beast that wants discourse of reason,
> Would have mourn'd longer)—married with mine uncle,
> My father's brother: but no more like my father,
> Than I to Hercules. Within a month!——
> Ere yet the salt of most unrighteous tears
> Had left the flushing in her gauled eyes.

She married——Oh, most wicked speed, to post
With such dexterity to incestuous sheets!
It is not, nor it cannot come to good.
But break, my heart, for I must hold my tongue. Act I. Sc 3.

The power of passion to falsify the computation of time is remarkable in this instance; because time, which hath an accurate measure, is less obsequious to our desires and wishes, than objects which have no precise standard of less or more.

155. Good news is greedily swallowed upon very slender evidence: our wishes magnify the probability of the event, as well as the veracity of the relater; and we believe as certain, what at best is doubtful:

Quel, che l'huom vede, amor li fa invisible
El l'invisibil fa veder amore
Questo creduto fu, che 'l miser suole
Dar facile credenza a' quel, che vuole.
Orland. Furios. Cant. I. St. 56.

For the same reason, bad news gains also credit upon the slightest evidence: fear, if once alarmed, has the same effect with hope, to magnify every circumstance that tends to conviction. Shakspeare, who shows more knowledge of human nature than any of our philosophers, hath in his *Cymbeline* (Act ii. Sc. 6) represented this bias of the mind; for he makes the person who alone was affected with the bad news, yield to evidence that did not convince any of his companions. And Othello (Act iii. Sc. 8) is convinced of his wife's infidelity from circumstances too light to move any person less interested.

If the news interest us in so low a degree as to give place to reason, the effect will not be altogether the same: judging of the probability or improbability of the story, the mind settles in a rational conviction either that it is true or not. But, even in that case, the mind is not allowed to rest in that degree of conviction which is produced by rational evidence: if the news be in any degree favorable, our belief is raised by hope to an improper height; and if unfavorable, by fear.

This observation holds equally with respect to future events: if a future event be either much wished or dreaded, the mind never fails to augment the probability beyond truth.

156. That easiness of belief with respect to wonders and prodigies, even the most absurd and ridiculous, is a strange phenomenon; because nothing can be more evident than the following proposition, that the more singular an event is, the more evidence is required to produce belief; a familiar event daily occurring, being in itself extremely probable, finds ready credit, and therefore is vouched by the slightest evidence; but to overcome the improbability of a

---

154. Examples, where passion makes us believe things to be otherwise than they are.—From *King Lear*, &c.

155. Why are good news and bad news received upon slight evidence? Examples —Belief of future events.

strange and rare event, contrary to the course of nature, the very strongest evidence is required. It is certain, however, that wonders and prodigies are swallowed by the vulgar, upon evidence that would not be sufficient to ascertain the most familiar occurrence. It has been reckoned difficult to explain that irregular bias of mind; but we are now made acquainted with the influence of passion upon opinion and belief: a story of ghosts or fairies, told with an air of gravity and truth, raiseth an emotion of wonder, and perhaps of dread; and these emotions imposing upon a weak mind, impress upon it a thorough conviction contrary to reason.

Opinion and belief are influenced by propensity as well as by passion. An innate propensity is all we have to convince us, that the operations of nature are uniform: influenced by that propensity, we often rashly think that good or bad weather will never have an end; and in natural philosophy, writers, influenced by the same propensity, stretch commonly their analogical reasonings beyond just bounds.

Opinion and belief are influenced by affection as well as by propensity. The noted story of a fine lady and a curate viewing the moon through a telescope, is a pleasant illustration: I perceive, says the lady, two shadows inclining to each other; they are certainly two happy lovers. Not at all, replies the curate, they are two steeples of a cathedral.

APPENDIX TO PART V.

Methods that Nature hath afforded for computing Time and Space.

157. THIS subject is introduced, because it affords several curious examples of the influence of passion to bias the mind in its conceptions and opinions; a lesson that cannot be too frequently inculcated, as there is not, perhaps, another bias in human nature that hath an influence so universal to make us wander from truth as well as from justice.

The question is, What was the measure of time before artificial measures were invented; and what is the measure at present, when these are not at hand? I speak not of months and days, which are computed by the moon and sun; but of hours, or in general of the time that passes between any two occurrences when there is not access to the sun. The only natural measure is the succession of our thoughts; for we always judge the time to be long or short, in pro-

---

156. Facility of belief with respect to wonders: how explained.—Opinion and belief influenced by propensity; e. g. to believe the uniformity of nature's operations.—Opinion and belief influenced by affection.—Story of the lady and the curate.

portion to the number of perceptions and ideas that have passed during that interval. This measure is indeed far from being accurate; because in a quick and in a slow succession, it must evidently produce different computations of the same time: but, however inaccurate, it is the only measure by which we naturally calculate time; and that measure is applied, on all occasions, without regard to any casual variation in the rate of succession.

That measure would, however, be tolerable, did it labor under no other imperfection besides that mentioned: but in many instances it is much more fallacious; in order to explain which distinctly, an analysis will be necessary. Time is computed at two different periods; one while it is passing, another after it is past: these computations shall be considered separately, with the errors to which each of them is liable. Beginning with computation of time while it is passing, it is a common and trite observation, That to lovers absence appears immeasurably long, every minute an hour, and every day a year: the same computation is made in every case where we long for a distant event; as where one is in expectation of good news, or where a profligate heir watches for the death of an old rich miser. Opposite to these are instances not fewer in number: to a criminal the interval between sentence and execution appears woefully short; and the same holds in every case where one dreads an approaching event; of which even a school-boy can bear witness: the hour allowed him for play, moves, in his apprehension, with a very swift pace; before he is thoroughly engaged, the hour is gone. Among the circumstances that terrify a condemned criminal, the short time he has to live is one; which time, by the influence of terror, is made to appear still shorter than it is in reality. In the same manner among the distresses of an absent lover, the time of separation is a capital circumstance, which for that reason is greatly magnified by his anxiety and impatience: he imagines that the time of meeting comes on very slow, or rather that it will never come: every minute is thought of an intolerable length. Here is a fair, and, I hope, satisfactory reason, why time is thought to be tedious when we long for a future event, and not less fleet when we dread the event. The reason is confirmed by other instances. Bodily pain, fixed to one part, produceth a slow train of perceptions, which, according to the common measure of time, ought to make it appear short: yet we know, that, in such a state, time has the opposite appearance; and the reason is, that bodily pain is always attended with a degree of impatience, which makes us think every minute to be an hour. The same holds where the pain shifts from place to place; but not so remarkably, because such a pain is not attended with the same degree

---

157. The natural measure of time.—Its inaccuracy.—Time computed (1) when it is passing. Instance of absent lovers; of longing for a distant event. Opposite instances.—When an approaching event is dreaded.—The computation of time while suffering bodily pain: also in travelling a bad road.

of impatience. The impatience a man hath in travelling through a barren country, or in a bad road, makes him think, during the journey, that time goes on with a very slow pace. We shall see afterwards, that a very different computation is made when the journey is over.

158. How ought it to stand with a person who apprehends bad news? It will probably be thought that the case of this person resembles that of a criminal, who, terrified at his approaching execution, believes every hour to be but a minute: yet the computation is directly opposite. Reflecting upon the difficulty, there appears one capital distinguishing circumstance: the fate of the criminal is determined; in the case under consideration, the person is still in suspense. Every one has felt the distress that accompanies suspense: we wish to get rid of it at any rate, even at the expense of bad news. This case, therefore, upon a more narrow inspection, resembles that of bodily pain: the present distress, in both cases, makes the time appear extremely tedious.

The reader probably will not be displeased, to have this branch of the subject illustrated, by an author who is acquainted with every maze of the human heart, and who bestows ineffable grace and ornament upon every subject he handles:

Rosalinda. I pray you, what is't a-clock?
Orlando. You should ask me, what time o' day; there's no clock in the forest.
Ros. Then there is no true lover in the forest; else, sighing every minute, and groaning every hour, would detect the lazy foot of Time, as well as a clock.
Orla. And why not the swift foot of Time? Had not that been as proper?
Ros. By no means, Sir. Time travels in divers paces with divers persons. I'll tell you who Time ambles withal, who Time trots withal, who Time gallops withal, and who he stands still withal?
Orla. I pr'ythee whom doth he trot withal?
Ros. Marry, he trots hard with a young maid between the contract of her marriage and the day it is solemnized: if the interim be but a se'ennight, Time's pace is so hard, that it seems the length of seven year.
Orla. Who ambles Time withal?
Ros. With a priest that lacks Latin, and a rich man that hath not the gout, for the one sleeps easily, because he cannot study; the other lives merrily, because he feels no pain: the one lacking the burthen of lean and wasteful learning; the other knowing no burthen of heavy tedious penury. These Time ambles withal.
Orla. Who doth he gallop withal?
Ros. With a thief to the gallows: for, though he go as softly as foot can fall, he thinks himself too soon there.
Orla. Who stays it still withal?
Ros. With lawyers in the vacation: for they sleep between term and term, and then they perceive not how Time moves.—*As You Like It*, Act III. Sc. 8.

159. The natural method of computing present time, shows how far from the truth we may be led by the irregular influence of passion; nor are our eyes immediately opened when the scene is past; for the deception continues while there remain any traces of the passion. But looking back upon past time when the joy or distress

158. Computation by a person who apprehends bad news.—How this case differs from that of a criminal approaching the time of execution.

is no longer remembered, the computation is very different: in that condition we coolly and deliberately make use of the ordinary measure, namely, the course of our perceptions. And I shall now proceed to the errors that this measure is subjected to. Here we must distinguish between a train of perceptions and a train of ideas: real objects make a strong impression, and are faithfully remembered: ideas, on the contrary, however entertaining at the time, are apt to escape a subsequent recollection. Hence it is, that in retrospection, the time that was employed upon real objects, appears longer than that employed upon ideas: the former are more accurately recollected than the latter; and we measure the time by the number that is recollected. This doctrine shall be illustrated by examples After finishing a journey through a populous country, the frequency of agreeable objects distinctly recollected by the traveller, makes the time spent in the journey appear to him longer than it was in reality; which is chiefly remarkable in the first journey, when every object is new, and makes a strong impression. On the other hand, after finishing a journey through a barren country thinly peopled, the time appears short, being measured by the number of objects, which were few, and far from interesting. Here in both instances a computation is made, directly opposite to that made during the journey. And this, by the way, serves to account for what may appear singular, that, in a barren country, a computed mile is always longer than near the capital, where the country is rich and populous: the traveller has no natural measure of the miles he has travelled, other than the time bestowed upon the journey; nor any natural measure of the time, other than the number of his perceptions: now these, being few from the paucity of objects in a waste country, lead him to compute that the time has been short, and consequently that the miles have been few: by the same method of computation, the great number of perceptions, from the quantity of objects in a populous country, make the traveller conjecture that the time has been long, and the miles many. The last step of the computation is obvious: in estimating the distance of one place from another, if the miles be reckoned few in number, each mile must of course be long: if many in number, each must be short.

160. Again, the travelling with an agreeable companion, produceth a short computation both of the road and of time; especially if there be few objects that demand attention, or if the objects be familiar: and the case is the same of young people at a ball, or of a joyous company over a bottle: the ideas with which they have been entertained, being transitory, escape the memory: after the journey and the entertainment are over, they reflect that they have been much diverted, but scarce can say about what.

---

159. (2.) When the time of an event has passed; how we compute.—The retrospection of time employed upon real objects, and upon ideas. Examples.—Computation of distance and of time in passing through a populous country; and through a barren one.

When one is totally occupied with any agreeable work that admits not many objects, time runs on without observation; and upon a subsequent recollection, must appear short, in proportion to the paucity of objects. This is still more remarkable in close contemplation and in deep thinking, where the train, composed wholly of ideas, proceeds with an extreme slow pace: not only are the ideas few in number, but are apt to escape an after reckoning. The like false reckoning of time may proceed from an opposite state of mind: in a reverie, where ideas float at random without making any impression, time goes on unheeded, and the reckoning is lost. A reverie may be so profound as to prevent the recollection of any one idea: that the mind was busied in a train of thinking may in general be remembered; but what was the subject, has quite escaped the memory. In such a case we are altogether at a loss about the time, having no *data* for making a computation. No cause produceth so false a reckoning of time as immoderate grief: the mind. in that state, is violently attached to a single object, and admits not a different thought: any other object breaking in, is instantly banished, so as scarce to give an appearance of succession. In a reverie, we are uncertain of the time that is past; but, in the example now given, there is an appearance of certainty, that the time must have been short, when the perceptions are so few in number.

PART VI.

THE RESEMBLANCE OF EMOTIONS TO THEIR CAUSES.

161. THAT many emotions have some resemblance to their causes is a truth that can be made clear by induction; though, as far as I know, the observation has not been made by any writer. Motion, in its different circumstances, is productive of feelings that resemble it: sluggish motion, for example, causeth a languid, unpleasant feeling; slow uniform motion, a feeling calm and pleasant; and brisk motion, a lively feeling that rouses the spirits and promotes activity. A fall of water through rocks raises in the mind a tumultuous confused agitation, extremely similar to its cause. When force is exerted with any effort, the spectator feels a similar effort, as of

---

160. Computation of road and time when travelling with an agreeable companion.—Computation of time passed at a ball; or when occupied with any agreeable work, admitting few objects; after a process of deep thinking; after a reverie; false reckoning arising from immoderate grief.

161. Emotions resemble their causes.—Effect on the mind of various degrees of motion and of force.—View of a large object; of an elevated one.

force exerted within his mind. A large object swells in the heart: an elevated object makes the spectator stand erect.

162. Sounds also produce emotions, or feelings that resemble them. A sound in a low key brings down the mind such a sound in a full tone hath a certain solemnity, which it communicates to the feeling produced by it. A sound in a high key cheers the mind by raising it: such a sound in a full tone both elevates and swells the mind.

Again, a wall or pillar that declines from the perpendicular produceth a painful feeling, as of a tottering and falling within the mind; and a feeling somewhat similar is produced by a tall pillar that stands so ticklish as to look like falling. A column with a base looks more firm and stable than upon the naked ground, and for that reason is more agreeable; and though the cylinder is a more beautiful figure, yet the cube for a base is preferred, its angles being extended to a greater distance from the centre than the circumference of a cylinder. This excludes not a different reason, that the base, the shaft, and the capital of a pillar ought, for the sake of variety, to differ from each other: if the shaft be round, the base and capital ought to be square.

A constrained posture, uneasy to the man himself, is disagreeable to the spectator; whence a rule in painting, that the drapery ought not to adhere to the body, but hang loose, that the figures may appear easy and free in their movements. The constrained posture of a French dancing-master in one of Hogarth's pieces is for that reason disagreeable; and it is also ridiculous, because the constraint is assumed as a grace.

163. The foregoing observation is not confined to emotions or feelings raised by still life: it holds also in what are raised by the qualities, actions, and passions of a sensible being. Love, inspired by a fine woman, assumes her qualities: it is sublime, soft, tender, severe, or gay, according to its cause. This is still more remarkable in emotions raised by human actions: it hath already been remarked, that any single instance of gratitude, besides procuring esteem for the author, raiseth in the spectator a vague emotion of gratitude, which disposeth him to be grateful; and I now further remark, that this vague emotion hath a strong resemblance to its cause, namely, the passion that produced the grateful action. Courage exerted inspires the reader as well as the spectator with a like emotion of courage; a just action fortifies our love of justice, and a generous action rouses our generosity. In short, with respect to all virtuous actions, it will be found by induction, that they lead us to imitation, by inspiring emotions resembling the passions that pro-

---

162. Emotions produced by various sounds; also by a view of a wall or pillar declining from a perpendicular.—Column resting on a base or on the ground.—Proper form of the base of a column.—A constrained posture disagreeable. Hence a rule in painting.

163. Emotions raised by the qualities, actions, and passions of a sensible being.—Effect of observing or reading of an instance of gratitude, &c. Practical inference.

duceth these actions. And hence the advantage of choice books and choice company.

164. Grief as well as joy is infectious: the emotions they raise in a spectator resemble them perfectly. Fear is equally infectious; and hence in an army, a few taking fright, even without cause, spread the infection till it becomes a universal panic. Pity is similar to its cause; a parting scene between lovers or friends produceth in the spectator a sort of pity, which is tender like the distress; the anguish of remorse produceth pity of a harsh kind; and if the remorse be extreme, the pity hath a mixture of horror. Anger I think is singular; for even where it is moderate, and causeth no disgust, it disposeth not the spectator to anger in any degree. Covetousness, cruelty, treachery, and other vicious passions, are so far from raising any emotion similar to themselves, to incite a spectator to imitation, that they have an opposite effect: they raise abhorrence, and fortify the spectator in his aversion to such actions. When anger is immoderate, it cannot fail to produce the same effect

---

PART VII.

FINAL CAUSES OF THE MORE FREQUENT EMOTIONS AND PASSIONS.

165. It is a law in our nature, that we never act but by the impulse of desire; which in other words is saying, that passion, by the desire included in it, is what determines the will. Hence in the conduct of life, it is of the utmost importance that our passions be directed to proper objects, tend to just and rational ends, and with relation to each other be duly balanced. The beauty of contrivance, so conspicuous in the human frame, is not confined to the rational part of our nature, but is visible over the whole. Concerning the passions in particular, however irregular, headstrong, and perverse, in a slight view, they may appear, I hope to demonstrate that they are by nature modelled and tempered with perfect wisdom, for the good of society as well as for private good.

In order to fulfil my engagement, it must be premised, that an agreeable cause produceth always a pleasant emotion; and a disagreeable cause, a painful emotion. This is a general law of nature which admits not a single exception: agreeableness in the cause is indeed so essentially connected with pleasure in the emotion, its effect, that an agreeable cause cannot be better defined, than by its

---

164. Remarks on grief and joy; fear; pity; anger; covetousness; cruelty, and other vicious passions

power of producing a pleasant emotion; and disagreeableness in the cause has the same necessary connection with pain in the emotion produced by it.

166. From this preliminary it appears, that in order to know for what end an emotion is made, pleasant or painful, we must begin with inquiring for what end its cause is made agreeable or disagreeable. And, with respect to inanimate objects, considered as the causes of emotions, many of them are made agreeable in order to promote our happiness; and it proves invincibly the benignity of the Deity, that we are placed in the midst of objects for the most part agreeable. But that is not all: the bulk of such objects being of real use in life, are made agreeable in order to excite our industry; witness a large tree, a well-dressed fallow, a rich field of grain, and others that may be named without end. On the other hand, it is not easy to specify a disagreeable object that is not at the same time hurtful. Some things are made disagreeable, such as a rotten carcass, because they are noxious; others, a dirty marsh, for example, or a barren heath, are made disagreeable, in order, as above, to excite our industry. And, with respect to the few things that are neither agreeable nor disagreeable, it will be made evident, that their being left indifferent is not a work of chance but of wisdom: of such I shall have occasion to give several instances.

167. Because inanimate objects that are agreeable fix our attention, and draw us to them, they in that respect are termed *attractive:* such objects inspire pleasant emotions, which are gratified by adhering to the objects and enjoying them. Because disagreeable objects of the same kind repel us from them, they in that respect are termed *repulsive;* and the painful emotions raised by such objects are gratified by flying from them. Thus, in general, with respect to things inanimate, the tendency of every pleasant emotion is to prolong the pleasure; and the tendency of every painful emotion is to end the pain.

168. Sensible beings, considered as objects of passion, lead into a more complex theory. A sensible being that is agreeable by its attributes, inspires us with a pleasant emotion accompanied with desire; and the question is, What is naturally the gratification of that desire? As man is endued with a principle of benevolence as well as of selfishness, he is prompted by his nature to desire the good of every sensible being that gives him pleasure; and the happiness of that being is the gratification of his desire. The final cause of desire so directed is illustrious: it contributes to a man's own happiness, by affording him means of gratification beyond what selfishness can afford; and, at the same time, it tends eminently to

---

165. What impels to action.—Rule in regard to our passions.—Agreeable and disagreeable cause defined.

166. Inanimate objects as causes of emotions.—Why the bulk of such objects are agreeable. Why some things are made disagreeable.

167. Why certain objects are termed attractive, others repulsive.

advance the happiness of others. This lays open a beautiful theory in the nature of man: a selfish action can only benefit myself; a benevolent action benefits myself as much as it benefits others. In a word, benevolence may not improperly be said to be the most refined selfishness; which, by the way, ought to silence certain shallow philosophers, who, ignorant of human nature, teach a disgustful doctrine—that to serve others, unless with a view to our own happiness, is weakness and folly; as if self-love only, and not benevolence, contributed to our happiness. With shallow thinkers, the selfish system naturally prevails in theory, I do not say in practice During infancy, our desires centre mostly in ourselves: every one perceives intuitively the comfort of food and raiment, of a snug dwelling, and of every convenience. But that the doing good to others will make us happy, is not so evident; feeding the hungry, for example, or clothing the naked. This truth is seen but obscurely by the gross of mankind, if at all seen: the superior pleasure that accompanies the exercise of benevolence, of friendship, and of every social principle, is not clearly understood till it be frequently felt. To perceive the social principle in its triumphant state, a man must forget himself, and turn his thoughts upon the character and conduct of his fellow-creatures: he will feel a secret charm in every passion that tends to the good of others, and a secret aversion against every unfeeling heart that is indifferent to the happiness and distress of others. In a word, it is but too common for men to indulge selfishness in themselves; but all men abhor it in others.

169. Next in order come sensible beings that are in distress. A person in distress, being so far a disagreeable object, must raise in a spectator a painful passion; and, were man purely a selfish being, he would desire to be relieved from that pain by turning from the object. But the principle of benevolence gives an opposite direction to his desire; it makes him desire to afford relief, and, by relieving the person from distress, his passion is gratified. The painful passion thus directed, is termed *sympathy;* which, though painful, is yet in its nature attractive. And, with respect to its final cause, we can be at no loss: it not only tends to relieve a fellow-creature from distress, but in its gratification is greatly more pleasant than if it were repulsive.

170. We, in the last place, bring under consideration persons hateful by vice or wickedness. Imagine a wretch who has lately perpetrated some horrid crime; he is disagreeable to every spectator, and consequently raiseth in every spectator a painful passion. What is the natural gratification of that passion? I must here again observe that, supposing man to be entirely a selfish being, he would

---

168. Sensible beings considered as objects of passion.—The final cause (or design) of desire directed to agreeable persons.—The comparative benefit of selfish and benevolent actions.—Censure upon the doctrine of certain shallow philosophers.—How we are to learn the pleasure that accompanies benevolent actions.

169. Rational beings in distress; emotions excited.—Sympathy.

be prompted by his nature to relieve himself from the pain by averting his eye and banishing the criminal from his thoughts. But man is not so constituted; he is composed of many principles, which, though seemingly contradictory, are perfectly concordant. His actions are influenced by the principle of benevolence, as well as by that of selfishness; and, in order to answer the foregoing question, I must introduce a third principle, no less remarkable in its influence than either of these mentioned: it is that principle, common to all, which prompts us to punish those who do wrong. An envious, a malicious, or a cruel action, being disagreeable, raiseth in the spectator the painful emotion of resentment, which frequently swells into a passion; and the natural gratification of the desire included in that passion is to punish the guilty person: I must chastise the wretch by indignation at least, and hatred, if not more severely. Here the final cause is self-evident.

171. An injury done to myself, touching me more than when done to others, raises my resentment to a higher degree. The desire, accordingly, included in this passion, is not satisfied with so slight a punishment as indignation or hatred: it is not fully gratified with retaliation; and the author must by my hand suffer mischief, as great at least as he has done to me. Neither can we be at any loss about the final cause of that higher degree of resentment: the whole vigor of the passion is required to secure individuals from the injustice and oppression of others.

172. A wicked or disgraceful action is disagreeable, not only to others, but even to the delinquent himself; and raises in both a painful emotion, including a desire of punishment. The painful emotion felt by the delinquent is distinguished by the name of *remorse*, which naturally excites him to punish himself. There cannot be imagined a better contrivance to deter us from vice; for remorse itself is a severe punishment. That passion, and the desire of self-punishment derived from it, are touched delicately by Terence (*Heautontimorumenos*, Act I. Sc. 1)

Otway reaches the same sentiment:

> *Monimia.* Let mischiefs multiply! let every hour
> Of my loathed life yield me increase of horror!
> Oh let the sun to these unhappy eyes
> Ne'er shine again, but be eclipsed forever!
> May every thing I look on seem a prodigy,
> To fill my soul with terror, till I quite
> Forget I ever had humanity,
> And grow a curser of the works of nature!—*Orphan*, Act IV.

173. In the cases mentioned, benevolence alone, or desire of punishment alone, governs without a rival; and it was necessary to

---

170. Persons hateful by vice. Man influenced in view of them by selfishness or by benevolence.—A third principle active in such cases. Its final cause.
171. Emotion excited by an injury done to myself. The final cause.
172. A wicked action disagreeable to the delinquent as well as to others. Emotion excited; its use.—Quotation from Otway's *Orphan*.

handle these cases separately, in order to elucidate a subject which by writers is left in great obscurity. But neither of these principles operates always without rivalship: cases may be figured, and cases actually exist, where the some person is an object both of sympathy and of punishment. Thus the sight of a profligate in the venereal disease, overrun with blotches and sores, puts both principles in motion: while his distress fixis my attention, sympathy prevails; but as soon as I think of his profligacy, hatred prevails, accompanied sometimes with a desire to punish. This, in general, is the case of distress occasioned by immoral actions that are not highly criminal; and if the distress and the immoral action make impressions equal or nearly so, sympathy and hatred, counterbalancing each other, will not suffer me either to afford relief or to inflict punishment What then will be the result? The principle of self-love solves the question: abhorring an object so loathsome, I naturally avert my eye, and walk off as fast as I can, in order to be relieved from the pain.

174. No action, right or wrong, is indifferent even to a mere spectator: if right, it inspires esteem; disgust, if wrong. But it is remarkable, that these emotions seldom are accompanied with desire: the abilities of man are limited, and he finds sufficient employment in relieving the distressed, in requiting his benefactors, and in punishing those who wrong him, without moving out of his sphere for the benefit or chastisement of those with whom he has no connection.

If the good qualities of others raise my esteem, the same qualities in myself must produce a similar effect in a superior degree, upon account of the natural partiality every man hath for himself; and this increases self-love. If these qualities be of a high rank, they produce a conviction of superiority, which excites me to assume some sort of government over others. Mean qualities, on the other hand, produce in me a conviction of inferiority, which makes me submit to others. These convictions, distributed among individuals. by measure and proportion, may justly be esteemed the solid basis of government; because upon them depend the natural submission of the many to the few, without which even the mildest government would be in a violent state, and have a constant tendency to dissolution.

175. No other branch of the human constitution shows more visibly our destination for society, nor tends more to our improvement, than appetite for fame or esteem: for as the whole conveniences of life are derived from mutual aid and support in society, it ought to be a capital aim to secure these conveni-

---

173. Cases where benevolence and desire of punishment alternately operate When they counterbalance each other, what is the result?

174. No action, right or wrong is indifferent.—Emotions raised by a view of good qualities in others: in myself. In view of mean qualities in myself.—The basis of government.

ences, by gaining the esteem and affection of others. Reason, indeed, dictates that lesson: but reason alone is not sufficient in a matter of such importance; and the appetite mentioned is a motive more powerful than reason, to be active in gaining esteem and affection. That appetite, at the same time, is finely adjusted to the moral branch of our constitution, by promoting all the moral virtues; for what means are there to attract love and esteem so effectual as a virtuous course of life?—if a man be just and beneficent, if he be temperate, modest, and prudent, he will infallibly gain the esteem and love of all who know him.*

176. Communication of passion to related objects, is an illustrious instance of the care of Providence to extend social connections as far as the limited nature of man can admit. That communication is so far hurtful, as to spread the malevolent passions beyond their natural bounds: but let it be remarked, that this unhappy effect regards savages only, who give way to malevolent passions; for under the discipline of society, these passions being subdued, are in a good measure eradicated; and in their place succeed the kindly affections, which, meeting with all encouragement, take possession of the mind, and govern all our actions. In that condition, the progress of passion along related objects, by spreading the kindly affections through a multitude of individuals, hath a glorious effect.

177. Nothing can be more entertaining to a rational mind, than the economy of the human passions, of which I have attempted to give some faint notion. It must, however, be acknowledged, that our passions, when they happen to swell beyond proper limits, take on a less regular appearance: reason may proclaim our duty, but the will, influenced by passion, makes gratification always welcome. Hence the power of passion, which, when in excess, cannot be resisted but by the utmost fortitude of mind: it is bent upon gratification; and where proper objects are wanting, it clings to any object at hand without distinction. Thus joy inspired by a fortunate event, is diffused upon every person around by acts of benevolence; and resentment for an atrocious injury done by one out of reach, seizes the first object that occurs to vent itself upon. Those who believe in prophecies, even wish the accomplishment; and a weak mind is disposed voluntarily to fulfil a prophecy, in order to gratify its wish. Shakspeare, whom no particle of human nature hath

* [The author presents here rather a low standard of moral virtue. The motive assigned may have a good effect in securing an external morality; but if moral virtues have no higher origin than a regard to human applause, they are, in the view of the Divine Law, only brilliant sins; for that requires supreme regard and love to God, as the basis of all true virtue.]

175. Tendency and uses of an appetite for fame or esteem.—Criticism on the author's views.
176. Communication of passion to related objects: in part hurtful; in part beneficial.

escaped, however remote from common observation, describes that weakness:

King Henry. Doth any name particular belong
Unto that lodging where I first did swoon?
Warwick. 'Tis call'd *Jerusalem*, my noble lord.
King Henry. Laud be to God! e'en there my life must end.
It hath been prophesied to me many years,
I should not die but in Jerusalem,
Which vainly I supposed the Holy Land.
But bear me to that chamber, there I'll lie:
In that Jerusalem shall Henry die.
Second Part, Henry IV. Act IV. Sc. last.

CHAPTER III.

BEAUTY.

178. HAVING discoursed in general of emotions and passions, I proceed to a more narrow inspection of such of them as serve to unfold the principles of the fine arts. It is the province of a writer upon ethics, to give a full enumeration of all the passions; and of each separately to assign the nature, the cause, the gratification, and the effects. But a treatise of ethics is not my province: I carry my view no farther than to the elements of criticism, in order to show, that the fine arts are a subject of reasoning as well as of taste. Instead of a painful and tedious examination of the several passions and emotions, I purpose to confine my inquiries to such attributes, relations, and circumstances, as in the fine arts are chiefly employed to raise agreeable emotions. Attributes of single objects, as the most simple, shall take the lead; to be followed with particulars, which, depending on relations, are not found in single objects. I begin with Beauty, the most noted of all the qualities that belong to single objects.

179. The term *beauty*, in its native signification, is appropriated to objects of sight: objects of the other senses may be agreeable, such as the sounds of musical instruments; the smoothness and softness of some surfaces; but the agreeableness denominated *beauty* belongs to objects of sight.

Of all the objects of external sense, an object of sight is the most complex: in the very simplest, color is perceived, figure and length, breadth and thickness. A tree is composed of a trunk, branches, and leaves; it has color, figure, size, and sometimes motion: by means of each of these particulars, separately considered, it appears

177. Power of passion when expressive; joy; resentment.—The wish to accomplish a prophecy illustrated from Shakspeare.

178. What the ethical writer has to say of the passions.—To what does Lord Kames propose to confine his inquiries?

beautiful; how much more so, when they are all united together! The beauty of the human figure is extraordinary, being a composition of numberless beauties arising from the parts and qualities of the object, various colors, various motions, figures, size, &c., all united in one complex object, and striking the eye with combined force. Hence it is, that beauty, a quality so remarkable in visible objects, lends its name to express every thing that is eminently agreeable: thus, by a figure of speech, we say a beautiful sound, a beautiful thought or expression, a beautiful theorem, a beautiful event, a beautiful discovery in art or science. But, as figurative expression is the subject of a following chapter, this chapter is confined to beauty in its proper signification.*

180. It is natural to suppose, that a perception so various as that of beauty, comprehending sometimes many particulars, sometimes few, should occasion emotions equally various; and yet all the various emotions of beauty maintain one common character, that of sweetness and gayety.†

Considering, attentively, the beauty of visible objects, we discover two kinds. The first may be termed *intrinsic* beauty, because it is

---

* [Cousin (in his Lectures on the Beautiful) offers some discriminating remarks upon this topic:

"Experience testifies that all agreeable things do not appear beautiful, and that, among agreeable things, those which are most so are not the most beautiful; a sure sign that the agreeable is not the beautiful, for if one is identical with the other, they should never be separated, but should always be commensurate with each other.

"Far from this, whilst all our senses give us agreeable sensations, only two have the privilege of awakening in us the idea of beauty. Does one ever say: This is a beautiful taste—This is a beautiful smell? Nevertheless one should say it, if the beautiful is the agreeable. On the other hand, there are certain pleasures of odor and taste, that move sensibility more than the greatest beauties of nature and art; and even among the perceptions of hearing and sight, those are not always the most vivid that most excite in us the idea of beauty." —*Cousin's Lectures*, VI.]

† [Cousin has the following just observations: "Place yourself before an object of nature, wherein men recognize beauty, and observe what takes place within you at the sight of this object. Is it not certain that at the same time that you judge that it is beautiful, you also feel its beauty, that is to say, that you experience at the sight of it a delightful emotion, and that you are attracted towards this object by a sentiment of sympathy and love? In other cases you judge otherwise and feel an opposite sentiment. Aversion accompanies the judgment of the ugly, as love accompanies the judgment of the beautiful. And this sentiment is awakened not only in presence of the objects of nature: all objects, whatever they may be, that we judge to be ugly or beautiful, have the power to excite in us this sentiment. Vary the circumstances as much as you please, place me before an admirable edifice, or before a beautiful landscape; represent to my mind the great discoveries of Descartes and Newton, the exploits of the great Condé, the virtue of St. Vincent de Paul; elevate me still higher; awaken in me the obscure and too much forgotten idea of the infinite Being; whatever you do, as often as you give birth within me to the idea of the beautiful, you give me an internal and exquisite joy, always followed by a sentiment of love for the object that caused it."]

---

179. To what class of objects is the term Beauty appropriated?—The complex structure of objects of external sense.—A tree; the human figure.—To what, figuratively, the term Beauty is applied.—Cousin's remarks.

discovered in a single object viewed apart without relation to any other: the examples above given are of that kind. The other may be termed *relative* beauty, being founded on the relation of objects. Intrinsic beauty is an object of sense merely: to perceive the beauty of a spreading oak, or of a flowing river, no more is required but singly an act of vision. The perception of relative beauty is accompanied with an act of understanding and reflection; for of a fine instrument or engine, we perceive not the relative beauty, until we be made acquainted with its use and destination. In a word, intrinsic beauty is ultimate; relative beauty is that of means relating to some good end or purpose. These different beauties agree in one capital circumstance, that both are equally perceived as belonging to the object. This is evident with respect to intrinsic beauty; but will not be so readily admitted with respect to the other: the utility of the plough, for example, may make it an object of admiration or of desire; but why should utility make it appear beautiful? A natural propensity mentioned (Chapter ii. part i. sect. 5) will explain that doubt: the beauty of the effect, by an easy transition of ideas, is transferred to the cause, and is perceived as one of the qualities of the cause. Thus a subject void of intrinsic beauty appears beautiful from its utility: an old Gothic tower, that has no beauty in itself, appears beautiful, considered as proper to defend against an enemy; a dwelling-house void of all regularity, is however beautiful in the view of convenience; and the want of form or symmetry in a tree, will not prevent its appearing beautiful, if it be known to produce good fruit.*

181. When these two beauties coincide in any object, it appears delightful: every member of the human body possesses both in a high degree: the fine proportions and slender make of a horse destined for running, please every eye; partly from symmetry, and partly from utility.

The beauty of utility, being proportioned accurately to the degree of utility, requires no illustration; but intrinsic beauty, so complex as I have said, cannot be handled distinctly without being analyzed into its constituent parts. If a tree be beautiful by means of its col-

---

* [Cousin, in his Lecture on The Beautiful in Objects, ignores the obvious distinction which Lord Kames makes between intrinsic and *relative* beauty. He says:—"No great effort of observation or reasoning is necessary to convince us that utility has nothing to do with beauty. What is useful is not always beautiful. What is beautiful is not always useful, and what is at once useful and beautiful is beautiful for some other reason than its utility. Observe a lever or a pulley: surely nothing is more useful. Nevertheless you are not tempted to say that this is beautiful. Have you discovered an antique vase admirably worked? You exclaim that this vase is beautiful, without thinking to seek of what use it may be to you."]

---

180. The common character of all the emotions of beauty.— Twofold beauty of visible objects: intrinsic; relative.—How these differ as to manner of perception; in what they agree.—Why should the utility of a plough make it appear beautiful?—Instances where a subject void of intrinsic beauty appears beautiful from its utility.—Cousin's observations

or, its figure, its size, its motion, it is in reality possessed of so many different beauties, which ought to be examined separately, in order to have a clear notion of them when combined. The beauty of color is too familiar to need explanation.* Do not the bright and cheerful colors of gold and silver contribute to preserve these metals in high estimation? The beauty of figure, arising from various circumstances and different views, is more complex: for example, viewing any body as a whole, the beauty of its figure arises from regularity and simplicity; viewing the parts with relation to each other, uniformity, proportion, and order contribute to its beauty. The beauty of motion deserves a chapter by itself; and another chapter is destined for grandeur, being distinguishable from beauty in its proper sense. Upon simplicity I must make a few cursory observations, such as may be of use in examining the beauty of single objects.

182. A multitude of objects crowding into the mind at once, disturb the attention, and pass without making any impression, or any distinct impression; in a group, no single object makes the figure it would do apart, when it occupies the whole attention. For the same reason, the impression made by an object that divides the attention by the multiplicity of its parts, equals not that of a more simple object comprehended in a single view: parts extremely complex must be considered in portions successively; and a number of impressions in succession, which cannot unite because not simultaneous, never touch the mind like one entire impression made as it were at one stroke. This justifies simplicity in works of art, as opposed to complicated circumstances and crowded ornaments. There is an additional reason for simplicity in works of dignity or elevation; which is, that the mind attached to beauties of a high rank, cannot descend to inferior beauties. The best artists accordingly have in all ages been governed by a taste for simplicity. How comes it then that we find profuse decoration prevailing in works of art? The reason

* ["Colors are beautiful, first, when they convey to the mind a lively sensation, as white and red; (2) when they cherish the organ of sight, as green; (3) when they have that character which we term delicacy, and yield a sensation both lively and gentle, as pale red and light blue. But (4) the beauty of a color depends chiefly on the agreeableness of the ideas it conveys to the mind; for the same color, which in one thing is very beautiful, may in another be very ugly. The verdure of the fields, for example, is delightful, because it leads us to think of fruitfulness, fragrance, and many other pleasant things; but greenness in the human face would be horrible, because it would suggest the notion of pain, of disease, or of something unnatural.

"In general, every color is beautiful, that brings along with it the agreeable idea of perfection, of health, of convenience, of intellectual or moral virtue, or of any other sort of excellence. Negroes love their own color for the same reason that we love ours; because they always see it; because all the people they love have it; and because none are without it but those who are thought to be strangers and enemies."—*Beattie.*]

181. Effect of the coincidence of intrinsic and relative beauty. Examples.—Why the beauty of utility requires no illustration.—Intrinsic beauty must be analyzed into constituent parts. Example of a tree.—Dr. Beattie's remarks on color.—Beauty of figure.

plainly is, that authors and architects, who cannot reach the higher beauties, endeavor to supply want of genius by multiplying those that are inferior.

183. These things premised, I proceed to examine the beauty of figure as arising from the above-mentioned particulars, namely, regularity, uniformity, proportion, order, and simplicity. To inquire why an object, by means of the particulars mentioned, appears beautiful, would, I am afraid, be a vain attempt: it seems the most probable opinion, that the nature of man was originally framed with a relish for them, in order to answer wise and good purposes. To explain these purposes or final causes, though a subject of great importance, has scarce been attempted by any writer. One thing is evident, that our relish for the particulars mentioned, adds much beauty to the objects that surround us, which of course tends to our happiness; and the Author of our nature has given many signal proofs that this final cause is not below his care. We may be confirmed in this thought upon reflecting, that our taste for these particulars is not accidental, but uniform and universal, making a branch of our nature. At the same time, it ought not to be overlooked, that regularity, uniformity, order, and simplicity, contribute each of them to readiness of apprehension; enabling us to form more distinct images of objects than can be done with the utmost attention where these particulars are not found. With respect to proportion, it is in some instances connected with a useful end, as in animals, where the best proportioned are the strongest and most active; but instances are still more numerous, where the proportions we relish have no connection with utility. Writers on architecture insist much on the proportions of a column, and assign different proportions to the Doric, Ionic, and Corinthian; but no architect will maintain, that the most accurate proportions contribute more to use, than several that are less accurate and less agreeable; neither will it be maintained, that the length, breadth, and height of rooms, assigned as the most beautiful proportions, tend also to make them the more commodious. With respect then to the final cause of proportion, I see not more to be made of it but to rest upon the final cause first mentioned, namely, its contributing to our happiness, by increasing the beauty of visible objects.*

* [Some remarks of Cousin throw considerable light on this subject:

"Symmetry and order are beautiful things, and at the same time are useful things, because they economize space, because objects symmetrically disposed are easier to find when one wants them; but that is not what makes for us the beauty of symmetry, for we immediately seize this kind of beauty, and it is often late enough before we recognize the utility that is found in it. It even sometimes happens, that after having admired the beauty of an object, we are

182. Reasons for simplicity in works of art.—Additional reason for it in works of dignity and elevation.—Why profuse decoration prevails in works of art.

183. Why an object appears beautiful, on account of its regularity, uniformity, &c. What beneficial purposes are answered by the relish we naturally have for these particulars.—Cousin's remarks

184. And now with respect to the beauty of figure, as far as it depends on the other circumstances mentioned; as to which, having room only for a slight specimen, I confine myself to the simplest figures. A circle and a square are each of them perfectly regular, being equally confined to a precise form, which admits not the slightest variation; a square, however, is less beautiful than a circle. And the reason seems to be, that the attention is divided among the sides and angles of a square; whereas the circumference of a circle, being a single object, makes one entire impression. And this simplicity contributes to beauty, which may be illustrated by another example: a square, though not more regular than a hexagon or octagon, is more beautiful than either; for what other reason, but that a square is more simple, and the attention less divided? This reasoning will appear still more conclusive, when we consider any regular polygon of very many sides; for of this figure the mind can never have any distinct perception.

A square is more regular than a parallelogram, and its parts more uniform; and for these reasons it is more beautiful. But that holds with respect to intrinsic beauty only; for in many instances utility turns the scale on the side of the parallelogram: this figure, for the doors and windows of a dwelling-house, is preferred, because of utility; and here we find the beauty of utility prevailing over that of regularity and uniformity.

A parallelogram again depends, for its beauty, on the proportion of its sides: a great inequality of sides annihilates its beauty; approximation towards equality hath the same effect, for proportion there degenerates into imperfect uniformity, and the figure appears an unsuccessful attempt towards a square; and thus proportion contributes to beauty.

185. An equilateral triangle yields not to a square in regularity nor in uniformity of parts, and it is more simple. But an equilateral

---

not able to divine its use, although it may have one. The useful is, then, entirely different from the beautiful, far from being its foundation.

"A celebrated and very ancient theory makes the beautiful consist in the perfect suitableness of means to their end. Here the beautiful is no longer the useful; it is the suitable. These two ideas must be distinguished. A machine produces excellent effects, economy of time, work, &c.; it is therefore useful. If, moreover, examining its construction, I find that each piece is in its place, and that all are skilfully disposed for the result which they should produce; even without regarding the utility of this result, as the means are well adapted to their end, I judge that there is suitableness in it. We are already approaching the idea of the beautiful; for we are no longer considering what is useful, but what is proper. Now we have not yet attained the true character of beauty; there are, in fact, objects very well adapted to their end, which we do not call beautiful. . . . . There is here always this difference between suitableness and utility, that an object to be beautiful has no need of being useful, but that it is not beautiful if it does not possess suitableness, if there is in it a disagreement between the end and the means."—Lect. VII. p. 141. Appleton's Ed.]

---

184. Beauty of a circle and square compared.—Comparison of a square with a hexagon, &c.

triangle is less beautiful than a square, which must be owing to inferiority of order in the position of its parts: the sides of an equilateral triangle incline to each other in the same angle, being the most perfect order they are susceptible of; but this order is obscure, and far from being so perfect as the parallelism of the sides of a square. Thus order contributes to the beauty of visible objects, no less than simplicity, regularity, or proportion.

A parallelogram exceeds an equilateral triangle in the orderly disposition of its parts; but being inferior in uniformity and simplicity, it is less beautiful.

186. Uniformity is singular in one capital circumstance, that it is apt to disgust by excess: a number of things destined for the same use, such as windows, chairs, spoons, buttons, cannot be too uniform; for supposing their figure to be good, utility requires uniformity: but a scrupulous uniformity of parts in a large garden or field, is far from being agreeable. Uniformity among connected objects belongs not to the present subject; it is handled in the chapter of uniformity and variety.

In all the works of nature, simplicity makes an illustrious figure. It also makes a figure in works of art: profuse ornament in painting, gardening, or architecture, as well as in dress or in language, shows a mean or corrupted taste:

> Poets, like painters, thus unskill'd to trace
> The naked nature and the living grace,
> With gold and jewels cover every part,
> And hide with ornaments their want of art.
>
> *Pope's Essay on Criticism.*

187. No single property recommends a machine more than its simplicity; not solely for better answering its purpose, but by appearing in itself more beautiful. Simplicity in behavior and manners has an enchanting effect, and never fails to gain our affection: very different are the artificial manners of modern times. General theorems, abstracting from their importance, are delightful by their simplicity, and by the easiness of their application to variety of cases. We take equal delight in the laws of motion, which, with the greatest simplicity, are boundless in their operations.

188. A gradual progress from simplicity to complex forms and profuse ornament, seems to be the fate of all the fine arts: in that progress these arts resemble behavior, which, from original candor and simplicity, has degenerated into artificial refinements. At present, literary productions are crowded with words, epithets, figures: in music, sentiment is neglected for the luxury of harmony, and for difficult movement: in taste, properly so called, poignant sauces,

---

185. An equilateral triangle compared with a square, and with a parallelogram.
186. When uniformity disgusts, and when it pleases.—Simplicity in the works of nature, and of art.
187. Simplicity in manners in general theorems · in laws of motion.

with complicated mixtures of different savors, prevail among people of condition: the French, accustomed to artificial red on a female cheek, think the modest coloring of nature altogether insipid.

The same tendency is discovered in the progress of the fine arts among the ancients. Some vestiges of the old Grecian buildings prove them to be of the Doric order: the Ionic succeeded, and seems to have been the favorite order, while architecture was in the height of glory: the Corinthian came next in vogue; and in Greece the buildings of that order appear mostly to have been erected after the Romans got footing there. At last came the Composite, with all its extravagances, where simplicity is sacrificed to finery and crowded ornament.

But what taste is to prevail next? for fashion is a continual flux, and taste must vary with it. After rich and profuse ornaments become familiar, simplicity appears lifeless and insipid; which would be an insurmountable obstruction, should any person of genius and taste endeavor to restore ancient simplicity.

189. The distinction between primary and secondary qualities in matter, seems now fully established. Heat and cold, smell and taste, though seeming to exist in bodies, are discovered to be effects caused by these bodies in a sensitive being: color, which appears to the eye as spread upon a substance, has no existence but in the mind of the spectator.* Qualities of that kind, which owe their existence to the percipient as much as to the object, are termed *secondary* qualities, and are distinguished from figure, extension, solidity, which, in contradistinction to the former, are termed *primary* qualities, because they inhere in subjects, whether perceived or not. This distinction suggests a curious inquiry, whether beauty be a primary or only a secondary quality of objects? The question is easily determined with respect to the beauty of color; for, if color be a secondary quality, existing nowhere but in the mind of the spectator, its beauty must exist there also. This conclusion equally holds with respect to the beauty of utility, which is plainly a conception of the mind, arising not from sight, but from reflecting that the thing is fitted for some good end or purpose. The question is more intricate with re-

* [Dr. James Beattie takes a more just and enlarged view of this topic, in saying: "Colors inhere not in the colored body, but in the light that falls upon it; and a body presents to our eye that color which predominates in the rays of light reflected by it; and different bodies reflect different sorts of rays, according to the texture and consistency of their minute parts. Now the component parts of bodies, and the rays of light, are not in the mind; and therefore colors, as well as bodies, are things external; and the word *color* denotes always an external thing, and never a sensation in the mind."

Again, he justly remarks: "We perceive colors and figures by the eye; we also perceive that some colors and figures are *beautiful*, and others not. This power of perceiving beauty, which the brutes have not, though they *see* as well as we, I call a secondary sense."]

188. **Progress from simplicity to complex forms and profuse ornament, illustrated in arts, conduct, literary style, &c. Also, among the ancients, in architecture.**

spect to the beauty of regularity; for, if regularity be a primary quality, why not also its beauty? That this is not a good inference will appear from considering, that beauty, in its very conception, refers to a percipient; for an object is said to be beautiful, for no other reason but that it appears so to a spectator: the same piece of matter that to a man appears beautiful, may possibly appear ugly to a being of a different species. Beauty, therefore, which for its existence depends on the percipient as much as on the object perceived, cannot be an inherent property in either. And hence it is wittily observed by the poet, that beauty is not in the person beloved, but in the lover's eye.

190. This reasoning is solid; and the only cause of doubt or hesitation is, that we are taught a different lesson by sense: a singular determination of nature makes us perceive both beauty and color as belonging to the object, and, like figure or extension, as inherent properties. This mechanism is uncommon; and when nature, to fulfil her intention, prefers any singular method of operation, we may be certain of some final cause that cannot be reached by ordinary means. For the beauty of some objects we are indebted entirely to nature; but, with respect to the endless variety of objects that owe their beauty to art and culture, the perception of beauty greatly promotes industry; being to us a strong additional incitement to enrich our fields, and improve our manufactures. These however are but slight effects, compared with the connections that are formed among individuals in society by means of this singular mechanism: the qualifications of the head and heart form undoubtedly the most solid and most permanent connections; but external beauty, which lies more in view, has a more extensive influence in forming these connections; at any rate, it concurs in an eminent degree with mental qualifications to produce social intercourse, mutual good-will, and consequently mutual aid and support, which are the life of society.

["That which in the smallest compass exhibits the greatest variety of beauty, is a fine human face. The features are of *various* sizes and forms; the corresponding ones exactly *uniform;* and each has that shape, size, position, and *proportion,* which is most *convenient.* Here too is the greatest beauty of *colors*, which are blended, varied, and disposed with marvellous *delicacy.* But the chief beauty of the countenance arises from its expression, of sagacity, good-nature, cheerfulness, modesty, and other moral and intellectual virtues. Without such expression, no face can be truly beautiful, and with it, none can be really ugly. Human beauty, therefore, at least that of the face, is not merely a corporeal quality; but derives its origin

---

189. Do heat and cold, smell, taste, and color, exist in material bodies?—Dr. Beattie's remarks on color.—*Secondary* qualities and primary distinguished.—Whether beauty is a primary or secondary quality of bodies.—What is said of beauty of color; of beauty of utility; of beauty of regularity.—What beauty, in its very conception, refers to.

and essential characters from the soul; and almost any person may, in some degree, acquire it, who is at pains to improve his understanding, to repress criminal thoughts, and to cherish good affections; as every one must lose it, whatever features or complexion there may be to boast of who leaves the mind uncultivated, or a prey to evil passions, or a slave to trifling pursuits."—*Beattie.*

Cole, the distinguished American painter, speaks thus of beauty:

"Irving was rather disappointed in the scenes in which Scott so much delighted. After all, *beauty is in the mind.* A scene is rather an index to feelings and associations. History and poetry made the barren hills of Scotland glorious to Scott: Irving remembered the majestic forests and the rich luxuriance of his own country. What a beautiful exemplification of the power of poetry was that remark of the old carpenter who had been a companion of Burns: 'and it seemed to him that the country had grown more beautiful since Burns had written his bonnie little sangs about it.'"

To the remarks made by our author on the subject of beauty, the following from Cousin make a valuable addition:

"Above real beauty, is a beauty of another order—*ideal beauty.* The ideal resides neither in an individual, nor in a collection of individuals. Nature or experience furnishes us the occasion of conceiving it, but it is essentially distinct. Let it once be conceived, and all natural figures, though never so beautiful, are only images of a superior beauty which they do not realize. Give me a beautiful action, and I will imagine one still more beautiful. The Apollo itself is open to criticism in more than one respect. The ideal continually recedes as we approach it. Its last termination is in the infinite, that is to say, in God; or, to speak more correctly, the true and absolute ideal is nothing else than God himself." . . . . .

"God is, *par excellence*, the beautiful—for what object satisfies more all our faculties, our reason, our imagination, our heart! He offers to reason the highest idea, beyond which it has nothing more to seek; to imagination the most ravishing contemplation; to the heart a sovereign object of love. He is, then, perfectly beautiful; but is he not sublime, also, in other ways? If he extends the horizon of thought, it is to confound it in the abyss of his greatness. If the soul blooms at the spectacle of his goodness, has it not also reason to be affrighted at the idea of his justice, which is not less present to it? At the same time that he is the life, the light, the movement, the ineffable grace of visible and finite nature, he is also called the Eternal, the Invisible, the Infinite, the Absolute Unity, and the Being of beings."—Lect. vii. p. 151, Appleton's Ed.] X

---

190. What lesson, on this subject, our senses teach.—The ends answered by this reference of beauty to the object and not to the percipient.—Connections formed among individuals in society.—Remarks on the human face.—Cole's remarks on beauty.—Cousin's remarks on ideal beauty.

PART II.

THE THEORY OF BEAUTY.

(Condensed from LORD JEFFREY's Review of Alison on Taste, 1841.)

191. THERE are some decisive *objections* against the notion of beauty being a simple sensation, or the object of a separate and peculiar faculty.

The *first*, is the want of agreement as to the presence and existence of beauty in particular objects, among men whose organization is perfect, and who are plainly possessed of the faculty, whatever it may be, by which beauty is discerned. Now no such thing happens, or can be conceived to happen, in the case of any other simple sensation, or the exercise of any other distinct faculty. Where one man sees light, all men who have eyes see light also. All men allow grass to be green, and sugar to be sweet. With regard to beauty, however, the case is entirely different. One man sees it perpetually, where to another it is quite invisible, or even where its reverse seems to be conspicuous. But how can we believe that beauty is the object of a peculiar sense or faculty, when persons undoubtedly possessed of the faculty, and even in an eminent degree, can discover nothing of it in objects where it is distinctly felt and perceived by others with the same use of the faculty? This consideration seems conclusive against the supposition of beauty being a real property of objects, addressing itself to the power of Taste, as a separate sense or faculty; and it suggests that our sense of it is the result of other more elementary feelings into which it may be resolved.

192. A *second* objection arises from the almost infinite variety of things to which the property of beauty is ascribed, and the impossibility of imagining any one inherent quality which can belong to them all, and yet at the same time possess so much unity as to pass universally by the same name, and be recognized as the peculiar object of a separate sense or faculty. The form of a fine tree is beautiful, and the form of a fine woman, and the form of a column, and a vase, and a chandelier; yet how can it be said that the form of a woman has any thing in common with that of a tree or a temple? or to which of the senses, by which forms are distinguished, can it appear that they have any resemblance or affinity?

The matter, however, becomes still more inextricable when we

---

191. The first objection urged against the notion of beauty being a simple sensation.

recollect that beauty does not belong merely to forms or colors, but to sounds, and perhaps to the objects of other senses; nay, that in all languages and in all nations it is not supposed to reside exclusively in material objects, but to belong also to sentiments and ideas, and intellectual and moral existences. But if things intellectual and totally segregated from matter may thus possess beauty, how can it possibly be a quality of material objects? or what sense or faculty can that be whose proper office it is to intimate to us the existence of some property which is common to a flower and a demonstration, a valley and an eloquent discourse?

193. If, in reply, it be said that all these objects, however various and dissimilar, agree at least in being agreeable, and that this *agreeableness*, which is the only quality they possess in common, may probably be the beauty which is ascribed to them all, we answer:—that though the agreeableness of such objects depends plainly enough upon their beauty, it by no means follows, but quite the contrary, that their beauty depends upon their agreeableness, the latter being the more comprehensive, or generic term, under which beauty must rank as one of the species.

(1) Agreeableness, in general, cannot be the same with beauty, because there are very many things in the highest degree agreeable that can in no sense be called beautiful. We learn nothing of the nature of beauty, therefore, by merely classing it among our pleasurable emotions.

(2) Among all the objects that are agreeable, whether they are also beautiful or not, scarcely any two are agreeable on account of the same qualities, or even suggest their agreeableness to the same faculty or organ. The truth is, that agreeableness is not properly a quality of any object whatsoever, but the effect or result of certain qualities, the nature of which, in any particular instance, we can generally define pretty exactly, or of which we know at least with certainly that they manifest themselves respectively to some one particular sense or faculty, and to no other; and consequently, it would be just as obviously ridiculous to suppose a faculty or organ, whose office it was to perceive agreeableness in general, as to suppose that agreeableness was a distinct quality that could thus be perceived. The words beauty and beautiful are universally felt to mean something much more definite than agreeableness or gratification in general; and the force and clearness of our perception of that something is demonstrated by the readiness with which we determine, in any particular instance, whether the object of a given pleasurable emotion is or is not properly described as beauty.

194. In our opinion, *our sense of beauty depends* entirely on our

---

192. The second objection.—Whether beauty belong to forms or colors alone.

193. It is replied that various objects of beauty are alike in one respect, that of agreeableness, and that this may be the beauty which is ascribed to them all. Two answers to this statement.

previous experience of simpler pleasures or emotions, and consists in the *suggestion* of agreeable or interesting sensations with which we had formerly been made familiar by the direct and intelligible agency of our common sensibilities; and that vast variety of objects to which we give the common name of beautiful, become entitled to that appellation merely because they all possess the power of recalling or reflecting those sensations of which they have been the accompaniments, or with which they have been associated in our imagination by any other more casual bond of connection.

According to this view of the matter, therefore, *beauty is not an inherent property or quality of objects at all, but the result of the accidental relations in which they may stand* to our experience of pleasures or emotions, and does not depend on any particular configuration of parts, proportions, or colors in external things, nor upon the unity, coherence, or simplicity of intellectual creations, but merely upon the associations which, in the case of every individual, may enable these inherent, and otherwise indifferent qualities, to suggest or recall to the mind emotions of a pleasurable or interesting description. It follows, therefore, that no object is beautiful in itself, or could appear so, antecedent to our experience of direct pleasures or emotions; and that, as an infinite variety of objects may thus reflect interesting ideas, so all of them may acquire the title of beautiful, although utterly diverse in their nature, and possessing nothing in common but this accidental power of reminding us of other emotions.

195. This theory serves to explain how objects which have no inherent resemblance, nor indeed any one quality in common, should yet be united in one common relation, and consequently acquire one common name; just as all the things that belonged to a beloved individual may serve to remind us of him, and thus to awake a kindred class of emotions, though just as unlike each other as any of the objects that are classed under the general name of beautiful.

We thus get rid of all the mystery of a peculiar sense or faculty imagined for the express purpose of perceiving beauty, and discover that the *power of taste* is nothing more than the habit of tracing those associations by which almost all objects may be connected with interesting emotions.

196. *The basis of our theory* is, that the beauty which we impute to outward objects, is nothing more than the reflection of our own inward emotions, and is made up entirely of certain little portions of love, pity, or other affections which have been connected with these objects, and still adhere, as it were, to them, and move us anew whenever they are presented to our observation. Two things here

---

194. On what our sense of beauty depends.—Beauty not an inherent property of objects, but the result of accidental relations.

195. What does this theory explain concerning objects that have no inherent resemblance? What mystery do we thus get rid of?—What thus appears to be the power of taste?

require explanation. First, what are the primary affections, by the suggestion of which we think the sense of beauty is produced? and, secondly, what is the nature of the connection by which we suppose that the objects we call beautiful are enabled to suggest these affections?

With regard to the first of these points—all sensations that are not absolutely indifferent, and are at the same time either agreeable when experienced by ourselves, or attractive when contemplated in others, may form the foundation of the emotions of sublimity or beauty. *The sum of the whole is*, that every feeling which it is agreeable to experience, to recall, or to witness, may become the source of beauty in external objects, when it is so connected with them as that their appearance reminds us of that feeling. Our proposition is, that *the emotions of sublimity or beauty are not original emotions*, nor produced directly by any material qualities in the objects that excite them, but are reflections, or images, of the more radical and familiar emotions to which we have alluded; and are occasioned, not by any inherent virtue in the objects before us, but by the accidents, if we may so express ourselves, by which these may have been enabled to suggest or recall to us our own past sensations or sympathies. It might almost be laid down as an axiom, that, except in the plain and palpable case of bodily pain or pleasure, we can never be *interested* in any thing but the fortunes of sentient beings, and that every thing partaking of the nature of mental emotion, must have for its object the *feelings*, past, present, or possible, of something capable of sensation. Independent, therefore, of all evidence, we should have been apt to conclude, that the emotions of beauty and sublimity must have for their objects the sufferings or enjoyments of sentient beings.

197. Secondly, as to the connection of our feelings with external objects by which they become beautiful—objects are sublime or beautiful, (1) when they are the natural signs and perpetual concomitants of pleasurable sensations; or, at any rate, of some lively feeling or emotion in ourselves or in some other sentient beings; or, (2) when they are the arbitrary or accidental concomitants of such feelings; or, (3) when they bear some analogy or fanciful resemblance to things with which these emotions are naturally connected.

198. The most obvious and the strongest association between inward feelings and external objects is, where the object is necessarily and universally connected with the feeling by the law of nature, so that it is always presented to the senses when the feeling is impressed upon the mind—as the sight or sound of laughter, with the feeling of gayety—of weeping with distress—of the sound of thunder with

---

196. The basis of our theory.—Two things requiring explanation.—What sensations may form the foundation of emotions of sublimity and beauty? Those emotions more particularly defined. How occasioned.—The axiom referred to.
197. When objects are sublime; when beautiful.

ideas of danger and power. In the last instance, it is obvious that the sense of sublimity is produced, not by any quality that is perceived by the ear, but altogether by the impression of power and of danger that is necessarily made upon the mind, whenever that sound is heard. The noise of a cart rattling over the stones, is often mistaken for thunder; and as long as the mistake lasts, this very vulgar and insignificant noise is actually felt to be prodigiously sublime, merely because it is then associated with ideas of prodigious power and undefined danger; and the sublimity is accordingly destroyed, the moment the association is dissolved, though the sound itself, and its effect on the organ, continue exactly the same. This, therefore, is an instance in which sublimity is distinctly proved to consist, not in any physical quality of the object to which it is ascribed, but in its necessary connection with that vast and uncontrolled Power which is the natural object of awe and veneration.

199. *The most beautiful object in nature*, perhaps, is the countenance of a young and beautiful woman: and we are apt at first to imagine, that, independent of all associations, the form and colors which it displays are, in themselves, lovely and engaging; and would appear charming to all beholders, with whatever other qualities or impressions they might happen to be connected. But reflection will satisfy us, that what we admire is not a combination of forms and colors (which could never excite any mental emotion), but a collection of signs and tokens of certain mental feelings and affections which are universally recognized as the proper objects of love and sympathy. Among the ingredients of female beauty, we should trace the signs of two different sets of qualities, neither of them the object of sight, but of a far higher faculty: in the first place, of youth and health; and, in the second place, of innocence gayety, sensibility, intelligence, delicacy, or vivacity.

200. It is easy enough to understand how the sight of a picture or statue should affect us nearly in the same way as the sight of the original; nor is it much more difficult to conceive, how the sight of a cottage should give us something of the same feeling as the sight of a peasant's family; and the aspect of a town raise many of the same ideas as the appearance of a multitude of persons. Take the case of a common English landscape—green meadows with grazing and ruminating cattle—canals or navigable rivers—well-fenced, well-cultivated fields—neat, clean, scattered cottages—humble, antique churches, with church-yard elms and crossing hedge-rows—all seen under bright skies and in good weather: there is much beauty in such a scene. But in what does the beauty consist? Not, certainly, in the mere mixture of colors and forms; for colors

---

198. The most obvious association between inward feelings and external objects.—Remarks on the sound of thunder.

199. The most beautiful object in nature.—The signs of two different sets of qualities in female beauty.

more pleasing and lines more graceful might be spread upon a board, or a painter's pallet, without engaging the eye to a second glance, or raising the least emotion in the mind; but in the picture of human happiness that is presented to our imaginations and affections—in the visible and unequivocal signs of comfort, and cheerful and peaceful enjoyment—and of that secure and successful industry that insures its continuance—and of the piety by which it is exalted—and of the simplicity by which it is contrasted with the guilt and the fever of a city life; in the images of health, and temperance, and plenty which it exhibits to every eye—and in the glimpses which it affords to warmer imaginations, of those primitive or fabulous times when man was uncorrupted by luxury and ambition, and of those humble retreats in which we still delight to imagine that love and philosophy may find an unpolluted asylum. At all events, however, it is human feeling that excites our sympathy, and forms the true object of our emotions. It is man, and man alone, that we see in the beauties of the earth which he inhabits; or, if a more sensitive and extended sympathy connect us with the lower families of animated nature, and make us rejoice with the lambs that bleat on the uplands, or the cattle that repose in the valley, or even with the *living* plants that drink the bright sun and the balmy air beside them, it is still the idea of enjoyment—of feelings that animate the existence of sentient beings—that calls forth all our emotions, and is the parent of all the beauty with which we proceed to invest the inanimate creation around us.

201. Instead of this quiet and tame *English* landscape, let us now take a Welsh or a Highland scene, and see whether its beauties will admit of being explained on the same principle. Here we shall have lofty mountains, and rocky and lonely recesses—tufted woods hung over precipices—lakes intersected with castled promontories—ample solitudes of unploughed and untrodden valleys—nameless and gigantic ruins—and mountain echoes repeating the scream of the eagle and the roar of the cataract. This, too, is beautiful; and, to those who can interpret the language it speaks, far more beautiful than the prosperous scene with which we have contrasted it. Yet, lonely as it is, it is to the recollection of man and the suggestion of human feelings that its beauty also is owing. The mere forms and colors that compose its visible appearance, are no more capable of exciting any emotion in the mind than the forms and colors of a Turkey carpet. It is sympathy with the present or the past, or the imaginary *inhabitants* of such a region, that alone gives it either interest or beauty; and the delight of those who behold it, will always be found to be in exact proportion to the force of their imaginations, and the warmth of their social affections. The leading

---

200. The emotions excited by a picture, by sight of a cottage, of a town, of an English landscape.

impressions here are those of romantic seclusion and primeval simplicity; lovers sequestered in these blissful solitudes, "from towns and toils remote,"—and rustic poets and philosophers communing with nature, and at a distance from the low pursuits and selfish malignity of ordinary mortals; then there is the sublime impression of the Mighty Power which piled the massive cliffs upon each other, and rent the mountains asunder, and scattered their giant fragments at their base; and all the images connected with the monuments of ancient magnificence and extinguished hostility—the feuds, and the combats, and the triumphs of its wild and primitive inhabitants, contrasted with the stillness and desolation of the scenes where they lie interred; and the romantic ideas attached to their ancient traditions, and the peculiarities of the actual life of their descendants—their wild and enthusiastic poetry—their gloomy superstitions—their attachment to their chiefs—the dangers and the hardships and enjoyments of their lonely huntings and fishings—their pastoral sheilings on the mountains in summer—and the tales and the sports that amuse the little groups that are frozen into their vast and trackless valleys in winter.

202. The forms and colors that are peculiar to *childhood*, are not necessarily or absolutely beautiful in themselves; for, in a grown person, the same forms and colors would be either ludicrous or disgusting. It is their indestructible connection with the engaging ideas of innocence—of careless gayety—of unsuspecting confidence; made still more tender and attractive by the recollection of helplessness, and blameless and happy ignorance—of the anxious affection that watches over all their ways—and of the hopes and fears that seek to pierce futurity for those who have neither fears nor cares nor anxieties for themselves.

203. But our general theory must be very greatly confirmed by considering the *second* class of cases, or those in which the external object is not the natural and necessary, but only the occasional or accidental concomitant of the emotion which it recalls. In the former instances (already given), some conception of beauty seems to be inseparable from the appearance of the objects; and being impressed, in some degree, upon all persons to whom they are presented, there is evidently room for insinuating that it is an independent and intrinsic quality of their nature, and does not arise from association with any thing else. In the instances, however, to which we now allude, this perception of beauty is not universal, but entirely dependent on the opportunities which each individual has had to associate ideas of emotion with the object to which it is ascribed; the same thing appearing beautiful to those who have been exposed

---

201. How the beauties of a Welsh or Highland landscape are to be explained.
202. The forms and colors that seem beautiful in childhood.
203. Our theory confirmed by the second class of cases. What these are; how they differ from those already considered.

to the influence of such associations, and indifferen to those who have not.

204. *The accidental or arbitrary relations that may thus be established between natural sympathies or emotions, and external objects*, may be either such as occur to whole classes of men, or are confined to particular individuals. Among the former, those that apply to different nations, or races of men, are the most important and remarkable, and constitute the basis of those peculiarities by which *national* tastes are distinguished. Take again, for example, the instance of female beauty, and think what different and inconsistent standards would be fixed for it in the different regions of the world : in Africa, in Asia, and in Europe ; in Tartary and in Greece : in Lapland, Patagonia, and Circassia. If there was any thing absolutely or intrinsically beautiful in any of the forms thus distinguished, it is inconceivable that men should differ so outrageously in their conceptions of it : if beauty were a real or independent quality, it seems impossible that it should be distinctly and clearly felt by one set of persons, where another set altogether as sensitive, could see nothing but its opposite ; and if it were actually and inseparably attached to certain forms, colors, or proportions, it must appear utterly inexplicable that it should be felt or perceived in the most opposite forms and proportions, in objects of the same description. On the other hand, if all beauty consist in reminding us of certain natural sympathies, and objects of emotion, with which they have been habitually connected, it is easy to perceive how the most different forms should be felt to be equally beautiful. If female beauty, for instance, consist in the visible signs and expressions of youth and health, and of gentleness, vivacity, and kindness, then it will necessarily happen, that the forms, and colors, and proportions which nature may have connected with those qualities, in the different climates or regions of the world, will all appear equally beautiful to those who have been accustomed to recognize them as the signs of such qualities ; while they will be respectively indifferent to those who have not learned to interpret them in this sense, and displeasing to those whom experience has led to consider them as the signs of opposite qualities.

205. The case is the same, though perhaps in a smaller degree, as to *the peculiarity of national taste* in other particulars. The style of dress and architecture in every nation, if not adopted from mere want of skill, or penury of materials, always appears beautiful to the natives, and somewhat monstrous and absurd to foreigners ;—and the general character and aspect of their landscape, in like manner, if not associated with substantial evils and inconveniences, always appears more beautiful and enchanting than the scenery of any

---

204. Accidental relations either occur to classes of men or to individuals.—National tastes.—Diversity of opinion respecting female beauty. Remarks upon this diversity other region. The fact is still more striking, perhaps, in the case of music; in the effects of those national airs, with which even the most uncultivated imaginations have connected so many interesting recollections; and in the delight with which all persons of sensibility catch the strains of their native melodies in strange or in distant lands. It is owing chiefly to the same sort of arbitrary and national association, that white is thought a gay color in Europe, where it is used at weddings; and a dismal color in China, where it is used for mourning; that we think yew-trees gloomy, because they are planted in church-yards, and large masses of powdered horse-hair majestic, because we see them on the heads of judges and bishops.

206. Again, our *ideas of beauty are modified by the differences of instruction or education.* If external objects were sublime or beautiful in themselves, it is plain that they would appear equally so to those who were acquainted with their origin, and to those to whom it was unknown. Yet it is not easy, perhaps, to calculate the degree to which the notions of beauty and sublimity are now influenced all over Europe, by the study of classical literature; or the number of impressions of this sort which the well-educated consequently receive, from objects that are utterly indifferent to uninstructed persons of the same natural sensibility. [See Alison on Taste, pp. 39–41.]

207. The influences of the same studies may be traced, indeed, through almost all our impressions of beauty—and especially in the feelings which we receive from the contemplation of *rural scenery;* where the images and recollections which have been associated with such objects, in the enchanting strains of the poets, are perpetually recalled by their appearance, and give an interest and a beauty to the prospect, of which the uninstructed cannot have the slightest perception. Upon this subject, also, Mr. Alison has expressed himself with his usual warmth and elegance. After observing that in childhood, the beauties of nature have scarcely any existence for those who have as yet but little general sympathy with mankind, he proceeds to state, that they are usually first recommended to notice by the poets, to whom we are introduced in the course of education; and who, in a manner, create them for us, by the associations which they enable us to form with their visible appearance. [See Alison on Taste, Mills' Edition, pp. 53–4.]

208. Before leaving this branch of the subject, let us pause for a moment on the familiar but very striking instance of our *varying and contradictory judgments, as to the beauty of the successive fashions of dress* that have existed within our own remembrance All persons who still continue to find amusement in society, and are

---

205. Peculiarities of national taste in regard to dress, architecture, music, colors appropriated to mourning, &c.
206. Ideas of beauty modified by instruction and education.
207. Contemplation of rural scenery.—Influence of the poets.

not old enough to enjoy only the recollections of their youth, think the prevailing fashions becoming and graceful, and the fashions of twenty or twenty-five years old intolerably ugly and ridiculous. It is plain, then, that there is, in the general case, no intrinsic beauty or deformity in any of those fashions; and that the forms, and colors, and materials, that are, we may say, universally and very strongly felt to be beautiful while they are in fashion, are sure to lose all their beauty as soon as the fashion has passed away.

Hitherto we have spoken of the beauty of external objects only. But the whole difficulty of the theory consists in its application to them. If that be once adjusted, the *beauty of immaterial objects* can occasion no perplexity. *Poems* and other compositions in words, are beautiful in proportion as they are conversant with beautiful objects—or, as they suggest to us, in a more direct way, the moral and social emotions on which the beauty of all objects depends. *Theorems and demonstrations* again are beautiful, according as they excite in us emotions of admiration for the genius and intellectual power of their inventors, and images of the magnificent and beneficial ends to which such discoveries may be applied;—and *mechanical contrivances* are beautiful when they remind us of similar talents and ingenuity, and at the same time impress us with a more direct sense of their vast utility to mankind, and of the great additional conveniences with which life is consequently adorned. In all cases, therefore, there is the suggestion of some interesting conception or emotion associated with a present perception, in which it is apparently confounded and embodied—and this, according to the whole of the preceding deduction, is the distinguishing characteristic of Beauty.

Necessary consequences of the adoption of this Theory.

(1.) We conceive that it establishes the substantial identity of the Sublime, the Beautiful, and the Picturesque; and consequently puts an end to all controversy that is not purely verbal, as to the difference of these several qualities. Every material object that interests us, without actually hurting or gratifying our bodily feelings, must do so, according to this theory, in one and the same manner,—that is, by suggesting or recalling some emotion or affection of ourselves, or some other sentient being, and presenting, to our imagination at least, some natural object of love, pity, admiration, or awe. Though material objects have but one means of exciting emotion, the emotions they do excite are infinite. They are mirrors that may reflect all shades and all colors; and, in point of fact, do seldom reflect the same hues twice. No two interesting objects, perhaps, whether known by the name of Beautiful, Sublime, or Picturesque, ever produced exactly the same emotion in the beholder; and no one object, it is most probable, ever moved any two persons to the very same conceptions

208. Varying judgments on successive fashions of dress.—Remarks on the beauty of immaterial objects.—Two consequences resulting from this theory.

(2.) Our theory seems calculated to put an end to all the perplexing questions about the *Standard of Taste.* If things are not beautiful in themselves, but only as they serve to suggest interesting conceptions to the mind, then *every thing which does in point of fact suggest such a conception* to any individual, *is beautiful* to that individual; and it is not only quite true that there is no room for disputing about tastes, but that all tastes are equally just and correct, in so far as each individual speaks his own emotions. What a man feels distinctly to be beautiful, is beautiful to him, whatever other people may think of it. All this follows clearly from the theory now in question; but it does not follow from it that all tastes are equally good, or desirable, or that there is any difficulty in describing that which is really the best, and the most to be envied. The only *use of the faculty of Taste*, is to afford an innocent delight, and to assist in the cultivation of a finer morality; and that man certainly will have the most delight from this faculty, who has the most numerous and the most powerful perceptions of Beauty. But, if beauty consist in the reflection of our affections and sympathies, it is plain that he will always see the most beauty whose affections are the warmest and the most exercised--whose imagination is the most powerful, and who has most accustomed himself to attend to the objects by which he is surrounded. The best taste, therefore, must be that which belongs to the best affections, the most active fancy, and the most attentive habits of observation. It will follow pretty exactly too, that all men's perceptions of beauty will be nearly in proportion to the degree of their sensibility and social sympathies; and that those who have no affections towards sentient beings, will be as certainly insensible to beauty in external objects, as he who cannot hear the sound of his friend's voice, must be deaf to its echo.

If, however, we aspire to be *creators* as well as observers of Beauty, and place any part of our happiness in ministering to the gratification of others—as artists, or poets, or authors of any sort,—then a more laborious system of cultivation will be necessary. We must be cautious to employ only such objects as are the natural signs, or the inseparable concomitants of emotions of which the greater part of mankind are susceptible; and our taste will then deserve to be called bad or false, if we intrude upon the public as beautiful, objects that are not likely to be associated in common minds with any interesting impressions. As all men must have some peculiar associations, all men must have some peculiar notions of beauty, and, of course, to a certain extent, a taste that the public would be entitled to consider as false or vitiated.

[Notwithstanding all that is here said about the Standard of Taste, it is thought best, for the sake of those who may not adopt Lord Jeffrey's Theory, to give, in chap. xxvi., Dr. Blair's views on that subject, being far superior to what Lord Kames had furnished.—Am. Ed.]

CHAPTER IV.

GRANDEUR AND SUBLIMITY.

209. NATURE hath not more remarkably distinguished us from other animals by an erect posture, than by a capacious and aspiring mind, attaching us to things great and elevated. The ocean, the sky, seize the attention, and make a deep impression; robes of state are made large and full, to draw respect: we admire an elephant for its magnitude, notwithstanding its unwieldiness.

The elevation of an object affects us no less than its magnitude: a high place is chosen for the statue of a deity or hero: a tree growing on the brink of a precipice looks charming when viewed from the plain below: a throne is erected for the chief magistrate; and a chair with a high seat for the president of a court. Among all nations, heaven is placed far above us, hell far below us.

In some objects, greatness and elevation concur to make a complicated impression: the Alps and the Peake of Teneriffe are proper examples; with the following difference, that in the former greatness seems to prevail, elevation in the latter.

210. The emotions raised by great and by elevated objects are clearly distinguishable, not only in internal feeling, but even in their external expressions. A great object makes the spectator endeavor to enlarge his bulk; which is remarkable in plain people who give way to nature without reserve; in describing a great object, they naturally expand themselves by drawing in air with all their force. An elevated object produces a different expression; it makes the spectator stretch upward and stand a-tiptoe.

Great and elevated objects considered with relation to the emotions produced by them, are termed *grand* and *sublime*. *Grandeur* and *sublimity* have a double signification; they commonly signify the quality or circumstance in objects by which the emotions of grandeur and sublimity are produced; sometimes the emotions themselves.

[The sentiment of the Beautiful, and the sentiment of the Sublime are thus distinguished by Cousin:

"When we have before our eyes an object whose forms are perfectly determined, and the whole easy to embrace,—a beautiful flower, a beautiful statue, an antique temple of moderate size,—each of our faculties attaches itself to this object, and rests upon it with unalloyed satisfaction. Our senses easily perceive its details: our reason seizes the happy harmony of all its parts. Should this object

---

209. How nature has distinguished us from other animals.—The mind affected by the elevation as well as by the magnitude of an object.

disappear, we can distinctly represent it to ourselves, so precise and fixed are its forms. The soul in this contemplation feels again a sweet and tranquil joy, a sort of efflorescence.

Let us consider, on the other hand, an object with vague and indefinite forms, which may nevertheless be very beautiful: the impression which we experience is without doubt a pleasure still, but it is a pleasure of a different order. This object does not call forth all our powers like the first. Reason conceives it, but the senses do not perceive the whole of it, and imagination does not distinctly represent it to itself. The senses and the imagination try in vain to attain its last limits: our faculties are enlarged, are inflated, thus to speak, in order to embrace it, but it escapes and surpasses them. The pleasure that we feel comes from the very magnitude of the object; but at the same time, this magnitude produces in us I know not what melancholy sentiment, because it is disproportionate to us. At the sight of the starry heavens, of the vast sea, of gigantic mountains, admiration is mingled with sadness. These objects, in reality finite, like the world itself, seem to us infinite, in our want of power to comprehend their immensity, and, resembling what is truly without bounds, they awaken in us the idea of the infinite, that idea which at once elevates and confounds our intelligence."—Lect. vi.]

211. In handling the present subject, it is necessary that the impression made on the mind by the magnitude of an object, abstracting from its other qualities, should be ascertained. And because abstraction is a mental operation of some difficulty, the safest method for judging is, to choose a plain object that is neither beautiful nor deformed, if such a one can be found. The plainest that occurs is a huge mass of rubbish, the ruins, perhaps, of some extensive building, or a large heap of stones, such as are collected together for keeping in memory a battle, or other remarkable event. Such an object, which in miniature would be perfectly indifferent, makes an impression by its magnitude, and appears agreeable. And supposing it so large as to fill the eye, and to prevent the attention from wandering upon other objects, the impression it makes will be so much the deeper.

212. But, though a plain object of that kind be agreeable, it is not termed *grand;* it is not entitled to that character unless, together with its size, it be possessed of other qualities that contribute to beauty, such as regularity, proportion, order, or color; and according to the number of such qualities combined with magnitude, it is more or less grand. Thus, St. Peter's church at Rome, the great Pyramid of Egypt, the Alps towering above the clouds, a great

---

210. Emotions raised by great and by elevated objects distinguishable.—Double signification of grandeur and sublimity.—How the beautiful and the sublime are distinguished by Cousin.

211. Impressions made on the mind by the *magnitude* of an object simply. Illustrations; those of the plainest sort.

arm of the sea, and, above all, a clear and serene sky, are grand, because, besides their size, they are beautiful in an eminent degree. On the other hand, an overgrown whale, having a disagreeable appearance, is not grand. A large building, agreeable by its regularity and proportion, is grand, and yet a much larger building destitute of regularity, has not the least tincture of grandeur. A single regiment in battle array, makes a grand appearance; which the surrounding crowd does not, though perhaps ten for one in number. And a regiment where the men are all in one livery, and the horses of one color, makes a grander appearance, and consequently strikes more terror than where there is confusion of colors and of dress. Thus greatness or magnitude is the circumstance that distinguishes grandeur from beauty: agreeableness is the genus of which beauty and grandeur are species.

213. The emotion of grandeur, duly examined, will be found an additional proof of the foregoing doctrine. That this emotion is pleasant in a high degree, requires no other evidence but once to have seen a grand object; and if an emotion of grandeur be pleasant, its cause or object, as observed above, must infallibly be agreeable in proportion.

The qualities of grandeur and beauty are not more distinct than the emotions are which these qualities produce in a spectator.* It is observed in the chapter immediately foregoing, that all the various emotions of beauty have one common character, that of sweetness and gayety. The emotion of grandeur has a different character: a large object that is agreeable, occupies the whole attention, and swells the heart into a vivid emotion, which though extremely pleasant, is rather serious than gay. And this affords a good reason for distinguishing in language these different emotions. The emotions raised by color, by regularity, by proportion, and by order,

* [*Definition of terms.*—GREAT simply designates extent; GRAND includes likewise the idea of excellence and superiority. A *great* undertaking characterizes only the extent of the undertaking; a *grand* undertaking bespeaks its superior excellence.

Grand and SUBLIME are both superior to *great;* but the former marks the dimension of *greatness;* the latter, from the Latin *sublimis*, designates that of height. A scene may be either *grand* or *sublime:* it is *grand* as it fills the imagination with its immensity; it is *sublime* as it elevates the imagination beyond the surrounding and less important objects. There is something *grand* in the sight of a vast army moving forward as it were by one impulse; there is something peculiarly *sublime* in the sight of huge mountains and craggy cliffs of ice, shaped into various fantastic forms. *Grand* may be said either of the works of art or nature. The Egyptian pyramids, or the ocean, are both *grand* objects; a tempestuous ocean is a *sublime* object. *Grand* is sometimes applied to the mind: *sublime* is applied both to the thoughts and the expressions. There is a *grandeur* of conception in the writings of Milton; there is a *sublimity* in the inspired writings, which far surpass all human productions.
Crabb's Synonymes.]

212. What besides magnitude is necessary to make an object *grand* Examples.—How grandeur is distinguished from beauty.

have such a resemblance to each other, as readily to come under one general term, viz., *the emotion of beauty ;* but the emotion of grandeur is so different from these mentioned, as to merit a peculiar name.

Though regularity, proportion, order, and color, contribute to grandeur as well as to beauty, yet these qualities are not by far so essential to the former as to the latter. To make out that proposition, some preliminaries are requisite. In the first place, the mind, not being totally occupied with a small object, can give its attention at the same time to every minute part; but in a great or extensive object, the mind being totally occupied with the capital and striking parts, has no attention left for those that are little or indifferent. In the next place, two similar objects appear not similar when viewed at different distances; the similar parts of a very large object cannot be seen but at different distances; and for that reason, its regularity, and the proportion of its parts, are in some measure lost to the eye; neither are the irregularities of a very large object so conspicuous as of one that is small. Hence it is, that a large object is not so agreeable by its regularity, as a small object, nor so disagreeable by its irregularities.

214. These considerations make it evident, that grandeur is satisfied with a less degree of regularity and of the other qualities mentioned, than is requisite for beauty; which may be illustrated by the following experiment. Approaching to a small conical hill, we take an accurate survey of every part, and are sensible of the slightest deviation from regularity and proportion. Supposing the hill to be considerably enlarged, so as to make us less sensible of its regularity, it will upon that account appear less beautiful. It will not, however, appear less agreeable, because some slight emotion of grandeur comes in place of what is lost in beauty. And at last, when the hill is enlarged to a great mountain, the small degree of beauty that is left, is sunk in its grandeur. Hence it is, that a towering hill is delightful, if it have but the slightest resemblance of a cone; and a chain of mountains no less so, though deficient in the accuracy of order and proportion. We require a small surface to be smooth; but in an extensive plain, considerable inequalities are overlooked. In a word, regularity, proportion, order, and color contribute to grandeur as well as to beauty; but with a remarkable difference, that, in passing from small to great, they are not required in the same degree of perfection. This remark serves to explain the extreme delight we have in viewing the face of nature, when sufficiently enriched and diversified with objects. The bulk of the objects in a natural landscape are beautiful, and some of them grand: a flowing river, a spreading oak, a round hill, an extended

---

213. Emotions of grandeur and beauty distinguished.—Why regularity, proportion, &c., are not so essential to grandeur as to beauty.—Terms *great*, *grand*, and *sublime*, defined and illustrated.

plain are delightful; and even a rugged rock or barren heath, though in themselves disagreeable, contribute by contrast to the beauty of the whole: joining to these the verdure of the fields, the mixture of light and shade, and the sublime canopy spread over all, it will not appear wonderful, that so extensive a group of splendid objects should swell the heart to its utmost bounds, and raise the strongest emotion of grandeur. The spectator is conscious of an enthusiasm, which cannot bear confinement, nor the strictness of regularity and order: he loves to range at large; and is so enchanted with magnificent objects, as to overlook slight beauties or deformities.

215. The same observation is applicable in some measure to works of art: in a small building, the slightest irregularity is disagreeable; but, in a magnificent palace, or a large Gothic church, irregularities are less regarded; in an epic poem we pardon many negligences that would not be permitted in a sonnet or epigram Notwithstanding such exceptions, it may be justly laid down for a rule, That in works of art, order and regularity ought to be governing principles: and hence the observation of Longinus (chapter xxx.), "In works of art we have regard to exact proportion; in those of nature, to grandeur and magnificence."

The same reflections are in a good measure applicable to sublimity; particularly, that, like grandeur, it is a species of agreeableness; that a beautiful object placed high, appearing more agreeable than formerly, produces in the spectator a new emotion, termed *the emotion of sublimity;* and that the perfection of order, regularity, and proportion, is less required in objects placed high, or at a distance, than at hand.

216. The pleasant emotion raised by large objects, has not escaped the poets:

> ——— He doth bestride the narrow world
> Like a Colossus; and we petty men
> Walk under his huge legs. *Julius Cæsar*, Act I. Sc. 3.

> *Cleopatra.* I dreamt there was an Emp'ror Antony:
> Oh such another sleep, that I might see
> But such another man!
> His face was as the heavens: and therein stuck
> A sun and moon, which kept their course, and lighted
> The little O o' the earth.
> His legs bestrid the ocean, his rear'd arm
> Crested the world. *Antony and Cleopatra*, Act V. Sc. 3.

> ——————— Majesty
> Dies not alone, but, like a gulf, doth draw
> What's near it with it. It's a massy wheel
> Fix'd on the summit of the highest mount;

---

214. Illustrated by the experiment of approaching a hill.—How it is in passing from the sight of small to that of great objects.—The delight found in viewing the face of nature explained.

215. Observations in regard to works of art. Also in regard to sublimity.

To whose huge spokes, ten thousand lesser things
Are mortised and adjoin'd; which when it falls,
Each small annexment, petty consequence,
Attends the boist'rous ruin. *Hamlet*, Act III. Sc. 8.

The poets have also made good use of the emotion produced by the elevated situation of an object:

Quod si me lyricis vatibus inseres,
Sublimi feriam sidera vertice.
Horat. Carm. L. I. Ode I.

Oh thou! the earthly author of my blood,
Whose youthful spirit, in me regenerate,
Doth with a twofold vigor lift me up,
To reach at victory above my head.
Richard II. Act I. Sc. 4.

Northumberland, thou ladder wherewithal
The mounting Bolingbroke ascends my throne.
Richard II. Act V. Sc. 2.

Antony. Why was I raised the meteor of the world,
Hung in the skies, and blazing as I travell'd,
Till all my fires were spent; and then cast downward,
To be trod out by Cæsar?—*Dryden*, *All for Love*, Act I.

The description of Paradise in the fourth book of *Paradise Lost*, is a fine illustration of the impression made by elevated objects:

So on he fares, and to the border comes
Of Eden, where delicious Paradise,
Now nearer, crowns with her inclosure green,
As with a rural mound, the champain head
Of a steep wilderness; whose hairy sides,
With thicket overgrown, grotesque and wild,
Access denied; and overhead up grew
Insuperable height of loftiest shade,
Cedar, and pine, and fir, and branching palm,
A sylvan scene; and as the ranks ascend,
Shade above shade, a woody theatre
Of stateliest view. Yet higher than their tops
The verd'rous wall of Paradise up sprung;
Which to our general sire gave prospect large
Into his nether empire neighb'ring round.
And higher than that wall a circling row
Of goodliest trees, loaden with fairest fruit,
Blossoms and fruits at once of golden hue,
Appear'd with gay enamell'd colors mix'd.—B. iv. l. 131.

217. Though a grand object is agreeable, we must not infer that a little object is disagreeable; which would be unhappy for man, considering that he is surrounded with so many objects of that kind. The same holds with respect to place: a body placed high is agreeable; but the same body placed low is not by that circumstance rendered disagreeable. Littleness and lowness of place are precisely similar in the following particular, that they neither give pleasure nor pain. And in this may visibly be discovered peculiar attention in fitting the internal constitution of man to his external circumstances: were littleness and lowness of place agreeable, greatness

---

216. Pleasant emotions raised by large objects illustrated from the poets; those also raised by high objects especially from Paradise Lost.

and elevation could not be so; were littleness and lowness of place disagreeable, they would occasion perpetual uneasiness.

The difference between great and little with respect to agreeableness, is remarkably felt in a series, when we pass gradually from the one extreme to the other. A mental progress from the capital to the kingdom, from that to Europe—to the whole earth—to the planetary system—to the universe, is extremely pleasant; the heart swells and the mind is dilated at every step. The returning in an opposite direction is not positively painful, though our pleasure lessens at every step till it vanish into indifference: such a progress may sometimes produce pleasure of a different sort, which arises from taking a narrower and narrower inspection. The same observation holds in a progress upward and downward. Ascent is pleasant because it elevates us: but descent is never painful; it is for the most part pleasant from a different cause, that it is according to the order of nature. The fall of a stone from any height is extremely agreeable by its accelerated motion. I feel it pleasant to descend from a mountain, because the descent is natural and easy. Neither is looking downward painful; on the contrary, to look down upon objects makes part of the pleasure of elevation. Looking down becomes then only painful when the object is so far below as to create dizziness; and even when that is the case we feel a sort of pleasure mixed with the pain. Witness Shakspeare's description of Dover Cliffs:

> ——————How fearful
> And dizzy 'tis to cast one's eyes so low!
> The crows and choughs, that wing the midway air,
> Show scarce so gross as beetles. Half-way down
> Hangs one that gathers samphire; dreadful trade!
> Methinks he seems no bigger than his head.
> The fishermen that walk upon the beach,
> Appear like mice; and yon tall anchoring bark
> Diminish'd to her cock; her cock, a buoy
> Almost too small for sight. The murmuring surge,
> That on the unnumber'd idle pebbles chafes,
> Cannot be heard so high. I'll look no more,
> Lest my brain turn, and the deficient sight
> Topple down headlong.—*King Lear*, Act. IV. Sc. 6.

218. A remark is made above that the emotions of grandeur and sublimity are nearly allied. And hence it is that the one term is frequently put for the other: an increasing series of numbers, for example, producing an emotion similar to that of mounting upward, is commonly termed *an ascending series;* a series of numbers gradually decreasing, producing an emotion similar to that of going downward, is commonly termed *a descending series.* We talk familiarly of going *up* to the capital, and of going *down* to the country: from a lesser kingdom we talk of going *up* to a greater; whence the *anabasis* in the Greek language, when one travels from Greece

---

217. Comparison between great and small, high and low objects, as to agreeableness.—Progress in an advancing series from one extreme to another, and in reverse order, as to agreeableness.—Progress upward and downward.—Shakspeare's description of Dover Cliffs to Persia. We discover the same way of speaking in the language even of Japan;* and it universally proves it the offspring of a natural feeling.

219. The foregoing observation leads us to consider grandeur and sublimity in a figurative sense, and as applicable to the fine arts Hitherto these terms have been taken in their proper sense as applicable to objects of sight only; and it was of importance to bestow some pains upon that article, because, generally speaking, the figurative sense of a word is derived from its proper sense, which holds remarkably at present. Beauty, in its original signification, is confined to objects of sight; but as many other objects, intellectual as well as moral, raise emotions resembling that of beauty, the resemblance of the effects prompts us to extend the term *beauty* to these objects.† This equally accounts for the terms *grandeur* and *sublimity* taken in a figurative sense. Every emotion, from whatever cause proceeding, that resembles an emotion of grandeur or elevation, is called by the same name: thus generosity is said to be an *elevated* emotion, as well as great courage; and that firmness of soul, which is superior to misfortunes, obtains the peculiar name of *magnanimity*. On the other hand, every emotion that contracts the mind and fixeth it upon things trivial or of no importance, is termed *low*, by its resemblance to an emotion produced by a little or low object of sight; thus an appetite for trifling amusements is called *a low taste*. The same terms are applied to characters and actions: we talk familiarly of an *elevated* genius, of a *great* man, and equally so of *littleness* of mind: some actions are *great* and *elevated*, and others are *little* and *grovelling*. Sentiments, and even expressions, are characterized in the same manner; an expression or sentiment

---

* Kempfer's History of Japan, b. v. chap. 2.

† [Cousin gives the following *classification of the objects of beauty:*

"Among sensible objects, colors, sounds, figures, movements, are capable of producing the idea and the sentiment of the beautiful. All these beauties are arranged under that species of beauty, which, right or wrong, is called *physical beauty*.

"If, from the world of sense, we elevate ourselves to that of mind, truth, and science, we shall find there beauties more severe, but not less real. The universal laws that govern bodies, those that govern intelligences, the great principles that contain and produce long deductions, the genius that creates in the artist, poet, or philosopher,—all these are beautiful, as well as nature herself: this is what is called *intellectual beauty*.

"Finally, if we consider the moral world and its laws, the idea of liberty, virtue, and devotedness; here the austere justice of an Aristides, there the heroism of a Leonidas, the prodigies of charity or of patriotism, we shall certainly find a third order of beauty that still surpasses the other two, to wit, *moral beauty*.

"Neither let us forget to apply to all these beauties the distinction between the beautiful and the sublime. There are, then, the beautiful and the sublime at once *in nature, in ideas, in sentiments, in actions*. What an almost infinite variety in beauty!"—Lect. vi. pp. 143 4.]

---

218. Emotions of grandeur and sublimity nearly allied. —Increasing series of numbers termed *ascending*, &c.

that raises the mind is denominated *great* or *elevated*, and hence the SUBLIME* in poetry. In such figurative terms we lose the distinction between *great* and *elevated* in their proper sense; for the resemblance is not so entire as to preserve these terms distinct in their figurative application. We carry this figure still farther. Elevation in its proper sense, imports superiority of place; and lowness, inferiority of place; and hence a man of *superior* talents, of *superior* rank, of *inferior* parts, of *inferior* taste, and such like. The veneration we have for our ancestors, and for the ancients in general, being similar to the emotion produced by an elevated object of sight, justifies the figurative expression of the ancients being *raised* above us, or possessing a *superior* place. And we may remark in passing, that as words are intimately connected with ideas, many, by this form of expression, are led to conceive their ancestors as really above them in place, and their posterity below them:

> A grandam's name is little less in love,
> Than is the doting title of a mother:
> They are as children but one step below.
> *Richard III.* Act IV. Sc. 5.

The notes of the gamut, proceeding regularly from the blunter or grosser sounds to the more acute and piercing, produce in the hearer a feeling somewhat similar to what is produced by mounting upward; and this gives occasion to the figurative expressions, *a high note, a low note.*

220. Such is the resemblance in feeling between real and figurative grandeur, that among the nations on the east coast of Africa, who are directed purely by nature, the officers of state are, with respect to rank, distinguished by the length of the batoon each carries in his hand; and in Japan, princes and great lords show their rank by the length and size of their sedan-poles.† Again, it is a rule in painting, that figures of a small size are proper for a grotesque piece; but that an historical subject, grand and important, requires figures as great as the life. The resemblance of these feelings is in reality so strong, that elevation, in a figurative sense, is observed to have the same effect, even externally, with real elevation.

> *K. Henry.* This day is call'd the feast of Crispian.
> He that outlives this day, and comes safe home,
> Will stand a-tiptoe when this day is named,
> And rouse him at the name of Crispian.—*Henry V.* Act IV. Sc. 8.

---

* Longinus gives a description of the Sublime that is not amiss, though far from being just in every circumstance: "That the mind is elevated by it, and so sensibly affected as to swell in transport and inward pride, as if what is only heard or read were its own invention."

† Kempfer's History of Japan.

---

219. Grandeur and sublimity in a figurative sense, as applied to the fine arts.—Beauty *originally* confined to what?—Cousin's classification of the objects of beauty.—Emotions resembling those of grandeur or sublimity are called by the same name.—Opposite emotions, how called.—Characters, actions, sentiments, and expressions characterized in the same manner.—How we speak of ancestors and of the ancients.—Notes of the gamut.

The resemblance in feeling between real and figurative grandeur is humorously illustrated by Addison in criticising upon English tragedy: "The ordinary method of making a hero, is to clap a huge plume of feathers upon his head, which rises so high, that there is often a greater length from his chin to the top of his head, than to the sole of his foot. One would believe, that we thought a great man and a tall man the same thing. As these superfluous ornaments upon the head make a great man, a princess generally receives her grandeur from those additional incumbrances that fall into her tail: I mean the broad sweeping train, that follows her in all her motions, and finds constant employment for a boy, who stands behind her to open and spread it to advantage." (Spectator, No. 42.) The Scythians, impressed with the fame of Alexander, were astonished when they found him a little man.

221. A gradual progress from small to great is no less remarkable in figurative than in real grandeur or elevation. Every one must have observed the delightful effect of a number of thoughts or sentiments artfully disposed like an ascending series, and making impressions deeper and deeper: such disposition of members in a period is termed a *climax*.

Within certain limits, grandeur and sublimity produce their strongest effects, which lessen by excess as well as by defect. This is remarkable in grandeur and sublimity taken in their proper sense: the grandest emotion that can be raised by a visible object, is where the object can be taken in at one view; if so immense as not to be comprehended but in parts, it tends rather to distract than satisfy the mind:* in like manner, the strongest emotion produced by elevation, is where the object is seen distinctly; a greater elevation lessens in appearance the object, until it vanishes out of sight with its pleasant emotion. The same is equally remarkable in figurative grandeur and elevation, which shall be handled together, because, as observed above, they are scarce distinguishable. Sentiments may be so strained as to become obscure, or to exceed the capacity of the human mind: against such license of imagination, every good writer will be upon his guard; and therefore it is of greater importance to observe, that even the true sublime may be carried beyond that pitch which produces the highest entertainment. We are undoubtedly susceptible of a greater elevation than can be inspired

* It is justly observed by Addison, that perhaps a man would have been more astonished with the majestic air that appeared in one of Lysippus's statues of Alexander, though no bigger than the life, than he might have been with Mount Athos, had it been cut into the figure of the hero, according to the proposal of Phidias, with a river in one hand, and a city in the other.—*Spectator*, No. 415.

220. How superiority of rank is expressed in Africa and Japan.—Rule in painting as to size of figures.—The resemblance in feeling between real and figurative grandeur, illustrated by Addison.

by human actions, the most heroic and magnanimous: witness what we feel from Milton's description of superior beings; yet every man must be sensible of a more constant and sweet elevation, when the history of his own species is the subject: he enjoys an elevation equal to that of the greatest hero, of an Alexander or a Cæsar, of a Brutus or an Epaminondas; he accompanies these heroes in their sublimest sentiments and most hazardous exploits, with a magnanimity equal to theirs; and finds it no stretch, to preserve the same tone of mind, for hours together, without sinking. The case is not the same in describing the actions or qualities of superior beings: the reader's imagination cannot keep pace with that of the poet; the mind, unable to support itself in a strained elevation, falls as if from a height; and the fall is immoderate, like the elevation: where that effect is not felt, it must be prevented by some obscurity in the conception, which frequently attends the description of unknown objects. Hence the St. Francises, St. Dominics, and other tutelary saints, among the Roman Catholics. A mind unable to raise itself to the Supreme Being, self-existent and eternal, or to support itself in a strained elevation, finds itself more at ease in using the intercession of some saint whose piety and penances while on earth are supposed to have made him a favorite in heaven.

222. A strained elevation is attended with another inconvenience, that the author is apt to fall suddenly as well as the reader: because it is not a little difficult to descend sweetly and easily from such elevation to the ordinary tone of the subject. The following passage is a good illustration of that observation:

> Sæpe etiam immensum cœlo venit agmen aquarum,
> Et fœdam glomerant tempestatem imbribus atris
> Conlectæ ex alto nubes. Ruit arduus æther,
> Et pluvia ingenti sata læta boumque labores
> Diluit. Inplentur fussæ, et cava flumina crescunt
> Cum sonitu, fervetque fretis spirantibus æquor.
> Ipse Pater, media nimborum in nocte, corruscâ
> Fulmina molitur dextra. Quo maxima motu
> Terra tremit: fugêre feræ! et mortalia corda
> Per gentes humilis stravit pavor. Ille flagranti
> Aut Atho, aut Rodopen, aut alta Ceraunia telo
> Dejicit: *ingeminant austri, et densissimus imber.*—*Virg. Georg.* l. 1

In the description of a storm, to figure Jupiter throwing down huge mountains with his thunderbolts, is hyperbolically sublime, if I may use the expression: the tone of mind produced by that image is so distant from the tone produced by a thick shower of rain, that the sudden transition must be unpleasant.

Objects of sight that are not remarkably great or high, scarce raise any emotion of grandeur or of sublimity: and the same holds in other objects; for we often find the mind roused and animated,

---

221. Climax.—Grandeur and sublimity produce their greatest effects only within certain limits.—Sentiments may be strained too far.—Elevation inspired by the actions of superhuman beings, compared with that inspired by our own species.

without being carried to that height. This difference may be discerned in many sorts of music, as well as in some musical instruments: a kettle-drum rouses, and a hautboy is animating; but neither of them inspires an emotion of sublimity: revenge animates the mind in a considerable degree; but I think it never produceth an emotion that can be termed *grand* or *sublime;* and I shall have occasion afterwards to observe, that no disagreeable passion ever has that effect. I am willing to put this to the test, by placing before my reader a most spirited picture of revenge: it is a speech of Antony wailing over the body of Cæsar:

> Woe to the hand that shed this cost.y blood!
> Over thy wounds now do I prophesy,
> (Which like dumb mouths, do ope their ruby lips,
> To beg the voice and utterance of my tongue,)
> A curse shall light upon the kind of men;
> Domestic fury, and fierce civil strife,
> Shall cumber all the parts of Italy;
> Blood and destruction shall be so in use,
> And dreadful objects so familiar,
> That mothers shall but smile, when they behold
> Their infants quarter'd by the hands of war.
> All pity choked with custom of fell deeds,
> And Cæsar's spirit, ranging for revenge,
> With *Até* by his side come hot from hell,
> Shall in these confines, with a monarch's voice,
> Cry, *Havoc!* and let slip the dogs of war.
>
> *Julius Cæsar*, Act III. Sc. 4.

223. No desire is more general than to be exalted and honored: and upon that account chiefly are we ambitious of power, riches, titles, fame, which would suddenly lose their relish, did they not raise us above others, and command submission and deference; and it may be thought that our attachment to things grand and lofty proceeds from their connection with our favorite passion. This connection has undoubtedly an effect: but that the preference given to things grand and lofty must have deeper root in human nature, will appear from considering, that many bestow their time upon low and trifling amusements, without having the least tincture of this favorite passion; yet these very persons talk the same language with the rest of mankind, and prefer the more elevated pleasures: they acknowledge a more refined taste, and are ashamed of their own as low and grovelling. This sentiment, constant and universal, must be the work of nature; and it plainly indicates an original attachment in human nature to every object that elevates the mind: some men may have a greater relish for an object not of the highest rank; but they are conscious of the preference given by mankind in general to things grand and sublime: and they are sensible that their peculiar taste ought to yield to the general taste.

---

222. Inconvenience of a strained elevation. No disagreeable passion raises an emotion of sublimity. Revenge does not.—Speech of Antony.

223. The desire to be honored. Its effects.—The preference of the human mind for things grand and lofty.

224. What is said above suggests a capital rule for reaching the sublime in such works of art as are susceptible of it: and that is, to present those parts or circumstances only which make the greatest figure, keeping out of view every thing low or trivial; for the mind, elevated by an important object, cannot, without reluctance, be forced down to bestow any share of its attention upon trifles. Such judicious selection of capital circumstances, is by an eminent critic styled *grandeur of manner* (Spectator, No 415). In none of the fine arts is there so great scope for that rule as in poetry; which, by that means, enjoys a remarkable power of bestowing upon objects and events an air of grandeur: when we are spectators, every minute object presents itself in its order: but, in describing at second hand, these are laid aside, and the capital objects are brought close together. A judicious taste in thus selecting the most interesting incidents, to give them a united force, accounts for a fact that may appear surprising; which is, that we are more moved by a spirited narrative at second hand, than by being spectators of the event itself, in all its circumstances.

Longinus exemplifies the foregoing rule by a comparison of two passages (Chapter viii. of the Sublime). The first, from Aristæus, is thus translated:

> Ye powers, what madness! how on ships so frail
> (Tremendous thought!) can thoughtless mortals sail?
> For stormy seas they quit the pleasing plain,
> Plant woods in waves, and dwell amidst the main.
> Far o'er the deep (a trackless path) they go,
> And wander oceans in pursuit of woe.
> No ease their hearts, no rest their eyes can find,
> On heaven their looks, and on the waves their mind,
> Sunk are their spirits, while their arms they rear,
> And gods are wearied with their fruitless prayer.

The other, from Homer, I shall give in Pope's translation:

> Burst as a wave that from the cloud impends,
> And swell'd with tempests on the ship descends.
> White are the decks with foam: the winds aloud
> Howl o'er the masts, and sing through every shroud.
> Pale, trembling, tired, the sailors freeze with fears,
> And instant death on every wave appears.

In the latter passage, the most striking circumstances are selected to fill the mind with terror and astonishment. The former is a collection of minute and low circumstances, which scatter the thought, and make no impression: it is at the same time full of verbal antitheses and low conceit, extremely improper in a scene of distress. But this last observation belongs to another head.

The following description of a battle is remarkably sublime, by collecting together in the fewest words, those circumstances which make the greatest figure.

Like Autumn's dark storms pouring from two echoing hills, towards each other approached the heroes; as two dark streams from high rocks meet and roar on the plain, loud, rough, and dark in battle, meet Lochlin and Innisfail. Chief mixes his strokes with chief, and man with man: steel sounds on steel, and helmets are cleft on high: blood bursts and smokes around; strings murmur on the polished yew: darts rush along the sky: spears fall like sparks of flame that gild the stormy face of night.

As the noise of the troubled ocean when roll the waves on high, as the last peal of thundering heaven, such is the noise of battle. Though Cormac's hundred bards were there, feeble were the voice of a hundred bards to send the deaths to future times; for many were the deaths of the heroes, and wide poured the blood of the valiant.—*Fingal.*

The following passage in the 4th book of the Iliad is a description of a battle, wonderfully ardent. "When now gathered on either side, the hosts plunged together in fight; shield is harshly laid to shield; spears crash on the brazen corslets; bossy buckler with buckler meets; loud tumult rages over all; groans are mixed with boasts of men; the slain and slayer join in noise; the earth is floating round with blood. As when two rushing streams from two mountains come roaring down, and throw together their rapid waters below, they roar along the gulfy vale: the startled shepherd hears the sound, as he stalks o'er the distant hills: so, as they mixed in fight, from both armies clamor with loud terror arose." But such general descriptions are not frequent in Homer. Even his single combats are rare. The fifth book is the longest account of a battle that is in the Iliad; and yet contains nothing but a long catalogue of chiefs killing chiefs, not in single combat neither, but at a distance, with an arrow or a javelin; and these chiefs named for the first time and the last. The same scene is continued through a great part of the sixth book. There is at the same time a minute description of every wound, which for accuracy may do honor to an anatomist, but in an epic poem is tiresome and fatiguing. There is no relief from horrid languor but the beautiful Greek language and melody of Homer's versification.

225. In the twenty-first book of the Odyssey, there is a passage which deviates widely from the rule above laid down: it concerns that part of the history of Penelope and her suitors, in which she is made to declare in favor of him who should prove the most dexterous in shooting with the bow of Ulysses:

Now gently winding up the fair ascent
By many an easy step, the matron went:
Then o'er the pavement glides with grace divine,
(With polish'd oak the level pavements shine;)
The folding gates a dazzling light display'd,
With pomp of various architrave o'erlay'd.
The bolt, obedient to the silken string,
Forsakes the staple as she pulls the ring;
The wards respondent to the key turn'd round;
The bars fall back; the flying valves resound
Loud as a bull makes hill and valley ring;
So roar'd the lock when it released the spring.

---

224. Rule for reaching the sublime in works of art. Scope for this rule in poetry—Effect of a spirited narration. Example from Fingal: from the Iliad.

225. Violation of the rule above given, in the Odyssey.

She moves majestic through the wealthy room,
Where treasured garments cast a rich perfume;
There from the column where aloft it hung,
Reach'd, in its splendid case, the bow unstrung

226. This rule is also applicable to other fine arts. In painting it is established, that the principal figure must be put in the strongest light; that the beauty of attitude consists in placing the nobler parts most in view, and in suppressing the smaller parts as much as possible; that the folds of the drapery must be few and large; that fore-shortenings are bad, because they make the parts appear little; and that the muscles ought to be kept as entire as possible, without being divided into small sections. Every one at present subscribes to that rule as applied to gardening, in opposition to parterres split into a thousand small parts in the stiffest regularity of figure. The most eminent architects have governed themselves by the same rule in all their works.

227. Another rule chiefly regards the sublime, though it is applicable to every sort of literary performance intended for amusement; and that is to avoid as much as possible abstract and general terms. Such terms, similar to mathematical signs, are contrived to express our thoughts in a concise manner; but images, which are the life of poetry, cannot be raised in any perfection but by introducing particular objects. General terms that comprehend a number of individuals, must be excepted from that rule: our kindred, our clan, our country, and words of the like import, though they scarce raise any image, have, however, a wonderful power over our passions: the greatness of the complex object overbalances the obscurity of the image. (See chap. xxii.)

228. Grandeur being an extremely vivid emotion, is not readily produced in perfection but by reiterated impressions. The effect of a single impression can be but momentary; and if one feel suddenly somewhat like a swelling or exaltation of mind, the emotion vanisheth as soon as felt. Single thoughts or sentiments, I know, are often cited as examples of the sublime; but their effect is far inferior to that of a grand subject displayed in its capital parts. I shall give a few examples, that the reader may judge for himself. In the famous action of Thermopylæ, where Leonidas, the Spartan king, with his chosen band fighting for their country, were cut off to the last man, a saying is reported of Dieneces, one of the band, which, expressing cheerful and undisturbed bravery, is well entitled to the first place in examples of that kind. Respecting the number of their enemies, it was observed, that the arrows shot by such a multitude would intercept the light of the sun. So much the better, says he, for we shall then fight in the shade. (*Herodotus*, Book vii.)

---

226. Grandeur of manner illustrated in painting and gardening.
227. Abstract and general terms An exception.

Somerset. Ah! Warwick, Warwick, wert thou as we are,
We might recover all our loss again.
The Queen from France hath brought a puissant power,
Even now we heard the news. Ah! couldst thou fly!
Warwick. Why, then I would not fly.
Third Part, Henry VI. Act V. Sc. 3

Such a sentiment from a man expiring of his wounds, is truly heroic and must elevate the mind to the greatest height that can be done by a single expression: it will not suffer in a comparison with the famous sentiment *Qu'il mourut* of Corneille: the latter is a sentiment of indignation merely, the former of firm and cheerful courage.

To cite in opposition many a sublime passage enriched with the finest images, and dressed in the most nervous expressions, would scarce be fair: I shall produce but one instance, from Shakspeare, which sets a few objects before the eye without much pomp of language; it operates its effect by representing these objects in a climax, raising the mind higher and higher till it feel the emotion of grandeur in perfection:

The cloud-capp'd towers, the gorgeous palaces,
The solemn temples, the great globe itself,
Yea, all which it inherit, shall dissolve, &c.

The cloud-capp'd towers produce an elevating emotion, heightened by the *gorgeous palaces*; and the mind is carried still higher and higher by the images that follow. Successive images making thus deeper and deeper impressions, must elevate more than any single image can do.

229. As, on the one hand, no means directly applied have more influence to raise the mind than grandeur and sublimity; so, on the other, no means indirectly applied have more influence to sink and depress it; for in a state of elevation, the artful introduction of an humbling object, makes the fall great in proportion to the elevation. Of this observation Shakspeare gives a beautiful example in the passage last quoted:

The cloud-capp'd towers, the gorgeous palaces,
The solemn temples, the great globe itself,
Yea, all which it inherit, shall dissolve,
And, like the baseless fabric of a vision,
Leave not a rack behind.——— *Tempest*, Act IV. Sc. 4.

The elevation of the mind in the former part of this beautiful passage, makes the fall great in proportion, when the most humbling of all images is introduced, that of an utter dissolution of the earth and its inhabitants. The mind, when warmed, is more susceptible of impressions than in a cool state; and a depressing or melancholy object listened to, makes the strongest impression when it reaches the mind in its highest state of elevation or cheerfulness.

But an humbling image is not always necessary to produce that

---

228. Grandeur produced by reiterated impressions.—Effect of a grand subject displayed in its capital parts.—The saying of Dieneces.—Example of climax from Shakspeare.

effect: a remark is made above, that in describing superior beings, the reader's imagination, unable to support itself in a strained elevation, falls often as from a height, and sinks even below its ordinary tone. The following instance comes luckily in view; for a better cannot be given: "God said, Let there be light, and there was light." Longinus quotes this passage from Moses as a shining example of the sublime; and it is scarce possible, in fewer words, to convey so clear an image of the infinite power of the Deity; but then it belongs to the present subject to remark that the emotion of sublimity raised by this image is but momentary; and that the mind, unable to support itself in an elevation so much above nature, immediately sinks down into humility and veneration for a being so far exalted above grovelling mortals. Every one is acquainted with a dispute about that passage between two French critics (Boileau and Huet), the one positively affirming it to be sublime, the other as positively denying. What I have remarked shows that both of them have reached the truth, but neither of them the whole truth: the primary effect of the passage is undoubtedly an emotion of grandeur; which so far justifies Boileau; but then every one must be sensible, that the emotion is merely a flash which, vanishing instantaneously, gives way to humility and veneration. That indirect effect of sublimity justifies Huet, who, being a man of true piety, and probably not much carried by imagination, felt the humbling passion more sensibly than his antagonist did. And, laying aside difference of character, Huet's opinion may, I think, be defended as the more solid; because in such images, the depressing emotions are the more sensibly felt, and have the longer endurance.

230. The straining an elevated subject beyond due bounds, is a vice not so frequent as to require the correction of criticism. But false sublime is a rock that writers of more fire than judgment commonly split on; and, therefore, a collection of examples may be of use as a beacon to future adventurers. One species of false sublime, known by the name of *bombast*, is common among writers of a mean genius: it is a serious endeavor, by strained description, to raise a low or familiar subject above its rank; which, instead of being sublime, becomes ridiculous. I am extremely sensible how prone the mind is, in some animating passions, to magnify its objects beyond natural bounds; but such hyperbolical description has its limits, and, when carried beyond the impulse of the propensity, it degenerates into burlesque. Take the following examples:

> *Sejanus.* ——————Great and high
> The world knows only two, that's Rome and I.
> My roof receives me not; 'tis air I tread,
> And at each step I feel my advanced head
> Knock out a star in heaven.—*Sejanus*, *Ben Jonson*, Act V.

---

229. The effect of introducing an humbling object when the mind is in a state of elevation. The reader's imagination unable long to sustain itself in a strained elevation, falls.—Remarks on the passage "Let there be light," &c. Dispute upon it between Boileau and Huet.

A writer who has no natural elevation of mind, deviates readily into bombast; he strains above his natural powers, and the violent effort carries him beyond the bounds of propriety. Boileau expresses this happily:

> L'autre à peur de ramper, il se perd dans la nue.

The same author, Ben Jonson, abounds in the bombast:

> ————————The mother,
> Th' expulsed Apicata, finds them there;
> Whom when she saw lie spread on the degrees,
> After a world of fury on herself,
> Tearing her hair, defacing of her face,
> Beating her breasts and womb, kneeling amazed,
> Crying to heaven, then to them; at last
> Her drowned voice got up above her woes;
> And with such black and bitter execrations,
> As might affright the gods, and force the sun
> Run backward to the east; nay, make the old
> Deformed chaos rise again t' overwhelm
> Them (us and all the world), she fills the air,
> Upbraids the heavens with their partial dooms,
> Defies their tyrannous powers, and demands
> What she and those poor innocents have transgress'd,
> That they must suffer such a share in vengeance.
>
> *Sejanus*, Act V. Sc. last.

I am sorry to observe that the following bombast stuff dropt from the pen of Dryden:

> To see this fleet upon the ocean move,
> Angels drew wide the curtains of the skies;
> And heaven, as if there wanted lights above,
> For tapers made two glaring comets rise.

231. Another species of false sublime is still more faulty than bombast; and that is, to force elevation by introducing imaginary beings without preserving any propriety in their actions, as if it were lawful to ascribe every extravagance and inconsistence to beings of the poet's creation. No writers are more licentious in that article than Jonson and Dryden:

> Methinks I see Death and the Furies waiting
> What we will do, and all the heaven at leisure
> For the great spectacle. Draw then your swords:
> And if our destiny envy our virtue
> The honor of the day, yet let us care
> To sell ourselves at such a price as may
> Undo the world to buy us, and make Fate,
> While she tempts ours, to fear her own estate.
>
> *Catiline*, Act V.

> ————————The Furies stood on hill
> Circling the place, and trembled to see men
> Do more than they; whilst Piety left the field,
> Grieved for that side that in so bad a cause
> They knew not what a crime their valor was.
> The sun stood still, and was, behind the cloud
> The battle made, seen sweating to drive up
> His frighted horse, whom still the noise drove backward.
>
> *Ibid.* Act V.

230. False sublime, known as bombast. Examples from Ben Jonson; from Dryden.

An actor on the stage may be guilty of bombast as well as an author in his closet; a certain manner of acting, which is grand when supported by dignity in the sentiment and force in the expression, is ridiculous where the sentiment is mean, and the expression flat.

232. This chapter shall be closed with some observations. When the sublime is carried to its due height, and circumscribed within proper bounds, it enchants the mind, and raises the most delightful of all emotions: the reader, engrossed by a sublime object, feels himself raised as it were to a higher rank. Considering that effect, it is not wonderful that the history of conquerors and heroes should be universally the favorite entertainment. And this fairly accounts for what I once erroneously suspected to be a wrong bias originally in human nature; which is, that the grossest acts of oppression and injustice scarce blemish the character of a great conqueror: we, nevertheless, warmly espouse his interest, accompany him in his exploits, and are anxious for his success: the splendor and enthusiasm of the hero, transfused into the readers, elevate their minds far above the rules of justice, and render them in a great measure insensible of the wrongs that are committed:

For in those days might only shall be admired,
And valor an heroic virtue call'd;
To overcome in battle, and subdue
Nations, and bring home spoils with infinite
Manslaughter, shall be held the highest pitch
Of human glory, and for glory done
Of triumph, to be styled great conquerors,
Patrons of mankind, gods, and sons of gods,
Destroyers rightlier call'd, and plagues of men.
Thus fame shall be achieved, renown on earth,
And what most merits fame in silence hid. *Milton*, B. xi.

The irregular influence of grandeur reaches also to other matters: however good, honest, or useful a man may be, he is not so much respected as is one of a more elevated character, though of less integrity; nor do the misfortunes of the former affect us so much as those of the latter. And I add, because it cannot be disguised, that the remorse which attends breach of engagement, is in a great measure proportioned to the figure that the injured person makes: the vows and protestations of lovers are an illustrious example; for these commonly are little regarded when made to women of inferior rank.

---

231. False sublime in introducing imaginary beings. Examples from Jonson and Dryden.—Bombast in an actor.

232. Closing observations.—Why the history of conquerors and heroes fascinates: why their crimes are palliated. Milton quoted.—The irregular influence of the sentiment of grandeur in other instances.

CHAPTER V.

MOTION AND FORCE.

233. THAT motion is agreeable to the eye without relation to purpose or design, may appear from the amusement it gives to infants: juvenile exercises are relished chiefly on that account.

If a body in motion be agreeable, one will be apt to conclude that at rest it must be disagreeable; but we learn from experience, that this would be a rash conclusion. Rest is one of those circumstances that are neither agreeable nor disagreeable, being viewed with perfect indifferency. And happy is it for mankind to have the matter so ordered: if rest were agreeable, it would disincline us to motion, by which all things are performed: if it were disagreeable, it would be a source of perpetual uneasiness; for the bulk of the things we see, appear to be at rest. A similar instance of designing wisdom I have had occasion to explain, in opposing grandeur to littleness, and elevation to lowness of place. (See chapter iv.) Even in the simplest matters, the finger of God is conspicuous: the happy adjustment of the internal nature of man to his external circumstances, displayed in the instances here given, is indeed admirable.

234. Motion is agreeable in all its varieties of quickness and slowness; but motion long continued admits some exceptions. That degree of continued motion which corresponds to the natural course of our perceptions is the most agreeable. The quickest motion is for an instant delightful; but soon appears to be too rapid: it becomes painful by forcibly accelerating the course of our perceptions. Slow continued motion becomes disagreeable from an opposite cause, that it retards the natural course of our perceptions. (See chapter ix.)

There are other varieties in motion, besides quickness and slowness, that make it more or less agreeable: regular motion is preferred before what is irregular; witness the motion of the planets in orbits nearly circular: the motion of the comets in orbits less regular, is less agreeable.

Motion uniformly accelerated, resembling an ascending series of numbers, is more agreeable than when uniformly retarded: motion upward is agreeable, by tendency to elevation. What then shall we say of downward motion regularly accelerated by the force of

---

233. Motion in itself agreeable.—Rest, a matter of indifference.—Advantage of this arrangement.

gravity, compared with upward motion regularly retarded by the same force? Which of these is the most agreeable? This question is not easily solved.

Motion in a straight line is agreeable; but we prefer undulating motion, as of waves, of a flame, of a ship under sail: such motion is more free, and also more natural. Hence the beauty of a serpentine river.

The easy and sliding motion of a fluid, from the lubricity of its parts, is agreeable upon that account; but the agreeableness chiefly depends upon the following circumstance, that the motion is perceived, not as of one body, but as of an endless number moving together with order and regularity. Poets, struck with that beauty, draw more images from fluids in motion than from solids.

Force is of two kinds; one quiescent, and one exerted in motion. The former, dead weight for example, must be laid aside; for a body at rest is not, by that circumstance, either agreeable or disagreeable. Moving force only is my province; and, though it is not separable from motion, yet by the power of abstraction, either of them may be considered independent of the other. Both of them are agreeable, because both of them include activity. It is agreeable to see a thing move: to see it moved, as when it is dragged or pushed along, is neither agreeable nor disagreeable, more than when at rest. It is agreeable to see a thing exert force; but it makes not the thing either agreeable or disagreeable to see force exerted upon it.

Though motion and force are each of them agreeable, the impressions they make are different. This difference, clearly felt, is not easily described. All we can say is, that the emotion raised by a moving body, resembling its cause, is felt as if the mind were carried along: the emotion raised by force exerted, resembling also its cause, is felt as if force were exerted within the mind.

To illustrate that difference, I give the following examples. It has been explained why smoke ascending in a calm day, suppose from a cottage in a wood, is an agreeable object (chapter i.); so remarkably agreeable, that landscape-painters introduce it upon all occasions. The ascent being natural, and without effort, is pleasant in a calm state of mind: it resembles a gently-flowing river, but is more agreeable, because ascent is more to our taste than descent. A fire-work, or a *jet d'eau*, rouses the mind more; because the beauty of force visibly exerted is superadded to that of upward motion. To a man reclining indolently upon a bank of flowers, ascending smoke in a still morning is charming; but a fire-work, or a *jet d'eau*, rouses him from that supine posture, and puts him in motion.

A *jet d'eau* makes an impression distinguishable from that of a waterfall. Downward motion being natural and without effort, tends rather to quiet the mind than to rouse it: upward motion, on the contrary, overcoming the resistance of gravity, makes an impres sion of a great effort, and thereby rouses and enlivens the mind.

235. The public games of the Greeks and Romans, which gave so much entertainment to the spectators, consisted chiefly in exerting force, wrestling, leaping, throwing great stones, and such-like trials of strength. When great force is exerted, the effort felt internally is animating. The effort may be such as in some measure to overpower the mind: thus the explosion of gunpowder, the violence of a torrent, the weight of a mountain, and the crush of an earthquake, create astonishment rather than pleasure.

No quality nor circumstance contributes more to grandeur than force, especially when exerted by sensible beings. I cannot make the observation more evident than by the following quotations

———— Him the almighty power
Hurl'd headlong flaming from th' ethereal sky,
With hideous ruin and combustion, down
To bottomless perdition, there to dwell
In adamantine chains and penal fire,
Who durst defy th' Omnipotent to arms.

Paradise Lost, **Book i.**

———— Now storming fury rose,
And clamor such as heard in heaven till now
Was never; arms on armor clashing bray'd
Horrible discord, and the madding wheels
Of brazen chariots raged; dire was the noise
Of conflict; overhead the dismal hiss
Of fiery darts in flaming volleys flew,
And flying, vaulted either host with fire.
So under fiery cone together rush'd
Both battles main, with ruinous assault
And inextinguishable rage; all heaven
Resounded; and had earth been then, all earth
Had to her centre shook. *Ibid.* **Book vi.**

They ended parle, and both address'd for fight
Unspeakable; for who, though with the tongue
Of angels, can relate, or to what things
Liken on earth conspicuous, that may lift
Human imagination to such height
Of godlike power? for likest gods they seem'd,
Stood they or moved, in stature, motion, arms,
Fit to decide the empire of great Heaven.
Now waved their fiery swords, and in the air
Made horrid circles: two broad suns their shields
Blazed opposite, while Expectation stood
In horror: from each hand with speed retired,
Where erst was thickest fight, th' angelic throng,
And left large field, unsafe within the wind
Of such commotion; such as, to set forth
Great things by small, if Nature's concord broke,
Among the constellations war were sprung,

234. Motion rapid and slow. Regular and irregular Uniformly accelerated, and uniformly retarded. In a straight line, and undulating.—Fluids in motion.—Force; quiescent and in motion.—Motion and force make different impressions on the mind.—Ascent of smoke from a cottage in a wood.—A fire-work or *jet d'eau.* The latter in its effect distinguished from a waterfall

235. Force exerted at Roman and Grecian games.—Forces that overpower the mind.—Force exerted by intelligent beings.—Quotations.

Two planets, rushing from aspect malign
Of fiercest opposition, in mid sky
Should combat, and their jarring spheres confound.
Ibid. Book vi.

236. We shall next consider the effect of motion and force in conjunction. In contemplating the planetary system, what strikes us the most, is the spherical figures of the planets, and their regular motions; the conception we have of their activity and enormous bulk being more obscure: the beauty accordingly of that system raises a more lively emotion than its grandeur. But if we could comprehend the whole system at one view, the activity and irresistible force of these immense bodies would fill us with amazement; nature cannot furnish another scene so grand.

Motion and force, agreeable in themselves, are also agreeable by their utility when employed as means to accomplish some beneficial end. Hence the superior beauty of some machines, where force and motion concur to perform the work of numberless hands. Hence the beautiful motions, firm and regular, of a horse trained for war: every single step is the fittest that can be for obtaining the purposed end. But the grace of motion is visible chiefly in man, not only for the reasons mentioned, but because every gesture is significant. The power, however, of agreeable motion is not a common talent: every limb of the human body has an agreeable and disagreeable motion; some motions being extremely graceful, others plain and vulgar; some expressing dignity, others meanness. But the pleasure here, arising, not singly from the beauty of motion, but from indicating character and sentiment, belongs to different chapters. (Chapters xi. and xv.)

I should conclude with the final cause of the relish we have for motion and force, were it not so evident as to require no explanation. We are placed here in such circumstances as to make industry essential to our well-being; for without industry the plainest necessaries of life are not obtained. When our situation, therefore, in this world requires activity and a constant exertion of motion and force, Providence indulgently provides for our welfare by making these agreeable to us: it would be a gross imperfection in our nature to make any thing disagreeable that we depend on for existence; and even indifference would slacken greatly that degree of activity which is indispensable.

---

236. The effect of motion and force conjoined. The planetary system.—Motion and force also agreeable from their utility.—Beauty of some machines.—Motion of the war-horse.—Grace of motion in man. Not a common talent.—Final cause of our relish for motion and force

CHAPTER VI.

NOVELTY, AND THE UNEXPECTED APPEARANCE OF OBJECTS.

237. Of all the circumstances that raise emotions, not excepting beauty, nor even greatness, novelty hath the most powerful influence. A new object produceth instantaneously an emotion termed *wonder*, which totally occupies the mind, and for a time excludes all other objects. Conversation among the vulgar never is more interesting than when it turns upon strange objects and extraordinary events. Men tear themselves from their native country in search of things rare and new; and novelty converts into a pleasure, the fatigues and even perils of travelling. To what cause shall we ascribe these singular appearances? To curiosity undoubtedly, a principle implanted in human nature for a purpose extremely beneficial, that of acquiring knowledge; and the emotion of wonder, raised by new and strange objects, inflames our curiosity to know more of them. This emotion is different from *admiration:* novelty, wherever found, whether in a quality or action, is the cause of wonder; admiration is directed to the person who performs any thing wonderful.

During infancy, every new object is probably the occasion of wonder, in some degree; because, during infancy, every object at first sight is strange as well as new: but as objects are rendered familiar by custom, we cease by degrees to wonder at new appearances, if they have any resemblance to what we are acquainted with: for a thing must be singular as well as new, to raise our wonder. To save multiplying words, I would be understood to comprehend both circumstances when I hereafter talk of novelty.

238. In an ordinary train of perceptions, where one thing introduces another, not a single object makes its appearance unexpectedly (see chap. i.): the mind, thus prepared for the reception of its objects, admits them one after another without perturbation. But when a thing breaks in unexpectedly, and without the preparation of any connection, it raises an emotion, known by the name of *surprise.* That emotion may be produced by the most familiar object, as when one unexpectedly meets a friend who was reported to be dead; or a man in high life lately a beggar. On the other hand, a new object, however strange, will not produce the emotion, if the spectator be prepared for the sight: an elephant in India will not surprise a traveller who goes to see one; and yet its novelty will raise his wonder: an Indian in Britain would be much surprised to

237. Emotion excited by a new object. Conversation that most interests the vulgar.—Motive for travelling.—Curiosity beneficial.—Wonder and admiration distinguished.—Wonder in infancy; in advancing years.

stumble upon an elephant feeding at large in the open fields: but the creature itself, to which he was accustomed, would not raise his wonder.

Surprise thus in several respects differs from wonder: unexpectedness is the cause of the former emotion; novelty is the cause of the latter. Nor differ they less in their nature and circumstances, as will be explained by and by. With relation to one circumstance they perfectly agree; which is, the shortness of their duration: the instantaneous production of these emotions in perfection may contribute to that effect, in conformity to a general law, That things soon decay which soon come to perfection: the violence of the emotions may also contribute; for an ardent emotion, which is not susceptible of increase, cannot have a long course. But their short duration is occasioned chiefly by that of their causes: we are soon reconciled to an object, however unexpected; and novelty soon degenerates into familiarity.

239. Whether these emotions be pleasant or painful, is not a clear point. It may appear strange, that our own feelings and their capital qualities should afford any matter for a doubt: but when we are engrossed by any emotion, there is no place for speculation; and when sufficiently calm for speculation, it is not easy to recall the emotion with accuracy. New objects are sometimes terrible, sometimes delightful: the terror which a tiger inspires is greatest at first, and wears off gradually by familiarity: on the other hand, even women will acknowledge that it is novelty which pleases the most in a new fashion. It would be rash, however, to conclude that wonder is in itself neither pleasant nor painful, but that it assumes either quality according to circumstances. An object, it is true, that hath a threatening appearance, adds to our terror by its novelty: but from that experiment it doth not follow that novelty is in itself disagreeable; for it is perfectly consistent that we be delighted with an object in one view, and terrified with it in another: a river in flood, swelling over its banks, is a grand and delightful object; and yet it may produce no small degree of fear when we attempt to cross it: courage and magnanimity are agreeable; and yet, when we view these qualities in an enemy, they serve to increase our terror. In the same manner, novelty may produce two effects clearly distinguishable from each other: it may, directly and in itself, be agreeable; and it may have an opposite effect indirectly, which is, to inspire terror: for when a new object appears in any degree dangerous, our ignorance of its powers and qualities affords ample scope for the imagination to dress it in the most frightful colors. The first sight of a lion, for example, may at the same instant produce two opposite feelings,—the pleasant emotion of wonder, and the painful passion

---

238. Emotion of surprise, how it arises. How it differs from wonder, in its nature and circumstances.

of terror: the novelty of the object produces the former directly and contributes to the latter indirectly. Thus, when the subject is analyzed, we find that the power which novelty hath indirectly to inflame terror, is perfectly consistent with its being in every circumstance agreeable. The matter may be put in the clearest light by adding the following circumstances:—If a lion be first seen from a place of safety, the spectacle is altogether agreeable, without the least mixture of terror. If, again, the first sight puts us within reach of that dangerous animal, our terror may be so great as quite to exclude any sense of novelty. But this fact proves not that wonder is painful: it proves only that wonder may be excluded by a more powerful passion. Every man may be made certain, from his own experience, that wonder raised by a new object which is inoffensive is always pleasant; and with respect to offensive objects, it appears from the foregoing deduction, that the same must hold as long as the spectator can attend to the novelty.

240. Whether surprise be in itself pleasant or painful, is a question no less intricate than the former. It is certain that surprise inflames our joy when unexpectedly we meet with an old friend, and our terror when we stumble upon any thing noxious. To clear that question, the first thing to be remarked is, that in some instances an unexpected object overpowers the mind, so as to produce a momentary stupefaction: where the object is dangerous, or appears so, the sudden alarm it gives, without preparation, is apt totally to unhinge the mind, and for a moment to suspend all its faculties, even thought itself;* in which state a man is quite helpless, and, if he move at all, is as like to run upon the danger as from it. Surprise carried to such a height cannot be either pleasant or painful; because the mind, during such a momentary stupefaction, is in a good measure, if not totally, insensible.

If we then inquire for the character of this emotion, it must be where the unexpected object or event produceth less violent effects When a man meets a friend unexpectedly, he is said to be agreeably surprised; and when he meets an enemy unexpectedly, he is said to be disagreeably surprised. It appears, then, that the sole effect of surprise is to swell the emotion raised by the object. And that effect can be clearly explained: a tide of connected perceptions glide gently into the mind, and produce no perturbation; but an object breaking in unexpectedly, sounds an alarm, rouses the mind out of its calm state, and directs its whole attention to the object, which, if agreeable, becomes doubly so. Several circumstances concur to produce that effect: on the one hand, the agitation of the mind,

* Hence the Latin names for surprise, *torpor*, *animi stupor*.

239. New objects sometimes terrible—sometimes agreeable: yet novelty not in itself disagreeable. Novelty may produce two effects—an agreeable one directly, a disagreeable one indirectly

and its keen attention, prepare it in the most effectual manner for receiving a deep impression: on the other hand, the object, by its sudden and unforeseen appearance, makes an impression, not gradually, as expected objects do, but as at one stroke with its whole force. The circumstances are precisely similar where the object is in itself disagreeable.*

241. The pleasure of novelty is easily distinguished from that of variety: to produce the latter, a plurality of objects is necessary; the former arises from a circumstance found in a single object. Again, where objects, whether coexistent or in succession, are sufficiently diversified, the pleasure of variety is complete, though every single object of the train be familiar; but the pleasure of novelty, directly opposite to familiarity, requires no diversification.

There are different degrees of novelty, and its effects are in proportion. The lowest degree is found in objects surveyed a second time after a long interval; and that in this case an object takes on some appearance of novelty, is certain from experience: a large building of many parts variously adorned, or an extensive field embellished with trees, lakes, temples, statues, and other ornaments, will appear new oftener than once: the memory of an object so complex is soon lost, of its parts at least, or of their arrangement. But experience teaches, that even without any decay of remembrance, absence alone will give an air of novelty to a once familiar object; which is not surprising, because familiarity wears off gradually by absence: thus a person with whom we have been intimate, returning after a long interval, appears like a new acquaintance. And distance of place contributes to this appearance, no less than distance of time: a friend, for example, after a short absence in a remote country, has the same air of novelty as if he had returned after a longer interval from a place near home: the mind forms a connection between him and the remote country, and bestows upon him

* What Marshal Saxe terms *le cœur humain* is no other than fear occasioned by surprise. It is owing to that cause that an ambush is generally so destructive: intelligence of it beforehand renders it harmless. The Marshal gives from Cæsar's Commentaries two examples of what he calls *le cœur humain*. At the siege of Amiens by the Gauls, Cæsar came up with his army, which did not exceed 7000 men, and began to intrench himself in such hurry, that the barbarians, judging him to be afraid, attacked his intrenchments with great spirit. During the time they were filling up the ditch, he issued out with his cohorts; and, by attacking them unexpectedly, struck a panic that made them fly with precipitation, not a single man offering to make a stand. At the siege of Alesia, the Gauls, infinitely superior in number, attacked the Roman lines of circumvallation, in order to raise the siege. Cæsar ordered a body of his men to march out silently, and to attack them on the one flank, while he with another body did the same on the other flank. The surprise of being attacked, when they expected a defence only, put the Gauls into disorder, and gave an easy victory to Cæsar.

240. Whether surprise be pleasant or painful: (1) when it produces violent effects (2) when effects are less violent Why surprise has the effect of swelling the emotion raised by the object.

the singularity of the objects he has seen. For the same reason when two things, equally new and singular, are presented, the spectator balances between them; but when told that one of them is the product of a distant quarter of the world, he no longer hesitates, but clings to it as the more singular. Hence the preference given to foreign luxuries, and to foreign curiosities, which appear rare in proportion to their original distance.

242. The next degree of novelty, mounting upward, is found in objects of which we have some information at second hand; for description, though it contribute to familiarity, cannot altogether remove the appearance of novelty when the object itself is presented: the first sight of a lion occasions some wonder after a thorough acquaintance with the correctest pictures and statues of that animal.

A new object that bears some distant resemblance to a known species, is an instance of a third degree of novelty: a strong resemblance among individuals of the same species, prevents almost entirely the effect of novelty, unless distance of place or some other circumstance concur; but where the resemblance is faint, some degree of wonder is felt, and the emotion rises in proportion to the faintness of the resemblance.

The highest degree of wonder ariseth from unknown objects that have no analogy to any species we are acquainted with. Shakspeare, in a simile, introduces that species of novelty:

> As glorious to the sight
> As is a winged messenger from heaven
> Unto the white up-turned wond'ring eye
> Of mortals, that fall back to gaze on him
> When he bestrides the lazy-pacing clouds,
> And sails upon the bosom of the air.
>
> *Romeo and Juliet.*

One example of that species of novelty deserves peculiar attention; and that is, when an object, altogether new, is seen by one person only, and but once. These circumstances heighten remarkably the emotion: the singularity of the spectator concurs with the singularity of the object, to inflame wonder to its highest pitch.

243. In explaining the effects of novelty, the place a being occupies in the scale of existence, is a circumstance that must not be omitted. Novelty in the individuals of a low class is perceived with indifference, or with a very slight emotion: thus a pebble, however singular in its appearance, scarce moves our wonder. The emotion rises with the rank of the object; and, other circumstances

---

241. Pleasure of novelty distinguished from that of variety.—Different degrees of novelty and their effects. The lowest degree.—Objects surveyed a second time after a long interval.

242. The next higher degree of novelty; the next; the highest.—Simile from Shakspeare.—A species of novelty demanding peculiar attention.

being equal, is strongest in the highest order of existence: a strange insect affects us more than a strange vegetable; and a strange quadruped more than a strange insect.

However natural novelty may be, it is a matter of experience, that those who relish it the most are careful to conceal its influence. Love of novelty it is true prevails in children, in idlers, and in men of shallow understanding; and yet, after all, why should one be ashamed of indulging a natural propensity? A distinction will afford a satisfactory answer. No man is ashamed of curiosity when it is indulged in order to acquire knowledge. But to prefer any thing merely because it is new, shows a mean taste, which one ought to be ashamed of: vanity is commonly at the bottom, which leads those who are deficient in taste to prefer things odd, rare, or singular, in order to distinguish themselves from others. And in fact, that appetite, as above mentioned, reigns chiefly among persons of a mean taste, who are ignorant of refined and elegant pleasures.

244. One final cause of wonder, hinted above, is, that this emotion is intended to stimulate our curiosity. Another, somewhat different, is, to prepare the mind for receiving deep impressions of new objects. An acquaintance with the various things that may affect us, and with their properties, is essential to our well-being: nor will a slight or superficial acquaintance be sufficient; they ought to be so deeply engraved on the mind, as to be ready for use upon every occasion. Now, in order to make a deep impression, it is wisely contrived, that things should be introduced to our acquaintance with a certain pomp and solemnity productive of a vivid emotion. When the impression is once fairly made, the emotion of novelty, being no longer necessary, vanisheth almost instantaneously; never to return, unless where the impression happens to be obliterated by length of time or other means; in which case the second introduction hath nearly the same solemnity with the first.

Designing wisdom is nowhere more legible than in this part of the human frame. If new objects did not affect us in a very peculiar manner, their impressions would be so slight as scarce to be of any use in life: on the other hand, did objects continue to affect us deeply as at first, the mind would be totally engrossed with them, and have no room left either for action or reflection.

The final cause of surprise is still more evident than of novelty. Self-love makes us vigilantly attentive to self-preservation; but self-love, which operates by means of reason and reflection, and impels not the mind to any particular object or from it, is a principle too cool for a sudden emergency: an object breaking in unexpectedly affords no time for deliberation; and, in that case, the agitation of

---

243. Emotion of wonder rises with the rank of its object.--Why and when are men ashamed of curiosity.

surprise comes in seasonably to rouse self-love into action: surprise gives the alarm; and, if there be any appearance of danger, our whole force is instantly summoned up to shun or to prevent it.

CHAPTER VII.

RISIBLE OBJECTS.

245. SUCH is the nature of man, that his powers and faculties are soon blunted by exercise. The returns of sleep, suspending all activity, are not alone sufficient to preserve him in vigor; during his waking hours, amusement by intervals is requisite to unbend his mind from serious occupation. To that end, nature hath kindly made a provision of many objects, which may be distinguished by the epithet of *risible*, because they raise in us a peculiar emotion expressed externally by *laughter:* that emotion is pleasant; and, being also mirthful, it most successfully unbends the mind and recruits the spirits. Imagination contributes a part by multiplying such objects without end.

Ludicrous is a general term, signifying, as may appear from its derivation, what is playsome, sportive, or jocular. *Ludicrous*, therefore, seems the genus, of which *risible* is a species, limited as above to what makes us laugh.

246. However easy it may be, concerning any particular object, to say whether it be risible or not, it seems difficult, if at all practicable, to establish any general character by which objects of that kind may be distinguished from others. Nor is that a singular case; for, upon a review, we find the same difficulty in most of the articles already handled. There is nothing more easy, viewing a particular object, than to pronounce that it is beautiful or ugly, grand or little; but were we to attempt general rules for ranging objects under different classes, according to these qualities, we should be much gravelled. A separate cause increases the difficulty of distinguishing risible objects by a general character: all men are not equally affected by risible objects, nor the same man at all times; for, in high spirits, a thing will make him laugh outright, which scarce provokes a smile in a grave mood. Risible objects, however, are circumscribed within certain limits which I shall suggest, without pretending to accuracy. And, in the first place, I observe that no object is risible but what appears slight, little, or trivial; for we laugh at nothing

244. Final causes of wonder.—Designing wisdom here shown.—Final cause of surprise
245. The use of risible objects. How multiplied.—Ludicrous and risible objects distinguished

that is of importance to our own interest or to that of others. A real distress raises pity and therefore cannot be risible; but a slight or imaginary distress, which moves not pity, is risible. The adventure of the fulling-mills in Don Quixote, is extremely risible; so is the scene where Sancho, in a dark night, tumbling into a pit, and, attaching himself to the side by hand and foot, hangs there in terrible dismay till the morning, when he discovers himself to be within a foot of the bottom. A nose remarkably long or short, is risible; but to want it altogether, far from provoking laughter, raises horror in the spectator. Secondly, With respect to works both of nature and of art, none of them are risible but what are out of rule, some remarkable defect or excess; a very long visage, for example, or a very short one. Hence nothing just, proper, decent, beautiful, proportioned, or grand, is risible.

247. Even from this slight sketch it will readily be conjectured that the emotion raised by a risible object is of a nature so singular as scarce to find place while the mind is occupied with any other passion or emotion; and the conjecture is verified by experience, for we scarce ever find that emotion blended with any other. One emotion I must except; and that is, contempt raised by certain improprieties: every improper act inspires us with some degree of contempt for the author; and if an improper act be at the same time risible to provoke laughter, of which blunders and absurdities are noted instances, the two emotions of contempt and of laughter unite intimately in the mind, and produce externally what is termed *a laugh of derision* or *of scorn*. Hence objects that cause laughter may be distinguished into two kinds; they are either *risible* or *ridiculous*. A risible object is mirthful only; a ridiculous object is both mirthful and contemptible. The first raises an emotion of laughter that is altogether pleasant; the pleasant emotion of laughter raised by the other, is blended with the painful emotion of contempt, and the mixed emotion is termed *the emotion of ridicule*. The pain a ridiculous object gives me is resented and punished by a laugh of derision. A risible object, on the other hand, gives me no pain; it is altogether pleasant by a certain sort of titillation, which is expressed externally by mirthful laughter. Ridicule will be more fully explained afterwards; the present chapter is appropriated to the other emotion.

Risible objects are so common, and so well understood, that it is unnecessary to consume paper or time upon them. Take the few following examples:

Falstaff. I do remember him at Clement's inn, like a man made after supper of a cheese-paring. When he was naked, he was for all the world like a forked radish, with a head fantastically carved upon it with a knife.

Second Part, Henry IV. Act III. Sc. 5.

---

246. Why difficult to distinguish risible objects by a general character.—Two limits assigned to risible objects.—Don Quixote.—A nose.—When are works both of nature and art risible?

The foregoing is of disproportion. The following examples are of slight or imaginary misfortunes:

Falstaff. Go fetch me a quart of sack; put a toast in 't. Have I lived to be carried in a basket, like a barrow of butcher's offal, and to be thrown into the Thames! Well, if I be served such another trick, I'll have my brains ta'en out and butter'd and give them to a dog for a new-year's gift. The rogues slided me into the river with as little remorse as they would have drown'd a bitch's blind puppies, fifteen i' th' litter: and you may know by my size that I have a kind of alacrity in sinking: if the bottom were as deep as hell, I should down. I had been drown'd, but that the shore was shelvy and shallow; a death that I abhor; for the water swells a man; and what a thing should I have been when I had been swell'd? I should have been a mountain of mummy. *Merry Wives of Windsor*, Act III. Sc. 15.

Falstaff. Nay, you shall hear, Master Brook, what I have suffered to bring this woman to evil for your good. Being thus crammed in the basket, a couple of Ford's knaves, his hinds, were called forth by their mistress, to carry me in the name of foul clothes to Datchet-lane. They took me on their shoulders, met the jealous knave their master in the door, who asked them once or twice what they had in their basket. I quaked for fear, lest the lunatic knave would have searched it; but Fate, ordaining he should be a cuckold, held his hand. Well, on went he for a search, and away went I for foul clothes. But mark the sequel, Master Brook. I suffered the pangs of three egregious deaths; first, an intolerable fright, to be detected by a jealous rotten bell-wether; next, to be compassed like a good bilbo, in the circumference of a peck, hilt to point, heel to head; and then to be stopped in, like a strong distillation, with stinking clothes that fretted in their own grease. Think of that, a man of my kidney; think of that, that am as subject to heat as butter; a man of continual dissolution and thaw; it was a miracle to 'scape suffocation. And in the height of this bath, when I was more than half stewed in grease, like a Dutch dish, to be thrown into the Thames, and cooled glowing hot, in that surge, like a horse-shoe; think of that; hissing hot; think of that, Master Brook. *Merry Wives of Windsor*, Act III. Sc. 17.

CHAPTER VIII.

RESEMBLANCE AND DISSIMILITUDE.

248. Having discussed those qualities and circumstances of single objects that seem peculiarly connected with criticism, we proceed, according to the method proposed in the chapter of beauty, to the relations of objects, beginning with the relations of resemblance and dissimilitude.

The connection that man hath with the beings around him, requires some acquaintance with their nature, their powers, and their qualities, for regulating his conduct. For acquiring a branch of knowledge so essential to our well-being, motives alone of reason and interest are not sufficient: nature hath providently superadded curiosity, a vigorous propensity, which never is at rest. This pro-

---

247. Emotion raised by risible objects not blended with other emotions; except what?—Two kinds of objects causing laughter.—Define emotion excited by a *risible* object; by a *ridiculous* one. Examples from Shakspeare.

pensity attaches us to every new object (see chapter vi.); and incites us to compare objects, in order to discover their differences and resemblances.

Resemblance among objects of the same kind, and dissimilitude among objects of different kinds, are too obvious and familiar to gratify our curiosity in any degree: its gratification lies in discovering differences among things where resemblance prevails, and resemblances where difference prevails. Thus a difference in individuals of the same kind of plants or animals is deemed a discovery; while the many particulars in which they agree are neglected: and in different kinds, any resemblance is greedily remarked, without attending to the many particulars in which they differ.

249. A comparison, however, may be too far stretched. When differences or resemblances are carried beyond certain bounds, they appear slight and trivial; and for that reason will not be relished by a man of taste: yet such propensity is there to gratify passion, curiosity in particular, that even among good writers we find many comparisons too slight to afford satisfaction. Hence the frequent instances among logicians of distinctions without any solid difference; and hence the frequent instances among poets and orators, of similes without any just resemblance. Shakspeare, with uncommon humor, ridicules such disposition to simile-making, by putting in the mouth of a weak man a resemblance that will illustrate the point before us:

Fluellen. I think it is in Macedon where Alexander is porn: I tell you, Captain, if you look in the maps of the orld, I warrant that you sall find, in the comparisons between Macedon and Monmouth, that the situations, look you, is both alike. There is a river in Macedon, there is also moreover a river in Monmouth: it is called *Wye* at Monmouth, but it is out of my prains what is the name of the other river: but it is all one, 'tis as like as my fingers to my fingers, and there is salmons in both. If you mark Alexander's life well, Harry of Monmouth's life is come after it indifferent well; for there is figures in all things. Alexander, God knows, and you know, in his rages, and his furies, and his wraths, and his cholars, and his moods, and his displeasures, and his indignations; and also being a little intoxicates in his prains, did, in his ales and his angers, look you, kill his pest friend Clytus.

Gower. Our king is not like him in that; he never killed any of his friends.

Fluellen. It is not well done, mark you now, to take the tales out of my mouth, ere it is made and finished. I speak but in figures, and comparisons of it: as Alexander killed his friend Clytus, being in his ales and his cups; so also Harry Monmouth, being in his right wits and his good judgments, turned away the fat knight with the great belly doublet; he was full of jests, and gypes, and knaveries, and mocks: I have forgot his name.

Gower. Sir John Falstaff.

Fluellen. That is he: I tell you there is good men porn at Monmouth.

King Henry V. Act IV. Sc. 13.

250. Instruction, no doubt, is the chief end of comparison; but that it is not the only end will be evident from considering, that a

---

248. What relations of objects to be considered.—What provision is made for securing our acquaintance with surrounding objects?—Why does curiosity incite us to compare objects?—Where does curiosity prompt us to look for differences and resemblances?

249. A comparison may be stretched too far. Example.

comparison may be employed with success to put a subject in a strong point of view. A lively idea is formed of a man's courage, by likening it to that of a lion; and eloquence is exalted in our imagination, by comparing it to a river overflowing its banks, and involving all in its impetuous course. The same effect is produced by contrast: a man in prosperity becomes more sensible of his happiness by opposing his condition to that of a person in want of bread. Thus comparison is subservient to poetry as well as to philosophy: and, with respect to both, the foregoing observation holds equally, that resemblance among objects of the same kind, and dissimilitude among objects of different kinds, have no effect: such a comparison neither tends to gratify our curiosity, nor to set the objects compared in a stronger light: two apartments in a palace, similar in shape, size, and furniture, make separately as good a figure as when compared; and the same observation is applicable to two similar compartments in a garden: on the other hand, oppose a regular building to a fall of water, or a good picture to a towering hill, or even a little dog to a large horse, and the contrast will produce no effect. But a resemblance between objects of different kinds, and a difference between objects of the same kind, have remarkably an enlivening effect. The poets, such of them as have a just taste, draw all their similes from things that in the main differ widely from the principal subject; and they never attempt the contrast but where the things have a common genus and a resemblance in the capital circumstances: place together a large and a small sized animal of the same species, the one will appear greater, the other less, than when viewed separately: when we oppose beauty to deformity, each makes a greater figure by the comparison. We compare the dress of different nations with curiosity, but without surprise; because they have no such resemblance in the capital parts as to please us by contrasting the smaller parts. But a new cut of a sleeve or of a pocket enchants by its novelty, and in opposition to the former fashion, raises some degree of surprise.

251. That resemblance and dissimilitude have an enlivening effect upon objects of sight, is made sufficiently evident; and that they have the same effect upon objects of the other senses, is also certain. Nor is that law confined to the external senses; for characters contrasted make a greater figure by the opposition: Iago, in the tragedy of *Othello*, says,

> He hath a daily beauty in his life
> That makes me ugly.

The character of a fop, and of a rough warrior, are nowhere more successfully contrasted than in Shakspeare:

---

250. The chief end of comparison: what other end?—How do we convey a strong idea of a man's courage: of a man's eloquence?—Resemblance among objects of the same kind and dissimilitude among objects of a different kind. The converse of this.

Hotspur. My liege, I did deny no prisoners;
But I remember, when the fight was done,
When I was dry with rage, and extreme toil,
Breathless and faint, leaning upon my sword,
Came there a certain lord, neat trimly dress'd,
Fresh as a bridegroom; and his chin, new-reap'd,
Show'd like a stubble-land at harvest-home.
He was perfumed like a milliner;
And 'twixt his finger and his thumb he held
A pouncet-box, which ever and anon
He gave his nose;—and still he smiled, and talk'd:
And as the soldiers bare dead bodies by,
He call'd them untaught knaves, unmannerly,
To bring a slovenly unhandsome corse
Betwixt the wind and his nobility!
With many holiday and lady terms
He question'd me: among the rest, demanded
My pris'ners, in your Majesty's behalf.
I then all smarting with my wound, being gall'd
To be so pester'd with a popinjay,
Out of my grief, and my impatience,
Answer'd neglectingly, I know not what:
He should, or should not; for he made me mad,
To see him shine so brisk, and smell so sweet,
And talk so like a waiting gentlewoman,
Of guns, and drums, and wounds; (God save the mark!)
And telling me, the sov'reignest thing on earth
Was parmacity, for an inward bruise;
And that it was great pity, so it was,
This villainous saltpetre should be digg'd
Out of the bowels of the harmless earth,
Which many a good tall fellow had destroy'd
So cowardly; and but for these vile guns
He would himself have been a soldier.———

First Part Henry IV. Act I. Sc. 4.

Passions and emotions are also inflamed by comparison. A man of high rank humbles the bystanders, even to annihilate them in their own opinion: Cæsar, beholding the statue of Alexander, was greatly mortified, that now at the age of thirty-two when Alexander died, he had not performed one memorable action.

252. Our opinions also are much influenced by comparison. A man whose opulence exceeds the ordinary standard, is reputed richer than he is in reality; and wisdom or weakness, if at all remarkable in an individual, is generally carried beyond the truth.

The opinion a man forms of his present distress is heightened by contrasting it with his former happiness.

Could I forget
What I have been, I might the better bear
What I am destined to. I'm not the first
That have been wretched: but to think how much
I have been happier. *Southern*. I.

The distress of a long journey makes even an indifferent inn agreeable; and in travelling, when the road is good, and the horseman well covered, a bad day may be agreeable by making him sensible how snug he is.

---

251. Characters contrasted make a greater figure by the opposition. Examples.—Passions and emotions inflamed by comparison.—Cæsar beholding Alexander's statue

The same effect is equally remarkable when a man opposes his condition to that of others. A ship tossed about in a storm, makes the spectator reflect upon his own ease and security, and puts these in the strongest light. A man in grief cannot bear mirth; it gives him a more lively notion of his unhappiness, and of course makes him more unhappy. Satan contemplating the beauties of the terrestrial paradise, has the following exclamation:

With what delight could I have walk'd thee round,
If I could joy in aught, sweet interchange
Of hill and valley, rivers, woods, and plains,
Now land, now sea, and shores with forest crown'd,
Rocks, dens, and caves! but I in none of these
Find place or refuge; and the more I see
Pleasures about me, so much more I feel
Torment within me, as from the hateful siege
Of contraries: all good to me becomes
Bane, and in heaven much worse would be my state.

Paradise Lost, Book IX. l. 114.

Gaunt. All places that the eye of heaven visits,
Are to the wise man ports and happy havens.
Teach thy necessity to reason thus:
There is no virtue like necessity.
Think not the King did banish thee;
But thou the King. Woe doth the heavier sit,
Where it perceives it is but faintly borne.
Go say, I sent thee forth to purchase honor;
And not, the King exiled thee. Or suppose,
Devouring pestilence hangs in our air,
And thou art flying to a fresher clime.
Look what thy soul holds dear, imagine it
To lie that way thou go'st, not whence thou comest.
Suppose the singing birds, musicians;
The grass whereon thou tread'st, the presence-floor;
The flowers, fair ladies; and thy steps, no more
Than a delightful measure, or a dance.
For snarling Sorrow hath less power to bite
The man that mocks it, and sets it light.
Bolingbroke. Oh, who can hold a fire in his hand,
By thinking on the frosty Caucasus?
Or cloy the hungry edge of Appetite,
By bare imagination of a feast?
Or wallow naked in December snow,
By thinking on fantastic summer's heat?
Oh, no! the apprehension of the good
Gives but the greater feeling to the worse.

King Richard II. Act I. Sc. 6.

253. The appearance of danger gives sometimes pleasure, sometimes pain. A timorous person upon the battlements of a high tower, is seized with fear, which even the consciousness of security cannot dissipate. But upon one of a firm head, this situation has a contrary effect; the appearance of danger heightens, by opposition, the consciousness of security, and consequently, the satisfaction that arises from security: here the feeling resembles that above mentioned, occasioned by a ship laboring in a storm.

---

252. Opinions influenced by comparison.—Opinion of the wealth of a rich man, &c.—Effect of opposing our condition to that of others.—A man in grief.—Satan surveying Paradise.—Quotation from *Richard II*

The effect of magnifying or lessening objects by means of comparison is so familiar, that no philosopher has thought of searching for a cause. The obscurity of the object may possibly have contributed to their silence; but luckily, we discover the cause to be a principle unfolded above, which is the influence of passion over our opinions. (Chapter ii. part v.)

254. We have had occasion to see many illustrious effects of that singular power of passion; and that the magnifying or diminishing objects by means of comparison proceeds from the same cause, will evidently appear by reflecting in what manner a spectator is affected when a very large animal is for the first time placed beside a very small one of the same species. The first thing that strikes the mind is the difference between the two animals, which is so great as to occasion surprise; and this, like other emotions, magnifying its object, makes us conceive the difference to be the greatest that can be: we see, or seem to see, the one animal extremely little, and the other extremely large. The emotion of surprise arising from any unusual resemblance, serves equally to explain why at first view we are apt to think such resemblance more entire than it is in reality. And it must not escape observation, that the circumstances of more and less, which are the proper subjects of comparison, raise a perception so indistinct and vague as to facilitate the effect described: we have no mental standard of great and little, nor of the several degrees of any attribute; and the mind thus unrestrained, is naturally disposed to indulge its surprise to the utmost extent.

255. To explain the influence of comparison upon the mind, by a familiar example: take a piece of paper, or of linen tolerably white, and compare it with a pure white of the same kind: the judgment we formed of the first object is instantly varied; and the surprise occasioned by finding it less white than was thought, produceth a hasty conviction that it is much less white than it is in reality: withdrawing now the pure white, and putting in its place a deep black, the surprise occasioned by that new circumstance carries us to the other extreme, and makes us conceive the object first mentioned to be a pure white: and thus experience compels us to acknowledge that our emotions have an influence even upon our eyesight. This experiment leads to a general observation, That whatever is found more strange or beautiful than was expected, is judged to be more strange or beautiful than it is in reality. Hence a common artifice, to depreciate beforehand what we wish to make a figure in the opinion of others.

256. The comparisons employed by poets and orators are of the

---

253. Appearance of danger

254. The effect of magnifying or lessening objects by comparison, explained.—Effect of seeing, for the first time, a very large animal placed beside a very small one of the same species.—The emotion of surprise arising from any unusual resemblance.

255. Influence of comparison on the mind illustrated.—General observation; common artifice.

kind last mentioned; for it is always a known object that is to be magnified or lessened. The former is effected by likening it to some grand object, or by contrasting it with one of an opposite character. To effectuate the latter, the method must be reversed: the object must be contrasted with something superior to it, or likened to something inferior. The whole effect is produced upon the principal object, which by that means is elevated above its rank, or depressed below it.

In accounting for the effects that any unusual resemblance or dissimilitude hath upon the mind, no cause has been mentioned but surprise; and to prevent confusion, it was proper to discuss that cause first. But surprise is not the only cause of the effect described: another concurs which operates perhaps not less powerfully, namely, a principle in human nature that lies still in obscurity, not having been unfolded by any writer, though its effects are extensive; and as it is not distinguished by a proper name, the reader must be satisfied with the following description. Every man who studies himself or others, must be sensible of a tendency or propensity in the mind, to complete every work that is begun, and to carry things to their full perfection. There is little opportunity to display that propensity upon natural operations, which are seldom left imperfect; but in the operations of art, it hath great scope: it impels us to persevere in our own work, and to wish for the completion of what another is doing: we feel a sensible pleasure when the work is brought to perfection; and our pain is no less sensible when we are disappointed. Hence our uneasiness, when an interesting story is broke off in the middle, when a piece of music ends without a close, or when a building or garden is left unfinished. The same propensity operates in making collections, such as the whole works good and bad of any author. A certain person attempted to collect prints of all the capital paintings, and succeeded except as to a few. La Bruyere remarks, that an anxious search was made for these; not for their value, but to complete the set.*

257. The final cause of the propensity is an additional proof of its existence: human works are of no significancy till they be completed; and reason is not always a sufficient counterbalance to indolence: some principle over and above is necessary, to excite our industry, and to prevent our stopping short in the middle of the course.

* The examples above given, are of things that can be carried to an end or conclusion. But the same uneasiness is perceptible with respect to things that admit not any conclusion: witness a series that has no end, commonly called *an infinite series*. The mind moving along such a series, begins soon to feel an uneasiness, which becomes more and more sensible, in continuing its progress without hope of an end.

256. How poets and orators magnify a known object; how they depress it.—Surprise, not the only cause of the effect which any unusual resemblance or dissimilitude has upon the mind.—Another cause described.—Great scope in operations of art. Examples.

We need not lose time to describe the co-operation of the foregoing propensity with surprise, in producing the effect that follows any unusual resemblance or dissimilitude. Surprise first operates, and carries our opinion of the resemblance or dissimilitude beyond truth. The propensity we have been describing carries us still farther; for it forces upon the mind a conviction that the resemblance or dissimilitude is complete. We need no better illustration, than the resemblance that is fancied in some pebbles to a tree or an insect; which resemblance, however faint in reality, is conceived to be wonderfully perfect. The tendency to complete a resemblance acting jointly with surprise, carries the mind sometimes so far, as even to presume upon future events. In the Greek tragedy entitled *Phineides*, those unhappy women, seeing the place where it was intended they should be slain, cried out with anguish, "They now saw their cruel destiny had condemned them to die in that place, being the same where they had been exposed in their infancy." (*Aristotle*, Poet. cap. 17.)

The propensity to advance every thing to its perfection, not only co-operates with surprise to deceive the mind, but of itself is able to produce that effect. Of this we see many instances where there is no place for surprise; and the first I shall give is of resemblance. *Unumquodque eodem modo dissolvitur quo colligatum est,* is a maxim in the Roman law that has no foundation in truth; for tying and loosing, building and demolishing, are acts opposite to each other, and are performed by opposite means: but when these acts are connected by their relation to the same subject, their connection leads us to imagine a sort of resemblance between them, which by the foregoing propensity is conceived to be as complete as possible. The next instance shall be of contrast. Addison observes, "That the palest features look the most agreeable in white; that a face which is overflushed appears to advantage in the deepest scarlet; and that a dark complexion is not a little alleviated by a black hood." (Spectator, No. 265.) The foregoing propensity serves to account for these appearances; to make which evident one of the cases shall suffice. A complexion, however dark, never approaches to black: when these colors appear together, their opposition strikes us: and the propensity we have to complete the opposition makes the darkness of complexion vanish out of sight.

258. The operation of this propensity, even where there is no ground for surprise, is not confined to opinion or conviction: so powerful it is, as to make us sometimes proceed to action, in order to complete a resemblance or dissimilitude. If this appear obscure, it will be made clear by the following instances. Upon what principle is the *lex talionis* founded, other than to make the punishment

257. Final cause of this tendency of mind.—Its co-operation with surprise to deceive the mind.—The same effect without the aid of surprise.—Maxim of Roman law.—Instance of contrast given by Addison.

resemble the mischief? Reason dictates, that there ought to be a conformity or resemblance between a crime and its punishment; and the foregoing propensity impels us to make the resemblance as complete as possible. Titus Livius, under the influence of that propensity, accounts for a certain punishment by a resemblance between it and the crime, too subtile for common apprehension. Treating of Mettus Fuffetius, the Alban general, who, for treachery to the Romans his allies, was sentenced to be torn in pieces by horses, he puts the following speech in the mouth of Tullus Hostilius, who decreed the punishment. "Mette Fuffeti, inquit, si ipse discere posses fidem ac fœdera servare, vivo tibi ea disciplina a me adhibita esset. Nunc, quoniam tuum insanabile ingenium est, at tu tuo supplicio doce humanum genus, ea sancta credere, quæ a te violata sunt. Ut igitur paulo ante animum inter Fidenatem Romanamque rem ancipitem gessisti, ita jam corpus passim distrahendum dabis." (Lib. i. sect. 28.)* By the same influence, the sentence is often executed upon the very spot where the crime was committed. In the *Electra* of Sophocles, Egistheus is dragged from the theatre into an inner room of the supposed palace, to suffer death where he murdered Agamemnon. Shakspeare, whose knowledge of nature is no less profound than extensive, has not overlooked this propensity:

Othello. Get me some poison, Iago, this night; I'll not expostulate with her, lest her body and her beauty unprovide my mind again; this night, Iago.
Iago. Do it not with poison; strangle her in bed, even in the bed she hath contaminated.
Othello. Good, good: The justice of it pleases: very good.
Othello, Act IV. Sc. 5.

Warwick. From off the gates of York fetch down the head,
Your father's head, which Clifford placed there.
Instead whereof let his supply the room.
Measure for measure must be answered.
Third Part of Henry VI. Act II. Sc. 9.

Persons in their last moments are generally seized with an anxiety to be buried with their relations. In the *Amynta* of Tasso, the lover, hearing that his mistress was torn to pieces by a wolf, expresses a desire to die the same death. (Act iv. Sc. 2.)

259. Upon the subject in general I have two remarks to add. The first concerns resemblance, which, when too entire, hath no effect, however different in kind the things compared may be. The

* ["Mettus Fuffetius, if you were capable of learning to preserve faith, and a regard to treaties, I should suffer you to live and supply you with instructions; but your disposition is incurable. Let your punishment, then, teach mankind to consider those things as sacred which you have dared to violate. As, therefore, you lately kept your mind divided between the interests of the Fidenatians and of the Romans, so shall you now have your body divided and torn in pieces."—*Baker's Livy*, B. i. sec. 28.]

258. This propensity often prompts to action; to complete a resemblance or dissimilitude.—Punishment of Mettus Fuffetius.—Case of Egistheus; words of Othello; of Warwick.

remark is applicable to works of art only; for natural objects o. different kinds have scarce ever an entire resemblance. To give an example in a work of art, marble is a sort of matter very different from what composes an animal; and marble cut into a human figure produces great pleasure by the resemblance; but, if a marble statue be colored like a picture, the resemblance is so entire, as at a distance to make the statue appear a person: we discover the mistake when we approach; and no other emotion is raised, but surprise occasioned by the deception. The figure still appears a real person, rather than an imitation; and we must use reflection to correct the mistake. This cannot happen in a picture; for the resemblance can never be so entire as to disguise the imitation.

The other remark relates to contrast. Emotions make the greatest figure when contrasted in succession; but the succession ought neither to be rapid, nor immoderately slow: if too slow, the effect of contrast becomes faint by the distance of the emotions; and if rapid, no single emotion has room to expand itself to its full size, but is stifled, as it were, in the birth, by a succeeding emotion. The funeral oration of the Bishop of Meaux, upon the Duchess of Orleans, is a perfect hodge-podge of cheerful and melancholy representations, following each other in the quickest succession. Opposite emotions are best felt in succession; but each emotion separately should be raised to its due pitch, before another be introduced.

260. What is above laid down will enable us to determine a very important question concerning emotions raised by the fine arts namely, Whether ought similar emotions to succeed each other, of dissimilar? The emotions raised by the fine arts are for the most part too nearly related to make a figure by resemblance; and for that reason their succession ought to be regulated as much as possible by contrast. This holds confessedly in epic and dramatic compositions; and the best writers, led perhaps by taste more than by reasoning, have generally aimed at that beauty. It holds equally in music: in the same cantata, all the variety of emotions that are within the power of music may not only be indulged, but, to make the greatest figure, ought to be contrasted. In gardening, there is an additional reason for the rule: the emotions raised by that art are at best so faint that every artifice should be employed to give them their utmost vigor. A field may be laid out in grand, sweet, gay, neat, wild, melancholy scenes; and when these are viewed in succession, grandeur ought to be contrasted with neatness, regularity with wildness, and gayety with melancholy, so as that each emotion may succeed its opposite: nay, it is an improvement to intermix in the succession rude uncultivated spots as well as unbounded views, which in themselves are disagreeable, but in succession heighten the

---

259. Remark concerning resemblance. Example.—Remark concerning contrast.—Rule for the succession of emotions in contrast.

feeling of the agreeable objects; and we have nature for our guide, which, in her most beautiful landscapes, often intermixes rugged rocks, dirty marshes, and barren stony heaths. The greatest masters of music have the same view in their compositions: the second part of an Italian song seldom conveys any sentiment; and, by its harshness, seems purposely contrived to give a greater relish for the interesting parts of the composition.

261. A small garden comprehended under a single view, affords little opportunity for that embellishment. Dissimilar emotions require different tones of mind, and therefore in conjunction can never be pleasant (see chapter ii. part iv.): gayety and sweetness may be combined, or wildness and gloominess, but a composition of gayety and gloominess is distasteful. The rude uncultivated compartment of furze and broom in Richmond garden hath a good effect in the succession of objects; but a spot of that nature would be insufferable in the midst of a polished parterre or flower-pot. A garden, therefore, if not of great extent, admits not dissimilar emotions; and in ornamenting a small garden, the safest course is to confine it to a single expression. For the same reason a landscape ought also to be confined to a single expression; and accordingly it is a rule in painting that, if the subject be gay, every figure ought to contribute to that emotion.

It follows from the foregoing train of reasoning that a garden near a great city ought to have an air of solitude. The solitariness again of a waste country ought to be contrasted in forming a garden; no temples, no obscure walks; but *jets d'eau*, cascades, objects active, gay, and splendid. Nay, such a garden should in some measure avoid imitating nature by taking on an extraordinary appearance of regularity and art, to show the busy hand of man, which, in a waste country, has a fine effect by contrast.

262. It may be gathered from what is said above (chapter ii. part iv.), that wit and ridicule make not an agreeable mixture with grandeur. Dissimilar emotions have a fine effect in a slow succession; but in a rapid succession, which approaches to coexistence, they will not be relished: in the midst of a labored and elevated description of a battle, Virgil introduces a ludicrous image, which is certainly out of its place. (*Æneid*, vii. 298.)

It would, however, be too austere to banish altogether ludicrous images from an epic poem. In its more familiar tones a ludicrous scene many be introduced without impropriety. This is done by Virgil in a foot-race (*Æn.* lib. v.); the circumstances of which, not excepting the ludicrous part, are copied from Homer. (*Iliad*, Book xxiii. l. 789.) After a fit of merriment we are, it is true, the

---

260. Ought similar or dissimilar emotions (raised by the fine arts) to succeed each other? —Succession by contrast sought by epic and dramatic writers; by composers of music by gardeners.—Italian songs.

261. Emotions proper to be excited in embellishing a large compared with a small garden.—A garden in a city; in a solitary region.

less disposed to the serious and sublime; but then a ludicrous scene by unbending the mind from severe application to more interesting subjects, may prevent fatigue and preserve our relish entire.

CHAPTER IX.

UNIFORMITY AND VARIETY.

263. THE necessary succession of perceptions may be examined in two different views; one with respect to order and connection, and one with respect to uniformity and variety. In the first view it is handled above (chapter i.), and I now proceed to the second. The world we inhabit is replete with things no less remarkable for their variety than for their number; these, unfolded by the wonderful mechanism of external sense, furnish the mind with many perceptions, which, joined with ideas of memory, of imagination, and of reflection, form a complete train that has not a gap or interval. This train of perceptions and ideas depends very little on will. The mind, as has been observed (Locke, Book ii. chap. 14), is so constituted "that it can by no effort break off the succession of its ideas, nor keep its attention long fixed upon the same object:" we can arrest a perception in its course; we can shorten its natural duration to make room for another; we can vary the succession by change of place or of amusement; and we can in some measure prevent variety by frequently recalling the same object after short intervals: but still there must be a succession and a change from one perception to another. By artificial means the succession may be retarded or accelerated, may be rendered more various or more uniform, but in one shape or another is unavoidable.

264. The train, even when left to its ordinary course, is not always uniform in its motion; there are natural causes that accelerate or retard it considerably. The first I shall mention is a peculiar constitution of mind. One man is distinguished from another by no circumstance more remarkably than his train of perceptions: to a cold languid temper belongs a slow course of perceptions, which occasions a dullness of apprehension and sluggishness in action; to a warm temper, on the contrary, belongs a quick course of perceptions, which occasions quickness of apprehension and activity in business. The Asiatic nations, the Chinese especially, are observed

262. Wit and ridicule with respect to grandeur.—Remarks on Virgil.
263. How the necessary succession of perceptions may be examined.—How our train of perceptions and ideas is acquired. Whether it depends on the will; and how far.—Succession and change of ideas unavoidable.

to be more cool and deliberate than the Europeans: may not the reason be that heat enervates by exhausting the spirits? and that a certain degree of cold, as in the middle regions of Europe, bracing the fibres, rouseth the mind, and produceth a brisk circulation of thought, accompanied with vigor in action? In youth is observable a quicker succession of perceptions than in old age; and hence, in youth, a remarkable avidity for variety of amusements, which in riper years give place to more uniform and more sedate occupation. This qualifies men of middle age for business, where activity is required, but with a greater proportion of uniformity than variety. In old age, a slow and languid succession makes variety unnecessary; and for that reason the aged, in all their motions, are generally governed by an habitual uniformity. Whatever be the cause, we may venture to pronounce that heat, in the imagination and temper, is always connected with a brisk flow of perceptions.

265. The natural rate of succession depends also in some degree upon the particular perceptions that compose the train. An agreeable object, taking a strong hold of the mind, occasions a slower succession than when the objects are indifferent: grandeur and novelty fix the attention for a considerable time, excluding all other ideas: and the mind thus occupied is sensible of no vacuity. Some emotions, by hurrying the mind from object to object, accelerate the succession. Where the train is composed of connected perceptions or ideas, the succession is quick; for it is ordered by nature that the mind goes easily and sweetly along connected objects. (See chapter i.) On the other hand, the succession must be slow where the train is composed of unconnected perceptions or ideas, which find not ready access to the mind; and that an unconnected object is not admitted without a struggle, appears from the unsettled state of the mind for some moments after such an object is presented, wavering between it and the former train: during that short period one or other of the former objects will intrude, perhaps oftener than once, till the attention be fixed entirely upon the new object. The same observations are applicable to ideas suggested by language: the mind can bear a quick succession of related ideas; but an unrelated idea, for which the mind is not prepared, takes time to make an impression; and therefore a train composed of such ideas ought to proceed with a slow pace. Hence an epic poem, a play, or any story connected in all its parts, may be perused in a shorter time than a book of maxims or apothegms, of which a quick succession creates both confusion and fatigue.

266. Such latitude hath nature indulged in the rate of succession; what latitude it indulges with respect to uniformity, we proceed to

---

264. Natural causes that accelerate or retard the train. (1) A peculiar constitution of mind. (2) Effect of climate. (3) Period of life.

265. Natural rate of succession depends on the particular perceptions that compose the train.—On the degree of connection between the ideas. Hence an epic poem, &c., can be read more rapidly than a book of maxims.

examine. The uniformity or variety of a train, so far as composed of perceptions, depends on the particular objects that surround the percipient at the time. The present occupation must also have an influence, for one is sometimes engaged in a multiplicity of affairs, sometimes altogether vacant. A natural train of ideas of memory is more circumscribed, each object being, by some connection, linked to what precedes and to what follows it: these connections, which are many, and of different kinds, afford scope for a sufficient degree of variety, and at the same time prevent that degree which is unpleasant by excess. Temper and constitution also have an influence here, as well as upon the rate of succession: a man of a calm and sedate temper, admits not willingly any idea but what is regularly introduced by a proper connection; one of a roving disposition embraces with avidity every new idea, however slender its relation be to those that preceded it. Neither must we overlook the nature of the perceptions that compose the train; for their influence is no less with respect to uniformity and variety, than with respect to the rate of succession. The mind engrossed by any passion, love or hatred, hope or fear, broods over its object, and can bear no interruption; and in such a state, the train of perceptions must not only be slow, but extremely uniform. Anger newly inflamed eagerly grasps its object, and leaves not a cranny in the mind for another thought but of revenge. In the character of Hotspur, that state of mind is represented to the life; a picture remarkable for likeness as well as for high coloring:

> *Worcester.* Peace, cousin, say no more.
> And now I will unclasp a secret book,
> And to your quick conceiving discontents
> I'll read you matter, deep and dangerous;
> As full of peril and adventurous spirit
> As to o'erwalk a current roaring loud,
> On the unsteadfast footing of a spear.
> *Hotspur.* If he fall in, good night. Or sink or swim
> Send danger from the east into the west,
> So honor cross it from the north to south;
> And let them grapple. Oh! the blood more stirs
> To rouse a lion than to start a hare.
> *Worcester.* Those same noble Scots,
> That are your prisoners——
> *Hotspur.* I'll keep them all;
> By heaven he shall not have a Scot of them:
> No; if a Scot would save his soul, he shall not;
> I'll keep them, by this hand.
> *Worcester.* You start away,
> And lend no ear unto my purpose:
> Those pris'ners you shall keep.
> *Hotspur.* I will, that's flat:
> He said he would not ransom Mortimer:
> Forbade my tongue to speak of Mortimer:
> But I will find him when he lies asleep,
> And in his ear I'll holla *Mortimer!*
> Nay, I will have a starling taught to speak

---

266. Uniformity or variety of a train of perceptions depends on what?

Nothing but *Mortimer*, and give it him,
To keep his anger still in motion.
Worcester. Hear you, cousin, a word.
Hotspur. All studies here I solemnly defy,
Save how to gall and pinch this Bolingbroke:
And that same sword-and-buckler Prince of Wales
(But that I think his father loves him not,
And would be glad he met with some mischance),
I'd have him poison'd with a pot of ale.
Worcester. Farewell, my kinsman, I will talk to you
When you are better temper'd to attend.
King Henry IV. Act I. Sc. 4.

267. Having viewed a train of perceptions as directed by nature, and the variations it is susceptible of from different necessary causes, we proceed to examine how far it is subjected to will: for that this faculty hath some influence, is observed above. And first, the rate of succession may be retarded by insisting upon one object, and propelled by dismissing another before its time. But such voluntary mutations in the natural course of succession, have limits that cannot be extended by the most painful efforts: which will appear from considering, that the mind circumscribed in its capacity, cannot, at the same instant, admit many perceptions; and when replete, that it hath not place for new perceptions, till others are removed; consequently, that a voluntary change of perceptions cannot be instantaneous, as the time it requires sets bounds to the velocity of succession. On the other hand, the power we have to arrest a flying perception is equally limited; and the reason is, that the longer we detain any perception, the more difficulty we find in the operation; till, the difficulty becoming insurmountable, we are forced to quit our hold, and to permit the train to take its usual course.

The power we have over this train, as to uniformity and variety, is in some cases very great, in others very little. A train composed of perceptions of external objects, depends entirely on the place we occupy, and admits not more nor less variety but by change of place. A train composed of ideas of memory is still less under our power, because we cannot at will call up any idea that is not connected with the train. (See chapter i.) But a train of ideas suggested by reading may be varied at will, provided we have books at hand.

268. The power that nature hath given us over our train of perceptions, may be greatly strengthened by proper discipline, and by an early application to business: witness some mathematicians, who go far beyond common nature in slowness and uniformity; and still more, persons devoted to religious exercises, who pass whole days in contemplation, and impose upon themselves long and severe penances. With respect to celerity and variety, it is not easily conceived what length a habit of activity in affairs will carry some men. Let a stranger, or let any person to whom the sight is not familiar, attend the Chancellor of Great Britain through the labors but of one

267. How far the train of perceptions is subjected to will.—Various trains, and the power we have over them.

day, during a session of parliament: how great will be his astonishment! what multiplicity of law business, what deep thinking, and what elaborate application to matters of government! The train of perceptions must in that great man be accelerated far beyond the ordinary course of nature, yet no confusion or hurry, but in every article the greatest order and accuracy. Such is the force of habit. How happy is man, to have the command of a principle of action that can elevate him so far above the ordinary condition of humanity!*

269. We are now ripe for considering a train of perceptions, with respect to pleasure and pain; and to that speculation peculiar attention must be given, because it serves to explain the effects that uniformity and variety have upon the mind. A man, when his perceptions flow in their natural course, feels himself free, light, and easy, especially after any forcible acceleration or retardation. On the other hand, the accelerating or retarding the natural course, excites a pain, which, though scarcely felt in small removes, becomes considerable towards the extremes. Aversion to fix on a single object for a long time, or to take in a multiplicity of objects in a short time, is remarkable in children, and equally so in men unaccustomed to business: a man languishes when the succession is very slow; and, if he grow not impatient, is apt to fall asleep: during a rapid succession, he hath a feeling as if his head were turning round; he is fatigued, and his pain resembles that of weariness after bodily labor.

But a moderate course will not satisfy the mind, unless the perceptions be also diversified: number without variety is not sufficient to constitute an agreeable train. In comparing a few objects, uniformity is pleasant; but the frequent reiteration of uniform objects becomes unpleasant: one tires of a scene that is not diversified; and soon feels a sort of unnatural restraint when confined within a narrow range, whether occasioned by a retarded succession, or by too great uniformity. An excess in variety is, on the other hand, fatiguing; which is felt even in a train of related perceptions, much more of unrelated perceptions, which gain not admittance without effort: the effort, it is true, is scarce perceptible in a single instance, but by frequent reiteration it becomes exceedingly painful. Whatever be the cause, the fact is certain, that a man never finds himself more at ease than when his perceptions succeed each other with a certain degree, not only of velocity, but also of variety. The pleasure that arises from a train of connected ideas, is remarkable in a reverie; especially where the imagination interposeth, and is active in coining new ideas, which is done with wonderful facility: one must be sensible that the serenity and ease of the mind, in that

* This chapter was composed in the year 1753.

268. The train varied by discipline and attention to business. Illustrations

state makes a great part of the enjoyment. The case is different where external objects enter into the train; for these, making their appearance without order and without connection, save that of contiguity, form a train of perceptions that may be extremely uniform or extremely diversified; which, for opposite reasons, are both of them painful.

270. To alter, by an act of will, that degree of variety which nature requires, is not less painful than to alter that degree of velocity which it requires. Contemplation, when the mind is long attached to one subject, becomes painful by restraining the free range of perception: curiosity, and the prospect of useful discoveries, may fortify one to bear that pain; but it is deeply felt by the bulk of mankind, and produceth in them aversion to all abstract sciences. In any profession or calling, a train of operation that is simple and reiterated without intromission, makes the operator languish, and lose vigor: he complains neither of too great labor, nor of too little action; but regrets the want of variety, and the being obliged to do the same thing over and over: where the operation is sufficiently varied, the mind retains its vigor, and is pleased with its condition. Actions again create uneasiness when excessive in number or variety, though in every other respect pleasant: thus a throng of business in law, in physic, or in traffic, distresses and distracts the mind, unless where a habit of application is acquired by long and constant exercise: the excessive variety is the distressing circumstance; and the mind suffers grievously by being kept constantly upon the stretch.

271. With relation to involuntary causes disturbing that degree of variety which nature requires, a slight pain affecting one part of the body without variation, becomes, by its constancy and long duration, almost insupportable: the patient, sensible that the pain is not increased in degree, complains of its constancy more than of its severity, of its engrossing his whole thoughts, and admitting no other object. A shifting pain is more tolerable, because change of place contributes to variety; and an intermitting pain, suffering other objects to intervene, still more so. Again, any single color or sound, often returning, becomes unpleasant; as may be observed in viewing a train of similar apartments in a great house painted with the same color, and in hearing the prolonged tollings of a bell. Color and sound varied within certain limits, though without any order, are pleasant; witness the various colors of plants and flowers in a field, and the various notes of birds in a thicket: increase the number of variety, and the feeling becomes unpleasant; thus a great variety of colors, crowded upon a small canvas, or in quick succession, create

---

269. The train, with respect to pleasure and pain. When natural. When greatly accelerated. When retarded.—Number of ideas without variety, not agreeable.—When uniformity is pleasant; when unpleasant.—Excess in variety.—Reverie.

270. The act of altering, by will, the degree of variety which nature requires.—Contemplation long confined to one object.—Where operations are simple and reiterated.—Effect of actions excessive in number and variety.

an uneasy feeling, which is prevented by putting the colors at a greater distance from each other, either of place or of time. A number of voices in a crowded assembly, a number of animals collected in a market, produce an unpleasant feeling; though a few of them together, or all of them in a moderate succession, would be pleasant. And because of the same excess in variety, a number of pains felt in different parts of the body, at the same instant or in a rapid succession, are an exquisite torture.

272. It is occasionally observed above, that persons of a phlegmatic temperament, having a sluggish train of perceptions, are indisposed to action; and that activity constantly accompanies a brisk flow of perceptions. To ascertain that fact, a man need not go abroad for experiments: reflecting on things passing in his own mind, he will find that a brisk circulation of thought constantly prompts him to action; and that he is averse to action when his perceptions languish in their course. But as a man by nature is formed for action, and must be active in order to be happy, nature hath kindly provided against indolence, by annexing pleasure to a moderate course of perceptions, and by making any remarkable retardation painful. A slow course of perceptions is attended with another bad effect: man, in a few capital cases, is governed by propensity or instinct; but in matters that admit deliberation and choice, reason is assigned him for a guide: now, as reasoning requires often a great compass of ideas, their succession ought to be so quick as readily to furnish every motive that may be necessary for mature deliberation; in a languid succession, motives will often occur after action is commenced, when it is too late to retreat.

273. Nature hath guarded man, her favorite, against a succession too rapid, no less carefully than against one too slow: both are equally painful, though the pain is not the same in both. Many are the good effects of that contrivance. In the first place, as the exertion of bodily faculties is by certain painful sensations confined within proper limits, Nature is equally provident with respect to the nobler faculties of the mind: the pain of an accelerated course of perceptions is Nature's admonition to relax our pace, and to admit a more gentle exertion of thought. Another valuable purpose is discovered upon reflecting in what manner objects are imprinted on the mind: to give the memory firm hold of an external object, time is required, even where attention is the greatest: and a moderate degree of attention, which is the common case, must be continued still longer to produce the same effect: a rapid succession, accordingly, must prevent objects from making an impression so deep as to be of real service in life; and Nature, for the sake of memory,

271. **Involuntary causes disturbing that degree of variety which nature requires.—Slight but unvarying pain; a shifting pain.—Any single color or sound often returning.—Color and sound varied within certain limits.**

272. **A sluggish train indisposes to action.—What provision is made against indolence.—Bad effect of a slow course of perceptions, in matters that require deliberation and choice.**

has, by a painful feeling, guarded against a rapid succession. But a still more valuable purpose is answered by the contrivance: as, on the one hand, a sluggish course of perceptions indisposeth to action; so, on the other, a course too rapid impels to rash and precipitant action: prudent conduct is the child of deliberation and clear conception, for which there is no place in a rapid course of thought. Nature therefore, taking measures for prudent conduct, has guarded us effectually from precipitancy of thought by making it painful.

274. Nature not only provides against a succession too slow or too quick, but makes the middle course extremely pleasant. Nor is that course confined within narrow bounds: every man can naturally, without pain, accelerate or retard in some degree the rate of his perceptions. And he can do it in a still greater degree by the force of habit: a habit of contemplation annihilates the pain of a retarded course of perceptions; and a busy life, after long practice, makes acceleration pleasant.

Concerning the final cause of our taste for variety, it will be considered, that human affairs, complex by variety as well as number, require the distributing our attention and activity in measure and proportion. Nature therefore, to secure a just distribution corresponding to the variety of human affairs, has made too great uniformity or too great variety in the course of perceptions, equally unpleasant: and, indeed, were we addicted to either extreme, our internal constitution would be ill suited to our external circumstances. At the same time, where great uniformity of operation is required, as in several manufactures, or great variety, as in law or physic, Nature, attentive to all our wants, hath also provided for these cases, by implanting in the breast of every person an efficacious principle that leads to habit: an obstinate perseverance in the same occupation, relieves from the pain of excessive uniformity; and the like perseverance in a quick circulation of different occupations, relieves from the pain of excessive variety. And thus we come to take delight in several occupations, that by nature, without habit, are not a little disgustful.

275. A middle rate also in the train of perceptions between uniformity and variety, is no less pleasant than between quickness and slowness. The mind of man, so framed, is wonderfully adapted to the course of human affairs, which are continually changing, but not without connection: it is equally adapted to the acquisition of knowledge, which results chiefly from discovering resemblances among differing objects, and differences among resembling objects: such occupation, even abstracting from the knowledge we acquire,

---

273. We are guarded against a succession too rapid.—Good effects of this to body and mind.

274. A moderate rate of succession agreeable; yet the rate may without pain be varied by force of habit.—Final cause of our taste for variety.—Where great uniformity or great variety of action is required, what provision is made for our comfort.

is in itself delightful, by preserving a middle rate between too great uniformity and too great variety.

We are now arrived at the chief purpose of the present chapter; which is to consider uniformity and variety with relation to the fine arts, in order to discover, if we can, when it is that the one ought to prevail, and when the other. And the knowledge we have obtained will even at first view suggest a general observation, That in every work of art it must be agreeable to find that degree of variety which corresponds to the natural course of our perceptions; and that an excess in variety or in uniformity must be disagreeable, by varying that natural course. For that reason, works of art admit more or less variety according to the nature of the subject: in a picture of an interesting event that strongly attaches the spectator to a single object, the mind relisheth not a multiplicity of figures nor of ornaments: a picture representing a gay subject, admits great variety of figures and ornaments; because these are agreeable to the mind in a cheerful tone. The same observation is applicable to poetry and to music.

276. It must at the same time be remarked, that one can bear a greater variety of natural objects, than of objects in a picture; and a greater variety in a picture, than in a description. A real object presented to view, makes an impression more readily than when represented in colors, and much more readily than when represented in words. Hence it is that the profuse variety of objects in some natural landscapes neither breeds confusion nor fatigue; and for the same reason, there is place for greater variety of ornament in a picture than in a poem. A picture, however, like a building, ought to be so simple as to be comprehended in one view.

From these general observations, I proceed to particulars. In works exposed continually to public view, variety ought to be studied. It is a rule accordingly in sculpture, to contrast the different limbs of a statue, in order to give it all the variety possible. In a landscape representing animals, those especially of the same kind, contrast ought to prevail: to draw one sleeping, another awake; one sitting, another in motion; one moving towards the spectator, another from him, is the life of such a performance.

277. In every sort of writing intended for amusement, variety is necessary in proportion to the length of the work. Want of variety is sensibly felt in Davila's history of the civil wars of France: the events are indeed important and various; but the reader languishes by a tiresome monotony of character, every person engaged being figured a consummate politician, governed by interest only. It is

---

275. A train between uniformity and variety, agreeable; adapted to the course of human affairs, and acquisition of knowledge. What degree of variety is agreeable in every work of art.

276. We can bear a greater variety of natural objects than in a picture, or description. In works exposed always to public view, variety should be studied.—Rule in sculpture: in painting animals on a landscape

hard to say, whether Ovid disgusts more by too great variety, or too great uniformity: his stories are all of the same kind, concluding invariably with the transformation of one being into another; and so far he is tiresome by excess in uniformity: he is not less fatiguing by excess in variety, hurrying his reader incessantly from story to story. Ariosto is still more fatiguing than Ovid, by exceeding the just bounds of variety: not satisfied, like Ovid, with a succession in his stories, he distracts the reader, by jumbling together a multitude of them without any connection. Nor is the Orlando Furioso less tiresome by its uniformity than the Metamorphoses, though in a different manner: after a story is brought to a crisis, the reader, intent on the catastrophe, is suddenly snatched away to a new story, which makes no impression so long as the mind is occupied with the former.

APPENDIX TO CHAPTER IX.

Concerning the Works of Nature, chiefly with respect to Uniformity and Variety.

278. In things of Nature's workmanship, whether we regard their internal or external structure, beauty and design are equally conspicuous. We shall begin with the outside of nature, as what first presents itself.

The figure of an organic body is generally regular. The trunk of a tree, its branches, and their ramifications, are nearly round, and form a series regularly decreasing from the trunk to the smallest fibre: uniformity is nowhere more remarkable than in the leaves, which, in the same species, have all the same color, size, and shape; the seeds and fruits are all regular figures, approaching, for the most part, to the globular form. Hence a plant, especially of the larger kind, with its trunk, branches, foliage, and fruit, is a charming object.

In an animal, the trunk, which is much larger than the other parts, occupies a chief place; its shape, like that of the stem of plants, is nearly round, a figure which of all is the most agreeable: its two sides are precisely similar; several of the under parts go off in pairs, and the two individuals of each pair are accurately uniform; the single parts are placed in the middle; the limbs, bearing a certain proportion to the trunk, serve to support it, and to give it a proper elevation: upon one extremity are disposed the neck and head, in the direction of the trunk: the head being the chief part,

---

277. In writing a work, how far variety is necessary. Remarks on Davila, Ovid, the Orlando Furioso.

possesses, with great propriety, the chief place. Hence, the beauty of the whole figure is the result of many equal and proportional parts orderly disposed; and the smallest variation in number, equality, proportion, or order, never fails to produce a perception of deformity.

279. Nature in no particular seems more profuse of ornament than in the beautiful coloring of her works. The flowers of plants, the furs of beasts, and the feathers of birds, vie with each other in the beauty of their colors, which in lustre as well as in harmony are beyond the power of imitation. Of all natural appearances, the coloring of the human face is the most exquisite; it is the strongest instance of the ineffable art of nature, in adapting and proportioning its colors to the magnitude, figure, and position of the parts. In a word, color seems to live in nature only, and to languish under the finest touches of art.

When we examine the internal structure of a plant or animal, a wonderful subtilty of mechanism is displayed. Man, in his mechanical operations, is confined to the surface of bodies; but the operations of nature are exerted through the whole substance, so as to reach even the elementary parts. Thus the body of an animal, and of a plant, are composed of certain great vessels; these of smaller; and these again of still smaller, without end, as far as we can discover. This power of diffusing mechanism through the most intimate parts, is peculiar to nature, and distinguishes her operations most remarkably from every work of art. Such texture continued from the grosser parts to the most minute, preserves all along the strictest regularity: the fibres of plants are a bundle of cylindric canals, lying in the same direction, and parallel, or nearly parallel to each other: in some instances, a most accurate arrangement of parts is discovered, as in onions, formed of concentric coats one within another, to the very centre. An animal body is still more admirable in the disposition of its internal parts, and in their order and symmetry; there is not a bone, a muscle, a blood-vessel, a nerve, that hath not one corresponding to it on the opposite side; and the same order is carried through the most minute parts: the lungs are composed of two parts, which are disposed upon the sides of the thorax; and the kidneys, in a lower situation, have a position no less orderly: as to the parts that are single, the heart is advantageously situated near the middle; the liver, stomach, and spleen, are disposed in the upper region of the abdomen, about the same height: the bladder is placed in the middle of the body, as well as the intestinal canal, which fills the whole cavity with its convolutions.

280. The mechanical power of nature, not confined to small bodies, reacheth equally those of the greatest size; witness the bodies

---

278. The figure of organic bodies. The trunk of a tree, its branches, &c. In an animal, the trunk, &c. In what the beauty of the whole figure consists.

279. Coloring of nature; of plants, &c.—Subtile or minute mechanism of plants and animals in their interior structure.—Fibres of plants.—In animals, correspondence and happy arrangement of parts.

that compose the solar system, which, however large, are weighed, measured, and subjected to certain laws, with the utmost accuracy. Their places round the sun, with their distances, are determined by a precise rule, corresponding to their quantity of matter. The superior dignity of the central body, in respect to its bulk and lucid appearance, is suited to the place it occupies. The globular figure of these bodies is not only in itself beautiful, but is above all others fitted for regular motion. Each planet revolves about its own axis in a given time; and each moves round the sun in an orbit nearly circular, and in a time proportioned to its distance. Their velocities, directed by an established law, are perpetually changing by regular accelerations and retardations. In fine, the great variety of regular appearances, joined with the beauty of the system itself, cannot fail to produce the highest delight in every one who is sensible of design, power, or beauty.

281. Nature hath a wonderful power of connecting systems with each other, and of propagating that connection through all her works. Thus the constituent parts of a plant, the roots, the stem, the branches, the leaves, the fruit, are really different systems, united by a mutual dependence on each other: in an animal, the lymphatic and lacteal ducts, the blood-vessels and nerves, the muscles and glands, the bones and cartilages, the membranes and bowels, with the other organs, form distinct systems, which are united into one whole. There are at the same time, other connections less intimate: every plant is joined to the earth by its roots: it requires rain and dews to furnish it with juices; and it requires heat to preserve these juices in fluidity and motion: every animal, by its gravity, is connected with the earth, with the element in which it breathes, and with the sun, by deriving from it cherishing and enlivening heat: the earth furnisheth aliment to plants, these to animals, and these again to other animals, in a long train of dependence: that the earth is part of a greater system comprehending many bodies mutually attracting each other, and gravitating all towards one common centre, is now thoroughly explored. Such a regular and uniform series of connections, propagated through so great a number of beings, and through such wide spaces, is wonderful; and our wonder must increase, when we observe these connections propagated from the minutest atoms to bodies of the most enormous size, and so widely diffused as that we can neither perceive their beginning nor their end. That these connections are not confined within our own planetary system, is certain: they are diffused over spaces still more remote, where new bodies and systems rise without end. All space is filled with the works of God, which are conducted by one plan, to answer unerringly one great end.

---

280. The solar system. Its variety and regularity.

281. Systems wonderfully connected with each other: the constituent parts of plants to of animals.—Other less intimate connections.—Some not confined to our own planetary system

282. But the most wonderful connection of all, though not the most conspicuous, is that of our internal frame with the works of nature: man is obviously fitted for contemplating these works, because in this contemplation he has great delight. The works of nature are remarkable in their uniformity no less than in their variety; and the mind of man is fitted to receive pleasure equally from both. Uniformity and variety are interwoven in the works of nature with surprising art: variety, however great, is never without some degree of uniformity; nor the greatest uniformity without some degree of variety: there is great variety in the same plant, by the different appearances of its stem, branches, leaves, blossoms, fruit, size, and color; and yet, when we trace that variety through different plants, especially of the same kind, there is discovered a surprising uniformity: again, where nature seems to have intended the most exact uniformity, as among individuals of the same kind, there still appears a diversity, which serves readily to distinguish one individual from another. It is indeed admirable, that the human visage, in which uniformity is so prevalent, should yet be so marked, as to leave no room, among millions, for mistaking one person for another; these marks, though clearly perceived, are generally so delicate, that words cannot be found to describe them. A correspondence so perfect between the human mind and the works of nature, is extremely remarkable. The opposition between variety and uniformity is so great that one would not readily imagine they could both be relished by the same palate: at least not in the same object, nor at the same time: it is however true, that the pleasures they afford, being happily adjusted to each other, and readily mixing in intimate union, are frequently produced by the same individual object. Nay, further, in the objects that touch us the most, uniformity and variety are constantly combined: witness natural objects, where this combination is always found in perfection. Hence it is, that natural objects readily form themselves into groups, and are agreeable in whatever manner combined: a wood with its trees, shrubs, and herbs, is agreeable: the music of birds, the lowing of cattle, and the murmuring of a brook, are in conjunction delightful; though they strike the ear without modulation or harmony. In short, nothing can be more happily accommodated to the inward constitution of man, than that mixture of uniformity with variety, which the eye discovers in natural objects; and, accordingly, the mind is never more highly gratified than in contemplating a natural landscape.

---

282. The wonderful connection of our internal frame with the works of nature. These afford pleasure to man from mingling uniformity with variety. For instance, in plants; in individuals of the same kind.—The human face.—Variety and uniformity relished at the same time and in the same object.—Natural objects form themselves into groups.—Natural landscape delightful.

CHAPTER X.

CONGRUITY AND PROPRIETY.

283. MAN is superior to the brute, not more by his rational faculties, than by his senses. With respect to external senses, brutes probably yield not to men; and they may also have some obscure perception of beauty: but the more delicate senses of regularity, order, uniformity, and congruity, being connected with morality and religion, are reserved to dignify the chief of the terrestrial creation. Upon that account, no discipline is more suitable to man, nor more *congruous* to the dignity of his nature, than that which refines his taste, and leads him to distinguish, in every subject, what is regular, what is orderly, what is suitable, and what is fit and proper. (*Cicero de Officiis*, l. i.)

It is clear from the very conception of the terms *congruity* and *propriety*, that they are not applicable to any single object: they imply a plurality, and obviously signify a particular *relation* between different objects. Thus we say currently, that a decent garb is suitable or *proper* for a judge, modest behavior for a young woman, and a lofty style for an epic poem: and, on the other hand, that it is unsuitable or *incongruous* to see a little woman sunk in an overgrown farthingale, a coat richly embroidered covering coarse and dirty linen, a mean subject in an elevated style, an elevated subject in a mean style, a first minister darning his wife's stocking, or a reverend prelate in lawn sleeves dancing a hornpipe.

284. The perception we have of this relation, which seems peculiar to man, cannot proceed from any other cause, but from a *sense* of congruity or propriety; for, supposing us destitute of that sense, the terms would be to us unintelligible.*

* From many things that pass current in the world without being generally condemned, one at first view would imagine, that the sense of congruity or propriety hath scarce any foundation in nature, and that it is rather an artificial refinement of those who affect to distinguish themselves from others. The fulsome panegyrics bestowed upon the great and opulent, in epistles dedicatory and other such compositions, would incline us to think so. Did there prevail in the world, it will be said, or did nature suggest, a taste of what is suitable, decent, or proper, would any good writer deal in such compositions, or any man of sense receive them without disgust? Can it be supposed that Louis XIV of France was endued by nature with any sense of propriety, when, in a dramatic performance purposely composed for his entertainment, he suffered himself, publicly and in his presence, to be styled the greatest king ever the earth produced? These, it is true, are strong facts; but luckily they do not prove the sense of propriety to be artificial: they only prove, that the sense of propriety is at times overpowered by pride and vanity; which is no singular case, for that sometimes is the fate even of the sense of justice.

283. Points in which man is superior to the brute.—Discipline suitable for man.—Terms *congruity* and *propriety*, not applicable to a single object.—Instances of what is *proper*, of what is *incongruous*.

It is a matter of experience, that congruity or propriety, wherever perceived, is agreeable; and that incongruity or impropriety where ever perceived, is disagreeable. The only difficulty is, to ascertain what are the particular objects that in conjunction suggest these relations; for there are many objects that do not: the sea, for example, viewed in conjunction with a picture, or a man viewed in conjunction with a mountain, suggest not either congruity or incongruity. It seems natural to infer, what will be found true by induction, that we never perceive congruity nor incongruity but among things that are connected by some relation; such as a man and his actions, a principle and its accessories, a subject and its ornaments. We are indeed so framed by nature, as, among things so connected, to require a certain suitableness or correspondence, termed *congruity* or *propriety;* and to be displeased when we find the opposite relation of *incongruity* or *impropriety.**

285. If things connected be the subject of congruity, it is reasonable beforehand to expect a degree of congruity proportioned to the degree of the connection. And, upon examination, we find our expectation to be well founded: where the relation is intimate, as between a cause and its effect, a whole and its parts, we require the strictest congruity; but where the relation is slight or accidental, as among things jumbled together, we require little or no congruity: the strictest propriety is required in behavior and manner of living; because a man is connected with these by the relation of cause and effect. The relation between an edifice and the ground it stands upon is of the most intimate kind, and therefore the situation of a great house ought to be lofty: its relation to neighboring hills, rivers, plains, being that of the propinquity only, demands but a small share of congruity. Among members of the same club, the congruity ought to be considerable, as well as among things placed for show in the same niche: among passengers in a stage-coach we require very little congruity; and less still at a public spectacle.

* In the chapter of beauty, qualities are distinguished into primary and secondary: and to clear some obscurity that may appear in the text, it is proper to be observed, that the same distinction is applicable to relations. Resemblance, equality, uniformity, proximity, are relations that depend not on us, but exist equally, whether perceived or not; and upon that account may justly be termed *primary* relations. But there are other relations, that only appear such to us, and that have not any external existence like primary relations; which is the case of congruity, incongruity, propriety, impropriety: these may be properly termed *secondary* relations. Thus it appears, from what is said in the text, that the secondary relations mentioned arise from objects connected by some primary relation. Property is an example of a secondary relation, as it exists nowhere but in the mind. I purchase a field or a horse: the covenant makes the primary relation; and the secondary relation built on it, is property.

284. The sense of congruity a constituent of our nature. Objections answered.—Congruity and propriety, agreeable, &c.—Among what things only congruity or incongruity is perceived.—Primary and secondary relations.

Congruity is so nearly allied to beauty as commonly to be held a species of it; and yet they differ so essentially as never to coincide: beauty, like color, is placed upon a single subject; congruity upon a plurality. Further, a thing beautiful in itself may, with relation to other things, produce the strongest sense of incongruity.

286. Congruity and propriety are commonly reckoned synonymous terms; and hitherto in opening the subject they have been used indifferently; but they are distinguishable, and the precise meaning of each must be ascertained. Congruity is the genus of which propriety is a species; for we call nothing *propriety* but that congruity or suitableness which ought to subsist between sensible beings and their thoughts, words, and actions.

In order to give a full view of these secondary relations, I shall trace them through some of the most considerable primary relations. The relation of a part to the whole, being extremely intimate, demands the utmost degree of congruity: even the slightest deviation is disgustful; witness the *Lutrin*, a burlesque poem, which is closed with a serious and warm panegyric on Lamoignon, one of the king's judges:

> ————Amphora cœpit
> Institui; currente rota, cur urceus exit?

287. Examples of congruity and incongruity are furnished in plenty by the relation between a subject and its ornaments. A literary performance, intended merely for amusement, is susceptible of much ornament, as well as a music-room or a playhouse; for in gayety the mind hath a peculiar relish for show and decoration. The most gorgeous apparel, however improper in tragedy, is not unsuitable to opera-actors: the truth is, an opera, in its present form, is a mighty fine thing; but, as it deviates from nature in its capital circumstances, we look not for nature nor propriety in those which are accessory. On the other hand, a serious and important subject admits not much ornament,* nor a subject that of itself is extremely beautiful; and a subject that fills the mind with its loftiness and grandeur, appears best in a dress altogether plain.

To a person of a mean appearance, gorgeous apparel is unsuitable; which, besides the incongruity, shows by contrast the meanness of appearance in the strongest light. Sweetness of look and manner requires simplicity of dress joined with the greatest elegance. A stately and majestic air requires sumptuous apparel, which ought

* Contrary to this rule, the introduction to the third volume of the *Characteristics*, is a continued chain of metaphors: these in such profusion are too florid for the subject; and have besides the bad effect of removing our attention from the principal subject, to fix it upon splendid trifles.

285. Congruity is expected in what degree? Instances.—Congruity nearly allied to beauty.
286. Congruity and propriety distinguishable.—Relation of a part to the whole demands congruity.

not to be gaudy, nor crowded with little ornaments. A woman of consummate beauty can bear to be highly adorned, and yet shows best in a plain dress.

> ——————For loveliness
> Needs not the foreign aid of ornament,
> But is, when unadorn'd, adorn'd the most.
> *Thomson's Autumn.*

288. Congruity regulates not only the quantity of ornament, but also the kind. The decorations of a dancing-room ought all of them to be gay. No picture is proper for a church but what has religion for its subject. Every ornament upon a shield should relate to war; and Virgil, with great judgment, confines the carvings upon the shield of Æneas to the military history of the Romans: that beauty is overlooked by Homer, for the bulk of the sculpture upon the shield of Achilles is of the arts of peace in general, and of joy and festivity in particular: the author of Telemachus betrays the same inattention in describing the shield of that young hero.

In judging of propriety with regard to ornaments, we must attend, not only to the nature of the subject that is to be adorned, but also to the circumstances in which it is placed: the ornaments that are proper for a ball will appear not altogether so decent at public worship; and the same person ought to dress differently for a marriage-feast and for a funeral.

289. Nothing is more intimately related to a man than his sentiments, words, and actions; and therefore we require here the strictest conformity. When we find what we thus require, we have a lively sense of propriety; when we find the contrary, our sense of impropriety is no less lively. Hence the universal distaste of affectation, which consists in making a show of greater delicacy and refinement than is suited either to the character or circumstances of the person. Nothing in epic or dramatic compositions is more disgustful than impropriety of manners. In Corneille's tragedy of *Cinna*, Æmilia, a favorite of Augustus, receives daily marks of his affection, and is loaded with benefits; yet all the while is laying plots to assassinate her benefactor, directed by no other motive than to avenge her father's death (see Act I. Sc. 2). Revenge against a benefactor, founded solely upon filial piety, cannot be directed by any principle but that of justice, and therefore never can suggest unlawful means; yet the crime here attempted, a treacherous murder, is what even a miscreant will scarce attempt against his bitterest enemy.

---

287. Instances of congruity and incongruity in a subject and its ornaments.—Dress required for different classes.

288. Congruity regulates not only the quantity of ornament, but the kind: in a dancing-room, &c.—Circumstances are to be considered in judging of propriety.

289. The close relation of a man to his sentiments, words, and actions.—Affectation, what, and why detested.—In epic or dramatic composition, what is most disgusting?—Remarks on the tragedy of *Cinna*.

290. What is said might be thought sufficient to explain the relations of congruity and propriety; and yet the subject is not exhausted; on the contrary, the prospect enlarges upon us, when we take under view the effects these relations produce in the mind Congruity and propriety, wherever perceived, appear agreeable; and every agreeable object produceth in the mind a pleasant emotion incongruity and impropriety, on the other hand, are disagreeable, and of course produce painful emotions. These emotions, whether pleasant or painful, sometimes vanish without any consequence; but more frequently occasion other emotions, to which I proceed.

When any slight incongruity is perceived in an accidental combination of persons or things, as of passengers in a stage-coach, or of individuals dining at an ordinary; the painful emotion of incongruity, after a momentary existence, vanisheth without producing any effect. But this is not the case of propriety and impropriety: voluntary acts, whether words or deeds, are imputed to the author: when proper, we reward him with our esteem; when improper, we punish him with our contempt. Let us suppose, for example, a generous action suited to the character of the author, which raises in him and in every spectator the pleasant emotion of propriety: this emotion generates in the author both self-esteem and joy; the former when he considers his relation to the action, and the latter when he considers the good opinion that others will entertain of him: the same emotion of propriety produceth in the spectators esteem for the author of the action; and when they think of themselves, it also produceth by contrast an emotion of humility. To discover the effects of an unsuitable action, we must invert each of these circumstances: the painful emotion of impropriety generates in the author of the action both humility and shame; the former when he considers his relation to the action, and the latter when he considers what others will think of him: the same emotion of impropriety produceth in the spectators contempt for the author of the action; and it also produceth, by contrast when they think of themselves, an emotion of self-esteem. Here, then, are many different emotions, derived from the same action considered in different views by different persons; a machine provided with many springs, and not a little complicated. Propriety of action, it would seem, is a favorite of Nature, or of the Author of Nature, when such care and solicitude is bestowed on it. It is not left to our own choice; but, like justice, is required at our hands: and, like justice, is enforced by natural rewards and punishments; a man cannot, with impunity, do any thing unbecoming or improper; he suffers the chastisement of contempt inflicted by others, and of shame inflicted by himself. An

290. The effects of the relations of congruity and propriety upon the mind of the beholder.—The effect of incongruity different from that of impropriety. Case of slight incongruity; of propriety and impropriety.—Effects of a suitable generous action, in the agent and spectator. Effects also of an unsuitable action.--Propriety of action, how enforced.

apparatus so complicated, and so singular, ought to rouse our attention: for nature doth nothing in vain; and we may conclude with certainty, that this curious branch of the human constitution is intended for some valuable purpose.

291. A gross impropriety is punished with contempt and indignation, which are vented against the offender by external expressions; nor is even the slightest impropriety suffered to pass without some degree of contempt. But there are improprieties of the slighter kind, that provoke laughter; of which we have examples without end in the blunders and absurdities of our own species: such improprieties receive a different punishment, as will appear by what follows. The emotions of contempt and of laughter occasioned by an impropriety of that kind, uniting intimately in the mind of the spectator, are expressed externally by a peculiar sort of laugh, termed *a laugh of derision or scorn.* (See chapter vii.) An impropriety that thus moves not only contempt but laughter, is distinguished by the epithet of *ridiculous;* and a laugh of derision or scorn is the punishment provided for it by nature. Nor ought it to escape observation, that we are so fond of inflicting that punishment, as sometimes to exert it even against creatures of an inferior species; witness a turkey-cock swelling with pride, and strutting with displayed feathers, which in a gay mood is apt to provoke a laugh of derision.

We must not expect that these different improprieties are separated by distinct boundaries; for of improprieties, from the slightest to the most gross, from the most risible to the most serious, there are degrees without end. Hence it is, that in viewing some unbecoming actions, too risible for anger, and too serious for derision, the spectator feels a sort of mixed emotion, partaking both of derision and of anger; which accounts for an expression, common with respect to the impropriety of some actions. Thus we know not whether to laugh or be angry.

292. It cannot fail to be observed, that in the case of a risible impropriety, which is always slight, the contempt we have for the offender is extremely faint, though derision, its gratification, is extremely pleasant. This disproportion between a passion and its gratification, may seem not conformable to the analogy of nature. In looking about for a solution, I reflect upon what is laid down above, that an improper action not only moves our contempt for the author, but also, by means of contrast, swells the good opinion we have of ourselves. This contributes, more than any other particular, to the pleasure we have in ridiculing follies and absurdities; and accordingly, it is well known that those who have the greatest share of vanity are the most prone to laugh at others. Vanity, which is a vivid passion, pleasant in itself, and not less so in its gratification,

291. How a gross impropriety is punished; how that of a slighter kind. Degrees of improprieties.

would singly be sufficient to account for the pleasure of ridicule, without borrowing any aid from contempt. Hence appears the reason of a noted observation, That we are the most disposed to ridicule the blunders and absurdities of others, when we are in high spirits; for in high spirits, self-conceit displays itself with more than ordinary vigor.

293. Having with wary steps traced an intricate road, not without danger of wandering, what remains to complete our journey, is to account for the final cause of congruity and propriety, which makes so great a figure in the human constitution. One final cause, regarding congruity, is pretty obvious, that the sense of congruity, as one principle of the fine arts, contributes in a remarkable degree to our entertainment, which is the final cause assigned above for our sense of proportion (see chapter iii.), and need not be enlarged upon here. Congruity, indeed, with respect to quantity, coincides with proportion; when the parts of a building are nicely adjusted to each other, it may be said indifferently, that it is agreeable by the congruity of its parts, or by the proportion of its parts. But propriety, which regards voluntary agents only, can never be the same with proportion: a very long nose is disproportioned, but cannot be termed *improper*. In some instances, it is true, impropriety coincides with disproportion in the same subject, but never in the same respect. I give for an example a very little man buckled to a long toledo: considering the man and the sword with respect to size, we perceive a disproportion: considering the sword as the choice of the man, we perceive an impropriety.

294. The sense of impropriety with respect to mistakes, blunders, and absurdities, is evidently calculated for the good of mankind. In the spectators it is productive of mirth and laughter, excellent recreation in an interval from business. But this is a trifle compared to what follows. It is painful to be the subject of ridicule; and to punish with ridicule the man who is guilty of an absurdity, tends to put him more on his guard in time coming. It is well ordered, that even the most innocent blunder is not committed with impunity; because, were errors licensed where they do no hurt, inattention would grow into habit, and be the occasion of much hurt.

The final cause of propriety as to moral duties, is of all the most illustrious. To have a just notion of it, the moral duties that respect others must be distinguished from those that respect ourselves. Fidelity, gratitude, and abstinence from injury, are examples of the first sort; temperance, modesty, firmness of mind, are examples of the other: the former are made duties by the sense of justice; the latter by the sense of propriety. Here is a final cause of the sense of propriety that will rouse our attention. It is undoubtedly the

---

292. Case of a risible impropriety.—Why derision is pleasant.

293. Final cause of congruity and propriety. Congruity often coincides with proportion; propriety never. Instance.—Instance of impropriety coinciding with disproportion

interest of every man to suit his behavior to the dignity of his nature, and to the station allotted him by Providence: for such rational conduct contributes in every respect to happiness, by preserving health, by procuring plenty, by gaining the esteem of others, and, which of all is the greatest blessing, by gaining a justly founded self-esteem. But in a matter so essential to our well-being, even self-interest is not relied on: the powerful authority of duty is superadded to the motive of interest. The God of Nature, in all things essential to our happiness, hath observed one uniform method: to keep us steady in our conduct, he hath fortified us with natural laws and principles, preventive of many aberrations, which would daily happen were we totally surrendered to so fallible a guide as is human reason. Propriety cannot rightly be considered in another light than as the natural law that regulates our conduct with respect to ourselves; as justice is the natural law that regulates our conduct with respect to others. I call propriety a law, no less than justice; because both are equally rules of conduct that *ought* to be obeyed: propriety includes that obligation; for to say an action is proper, is in other words to say, that it *ought* to be performed; and to say it is improper, is in other words to say, that it *ought* to be forborne. It is that very character of *ought* and *should* which makes justice a law to us; and the same character is applicable to propriety, though perhaps more faintly than to justice; but the difference is in degree only, not in kind; and we ought, without hesitation and reluctance, to submit equally to the government of both.

295. But I have more to urge upon that head. To the sense of propriety as well as of justice, are annexed the sanctions of rewards and punishments; which evidently prove the one to be a law as well as the other. The satisfaction a man hath in doing his duty, joined to the esteem and good-will of others, is the reward that belongs to both equally. The punishments also, though not the same, are nearly allied; and differ in degree more than in quality. Disobedience to the law of justice is punished with remorse; disobedience to the law of propriety, with shame, which is remorse in a lower degree. Every transgression of the law of justice raises indignation in the beholder; and so doth every flagrant transgression of the law of propriety. Slighter improprieties receive a milder punishment: they are always rebuked with some degree of contempt, and frequently with derision. In general, it is true, that the rewards and punishments annexed to the sense of propriety are slighter in degree than those annexed to the sense of justice; which is wisely ordered, because duty to others is still more essential to society than duty to ourselves: society, in-

---

294. Sense of impropriety with respect to blunders, &c., beneficial.—Final cause of propriety as to moral duties; those that respect others and ourselves distinguished.—The conduct which self-interest prompts.—What motive is added to self-interest.—Propriety and justice, natural laws of conduct.

295. Sanctions of rewards and punishments, appended to propriety and justice. Their kinds and degrees.

deed, could not subsist a moment, were individuals not protected from the headstrong and turbulent passions of their neighbors.

296. The final cause now unfolded of the sense of propriety, must, to every discerning eye, appear delightful; and yet this is but a partial view; for that sense reaches another illustrious end, which is, in conjunction with the sense of justice, to enforce the performance of social duties. In fact, the sanctions visibly contrived to compel a man to be just to himself, are equally serviceable to compel him to be just to others; which will be evident from a single reflection, that an action, by being unjust, ceases not to be improper: an action never appears more eminently improper, than when it is unjust: it is obviously becoming and suitable to human nature, that each man do his duty to others; and, accordingly, every transgression of duty to others, is at the same time a transgression of duty to one's self. This is a plain truth without exaggeration; and it opens a new and enchanting view in the moral landscape, the prospect being greatly enriched by the multiplication of agreeable objects. It appears now, that nothing is overlooked, nothing left undone, that can possibly contribute to the enforcing social duty; for to all the sanctions that belong to it singly, are superadded the sanctions of self-duty. A familiar example shall suffice for illustration. An act of ingratitude, considered in itself, is to the author disagreeable, as well as to every spectator: considered by the author with relation to himself, it raises self-contempt: considered by him with relation to the world, it makes him ashamed: considered by others, it raises their contempt and indignation against the author. These feelings are all of them occasioned by the impropriety of the action. When the action is considered as unjust, it occasions another set of feelings: in the author it produces remorse, and a dread of merited punishment; and in others, the benefactor chiefly, indignation and hatred directed to the ungrateful person. Thus shame and remorse united in the ungrateful person, and indignation united with hatred in the hearts of others, are the punishments provided by nature for injustice. Stupid and insensible must he be, who, in a contrivance so exquisite, perceives not the benevolent hand of our Creator.

CHAPTER XI.

DIGNITY AND GRACE.

297. The terms *dignity* and *meanness* are applied to man in point of character, sentiment, and behavior: we say, for example, of one

296. Sense of propriety and of justice enforces social duties.—Duty to others is also self duty. Example; an act of ingratitude.

man, that he hath natural dignity in his air and manner; of another, that he makes a mean figure: we perceive dignity in every action and sentiment of some persons; meanness and vulgarity in the actions and sentiments of others. With respect to the fine arts, some performances are said to be manly, and suitable to the dignity of human nature; others are termed low, mean, trivial. Such expressions are common, though they have not always a precise meaning. With respect to the art of criticism, it must be a real acquisition to ascertain what these terms truly import; which possibly may enable us to rank every performance in the fine arts according to its dignity.

Inquiring first to what subjects the terms *dignity* and *meanness* are appropriated, we soon discover, that they are not applicable to any thing inanimate: the most magnificent palace that ever was built may be lofty, may be grand, but it has no relation to dignity: the most diminutive shrub may be little, but it is not mean. These terms must belong to sensitive beings, probably to man only; which will be evident when we advance in the inquiry.

298. Human actions appear in many different lights: in themselves they appear grand or little; with respect to the author, they appear proper or improper; with respect to those affected by them, just or unjust; and I now add, that they are also distinguished by dignity and meanness. If any one incline to think, that, with respect to human actions, dignity coincides with grandeur, and meanness with littleness, the difference will be evident upon reflecting, that an action may be grand without being virtuous, and little without being faulty; but that we never attribute dignity to any action but what is virtuous, nor meanness to any but what is faulty. Every action of dignity creates respect and esteem for the author; and a mean action draws upon him contempt. A man is admired for a grand action, but frequently is neither loved nor esteemed for it: neither is a man always contemned for a low or little action. The action of Cæsar passing the Rubicon was grand; but there was no dignity in it, considering that his purpose was to enslave his country: Cæsar, in a march, taking opportunity of a rivulet to quench his thirst, did a low action, but the action was not mean.

299. As it appears to me, dignity and meanness are founded on a natural principle not hitherto mentioned. Man is endowed with a SENSE of the worth and excellence of his nature: he deems it more perfect than that of the other beings around him; and he perceives that the perfection of his nature consists in virtue, particularly in virtues of the highest rank. To express that sense, the term *dignity* is appropriated. Further, to behave with dignity and to refrain from all mean actions, is felt to be not a virtue only, but a duty: it is a

---

297. In what respects the terms dignity and meanness are applied to man; and to the fine arts. Not applicable to inanimate things.

298. Different lights in which human actions may be viewed.—The dignity of an action not coincident with grandeur.—Cæsar.

duty every man owes to himself. By acting in that manner, he attracts love and esteem: by acting meanly, or below himself, he is disapproved and contemned.

According to the description here given of dignity and meanness, they appear to be a species of propriety and impropriety. Many actions may be proper or improper, to which dignity or meanness cannot be applied: to eat when one is hungry, is proper, but there is no dignity in that action: revenge fairly taken, if against law, is improper, but not mean. But every action of dignity is also proper, and every mean action is also improper.

300. This sense of the dignity of human nature reaches even our pleasures and amusements: if they enlarge the mind by raising grand or elevated emotions, or if they humanize the mind by exercising our sympathy, they are approved as suited to the dignity of our nature; if they contract the mind by fixing it on trivial objects, they are contemned as not suited to the dignity of our nature. Hence, in general, every occupation, whether of use or amusement, that corresponds to the dignity of man, is termed *manly;* and every occupation below his nature, is termed *childish.*

To those who study human nature, there is a point which has always appeared intricate: How comes it that generosity and courage are more esteemed, and bestow more dignity, than good-nature, or even justice; though the latter contribute more than the former to private as well as to public happiness? This question, bluntly proposed, might puzzle a cunning philosopher; but, by means of the foregoing observations, will easily be solved. Human virtues, like other objects, obtain a rank in our estimation, not from their utility, which is a subject of reflection, but from the direct impression they make on us. Justice and good-nature are a sort of negative virtues, that scarce make any impression but when they are transgressed: courage and generosity, on the contrary, producing elevated emotions, enliven greatly the sense of a man's dignity, both in himself and in others; and for that reason, courage and generosity are in higher regard than the other virtues mentioned: we describe them as grand and elevated, as of greater dignity, and more praiseworthy.

301. This leads us to examine more directly emotions and passions with respect to the present subject; and it will not be difficult to form a scale of them, beginning with the meanest, and ascending gradually to those of the highest rank and dignity. Pleasure felt at the organ of sense, named *corporeal pleasure,* is perceived to be low; and, when indulged to excess, is perceived also to be mean: for that reason, persons of any delicacy dissemble the pleasure they take in eating and drinking. The pleasures of the eye and ear, having no

299 Dignity and meanness founded on a certain natural principle.—Dignity and meanness are a species of propriety and impropriety.

300. Pleasures and amusements, when dignified and manly.—How it happens that generosity and courage are more esteemed and bestow more dignity than good-nature, or even justice.

organic feeling (see the Introduction), and being free from any sense of meanness, are indulged without any shame: they even rise to a certain degree of dignity when their objects are grand or elevated. The same is the case of the sympathetic passions: a virtuous person behaving with fortitude and dignity under cruel misfortunes, makes a capital figure; and the sympathizing spectator feels in himself the same dignity. Sympathetic distress at the same time never is mean: on the contrary, it is agreeable to the nature of a social being, and has general approbation. The rank that love possesses in the scale, depends in a great measure on its object: it possesses a low place when founded on external properties merely; and is mean when bestowed on a person of inferior rank without any extraordinary qualification: but when founded on the more elevated internal properties, it assumes a considerable degree of dignity. The same is the case of friendship. When gratitude is warm, it animates the mind; but it scarce rises to dignity. Joy bestows dignity when it proceeds from an elevated cause.

302. If I can depend upon induction, dignity is not a property of any disagreeable passion: one is slight, another severe; one depresses the mind, another animates it; but there is no elevation, far less dignity, in any of them. Revenge in particular, though it inflame and swell the mind, is not accompanied with dignity, nor even with elevation: it is not, however, felt as mean or grovelling, unless when it takes indirect measures for gratification. Shame and remorse, though they sink the spirits, are not mean. Pride, a disagreeable passion, bestows no dignity in the eye of a spectator. Vanity always appears mean; and extremely so where founded, as commonly happens, on trivial qualifications.

303. I proceed to the pleasures of the understanding, which possess a high rank in point of dignity. Of this every one will be sensible, when he considers the important truths that have been laid open by science; such as general theorems, and the general laws that govern the material and moral worlds. The pleasures of the understanding are suited to man as a rational and contemplative being; and they tend not a little to ennoble his nature: even to the Deity he stretcheth his contemplations, which, in the discovery of infinite power, wisdom, and benevolence, afford delight of the most exalted kind. Hence it appears that the fine arts, studied as a rational science, afford entertainment of great dignity; superior far to what they afford as a subject of taste merely.

But contemplation, however in itself valuable, is chiefly respected as subservient to action; for man is intended to be more an active than a contemplative being. He accordingly shows more dignity in action than in contemplation: generosity, magnanimity, heroism,

---

301. Scale of emotions and passions with respect to dignity
302. Dignity does not belong to any disagreeable passion.

raise his character to the highest pitch; these best express the dignity of his nature, and advance him nearer to divinity than any other of his attributes.

304. By every production that shows art and contrivance, our curiosity is excited upon two points: first, how it was made; and next, to what end. Of the two, the latter is the more important inquiry, because the means are ever subordinate to the end; and, in fact, our curiosity is always more inflamed by the *final* than by the *efficient* cause This preference is nowhere more visible than in contemplating the works of nature: if in the efficient cause wisdom and power be displayed, wisdom is no less conspicuous in the final cause; and from it only can we infer benevolence, which, of all the divine attributes, is to man the most important.

305. Having endeavored to assign the efficient cause of dignity and meanness, by unfolding the principle on which they are founded, we proceed to explain the final cause of the dignity or meanness bestowed upon the several particulars above mentioned, beginning with corporeal pleasures. These, as far as usual, are, like justice, fenced with sufficient sanctions to prevent their being neglected: hunger and thirst are painful sensations; and we are incited to animal love by a vigorous propensity: were corporeal pleasures dignified over and above with a place in a high class, they would infallibly disturb the balance of the mind by outweighing the social affections. This is a satisfactory final cause for refusing to these pleasures any degree of dignity; and the final cause is no less evident of their meanness when they are indulged to excess. The more refined pleasures of external sense, conveyed by the eye and the ear from natural objects and from the fine arts, deserve a high place in our esteem, because of their singular and extensive utility: in some cases they rise to a considerable dignity, and the very lowest pleasures of the kind are never esteemed mean or grovelling. The pleasure arising from wit, humor, ridicule, or from what is simply ludicrous, is useful, by relaxing the mind after the fatigue of more manly occupation; but the mind, when it surrenders itself to pleasure of that kind, loses its vigor, and sinks gradually into sloth.* The place this pleasure occupies in point of dignity, is adjusted to these views; to make it useful as a relaxation, it is not branded with meanness; to prevent its usurpation, it is removed from that place but a single degree: no man values himself for that pleasure, even during gratification; and

* Neque enim ita generati à natura sumus, ut ad ludum et jocum facti esse videamur, sed ad severitatem potius et ad quædam studia graviora atque majora. Ludo autem et joco, uti illis quidem licet, sed sicut somno et quietibus cæteris, tum cum gravibus seriisque rebus satisfecerimus.—*Cicero de offic.* lib. 1

303. The pleasures of the understanding.—Man shows more dignity in action than in contemplation

304. Final and efficient causes.

if it have engrossed more of his time than is requisite for relaxation, he looks back with some degree of shame.

306. In point of dignity, the social emotions rise above the selfish, and much above those of the eye and ear: man is by his nature a social being, and to qualify him for society it is wisely contrived that he should value himself more for being social than selfish.

The excellency of man is chiefly discernible in the great improvements he is susceptible of in society; these, by perseverance, may be carried on progressively above any assignable limits; and, even abstracting from revelation, there is great probability that the progress begun here will be completed in some future state. Now, as all valuable improvements proceed from the exercise of our rational faculties, the Author of our nature, in order to excite us to a due sense of these faculties, hath assigned a high rank to the pleasures of the understanding: their utility, with respect to this life as well as a future, entitles them to that rank.

But as action is the aim of all our improvements, virtuous actions justly possess the highest of all the ranks. These, we find, are by nature distributed into different classes, and the first in point of dignity assigned to actions that appear not the first in point of use: generosity, for example, in the sense of mankind, is more respected than justice, though the latter is undoubtedly more essential to society; and magnanimity, heroism, undaunted courage, rise still higher in our esteem. One would readily think that the moral virtues should be esteemed according to their importance. Nature has here deviated from her ordinary path, and great wisdom is shown in the deviation: the efficient cause is explained above, and the final cause explained in the *Essays of Morality and Natural Religion.* (Part I. Essay ii. chapter iv.)

307. We proceed to analyze *grace*, which, being in a good measure an uncultivated field, requires more than ordinary labor.

Graceful is an attribute: *grace* and *gracefulness* express that attribute in the form of a noun.

That this attribute is agreeable, no one doubts.

As grace is displayed externally, it must be an object of one or other of our five senses. That it is an object of sight, every person of taste can bear witness; and that it is confined to that sense, appears from induction; for it is not an object of smell, nor of taste, nor of touch. Is it an object of hearing? Some music, indeed, is termed graceful; but that expression is metaphorical, as when we say of other music that it is beautiful: the latter metaphor, at the same time, is more sweet and easy, which shows how little applica-

---

305. Final cause of the meanness of corporeal pleasures; especially when indulged to excess.—Pleasures of the eye and ear, how to be regarded. Those from wit, humor, &c., when are they dignified?

306. Why the social emotions rise in our estimation above the selfish.—Why a high rank is assigned to the pleasures of the understanding.—The rank which virtuous actions occupy.

ble to music or to sound the former is when taken in its proper sense.

That it is an attribute of man, is beyond dispute. But of what other beings is it also an attribute? We perceive at first sight that nothing inanimate is entitled to that epithet. What animal, then, besides man, is entitled? Surely not an elephant, nor even a lion. A horse may have a delicate shape with a lofty mien, and all his motions may be exquisite; but he is never said to be graceful. Beauty and grandeur are common to man with some other beings; but dignity is not applied to any being inferior to man; and, upon the strictest examination, the same appears to hold in grace.

308. Confining then grace to man, the next inquiry is whether, like beauty, it makes a constant appearance, or in some circumstances only. Does a person display this attribute at rest as well as in motion, asleep as when awake? It is undoubtedly connected with motion; for when the most graceful person is at rest, neither moving nor speaking, we lose sight of that quality as much as of color in the dark. Grace then is an agreeable attribute, inseparable from motion as opposed to rest, and as comprehending speech, looks, gestures, and locomotion.

As some motions are homely, the opposite to graceful, the next inquiry is, with what motions is this attribute connected? No man appears graceful in a mask; and, therefore, laying aside the expressions of the countenance, the other motions may be genteel, may be elegant, but of themselves never are graceful. A motion adjusted in the most perfect manner to answer its end, is elegant; but still somewhat more is required to complete our idea of grace or gracefulness.

What this unknown *more* may be, is the nice point. One thing is clear from what is said, that this *more* must arise from the expression of the countenance: and from what expressions so naturally as from those which indicate mental qualities, such as sweetness, benevolence, elevation, dignity? This promises to be a fair analysis, because of all objects, mental qualities affect us the most; and the impression made by graceful appearance upon every spectator of taste, is too deep for any cause purely corporeal.

309. The next step is, to examine what are the mental qualities, that, in conjunction with elegance of motion, produce a graceful appearance. Sweetness, cheerfulness, affability, are not separately sufficient, nor even in conjunction. As it appears to me, dignity alone, with elegant motion, may produce a graceful appearance; but still more graceful with the aid of other qualities, those especially that are the most exalted.

But this is not all. The most exalted virtues may be the lot of a

---

307. Grace an object of sight. Applicable only to man.

308. Grace inseparable from motion. Definition given.—Not all motions are graceful. Those of the countenance indicating mental qualities.

person whose countenance has little expression: such a person cannot be graceful. Therefore, to produce this appearance, we must add another circumstance, namely, an expressive countenance, displaying to every spectator of taste, with life and energy, every thing that passes in the mind.

Collecting these circumstances together, grace may be defined, that agreeable appearance which arises from elegance of motion, and from a countenance expressive of dignity. Expressions of other mental qualities are not essential to that appearance, but they heighten it greatly.

Of all external objects, a graceful person is the most agreeable.

Dancing affords great opportunity for displaying grace, and haranguing still more.

I conclude with the following reflection: That in vain will a person attempt to be graceful, who is deficient in amiable qualities. A man, it is true, may form an idea of qualities he is destitute of; and, by means of that idea, may endeavor to express those qualities by looks and gestures; but such studied expression will be too faint and obscure to be graceful.

CHAPTER XII.

RIDICULE.

310. To define ridicule has puzzled and vexed every critic. The definition given by Aristotle is obscure and imperfect. (*Poet.* cap. v.) Cicero handles it at great length (L. ii. *De Oratore*), but without giving any satisfaction: he wanders in the dark, and misses the distinction between risible and ridiculous. Quintilian is sensible of the distinction,* but has not attempted to explain it. Luckily this subject lies no longer in obscurity: a risible object produceth an emotion of laughter merely (see chapter vii.): a ridiculous object is improper as well as risible, and produceth a mixed emotion, which is vented by a laugh of derision or scorn. (See chapter x.)

Having, therefore, happily unravelled the knotty part, I proceed to other particulars.

Burlesque, though a great engine of ridicule, is not confined to

---

* Ideoque anceps ejus rei ratio est, quod a derisu non procul abest risus.—Lib. VI. cap. iii. sect. 1.

---

309. What mental qualities, joined with elegance of motion, produce a graceful appearance.—Grace defined.—Concluding reflection.

that subject; for it is clearly distinguishable into burlesque that excites laughter merely, and burlesque that provokes derision or ridicule. A grave subject in which there is no impropriety, may be brought down by a certain coloring so as to be risible; which is the case of *Virgil Travestie*, and also the case of the *Secchia Rapita:* the authors laugh first, in order to make their readers laugh. The *Lutrin* is a burlesque poem of the other sort, laying hold of a low and trifling incident, to expose the luxury, indolence, and contentious spirit of a set of monks. Boileau, the author, gives a ridiculous air to the subject by dressing it in the heroic style, and affecting to consider it as of the utmost dignity and importance. In a composition of this kind, no image professedly ludicrous ought to find quarter, because such images destroy the contrast; and, accordingly, the author shows always the grave face, and never once betrays a smile.

311. Though the burlesque that aims at ridicule produces its effect by elevating the style far above the subject, yet it has limits beyond which the elevation ought not to be carried: the poet, consulting the imagination of his readers, ought to confine himself to such images as are lively, and readily apprehended: a strained elevation, soaring above an ordinary reach of fancy, makes not a pleasant impression: the reader, fatigued with being always upon the stretch, is soon disgusted; and if he persevere, becomes thoughtless and indifferent. Further, a fiction gives no pleasure unless it be painted in colors so lively as to produce some perception of reality; which never can be done effectually where the images are formed with labor or difficulty. For these reasons, I cannot avoid condemning the *Batrachomuomachia*, said to be the composition of Homer: it is beyond the power of imagination to form a clear and lively image of frogs and mice, acting with the dignity of the highest of our species; nor can we form a conception of the reality of such an action, in any manner so distinct as to interest our affections even in the slightest degree.

The *Rape of the Lock* is of a character clearly distinguishable from those now mentioned: it is not properly a burlesque performance, but what may rather be termed *a heroi-comical poem:* it treats a gay and familiar subject with pleasantry, and with a moderate degree of dignity; the author puts not on a mask like Boileau, nor professes to make us laugh like Tassoni. The *Rape of the Lock* is a genteel species of writing, less strained than those mentioned; and is pleasant or ludicrous without having ridicule for its chief aim; giving way, however, to ridicule where it arises naturally from a particular character, such as that of Sir Plume. Addison's *Specta-*

---

310. A risible distinguished from a ridiculous object.—Burlesque of two kinds. Examples.

311. Of the burlesque that aims at ridicule, its appropriate style.—*Rape of the Lock* criticised.

tor upon the exercise of the fan (No. 102), is extremely gay and ludicrous, resembling in its subject the *Rape of the Lock.*

312. Humor belongs to the present chapter, because it is connected with ridicule. Congreve defines humor to be "a singular and unavoidable manner of doing or saying any thing, peculiar and natural to one man only, by which his speech and actions are distinguished from those of other men." Were this definition just, a majestic and commanding air, which is a singular property, is humor; as also a natural flow of correct and commanding eloquence, which is no less singular. Nothing just or proper is denominated humor; nor any singularity of character, words, or actions, that is valued or respected. When we attend to the character of a humorist, we find that it arises from circumstances both risible and improper, and therefore that it lessens the man in our esteem, and makes him in some measure ridiculous. [Wordsworth gives the following representation of a true English ploughboy.

His joints are stiff;
Beneath a cumbrous frock, that to the knees
Invests the thriving churl, his legs appear,
Fellows to those which lustily upheld
The wooden stools, for everlasting use,
On which our fathers sate. And mark his brow!
Under whose shaggy canopy are set
Two eyes, not dim, but of a healthy stare;
Wide, sluggish, blank, and ignorant, and strange;
Proclaiming boldly that they never drew
A look or motion of intelligence
From infant conning of the Christ-cross row,
Or puzzling through a primer, line by line,
Till perfect mastery crown the pains at last. *Excursion.*

There is, says Prof. Wilson, in the above lines, a kind of forcible humor which may remind the reader of Cowper's manner in the Task. The versification is good, and gives so much point to the thoughts, that it should seem as if custom, rather than necessity, had caused all satires, from Donne to Churchill, to be written in rhyme.]

Humor in writing is very different from humor in character. When an author insists upon ludicrous subjects with a professed purpose to make his readers laugh, he may be styled *a ludicrous writer;* but is scarce entitled to be styled *a writer of humor.* This quality belongs to an author, who, affecting to be grave and serious, paints his objects in such colors as to provoke mirth and laughter. A writer that is really a humorist in character, does this without design: if not, he must affect the character in order to succeed. Swift and Fontaine were humorists in character, and their writings are full of humor. Addison was not a humorist in character; and yet in his prose writings a most delicate and refined humor prevails. Arbuthnot exceeds them all in drollery and humorous painting; which shows a great genius, because, if I am not misinformed, he had nothing of that peculiarity in his character.

There remains to show by examples the manner of treating subjects, so as to give them a ridiculous appearance.

Il ne dit jamais, je vous donne, mais, je vous prête le bon jour.—*Molière.*

Orleans. I know him to be valiant.
Constable. I was told that by one that knows him better than you.
Orleans. What's he?
Constable. Marry, he told me so himself; and he said he car'd not who knew it. *Henry V. Shakspeare.*

He never broke any man's head but his own, and that was against a post when he was drunk. *Ibid.*

Millament. Sententious Mirabell! Pr'ythee don't look with that violent and flexible wise face, like Solomon at the dividing of the child, in an old tapestry hanging. (Congreve.) *Way of the World.*

A true critic, in the perusal of a book, is like a dog at a feast, whose thoughts and stomach are wholly set upon what the guests fling away, and consequently is apt to snarl most when there are the fewest bones. *Tale of a Tub.*

313. In the following instances, the ridicule arises from absurd conceptions in the persons introduced:

Valentine. Your blessing, Sir.
Sir Sampson. You've had it already, Sir; I think I sent it you to-day in a bill for four thousand pound; a great deal of money, Brother Foresight.
Foresight. Ay indeed, Sir Sampson, a great deal of money for a young man; I wonder what can he do with it. *Love for Love*, Act II. Sc. 7.

Millament. I nauseate walking; 'tis a country-diversion; I loathe the country, and every thing that relates to it.
Sir Wilful. Indeed! hah! look ye, look ye, you do? nay, 'tis like you may —— here are choice of pastimes here in town, as plays and the like; that must be confess'd indeed.
Millament. Ah l'étourdie! I hate the town too.
Sir Wilful. Dear heart, that's much —— hah! that you should hate 'em both! hah! 'tis like you may, there are some can't relish the town, and others can't away with the country —— 'tis like you may be one of these, Cousine.
Way of the World, Act IV. Sc. 4.

Lord Froth. I assure you, Sir Paul, I laugh at nobody's jests but my own, or a lady's: I assure you, Sir Paul.
Brisk. How? how, my lord? what, affront my wit? Let me perish, do I never say any thing worthy to be laugh'd at?
Lord Froth. O foy, don't misapprehend me, I don't say so, for I often smile at your conceptions. But there is nothing more unbecoming a man of quality than to laugh; 'tis such a vulgar expression of the passion! everybody can laugh. Then especially to laugh at the jest of an inferior person, or when anybody else of the same quality does not laugh with one; ridiculous! To be pleas'd with what pleases the crowd! Now, when I laugh I always laugh alone. *Double Dealer*, Act I. Sc. 4.

So sharp-sighted is pride in blemishes, and so willing to be gratified, that it takes up with the very slightest improprieties; such as a blunder by a foreigner in speaking our language, especially if the blunder can bear a sense that reflects on the speaker:

Quickly. The young man is an honest man.
Caius. What shall de honest man do in my closet? dere is no honest man dat shall come in my closet. *Merry Wives of Windsor.*

---

312. Humor (in character) defined.—A ludicrous writer distinguished from a writer of humor.—Swift, Fontaine, Addison, Arbuthnot.—Examples.

Love speeches are finely ridiculed in the following passage:

Quoth he, My faith as adamantine,
As chains of destiny, I'll maintain;
True as Apollo ever spoke,
Or oracle from heart of oak;
And if you'll give my flame but vent,
Now in close hugger mugger pent,
And shine upon me but benignly,
With that one and that other pigsney,
The sun and day shall sooner part,
Than love, or you, shake off my heart;
The sun that shall no more dispense
His own but your bright influence:
I'll carve your name on barks of trees,
With true love-knots, and flourishes;
That shall infuse eternal spring,
And everlasting flourishing:
Drink ev'ry letter on't in stum,
And make it brisk champaign become.
Where'er you tread, your foot shall set
The primrose and the violet;
All spices, perfumes, and sweet powders,
Shall borrow from your breath their odors
Nature her charter shall renew,
And take all lives of things from you;
The world depend upon your eye,
And when you frown upon it, die.
Only our loves shall still survive,
New worlds and natures to outlive,
And, like to herald's moons, remain
All crescents, without change or wane.

Hudibras, Part II. canto I.

314. Irony turns things into ridicule in a peculiar manner; it consists in laughing at a man under disguise of appearing to praise or speak well of him. Swift affords us many illustrious examples of that species of ridicule. Take the following:

By these methods, in a few weeks, there starts up many a writer, capable of managing the profoundest and most universal subjects. For what though his head be empty, provided his common-place book be full! And if you will bate him but the circumstances of method, and style, and grammar, and invention; allow him but the common privileges of transcribing from others, and digressing from himself, as often as he shall see occasion; he will desire no more ingredients towards fitting up a treatise that shall make a very comely figure on a bookseller's shelf, there to be preserved neat and clean, for a long eternity, adorned with the heraldry of its title, fairly inscribed on a label; never to be thumbed or greased by students, nor bound to everlasting chains of darkness in a library; but when the fullness of time is come, shall happily undergo the trial of purgatory, in order to ascend the sky.—*Tale of a Tub*, sect. vii.

I cannot but congratulate our age on this peculiar felicity, that though we have indeed made great progress in all other branches of luxury, we are not yet debauched with any *high relish* in poetry, but are in this one taste less *nice* than our ancestors.

If the reverend clergy showed more concern than others, I charitably impute it to their great charge of souls: and what confirmed me in this opinion was, that the degrees of apprehension and terror could be distinguished to be greater or less, according to their ranks and degrees in the church.*

* A true and faithful narrative of what passed in London, during the general consternation of all ranks and degrees of mankind.

"Casabianca" Mrs. Hemans.
"The old oaken bucket" ("The old straw hat")
"Excelsior" Longfellow ("Upidee") Parody.

315. A parody must be distinguished from every species of ridicule: it enlivens a gay subject by imitating some important incident that is serious: it is ludicrous, and may be risible; but ridicule is not a necessary ingredient. Take the following examples, the first of which refers to an expression of Moses:

> The skilful nymph reviews her force with care:
> Let spades be trumps! she said, and trumps they were.
>
> *Rape of the Lock*, Canto iii. 45.

The next is in imitation of Achilles' oath in Homer:

> But by this lock, this sacred lock, I swear,
> (Which never more shall join its parted hair,
> Which never more its honors shall renew,
> Clipp'd from the lovely head where late it grew),
> That while my nostrils draw the vital air,
> This hand which won it, shall forever wear.
> He spoke, and speaking, in proud triumph spread
> The long-contended honors of her head.—*Ibid.* Canto iv. 133.

The following imitates the history of Agamemnon's sceptre in Homer:

> Now meet thy fate, incensed Belinda cried,
> And drew a deadly bodkin from her side,
> (The same, his ancient personage to deck,
> Her great-great-grandsire wore about his neck,
> In three seal rings: which after, melted down,
> Form'd a vast buckle for his widow's gown:
> Her infant grandame's whistle next it grew,
> The bells she jingled, and the whistle blew:
> Then in a bodkin graced her mother's hairs,
> Which long she wore and now Belinda wears).
>
> *Ibid.* Canto v. 87.

Though ridicule, as observed above, is no necessary ingredient in a parody, yet there is no opposition between them: ridicule may be successfully employed in a parody; and a parody may be employed to promote ridicule.

The interposition of the gods, in the manner of Homer and Virgil, ought to be confined to ludicrous subjects, which are much enlivened by such interposition handled in the form of a parody, witness the Cave of Spleen, *Rape of the Lock*, canto iv.; the goddess of Discord, *Lutrin*, canto i.; and the goddess of Indolence, canto ii.

["The secret of parody lies merely in transposing or applying at a venture to any thing, or to the lowest objects, that which is applicable only to certain given things, or to the highest matters. 'From the sublime to the ridiculous there is but a step.' The slightest want of unity of impression destroys the sublime; the detection of the smallest incongruity is an infallible ground to rest the ludicrous upon. But in serious poetry, which aims at riveting our affections, every blow must tell home. The missing a single time is fatal, and undoes the spell. We see how difficult it is to sustain a continued flight of impressive sentiment: how easy it must be then to travesty or burlesque it, to flounder into nonsense, and be witty by playing the fool. It is a common mistake, however, to suppose that parodies degrade, or imply a stigma on the subject; on the contrary, they in general imply something serious or sacred in the originals. Without this they would be good for nothing; for the immediate contrast would be wanting, and with this they are sure to tell. The best parodies are, accordingly, the best and most striking things reversed. Witness the common travesties of Homer and Virgil."—*Hazlitt*, Lect. I.]

316 Those who have a talent for ridicule, which is seldom united with a taste for delicate and refined beauties, are quick-sighted in improprieties; and these they eagerly grasp in order to gratify their favorite propensity. Persons galled are provoked to maintain, that ridicule is improper for grave subjects. Subjects really grave are by no means fit for ridicule: but then it is urged against them, that when it is called in question whether a certain subject be really grave, ridicule is the only means of determining the controversy. Hence a celebrated question, Whether ridicule be or be not a test of truth? I give this question a place here, because it tends to illustrate the nature of ridicule.

The question stated in accurate terms is, Whether the sense of ridicule be the proper test for distinguishing ridiculous objects, from what are not so. Taking it for granted, that ridicule is not a subject of reasoning, but of sense or taste (see chap. x. compared with chap. vii.), I proceed thus. No person doubts but that our sense of beauty is the true test of what is beautiful; and our sense of grandeur, of what is great or sublime. Is it more doubtful whether our sense of ridicule be the true test of what is ridiculous? It is not only the true test, but indeed the only test; for this subject comes not, more than beauty or grandeur, under the province of reason. If any subject, by the influence of fashion or custom, have acquired a degree of veneration to which naturally it is not entitled, what are the proper means for wiping off the artificial coloring, and displaying the subject in its true light? A man of true taste sees the subject without disguise; but if he hesitate, let him apply the test of ridicule, which separates it from its artificial connections, and exposes it naked with all its native improprieties.

317. But it is urged, that the gravest and most serious matters may be set in a ridiculous light. Hardly so; for where an object is neither risible nor improper, it lies not open in any quarter to an attack from ridicule. But supposing the fact, I foresee not any harmful consequence. By the same sort of reasoning, a talent for wit ought to be condemned, because it may be employed to burlesque a great or lofty subject. Such irregular use made of a talent for wit or ridicule, cannot long impose upon mankind: it cannot stand the test of correct and delicate taste; and truth will at last

---

315. A parody. Example from the Rape of the Lock.—Remarks of Hazlitt.

316. Whether ridicule is a test of truth. Question stated in accurate terms. The author's argument

"Knickerbocker's History of N. Y." Irving. Humorous.

prevail even with the vulgar. To condemn a talent for ridicule because it may be perverted to wrong purposes, is not a little ridiculous: could one forbear to smile, if a talent for reasoning were condemned because it also may be perverted? and yet the conclusion in the latter case, would be not less just than in the former: perhaps more just; for no talent is more frequently perverted than that of reason.

We had best leave nature to her own operations: the most valuable talents may be abused, and so may that of ridicule: let us bring it under proper culture if we can, without endeavoring to pluck it up by the root. Were we destitute of this test of truth, I know not what might be the consequences: I see not what rule would be left us to prevent splendid trifles passing for matters of importance, and show and form for substance, and superstition or enthusiasm for pure religion.

318. [(While there is much truth in the statements above made concerning Ridicule, there is also much and dangerous error.) Boyd.

As Dr. Blair observes: "Many vices might be more successfully exploded by employing ridicule against them, than by serious attacks and arguments. At the same time it must be confessed, that ridicule is an instrument of such a nature, that when managed by unskilful or improper hands, there is hazard of its doing mischief, instead of good, to society. For *ridicule is far from being*, as some have maintained it to be, *a test of truth*. On the contrary, it is apt to mislead and seduce, by the colors which it throws upon its objects; and it is often more difficult to judge whether these colors be natural and proper, than it is to distinguish between simple truth and error. Licentious writers, therefore, of the comic class, have too often had it in their power to cast a ridicule upon characters and objects which did not deserve it."

319. Lord Shaftesbury advocated the same false doctrine as Lord Kames; but Dr. Leland has clearly exposed his error, in the following remarks: "The best and wisest men in all ages have always recommended a calm attention and sobriety of mind, a cool and impartial examination and inquiry, as the properest disposition for finding out truth, and judging concerning it. But according to his lordship's representation of the case, those that apply themselves to the searching out of truth, or judging what is really true, serious, and excellent, must endeavor to put themselves in a merry humor, to raise up a gayety of spirit, and seek whether in the object they are examining they cannot find out something that may be justly laughed at. And it is great odds that a man who is thus disposed will find out something fit, as he imagines, to excite his mirth, in the most serious and important subject in the world. Such a temper is so far from being a help to a fair and unprejudiced inquiry, that it is

317. Objection stated and replied to.—Is ridicule to be abandoned?—Importance of a talent for ridicule.

318. Remark on Kames' doctrine concerning ridicule.—Dr. Blair's observations.

one of the greatest hindrances to it. A strong turn to ridicule has a tendency to disqualify a man for cool and sedate reflection, and to render him impatient of the pains that are necessary to a rational and deliberate search." * * * *

320. Dr. Leland proceeds to say:—"Our noble author, indeed, frequently observes that truth cannot be hurt by ridicule, since, when the ridicule is wrong placed, it will not hold. It will readily be allowed that truth and honesty cannot be the subject of *just* ridicule; but then this supposes that ridicule itself must be brought to the test of cool reason; and accordingly his lordship acknowledges, that it is in reality a serious study to temper and regulate that humor. And thus, after all, we are to return to gravity and serious *reason, as the ultimate test and criterion of ridicule*, and of every thing else. But though the most excellent things cannot be justly ridiculed, and ridicule, when thus applied, will, in the judgment of thinking men, render him that uses it ridiculous; yet there are many persons on whom it will have a different effect. The *ridicule will be apt to create prejudices* in their minds, and to inspire them with a contempt, or at least a disregard of things, which, when represented in a proper light, appear to be of the greatest worth and importance. . . . . . Weak and unstable minds have been driven into atheism, profaneness, and vice, by the force of ridicule, and have been made ashamed of that which they ought to esteem their glory."]

CHAPTER XIII.

WIT.

321. Wit is a quality of certain thoughts and expressions: the term is never applied to an action nor a passion, and as little to an external object.

However difficult it may be, in many instances, to distinguish a witty thought or expression from one that is not so, yet, in general, it may be laid down that the term *wit* is appropriated to such thoughts and expressions as are ludicrous, and also occasion some degree of surprise by their singularity. Wit, also, in a figurative sense, expresses a talent for inventing ludicrous thoughts or expressions: we say commonly *a witty man*, or *a man of wit*.

---

319. Dr. Leland's strictures upon Shaftesbury.—The method of searching out truth suggested by the wisest men.—Lord Shaftesbury's proposed method. Objections to his method.—Effect of a strong turn for ridicule.

320. Remarks on the statement that truth cannot be hurt by ridicule.—Reason the ultimate test, of what?—Bad effect of ridiculing sacred things.

Wit in its proper sense, as explained above, is distinguishable into two kinds: wit in the thought, and wit in the words or expression. Again, wit in the thought is of two kinds: *ludicrous images,* and *ludicrous combinations of things that have little or no natural relation.*

Ludicrous images that occasion surprise by their singularity, as having little or no foundation in nature, are fabricated by the imagination: and the imagination is well qualified for the office; being of all our faculties the most active, and the least under restraint. Take the following example:

Shylock. You knew (none so well, none so well as you) of my daughter's flight.

Salino. That's certain: I for my part knew the tailor that made the wings she flew withal. *Merchant of Venice,* Act III. Sc. 1.

The image here is undoubtedly witty. It is ludicrous: and it must occasion surprise; for having no natural foundation, it is altogether unexpected.

[According to Hazlitt, "the ludicrous is where there is a contradiction between the object and our expectations, heightened by some deformity or inconvenience, that is, by its being contrary to what is customary or desirable; as the ridiculous, which is the highest degree of the laughable, is that which is contrary not only to custom, but to sense and reason, or is a voluntary departure from what we have a right to expect from those who are conscious of absurdity and propriety in words, looks, and actions."]

322. The other branch, of wit in the thought, is that only which is taken notice of by Addison, following Locke, who defines it "to lie in the assemblage of ideas; and putting those together, with quickness and variety, wherein can be found any resemblance or congruity, thereby to make up pleasant pictures and agreeable visions in the fancy." (B. ii. ch. xi. sect. 2.) It may be defined more concisely, and perhaps more accurately, "A junction of things by distant and fanciful relations, which surprise because they are unexpected." (See chapter i.) The following is a proper example:

> We grant, although he had much wit,
> He was very shy of using it,
> As being loth to wear it out;
> And, therefore, bore it not about,
> Unless on holidays, or so,
> As men their best apparel do.—*Hudibras,* Canto i.

Wit is of all the most elegant recreation: the image enters the mind with gayety, and gives a sudden flash, which is extremely pleasant. Wit thereby gently elevates without straining, raises mirth without dissoluteness, and relaxes while it entertains.

---

321. To what the term wit is appropriated.—In a figurative sense, to what applied.—Two kinds of wit in the proper sense. Two kinds of wit in thought.—The source of ludicrous images.—Hazlitt's account of the ludicrous.

[*Wit and humor compared.*—"Humor is describing the ludicrous as it is in itself; wit is the exposing it, by comparing or contrasting it with something else. Humor is the growth of nature and accident; wit is the product of art and fancy. Humor, as it is shown in books, is an imitation of the natural or acquired absurdities of mankind, or of the ludicrous in accident, situation, and character, wit is the illustrating and heightening the sense of that absurdity by some sudden and unexpected likeness or opposition of one thing to another, which sets off the quality we laugh at or despise in a still more contemptible or striking point of view. Wit, *as distinguished from poetry*, is the imagination or fancy inverted, and so applied to given objects as to make the little look less, the mean more light and worthless; or to divert our admiration or wean our affections from that which is lofty and impressive, instead of producing a more intense admiration and exalted passion, as poetry does. Wit hovers round the borders of the light and trifling, whether in matters of pleasure or pain; for as soon as it describes the serious seriously, it ceases to be wit, and passes into a different form. The favorite employment of wit is to add littleness to littleness, and heap contempt on insignificance by all the arts of petty and incessant warfare; or if it ever affects to aggrandize and use the language of hyperbole, it is only to betray into derision by a fatal comparison, as in the mock-heroic; or if it treats of serious passion, it must do so as to lower the tone of intense and high-wrought sentiment by the introduction of burlesque and familiar circumstances."—*Hazlitt.*]

323. Wit in the expression, commonly called *a play of words*, being a bastard sort of wit, is reserved for the last place. I proceed to examples of wit in the thought; and first of ludicrous images.

Falstaff, speaking of his taking Sir John Coleville of the Dale:

Here he is, and here I yield him; and I beseech your Grace, let it be book'd with the rest of this day's deeds: or, by the Lord, I will have it in a particular ballad else, with mine own picture on the top of it, Coleville kissing my foot: to the which course if I be enforced, if you do not all show like gilt twopences to me; and I, in the clear sky of fame, o'ershine you as much as the full moon doth the cinders of the element, which show like pin's-heads to her; believe not the word of the Noble. Therefore let me have right, and let desert mount. —*Second Part Henry IV.* Act IV. Sc. 6.

I knew, when seven justices could not take up a quarrel, but when the parties were met themselves, one of them thought but of an *if;* as, If you said so, then I said so; and they shook hands, and swore brothers. Your *if* is the only peacemaker; much virtue in *if.—Shakspeare.*

An I have forgotten what the inside of a church is made of, I am a peppercorn, a brewer's horse: The inside of a church! Company, villanous company, hath been the spoil of me.—*Ib.*

The war hath introduced abundance of polysyllables, which will never be able to live many more campaigns. Speculations, operations, preliminaries,

---

322. Definitions of the other branch of wit in the thought. Example from Hudibras.—Wit, as a recreation.—Wit. distinguished from humor, and from poetry.

ambassadors, palisadoes, communication, circumvallation, battalions, as numerous as they are, if they attack us too frequently in our coffee-houses, we shall certainly put them to flight, and cut off the rear.—*Tatler*, No. 330.

Speaking of Discord:

She never went abroad but she brought home such a bundle of monstrous lies as would have amazed any mortal but such as knew her: of a whale that had swallowed a fleet of ships; of the lions being let out of the Tower to destroy the Protestant religion; of the Pope's being seen in a brandy-shop at Wapping, &c.—*History of John Bull*, part i. ch. xvi.

324. The other branch, of wit in the thought, namely, ludicrous combinations and oppositions, may be traced through various ramifications. And, first, fanciful causes assigned that have no natural relation to effects produced:

Lancast. Fare you well, Falstaff; I, in my condition, shall better speak of you than you deserve. [*Exit.*

Falstaff. I would you had but the wit; 'twere better than your dukedom. Good faith, this same young sober-blooded boy doth not love me; nor a man cannot make him laugh; but that's no marvel, he drinks no wine. There's never any of these demure boys come to any proof; for thin drink doth so overcool their blood, and making many fish-meals, that they fall into a kind of male green-sickness; and then, when they marry, they get wenches. They are generally fools and cowards; which some of us should be too, but for inflammation. A good sherris-sack hath a twofold operation in it: it ascends me into the brain; dries me there all the foolish, dull, and crudy vapors which environ it; makes it apprehensive, quick, forgetive, full of nimble, fiery, and delectable shapes; which delivered o'er to the voice, the tongue, which is the birth, becomes excellent wit. The second property of your excellent sherris is, the warming of the blood; which, before cold and settled, left the liver white and pale; which is the badge of pusillanimity and cowardice: but the sherris warms it, and makes it course from the inwards to the parts extreme; it illuminateth the face, which, as a beacon, gives warning to all the rest of this little kingdom, man, to arm; and then the vital commoners and inland petty spirits muster me all to their captain, the heart, who, great and puff'd up with this retinue, doth any deed of courage: and thus valor comes of sherris. So that skill in the weapon is nothing without sack, for that sets it a-work; and learning a mere hoard of gold kept by a devil, till sack commences it, and sets it in act and use. Hereof comes it that Prince Harry is valiant; for the cold blood he did naturally inherit of his father, he hath, like lean, sterile, and bare land, manured, husbanded, and till'd, with excellent endeavor of drinking good and good store of fertile sherris, that he is become very hot and valiant. If I had a thousand sons, the first human principle I would teach them, should be to forswear thin potations, and to addict themselves to sack.—*Second Part Henry IV.* Act IV. Sc. 7.

The trenchant blade Toledo trusty,
For want of fighting was grown rusty,
And ate into itself, for lack
Of somebody to hue and hack.
The peaceful scabbard where it dwelt,
The rancor of its edge had felt;
For of the lower end two handful
It had devour'd, 'twas so manful;
And so much scorn'd to lurk in case,
As if it durst not show its face.—*Hudibras*, Canto i

Speaking of Physicians:

Le bon de cette profession est, qu'il y a parmi les morts une honnêteté, une

---

323. Examples of ludicrous images.

discrétion la plus grande du monde; jamais on n'en voit se plaindre du médecin qui l'a tué.—*Le médecin malgré lui.*

325. To account for effects by such fantastical causes, being highly ludicrous, is quite improper in any serious composition. Therefore the following passage from Cowley, in his poem on the death of Sir Henry Wooton, is in a bad taste:

He did the utmost bounds of knowledge find,
He found them not so large as was his mind.
But, like the brave Pellæan youth, did moan,
Because that art had no more worlds than one.
And when he saw that he through all had past,
He dyed, lest he should idle grow at last.

Fanciful reasoning:

Falstaff. Imbowell'd!——if thou imbowel me to-day, I'll give you leave to powder me, and eat me to-morrow! 'Sblood 'twas time to counterfeit, or that hot termagant Scot had paid me scot and lot too. Counterfeit! I lie, I am no counterfeit; to die is to be a counterfeit; for he is but the counterfeit of a man who hath not the life of a man; but to counterfeit dying, when a man thereby liveth, is to be no counterfeit, but the true and perfect image of life indeed.—*First Part Henry IV.* Act I. Sc. 10.

Jessica. I shall be saved by my husband; he hath made me a Christian.
Launcelot. Truly the more to blame he; we were Christians enough before, e'en as many as could well live by one another: this making of Christians will raise the price of hogs; if we grow all to be pork-eaters, we shall not have a rasher on the coals for money.—*Merchant of Venice*, Act III. Sc. 6

In western clime there is a town,
To those that dwell therein well known;
Therefore there needs no more be said here,
We unto them refer our reader:
For brevity is very good
When we are, or are not understood.

Hudibras, Canto i.

326. Ludicrous junction of small things with great, as of equal importance:

This day black omens threat the brightest fair
That e'er deserved a watchful spirit's care:
Some dire disaster, or by force or slight;
But what, or where, the fates have wrapt in night:
Whether the nymph shall break Diana's law;
Or some frail china jar receive a flaw;
Or stain her honor, or her new brocade;
Forget her prayers, or miss a masquerade;
Or lose her heart, or necklace, at a ball;
Or whether Heaven has doom'd that Shock must fall.

Rape of the Lock, Canto ii. 101.

One speaks the glory of the British queen,
And one describes a charming Indian screen.

Ibid. Canto iii. 13.

---

324. First class of ludicrous combinations and oppositions.—Examples of fanciful causes assigned.
325. Assigning effects to fantastical causes improper in a serious composition.—Example of Cowley's bad taste.—Examples of fanciful reasoning.

Then flash'd the living lightr. ng from her eyes,
And screams of horror rend tl.' affrighted skies.
Not louder shrieks to pitying heaven are cast,
When husbands, or when lapdogs, breathe their last;
Or when rich china vessels fallen from high,
In glittering dust and painted fragments lie!
Ibid. Canto iii. 155.

327. Joining things that in appearance are opposite. As, for example, where Sir Roger de Coverly, in the Spectator, speaking of his widow,

That he would have given her a coal-pit to have kept her in clean linen; and that her finger should have sparkled with one hundred of his richest acres.

Premises that promise much and perform nothing. Cicero upon that article says,

Sed scitis esse notissimum ridiculi genus, cum aliud expectamus, aliud dicitur: hic nobismetipsis noster error risum movet.—*De Oratore*, l. ii. cap. 63.

Beatrice.——With a good leg and a good foot, uncle, and money enough in his purse, such a man would win any woman in the world, if he could get her good-will.—*Much Ado about Nothing*, Act II. Sc. 1.

Beatrice. I have a good eye, uncle, I can see a church by daylight.—*Ibid.*

Le médicin que l'on m'indique
Sait le Latin, le Grec, l'Hebreu,
Les belles lettres, la physique,
La chimie et la botanique.
Chacun lui donne son aveu:
Il auroit aussi ma pratique;
Mais je veux vivre encore un peu.

[Example (adduced by Hazlitt) of *lowering the tone of high-wrought sentiment by introducing burlesque and familiar circumstances.* Butler, in his "Hudibras," compares the change of night into day to the change of color in a boiled lobster:

The sun had long since, in the lap
Of Thetis, taken out his nap;
And like a lobster boil'd, the morn
From black to red began to turn,
When Hudibras, &c.

Wit, or ludicrous invention, produces its effect oftenest by comparison, but not always. It frequently effects its purposes by *unexpected and subtile distinctions.* A happy instance of the kind of wit which consists in sudden retorts, in turns upon an idea, and diverting the train of your adversary's argument abruptly and adroitly into some other channel, may be seen in the sarcastic reply of Porson, who hearing some one observe, that "certain modern poets would be read and admired when Homer and Virgil were forgotten," made answer —"And not till then!"

Voltaire's saying, in answer to a stranger who was observing how tall his trees grew—"that they had nothing else to do," was a quaint

326. Ludicrous junction of small things with great as of equal importance.

mixture of wit and humor, making it out as if they really led a lazy laborious life; but there was here neither allusion nor metaphor. The same principle of nice distinction must be allowed to prevail in those lines of "Hudibras," where he is professing to expound the dreams of judicial astrology:

There's but a twinkling of a star
Betwixt a man of peace and war,
A thief and justice, fool and knave,
A huffing officer and a slave,
A crafty lawyer and pickpocket;
A great philosopher and a blockhead;
A formal preacher and a player;
A learned physician and man-slayer.

Hazlitt, Lect. I.]

328. Having discussed wit in the thought, we proceed to what is verbal only, commonly called a *play of words*. This sort of wit depends, for the most part, upon choosing a word that hath different significations: by that artifice hocus-pocus tricks are played in language, and thoughts plain and simple take on a very different appearance. Play is necessary for man, in order to refresh him after labor; and, accordingly, man loves play, even so much as to relish a play of words: and it is happy for us, that words can be employed, not only for useful purposes, but also for our amusement. This amusement, though humble and low, unbends the mind; and is relished by some at all times, and by all at some times.*

It is remarkable, that this low species of wit has among all nations been a favorite entertainment, in a certain stage of their progress towards refinement of taste and manners, and has gradually gone into disrepute. As soon as a language is formed into a system, and the meaning of words is ascertained with tolerable accuracy, opportunity is afforded for expressions that, by the double meaning of some words, give a familiar thought the appearance of being new; and the penetration of the reader or hearer is gratified in detecting the true sense disguised under the double meaning. That this sort of wit was in England deemed a reputable amusement, during the reigns of Elizabeth and James I., is vouched by the works of Shakspeare, and even by the writings of grave divines. But it cannot have any long endurance: for as language ripens, and the meaning

* [Hazlitt observes:— "Man is the only animal that laughs and weeps; for he is the only animal that is struck with the difference between what things are, and what they ought to be. We weep at what thwarts or exceeds our desires in serious matters; we laugh at what only disappoints our expectations in trifles. We shed tears from sympathy with real and necessary distress; as we burst into laughter from want of sympathy with that which is unreasonable and unnecessary, the absurdity of which provokes our spleen or mirth, rather than any serious reflections on it."]

327. Joining things that in appearance are opposite. Example.—Premises that promise much and perform nothing.—Introducing burlesque circumstances.—Unexpected and subtle distinctions.

328. Play of words: its nature and advantage. When in repute.

of words is more and more ascertained, words held to be synonymous diminish daily; and when those that remain have been more than once employed, the pleasure vanisheth with the novelty.

329. I proceed to examples, which, as in the former case, shall be distributed into different classes.

A seeming resemblance from the double meaning of a word:

> Beneath this stone my wife doth lie;
> She's now at rest, and so am I.

A seeming contrast from the same cause, termed *a verbal antithesis*, which hath no despicable effect in ludicrous subjects:

> Whilst Iris his cosmetic wash would try
> To make her bloom revive, and lovers die,
> Some ask for charms, and others philters choose,
> To gain Corinna, and their quartans lose.
> *Dispensary*, Canto ii.

> And how frail nymphs, oft by abortion, aim
> To lose a substance, to preserve a name.—*Ibid.* Canto iii.

> While nymphs take treats, or assignations give.
> *Rape of the Lock*

Other seeming connections from the same cause:

> Will you employ your conquering sword,
> To break a fiddle, and your word?—*Hudibras*, Canto ii.

> To whom the knight with comely grace
> Put off his hat to put his case.—*Ibid.* Part III. Canto iii.

> Here Britain's statesmen oft the fall foredoom
> Of foreign tyrants, and of nymphs at home;
> Here thou, great Anna! whom three realms obey,
> Dost sometimes counsel take—and sometimes tea.
> *Rape of the Lock*, Canto iii. l. 5

> O'er their quietus where fat judges dose,
> And lull their cough and conscience to repose.
> *Dispensary*, Canto i.

Speaking of Prince Eugene:

> This general is a great taker of snuff as well as of towns.
> *Pope*, *Key to the Lock.*

> Exul mentisque domusque.—*Metamorphosis*, l. ix. 409.

A seeming opposition from the same cause:

> Hic quiescit qui nunquam quievit.

Again.

> So like the chances are of love and war,
> That they alone in this distinguish'd are:
> In love the victors from the vanquish'd fly,
> They fly that wound, and they pursue that die.—*Waller.*

> What new-found witchcraft was in thee,
> With thine own cold to kindle me?
> Strange art; like him that should devise
> To make a burning-glass of ice.—*Cowley.*

330. Wit of this kind is unsuitable in a serious poem; witness the following line in Pope's Elegy to the memory of an unfortunate lady:

---

329. Examples of seeming resemblance; seeming contrast; seeming connections; seeming opposition.

Cold is that breast which warm'd the world before.

This sort of writing is finely burlesqued by Swift:

Her hands the softest ever felt,
Though cold would burn, though dry would melt.
Strephon and Chloe.

Taking a word in a different sense from what is meant, comes under wit, because it occasions some slight degree of surprise:

Beatrice. I may sit in a corner, and cry *Heigh ho!* for a husband.
Pedro. Lady Beatrice, I will get you one.
Beatrice. I would rather have one of your father's getting. Hath your grace ne'er a brother like you? Your father got excellent husbands, if a maid could come by them. *Much Ado about Nothing*, Act II Sc. 5.

Falstaff. My honest lads, I will tell you what I am about.
Pistol. Two yards and more.
Falstaff. No quips, now, Pistol; indeed I am in the waist two yards about; but I am now about no waste; I am about thrift.
Merry Wives of Windsor, Act I. Sc. 7.

331. An assertion that bears a double meaning, one right, one wrong, but so introduced as to direct us to the wrong meaning, is a species of bastard wit, which is distinguished from all others by the name *pun*. For example:

Paris. ———Sweet Helen, I must woo you,
To help unarm our Hector: his stubborn buckles,
With these your white enchanting fingers touch'd,
Shall more obey, than to the edge of steel,
Or force of Greekish sinews; you shall do more
Than all the island kings, disarm great Hector.
Troilus and Cressida, Act III. Sc. 2.

The pun is in the close. The word *disarm* has a double meaning: it signifies to take off a man's armor, and also to subdue him in fight. We are directed to the latter sense by the context; but, with regard to Helen, the word holds only true in the former sense. I go on with other examples:

Chief Justice. Well! the truth is, Sir John, you live in great infamy.
Falstaff. He that buckles him in my belt, cannot live in less.
Chief Justice. Your means are very slender, and your waste is great.
Falstaff. I would it were otherwise: I would my means were greater, and my waist slenderer. *Second Part Henry IV.* Act I. Sc. 1.

Celia. I pray you bear with me, I can go no further.
Clown. For my part, I had rather bear with you than bear you; yet I should bear no cross if I did bear you; for I think you have no money in your purse.
As You Like It, Act II. Sc. 4.

He that imposes an oath makes it,
Not he that for convenience takes it;
Then how can any man be said
To break an oath he never made?
Hudibras, Part II. Canto ii.

[The greatest single production of wit, in England, is Butler's "Hudibras." It contains specimens of every variety of drollery and satire, and those specimens crowded together in almost every page. Butler is equally in the hands of the learned and the vulgar, for the

---

330. Wit of this kind, where unsuitable.—Taking a word in a different sense from what is meant.

sense is generally as solid as the images are amusing and grotesque Though his subject was local and temporary, his fame was not circumscribed within his own age. He was admired by Charles II., and has been rewarded by posterity. . . . . He in general ridicules not persons, but things; not a party, but their principles, which may belong, as time and occasion serve, to one set of solemn pretenders or another. He has exhausted the moods and figures of satire and sophistry. It would be possible to deduce the different forms of syllogism in Aristotle, from the different violations or mock imitations of them in Butler. He makes you laugh or smile, *by comparing the high to the low*:

> No Indian prince has to his palace
> More followers than a thief to the gallows.

Or, *by pretending to raise the low to the lofty*:

> And in his nose, like Indian king,
> He (Bruin) wore for ornament a ring.

He succeeds equally *in the familiarity of his illustrations*:

> Whose noise whets valor sharp, like beer
> By thunder turned to vinegar.

Or, *their incredible extravagance*, by comparing things that are alike or not alike:

> Replete with strange hermetic powder,
> That wounds nine miles point-blank would solder.

He surprises equally by his coincidences or contradictions, by spinning out a long-winded flimsy excuse, or by turning short upon you with the point-blank truth. His rhymes are as witty as his reasons, equally remote from what common custom would suggest:

> That deals in destiny's dark counsels,
> And sage opinions of the moon sells.

He startles you sometimes by an empty sound like a blow upon a drum-head:

> The mighty Totipotimoy
> Sent to our elders an envoy.

Sometimes, also, by *a pun upon one word*:

> For Hebrew *roots*, although they are found
> To flourish most in barren ground.

Sometimes, by *splitting another in two at the end of a verse*, with the same alertness and power over the odd and unaccountable, in the combinations of sounds as of images:

> Those wholesale critics, that in coffee-
> Houses cry down all philosophy.

There are as many shrewd aphorisms in his works, clenched by as many quaint and individual allusions, as perhaps in any author whatever. He makes none but palpable hits, that may be said to give one's understanding a rap on the knuckles:

This we among ourselves may speak,
But to the wicked or the weak,
We must be cautious to declare
Perfection-truths, such as these are.

He is, indeed, sometimes too prolific, and spins his antithetical sentences out, one after another, till the reader, not the author, is wearied

The vulgarity and meanness of sentiment which Butler complains of in the Presbyterians, seems at last, from long familiarity and close contemplation, to have tainted his own mind. Their worst vices appear to have taken root in his imagination. He has, indeed, carried his private grudge too far into his general speculations. He even makes out the rebels to be cowards, and well beaten, which does not accord with the history of the times. In an excess of zeal for Church and State, he is too much disposed to treat religion as a cheat, and liberty as a farce.

There are (in "Hudibras") occasional indications of poetical fancy, and an eye for natural beauty; but these are kept under, or soon discarded, judiciously enough, but it should seem, not for lack of power, for they are certainly as masterly as they are rare. Such is the description of the moon going down in the early morning, which is as pure, original, and picturesque as possible:

The queen of night, whose large command
Rules all the sea and half the land,
And over moist and crazy brains
In high spring-tides at midnight reigns,
Was now declining to the west,
To go to bed and take her rest.

Butler is sometimes scholastic, but he makes his learning tell to good account; and for the purposes of burlesque, nothing can be better fitted than the scholastic style."—*Hazlitt*, Lect. III.]

332. Though playing with words is a mark of a mind at ease, and disposed to any sort of amusement, we must not thence conclude that playing with words is always ludicrous. Words are so intimately connected with thought, that if the subject be really grave, it will not appear ludicrous even in that fantastic dress. I am, however, far from recommending it in any serious performance: on the contrary, the discordance between the thought and expression must be disagreeable: witness the following specimen:

He hath abandoned his physicians, madam, under whose practices he hath persecuted time with hope: and finds no other advantage in the process, but only the losing of hope by time.

All's Well that Ends Well, Act I. Sc. 1

K. Henry. O my poor kingdom, sick with civil blows!
When that my care could not withhold thy riots,
What wilt thou do when riot is thy care?

Second Part K. Henry IV.

331. Define the *pun*. Examples.—Butler's Hudibras. Its peculiarities.—Specimens of wit.—Faults.

If any one shall observe, that there is a third species of wit, different from those mentioned, consisting in sounds merely, I am willing to give it place. And indeed it must be admitted, that many of Hudibras's double rhymes come under the definition of wit given in the beginning of this chapter; they are ludicrous, and their singularity occasions some degree of surprise. Swift is no less successful than Butler in this sort of wit; witness the following instances: *Goddess—Boddice. Pliny—Nicolina. Iscariots—Chariots. Mitre—Nitre. Dragon—Suffragan.*

A repartee may happen to be witty; but it cannot be considered as a species of wit, because there are many repartees extremely smart, and yet extremely serious. I give the following example: A certain petulant Greek, objecting to Anacharsis that he was a Scythian—True, says Anacharsis, my country disgraces me, but you disgrace your country. This fine turn gives surprise, but it is far from being ludicrous.

[Lastly, there is a wit of sense and observation, which consists in the acute illustration of good sense and practical wisdom, by means of some far-fetched conceit or quaint imagery. Thus the lines in Pope—

> 'Tis with our judgments as our watches; none
> Go just alike, yet each believes his own—

are witty rather than poetical, because the truth they convey is a mere dry observation on human life, without elevation or enthusiasm, and the illustration of it is of that quaint and familiar kind that is merely curious and fanciful. Cowley is an instance of the same kind in almost all his writings. Many of the jests and witticisms in the best comedies are moral aphorisms and rules for the conduct of life, sparkling with wit and fancy in the mode of expression. The ancient philosophers also abounded in the same kind of wit, in telling home truths in the most unexpected manner. In this sense *Æsop* was the greatest wit and moralist that ever lived. Ape and slave, he looked askance at human nature, and beheld its weaknesses and errors transferred to another species. Vice and virtue were to him as plain as any objects of sense. He saw in man a talking, absurd, obstinate, proud, angry animal, and clothed these abstractions with wings, or a beak, or tail, or claws, or long ears, as they appeared embodied in these hieroglyphics in the brute creation. His moral philosophy is natural history. He makes an ass bray wisdom, and a frog croak humanity. The store of moral truth, and the fund of invention in exhibiting it in eternal forms, palpable, and intelligible, and delightful to children and grown persons, and to all ages and nations, are almost miraculous. The in-

---

332. Playing with words not always ludicrous.—Wit, consisting in sounds.—Repartee.—The last kind of wit described.—Witticisms of the best comedies.—Remarks on Æsop's Fables.

vention of a fable is to me the most enviable exertion of human genius: it is the discovering a truth to which there is no clue, and which, when once found out, can never be forgotten. I would rather have been the author of 'Æsop's Fables,' than of 'Euclid's Elements.'"—*Hazlitt*, Lect. I.]

CHAPTER XIV.

CUSTOM AND HABIT.

333. VIEWING man as under the influence of novelty, would one suspect that custom also should influence him? and yet our nature is equally susceptible of each; not only in different objects, but frequently in the same. When an object is new, it is enchanting; familiarity renders it indifferent; and custom, after a longer familiarity, makes it again disagreeable. Human nature, diversified with many and various springs of action, is wonderfully, and, indulging the expression, intricately constructed.

Custom respects the action, *habit* the agent. By *custom* we mean a frequent reiteration of the same act; and by *habit*, the effect that custom has on the agent. This effect may be either active, witness the dexterity produced by custom in performing certain exercises; or passive, as when a thing makes an impression on us different from what it did originally. The latter only, as relative to the sensitive part of our nature, comes under the present undertaking.

334. This subject is intricate: some pleasures are fortified by custom; and yet custom begets familiarity, and consequently indifference:* in many instances, satiety and disgust are the consequences of reiteration; again, though custom blunts the edge of distress and of pain, yet the want of any thing to which we have been long accustomed, is a sort of torture. A clue to guide us through all the intricacies of this labyrinth, would be an acceptable present.

Whatever be the cause, it is certain that we are much influenced by custom: it hath an effect upon our pleasures, upon our actions,

* If all the year were playing holidays,
To sport would be as tedious as to work;
But when they seldom come, they wish'd for come,
And nothing pleaseth but rare accidents.
First Part Henry IV. Act I. Sc. 3.

333. Influence of novelty and custom.—Custom and habit distinguished.—Active and passive effects of habit.

and even upon our thoughts and sentiments. Habit makes no figure during the vivacity of youth: in middle age it gains ground; and in old age governs without control. In that period of life, generally speaking, we eat at a certain hour, take exercise at a certain hour, go to rest at a certain hour, all by the direction of habit; nay, a particular seat, table, bed, comes to be essential; and a habit in any of these cannot be controlled without uneasiness.

335. Any slight or moderate pleasure frequently reiterated for a long time, forms a peculiar connection between us and the thing that causes the pleasure. This connection, termed *habit*, has the effect to awaken our desire or appetite for that thing when it returns not as usual. During the course of enjoyment, the pleasure rises insensibly higher and higher till a habit be established; at which time the pleasure is at its height. It continues not however stationary: the same customary reiteration which carried it to its height, brings it down again by insensible degrees, even lower than it was at first; but of that circumstance afterward. What at present we have in view, is to prove by experiments, that those things which at first are but moderately agreeable, are the aptest to become habitual. Spirituous liquors, at first scarce agreeable, readily produce an habitual appetite: and custom prevails so far, as even to make us fond of things originally disagreeable, such as coffee, asafœtida, and tobacco; which is pleasantly illustrated by Congreve. (*The Way of the World*, Act I. Sc. 3.)

A walk upon the quarter-deck, though intolerably confined, becomes however so agreeable by custom, that a sailor in his walk on shore, confines himself commonly within the same bounds. I knew a man who had relinquished the sea for a country life: in the corner of his garden he reared an artificial mount with a level summit, resembling most accurately a quarter-deck, not only in shape but in size; and here he generally walked. In Minorca, Governor Kane made an excellent road the whole length of the island; and yet the inhabitants adhered to the old road, though not only longer but extremely bad.* Play or gaming, at first barely amusing by the occupation it affords, becomes in time extremely agreeable; and is frequently prosecuted with avidity, as if it were the chief business of life. The same observation is applicable to the pleasures of the internal senses, those of knowledge and virtue in particular: children have scarce any sense of these pleasures; and men very little who are in the state of nature without culture: our taste for virtue

* Custom is second nature. Formerly, the merchants of Bristol had no place for meeting but the street, open to every variety of weather. An exchange was erected for them with convenient piazzas. But so riveted were they to their accustomed place, that in order to dislodge them, the magistrates were forced to break up the pavement, and to render the place a heap of rough stones.

334. Effect of custom upon our pleasures, &c.—Habit in youth, middle age, old age.

and knowledge improves slowly; but is capable of growing stronger than any other appetite in human nature.

336. To introduce an active habit, frequency of acts is not sufficient without length of time: the quickest succession of acts in a short time, is not sufficient; nor a slow succession in the longest time. The effect must be produced by a moderate soft action, and a long series of easy touches, removed from each other by short intervals. Nor are these sufficient without regularity in the time, place, and other circumstances of the action: the more uniform any operation is, the sooner it becomes habitual. And this holds equally in a passive habit; variety in any remarkable degree, prevents the effect: thus any particular food will scarce ever become habitual, where the manner of dressing is varied. The circumstances then requisite to augment a moderate pleasure, and at the long run to form a habit, are weak uniform acts, reiterated during a long course of time without any considerable interruption: every agreeable cause that operates in this manner, will grow habitual.

337. *Affection* and *aversion*, as distinguished from passion on the one hand, and on the other from original disposition, are in reality habits respecting particular objects, acquired in the manner above set forth. The pleasure of social intercourse with any person must originally be faint, and frequently reiterated, in order to establish the habit of affection. Affection thus generated, whether it be friendship or love, seldom swells into any tumultuous or vigorous passion; but is, however, the strongest cement that can bind together two individuals of the human species. In like manner, a slight degree of disgust often reiterated with regularity, grows into the habit of aversion, which commonly subsists for life.

Objects of taste that are delicious, far from tending to become habitual, are apt, by indulgence, to produce satiety and disgust: no man contracts a habit of sugar, honey, or sweetmeats, as he doth of tobacco:

> Dulcia non ferimus: succo renovamur amaro.
>
> *Ovid*, *Art. Amand.* l. iii

> Insipido è quel dolce, che condito
> Non è di qualche amor a, è tosto satia.
>
> *Aminta di Tasso.*

> These violent delights have violent ends,
> And in their triumph die. The sweetest honey
> Is loathsome in its own deliciousness,
> And in the taste confounds the appetite;
> Therefore love mod'rately, long love doth so;
> Too swift arrives as tardy as too slow.
>
> *Romeo and Juliet*, Act II. Sc. 6.

---

335. Desire awakened by habit.—Effect of habit on our pleasures.—Things apt to become habitual. Instances.—Walk upon a quarter-deck.—Governor Kane's new road.—Exchange at Bristol, &c.

336. How an active habit must be introduced; how a passive habit is formed.

The same observation holds with respect to all objects, that being extremely agreeable, raise violent passions: such passions are incompatible with a habit of any sort; and in particular they never produce affection or aversion. A man who is surprised with an unexpected favor, burns for an opportunity to exert his gratitude, without having any affection for his benefactor: neither does desire of vengeance for an atrocious injury involve aversion.

338. It is perhaps not easy to say why moderate pleasures gather strength by custom; but two causes concur to prevent that effect in the more intense pleasures. These, by an original law in our nature, increase quickly to their full growth, and decay with no less precipitation (see chap. ii. part iii.); and custom is too slow in its operation to overcome that law. The other cause is no less powerful: exquisite pleasure is extremely fatiguing; occasioning, as a naturalist would say, great expense of animal spirits;* and of such the mind cannot bear so frequent gratification, as to superinduce a habit: if the thing that raises the pleasure return before the mind have recovered its tone and relish, disgust ensues instead of pleasure.

A habit never fails to admonish us of the wonted time of gratification, by raising a pain for want of the object, and a desire to have it. The pain of want is always first felt; the desire naturally follows: and upon presenting the object, both vanish instantaneously. Thus a man accustomed to tobacco, feels, at the end of the usual interval, a confused pain of want; which at first points at nothing in particular, though it soon settles upon its accustomed object: and the same may be observed in persons addicted to drinking, who are often in an uneasy restless state before they think of the bottle. In pleasures indulged regularly, and at equal intervals, the appetite, remarkably obsequious to custom, returns regularly with the usual time of gratification; not sooner, even though the object be presented. This pain of want arising from habit, seems directly opposite to that of satiety; and it must appear singular, that frequency of gratification should produce effects so opposite, as are the pains of excess and of want.

339. The appetites that respect the preservation of our species, are attended with a pain of want similar to that occasioned by habit: hunger and thirst are uneasy sensations of want, which always precede the desire of eating or drinking. The natural appetites differ from habit in the following particular: they have an undetermined direction towards all objects of gratification in general; whereas an

* Lady Easy, upon her husband's reformation expresses to her friend the following sentiment: "Be satisfied: Sir Charles has made me happy, even to a pain of joy."

337. How affection or aversion is formed into a habit.—What is said of delicious objects of taste; what of agreeable objects that raise violent passions.

338. Two causes preventing intense pleasures from gaining strength by custom.—A habit admonishes of what?—Regular return of appetite.

habitual appetite is directed to a particular object. The habitual relish for a particular dish is far from being the same with a vague appetite for food. That difference notwithstanding, it is still remarkable that nature hath enforced the gratification of certain natural appetites essential to the species, by a pain of the same sort with that which habit produceth.

340. The pain of habit is less under our power than any other pain that arises from want of gratification; hunger and thirst are more easily endured, especially at first, than an unusual intermission of any habitual pleasure: persons are often heard declaring they would forego sleep or food, rather than tobacco. We must not, however, conclude that the gratification of an habitual appetite affords the same delight with the gratification of one that is natural; far from it; the pain of want only is greater.

The slow and reiterated acts that produce a habit, strengthen the mind to enjoy the habitual pleasure in greater quantity and more frequency than originally; and by that means a habit of intemperate gratification is often formed: after unbounded acts of intemperance the habitual relish is soon restored, and the pain for want of enjoyment returns with fresh vigor.

341. The causes of the present emotions hitherto in view are either an individual, such as a companion, a certain dwelling-place, a certain amusement, or a particular species, such as coffee, mutton, or any other food. But habit is not confined to such. A constant train of trifling diversions, may form such a habit in the mind, that it cannot be easy a moment without amusement: a variety in the objects prevents a habit as to any one in particular; but as the train is uniform with respect to amusement, the habit is formed accordingly; and that sort of habit may be denominated *a generic habit*, in opposition to the former, which is *a specific habit*. A habit of a town life, of country sports, of solitude, of reading, or of business, where sufficiently varied, are instances of generic habits. Every specific habit hath a mixture of the generic; for the habit of any one sort of food makes the taste agreeable, and we are fond of that taste wherever found. Thus a man, deprived of an habitual object, takes up with what most resembles it: deprived of tobacco, any bitter herb will do, rather than want: a habit of punch, makes wine a good resource: accustomed to the sweet society and comforts of matrimony, the man, unhappily deprived of his beloved object, inclines the sooner to a second. In general, when we are deprived of an habitual object, we are fond of its qualities in any other object.

342. The reasons are assigned above, why the causes of intense pleasure become not readily habitual; but now we discover that

---

339. The natural appetites attended with the pain of want. How they differ from habit.
340. The pain of habit.—How a habit of intemperate gratification is formed.
341. Difference between a generic and a specific habit. Instances.—Every specific habit partakes of the generic.—The effect of being deprived of an habitual object.

these reasons conclude only against specific habits. In the case of a weak pleasure, a habit is formed by frequency and uniformity of reiteration, which, in the case of an intense pleasure, produceth satiety and disgust. But it is remarkable, that satiety and disgust have no effect, except as to that thing singly which occasions them: a surfeit of honey produceth not a loathing of sugar; and intemperance with one woman produceth no disrelish of the same pleasure with others. Hence it is easy to account for a generic habit in any intense pleasure: the delight we had in the gratification of the appetite inflames the imagination, and makes us, with avidity, search for the same gratification in whatever other subject it can be found. And thus uniform frequency in gratifying the same passion upon different objects, produceth at length a generic habit. In this manner, one acquires an habitual delight in high and poignant sauces, rich dress, fine equipages, crowds of company, and in whatever is commonly termed *pleasure.* There concurs, at the same time, to introduce this habit, a peculiarity observed above, that reiteration of acts enlarges the capacity of the mind to admit a more plentiful gratification than originally, with regard to frequency as well as quantity.

343. Hence it appears, that though a specific habit cannot be formed but upon a moderate pleasure, a generic habit may be formed upon any sort of pleasure, moderate or immoderate, that hath variety of objects. The only difference is, that a weak pleasure runs naturally into a specific habit; whereas an intense pleasure is altogether averse to such a habit. In a word, it is only in singular cases that a moderate pleasure produces a generic habit; but an intense pleasure cannot produce any other habit.

The appetites that respect the preservation of the species, are formed into habit in a peculiar manner: the time as well as measure of their gratification are much under the power of custom, which, by introducing a change upon the body, occasions a proportional change in the appetites. Thus, if the body be gradually formed to a certain quantity of food at stated times, the appetite is regulated accordingly; and the appetite is again changed, when a different habit of body is introduced by a different practice. Here it would seem, that the change is not made upon the mind, which is commonly the case in passive habits, but upon the body.

When rich food is brought down by ingredients of a plainer taste, the composition is susceptible of a specific habit. Thus the sweet taste of sugar, rendered less poignant in a mixture, may, in course of time, produce a specific habit for such mixture. As moderate pleasures, by becoming more intense, tend to generic habits; so intense pleasures, by becoming more moderate, tend to specific habits

---

342. Weak pleasures produce a habit: intense pleasures produce satiety and disgust How far this satiety extends.—How a generic habit in any intense pleasure is accounted for.—Reiteration of acts attended with what effect?

343. Specific habit peculiar to a moderate pleasure: generic, to any sort of pleasure.—The appetites under the power of custom. Instance of food, as to time, quantity, quality

344. One effect of custom, different from any that have been explained, must not be omitted, because it makes a great figure in human nature: Though custom augments moderate pleasures, and lessens those that are intense, it has a different effect with respect to pain; for it blunts the edge of every sort of pain and distress, faint or acute. Uninterrupted misery, therefore, is attended with one good effect: if its torments be incessant, custom hardens us to bear them.

The changes made in forming habits are curious. Moderate pleasures are augmented gradually by reiteration, till they become habitual; and then are at their height: but they are not long stationary; for from that point they gradually decay, till they vanish altogether. The pain occasioned by want of gratification, runs a different course: it increases uniformly; and at last becomes extreme, when the pleasure of gratification is reduced to nothing:

> ——————It so falls out,
> That what we have we prize not to the worth,
> While we enjoy it; but being lack'd and lost,
> Why then we rack the value; then we find
> The virtue that possession would not show us
> Whilst it was ours.—*Much Ado about Nothing*, Act IV. Sc. 2.

The effect of custom with relation to specific habit, is displayed through all its varieties in the use of tobacco. The taste of that plant is at first extremely unpleasant: our disgust lessens gradually till it vanishes altogether; at which period the taste is neither agreeable nor disagreeable: continuing the use of the plant, we begin to relish it; and our relish improves by use, till it arrives at perfection: from that period it gradually decays while the habit is in a state of increment, and consequently the pain of want. The result is, that when the habit has acquired its greatest vigor, the relish is gone; and accordingly we often smoke and take snuff habitually, without so much as being conscious of the operation. We must except gratification after the pain of want; the pleasure of which gratification is the greatest when the habit is the most vigorous: it is of the same kind with the pleasure one feels upon being delivered from the rack. This pleasure, however, is but occasionally the effect of habit; and, however exquisite, is avoided as much as possible because of the pain that precedes it.

345. With regard to the pain of want, I can discover no difference between a generic and a specific habit. But these habits differ widely with respect to the positive pleasure. I have had occasion to observe, that the pleasure of a specific habit decays gradually till it turns imperceptible: the pleasure of a generic habit, on the contrary, being supported by variety of gratification, suffers little or no decay after it comes to its height. However it may be with other generic habits, the observation, I am certain, holds with respect to

---

344. Effect of custom with respect to pain.—Changes made in forming habits.—Effect of custom in the use of tobacco.

the pleasures of virtue and of knowledge: the pleasure of doing good has an unbounded scope, and may be so variously gratified that it can never decay; science is equally unbounded; our appetite for knowledge having an ample range of gratification, where discoveries are recommended by novelty, by variety, by utility, or by all of them.

In this intricate inquiry I have endeavored, but without success, to discover by what particular means it is that custom hath influence upon us; and now nothing seems left but to hold our nature to be so framed as to be susceptible of such influence. And supposing it purposely so framed, it will not be difficult to find out several important final causes. That the power of custom is a happy contrivance for our good, cannot have escaped any one who reflects that business is our province, and pleasure our relaxation only. Now satiety is necessary to check exquisite pleasure, which otherwise would engross the mind, and unqualify us for business. On the other hand, as business is sometimes painful, and is never pleasant beyond moderation, the habitual increase of moderate pleasure and the conversion of pain into pleasure, are admirably contrived for disappointing the malice of Fortune, and for reconciling us to whatever course of life may be our lot:

> How use doth breed a habit in a man!
> This shadowy desert, unfrequented woods,
> I better brook than flourishing peopled towns.
> Here I can sit alone, unseen of any,
> And to the nightingale's complaining notes
> Tune my distresses, and record my woes.
>
> *Two Gentlemen of Verona*, Act V. Sc. 4.

As the foregoing distinction between intense and moderate holds in pleasure only, every degree of pain being softened by time, custom is a catholicon for pain and distress of every sort; and of that regulation the final cause requires no illustration.

346. Another final cause of custom will be highly relished by every person of humanity, and yet has in a great measure been overlooked; which is, that custom hath a greater influence than any other known cause to put the rich and the poor upon a level: weak pleasures, the share of the latter, become fortunately stronger by custom; while voluptuous pleasures, the share of the former, are continually losing ground by satiety. Men of fortune, who possess palaces, sumptuous gardens, rich fields, enjoy them less than passengers do. The goods of Fortune are not unequally distributed: the opulent possess what others enjoy.

And indeed, if it be the effect of habit to produce the pain of want in a high degree, while there is little pleasure in enjoyment, a voluptuous life is of all the least to be envied. Those who are habituated to high feeling, easy vehicles, rich furniture, a crowd of valets, much

---

345. The pleasure of a specific habit, compared with that of a generic one.—Final causes of the power of custom.

deference and flattery, enjoy but a small share of happiness, while they are exposed to manifold distresses. To such a man, enslaved by ease and luxury, even the petty inconvenience in travelling, of a rough road, bad weather, or homely fare, are serious evils: he loses his tone of mind, turns peevish, and would wreak his resentment even upon the common accidents of life. Better far to use the goods of Fortune with moderation: a man who by temperance and activity hath acquired a hardy constitution, is, on the one hand, guarded against external accidents; and, on the other, is provided with great variety of enjoyment ever at command.

347. I shall close this chapter with an article more delicate than abstruse, namely, what authority custom ought to have over our taste in the fine arts. One particular is certain, that we cheerfully abandon to the authority of custom things that nature hath left indifferent. It is custom, not nature, that hath established a difference between the right hand and the left, so as to make it awkward and disagreeable to use the left where the right is commonly used. The various colors, though they affect us differently, are all of them agreeable in their purity; but custom has regulated that matter in another manner: a black skin upon a human being is to us disagreeable, and a white skin probably no less so to a negro. Thus things, originally indifferent, become agreeable or disagreeable by the force of custom. Nor will this be surprising after the discovery made above, that the original agreeableness or disagreeableness of an object is, by the influence of custom, often converted into the opposite quality.

Proceeding to matters of taste, where there is naturally a preference of one thing before another, it is certain, in the first place, that our faint and more delicate feelings are readily susceptible of a bias from custom; and therefore that it is no proof of a defective taste to find these in some measure influenced by custom: dress and the modes of external behavior are regulated by custom in every country: the deep red or vermilion with which the ladies in France cover their cheeks, appears to them beautiful in spite of nature; and strangers cannot altogether be justified in condemning that practice, considering the lawful authority of custom, or of the *fashion*, as it is called. It is told of the people who inhabit the skirts of the Alps facing the north, that the swelling they have universally in the neck is to them agreeable. So far has custom power to change the nature of things, and to make an object originally disagreeable take on an opposite appearance.*

* [Perhaps a more satisfactory account of this matter will be found in the following observations from the pen of Dr. Mark Hopkins:

"Association is the sole foundation of the value which we put upon some articles, and of the beauty which we find in others. Thus, a lock of hair,

346. Power of custom to put rich and poor on a level.—A voluptuous life not to be envied.
347. The authority that custom ought to have over our taste in the fine arts.—Things originally indifferent, become agreeable or disagreeable by force of custom.—Dress, &c.—The effect of association.

348. But, as to every particular that can be denominated proper or improper, right or wrong, custom has little authority, and ought to have none. The principle of duty takes naturally place of every other; and it argues a shameful weakness or degeneracy of mind to find it in any case so far subdued as to submit to custom.

These few hints may enable us to judge in some measure of foreign manners, whether exhibited by foreign writers or our own. A comparison between the ancients and the moderns was some time ago a favorite subject: those who declared for ancient manners thought it sufficient that these manners were supported by custom: their antagonists, on the other hand, refusing submission to custom as a standard of taste, condemned ancient manners as in several instances irrational. In that controversy, an appeal being made to different principles, without the slightest attempt to establish a common standard, the dispute could have no end. The hints above given tend to establish a standard for judging how far the authority of custom ought to be held lawful; and, for the sake of illustration, we shall apply that standard in a few instances.

349. Human sacrifices, the most dismal effect of blind and grovelling superstition, wore gradually out of use by the prevalence of reason and humanity. In the days of Sophocles and Euripides, traces of that practice were still recent; and the Athenians, through the prevalence of custom, could without disgust suffer human sacrifices to be represented in their theatre, of which the *Iphigenia* of Euripides is a proof. But a human sacrifice, being altogether inconsistent with modern manners as producing horror instead of pity, cannot with any propriety be introduced upon a modern stage. I must therefore condemn the *Iphigenia* of Racine, which, instead of the tender and sympathetic passions, substitutes disgust and horror. Another objection occurs against every fable that deviates so remarkably from improved notions and sentiments; which is, that if it should even command our belief by the authority of history, it appears too fictitious and unnatural to produce a perception of reality (see chapter ii. part i. sec. 7): a human sacrifice is so unnatural, and to us so improbable, that few will be affected with the representation of it more than with a fairy tale.

---

valueless in itself, may, from associations connected with it, have a value which money cannot measure; and articles of dress, which would otherwise be to us indifferent or odious, become beautiful by their association with those persons whom we have been accustomed to consider as models of elegance. It is indeed astonishing what an effect this principle will have upon our feelings; and from looking too exclusively at facts connected with it, some have been led to doubt whether there is any such thing as a permanent principle of taste. It would really seem that, within the bounds of comfort and decency both of which are often outraged by fashion, one mode of dress may come to be as becoming as another."]

---

348. Authority of custom in matters of right and wrong.—Of ancient manners as compared with modern.—How far custom ought to justify certain manners.

349. Human sacrifices represented before the Athenians.—The *Iphigenia* of Euripides and that of Racine.

CHAPTER XV.

EXTERNAL SIGNS OF EMOTIONS AND PASSIONS.

350. So intimately connected are the soul and body, that every agitation in the former produceth a visible effect upon the latter. There is, at the same time, a wonderful uniformity in that operation; each class of emotions and passions being invariably attended with an external appearance peculiar to itself.* These external appearances or signs may not improperly be considered as a natural language, expressing to all beholders emotions and passions as they arise in the heart. Hope, fear, joy, grief, are displayed externally: the character of a man can be read in his face: and beauty, which makes so deep an impression, is known to result, not so much from regular features, or a fine complexion, as from good-nature, good sense, sprightliness, sweetness, or other mental quality, expressed upon the countenance. Though perfect skill in that language be rare, yet what is generally known is sufficient for the ordinary purposes of life. But by what means we come to understand the language, is a point of some intricacy: it cannot be by sight merely; for upon the most attentive inspection of the human face, all that can be discerned, are figure, color, and motion, which, singly or combined, never can represent a passion, nor a sentiment: the external sign is indeed visible; but to understand its meaning we must be able to connect it with the passion that causes it, an operation far beyond the reach of eyesight. Where, then, is the instructor to be found that can unveil this secret connection? If we apply to experience, it is yielded, that from long and diligent observation, we may gather, in some measure, in what manner those we are acquainted with express their passions externally; but with respect to strangers, we are left in the dark; and yet we are not puzzled about the meaning of these external expressions in a stranger, more than in a bosom-companion. Further, had we no other means but experience for understanding the external signs of passion, we could not expect any degree of skill in the bulk of individuals: yet matters are so much better ordered, that the external expressions of passions form a language understood by all, by the young as well as the old, by the ignorant as well as the learned: I talk of the plain

---

* Omnis enim motus animi, suum quemdam a natura habet vultum et sonum et gestum.—*Cicero*, l. iii. *De Oratore*.

---

350. Effect of the mind upon the body.—Natural language of passion.—What beauty results from.—How we come to understand this natural language.—Cousin's remarks.

and legible characters of that language; for undoubtedly we are much indebted to experience in deciphering the dark and more delicate expressions.*

351. The external signs of passion are of two kinds, voluntary and involuntary. The voluntary signs are also of two kinds: some are arbitrary, some natural. Words are obviously voluntary signs: and they are also arbitrary; excepting a few simple sounds expressive of certain internal emotions, which sounds being the same in all languages, must be the work of nature: thus the unpremeditated tones of admiration are the same in all men; as also of compassion, resentment, and despair. Dramatic writers ought to be well acquainted with this natural language of passion: the chief talent of such a writer is a ready command of the expressions that nature dictates to every person, when any vivid emotion struggles for utterance; and the chief talent of a fine reader is a ready command of tones suited to these expressions.

352. The other kind of voluntary signs comprehends certain attitudes or gestures that naturally accompany certain emotions with a surprising uniformity: excessive joy is expressed by leaping, dancing, or some elevation of the body; excessive grief, by sinking or depressing it; and prostration and kneeling have been employed by all nations, and in all ages, to signify profound veneration. Another circumstance, still more than uniformity, demonstrates these gestures to be natural, viz. their remarkable conformity or resemblance to the passions that produce them. (See chapter ii. part vi.) Joy, which is a cheerful elevation of mind, is expressed by an elevation of body: pride, magnanimity, courage, and the whole tribe of elevating passions, are expressed by external gestures that are the same as to the circumstance of elevation, however distinguishable in other respects; and hence an erect posture is a sign or expression of dignity:

> Two of far nobler shape, erect and tall,
> Godlike erect, with native honor clad,
> In naked majesty, seem'd lords of all.—*Paradise Lost*, Book iv.

* [Well has Cousin remarked:—"Instead of a statue, observe a real and living man. Regard that man who, solicited by the strongest motives to sacrifice duty to fortune, triumphs over interest, after a heroic struggle, and sacrifices fortune to virtue. Regard him at the moment when he is about to take this magnanimous resolution; his face will appear to me beautiful, because it expresses the beauty of his soul. Perhaps, under all other circumstances, the face of the man is common, even trivial; here, illustrated by the soul which it manifests, it is ennobled and takes an imposing character of beauty. So, the natural face of Socrates contrasts strongly with the type of Grecian beauty; but look at him on his death-bed, at the moment of drinking the hemlock, conversing with his disciples on the immortality of the soul, and his face will appear to you sublime."—*Lect.* vii. p. 147.]

351. External signs of passion twofold.—The voluntary, of two kinds; arbitrary and natural.—The chief talent of dramatic writers and of fine readers.

352. Natural attitudes and gestures.—Their conformity to the passions producing them.

Grief, on the other hand, as well as respect, which depress the mind, cannot, for that reason, be expressed more significantly than by a similar depression of the body; and hence, *to be cast down*, is a common phrase, signifying to be grieved or dispirited.*

353. One would not imagine, who has not given peculiar attention, that the body should be susceptible of such variety of attitude and motion as readily to accompany every different emotion with a corresponding expression. Humility, for example, is expressed naturally by hanging the head; arrogance, by its elevation; and languor or despondence by reclining it to one side. The expressions of the hands are manifold: by different attitudes and motions, they express desire, hope, fear; they assist us in promising, in inviting, in keeping one at a distance; they are made instruments of threatening, of supplication, of praise, and of horror; they are employed in approving, in refusing, in questioning; in showing our joy, our sorrow, our doubts, our regret, our admiration. These expressions, so obedient to passion, are extremely difficult to be imitated in a calm state: the ancients, sensible of the advantage as well as difficulty of having these expressions at command, bestowed much time and care in collecting them from observation, and in digesting them into a practical art, which was taught in their schools as an important branch of education. Certain sounds are by nature allotted to each passion for expressing it externally. The actor who has these sounds at command to captivate the ear, is mighty; if he have also proper gestures at command to captivate the eye, he is irresistible.

354. The foregoing signs, though in a strict sense voluntary, cannot, however, be restrained but with the utmost difficulty when prompted by passion. We scarce need a stronger proof than the gestures of a keen player at bowls: observe only how he writhes his body, in order to restore a stray bowl to the right track. It is one article of good-breeding to suppress, as much as possible, these external signs of passion, that we may not in company appear too warm, or too interested. The same observation holds in speech: a passion, it is true, when in extreme, is silent (see chap. xvii.); but when less violent it must be vented in words, which have a peculiar force not to be equalled in a sedate composition. The ease and security we have in a confidant, may encourage us to talk of ourselves and of our feelings; but the cause is more general; for it operates

* Instead of a complimental speech in addressing a superior, the Chinese deliver the compliment in writing, the smallness of the letters being proportioned to the degree of respect; and the highest compliment is to make the letters so small as not to be legible. Here is a clear evidence of a mental connection between respect and littleness: a man humbles himself before his superior, and endeavors to contract himself and his handwriting within the smallest bounds.

353. The great variety of attitude and gesture of which the body is susceptible for expressing emotion. What the head and the hands may express.

when we are alone as well as in company. Passion is the cause for in many instances it is no slight gratification to vent a passion externally by words as well as by gestures. Some passions, when at a certain height, impel us so strongly to vent them in words, that we speak with an audible voice even when there is none to listen. It is that circumstance in passion which justifies soliloquies; and it is that circumstance which proves them to be natural. The mind sometimes favors this impulse of passion, by bestowing a temporary sensibility upon any object at hand, in order to make it a confidant. Thus in the *Winter's Tale* (Act III. Sc. 6), Antigonus addresses himself to an infant whom he was ordered to expose:

> Come, poor babe,
> I have heard, but not believed, that spirits of the dead
> May walk again: if such things be, thy mother
> Appear'd to me last night; for ne'er was dream
> So like a waking.

355. The involuntary signs, which are all of them natural, are either peculiar to one passion, or common to many. Every vivid passion hath an external expression peculiar to itself, not excepting pleasant passions; witness admiration and mirth. The pleasant emotions that are less vivid have one common expression; from which we may gather the strength of the emotion, but scarce the kind: we perceive a cheerful or contented look; and we can make no more of it. Painful passions, being all of them violent, are distinguishable from each other by their external expressions; thus fear, shame, anger, anxiety, dejection, despair, have each of them peculiar expressions, which are apprehended without the least confusion: some painful passions produce violent effects upon the body, trembling, for example, starting, and swooning; but these effects, depending in a good measure upon singularity of constitution, are not uniform in all men.

356. The involuntary signs, such of them as are displayed upon the countenance, are of two kinds: some are temporary, making their appearance with the emotions that produce them, and vanishing with these emotions; others, being formed gradually by some violent passion often recurring, become permanent signs of that passion, and serve to denote the disposition or temper. The face of an infant indicates no particular disposition, because it cannot be marked with any character, to which time is necessary: even the temporary signs are extremely awkward, being the first rude essays of Nature to discover internal feelings; thus the shrieking of a new-born infant, without tears or sobbings, is plainly an attempt to weep; and some of these temporary signs, as smiling and frowning, cannot be observed for some months after birth. Permanent signs, formed in

---

354. The foregoing signs difficult to restrain when prompted by passion.—What good-breeding requires.—Passion prone to vent itself in words and gestures; even to irrational objects.—Soliloquy.

355. The involuntary signs, either peculiar to one passion, or common to many.

youth while the body is soft and flexible, are preserved entire by the firmness and solidity that the body acquires, and are never obliterated even by a change of temper. Such signs are not produced after the fibres become rigid; some violent cases excepted, such as reiterated fits of the gout or stone through a course of time: but these signs are not so obstinate as what are produced in youth; for when the cause is removed, they gradually wear away, and at last vanish.

357. The natural signs of emotions, voluntary and involuntary, being nearly the same in all men, form a universal language, which no distance of place, no difference of tribe, no diversity of tongue, can darken or render doubtful: even education, though of mighty influence, hath not power to vary or sophisticate, far less to destroy, their signification. This is a wise appointment of Providence; for if these signs were like words, arbitrary and variable, the thoughts and volitions of strangers would be entirely hid from us; which would prove a great, or rather invincible, obstruction to the formation of societies; but as matters are ordered, the external appearances of joy, grief, anger, fear, shame, and of the other passions, forming a universal language, open a direct avenue to the heart. As the arbitrary signs vary in every country, there could be no communication of thoughts among different nations, were it not for the natural signs, in which all agree: and as the discovering passions instantly at their birth is essential to our well-being, and often necessary for self-preservation, the Author of our nature, attentive to our wants, hath provided a passage to the heart, which never can be obstructed while eyesight remains.

358. In an inquiry concerning the external signs of passion, actions must not be overlooked: for though singly they afford no clear light, they are, upon the whole, the best interpreters of the heart. By observing a man's conduct for a course of time, we discover unerringly the various passions that move him to action, what he loves and what he hates. In our younger years, every single action is a mark, not at all ambiguous of the temper; for in childhood there is little or no disguise: the subject becomes more intricate in advanced age; but even there, dissimulation is seldom carried on for any length of time. And thus the conduct of life is the most perfect expression of the internal disposition. It merits not indeed the title of a universal language; because it is not thoroughly understood but by those of penetrating genius or extensive observation: it is a language, however, which every one can decipher in some measure, and which, joined with the other external signs, affords sufficient means for the direction of our conduct with regard to others: if we commit any mistake when such light is afforded,

---

356. Signs, temporary or permanent. Temporary signs in infancy. Permanent signs formed in youth.

357. The natural signs form a universal language.—A wise appointment of Providence.

it can never be the effect of unavoidable ignorance, but of rashness or inadvertence.

359. Reflecting on the various expressions of our emotions, we recognize the anxious care of Nature to discover men to each other. Strong emotions, as above hinted, beget an impatience to express them externally by speech and other voluntary signs, which cannot be suppressed without a painful effort: thus a sudden fit of passion is a common excuse for indecent behavior or opprobrious language. As to involuntary signs, these are altogether unavoidable: no volition or effort can prevent the shaking of the limbs or a pale visage, in a fit of terror: the blood flies to the face upon a sudden emotion of shame, in spite of all opposition:

> Vergogna, che'n altrui stampo natura,
> Non si puo' rinegar: che se tu' tenti
> Di cacciarla dal cor, fugge nel volto.
>
> *Pastor Fido*, Act II. Sc. 5.

Emotions, indeed, properly so called, which are quiescent, produce no remarkable signs externally. Nor is it necessary that the more deliberate passions should, because the operation of such passions is neither sudden nor violent: these, however, remain not altogether in obscurity; for being more frequent than violent passion, the bulk of our actions are directed by them. Actions, therefore, display, with sufficient evidence, the more deliberate passions; and complete the admirable system of external signs, by which we become skilful in human nature.

360. What comes next in order is, to examine the effects produced upon a spectator by external signs of passion. None of these signs are beheld with indifference; they are productive of various emotions, tending all of them to ends wise and good. This curious subject makes a capital branch of human nature: it is peculiarly useful to writers who deal in the pathetic; and to history-painters it is indispensable.

It is mentioned above, that each passion, or class of passions, hath its peculiar signs; and, with respect to the present subject, it must be added, that these invariably make certain impressions on a spectator: the external signs of joy, for example, produce a cheerful emotion; the external signs of grief produce pity; and the external signs of rage produce a sort of terror even in those who are not aimed at.

361. Secondly, it is natural to think, that pleasant passions should express themselves externally by signs that to a spectator appear agreeable, and painful passions by signs that to him appear dis-

---

358. Action, the best interpreter of the heart; especially in our earlier years.—The language of action in more advanced years not easily understood.

359. The care of nature to discover men to each other.—Quiescent emotions produce no remarkable external sign.—The more deliberate passions, how expressed.

360. Effects produced upon a spectator by external signs of passion; by those of joy, &c

agreeable. This conjecture, which Nature suggests, is confirmed by experience. Pride possibly may be thought an exception, the external signs of which are disagreeable, though it be commonly reckoned a pleasant passion; but pride is not an exception, being in reality a mixed passion, partly pleasant, partly painful; for when a proud man confines his thoughts to himself, and to his own dignity or importance, the passion is pleasant, and its external signs agreeable; but as pride chiefly consists in undervaluing or contemning others, it is so far painful, and its external signs disagreeable.

Thirdly, it is laid down above, that an agreeable object produceth always a pleasant emotion, and a disagreeable object one that is painful. (See chapter ii. part vii.) According to this law, the external signs of a pleasant passion, being agreeable, must produce in the spectator a pleasant emotion; and the external signs of a painful passion, being disagreeable, must produce in him a painful emotion.

362. Fourthly, in the present chapter it is observed, that pleasant passions are, for the most part, expressed externally in one uniform manner; but that all the painful passions are distinguishable from each other by their external expressions. The emotions accordingly raised in a spectator by external signs of pleasant passions, have little variety: these emotions are pleasant or cheerful, and we have not words to reach a more particular description. But the external signs of painful passions produce in the spectator emotions of different kinds: the emotions, for example, raised by external signs of grief, of remorse, of anger, of envy, of malice, are clearly distinguishable from each other.

363. Fifthly, external signs of painful passions are some of them *attractive*, some *repulsive*. Of every painful passion that is also disagreeable,* the external signs are repulsive, repelling the spectator from the object; and the passion raised by such external signs may be also considered as repulsive. Painful passions that are agreeable produce an opposite effect: their external signs are attractive, drawing the spectator to them, and producing in him benevolence to the person upon whom these signs appear; witness distress painted on the countenance, which instantaneously inspires the spectator with pity, and impels him to afford relief. And the passion raised by such external signs may also be considered as attractive. The cause of this difference among the painful passions raised by their external signs may be readily gathered from what is laid down, chapter ii. part vii.

* See passions explained as agreeable, chapter ii. part ii.

361. Signs of pleasant passions, agreeable to a spectator, &c.—Pride, no exception.—An agreeable object produces a pleasant emotion, &c.
362. Emotions raised by external signs of pleasant passions have little variety; not so by those of painful passions.
363. External signs of painful passions either attractive or repulsive.

364. It is now time to look back to the question proposed in the beginning, How we come to understand external signs, so as to refer each sign to its proper passion? We have seen that this branch of knowledge cannot be derived originally from sight, nor from experience. Is it then implanted in us by nature? The following considerations will incline us to answer the question in the affirmative. In the first place, the external signs of passion must be natural; for they are invariably the same in every country, and among the different tribes of men: pride, for example, is always expressed by an erect posture, reverence by prostration, and sorrow by a dejected look. Secondly, we are not even indebted to experience for the knowledge that these expressions are natural and universal; for we are so framed as to have an innate conviction of the fact: let a man change his habitation to the other side of the globe, he will, from the accustomed signs, infer the passion of fear among his new neighbors with as little hesitation as he did at home. But why, after all, involve ourselves in preliminary observations, when the doubt may be directly solved as follows? That, if the meaning of external signs be not derived to us from sight, nor from experience, there is no remaining source whence it can be derived but from nature.

365. We may then venture to pronounce, with some degree of assurance, that man is provided by nature with a sense or faculty that lays open to him every passion by means of its external expressions. And we cannot entertain any reasonable doubt of this, when we reflect that the meaning of external signs is not hid even from infants: an infant is remarkably affected with the passions of its nurse expressed in her countenance; a smile cheers it, a frown makes it afraid: but fear cannot be without apprehending danger; and what danger can the infant apprehend, unless it be sensible that its nurse is angry? We must, therefore, admit that a child can read anger in its nurse's face; of which it must be sensible intuitively, for it has no other means of knowledge. I do not affirm that these particulars are clearly apprehended by the child, for to produce clear and distinct perceptions, reflection and experience are requisite; but that even an infant, when afraid, must have some notion of its being in danger, is evident.

That we should be conscious intuitively of a passion from its external expressions, is conformable to the analogy of nature: the knowledge of that language is of too great importance to be left upon experience; because a foundation so uncertain and precarious would prove a great obstacle to the formation of societies. Wisely, therefore, is it ordered, and agreeably to the system of Providence, that we should have nature for our instructor.

---

364. How we refer each sign to its proper passion. Considerations which show that this knowledge is implanted by nature.

365. Infants affected by external signs. Argument from analogy.

366. Manifold and admirable are the purposes to which the external signs of passion are made subservient by the Author of our nature: those occasionally mentioned above make but a part. Several final causes remain to be unfolded; and to that task I proceed with alacrity. In the first place, the signs of internal agitation displayed externally to every spectator, tend to fix the signification of many words. The only effectual means to ascertain the meaning of any doubtful word, is an appeal to the thing it represents; and hence the ambiguity of words expressive of things that are not objects of external sense, for in that case an appeal is denied. Passion, strictly speaking, is not an object of external sense, but its external signs are; and by means of these signs passions may be appealed to with tolerable accuracy: thus the words that denote our passions, next to those that denote external objects, have the most distinct meaning. Words signifying internal action and the more delicate feelings, are less distinct. This defect with regard to internal action is what chiefly occasions the intricacy of logic: the terms of that science are far from being sufficiently ascertained, even after much care and labor bestowed by Locke; to whom, however, the world is greatly indebted for removing a mountain of rubbish, and moulding the subject into a rational and correct form. The same defect is remarkable in criticism, which has for its object the more delicate feelings; the terms that denote these feelings being not more distinct than those of logic. To reduce the science of criticism to any regular form, has never once been attempted: however rich the ore may be, no critical chemist has been found to analyze its constituent parts, and to distinguish each by its own name.

367. In the second place, society among individuals is greatly promoted by that universal language. Looks and gestures give direct access to the heart, and lead us to select, with tolerable accuracy, the persons who are worthy of our confidence. It is surprising how quickly, and for the most part how correctly, we judge of character from external appearance.

Thirdly, After social intercourse is commenced, these external signs, which diffuse through a whole assembly the feelings of each individual, contribute above all other means to improve the social affections. Language, no doubt, is the most comprehensive vehicle for communicating emotions: but in expedition, as well as in power of conviction, it falls short of the signs under consideration; the involuntary signs especially, which are incapable of deceit. Where the countenance, the tones, the gestures, the actions, join with the words in communicating emotions, these united have a force irresistible: thus all the pleasant emotions of the human heart, with all the social and virtuous affections, are, by means of these external signs, not only perceived but felt. By this admirable contrivance, conver-

366. Purposes to which the external signs of passion are made subservient.

sation becomes that lively and animating amusement without which life would at best be insipid; one joyful countenance spreads cheerfulness instantaneously through a multitude of spectators.

368. Fourthly, Dissocial passions, being hurtful by prompting violence and mischief, are noted by the most conspicuous external signs, in order to put us upon our guard: thus anger and revenge, especially when sudden, display themselves on the countenance in legible characters.* The external signs again of every passion that threatens danger raise in us the passion of fear; which, frequently operating without reason or reflection, moves us by a sudden impulse to avoid the impending danger. (See chapter ii. part i. sec. 6.)

369. In the fifth place, These external signs are remarkably subservient to morality. A painful passion, being accompanied with disagreeable external signs, must produce in every spectator a painful emotion; but then, if the passion be social, the emotion it produces is attractive, and connects the spectator with the person who suffers. Dissocial passions only are productive of repulsive emotions, involving the spectator's aversion, and frequently his indignation. This beautiful contrivance makes us cling to the virtuous, and abhor the wicked.

370. Sixthly, Of all the external signs of passion, those of affliction or distress are the most illustrious with respect to a final cause. They are illustrious by the singularity of their contrivance, and also by inspiring sympathy, a passion to which human society is indebted for its greatest blessing, that of providing relief for the distressed. A subject so interesting deserves a leisurely and attentive examination. The conformity of the nature of man to his external circumstances is in every particular wonderful; his nature makes him prone to society; and society is necessary to his well-being, because in a solitary state he is a helpless being, destitute of support, and in his manifold distresses destitute of relief: but mutual support, the shining attribute of society, is of too great moment to be left dependent upon

* Rough and blunt manners are allied to anger by an internal feeling, as well as by external expressions resembling in a faint degree those of anger; therefore such manners are easily heightened into anger, and savages for that reason are prone to anger. Thus rough and blunt manners are unhappy in two respects: first, they are readily converted into anger; and next, the change being imperceptible because of the similitude of their external signs, the person against whom the anger is directed is not put upon his guard. It is for these reasons a great object in society to correct such manners, and to bring on a habit of sweetness and calmness. This temper has two opposite good effects. First, it is not easily provoked to wrath. Next, the interval being great between it and real anger, a person of that temper who receives an affront has many changes to go through before his anger be inflamed: these changes have each of them their external sign; and the offending party is put upon his guard, to retire, or to endeavor a reconciliation.

367. Society among individuals thus promoted.—The social affections improved; not only by language, but signs.—What enlivens conversation.

368. Signs of dissocial passions put us on our guard.—Rough and blunt manners unhappy in two respects.—Opposite good effects of a sweet temper.

369. External signs promote morality.

cool reason; it is ordered more wisely, and with greater conformity to the analogy of nature, that it should be enforced even instinctively by the passion of sympathy. Here sympathy makes a capital figure, and contributes, more than any other means, to make life easy and comfortable. But, however essential the sympathy of others may be to our well-being, one beforehand would not readily conceive how it could be raised by external signs of distress: for considering the analogy of nature, if these signs be agreeable, they must give birth to a pleasant emotion leading every beholder to be pleased with human woes; if disagreeable, as they undoubtedly are, ought they not naturally to repel the spectator from them, in order to be relieved from pain? Such would be the reasoning beforehand; and such would be the effect were man purely a selfish being. But the benevolence of our nature gives a very different direction to the painful passion of sympathy, and to the desire involved in it: instead of avoiding distress, we fly to it in order to afford relief; and our sympathy cannot be otherwise gratified but by giving all the succor in our power. (See chap. ii. part vii.) Thus external signs of distress, though disagreeable, are attractive; and the sympathy they inspire is a powerful cause, impelling us to afford relief even to a stranger, as if he were our friend or relation.*

371. The effects produced in all beholders by external signs of passion, tend so visibly to advance the social state, that I must indulge my heart with a more narrow inspection of this admirable branch of the human constitution. These external signs, being all of them resolvable into color, figure, and motion, should not naturally make any deep impression on a spectator; and supposing them qualified for making deep impressions, we have seen above that the effects they produce are not such as might be expected. We cannot therefore account otherwise for the operation of these external signs, but by ascribing it to the original constitution of human nature: to improve the social state by making us instinctively rejoice

* It is a noted observation, that the deepest tragedies are the most crowded; which in a slight view will be thought an unaccountable bias in human nature. Love of novelty, desire of occupation, beauty of action, make us fond of theatrical representations; and, when once engaged, we must follow the story to the conclusion, whatever distress it may create. But we generally become wise by experience; and when we foresee what pain we shall suffer during the course of the representation, is it not surprising that persons of reflection do not avoid such spectacles altogether? And yet one who has scarce recovered from the distress of a deep tragedy, resolves coolly and deliberately to go to the very next, without the slightest obstruction from self-love. The whole mystery is explained by a single observation. That sympathy, though painful, is attractive, and attaches us to an object in distress, the opposition of self-love notwithstanding, which should prompt us to fly from it. And by this curious mechanism it is, that persons of any degree of sensibility are attracted by affliction still more than by joy.

370. Final cause of external signs of distress.—Nature of man conformed to his circumstances.—Sympathy.—Why distress does not repel.—Why the deepest tragedies are attractive.

with the glad of heart, weep with the mourner, and shun those who threaten danger, is a contrivance no less illustrious for its wisdom than for its benevolence.

372. I add a reflection, with which I shall conclude. The external signs of passion are a strong indication that man, by his very constitution, is framed to be open and sincere. A child, in all things obedient to the impulse of nature, hides none of its emotions: the savage and clown, who have no guide but pure nature, expose their hearts to view, by giving way to all the natural signs. And even when men learn to dissemble their sentiments, and when behavior degenerates into art, there still remain checks that keep dissimulation within bounds, and prevent a great part of its mischievous effects: the total suppression of the voluntary signs during any vivid passion, begets the utmost uneasiness, which cannot be endured for any considerable time: this operation becomes indeed less painful by habit; but, luckily, the involuntary signs cannot, by any effort, be suppressed, nor even dissembled. An absolute hypocrisy, by which the character is concealed, and a fictitious one assumed, is made impracticable; and nature has thereby prevented much harm to society. We may pronounce, therefore, that Nature, herself sincere and candid, intends that mankind should preserve the same character, by cultivating simplicity and truth, and banishing every sort of dissimulation that tends to mischief.

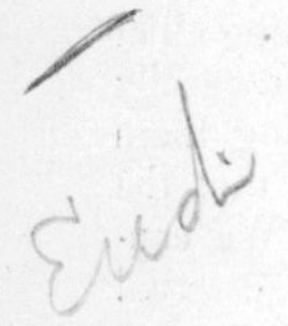

CHAPTER XVI.

SENTIMENTS.

373. Every thought prompted by passion, is termed *a sentiment* (see Introd. sec. 33). To have a general notion of the different passions, will not alone enable an artist to make a just representation of any passion: he ought, over and above, to know the various appearances of the same passion in different persons. Passions receive a tincture from every peculiarity of character; and for that reason it rarely happens that a passion, in the different circumstances of feeling, of sentiment, and of expression, is precisely the same in any two persons. Hence the following rule concerning dramatic and epic compositions: that a passion be adjusted to the character, the sentiments to the passion, and the language to the sentiments. If nature be not faithfully copied in each of these, a defect in execution is per-

371. The operation of external signs of emotion, attributable to the original constitution of human nature. Wisdom and benevolence of the contrivance.

372. Concluding reflection; what the external signs of passion indicate. Illustrated in the child; the savage; and even in men that have learned to dissemble their sentiments.

ceived: there may appear some resemblance; but the picture, upon the whole, will be insipid, through want of grace and delicacy. A painter, in order to represent the various attitudes of the body, ought to be intimately acquainted with muscular motion: no less intimately acquainted with emotions and characters ought a writer to be, in order to represent the various attitudes of the mind. A general notion of the passions, in their grosser differences of strong and weak, elevated and humble, severe and gay, is far from being sufficient: pictures formed so superficially have little resemblance, and no expression; yet it will appear by and by, that in many instances our artists are deficient even in that superficial knowledge.

In handling the present subject, it would be endless to trace even the ordinary passions through their nice and minute differences. Mine shall be an humbler task; which is, to select from the best writers instances of faulty sentiments, after paving the way by some general observations.

374. To talk in the language of music, each passion hath a certain tone, to which every sentiment proceeding from it ought to be tuned with the greatest accuracy; which is no easy work, especially where such harmony ought to be supported during the course of a long theatrical representation. In order to reach such delicacy of execution, it is necessary that a writer assume the precise character and passion of the personage represented; which requires an uncommon genius. But it is the only difficulty; for the writer, who, annihilating himself, can thus become another person, need be in no pain about the sentiments that belong to the assumed character: these will flow without the least study, or even preconception; and will frequently be as delightfully new to himself as to his reader. But if a lively picture even of a single emotion require an effort of genius, how much greater the effort to compose a passionate dialogue with as many different tones of passion as there are speakers! With what ductility of feeling must that writer be endowed, who approaches perfection in such a work: when it is necessary to assume different and even opposite characters and passions, in the quickest succession! Yet this work, difficult as it is, yields to that of composing a dialogue in genteel comedy, exhibiting characters without passion. The reason is, that the different tones of character are more delicate and less in sight, than those of passion; and accordingly, many writers, who have no genius for drawing characters, make a shift to represent tolerably well an ordinary passion in its simple movements. But of all works of this kind, what is truly the most difficult, is a characteristical dialogue upon any philosophical subject: to interweave characters with reasoning, by suiting to the character

---

373. Define *sentiment*.—How passions are modified.—Rule for dramatic and epic compositions

374. Sentiment to be adapted to each passion.—The writer must assume the character and passion of the personage represented.—Difficulty of composing dialogue. Three kinds compared.

of each speaker a peculiarity, not only of thought, but of expression requires the perfection of genius, taste, and judgment.

375. How nice dialogue-writing is, will be evident, even without reasoning, from the miserable compositions of that kind found without number in all languages. The art of mimicking any singularity in gesture or in voice, is a rare talent, though directed by sight and hearing, the acutest and most lively of our external senses: how much more rare must the talent be, of imitating characters and internal emotions, tracing all their different tints, and representing them in a lively manner by natural sentiments properly expressed! The truth is, such execution is too delicate for an ordinary genius: and for that reason, the bulk of writers, instead of expressing a passion as one does who feels it, content themselves with describing it in the language of a spectator. To awake passion by an internal effort merely, without any external cause, requires great sensibility: and yet that operation is necessary, no less to the writer than to the actor; because none but those who actually feel a passion, can represent it to the life. The writer's part is the more complicated: he must add composition to passion; and must, in the quickest succession, adopt every different character. But a very humble flight of imagination, may serve to convert a writer into a spectator; so as to figure, in some obscure manner, an action as passing in his sight and hearing. In that figured situation, being led naturally to write like a spectator, he entertains his readers with his own reflections, with cool description, and florid declamation; instead of making them eye-witnesses, as it were, to a real event, and to every movement of genuine passion.* Thus most of our plays appear to be cast in the same mould; personages without character, the mere outlines of passion, a tiresome monotony, and a pompous declamatory style.†

376. This descriptive manner of representing passion, is a very cold entertainment: our sympathy is not raised by description; we must first be lulled into a dream of reality, and every thing must appear as passing in our sight (see chap. ii. part i. sect. 7). Un-

* In the *Æneid*, the hero is made to describe himself in the following words: *Sum pius Æneas, fama super æthera notus.* Virgil could never have been guilty of an impropriety so gross, had he assumed the personage of his hero, instead of uttering the sentiments of a spectator. Nor would Xenophon have made the following speech for Cyrus the younger, to his Grecian auxiliaries, whom he was leading against his brother Artaxerxes: "I have chosen you, O Greeks! my auxiliaries, not to enlarge my army, for I have *Barbarians* without number; but because you surpass all the *Barbarians* in valor and military discipline." This sentiment is Xenophon's, for surely Cyrus did not reckon his countrymen Barbarians.

† "Chez Racine tout est sentiment; il a su faire parler *chacun pour soi*, et c'est en cela qu'il est vraiment unique parmi les auteurs dramatiques de sa nation."—*Rousseau.*

375. Rare talent required in imitating characters and internal emotions.—Most writers merely describe passion.—More easy to write as a spectator than to feel the passion described.—Remarks on Virgil and Xenophon.

happy is the player of genius who acts a capital part in what may be termed a *descriptive tragedy;* after assuming the very passion that is to be represented, how is he cramped in action, when he must utter, not the sentiments of the passion he feels, but a cold description in the language of a bystander! It is that imperfection, I am persuaded, in the bulk of our plays, which confines our stage almost entirely to Shakspeare, notwithstanding his many irregularities. In our late English tragedies, we sometimes find sentiments tolerably well adapted to a plain passion: but we must not, in any of them, expect a sentiment expressive of character; and, upon that very account, our late performances of the dramatic kind are for the most part intolerably insipid.

377. Looking back upon what is said, I am in some apprehension of not being perfectly understood; for it is not easy to avoid obscurity in handling a matter so complicated; but I promise to set it in the clearest light, by adding example to precept. The first examples shall be of sentiments that appear the legitimate offspring of passion; to which shall be opposed what are descriptive only, and illegitimate: and in making this comparison, I borrow my instances from Shakspeare and Corneille, who for genius in dramatic composition stand uppermost in the rolls of fame.

Shakspeare shall furnish the first example, being of sentiments dictated by a violent and perturbed passion:

> *Lear.* ——————— Filial ingratitude!
> Is it not, as if this mouth should tear this hand
> For lifting food to't?—But I'll punish home;
> No, I'll weep no more.——In such a night,
> To shut me out!——Pour on, I will endure.
> In such a night as this! O Regan, Goneril,
> Your old kind father, whose frank heart gave all—
> O! that way madness lies: let me shun that;
> No more of that. ———————
> *Kent.* Good, my lord, enter here.
> *Lear.* Pr'ythee, go in thyself, seek thine own ease,
> This tempest will not give me leave to ponder
> On things would hurt me more:—but I'll go in;
> In, boy, go first. You houseless poverty——
> Nay, get thee in; I'll pray, and then I'll sleep—
> Poor naked wretches, wheresoe'er you are,
> That bide the pelting of this pitiless storm!
> How shall your houseless heads, and unfed sides,
> Your loop'd and window'd raggedness defend you
> From seasons such as these?——O I have ta'en
> Too little care of this! Take physic, Pomp;
> Expose thyself to feel what wretches feel,
> That thou may'st shake the superflux to them,
> And show the heavens more just.
>
> *King Lear,* Act III. Sc. 5.

I give another example of the same kind, expressing sentiments arising from remorse and despair:

---

376. Defects of the descriptive manner of representing passion.—Merit of Shakspeare's plays.

Othello. Lo! I have a weapon:
A better never did itself sustain
Upon a soldier's thigh. I've seen the day,
That with this little arm, and this good sword,
I've made my way through more impediment
Than twenty times your stop. But, oh vain boast!
Who can control his fate? 'tis not so now.
Be not afraid, though you do see me weapon'd;
Here is my journey's end, here is my butt,
The very sea-mark of my utmost sail.
Do you go back dismay'd? 'tis a lost fear.
Man but a rush against Othello's breast,
And he retires. Where should Othello go?
Now—how dost thou look now? Oh ill-starr'd wench
Pale as thy smock! When we shall meet at compt,
This look of thine will hurl my soul from heaven,
And fiends will snatch at it. Cold, cold, my girl;
Ev'n like thy chastity. O cursed slave!
Whip me, ye devils,
From the possession of this heavenly sight;
Blow me about in winds, roast me in sulphur,
Wash me in steep down gulfs of liquid fire——
Oh, Desdemona! Desdemona! dead! dead! oh! oh!

Othello, Act V. Sc. 9.

The sentiments here displayed flow so naturally from the passions represented, that we cannot conceive any imitation more perfect.

378. With regard to the French author, truth obliges me to acknowledge, that he describes in the style of a spectator, instead of expressing passion like one who feels it; which naturally betrays him into a tiresome monotony, and a pompous declamatory style.* It is scarce necessary to give examples, for he never varies from that tone. I shall, however, take two passages at a venture, in order to be confronted with those transcribed above. In the tragedy of *Cinna*, Æmilia, after the conspiracy was discovered, having nothing in view but racks and death to herself and her lover, receives a pardon from Augustus, attended with the brightest circumstances of

* This criticism reaches the French dramatic writers in general, with very few exceptions: their tragedies, excepting those of Racine, are mostly, if not totally, descriptive. Corneille led the way; and later writers, imitating his manner, have accustomed the French ear to a style, formal, pompous, declamatory, which suits not with any passion. Hence, to burlesque a French tragedy, is not more difficult than to burlesque a stiff solemn fop. The facility of the operation has in Paris introduced a singular amusement, which is, to burlesque the more successful tragedies in a sort of farce, called *a parody*. La Motte, who himself appears to have been sorely galled by some of these productions, acknowledges, that no more is necessary to give them currency but barely to vary the *dramatis personæ*, and instead of kings and heroes, queens and princesses, to substitute tinkers and tailors, milkmaids and seamstresses. The declamatory style, so different from the genuine expression of passion, passes in some measure unobserved, when great personages are the speakers: but in the mouths of the vulgar the impropriety with regard to the speaker as well as to the passion represented, is so remarkable as to become ridiculous. A tragedy, where every passion is made to speak in its natural tone, is not liable to be thus burlesqued: the same passion is by all men expressed nearly in the same manner; and, therefore, the genuine expressions of a passion cannot be ridiculous in the mouth of any man who is susceptible of the passion.

377. Example of sentiments dictated by passion; by remorse and despair

magnanimity and tenderness. This is a lucky situation for representing the passions of surprise and gratitude in their different stages, which seem naturally to be what follow. These passions, raised at once to the utmost pitch, and being at first too big for utterance, must, for some moments, be expressed by violent gestures only: as soon as there is vent for words, the first expressions are broken and interrupted: at last we ought to expect a tide of intermingled sentiments, occasioned by the fluctuation of the mind between the two passions. Æmilia is made to behave in a very different manner: with extreme coolness she describes her own situation, as if she were merely a spectator, or rather the poet takes the task off her hands. (Act V. Sc. 3.)

In the tragedy of *Sertorius*, the queen, surprised with the news that her lover was assassinated, instead of venting any passion, degenerates into a cool spectator, and undertakes to instruct the bystanders how a queen ought to behave on such an occasion. (Act V. Sc. 3.)

379. So much in general upon the genuine sentiments of passion. I proceed to particular observations. And, first, passions seldom continue uniform any considerable time: they generally fluctuate, swelling and subsiding by turns, often in a quick succession (see chapter ii. part iii.); and the same sentiments cannot be just unless they correspond to such fluctuation. Accordingly, climax never shows better than in expressing a swelling passion: the following passages may suffice for an illustration:

> *Oroonoko.*———Can you raise the dead?
> Pursue and overtake the wings of time?
> And bring about again the hours, the days,
> The years that made me happy?—*Oroonoko*, Act II. Sc. 2.

> *Almeria.*———How hast thou charm'd
> The wildness of the waves and rocks to this?
> That thus relenting they have given thee back
> To earth, to light and life, to love and me?
> *Mourning Bride*, Act I. Sc. 7.

> I would not be the villain that thou think'st
> For the whole space that's in the tyrant's grasp,
> And the rich earth to boot.—*Macbeth*, Act IV. Sc. 4.

The following passage expresses finely the progress of conviction:

> Let me not stir, nor breathe, lest I dissolve
> That tender, lovely form of painted air,
> So like Almeria. Ha! it sinks, it falls;
> I'll catch it ere it goes, and grasp her shade.
> 'Tis life! 'tis warm! 'tis she! 'tis she herself!
> It is Almeria, 'tis, it is my wife!—*Mourning Bride*, Act II. Sc. 6.

In the progress of thought, our resolutions become more vigorous as well as our passions:

---

378. Peculiarities of Corneille.—French tragedies easily burlesqued. How this is done—Remarks on the tragedies of *Cinna* and *Sertorius*.

379. Passions seldom uniform for a long time.—Climax, expressive of a swelling passion Examples.

If ever I do yield or give consent,
By an action, word, or thought, to wed
Another lord; may then just heaven shower down, &c.
Ibid. Act I. Sc. 1.

380. And this leads to a second observation. That the different stages of a passion, and its different directions, from birth to extinction, must be carefully represented in their order; because otherwise the sentiments, by being misplaced, will appear forced and unnatural. Resentment, for example, when provoked by an atrocious injury, discharges itself first upon the author: sentiments therefore of revenge come always first, and must in some measure be exhausted before the person injured thinks of grieving for himself. In the *Cid* of Corneille, Don Diegue, having been affronted in a cruel manner, expresses scarce any sentiment of revenge, but is totally occupied in contemplating the low situation to which he is reduced by the affront:

O rage! ô désespoir! ô vieillesse ennemie!
N'ai-je donc tant vécu que pour cette infamie?
Et ne suis-je blanchi dans les trauvaux guerriers,
Que pour voir en un jour flêtrir tant de lauriers?
Mon bras, qu'avec respect toute l'Espagne admire,
Mon bras, qui tant de fois a suavé cet empire,
Tant de fois affermi le trône de son Roi,
Trahit donc ma querelle, et ne fait rien pour moi!
O cruel souvenir de ma gloire passée!
Œuvre de tant de jours en un jour effacée!
Nouvelle dignité fatale à mon bonheur!
Précipice élevé d'où tombe mon honneur!
Faut-il de votre eclat voir triompher le Comte.
Et mourir sans vengeance, ou vivre dans la honte?
Le Cid, Act I. Sc. 7.

These sentiments are certainly not the first that are suggested by the passion of resentment. As the first movements of resentment are always directed to its object, the very same is the case of grief. Yet with relation to the sudden and severe distemper that seized Alexander bathing in the river Cydnus, Quintus Curtius describes the first emotions of the army as directed to themselves, lamenting that they were left without a leader, far from home, and had scarce any hopes of returning in safety: their king's distress, which must naturally have been their first concern, occupies them but in the second place, according to that author. In the *Aminta* of Tasso, Sylvia, upon a report of her lover's death, which she believed certain, instead of bemoaning the loss of her beloved, turns her thoughts upon herself, and wonders her heart does not break:

Ohime, ben son di sasso,
Poi che questa novella non m'uccide.—Act IV. Sc. 2.

381. A person sometimes is agitated at once by different passions; and the mind, in that case, vibrating like a pendulum, vents itself

380. The different stages of a passion to be represented in order. For instance, resentment.—The *Cid* of Corneille.—Resentment first directed to its object: so with grief.—Description of Alexander's death, by Q. Curtius, faulty.—Sylvia, &c.

in sentiments that partake of the same vibration. This I give as a third observation:

> *Queen.* Would I had ne'er trod this English earth,
> Or felt the flatteries that grow upon it!
> Ye've angels' faces, but heaven knows your hearts.
> What shall become of me now? wretched lady!
> I am the most unhappy woman living.
> Alas! poor wenches, where are now your fortunes? [*To her women.*
> Shipwreck'd upon a kingdom, where no pity,
> No friends, no hope! no kindred weep for me!
> Almost no grave allow'd me. *Henry VIII.* Act III. Sc. 1.

> *Othello.* Oh devil, devil!
> If that the earth could teem with woman's tears,
> Each drop she falls would prove a crocodile.
> Out of my sight!
> *Desdemona.* I will not stay t' offend you. [*Going.*
> *Ludovico.* Truly, an obedient lady:
> I do beseech your lordship, call her back.
> *Oth.* Mistress———
> *Des.* My lord.
> *Oth.* What would you with her, sir?
> *Lud.* Who, I, my lord?
> *Oth.* Aye; you did wish that I would make her turn:
> Sir, she can turn and turn, and yet go on;
> And turn again. And she can weep, sir, weep:
> And she's obedient: as you say, obedient;
> Very obedient—proceed you in your tears—
> Concerning this, sir—oh well painted passion!
> I am commanded home—get you away,
> I'll send for you anon—sir, I obey the mandate,
> And will return to Venice.——Hence, avaunt! [*Exit Desdemona.*
> *Othello*, Act IV. Sc. 6.

> *Emilia.* Oh, my good lord, I would speak a word with you.
> *Othello.* Yes, 'tis Emilia—By and by—She's dead.
> 'Tis like she comes to speak of Cassio's death:
> The noise was high—Ha! no more moving?
> Still as the grave. Shall she come in? were't good?
> I think she stirs again—No—What's the best?
> If she come in, she'll sure speak to my wife;
> My wife! my wife! What wife? I have no wife;
> Oh, insupportable! Oh, heavy hour!—*Othello*, Act IV. Sc. 7.

382 A fourth observation is, That nature, which gave us passions, and made them extremely beneficial when moderate, intended undoubtedly that they should be subjected to the government of reason and conscience. (See chap. ii. part vii.) It is therefore against the order of nature, that passion in any case should take the lead in contradiction to reason and conscience: such a state of mind is a sort of anarchy, which every one is ashamed of, and endeavors to hide or dissemble. Even love, however laudable, is attended with a conscious shame when it becomes immoderate: it is covered from the world, and disclosed only to the beloved object:

> Et que l'amour souvent de remors combattu,
> Paroisse une foiblesse, et non une vertu.
> *Boileau, L'art Poet.* Chant. iii. l. 101.

---

381 The mind, agitated at once by different passions.—*Henry VIII.—Othello*

Oh, they love least that let men know their love.
Two Gentlemen of Verona, Act I. Sc. 3.

Hence a capital rule in the representation of immoderate passions, that they ought to be hid or dissembled as much as possible. And this holds in an especial manner with respect to criminal passions: one never counsels the commission of a crime in plain terms: guilt must not appear in its native colors, even in thought; the proposal must be made by hints, and by representing the action in some favorable light. Of the propriety of sentiment upon such an occasion, Shakspeare, in the *Tempest*, has given us a beautiful example, in a speech by the usurping Duke of Milan, advising Sebastian to murder his brother, the King of Naples:

Antonio.————————What might,
Worthy Sebastian—O, what might—no more.
And yet, methinks, I see it in thy face,
What thou shouldst be: th' occasion speaks thee, and
My strong imagination sees a crown
Dropping upon thy head. Act II. Sc. 1.

There never was drawn a more complete picture of this kind, than that of King John soliciting Hubert to murder the young Prince Arthur:

K. John. Come hither, Hubert. O my gentle Hubert,
We owe thee much; within this wall of flesh
There is a soul counts thee her creditor,
And with advantage means to pay thy love.
And, my good friend, thy voluntary oath
Lives in this bosom, dearly cherish'd.
Give me thy hand, I had a thing to say———
But I will fit it with some better time.
By Heaven, Hubert, I'm almost ashamed
To say what good respect I have of thee.
Hubert. I am much bounden to your majesty.
K. John. Good friend, thou hast no cause to say so yet—
But thou shalt have—and creep time ne'er so slow,
Yet it shall come for me to do thee good.
I had a thing to say——but let it go;
The sun is in the heaven: and the proud day,
Attended with the pleasures of the world,
Is all too wanton, and too full of gawds,
To give me audience. If the midnight bell
Did with his iron tongue and brazen mouth
Sound one in the drowsy race of night;
If this same were a church-yard where we stand,
And thou possessed with a thousand wrongs;
Or if that surly spirit Melancholy
Had baked thy blood, and made it heavy-thick,
Which else runs tickling up and down the veins,
Making that idiot Laughter keep men's eyes,
And strain their cheeks to idle merriment,
(A passion hateful to my purposes;)
Or if that thou couldst see me without eyes,
Hear me without thine ears, and make reply
Without a tongue, using conceit alone,
Without eyes, ears, and harmful sounds of words:
Then, in despite of broad-eyed watchful day,
I would into thy bosom pour my thoughts.
But ah, I will not—Yet I love thee well;
And by my troth, I think thou lovest me well.

Hubert. So well, that what you bid me undertake,
Though that my death were adjunct to my act,
By heaven I'd do it.
K. John. Do not I know thou wouldst?
Good Hubert, Hubert, Hubert, throw thine eye
On yon young boy. I tell thee what, my friend;
He is a very serpent in my way,
And wheresoe'er this foot of mine doth tread,
He lies before me. Dost thou understand me?
Thou art his keeper. *King John*, Act III. Sc. 5.

383. As things are best illustrated by their contraries, I proceed to faulty sentiments, disdaining to be indebted for examples to any but the most approved authors. The first class shall consist of sentiments that accord not with the passion; or, in other words, sentiments that the passion does not naturally suggest. In the second class shall be ranged sentiments that may belong to an ordinary passion, but unsuitable to it as tinctured by a singular character. Thoughts that properly are not sentiments, but rather descriptions, make a third. Sentiments that belong to the passion represented, but are faulty as being introduced too early or too late, make a fourth. Vicious sentiments exposed in their native dress, instead of being concealed or disguised, make a fifth. And in the last class shall be collected sentiments suited to no character or passion, and therefore unnatural.

384. The first class contains faulty sentiments of various kinds, which I shall endeavor to distinguish from each other; beginning with sentiments that are faulty by being above the tone of the passion:

Othello. ——————O my soul's joy!
If after every tempest come such calms,
May the winds blow till they have waken'd death!
And let the laboring bark climb hills of seas
Olympus high, and duck again as low
As hell's from heaven. *Othello*, Act II. Sc. 6.

This sentiment may be suggested by violent and inflamed passion, but is not suited to the calm satisfaction that one feels upon escaping danger.

Philaster. Place me, some god, upon a pyramid
Higher than hills of earth, and lend a voice
Loud as your thunder to me, that from thence
I may discourse to all the under-world
The worth that dwells in him.
Philaster of Beaumont and Fletcher, Act IV.

385. Second. Sentiments below the tone of the passion. Ptolemy, by putting Pompey to death, having incurred the displeasure of Cæsar, was in the utmost dread of being dethroned: in that agitating situation, Corneille makes him utter a speech full of cool reflection, that is in no degree expressive of the passion:

---

382. Passion should be subjected to reason and conscience.—The feeling that attends the immoderate indulgence of passion.—Rule for representing immoderate passions. Examples from the *Tempest*, &c.

383. Faulty sentiments: those that do not accord with the passion, &c.

384. Sentiments above the tone of the passion. *Othello*, &c.

Ah! si je t'avois crû, je n'aurois pas de maître,
Je serois dans le trône où le Ciel m'a fait naître;
Mais c'est une imprudence assez commune aux rois,
D'écouter trop d'avis, et se tromper aux choix.
Le Destin les aveugle au bord du précipice,
Où si quelque lumière en leur ame se glisse,
Cette fausse clarté dont il les éblouit,
Le plonge dans une gouffre, et puis s'évanouit.
La Morte de Pompée, Act IV. Sc. 1.

In *Les Frères ennemis* of Racine, the second act is opened with a love-scene: Hemon talks to his mistress of the torments of absence, of the lustre of her eyes, that he ought to die nowhere but at her feet, and that one moment of absence is a thousand years. Antigone, on her part, acts the coquette: pretends she must be gone to wait on her mother and brother, and cannot stay to listen to his courtship. This is odious French gallantry, below the dignity of the passion of love: it would be excusable in painting modern French manners; and is insufferable where the ancients are brought upon the stage.

386. Third. Sentiments that agree not with the tone of the passion; as where a pleasant sentiment is grafted upon a painful passion, or the contrary. In the following instances the sentiments are too gay for a serious passion:

No happier task these faded eyes pursue;
To read and weep is all they now can do.
Eloisa to Abelard, l. 47.

Again:

Heaven first taught letters for some wretch's aid,
Some banish'd lover, or some captive maid;
They live, they speak, they breathe what love inspires,
Warm from the soul, and faithful to its fires;
The virgin's wish without her fears impart,
Excuse the blush, and pour out all the heart;
Speed the soft intercourse from soul to soul,
And waft a sigh from Indus to the pole.
Eloisa to Abelard, l. 51.

These thoughts are pretty: they suit Pope, but not Eloisa.

Satan, enraged by a threatening of the angel Gabriel, answers thus:

Then when I am thy captive, talk of chains,
Proud limitary cherub; but ere then,
Far heavier load thyself expect to feel
From my prevailing arm, though Heaven's King
Ride on thy wings, and thou with thy compeers,
Used to the yoke, draw'st his triumphant wheels
In progress through the road of heaven *star-paved.*
Paradise Lost, Book iv.

The concluding epithet forms a grand and delightful image, which cannot be the genuine offspring of rage.

---

385. Sentiments below the tone of the passion Ptolemy's speech.
386. Sentiments that agree not with the tone of the passion, as to gayety or seriousness. *Eloise to Abelard*, &c.

387. Fourth. Sentiments too artificial for a serious passion. I give for the first example a speech of Percy expiring:

> O Harry, thou hast robb'd me of my growth;
> I better brook the loss of brittle life,
> Than those proud titles thou hast won of me;
> They wound my thoughts, worse than thy sword my flesh.
> But thought's the slave of life, and life time's fool:
> And time, that takes survey of all the world,
> Must have a stop. *First Part of Henry IV.* Act V. Sc. 9.

The sentiments of the *Mourning Bride* are, for the most part, no less delicate than just copies of nature: in the following exception the picture is beautiful, but too artful to be suggested by severe grief:

> *Almeria.* O no! Time gives increase to my afflictions
> The circling hours, that gather all the woes
> Which are diffused through the revolving year,
> Come heavy laden with th' oppressive weight
> To me; with me, successively they leave
> The sighs, the tears, the groans, the restless cares,
> And all the damps of grief, that did retard their flight;
> They shake their downy wings, and scatter all
> The dire collected dews on my poor head;
> They fly with joy and swiftness from me. Act I. Sc. 1.

In the same play, Almeria seeing a dead body, which she took to be Alphonso's, expresses sentiments strained and artificial, which nature suggests not to any person upon such an occasion:

> Had they or hearts or eyes, that did this deed?
> Could eyes endure to guide such cruel hands?
> Are not my eyes guilty alike with theirs,
> That thus can gaze, and yet not turn to stone?
> —I do not weep! The springs of tears are dried,
> And of a sudden I am calm, as if
> All things were well; and yet my husband's murder'd!
> Yes, yes, I know to mourn: I'll sluice this heart,
> The source of woe, and let the torrent loose. Act V. Sc. II.

Lady Trueman. How could you be so cruel to defer giving me that joy which you knew I must receive from your presence? You have robbed my life of some hours of happiness that ought to have been in it.—*Drummer*, Act V.

Pope's Elegy to the memory of an unfortunate lady, expresses delicately the most tender concern and sorrow that one can feel for the deplorable fate of a person of worth. Such a poem, deeply serious and pathetic, rejects with disdain all fiction. Upon that account, the following passage deserves no quarter; for it is not the language of the heart, but of the imagination indulging its flights at ease, and by that means is eminently discordant with the subject. It would be a still more severe censure, if it should be ascribed to imitation, copying indiscreetly what has been said by others:

> What though no weeping loves thy ashes grace,
> Nor polish'd marble emulate thy face?
> What though no sacred earth allow thee room,
> Nor hallow'd dirge be mutter'd o'er thy tomb?
> Yet shall thy grave with rising flow'rs be drest,
> And the green turf lie lightly on thy breast:

There shall the morn her earliest tears bestow,
There the first roses of the year shall blow;
While angels, with their silver wings, o'ershade
The ground, now sacred by thy relics made.

388. Fifth. Fanciful or finical sentiments. Sentiments that degenerate into point or conceit, however they may amuse in an idle hour, can never be the offspring of any serious or important passion. In the *Jerusalem* of Tasso, Tancred, after a single combat, spent with fatigue and loss of blood, falls into a swoon; in which situation, understood to be dead, he is discovered by Erminia, who was in love with him to distraction. A more happy situation cannot be imagined, to raise grief in an instant to its height; and yet, in venting her sorrow, she descends most abominably into antithesis and conceit even of the lowest kind. (Canto xix. stan. 105.) Armida's lamentation respecting her lover Rinaldo, is in the same vicious taste. (Canto xx. stan. 124, 125, and 126.)

Queen. Give me no help in lamentation,
I am not barren to bring forth complaints:
All springs reduce their currents to mine eyes,
That I, being govern'd by the wat'ry moon,
May send forth plenteous tears to drown the world,
Ah, for my husband, for my dear Lord Edward.
King Richard III. Act II. Sc 2.

Jane Shore. Let me be branded for the public scorn,
Turn'd forth, and driven to wander like a vagabond,
Be friendless and forsaken, seek my bread
Upon the barren wild, and desolate waste;
Feed on my sighs and drink my falling tears,
Ere I consent to teach my lips injustice,
Or wrong the orphan who has none to save him.
Jane Shore, Act IV

Give me your drops, ye soft-descending rains;
Give me your streams, ye never-ceasing springs,
That my sad eyes may still supply my duty,
And feed an everlasting flood of sorrow.—*Jane Shore,* Act V.

Jane Shore utters her last breath in a witty conceit:

Then all is well, and I shall sleep in peace—
'Tis very dark, and I have lost you now—
Was there not something I would have bequeath'd you?
But I have nothing left me to bestow,
Nothing but one sad sigh. Oh mercy, Heaven! [*Dies.*
Act V

Gilford to Lady Jane Gray, when both were condemned to die:

Thou stand'st unmoved;
Calm temper sits upon thy beauteous brow:
Thy eyes, that flow'd so fast for Edward's loss,
Gaze unconcern'd upon the ruin round thee,
As if thou hadst resolved to brave thy fate,
And triumph in the midst of desolation.
Ha! see, it swells, the liquid crystal rises,
It starts in spite of thee—but I will catch it,
Nor let the earth be wet with dew so rich.
Lady Jane Gray, Act IV. near the end.

---

387. Sentiments too artificial for a serious passion. Speech of Percy, &c.

The concluding sentiment is altogether finical, unsuitable to the importance of the occasion, and even to the dignity of the passion of love.

389. Corneille, in his *Examen of the Cid*, answering an objection, That his sentiments are sometimes too much refined for persons in deep distress, observes, that if poets did not indulge sentiments more ingenious or refined than are prompted by passion, their performances would often be low, and extreme grief would never suggest but exclamations merely. This is, in plain language, to assert that forced thoughts are more agreeable than those that are natural, and ought to be preferred.

390. The second class is of sentiments that may belong to an ordinary passion, but are not perfectly concordant with it, as tinctured by a singular character.

In the last act of that excellent comedy, *The Careless Husband*, Lady Easy, upon Sir Charles's reformation, is made to express more violent and turbulent sentiments of joy than are consistent with the mildness of her character:

Lady Easy. O the soft treasure! O the dear reward of long-desiring love.—Thus! thus to have you mine, is something more than happiness; 'tis double life, and madness of abounding joy.

If the sentiments of a passion ought to be suited to a peculiar character, it is still more necessary that actions be suited to the character. In the fifth act of the *Drummer*, Addison makes his gardener act even below the character of an ignorant, credulous rustic: he gives him the behavior of a gaping idiot.

391. The following instances are descriptions rather than sentiments, which compose a third class.

Of this descriptive manner of painting the passions, there is in the *Hippolytus* of Euripides (Act V.) an illustrious instance, namely, the speech of Theseus, upon hearing of his son's dismal exit. In Racine's tragedy of *Esther*, the queen, hearing of the decree issued against her people, instead of expressing sentiments suitable to the occasion, turns her attention upon herself, and describes with accuracy her own situation:

Juste Ciel! tout mon sang dans mes veines se glace.
Act I. Sc. 3.

A man stabbed to the heart in a combat with his enemy, expresses himself thus:

So, now I am at rest:———
I feel death rising higher still, and higher,
Within my bosom; every breath I fetch
Shuts up my life within a shorter compass:

---

388. Fanciful sentiments.—*Jerusalem* of Tasso. *Richard III.*, &c.
389. Corneille's answer to the objection that his sentiments are too refined.
390. Sentiments not concordant with an ordinary passion.—*Lady Easy.*– Actions should be suited to the character.
391. Instances of descriptions rather than sentiments. Example from Dryden; from Paradise Lost.

And like the vanishing sound of bells, grows less
And less each pulse, till it be lost in air.—*Dryden.*

An example is given above of remorse and despair expressed by genuine and natural sentiments. In the fourth book of *Paradise Lost*, Satan is made to express his remorse and despair in sentiments which, though beautiful, are not altogether natural: they are rather the sentiments of a spectator, than of a person who actually is tormented with these passions.

392. The fourth class is of sentiments introduced too early or too late.

Some examples mentioned above belong to this class. Add the following from *Venice Preserved* (Act V.), at the close of the scene between Belvidera and her father Priuli. The account given by Belvidera of the danger she was in, and of her husband's threatening to murder her, ought naturally to have alarmed her relenting father, and to have made him express the most perturbed sentiments. Instead of which he dissolves into tenderness and love for his daughter, as if he had already delivered her from danger, and as if there were a perfect tranquillity:

Canst thou forgive me all my follies past?
I'll henceforth be indeed a father; never,
Never more thus expose, but cherish thee,
Dear as the vital warmth that feeds my life,
Dear as those eyes that weep in fondness o'er thee:
Peace to thy heart.

393. Immoral sentiments exposed in their native colors, instead of being concealed or disguised, compose the fifth class.

The Lady Macbeth, projecting the death of the king, has the following soliloquy:

——————The raven himself is hoarse
That croaks the fatal entrance of Duncan
Under my battlements. Come, all you spirits
That tend on mortal thoughts, unsex me here,
And fill me from the crown to th' toe, top-full
Of direst cruelty; make thick my blood,
Stop up th' access and passage to remorse,
That no compunctious visitings of nature
Shake my fell purpose. *Macbeth*, Act I. Sc. 7.

This speech is not natural. A treacherous murder was never perpetrated even by the most hardened miscreant, without compunction: and that the lady here must have been in horrible agitation, appears from her invoking the infernal spirits to fill her with cruelty, and to stop up all avenues to remorse. But in that state of mind, it is a never-failing artifice of self-deceit, to draw the thickest veil over the wicked action, and to extenuate it by all the circumstances that imagination can suggest; and if the crime cannot bear disguise, the next attempt is to thrust it out of mind altogether, and to rush on to action without thought. This last was the husband's method:

---

392. Sentiments introduced unseasonably.—*Venice Preserved.*

> Strange things I have in head, that will to hand;
> Which must be acted ere they must be scann'd.—Act III. Sc. 5.

The lady follows neither of these courses, but in a deliberate manner endeavors to fortify her heart in the commission of an execrable crime, without even attempting to color it. This I think is not natural: I hope there is no such wretch to be found as is here represented.

In Congreve's *Double-dealer*, Maskwell, instead of disguising or coloring his crimes, values himself upon them in a soliloquy:

> Cynthia, let thy beauty gild my crimes; and whatsoever I commit of treachery or deceit, shall be imputed to me as a merit.——Treachery! what treachery? Love cancels all the bonds of friendship, and sets men right upon their first foundations.

In French plays, love, instead of being hid or disguised, is treated as a serious concern, and of greater importance than fortune, family, or dignity. I suspect the reason to be, that, in the capital of France, love, by the easiness of intercourse, has dwindled down from a real passion to be a connection that is regulated entirely by the mode or fashion.

394. The last class comprehends sentiments that are unnatural, as being suited to no character or passion. These may be subdivided into three branches: first, sentiments unsuitable to the constitution of man, and to the laws of his nature; second, inconsistent sentiments; third, sentiments that are pure rant and extravagance.

When the fable is of human affairs, every event, every incident, and every circumstance, ought to be natural, otherwise the imitation is imperfect. But an imperfect imitation is a venial fault, compared with that of running cross to nature. In the *Hippolytus* of Euripides (Act IV. Sc. 5), Hippolytus, wishing for another self in his own situation, "How much," says he, "should I be touched with his misfortune!" as if it were natural to grieve more for the misfortunes of another than for one's own.

> *Osmyn.* Yet I behold her—yet—and now no more.
> Turn your lights inward, eyes, and view my thought.
> So shall you still behold her—'twill not be.
> O impotence of sight! mechanic sense
> Which to exterior objects owest thy faculty,
> Not seeing of election, but necessity.
> Thus do our eyes, as do all common mirrors,
> Successively reflect succeeding images.
> Nor what they would, but must; a star or toad;
> Just as the hand of chance administers!
>
> *Mourning Bride*, Act II. Sc. 8.

No man in his senses, ever thought of applying his eyes to discover what passes in his mind; far less of blaming his eyes for not seeing a thought or idea. In Molière's *L'Avare* (Act IV. Sc. 7), Harpagon being robbed of his money, seizes himself by the arm, mistaking it for that of the robber. And again he expresses himself as follows:

---

393. Immoral sentiments exposed instead of being concealed.—Lady Macbeth's soliloquy. Not natural.—Remarks on French plays.

394. Sentiments unnatural. Three branches.—Examples of sentiments unsuitable to the constitution of man.

Je veux aller quérir la justice, et faire donner la question à toute ma maison à servantes, à valets, à fils, à fille, et à moi aussi.

395. Of the second branch the following are examples.

——————Now bid me run,
And I will strive with things impossible,
Yea, get the better of them.—*Julius Cæsar*, Act II. Sc. 3.

Vos mains seule sont droit de vaincre un invincible.
Le Cid, Act V. Sc. last.

Que son nom soit béni. Que son nom soit chanté,
Que l'on célèbre ses ouvrages
Au de là de l'éternité.—*Esther*, Act V. Sc. last.

Me miserable! which way shall I fly
Infinite wrath and infinite despair?
Which way I fly is hell: myself am hell;
And in the *lowest* deep, a *lower* deep
Still threatening to devour me, opens wide;
To which the hell I suffer seems a heaven.
Paradise Lost, Book IV.

396. Of the third branch, take the following samples, which are pure rant. Coriolanus, speaking to his mother—

What is this?
Your knees to me? to your corrected son?
Then let the pebbles on the hungry beach
Fillip the stars: then let the mutinous winds
Strike the proud cedars 'gainst the fiery sun:
Murd'ring impossibility, to make
What cannot be, slight work.—*Coriolanus*, Act V. Sc. 3.

Cæsar. ———Danger knows full well,
That Cæsar is more dangerous than he.
We were two lions litter'd in one day,
And I the elder and more terrible.
Julius Cæsar, Act II. Sc. 4

Almanzor. ————I'll hold it fast
As life: and when life's gone, I'll hold this last,
And if thou tak'st it after I am slain,
I'll send my ghost to fetch it back again.
Conquest of Granada, Part II. Act 3.

So much upon sentiments; the language proper for expressing them, comes next in order.

CHAPTER XVII.

LANGUAGE OF PASSION.

397. Among the particulars that compose the social part of our nature, a propensity to communicate our opinions, our emotions, and every thing that affects us, is remarkable. Bad fortune and injustice affect us greatly; and of these we are so prone to complain, that if we have no friend or acquaintance to take part in our sufferings,

395. Examples of inconsistent sentiments.
396. Examples of sentiments that are pure rant.

we sometimes utter our complaints aloud, even where there are none to listen.

But this propensity operates not in every state of mind. A man immoderately grieved, seeks to afflict himself, rejecting all consolation: immoderate grief accordingly is mute: complaining is struggling for consolation.

> It is the wretch's comfort still to have
> Some small reserve of near and inward woe.
> Some unsuspected hoard of inward grief,
> Which they unseen may wail, and weep, and mourn,
> And glutton-like alone devour.—*Mourning Bride*, Act I. Sc. 1.

When grief subsides, it then, and no sooner, finds a tongue: we complain, because complaining is an effort to disburden the mind of its distress.*

398. Surprise and terror are silent passions for a different reason: they agitate the mind so violently as for a time to suspend the exercise of its faculties, and among others the faculty of speech.

Love and revenge, when immoderate, are not more loquacious than immoderate grief. But when these passions become moderate, they set the tongue free, and, like moderate grief, become loquacious: moderate love, when unsuccessful, is vented in complaints; when successful, is full of joy expressed by words and gestures.

As no passion hath any long uninterrupted existence (see chap. ii. part iii.), nor beats away with an equal pulse, the language suggested by passion is not only unequal, but frequently interrupted: and even during an uninterrupted fit of passion, we only express in words the more capital sentiments. In familiar conversation, one who vents every single thought is justly branded with the character of *loquacity;* because sensible people express no thoughts but what make some figure: in the same manner, we are only disposed to express the strongest pulses of passion, especially when it returns with impetuosity after interruption.

---

* This observation is finely illustrated by a story which Herodotus records, b. iii. Cambyses, when he conquered Egypt, made Psammenitus, the king, prisoner; and for trying his constancy, ordered his daughter to be dressed in the habit of a slave, and to be employed in bringing water from the river; his son also was led to execution with a halter about his neck. The Egyptians vented their sorrow in tears and lamentations; Psammenitus only, with a downcast eye, remained silent. Afterwards meeting one of his companions, a man advanced in years, who, being plundered of all, was begging alms, he wept bitterly, calling him by his name. Cambyses, struck with wonder, demanded an answer to the following question: "Psammenitus, thy master, Cambyses, is desirous to know why, after thou hadst seen thy daughter so ignominiously treated, and thy son led to execution, without exclaiming or weeping, thou shouldst be so highly concerned for a poor man, no way related to thee?" Psammenitus returned the following answer: "Son of Cyrus, the calamities of my family are too great to leave me the power of weeping; but the misfortunes of a companion, reduced in his old age to want of bread, is a fit subject for lamentation."

---

397. Man's propensity to communicate opinions and emotions Not in every state of mind. Illustrate.—Why we utter comp'aints. Story from Herodotus.

398. Surprise and terror, silent passions; why?—Love and revenge, when silent.—The language suggested by passion.—Loquacity.

399 I had occasion to observe (chap. xvi.), that the sentiments ought to be tuned to the passion, and the language to both. Elevated sentiments require elevated language: tender sentiments ought to be clothed in words that are soft and flowing: when the mind is depressed with any passion, the sentiments must be expressed in words that are humble, not low. Words being intimately connected with the ideas they represent, the greatest harmony is required between them: to express, for example, an humble sentiment in high sounding words, is disagreeable by a discordant mixture of feelings; and the discord is not less when elevated sentiments are dressed in low words:

> Versibus exponi tragicis res comica non vult.
> Indignatur item privatis ac prope socco
> Dignis carminibus narrari cœna Thyestæ.—*Horace*, *Ars Poet.* l. 89.

This, however, excludes not figurative expression, which, within moderate bounds, communicates to the sentiment an agreeable elevation. We are sensible of an effect directly opposite, where figurative expression is indulged beyond a just measure: the opposition between the expression and the sentiment, makes the discord appear greater than it is in reality. (See chap. viii.)

400. At the same time, figures are not equally the language of every passion: pleasant emotions, which elevate or swell the mind, vent themselves in strong epithets and figurative expression; but humbling and dispiriting passions affect to speak plain:

> Et tragicus plerumque dolet sermone pedestri.
> Telephus et Peleus, cum pauper et exul uterque;
> Projicit ampullas et sesquipedalia verba,
> Si curat cor spectantis tetigisse querela.—*Horace*, *Ars Poet.* l. 95.

Figurative expression, being the work of an enlivened imagination, cannot be the language of anguish or distress. Otway, sensible of this, has painted a scene of distress in colors finely adapted to the subject: there is scarce a figure in it, except a short and natural simile with which the speech is introduced. Belvidera talking to her father of her husband:

> Think you saw what pass'd at our last parting;
> Think you beheld him like a raging lion,
> Pacing the earth, and tearing up his steps,
> Fate in his eyes, and roaring with the pain
> Of burning fury; think you saw his one hand
> Fix'd on my throat, while the extended other
> Grasp'd a keen threat'ning dagger; oh, 'twas thus
> We last embraced, when, trembling with revenge,
> He dragg'd me to the ground, and at my bosom
> Presented horrid death: cried out, My friends!
> Where are my friends? swore, wept, raged, threaten'd, loved;
> For he yet loved, and that dear love preserved me
> To this last trial of a father's pity.

---

399. The sentiments should be suited to the passion, and the language to both.—The use of figurative expression

I fear not death, but cannot bear a thought
That that dear hand should do the unfriendly office;
If I was ever then your care, now hear me;
Fly to the senate, save the promised lives
Of his dear friends, ere mine be made the sacrifice.
Venice Preserved, Act V.

401. To preserve the aforesaid resemblance between words and their meaning, the sentiments of active and hurrying passions ought to be dressed in words where syllables prevail that are pronounced short or fast; for these make an impression of hurry and precipitation. Emotions, on the other hand, that rest upon their objects, are best expressed by words where syllables prevail that are pronounced long or slow. A person affected with melancholy has a languid and slow train of perceptions: the expression best suited to that state of mind, is where words, not only of long but of many syllables, abound in the composition; and for that reason nothing can be finer than the following passage:

In those deep solitudes, and awful cells,
Where heavenly pensive Contemplation dwells,
And ever-musing melancholy reigns.—*Pope*, *Eloisa to Abelard.*

To preserve the same resemblance, another circumstance is requisite, that the language, like the emotion, be rough or smooth, broken or uniform. Calm and sweet emotions are best expressed by words that glide softly: surprise, fear, and other turbulent passions, require an expression both rough and broken.

It cannot have escaped any diligent inquirer into nature, that, in the hurry of passion, one generally expresses that thing first which is most at heart; which is beautifully done in the following passage:

Me, me; adsum qui feci: in me convertite ferrum,
O Rutuli, mea fraus omnis.—*Æneid*, ix. 427.

402. Passion has also the effect of redoubling words, the better to make them express the strong conception of the mind. This is finely imitated in the following examples:

————Thou sun, said I, fair light!
And thou enlighten'd earth, so fresh and gay!
Ye hills and dales, ye rivers, woods, and plains!
And ye that live, and move, fair creatures! tell,
Tell if ye saw, how came I thus, how here.——
Paradise Lost, Book viii. 27.

————Both have sinn'd! but thou
Against God only; I, 'gainst God and thee:
And to the place of judgment will return.
There with my cries importune heaven, that all
The sentence, from thy head removed, may light
On me, sole cause to thee of all this woe;
Me! me! only just object of his ire.
Paradise Lost, Book x. 980.

---

400. Figures not equally the language of every passion. Not the language of anguish *Otway.*

401. Class of words adapted to sentiments of hurrying passions: to passions that rest on their objects to melancholy.—Language should resemble the emotion, as rough or smooth, &c.—What we express first in the hurry of passion.

Shakspeare is superior to all other writers in delineating passion. It is difficult to say in what part he most excels, whether in moulding every passion to peculiarity of character, in discovering the sentiments that proceed from various tones of passion, or in expressing properly every different sentiment: he disgusts not his reader with general declamation and unmeaning words, too common in other writers; his sentiments are adjusted to the peculiar character and circumstances of the speaker; and the propriety is no less perfect between his sentiments and his diction. That this is no exaggeration, will be evident to every one of taste, upon comparing Shakspeare with other writers in similar passages. If upon any occasion he fall below himself, it is in those scenes where passion enters not: by endeavoring in that case to raise his dialogue above the style of ordinary conversation, he sometimes deviates into intricate thought and obscure expression:* sometimes, to throw his language out of the familiar, he employs rhyme. But may it not in some measure excuse Shakspeare, I shall not say his works, that he had no pattern, in his own or in any living language, of dialogue fitted for the theatre? At the same time it ought not to escape observation, that the stream clears in its progress, and that in his later plays he has attained to purity and perfection of dialogue: an observation that, with greater certainty than tradition, will direct us to arrange his plays in the order of time. This ought to be considered by those who rigidly exaggerate every blemish of the finest genius for the drama ever the world enjoyed: they ought also for their own sake to consider, that it is easier to discover his blemishes, which lie generally at the surface, than his beauties, which cannot be truly relished but by those who dive deep into human nature. One thing must be evident to the meanest capacity, that wherever passion is to be displayed, Nature shows itself mighty in him, and is conspicuous by the most delicate propriety of sentiment and expression.†

---

* Of this take the following specimen:

They clepe us drunkards, and with swinish phrase
Soil our ambition; and, indeed it takes
From our achievements, though perform'd at height,
The pith and marrow of our attribute.
So, oft it chances in particular men,
That for some vicious mole of nature in them
As, in their birth (wherein they are not guilty,
Since nature cannot choose his origin),
By the o'ergrowth of some complexion
Oft breaking down the pales and forts of reason
Or by some habit that too much o'er-leavens
The form of plausive manners; that these men
Carrying, I say, the stamp of one defect
(Being Nature's livery, or Fortune's scar),
Their virtues else, be they as pure as grace,
As infinite as man may undergo,
Shall in the general censure take corruption
For that particular fault. *Hamlet*, Act I. Sc. 7.

† The critics seem not perfectly to comprehend the genius of Shakspeare. His plays are defective in the mechanical part; which is less the work of genius

[It would please us to introduce here nearly all of *Hazlitt's observations upon Shakspeare*; but we have space only for the following:

"The striking peculiarity of Shakspeare's mind was its power of communication with all other minds—so that it contained a universe of thought and feeling within itself, and had no one peculiar bias, or exclusive excellence more than another..... He not only had in himself the germs of every faculty and feeling, but he could follow them by anticipation, intuitively, into all their conceivable ramifications, through every change of fortune or conflict of passion, or turn of thought. He 'had a mind reflecting ages past,' and present: all the people that ever lived are there. He turned the globe round for his amusement, and surveyed the generations of men, and the individuals as they passed, with their different concerns, passions, follies, vices, virtues, actions, and motives—as well those that they knew, as those which they did not know or acknowledge to themselves...... He had only to think of any thing in order to become that thing with all the circumstances belonging to it..... In reading this author, you do not merely learn what his characters say; you see their persons...... A word, an epithet paints a whole scene, or throws us back whole years in the history of the person represented."

"That which, perhaps, more than any thing else distinguishes the dramatic productions of Shakspeare from all others, is this *wonderful truth and individuality of conception.* Each of his characters is as much itself, and as absolutely independent of the rest, as well as of the author, as if they were living persons, not fictions of the mind. The poet may be said, for the time, to identify himself with the character he wishes to represent, and to pass from one to another, like the same soul successively animating different bodies. His plays alone are properly *expressions of the passions, not descriptions of them.* His characters are real beings of flesh and blood: they speak like men, not like authors."

"The passion in Shakspeare is of the same nature as his delineation of character. It is not some one habitual feeling or sentiment, preying upon itself, growing out of itself: it is passion modified by passion, by all the other feelings to which the individual is liable, and to which others are liable with him; subject to all the fluctuations of caprice and accident; calling into play all the resources of the understanding, and all the energies of the will; irritated by obstacles, or yielding to them; rising from small beginnings to its

---

man of experience, and is not otherwise brought to perfection but by diligently observing the errors of former compositions. Shakspeare excels all the ancients and moderns in knowledge of human nature, and in unfolding even the most obscure and refined emotions. This is a rare faculty, which makes him surpass all other writers in the comic as well as tragic vein.

---

402. Passion redoubles words. *Paradise Lost.*—Shakspeare excels in delineating passion. Sometimes fails in scenes where passion enters not. Apologies for him. In what he excels all the ancients and moderns. Hazlitt's observations.

utmost height; now drunk with hope, now stung to madness, now sunk in despair, now blown to air with a breath, now raging like a torrent."]

403. I return to my subject. That perfect harmony which ought to subsist among all the constituent parts of a dialogue, is a beauty no less rare than conspicuous: as to expression in particular, were I to give instances, where, in one or other of the respects above mentioned, it corresponds not precisely to the characters, passions, and sentiments, I might from different authors collect volumes. Following therefore the method laid down in the chapter of sentiments, I shall confine my quotations to the grosser errors, which every writer ought to avoid.

And, first, of passion expressed in words flowing in an equal course without interruption.

In the chapter above cited, Corneille is censured for the impropriety of his sentiments; and here, for the sake of truth, I am obliged to attack him a second time. Were I to give instances from that author of the fault under consideration, I might transcribe whole tragedies; for he is no less faulty in this particular, than in passing upon us his own thoughts as a spectator, instead of the genuine sentiments of passion. Nor would a comparison between him and Shakspeare, upon the present article, redound more to his honor, than the former upon the sentiments.

If, in general, the language of violent passion ought to be broken and interrupted, soliloquies ought to be so in a peculiar manner: language is intended by nature for society; and a man when alone, though he always clothes his thoughts in words, seldom gives his words utterance, unless when prompted by some strong emotion; and even then by starts and intervals only. (Chapter xv.) Shakspeare's soliloquies may justly be established as a model; for it is not easy to conceive any model more perfect: of his many incomparable soliloquies, I confine myself to the two following, being different in their manner:

Hamlet. Oh, that this too solid flesh would melt,
Thaw, and resolve itself into a dew!
Or that the Everlasting had not fix'd
His canon 'gainst self-slaughter! O God! O God!
How weary, stale, flat, and unprofitable
Seem to me all the uses of this world!
Fie on't! O fie! 'tis an unweeded garden,
That grows to seed: things rank and gross in nature
Possess it merely.——That it should come to this!
But two months dead! nay, not so much; not two;—
So excellent a king, that was, to this,
Hyperion to a satyr: so loving to my mother,
That he permitted not the winds of heaven
Visit her face too roughly. Heaven and earth!
Must I remember—why, she would hang on him,
As if increase of appetite had grown
By what it fed on: yet, within a month——
Let me not think—Frailty, thy name is *Woman!*

A little month! or ere those shoes were old,
With which she followed my poor father's body,
Like Niobe, all tears——Why she, even she—
(O heaven! a beast that wants discourse of reason,
Would have mourn'd longer)— married with mine uncle,
My father's brother; but no more like my father,
Than I to Hercules. Within a month!
Ere yet the salt of most unrighteous tears
Had left the flushing in her gauled eyes,
She married——Oh, most wicked speed, to post
With such dexterity to incestuous sheets!
It is not, nor it cannot come to good.
But break, my heart, for I must hold my tongue.

Hamlet, Act I. Sc. 3

Ford. Hum! ha! is this a vision? is this a dream? do I sleep? Mr. Ford, awake; awake, Mr. Ford; there's a hole made in your best coat, Mr. Ford! this 'tis to be married! this 'tis to have linen and buck-baskets! Well, I will proclaim myself what I am; I will now take the lecher; he is at my house; he cannot 'scape me: 'tis impossible he should; he cannot creep into a halfpenny purse, nor into a pepper-box. But lest the devil that guides him should aid him, I will search impossible places, though what I am I cannot avoid, yet to be what I would not, shall not make me tame

Merry Wives of Windsor, Act III. Sc. last.

404. These soliloquies are accurate and bold copies of nature: in a passionate soliloquy one begins with thinking aloud; and the strongest feelings only are expressed; as the speaker warms, he begins to imagine one listening, and gradually slides into a connected discourse.

How far distant are soliloquies generally from these models? So far, indeed, as to give disgust instead of pleasure. The first scene of *Iphigenia* in Tauris discovers that princess, in a soliloquy, gravely reporting to herself her own history. There is the same impropriety in the first scene of *Alcestes*, and in the other introductions of Euripides, almost without exception. Nothing can be more ridiculous: it puts one in mind of a most curious device in Gothic paintings, that of making every figure explain itself by a written label issuing from its mouth.

Corneille is not more happy in his soliloquies than in his dialogues. Take for a specimen the first scene of *Cinna.*

Racine also is extremely faulty in the same respect. His soliloquies are regular harangues, a chain completed in every link, without interruption or interval.

Soliloquies upon lively or interesting subjects, but without any turbulence of passion, may be carried on in a continued chain of thought. If, for example, the nature and sprightliness of the subject prompt a man to speak his thoughts in the form of a dialogue, the expression must be carried on without break or interruption, as in a dialogue between two persons; which justifies Falstaff's soliloquy upon honor:

---

403. Perfect harmony in parts of a dialogue a rare beauty. Errors to be avoided; first, words flowing too equably.—Soliloquies. Shakspeare's, a model.

What need I be so forward with Death, that calls not on me? Well, 'tis no matter, Honor pricks me on. But how if Honor prick me off, when I come on? how then? Can Honor set a leg? No: or an arm? No: or take away the grief of a wound? No. Honor hath no skill in surgery then? No. What is honor? a word. What is that word *honor?* Air: a trim reckoning. Who hath it? He that died a Wednesday. Doth he feel it? No. Doth he hear it? No. Is it insensible then? Yea, to the dead. But will it not live with the living? No. Why? Detraction will not suffer it. Therefore I'll none of it; honor is a mere scutcheon; and so ends my catechism.

First Part of Henry IV. Act V. Sc. 2.

And even without dialogue, a continued discourse may be justified, where a man reasons in a soliloquy upon an important subject; for if in such a case it be at all excusable to think aloud, it is necessary that the reasoning be carried on in a chain; which justifies that admirable soliloquy in *Hamlet* upon life and immortality, being a serene meditation upon the most interesting of all subjects. And the same consideration will justify the soliloquy which introduces the 5th act of Addison's *Cato.*

405. The next class of the grosser errors which all writers ought to avoid, shall be of language elevated above the tone of the sentiment; of which take the following instances:

Zara. Swift as occasion, I
Myself will fly; and earlier than the morn
Wake thee to freedom. Now 'tis late; and yet
Some news few minutes past arrived, which seem'd
To shake the temper of the King——Who knows
What racking cares disease a monarch's bed?
Or love, that late at night still lights his lamp,
And strikes his rays through dusk, and folded lids,
Forbidding rest, may stretch his eyes awake,
And force their balls abroad at this dead hour.
I'll try. *Mourning Bride,* Act III. Sc. 4.

The language here is undoubtedly too pompous and labored for describing so simple a circumstance as absence of sleep.

406. Language too artificial or too figurative for the gravity, dignity, or importance of the occasion, may be put in a third class.

Chimène demanding justice against Rodrigue who killed her father, instead of a plain and pathetic expostulation, makes a speech stuffed with the most artificial flowers of rhetoric:

Sire, mon père est mort, mes yeux ont vu son sang
Couler à gros bouillons de son généreux flanc:
Ce sang qui tant de fois garantit vos murailles,
Ce sang qui tant de fois vous gagna des batailles,
Ce sang qui, tout sorti, fume encore de courroux
De se voir répandu pour d'autres que pour vous,
Qu'au milieu des hasards n'osait verser la guerre,
Rodrigue en votre cour vient d'en couvrir la terre.
J'ai couru sur le lieu sans force, et sans couleur:
Je l'ai trouvé sans vie. Excusez ma douleur,
Sire; la voix me manque à ce récit funeste,
Mes pleurs et mes soupirs vous diront mieux le reste.

---

404. Properties of a natural soliloquy. Authors that fail in this.—Soliloquies without turbulence of passion how constructed. *Falstaff. Hamlet.*

405. Error of language elevated above the tone of the sentiment. *Mourning Bride.*

Nothing can be contrived in language more averse to the tone of the passion than this florid speech: I should imagine it more apt to provoke laughter than to inspire concern or pity.

407. In a fourth class shall be given specimens of language too light or airy for a severe passion.

Imagery and figurative expression are discordant, in the highest degree, with the agony of a mother who is deprived of two hopeful sons by a brutal murder. Therefore the following passage is undoubtedly in a bad taste:

> *Queen.* Ah, my poor princes! ah, my tender babes!
> My unblown flowers, new appearing sweets!
> If yet your gentle souls fly in the air,
> And be not fixt in doom perpetual,
> Hover about me with your airy wings,
> And hear your mother's lamentation.—*Richard III.* Act IV.

Again:

> *K. Philip.* You are as fond of grief as of your child.
> *Constance.* Grief fills the room up of my absent child,
> Lies in his bed, walks up and down with me,
> Puts on his pretty looks, repeats his words,
> Remembers me of all his gracious parts,
> Stuffs out his vacant garment with his form;
> Then have I reason to be fond of grief.
> *King John*, Act III. Sc. 6.

408. A thought that turns upon the expression instead of the subject, commonly called *a play of words*, being low and childish, is unworthy of any composition, whether gay or serious, that pretends to any degree of elevation: thoughts of this kind make a fifth class.

> To die is to be banish'd from myself:
> And Sylvia is myself: banish'd from her,
> Is self from self; a deadly banishment!
> *Two Gentlemen of Verona*, Act III. Sc. 3.

> *Countess.* I pray thee, lady, have a better cheer:
> If thou engrossest all the griefs as thine,
> Thou robb'st me of a moiety.
> *All's Well that Ends Well*, Act III. Sc. 3.

> *K. Henry.* O my poor kingdom, sick with civil blows!
> When that my care could not withhold thy riot,
> What wilt thou do when riot is thy care?
> Oh, thou wilt be a wilderness again,
> Peopled with wolves, thy old inhabitants.
> *Second Part Henry IV.* Act IV. Sc. 4.

> Cruda Amarilla, che col nome ancora
> D'amar, ahi lasso, amaramente insegni.
> *Pastor Fido*, Act I. Sc. 1

Antony, speaking of Julius Cæsar:

> O world! thou wast the forest of this hart:
> And this, indeed, O world, the heart of thee.
> How like a deer, stricken by many princes,
> Dost thou here lie! *Julius Cæsar*, Act III. Sc. 3.

---

406. Language too artificial or figurative for the occasion.
407. Too light or airy for a severe passion.—*Richard III. King John.*

Playing thus with the sound of words, which is still worse than a pun, is the meanest of all conceits. But Shakspeare, when he descends to a play of words, is not always in the wrong; for it is done sometimes to denote a peculiar character, as in the following passage:

K. Philip. What say'st thou, boy? look in the lady's face.
Lewis. I do, my lord, and in her eye I find
A wonder, or a wond'rous miracle;
The shadow of myself form'd in her eye;
Which, being but the shadow of your son,
Becomes a sun, and makes your son a shadow.
I do protest, I never loved myself
Till now infixed I beheld myself
Drawn in the flatt'ring table of her eye.
Faulconbridge. Drawn in the flatt'ring table of her eye!
Hang'd in the frowning wrinkle of her brow!
And quarter'd in her heart! he doth espy
Himself Love's traitor: this is pity now;
That hang'd, and drawn, and quarter'd, there should be
In such a love so vile a lout as he.—*King John*, Act II. Sc. 5.

409. A jingle of words is the lowest species of that low wit: which is scarce sufferable in any case, and least of all in an heroic poem; and yet Milton, in some instances, has descended to that puerility:

And brought into the world a world of woe.
——begirt th' Almighty throne
Beseeching or besieging———
Which tempted our attempt———
At one slight bound high overleap'd all bound.
——————With a shout
Loud as from number without numbers.

One should think it unnecessary to enter a caveat against an expression that has no meaning, or no distinct meaning; and yet somewhat of that kind may be found even among good writers. Such make a sixth class.

Cleopatra. Now, what news, my Charmion?
Will he be kind? and will he not forsake me?
Am I to live or die? nay, do I live?
Or am I dead? for when he gave his answer,
Fate took the word, and then I lived or died.
Dryden, *All for Love*, Act II

If she be coy, and scorn my noble fire,
If her chill heart I cannot move;
Why, I'll enjoy the very love,
And make a mistress of my own desire.
Cowley, poem inscribed *The Request*.

His whole poem, inscribed *My Picture*, is a jargon of the same kind.

——————'Tis he, they cry, by whom
Not men, but war itself is overcome.—*Indian Queen*.

Such empty expressions are finely ridiculed in the *Rehearsal:*

Was't not unjust to ravish hence her breath,
And in life's stead to leave us naught but death.—Act IV. Sc. 1.

---

408. Play of words. Examples from Shakspeare. When justifiable.
409. Jingle of words. Instance from Milton.—Expressions that have no distinct meaning to be avoided.

CHAPTER XVIII.

BEAUTY OF LANGUAGE.

410. Of all the fine arts, painting only and sculpture are in their nature imitative.* An ornamented field is not a copy or imitation

* [This remark of our author requires some qualification. A masterly view of the case is presented in the Third Discourse of Sir Joshua Reynolds, from which the following extracts are taken.—*Ed.*

"Nature herself is not to be too closely copied. There are excellencies in the art of painting beyond what is commonly called the imitation of nature. . . . . . A mere copier of nature can never produce any thing great; can never raise and enlarge the conceptions, or warm the heart of the spectator.

"The principle now laid down, that the perfection of this art does not consist in mere imitation, is far from being new or singular. It is, indeed, supported by the general opinion of the enlightened part of mankind. The poets, orators, and rhetoricians of antiquity are continually enforcing this position, that all the arts receive their perfection from an ideal beauty, superior to what is to be found in individual nature."

"All the objects which are exhibited to our view by nature, upon close examination will be found to have their blemishes and defects. The most beautiful forms have something about them like weakness, minuteness, or imperfection. But it is not every eye that perceives these blemishes. It must be an eye long used to the contemplation and comparison of these forms; and which, by a long habit of observing what any set of objects of the same kind have in common, has acquired the power of discerning what each wants in particular. This long laborious comparison should be the first study of the painter who aims at the "great style" (the *beau idéal* of the French). By this means he acquires a just idea of beautiful forms; he corrects nature by herself, her imperfect state by her more perfect. His eye being enabled to distinguish the accidental deficiencies, excrescences, and deformities of things from their general figures, he makes out an abstract idea of their forms more perfect than any one original; and, what may seem a paradox, he learns *to design naturally by drawing his figures unlike to any one object.* This idea of the perfect state of nature, which the artist calls the Ideal Beauty, is the great leading principle by which works of genius are conducted. By this Phidias acquired his fame."

"Thus it is from a reiterated experience and a close comparison of the objects in nature, that an artist becomes possessed of the idea of that central form, if I may so express it, from which every deviation is deformity. But the investigation of this form, I grant, is painful, and I know but of one method of shortening the road; that is by a careful study of the works of the ancient sculptors; who, being indefatigable in the school of nature, have left models of that perfect form behind them which an artist would prefer as supremely beautiful, who had spent his whole life in that single contemplation."—*Works*, vol. i. discourse iii.

Upon statuary, the same critical writer, in a similar strain, remarks:

"In strict propriety, the Grecian statues only excel nature by bringing together such an assemblage of beautiful parts as nature was never known to bestow on one object:

For earth-born graces sparingly impart
The symmetry supreme of perfect art.

It must be remembered that the component parts of the most perfect statue never can excel nature,—that we can form no idea of beauty beyond her works; we can only make this rare assemblage an assemblage so rare that if we are to of nature, but nature itself embellished. Architecture is productive of originals, and copies not from nature. Sound and motion may in some measure be imitated by music; but for the most part music, like architecture, is productive of originals. Language copies not from nature more than music or architecture; unless where, like music, it is imitative of sound or motion. Thus, in the description of particular sounds, language sometimes furnisheth words, which, besides their customary power of exciting ideas, resemble by their softness or harshness the sounds described; and there are words which, by the celerity or slowness of pronunciation, have some resemblance to the motion they signify. The imitative power of words goes one step farther: the loftiness of some words makes them proper symbols of lofty ideas; a rough subject is imitated by harsh-sounding words; and words of many syllables, pronounced slow and smooth, are expressive of grief and melancholy. Words have a separate effect on the mind, abstracting from their signification and from their imitative power: they are more or less agreeable to the ear by the fulness, sweetness, faintness, or roughness of their tones.

411. These are but faint beauties, being known to those only who have more than ordinary acuteness of perception. Language possesseth a beauty superior greatly in degree, of which we are eminently sensible when a thought is communicated with perspicuity and sprightliness. This beauty of language, arising from its power of expressing thought, is apt to be confounded with the beauty of the thought itself: the beauty of thought, transferred to the expression, makes it appear more beautiful.* But these beauties, if we wish to think accurately, must be distinguished from each other. They are in reality so distinct that we sometimes are conscious of the highest pleasure language can afford, when the subject expressed is disagreeable: a thing that is loathsome, or a scene of horror to make one's hair stand on end, may be described in a manner so lively as that the disagreeableness of the subject shall not even obscure the agreeableness of the description. The causes of the original beauty of language, considered as significant, which is a branch

give the name of Monster to what is uncommon, we might, in the words of the Duke of Buckingham, call it

A faultless Monster which the world ne'er saw."

Sir J. Reynolds' Works, vol. ii. p. 311.]

* Chapter ii. part i. sec. 5. Demetrius Phalereus (*of Elocution*, sec. 75) makes the same observation. We are apt, says that author, to confound the language with the subject; and if the latter be nervous, we judge the same of the former. But they are clearly distinguishable; and it is not uncommon to find subjects of great dignity dressed in mean language. Theopompus is celebrated for the force of his diction, but erroneously; his subject indeed has great force, but his style very little.

410. The fine arts that are imitative. Sir Joshua Reynold's observations on this point. -The author's remarks on gardening, architecture, language, music.—Imitative power of words.—Agreeableness to the ear.

of the present subject, will be explained in their order. I shall only at present observe that this beauty is the beauty of means fitted to an end, that of communicating thought; and hence it evidently appears, that of several expressions all conveying the same thought, the most beautiful, in the sense now mentioned, is that which in the most perfect manner answers its end.

The several beauties of language above mentioned, being of different kinds, ought to be handled separately. I shall begin with those beauties of language that arise from sound; after which will follow the beauties of language considered as significant; this order appears natural, for the sound of a word is attended to before we consider its signification. In a third section come those singular beauties of language that are derived from a resemblance between sound and signification. The beauties of verse are handled in the last section; for though the foregoing beauties are found in verse as well as in prose, yet verse has many peculiar beauties, which, for the sake of connection, must be brought under one view; and versification, at any rate, is a subject of so great importance as to deserve a place by itself.

SECTION I.

Beauty of Language with respect to Sound.

412. THIS subject requires the following order: The sounds of the different letters come first; next, these sounds as united in syllables; third, syllables united in words; fourth, words united in a period; and, in the last place, periods united in a discourse.

With respect to the first article, every vowel is sounded with a single expiration of air from the windpipe through the cavity of the mouth. By varying this cavity, the different vowels are sounded; for the air in passing through cavities differing in size, produceth various sounds, some high or sharp, some low or flat: a small cavity occasions a high sound, a large cavity a low sound. The five vowels accordingly, pronounced with the same extension of the windpipe, but with different openings of the mouth, form a regular series of sounds, descending from high to low, in the following order, *i*, *e*, *a*, *o*, *u*.* Each of these sounds is agreeable to the ear; and if it be required which of them is the most agreeable, it is perhaps safest to hold that those vowels which are the farthest removed from the ex-

* In this scale of sounds, the letter *i* must be pronounced as in the word *interest*, and as in other words beginning with the syllable *in*; the letter *e* as in *persuasion*; the letter *a* as in *bat*; and the letter *u* as in *number*.

411. A superior beauty of language; apt to be confounded with what?—Remark of Demetrius Phalereus.—Beauty of language and of thought to be distinguished.—The several beauties of language that are to be handled.

tremes will be the most relished. This is all I have to remark upon the first article: for consonants being letters that of themselves have no sound, serve only in conjunction with vowels to form articulate sounds; and as every articulate sound makes a syllable, consonants come naturally under the second article, to which we proceed.

A consonant is pronounced with a less cavity than any vowel; and consequently every syllable into which a consonant enters, must have more than one sound, though pronounced with one expiration of air, or with one breath, as commonly expressed; for however readily two sounds may unite, yet where they differ in tone, both of them must be heard if neither of them be suppressed. For the same reason, every syllable must be composed of as many sounds as there are letters, supposing every letter to be distinctly pronounced.

413. We next inquire how far syllables are agreeable to the ear. Few tongues are so polished as entirely to have rejected sounds that are pronounced with difficulty; and it is a noted observation, That such sounds are to the ear harsh and disagreeable. But with respect to agreeable sounds, it appears that a double sound is always more agreeable than a single sound: every one who has an ear must be sensible that the diphthong *oi* or *ai* is more agreeable than any of these vowels pronounced singly: the same holds where a consonant enters into the double sound; the syllable *le* has a more agreeable sound than the vowel *e*, or than any other vowel.

Having discussed syllables, we proceed to words; which make the third article. Monosyllables belong to the former head; polysyllables open a different scene. In a cursory view, one would imagine, that the agreeableness or disagreeableness of a word with respect to its sound, should depend upon the agreeableness or disagreeableness of its component syllables, which is true in part, but not entirely; for we must also take under consideration the effect of syllables in succession. In the first place, syllables in immediate succession, pronounced each of them with the same or nearly the same aperture of the mouth, produce a succession of weak and feeble sounds; witness the French words *dit-il*, *pathétique:* on the other hand, a syllable of the greatest aperture succeeding one of the smallest, on the contrary, makes a succession which, because of its remarkable disagreeableness, is distinguished by a proper name, *hiatus.* The most agreeable succession is, where the cavity is increased and diminished alternately within moderate limits. Examples, *alternative*, *longevity*, *pusillanimous.* Secondly, words consisting wholly of syllables pronounced slow, or of syllables pronounced quick, commonly called *long* and *short syllables*, have little melody in them: witness the words *petitioner*, *fruiterer*, *dizziness:* on the other hand, the intermixture of long and short syllables is remarkably agreeable; for example, *degree*, *repent*, *wonderful*, *altitude*, *rapidity*, *independent*,

---

412. The order of the subject.—The vowel sounds. How pronounced. The consonant sound.

*impetuosity.** The cause will be explained afterwards, in treating of versification.

Distinguishable from the beauties above mentioned, there is a beauty of some words which arises from their signification: when the emotion raised by the length or shortness, the roughness or smoothness of the sound, resembles in any degree what is raised by the sense, we feel a very remarkable pleasure. But this subject belongs to the third section.

414. The foregoing observations afford a standard to every nation, for estimating, pretty accurately, the comparative merit of the words that enter into their own language; but they are not equally useful in comparing the words of different languages, which will thus appear. Different nations judge differently of the harshness or smoothness of articulate sounds; a sound, for example, harsh and disagreeable to an Italian, may be abundantly smooth to a northern ear; here every nation must judge for itself; nor can there be any solid ground for a preference, when there is no common standard to which we can appeal. The case is precisely the same as in behavior and manners; plain-dealing and sincerity, liberty in words and actions, form the character of one people; politeness, reserve, and a total disguise of every sentiment that can give offence, form the character of another people: to each the manners of the other are disagreeable. An effeminate mind cannot bear the least of that roughness and severity which is generally esteemed manly, when exerted upon proper occasions; neither can an effeminate ear bear the harshness of certain words, that are deemed nervous and sounding by those accustomed to a rougher tone of speech. Must we then relinquish all thoughts of comparing languages in point of roughness and smoothness, as a fruitless inquiry? Not altogether; for we may proceed a certain length, though without hope of an ultimate decision. A language pronounced with difficulty even by natives, must yield to a smoother language; and supposing two languages pronounced with equal facility by natives, the rougher language, in my judgment, ought to be preferred, provided it be also stored with a competent share of more mellow sounds, which will be evident from attending to the different effects that articulate sound hath on the mind. A smooth gliding sound is agreeable, by calming the mind and lulling it to rest: a rough, bold sound, on the contrary, animates the mind; the effect perceived in pronouncing, is communicated to the hearers, who feel in their own minds a simi-

* Italian words, like those of Latin and Greek, have this property almost universally: English and French words are generally deficient. In the former, the long syllable is removed from the end, as far as the sound will permit; and in the latter, the last syllable is generally long. For example, Sēnator, in English; Senātor, in Latin; and Senateūr in French.

413. How far syllables are agreeable to the ear.—The agreeableness of words not dependent on that of the component syllables.—Effect of syllables in succession.—Various kinds of successions.

lar effort, rousing their attention, and disposing them to action I add another consideration: the agreeableness of contrast in the rougher language, for which the great variety of sounds gives ample opportunity, must, even in an effeminate ear, prevail over the more uniform sounds of the smoother language.* This appears all that can be safely determined upon the present point.

That the English tongue, originally harsh, is at present much softened by dropping in the pronunciation many redundant consonants, is undoubtedly true: that it is not capable of being further mellowed without suffering in its force and energy, will scarce be thought by any one who possesses an ear; and yet such in Britain is the propensity for dispatch, that overlooking the majesty of words composed of many syllables aptly connected, the prevailing taste is to shorten words, even at the expense of making them disagreeable to the ear, and harsh in the pronunciation.

["There is little reason to doubt that the guttural sounds formerly made a part of the most approved pronunciation of English. The analogy, in this respect, of the German, Swedish, Danish, and Saxon, the prevalence of these sounds in some of the provinces of England, and their general use in the Lowland part of Scotland, which certainly derived its language from England, concur to support this opinion. The expulsion of the guttural sounds from the polite pronunciation of English, whilst they are retained in all the other tongues of Saxon original, cannot be accounted for so plausibly as from the superior refinement of the English ear, to that of the other nations who employ languages descended from the same source.—*Barron's Lect.* vol. i. p. 35."]

415. The article next in order, is the music of words as united in a period. We may assume as a maxim, which will hold in the composition of language as well as of other subjects, That a strong impulse succeeding a weak, makes double impression on the mind: and that a weak impulse succeeding a strong, makes scarce any impression.

After establishing this maxim, we can be at no loss about its application to the subject in hand. The following rule is laid down by Diomedes. "In verbis observandum est, ne a majoribus ad minora descendat oratio; melius enim dicitur, *Vir est optimus*, quam *Vir optimus est*." This rule is also applicable to entire members of a period, which, according to our author's expression, ought not, more than single words, to proceed from the greater to the less, but from the less to the greater. In arranging the members of a period,

* That the Italian tongue is too smooth, seems probable, from considering that in versification, vowels are frequently suppressed, in order to produce a rougher and bolder tone.

414. A national standard for comparative merit of words that compose a language.—Advantage of smooth sounds; of rough sounds.—The English language less rough than formerly.

no writer equals Cicero: the beauty of the following examples, out of many, will not suffer me to slur them over by a reference:

> Quicum quæstor fueram,
> Quicum me sors consuetudoque majorum,
> Quicum me deorum hominumque judicium conjunxerat.

Again:

> Habet honorem quem petimus.
> Habet spem quam præpositam nobis habemus,
> Habet existimationem, multo sudore, labore, vigiliisque, collectam.

Again:

> Eripite nos ex miseriis,
> Eripite nos ex faucibus eorum,
> Quorum crudelitas nostro sanguine non potest expleri.
> *De Oratore*, l. i. sect. 52.

This order of words or members gradually increasing in length, may, as far as concerns the pleasure of sound, be denominated *a climax in sound*.

416. The last article is the music of periods as united in a discourse; which shall be dispatched in a very few words. By no other human means is it possible to present to the mind such a number of objects, and in so swift a succession, as by speaking or writing; and for that reason, variety ought more to be studied in these, than in any other sort of composition. Hence a rule for arranging the members of different periods with relation to each other, That to avoid a tedious uniformity of sound and cadence, the arrangement, the cadence, and the length of the members, ought to be diversified as much as possible: and if the members of different periods be sufficiently diversified, the periods themselves will be equally so.

SECTION II.

Beauty of Language with respect to Signification.

417. It is well said by a noted writer (Scott's *Christian Life*), "That by means of speech we can divert our sorrows, mingle our mirth, impart our secrets, communicate our counsels, and make mutual compacts and agreements to supply and assist each other." Considering speech as contributing to so many good purposes, words that convey clear and distinct ideas, must be one of its capital beauties.

In every period, two things are to be regarded: first, the words of which it is composed; next the arrangement of these words: the former resembling the stones that compose a building, and the latter resembling the order in which they are placed. Hence the beauties of language, with respect to signification, may not improperly be

---

415. Music of words in a period.—Maxim concerning strong or weak impulses succeeding each other.—Arrangement of the members of a period.—Climax in sound.
416. Rule for arranging members of different periods in discourse.

distinguished into two kinds: first, the beauties that arise from a right choice of words or materials for constructing the period; and next, the beauties that arise from a due arrangement of these words or materials. I begin with rules that direct us to a right choice of words, and then proceed to rules that concern their arrangement.

418. And with respect to the former, communication of thought being the chief end of language, it is a rule, That perspicuity ought not to be sacrificed to any other beauty whatever: if it should be doubted whether perspicuity be a positive beauty, it cannot be doubted that the want of it is the greatest defect. Nothing therefore in language ought more to be studied, than to prevent all obscurity in the expression; for to have no meaning, is but one degree worse than to have a meaning that is not understood. Want of perspicuity from a wrong arrangement, belongs to the next branch. I shall here give a few examples where the obscurity arises from a wrong choice of words; and as this defect is too common in the ordinary herd of writers to make examples from them necessary, I confine myself to the most celebrated authors.

Livy speaking of a rout after a battle,

> Multique in ruina *Majore* quam fuga oppressi obtruncatique.
> L. iv. sect. 46.

This author is frequently obscure, by expressing but part of his thought, leaving it to be completed by his reader. His description of the sea-fight (l. xxviii. cap. 30) is extremely perplexed.

> Unde tibi reditum *certo subtemine* Parcæ
> Rupere. *Horace*, epod. xiii. 22.

> Qui persæpe cava testudine flevit amorem,
> *Non elaboratum ad pedem.* *Horace*, epod. xiv. 11.

> Me fabulosæ Vulture in Appulo,
> Altricis extra limen Apuliæ,
> Ludo, fatigatumque *somno*,
> Fronde nova puerum palumbes
> Texere. *Horace*, Carm. l. iii. ode 4.

419. There may be a defect in perspicuity proceeding even from the slightest ambiguity in construction; as where the period commences with a member conceived to be in the nominative case, which afterwards is found to be in the accusative. Example: "Some emotions more peculiarly connected with the fine arts, I propose to handle in separate chapters."* Better thus: "Some emotions more peculiarly connected with the fine arts are proposed to be handled in separate chapters."

I add another error against perspicuity; which I mention the

* Elements of Criticism, vol. i. p. 43, first edition.

417. Purposes answered by speech.—One of the capital beauties of speech.—In every period, two things to be regarded.—Beauties of language with respect to signification: two kinds.
418. Rule in regard to perspicuity.

rather because with some writers it passes for a beauty. It is the giving different names to the same object, mentioned oftener than once in the same period. Example: speaking of the English adventurers who first attempted the conquest of Ireland, "and instead of reclaiming the natives from their uncultivated manners, they were gradually assimilated to the ancient inhabitants, and degenerated from the customs of their own nation." From this mode of expression, one would think the author meant to distinguish *the ancient inhabitants* from *the natives;* and we cannot discover otherwise than from the sense, that these are only different names given to the same object for the sake of variety. But perspicuity ought never to be sacrificed to any other beauty, which leads me to think that the passage may be improved as follows: "and degenerating from the customs of their own nation, they were gradually assimilated to the natives, instead of reclaiming them from their uncultivated manners."

420. The next rule in order, because next in importance, is, That the language ought to correspond to the subject: heroic actions or sentiments require elevated language; tender sentiments ought to be expressed in words soft and flowing, and plain language void of ornament is adapted to subjects grave and didactic. Language may be considered as the dress of thought; and where the one is not suited to the other, we are sensible of incongruity, in the same manner as where a judge is dressed like a fop, or a peasant like a man of quality. Where the impression made by the words resembles the impression made by the thought, the similar emotions mix sweetly in the mind, and double the pleasure (chapter ii. part iv.); but where the impressions made by the thought and the words are dissimilar, the unnatural union they are forced into is disagreeable.

421. This concordance between the thought and the words has been observed by every critic, and is so well understood as not to require any illustration. But there is a concordance of a peculiar kind, that has scarcely been touched in works of criticism, though it contributes to neatness of composition. It is what follows. In a thought of any extent, we commonly find some parts intimately united, some slightly, some disjointed, and some directly opposed to each other. To find these conjunctions and disjunctions imitated in the expression, is a beauty; because such imitation makes the words concordant with the sense. This doctrine may be illustrated by a familiar example. When we have occasion to mention the intimate connection that the soul hath with the body, the expression ought to be, *the soul and body;* because the particle *the*, relative to both, makes a connection in the expression, resembling in some degree the connection in the thought; but when the soul is distinguished

---

419. Ambiguity in construction. Example.—Another error against perspicuity. Example.

420. Next rule for language.—The dress of thought.—Impression made by the words and the thought.

from the body, it is better to say *the soul and the body;* because the disjunction in the words resembles the disjunction in the thought.

422. Two members of a thought connected by their relation to the same action, will naturally be expressed by two members of the period governed by the same verb: in which case these members, in order to improve their connection, ought to be constructed in the same manner. This beauty is so common among good writers, as to have been little attended to; but the neglect of it is remarkably disagreeable. For example, "He did not mention Leonora, nor that her father was dead." Better thus: "He did not mention Leonora, nor her father's death."

Where two ideas are so connected as to require but a copulative, it is pleasant to find a connection in the words that express these ideas, were it even so slight as where both begin with the same letter:

The peacock, in all his pride, does not display half the color that appears in the garments of a British lady, when she is either dressed for a ball or a birth-day. *Spectator*, No. 265.

Had not my dog of a steward run away as he did, without making up his accounts, I had still been immersed in sin and sea-coal. *Ibid.* No. 530.

My life's companion, and my bosom-friend,
One faith, one fame, one fate shall both attend.
Dryden, Translation of Æneid.

There is sensibly a defect in neatness when uniformity in this case is totally neglected; witness the following example, where the construction of two members connected by a copulative is unnecessarily varied.

For it is confidently reported, that two young gentlemen of real hopes, bright wit, and profound judgment, who, upon a thorough examination of causes and effects, and by the mere force of natural abilities, without the least tincture of learning, have made a discovery that there was no God, and *generously communicating* their thoughts for the good of the public, were some time ago, by an unparalleled severity, and upon I know not what obsolete law, broke for blasphemy. (*Swift.*) [Better thus:]—having made a discovery that there was no God, and having generously communicated their thoughts for the good of the public, were some time ago, &c.

He had been guilty of a fault, for which his master would have put him to death, had he not found an opportunity to escape out of his hands, and *fled* into the deserts of Numidia. *Guardian*, No. 139.

If all the ends of the Revolution are already obtained, it is not only impertinent to argue for obtaining any of them, but *factious designs might be imputed*, and the name of incendiary be applied with some color, perhaps, to any one who should persist in pressing this point.
Dissertation upon Parties, Dedication.

---

421. A peculiar concordance of word and thought.—Example.
422. Two members of a thought relating to the same action. Example.—Connected ideas, expressed by words somewhat related to each other.—Two members connected by copulative. Examples.

423. Next as to examples of disjunction and opposition in the parts of the thought, imitated in the expression; an imitation that is distinguished by the name of *antithesis*.

Speaking of Coriolanus soliciting the people to be made consul:

> With a proud heart he wore his humble weeds.—*Coriolanus.*

> Had you rather Cæsar were living, and die all slaves, than that Cæsar were dead, to live all freemen? *Julius Cæsar.*

> He hath cool'd my friends and heated mine enemies.—*Shakspeare.*

An artificial connection among the words, is undoubtedly a beauty when it represents any peculiar connection among the constituent parts of the thought; but where there is no such connection, it is a positive deformity, as above observed, because it makes a discordance between the thought and expression. For the same reason we ought also to avoid every artificial opposition of words where there is none in the thought. This last, termed *verbal antithesis*, is studied by low writers, because of a certain degree of liveliness in it. They do not consider how incongruous it is, in a grave composition, to cheat the reader, and to make him expect a contrast in the thought, which upon examination is not found there.

> A *light* wife doth make a *heavy* husband.
> *Merchant of Venice*

Here is a studied opposition in the words, not only without any opposition in the sense, but even where there is a very intimate connection, that of cause and effect; for it is the levity of the wife that torments the husband.

> ———————— Will maintain
> Upon his *bad* life to make all this *good*.
> *King Richard II.* Act I. Sc. 3

> *Lucetta.* What, shall these papers lie like tell-tales here?
> *Julia.* If thou respect them, best to take them up.
> *Lucetta.* Nay, I was *taken up* for *laying them down*.
> *Two Gentlemen of Verona*, Act I. Sc. 3.

424. A fault directly opposite to that last mentioned, is to conjoin artificially words that express ideas opposed to each other. This is a fault too gross to be in common practice; and yet writers are guilty of it in some degree, when they conjoin by a copulative things transacted at different periods of time. Hence a want of neatness in the following expression:

> The nobility too, whom the king had no means of retaining by suitable offices and preferments, had been seized with the general discontent, and unwarily threw themselves into the scale which began already too much to preponderate
> *History of Great Britain*, vol. i. p. 250.

In periods of this kind, it appears more neat to express the past time by the participle passive, thus:

---

423. Examples of disjunction and opposition in the parts of the thought.—Verbal antithesis where there is none in thought. Example.

The nobility having been seized with the general discontent, unwarily threw themselves, &c. (or) The nobility, who had been seized, &c., unwarily threw themselves, &c.

It is unpleasant to find even a negative and affirmative proposition connected by a copulative:

> If it appear not plain, and prove untrue,
> Deadly divorce step between me and you.—*Shakspeare.*

In mirth and drollery it may have a good effect to connect verbally things that are opposite to each other in the thought. Example: Henry IV., of France, introducing the Mareschal Biron to some of his friends, "Here, gentlemen," says he, "is the Mareschal Biron, whom I freely present both to my friends and enemies."

425. This rule of studying uniformity between the thought and expression, may be extended to the construction of sentences or periods. A sentence or period ought to express one entire thought or mental proposition; and different thoughts ought to be separated in the expression by placing them in different sentences or periods. It is therefore offending against neatness, to crowd into one period entire thoughts requiring more than one; which is joining in language things that are separated in reality. Of errors against this rule take the following examples:

Behold, thou art fair, my beloved, yea, pleasant; also our bed is green.

Burnet, in the History of his own Times, giving Lord Sunderland's character, says,

His own notions were always good; but he was a man of great expense.

I have seen a woman's face break out in heats, as she has been talking against a great lord, whom she had never seen in her life; and indeed never knew a party-woman that kept her beauty for a twelvemonth.—*Spectator*, No. 57.

Lord Bolingbroke, speaking of Strada:

I single him out among the moderns, because he had the foolish presumption to censure Tacitus, and to write history himself; and your lordship will forgive this short excursion in honor of a favorite writer.

Letters on History, vol. i. Let. v.

To crowd in a single member of a period different subjects, is still worse than to crowd them into one period.

426. From conjunctions and distinctions in general, we proceed to comparisons, which make one species of them, beginning with similes. And here, also, the intimate connection that words have with their meaning, requires that in describing two resembling objects, a resemblance in the two members of the period ought to be studied. To illustrate the rule in this case, I shall give various examples of deviations from it; beginning with resemblances expressed in words that have no resemblance.

---

424. Conjoining artificially words that express opposite ideas. Example.—Negative and affirmative propositions.
425. Rule for the distribution of thought. Violations of this rule.

I have observed of late, the style of some great *ministers* very much to exceed that of any other *productions.—Letter to the Lord High Treasurer.* Swift.

This, instead of studying the resemblance of words in a period that expresses a comparison, is going out of one's road to avoid it. Instead of *productions*, which resemble not ministers great or small, the proper word is *writers* or *authors*.

If men of eminence are exposed to censure on the one hand, they are as much liable to flattery on the other. If they receive reproaches which are not due to them, they likewise receive praises which they do not deserve.—*Spectator.*

Here the subject plainly demands uniformity in expression instead of variety; and therefore it is submitted, whether the period would not do better in the following manner:

If men of eminence be exposed to censure on the one hand, they are as much exposed to flattery on the other. If they receive reproaches that are not due, they likewise receive praises that are not due.

I cannot but fancy, however, that this imitation, which passes so currently with *other judgments*, must at some time or other have stuck a little with your *lordship*. (Shaftesbury.) [Better thus:] I cannot but fancy, however, that this imitation, which passes so currently with others, must at some time or other have stuck a little with your *lordship*.

They wisely prefer *the generous efforts of good-will and affection* to the reluctant compliances *of such as* obey by force.
Remarks on the History of England, letter v. Bolingbroke.

Speaking of Shakspeare:

There may remain a suspicion that we overrate the greatness of his genius, in the same manner as bodies appear more gigantic on account of their being disproportioned and misshapen.—*History of G. Britain*, vol. i. p. 138.

This is studying variety in a period where the beauty lies in uniformity. Better thus:

There may remain a suspicion that we overrate the greatness of his genius, in the same manner as we overrate the greatness of bodies that are disproportioned and misshapen.

427. Next as to the length of the members that signify the resembling objects. To produce a resemblance between such members, they ought not only to be constructed in the same manner, but as nearly as possible be equal in length. By neglecting this circumstance, the following example is defective in neatness:

As the performance of all other religious duties will not avail in the sight of God, *without charity;* so neither will the discharge of all other ministerial duties avail in the sight of men, *without a faithful discharge of this principal duty.*
Dissertation upon Parties, *Dedication.*

In the following passage are accumulated all the errors that a period expressing a resemblance can well admit:

Ministers are answerable for every thing done to the prejudice of the constitution, in the same proportion as the preservation of the constitution in its purity and vigor, or the perverting and weakening it, are of greater consequence to the nation, than any other instances of good or bad government.
Dissertation upon Parties, Dedication.

---

426. Rule for describing *resembling* objects. Examples of deviations.
427 Rule for the length of the members that signify resembling objects. Examples.

428. Next of a comparison where things are opposed to each other. And here it must be obvious, that if resemblance ought to be studied in the words which express two resembling objects, there is equal reason for studying opposition in the words which express contrasted objects. This rule will be best illustrated by examples of deviations from it:

A friend exaggerates a man's virtues, an enemy inflames his crimes.
Spectator, No. 399.

Here the opposition in the thought is neglected in the words, which at first view seem to import, that the friend and the enemy are employed in different matters, without any relation to each other, whether of resemblance or of opposition, and therefore the contrast or opposition will be better marked by expressing the thought as follows:

A friend exaggerates a man's virtues, an enemy his crimes.

The following are examples of the same kind:

The wise man is happy when he gains his own approbation; the fool when he recommends himself to the applause of those about him.—*Ibid.* No. 73.

Better:

The wise man is happy when he gains his own approbation; the fool when he gains that of others.

429. We proceed to a rule of a different kind. During the course of a period, the scene ought to be continued without variation: the changing from person to person, from subject to subject, or from person to subject, within the bounds of a single period, distracts the mind, and affords no time for a solid impression. I illustrate this rule by giving examples of deviations from it.

Hook, in his Roman history, speaking of Eumenes, who had been beat to the ground with a stone, says,

After a short time *he* came to himself; and the next day *they* put him on board his ship, *which* conveyed him first to Corinth, and thence to the island of Ægina.

I give another example of a period which is unpleasant, even by a very slight deviation from the rule:

That sort of instruction, which is acquired by inculcating an important moral truth, &c.

This expression includes two persons, one acquiring and one inculcating; and the scene is changed without necessity. To avoid this blemish, the thought may be expressed thus:

That sort of instruction which is afforded by inculcating, &c.

The bad effect of such change of person is remarkable in the following passage:

The *Britons*, daily harassed by cruel inroads from the Picts, were forced to call in the Saxons for their defence, *who* consequently reduced the greatest

---

428. Comparison where things are opposed.

part of the island to their own power, drove the Britons into the most remote and mountainous parts, and *the rest of the country*, in customs, religion, and language, became wholly Saxon.—*Letter to the Lord High Treasurer.* Swift.

430. The present head, which relates to the choice of materials, shall be closed with a rule concerning the use of copulatives. Longinus observes, that it animates a period to drop the copulatives; and he gives the following example from Xenophon:

Closing their shields together, they were pushed, they fought, they slew, they were slain. *Treatise of the Sublime*, cap. xvi.

The reason I take to be what follows. A continued sound, if not loud, tends to lay us asleep: an interrupted sound rouses and animates by its repeated impulses. Thus feet composed of syllables, being pronounced with a sensible interval between each, make more lively impressions than can be made by a continued sound. A period of which the members are connected by copulatives, produceth an effect upon the mind approaching to that of a continued sound; and therefore the suppressing of copulatives must animate a description. It produces a different effect akin to that mentioned: the members of a period connected by proper copulatives, glide smoothly and gently along; and are a proof of sedateness and leisure in the speaker: on the other hand, one in the hurry of passion, neglecting copulatives and other particles, expresses the principal image only; and for that reason, hurry or quick action is best expressed without copulatives:

Veni, vidi, vici.

————————Ite:
Ferte citi flammas, date vela, impellite remos.—*Æneid*, iv. 593.

Quis globus, O civis, caligine volvitur atra?
Ferte citi ferrum, dete tela, scandite muros.
Hostis adest, eja. *Æneid*, ix. 37.

431. It follows that a plurality of copulatives in the same period ought to be avoided; for if the laying aside copulatives gives force and liveliness, a redundancy of them must render the period languid. I appeal to the following instance, though there are but two copulatives:

Upon looking over the letters of my female correspondents, I find several from women complaining of jealous husbands; and at the same time protesting their own innocence, and desiring my advice upon this occasion.
Spectator, No. 170.

I except the case where the words are intended to express the coldness of the speaker; for there the redundancy of copulatives is a beauty.

Dining one day at an alderman's in the city, Peter observed him expatiating after the manner of his brethren, in the praises of a sirloin of beef. "Beef," said the sage magistrate, "is the king of meat: Beef comprehends in it the quintessence of partridge, and quail, and venison, and pheasant, and plumb-pudding, and custard." *Tale of a Tub*, sect. 4.

---

429. In a period the scene should not vary.
430. Rule for use of copulatives.—Remark of Longinus.

And the author shows great delicacy of taste by varying the expression in the mouth of Peter, who is represented more animated:

"Bread," says he, "dear brothers, is the staff of life, in which bread is contained, *inclusive*, the quintessence of beef, mutton, veal, venison, partridges, plum-pudding, and custard."

Another case must also be excepted: copulatives have a good effect where the intention is to give an impression of a great multitude consisting of many divisions; for example, "The army was composed of Grecians, and Carians, and Lycians, and Pamphylians, and Phrygians." The reason is, that a leisurely survey, which is expressed by the copulatives, makes the parts appear more numerous than they would do by a hasty survey: in the latter case the army appears in one group; in the former, we take as it were an accurate survey of each nation and of each division. (See *Demetrius Phalereus*, Of Elocution, sect. 63.)

432. We proceed to the second kind of beauty; which consists in a due arrangement of words or materials. This branch of the subject is no less nice than extensive; and I despair of setting it in a clear light, except to those who are well acquainted with the general principles that govern the structure or composition of language.

In a thought, generally speaking, there is at least one capital object considered as acting or as suffering. This object is expressed by a substantive noun; its action is expressed by an active verb; and the thing affected by the action is expressed by another substantive noun: its suffering or passive state is expressed by a passive verb; and the thing that acts upon it, by a substantive noun. Besides these, which are the capital parts of a sentence or period, there are generally under-parts; each of the substantives, as well as the verb, may be qualified: time, place, purpose, motive, means, instrument, and a thousand other circumstances, may be necessary to complete the thought. And in what manner these several parts are connected in the expression, will appear from what follows.

In a complete thought or mental proposition, all the members and parts are mutually related, some slightly, some intimately. To put such a thought in words, it is not sufficient that the component ideas be clearly expressed; it is also necessary that all the relations contained in the thought be expressed according to their different degrees of intimacy. To annex a certain meaning to a certain sound or word, requires no art: the great nicety in all languages is, to express the various relations that connect the parts of the thought. Could we suppose this branch of language to be still a secret, it would puzzle, I am apt to think, the acutest grammarian to invent an expeditious method: and yet, by the guidance merely of nature, the rude and illiterate have been led to a method so perfect, as to

---

431. Redundancy of copulatives in the same period. Cases where it is proper.

432. Due arrangement of words.—The capital and under-parts of a sentence.—Members and parts of a complete thought mutually related.—The great nicety in all languages.

appear not susceptible of any improvement; and the next step in our progress shall be to explain that method.

433. Words that import a relation must be distinguished from such as do not. Substantives commonly imply no relation; such as *animal*, *man*, *tree*, *river*. Adjectives, verbs, and adverbs imply a relation; the adjective *good* must relate to some being possessed of that quality; the verb *write* is applied to some person who writes; and the adverbs *moderately*, *diligently*, have plainly a reference to some action which they modify. When a relative word is introduced, it must be signified by the expression to what word it relates, without which the sense is not complete. For answering that purpose, I observe in Greek and Latin two different methods. Adjectives are declined as well as substantives; and declensions serve to ascertain their connection: If the word that expresses the subject be, for example, in the nominative case, so also must the word be that expresses its quality; example, *vir bonus*. Again, verbs are related, on the one hand to the agent, and on the other to the subject upon which the action is exerted; and a contrivance similar to that now mentioned, serves to express the double relation: the nominative case is appropriated to the agent, the accusative to the passive subject; and the verb is put in the first, second, or third person to intimate the connection with the word that signifies the agent: examples, *Ego amo Tulliam; tu amas Semproniam; Brutus amat Portiam.* The other method is by juxtaposition, which is necessary with respect to such words only as are not declined; adverbs, for example, articles, prepositions, and conjunctions. In the English language there are few declensions, and therefore juxtaposition is our chief resource: adjectives accompany their substantives; an adverb accompanies the word it qualifies; and the verb occupies the middle place between the active and passive subjects to which it relates.

434. It must be obvious that those terms which have nothing relative in their signification, cannot be connected in so easy a manner. When two substantives happen to be connected, as cause and effect, as principal and accessory, or in any other manner, such connection cannot be expressed by contiguity solely; for words must often in a period be placed together which are not thus related: the relation between substantives, therefore, cannot otherwise be expressed but by particles denoting the relation. Latin indeed and Greek, by their declensions, go a certain length to express such relations without the aid of particles. The relation of property, for example, between Cæsar and his horse, is expressed by putting the latter in the nominative case, the former in the genitive: *equus Cæsaris;* the same is also expressed in English without the aid of a particle, *Cæsar's horse.* But in other instances, declensions not

---

433. Words implying relation. Two methods of indicating relation.

being used in the English language, relations of this kind are commonly expressed by prepositions. Examples: That wine came *from* Cyprus. He is going *to* Paris. The sun is *below* the horizon.

This form of connecting by prepositions is not confined to substantives. Qualities, attributes, manner of existing or acting, and all other circumstances may in the same manner be connected with the substances to which they relate. This is done artificially by converting the circumstance into a substantive; in which condition it is qualified to be connected with the principal subject by a preposition in the manner above described. For example, the adjective *wise* being converted into the substantive *wisdom*, gives opportunity for the expression "a man *of* wisdom," instead of the more simple expression *a wise man;* this variety in the expression enriches language. I observe, besides, that the using a preposition in this case is not always a matter of choice; it is indispensable with respect to every circumstance that cannot be expressed by a single adjective or adverb.

435. To pave the way for the rules of arrangement, one other preliminary is necessary; which is, to explain the difference between a natural style and that where transposition or inversion prevails. There are, it is true, no precise boundaries between them, for they run into each other like the shades of different colors. No person, however, is at a loss to distinguish them in their extremes; and it is necessary to make the distinction, because though some of the rules I shall have occasion to mention are common to both, yet each has rules peculiar to itself. In a natural style, relative words are by juxtaposition connected with those to which they relate, going before or after according to the peculiar genius of the language. Again, a circumstance connected by a preposition follows naturally the word with which it is connected. But this arrangement may be varied when a different order is more beautiful: a circumstance may be placed before the word with which it is connected by a preposition; and may be interjected even between a relative word and that to which it relates. When such liberties are frequently taken, the style becomes inverted or transposed.*

* [The imagination and the understanding are the powers of the mind that chiefly influence the arrangement of words in sentences. The grammatical order is dictated by the understanding; the inverted order results from the prevalence of the imagination. In the grammatical order of words it is required that the agent or nominative shall first make its appearance; the agent is succeeded by the action, or the verb; and the verb is followed by the object or accusative, on which the action is exerted. The other parts of speech, consisting of adjectives, &c., are intermixed with these capital parts, and are associated with them respectively, according as they are necessary to restrict or explain them.

The inverted order is prompted by the imagination, a keen and sprightly

434. The relation between substantives, how expressed.—Qualities and attributes, &c. how connected with the substances to which they relate.

435. Difference between a natural and inverted style. The inverted style and the natural explained in the Note.

436. But as the liberty of inversion is a capital point in the present subject, it will be necessary to examine it more narrowly, and in particular to trace the several degrees in which an inverted style recedes more and more from that which is natural. And first, as to the placing a circumstance before the word with which it is connected, I observe that it is the easiest of all inversion, even so easy as to be consistent with a style that is properly termed natural; witness the following examples:

In the sincerity of my heart, I profess, &c.

By our own ill management we are brought to so low an ebb of wealth and credit, that, &c.

On Thursday morning there was little or nothing transacted in Change-alley.

At St. Bride's church in Fleet-street, Mr. Woolston (who writ against the miracles of our Saviour), in the utmost terrors of conscience, made a public recantation.

The interjecting a circumstance between a relative word and that to which it relates, is more properly termed inversion; because, by a disjunction of words intimately connected, it recedes farther from a natural style.

The degree of inversion depends greatly on the order in which the related words are placed: when a substantive occupies the first place, the idea it suggests must subsist in the mind at least for a moment, independent of the relative words afterwards introduced; and that moment may without difficulty be prolonged by interjecting a circumstance between the substantive and its connections. This liberty, therefore, however frequent, will scarce alone be sufficient to denominate a style inverted. The case is very different, where the word that occupies the first place denotes a quality or an action: for as these cannot be conceived without a subject, they cannot without great violence be separated from the subject that follows; and for that reason, every such separation, by means of an interjected circumstance, belongs to an inverted style.

To illustrate this doctrine, examples are necessary; and I shall

---

faculty, which attaches itself strongly to its objects, and to those the most that affect it most forcibly. A sentence constructed according to the order dictated by this faculty, presents the object or accusative first, the agent or recipient next, and the action or verb last. The other parts of speech are interwoven, as in the former case, with these capital words with which they are naturally connected. The reason of this arrangement is, that the imagination attaches itself principally to the object, in an inferior degree to the subject or recipient, least of all to the action; and they are accordingly disposed agreeably to these degrees of attachment.

In the early periods of society, and even in the early part of life, we observe the mind disposed to inversion, because in these times the imagination is more vivid and active, and the powers of reason are more languid and ineffectual.—*Barron's Lect.* 3.]

---

436. Several degrees of departure from a natural style; in the placing of a circumstance. On what the degree of inversion depends. Examples.

begin with those where the word first introduced does not imply a relation.

> ——————Nor Eve to iterate
> Her former trespass fear'd.

> ——————Hunger and thirst at once,
> Powerful persuaders, quicken'd at the scent
> Of that alluring fruit, urged me so keen.

> Moon that now meet'st the orient sun, now fliest
> With the fix'd stars, fix'd in their orb that flies,
> And ye five other wand'ring fires that move
> In mystic dance not without song, resound
> His praise.

In the following examples, where the word first introduced imports a relation, the disjunction will be found more violent:

> Of man's first disobedience, and the fruit
> Of that forbidden tree, whose mortal taste
> Brought death into the world, and all our woe,
> With loss of Eden, till one greater man
> Restore us, and regain the blissful seat,
> Sing, heavenly muse.

> ——————Upon the firm opacous globe
> Of this round world, whose first convex divides
> The luminous inferior orbs inclosed
> From chaos and th' inroad of darkness old,
> Satan alighted walks.

> ——————On a sudden open fly
> With impetuous recoil and jarring sound,
> Th' infernal doors.

> ——————Wherein remain'd,
> For what could else? to our almighty foe
> Clear victory, to our part loss and rout.

> ——————Forth rush'd, with whirlwind sound,
> The chariot of paternal Deity.

437. Language would have no great power, were it confined to the natural order of ideas. I shall soon have opportunity to make it evident, that by inversion a thousand beauties may be compassed, which must be relinquished in a natural arrangement. In the mean time, it ought not to escape observation, that the mind of man is happily so constituted as to relish inversion, though in one respect unnatural; and to relish it so much, as in many cases to admit a separation between words the most intimately connected. It can scarce be said that inversion has any limits; though I may venture to pronounce, that the disjunction of articles, conjunctions, or prepositions, from the words to which they belong, has very seldom a good effect. The following example with relation to a preposition, is perhaps as tolerable as any of the kind:

He would neither separate *from*, nor act against *them.*

---

437. Effect of inversion upon language.—Effect of separating articles, conjunctions, and prepositions, from the words to which they belong.

438. I give notice to the reader, that I am now ready to enter on the rules of arrangement: beginning with a natural style, and proceeding gradually to what is the most inverted. And in the arrangement of a period, as well as in a right choice of words, the first and great object being perspicuity, the rule above laid down, that perspicuity ought not to be sacrificed to any other beauty, holds equally in both. Ambiguities occasioned by a wrong arrangement are of two sorts; one where the arrangement leads to a wrong sense, and one where the sense is left doubtful. The first, being more culpable, shall take the lead, beginning with examples of words put in a wrong place.

How much the imagination of such a presence must exalt a genius, we may observe *merely* from the influence which an ordinary presence has over men. *Characteristics*, vol. i. p. 7.

This arrangement leads to a wrong sense: the adverb *merely* seems by its position to affect the preceding word; whereas it is intended to affect the following words, *an ordinary presence;* and therefore the arrangement ought to be thus:

How much the imagination of such a presence must exalt a genius, we may observe from the influence which an ordinary presence merely has over men. [Or better]—which even an ordinary presence has over men.

The time of the election of a poet-laureat being now at hand, it may be proper to give some account of the rites and ceremonies anciently used at that solemnity, and *only* discontinued through the neglect and degeneracy of later times. *Guardian.*

The term *only* is intended to qualify the noun *degeneracy*, and not the participle *discontinued;* and therefore the arrangement ought to be as follows:

————and discontinued through the neglect and degeneracy only of later times.

Sixtus the Fourth was, if I mistake not, a great collector of books at least. *Letters on History*, vol. i. Lect. 6.—Bolingbroke.

The expression here leads evidently to a wrong sense; the adverb *at least*, ought not to be connected with the substantive *books*, but with *collector*, thus:

Sixtus the Fourth was a great collector at least of books.

Speaking of Louis XIV.

If he was not the greatest king, he was the best actor of majesty at least that ever filled a throne.—*Ibid.* Letter vii.

Better thus:

If he was not the greatest king, he was at least the best actor of majesty, &c

This arrangement removes the wrong sense occasioned by the juxtaposition of *majesty* and *at least.*

---

438. Two sorts of ambiguity from a wrong arrangement. First, of words.

439. The following examples are of a wrong arrangement of members:

I have confined myself to those methods for the advancement of piety, which are in the power of a prince limited like ours by a strict execution of the laws.
A Project for the Advancement of Religion.—Swift.

The structure of this period leads to a meaning which is not the author's, viz. power limited by a strict execution of the laws. That wrong sense is removed by the following arrangement:

I have confined myself to those methods for the advancement of piety, which, by a strict execution of the laws, are in the power of a prince limited like ours.

This morning, when one of Lady Lizard's daughters was looking over some hoods and ribands brought by her tirewoman, with great care and diligence, I employed no less in examining the box which contained them.
Guardian, No. 4.

The wrong sense occasioned by this arrangement, may be easily prevented by varying it thus:

This morning when, with great care and diligence, one of Lady Lizard's daughters was looking over some hoods and ribands, &c.

A great stone that I happened to find after a long search by the seashore, served me for an anchor.—*Gulliver's Travels*, part i. chap. viii.

One would think that the search was confined to the seashore: but as the meaning is, that the great stone was found by the seashore, the period ought to be arranged thus:

A great stone, that, after a long search, I happened to find by the seashore, served me for an anchor.

440. Next of a wrong arrangement where the sense is left doubtful; beginning, as in the former sort, with examples of wrong arrangement of words in a member.

These forms of conversation *by degrees* multiplied and grew troublesome.—*Spectator*, No. 119.

Here it is left doubtful whether the modification *by degrees* relates to the preceding member or to what follows: it should be,

These forms of conversation multiplied by degrees.

Nor does this false modesty expose us *only* to such actions as are indiscreet, but very often to such as are highly criminal.—*Spectator*, No. 458.

The ambiguity is removed by the following arrangement:

Nor does this false modesty expose us to such actions only as are indiscreet, &c.

The empire of Blefuscu is an island situated to the northeast side of Lilliput, from whence it is parted *only* by a channel of 800 yards wide.—*Gulliver's Travels*, part i. chap. v.

The ambiguity may be removed thus:

———— from whence it is parted by a channel of 800 yards wide only.

---

439. Of a wrong arrangement of members.

In the following examples the sense is left doubtful by wrong arrangement of members:

The minister who grows less by his elevation, *like a little statue placed on a mighty pedestal*, will always have his jealousy strong about him.—*Dissertation upon Parties. Dedication.*—Bolingbroke.

Here, as far as can be gathered from the arrangement, it is doubtful whether the object, introduced by way of simile, relates to what goes before or to what follows: the ambiguity is removed by the following arrangement:

The minister, who, like a little statue placed on a mighty pedestal, grows less by his elevation, will always, &c.

Since this is too much to ask of freemen, nay of slaves, *if his expectation be not answered*, shall he form a lasting division upon such transient motives?—*Ibid.*

Better thus:

Since this is too much to ask of freemen, nay of slaves, shall he, if his expectations be not answered, form, &c.

Speaking of the superstitious practice of locking up the room where a person of distinction dies:

The knight, seeing his habitation reduced to so small a compass, and himself in a manner shut out of his own house, *upon the death of his mother*, ordered all the apartments to be flung open, and exorcised by his chaplain.—*Spectator*, No. 110.

Better thus:

The knight, seeing his habitation reduced to so small a compass, and himself in a manner shut out of his own house, ordered, upon the death of his mother, all the apartments to be flung open.

Speaking of some indecencies in conversation:

As it is impossible for such an irrational way of conversation to last long among a people that make any profession of religion, or show of modesty, *if the country gentlemen get into it*, they will certainly be left in the lurch.—*Spectator*, No. 119.

The ambiguity vanishes in the following arrangement:

——— the country gentlemen, if they get into it, will certainly be left in the lurch.

Speaking of a discovery in natural philosophy, that color is not a quality of matter:

As this is a truth which has been proved incontestably by many modern philosophers, and is indeed one of the finest speculations in that science, *if the English reader would see the notion explained at large*, he may find it in the eighth chapter in the second book of Mr. Locke's Essay on the Human Understanding. —*Spectator*, No. 413.

Better thus:

As this is a truth, &c., the English reader, if he would see the notion explained at large, may find it, &c.

A woman seldom asks advice before she has bought her wedding-clothes

When she has made her own choice, *for form's sake*, she sends a *conge d'elire* to her friends.—*Ibid.* No. 475.

Better thus:

—————— she sends, for form's sake, a *conge d'elire* to her friends.

And since it is necessary that there should be a perpetual intercourse of buying and selling, and dealing upon credit, *where fraud is permitted or connived at, or hath no law to punish it*, the honest dealer is always undone, and the knave gets the advantage.—*Gulliver's Travels*, part i. chap. vi.

Better thus:

And since it is necessary that there should be a perpetual intercourse of buying and selling, and dealing upon credit, the honest dealer, where fraud is permitted or connived at, or hath no law to punish it, is always undone, and the knave gets the advantage.

441. From these examples, the following observation will occur, that a circumstance ought never to be placed between two capital members of a period; for by such situation it must always be doubtful, as far as we gather from the arrangement, to which of the two members it belongs: where it is interjected, as it ought to be, between parts of the member to which it belongs, the ambiguity is removed, and the capital members are kept distinct, which is a great beauty in composition. In general, to preserve members distinct that signify things distinguished in the thought, the best method is, to place first in the consequent member, some word that cannot connect with what precedes it.

If it shall be thought, that the objections here are too scrupulous, and that the defect of perspicuity is easily supplied by accurate punctuation; the answer is, That punctuation may remove an ambiguity, but will never produce that peculiar beauty which is perceived when the sense comes out clearly and distinctly by means of a happy arrangement.

442. A rule deservedly occupying the second place, is, That words expressing things connected in the thought, ought to be placed as near together as possible. This rule is derived immediately from human nature, prone in every instance to place together things in any manner connected (see chapter i.): where things are arranged according to their connections, we have a sense of order: otherwise we have a sense of disorder, as of things placed by chance: and we naturally place words in the same order in which we would place the things they signify. The bad effect of a violent separation of words or members thus intimately connected will appear from the following examples:

For the English are naturally fanciful, and very often disposed, by that gloominess and melancholy of temper which is so frequent in our nation, to many wild notions and visions, to which others are not so liable.

Spectator, No. 419.

---

440. Where thus the sense is left doubtful. Examples.
441. Where a capital circumstance should not be placed. The best method.

Here the verb or assertion is, by a pretty long circumstance, violently separated from the subject to which it refers: this makes a harsh arrangement; the less excusable that the fault is easily prevented by placing the circumstances before the verb, after the following manner:

For the English are naturally fanciful, and, by that gloominess and melancholy of temper which is so frequent in our nation, are often disposed to many wild notions, &c.

For as no mortal author, in the ordinary fate and vicissitude of things, knows to what use his works may, some time or other, be applied, &c.
Spectator, No. 85.

Better thus:

For as, in the ordinary fate and vicissitude of things, no mortal author knows to what use, some time or other, his works may be applied, &c.

From whence we may date likewise the rivalship of the house of France, for we may reckon that of Valois and that of Bourbon as one upon this occasion, and the house of Austria that continues at this day, and has oft cost so much blood and so much treasure in the course of it.
Letters on History, vol. i. let. vi.—*Bolingbroke*.

It cannot be impertinent or ridiculous, therefore, in such a country, whatever it might be in the Abbot of St. Real's, which was Savoy, I think; or in Peru, under the Incas, where Garcilasso de la Vega says it was lawful for none but the nobility to study—for men of all degrees to instruct themselves, in those affairs wherein they may be actors, or judges of those who act, or controllers of those that judge.—*Ibid.* let. v.

If Scipio, who was naturally given to women, for which anecdote we have, if I mistake not, the authority of Polybius, as well as some verses of Nevius, preserved by Aulus Gellius, had been educated by Olympias at the court of Philip, it is improbable that he would have restored the beautiful Spaniard.
Ibid. let. iii.

If any one have a curiosity for more specimens of this kind, they will be found without number in the works of the same author.

443. A pronoun, which saves the naming a person or thing a second time, ought to be placed as near as possible to the name of that person or thing. This is a branch of the foregoing rule; and with the reason there given another concurs, viz., That if other ideas intervene, it is difficult to recall the person or thing by reference:

If I had leave to print the Latin letters transmitted to me from foreign parts, they would fill a volume, and be a full defence against all that Mr. Partridge or his accomplices of the Portugal inquisition, will be ever able to object; *who*, by the way, are the only enemies my predictions have ever met with at home or abroad.

Better thus:

————————and be a full defence against all that can be objected by Mr. Partridge, or his accomplices of the Portugal inquisition; who, by the way, are, &c.

There being a round million of creatures in human figure, throughout this kingdom, *whose* whole subsistence, &c.—*A Modest Proposal*, &c. Swift.

---

442. **Second rule; relating to words expressing things connected in thought. The basis of this rule. Examples of a violation of this rule.**

Better:

There being throughout this kingdom a round million of creatures in human figure, whose whole subsistence, &c.

Tom is a lively impudent clown, and has wit enough to have made him a pleasant companion, had it been polished and rectified by good manners.
Guardian, No. 162.

It is the custom of the Mahometans, if they see any printed or written paper upon the ground, to take it up, and lay it aside carefully, as not knowing but it may contain some piece of their Alcoran.—*Spectator*, No. 85.

The arrangement here leads to a wrong sense, as if the ground were taken up, not the paper.—Better thus:

It is the custom of the Mahometans, if they see upon the ground any printed or written paper, to take it up, &c.

444. The following rule depends on the communication of emotions to related objects, a principle in human nature that hath an extensive operation; and we find this operation even where the objects are not otherwise related than by juxtaposition of the words that express them. Hence, to elevate or depress an object, one method is, to join it in the expression with another that is naturally high or low: witness the following speech of Eumenes to the Roman Senate:

Causam veniendi sibi Romam fuisse, præter cupiditatem visendi *deos hominesque*, quorum beneficio in ea fortuna esset, supra quam ne optare quidem auderet, etiam ut coram moneret senatum ut Persei conatus obviam iret.
Livy, l. xiii. cap. xi.

To join the Romans with the gods in the same enunciation, is an artful stroke of flattery, because it tacitly puts them on a level. On the other hand, the degrading or vilifying an object, is done successfully by ranking it with one that is really low:

I hope to have this entertainment in a readiness for the next winter; and doubt not but it will please more than the opera or puppet-show.
Spectator, No. 28.

Manifold have been the judgments which Heaven from time to time, for the chastisement of a sinful people, has inflicted upon whole nations. For when the degeneracy becomes common, 'tis but just the punishment should be general. Of this kind, in our own unfortunate country, was that destructive pestilence, whose mortality was so fatal as to sweep away, if Sir William Petty may be believed, five millions of Christian souls, besides women and Jews.
God's Revenge against Punning. Arbuthnot.

Such also was that dreadful conflagration ensuing in this famous metropolis of London, which consumed, according to the computation of Sir Samuel Moreland, 100,000 houses, not to mention churches and stables.—*Ibid.*

But on condition it might pass into a law, I would gladly exempt both lawyers of all ages, subaltern and field-officers, young heirs, dancing-masters, pick pockets, and players.—*An infallible Scheme to pay the Public Debt.* Swift.

---

443. The proper place for the pronoun.
444. Rule depending on the communication of emotions to related objects.—How to elevate or depress an object.

Sooner let earth, air, sea, to chaos fall,
Men, monkeys, lap-dogs, parrots, perish all.
Rape of the Lock.

445. Circumstances in a period resemble small stones in a building, employed to fill up vacuities among those of a larger size. In the arrangement of a period, such underparts crowded together make a poor figure, and never are graceful but when interspersed among the capital parts. I illustrate this rule by the following example:

It is likewise urged that there are, by computation, in this kingdom, above 10,000 parsons, whose revenues, added to those of my lords the bishops, would suffice to maintain, &c.
Argument against abolishing Christianity. Swift.

Here two circumstances, viz., *by computation*, and *in this kingdom*, are crowded together unnecessarily: they make a better appearance separated in the following manner:

It is likewise urged that in this kingdom there are, by computation, above 10,000 parsons, &c.

If there be room for a choice, the sooner a circumstance is introduced the better; because circumstances are proper for that coolness of mind with which we begin a period as well as a volume: in the progress, the mind warms, and has a greater relish for matters of importance. When a circumstance is placed at the beginning of the period, or near the beginning, the transition from it to the principal subject is agreeable: it is like ascending or going upward. On the other hand, to place it late in the period has a bad effect; for after being engaged in the principal subject, one is with reluctance brought down to give attention to a circumstance. Hence evidently the preference of the following arrangement,

Whether in any country a choice altogether unexceptionable has been made, seems doubtful.

Before this other,

Whether a choice altogether unexceptionable has in any country been made, &c.

For this reason the following period is exceptionable in point of arrangement:

I have considered formerly, with a good deal of attention, the subject upon which you command me to communicate my thoughts to you.—*Bolingbroke on the Study of History*, Letter I.

Which, with a slight alteration, may be improved thus:

I have formerly, with a good deal of attention, considered the subject, &c.

Swift, speaking of a virtuous and learned education:

And although they may be, and too often are drawn, by the temptations of youth, and the opportunities of a large fortune, into some irregularities, *when they come forward into the great world;* it is ever with reluctance and compunction of mind, because their bias to virtue still continues.—*The Intelligencer* No. 9.

Better:

And although, *when they come forward into the great world*, they may be, and too often, &c.

The bad effect of placing a circumstance last or late in a period, will appear from the following examples:

Let us endeavor to establish to ourselves an interest in him who holds the reins of the whole creation in his hand.—*Spectator*, No. 12.

Better thus:

Let us endeavor to establish to ourselves an interest in him, who, in his hand, holds the reins of the whole creation.

Virgil, who has cast the whole system of Platonic philosophy, so far as it relates to the soul of man, into beautiful allegories, *in the sixth book of his Æneid*, gives us the punishment, &c.—*Spectator*, No. 90.

Better thus:

Virgil, who, in the sixth book of his Æneid, has cast, &c.

And Philip the Fourth was obliged at last to conclude a peace on terms repugnant to his inclination, to that of his people, to the interest of Spain, and to that of all Europe, in the Pyrenean treaty.—*Letters on History*, vol. i. let. vi. *Bolingbroke.*

Better thus:

And at last in the Pyrenean treaty, Philip the Fourth was obliged to conclude a peace, &c.

446. In arranging a period, it is of importance to determine in what part of it a word makes the greatest figure; whether at the beginning, during the course, or at the close. The breaking silence rouses the attention, and prepares for a deep impression at the beginning: the beginning, however, must yield to the close; which being succeeded by a pause, affords time for a word to make its deepest impression. Hence the following rule, That to give the utmost force to a period, it ought if possible to be closed with that word which makes the greatest figure. The opportunity of a pause should not be thrown away upon accessories, but reserved for the principal object, in order that it may make a full impression; which is an additional reason against closing a period with a circumstance. There are however periods that admit not such a structure; and in that case, the capital word ought, if possible, to be placed in the front, which next to the close is the most advantageous for making an impression. Hence, in directing our discourse to a man of figure, we ought to begin with his name; and one will be sensible of a degradation, when this rule is neglected, as it frequently is for the sake of verse. I give the following examples:

---

445. Circumstances, how to be disposed of. Example The best plan for them. Transition from it to the principal subject, agreeable. Example

Integer vitæ, scelerisque purus,
Non eget Mauri jaculis, neque arcu,
Nec venenatis gravidâ sagittis,
Fusce, pharetrâ. *Horat. Carm.* l. 1 ode 22.

Je crains Dieu, cher Abner, et n'ai point d'autre crainte

In these examples, the name of the person addressed to, makes a mean figure, being like a circumstance slipt into a corner. That this criticism is well founded, we need no further proof than Addison's translation of the last example:

O Abner! I fear my God, and I fear none but him.
Guardian, No. 117.

O father, what intends thy hand, she cried,
Against thy only son? What fury, O son,
Possesses thee to bend that mortal dart
Against thy father's head?
Paradise Lost, book ii. l. 727.

Every one must be sensible of a dignity in the invocation at the beginning, which is not attained by that in the middle. I mean not, however, to censure this passage: on the contrary, it appears beautiful, by distinguishing the respect that is due to a father from that which is due to a son.

447. The substance of what is said in this and the foregoing section, upon the method of arranging words in a period, so as to make the deepest impression with respect to sound as well as signification, is comprehended in the following observation: That order of words in a period will always be the most agreeable, where, without obscuring the sense, the most important images, the most sonorous words, and the longest members, bring up the rear.

Hitherto of arranging single words, single members, and single circumstances. But the enumeration of many particulars in the same period is often necessary; and the question is, In what order they should be placed? It does not seem easy, at first view, to bring a subject apparently so loose under any general rule; but luckily, reflecting upon what is said in the first chapter about order, we find rules laid down to our hand, which leave us no task but that of applying them to the present question. And, first, with respect to the enumerating particulars of equal rank, it is laid down in the place quoted, that as there is no cause for preferring any one before the rest, it is indifferent to the mind in what order they be viewed. And it is only necessary to be added here, that for the same reason, it is indifferent in what order they be named. 2dly, If a number of objects of the same kind, differing only in size, are to be ranged along a straight line, the most agreeable order to the eye is that of an increasing series. In surveying a number of such ob-

446. How to give the utmost force to a period.—The second best place for the capital word.—How to begin a discourse to a person of consequence.

jects, beginning at the least, and proceeding to greater and greater, the mind swells gradually with the successive objects, and in its progress has a very sensible pleasure. Precisely for the same reason, words expressive of such objects ought to be placed in the same order. The beauty of this figure, which may be termed *a climax in sense*, has escaped Lord Bolingbroke in the first member of the following period:

Let but one great, brave, disinterested, active man arise, and he will be received, followed, and almost adored.

The following arrangement has sensibly a better effect:

Let but one brave, great, active, disinterested man arise, &c.

Whether the same rule ought to be followed in enumerating men of different ranks, seems doubtful: on the one hand, a number of persons presented to the eye in form of an increasing series, is undoubtedly the most agreeable order: on the other hand, in every list of names, we set the person of the greatest dignity at the top, and descend gradually through his inferiors. Where the purpose is to honor the persons named according to their rank, the latter order ought to be followed; but every one who regards himself only, or his reader, will choose the former order. 3dly, As the sense of order directs the eye to descend from the principal to its greatest accessory, and from the whole to its greatest part, and in the same order through all the parts and accessories till we arrive at the minutest; the same order ought to be followed in the enumeration of such particulars.

448. When force and liveliness of expression are demanded, the rule is, to suspend the thought as long as possible, and to bring it out full and entire at the close; which cannot be done but by inverting the natural arrangement. By introducing a word or member before its time, curiosity is raised about what is to follow; and it is agreeable to have our curiosity gratified at the close of the period: the pleasure we feel resembles that of seeing a stroke exerted upon a body by the whole collected force of the agent. On the other hand, where a period is so constructed as to admit more than one complete close in the sense, the curiosity of the reader is exhausted at the first close, and what follows appears languid or superfluous: his disappointment contributes also to that appearance, when he finds, contrary to expectation, that the period is not yet finished. Cicero, and after him Quintilian, recommend the verb to the last place. This method evidently tends to suspend the sense till the close of the period; for without the verb the sense cannot be complete; and when the verb happens to be the capital word, which it frequently is, it ought at any rate to be the last, according to an-

447 The best order of words in a period.—Rule for enumerating *particulars* of equal rank in a period.—2d, Where they differ in size.—Order when enumerating men of different ranks.—3d, What the sense of order directs.
operation

other rule, above laid down. I proceed as usual to illustrate this rule by examples. The following period is placed in its natural order.

Were instruction an essential circumstance in epic poetry, I doubt whether a single instance could be given of this species of composition, in any language.

The period thus arranged admits a full close upon the word *composition;* after which it goes on languidly, and closes without force. This blemish will be avoided by the following arrangement:

Were instruction an essential circumstance in epic poetry, I doubt whether, in any language, a single instance could be given of this species of composition.

Some of our most eminent divines have made use of this Platonic notion, as far as it regards the subsistence of our passions after death, with great beauty and strength of reason.—*Spectator*, No. 90.

Better thus:

Some of our most eminent divines have, with great beauty and strength of reason, made use of this Platonic notion, &c.

Men of the best sense have been touched more or less with these groundless horrors and presages of futurity, upon surveying the most indifferent works of nature.—*Ibid.* No. 505.

Better,

Upon surveying the most indifferent works of nature, men of the best sense, &c.

She soon informed him of the place he was in, which, notwithstanding all its horrors, appeared to him more sweet than the bower of Mahomet, in the company of his Balsora.—*Guardian*, No. 167.

Better,

She soon, &c., appeared to him, in the company of his Balsora, more sweet, &c.

The emperor was so intent on the establishment of his absolute power in Hungary, that he exposed the empire doubly to desolation and ruin for the sake of it.—*Letters on History*, vol. i. let. vii. Bolingbroke.

Better,

———that for the sake of it he exposed the empire doubly to desolation and ruin.

None of the rules for the composition of periods are more liable to be abused, than those last mentioned; witness many Latin writers, among the moderns especially, whose style, by inversions too violent, is rendered harsh and obscure. Suspension of the thought till the close of the period, ought never to be preferred before perspicuity. Neither ought such suspension to be attempted in a long period; because in that case the mind is bewildered amidst a profusion of words: a traveller, while he is puzzled about the road, relishes not the finest prospect:

---

448. Rule, when force and liveliness of expression are demanded.—Disadvantage of constructing a period with more than one complete close in the sense. Examples.—When the suspension of thought to the close of a period should not be attempted.

All the rich presents which Astyages had given him at parting, keeping only some Median horses, in order to propagate the breed of them in Persia, he distributed among his friends whom he left at the court of Ecbatana.
Travels of Cyrus, Book i.

449. The foregoing rules concern the arrangement of a single period: I add one rule more concerning the distribution of a discourse into different periods. A short period is lively and familiar: a long period, requiring more attention, makes an impression grave and solemn. In general, a writer ought to study a mixture of long and short periods, which prevent an irksome uniformity, and entertain the mind with a variety of impressions. In particular, long periods ought to be avoided till the reader's attention be thoroughly engaged; and therefore a discourse, especially of the familiar kind, ought never to be introduced with a long period. For that reason the commencement of a letter to a very young lady on her marriage is faulty:

Madam, the hurry and impertinence of receiving and paying visits on account of your marriage, being now over, you are beginning to enter into a course of life, where you will want much advice to divert you from falling into many errors, fopperies, and follies, to which your sex is subject.—*Swift.*

See another example still more faulty, in the commencement of Cicero's oration, *Pro Archia Poeta.*

450. Before proceeding farther, it may be proper to review the rules laid down in this and the preceding section, in order to make some general observations. That order of the words and members of a period is justly termed natural, which corresponds to the natural order of the ideas that compose the thought. The tendency of many of the foregoing rules is to substitute an artificial arrangement in order to catch some beauty either of sound or meaning for which there is no place in the natural order. But seldom it happens, that in the same period there is place for a plurality of these rules: if one beauty can be retained, another must be relinquished; and the only question is, Which ought to be preferred? This question cannot be resolved by any general rule: if the natural order be not relished, a few trials will discover that artificial order which has the best effect; and this exercise, supported by a good taste, will in time make the choice easy. All that can be said in general is, that in making a choice, sound ought to yield to signification.

The transposing words and members out of their natural order, so remarkable in the learned languages, has been the subject of much speculation.* It is agreed on all hands, that such transposi-

* [The very great difference of the genius of the ancient and modern languages in this respect has been thus illustrated by Prof. Barron, Lect. III.:

"Suppose an English historian were to address his readers, in the introduction of a work from which he expected high literary fame, in the following style:—'All men who themselves wish to exceed the inferior animals, by every effort to endeavor ought,' he would find himself disappointed; as few read-

449. Rule for the distribution of discourse into different periods. Long and short periods.

tion or inversion bestows upon a period a very sensible degree of force and elevation; and yet writers seem to be at a loss how to account for this effect. Cerceau ascribes so much power to inversion, as to make it the characteristic of French verse, and the single circumstance which in that language distinguishes verse from prose: and yet he pretends not to say, that it hath any other effect but to raise surprise; he must mean curiosity, which is done by suspending the thought during the period, and bringing it out entire at the close. This indeed is one effect of inversion; but neither its sole effect, nor even that which is the most remarkable, as is made evident above. But waiving censure, which is not an agreeable task, I enter into the matter; and begin with observing, that if conformity between words and their meaning be agreeable, it must of course be agreeable to find the same order or arrangement in both. Hence the beauty of a plain or natural style, where the order of the words corresponds precisely to the order of the ideas. Nor is this the single beauty of a natural style: it is also agreeable by its simplicity and perspicuity. This observation throws light upon the subject for if a natural style be in itself agreeable, a transposed style cannot be so; and therefore its agreeableness must arise from admitting some positive beauty that is excluded in a natural style. To be confirmed in this opinion, we need but reflect upon some of the foregoing rules, which make it evident, that language by means of inversion, is susceptible of many beauties that are totally excluded in a natural arrangement. From these premises it clearly follows, that inversion ought not to be indulged, unless in order to reach some beauty superior to those of a natural style. It may with great certainty be pronounced, that every inversion which is not governed by this rule, will appear harsh and strained, and be disrelished by every one of taste. Hence the beauty of inversion when happily conducted; the beauty, not of an end, but of means, as furnishing opportunity for numberless ornaments that find no place in a natural style: hence the force, the elevation, the harmony, the cadence, of some compositions: hence the manifold beauties of the Greek and Roman tongues, of which living languages afford but faint imitations.

["If we attend to the history of our own language," says Prof. Barron, "we may discover a strong disposition in some of our prose

ers, I believe, unless to indulge a little mirth, would be induced to proceed further than the first sentence; yet a Roman historian could express these ideas in that very arrangement with full energy and propriety: 'Omnes homines, qui sese student præstare cæteris animalibus, summa ope niti decet.'

"Little less surprising and uncouth would be the following exordium on a similar occasion: 'Whether I shall execute a work of merit, if, from the building of the city, the affairs of the people of Rome I shall relate, neither sufficiently know I, nor if I knew declare durst I.' The reader perhaps would not suspect such language to be a literal translation of the first sentence of the most finished historical production of antiquity, which runs thus in the elegant diction of Livy: 'Facturusne sum operæ pretium si a primordio urbis, res populi Romani perscripserim; nec satis scio, nec, si scirem, dicere ausim.' "]

writers, to accommodate its arrangement to that of the languages of Greece and Rome. But, in executing the design, they disfigured our language in every respect. They Latinized our words and our terminations. They introduced inversions so violent, as to render the sense often obscure, in some cases unintelligible; and they extended their periods to a length which extinguished every spark of patience in the reader. Hobbes, Clarendon, and even Milton in his prose writings, afford numberless instances of this bad taste; and it is remarkable, that it prevailed chiefly during the latter part of the seventeenth century. In the beginning of that century, and in the end of the preceding one, during the reigns of Queen Elizabeth and James I., the purity of the English language, and a correct taste in writing it, were perhaps farther advanced, both in England and Scotland, than in the succeeding period. The works of Shakspeare Hooker, Melvil, and the translation of the Bible, have scarcely been equalled for good style, by any productions of the seventeenth century; and, in point of grammatical correctness, have not yet been often surpassed. The fanaticism and violence of the civil wars corrupted the taste, and the imitation of Latin composition in theological controversy, seems to have disfigured the language of England." —Lect. III.]*

SECTION III.

Beauty of Language from a Resemblance between Sound and Signification.

451. A RESEMBLANCE between the sound of certain words and their signification, is a beauty that has escaped no critical writer, and yet is not handled with accuracy by any of them. They have probably been of opinion, that a beauty so obvious to the feeling requires no explanation. This is an error; and to avoid it, I shall give examples of the various resemblances between sound and signification, accompanied with an endeavor to explain why such resemblances are beautiful. I begin with examples where the resemblance between the sound and signification is the most entire; and next examples where the resemblance is less and less so.

There being frequently a strong resemblance of one sound to another, it will not be surprising to find an articulate sound resembling

* [In connection with the above, may be read with great advantage, the first of chap. xxii. on the Philosophy of Style.]

450. The order of words and members that may be called natural. Rule for choice between it and an artificial order.—Transposition in the learned languages. Illustration.—Whence the beauty of a natural style. Whence, then, the agreeableness of a transposed style. When, only such a style should be used.—Style of the latter part of the seventeenth century

one that is not articulate: thus the sound of a bowstring is imitated by the words that express it:

> ———————The string let fly,
> *Twang'd short and sharp*, like the shrill swallow's cry.
>
> *Odyssey*, xxi. 449.

The sound of felling trees in a wood:

> Loud sounds the axe, redoubling strokes on strokes,
> On all sides round the forest hurls her oaks
> Headlong. Deep echoing groan the thickets brown,
> Then *rustling*, *crackling*, *crashing*, thunder down.
>
> *Iliad*, xxiii. 144.

> But when loud surges lash the sounding shore,
> The hoarse rough verse should like the torrent roar.
>
> *Pope's Essay on Criticism*, 369.

> Dire Scylla there a scene of horror forms,
> And here Charybdis fills the deep with storms;
> When the tide rushes from her rumbling caves,
> The rough rock roars; tumultuous boil the waves.—*Pope.*

No person can be at a loss about the cause of this beauty: it is obviously that of imitation.

452. That there is any other natural resemblance of sound to signification, must not be taken for granted. There is no resemblance of sound to motion, nor of sound to sentiment. We are however apt to be deceived by artful pronunciation; the same passage may be pronounced in many different tones, elevated or humble, sweet or harsh, brisk or melancholy, so as to accord with the thought or sentiment; such concord must be distinguished from that concord between sound and sense, which is perceived in some expressions independent of artful pronunciation: the latter is the poet's work; the former must be attributed to the reader. Another thing contributes still more to the deceit: in language, sound and sense being intimately connected, the properties of the one are readily communicated to the other; for example, the quality of grandeur, of sweetness, or of melancholy, though belonging to the thought solely, is transferred to the words, which by that means resemble in appearance the thought that is expressed by them (see chap. ii. part i. sec. 5).

["Wordsworth has not only presented the hues of nature to the eye, but has also imitated her harmonies to the ear. Of this I will adduce an instance:

> Astounded in the mountain gap
> By peals of thunder, clap on clap,
> And many a terror-striking flash,
> *And somewhere, as it seems, a crash*
> *Among the rocks; with weight of rain,*
> *And sullen motions, long and slow,*
> *That to a dreary distance go—*
> Till breaking in upon the dying strain,
> A rending o'er his head begins the fray again.—*Waggoner.*

---

451. Resemblances between sound and signification. Its beauty.—Articulate sound resembling one that is not so. The cause of this beauty.

Surely the four lines marked by the italic character would alone be sufficient to decide the question, whether such a grace as imitative harmony really exists. I own that it is difficult to determine how much of the effect upon the mind depends upon the meaning associated with the words; but let it be remembered, that words designative of sound have naturally derived their birth from an attempt, in the infancy of language, actually to imitate the sounds of which they are symbolical. After God's own language—the Hebrew—and the affluent Greek, there is probably no tongue so rich in imitative harmonies as our own. Let any person with a true ear, observe the difference between the two words *snow* and *rain*. The hushing sound of the sibilant, in the first, followed by the soft liquid and by the round full vowel, is not less indicative of the still descent of snow, than the harsher liquid and vowel, in the second, are of the falling shower. I fear that I shall be considered fanciful, yet I cannot help remarking that the letter R, the sound of which, when lengthened out, is so expressive of the murmur of streams and brooks, is generally to be found in words relating to the element of water, and in such combinations as, either single or reduplicated, suit precisely its different modifications. The words "*long*" and "*slow*" are, if pronounced in a natural manner, actually of a longer time than the words *short* and *quick*. There is a drag upon the nasal *N* and *G*; there is a protracted effect in the vowel followed by a double vowel in the first two words, not to be found in the two last."—*Prof. Wilson.*]

453. Resembling causes may produce effects that have no resemblance; and causes that have no resemblance may produce resembling effects. A magnificent building, for example, resembles not in any degree an heroic action: and yet the emotions they produce, are concordant, and bear a resemblance to each other. We are still more sensible of this resemblance in a song, when the music is properly adapted to the sentiment: there is no resemblance between thought and sound; but there is the strongest resemblance between the emotion raised by music tender and pathetic, and that raised by the complaint of an unsuccessful lover. Applying this observation to the present subject, it appears that, in some instances, the sound even of a single word makes an impression resembling that which is made by the thing it signifies: witness the word *running*, composed of two short syllables; and more remarkably the words *rapidity, impetuosity, precipitation*. Brutal manners produce in the spectator an emotion not unlike what is produced by a harsh and rough sound; and hence the beauty of the figurative expression *rugged* manners. Again, the word *little*, being pronounced with a very small aperture of the mouth, has a weak and faint sound, which

---

452. Concord between words and thought, sometimes due to pronunciation.—Sound and sense being connected, the properties of the one are readily attributed to the other

makes an impression resembling that made by a diminutive object. This resemblance of effect is still more remarkable where a number of words are connected in a period: words pronounced in succession make often a strong impression; and when this impression happens to accord with that made by the sense, we are sensible of a complex emotion, peculiarly pleasant; one proceeding from the sentiment, and one from the melody or sound of the words. But the chief pleasure proceeds from having these two concordant emotions combined in perfect harmony, and carried on in the mind to a full close (see chap. ii. part iv.). Except in the single case where sound is described, all the examples given by critics of sense being imitated in sound, resolve into a resemblance of effects: emotions raised by sound and signification may have a resemblance; but sound itself cannot have a resemblance to any thing but sound.*

454. Proceeding now to particulars, and beginning with those cases where the emotions have the strongest resemblance, I observe, first, That by a number of syllables in succession, an emotion is sometimes raised extremely similar to that raised by successive motion; which may be evident even to those who are defective in taste, from the following fact, that the term *movement* in all languages is equally applied to both. In this manner successive motion, such as walking, running, galloping, can be imitated by a succession of long or short syllables, or by a due mixture of both. For example, slow motion may be justly imitated in a verse where long syllables prevail; especially when aided by a slow pronunciation:

> Illi inter sese magnâ vi brachia tollunt.—*Georg.* iv. 174.

On the other hand, swift motion is imitated by a succession of short syllables:

> Quadrupedante putrem sonitu quatit ungula campum.

Again:

> Radit iter liquidum, celeres neque commovet alas.

Thirdly, A line composed of monosyllables, makes an impression, by the frequency of its pauses, similar to what is made by laborious interrupted motion:

> With many a weary step and many a groan,
> Up the high hill he heaves a huge round stone.—*Odyssey*, xi 736.

> First march the heavy mules securely slow;
> O'er hills, o'er dales, o'er crags, o'er rocks they go.
> *Iliad*, xxiii. 138.

Fourthly, the impression made by rough sounds in succession, resembles that made by rough or tumultuous motion: on the other

* [See an excellent chapter on the Poetry of Language in Mrs. Ellis's "Poetry of Life."]

453. Resembling causes and their effects.—Non-resembling causes. Example: a building and an heroic action produce concordant emotions. A song, and the sentiment, &c. Example: Resemblance of effects from words connected in a period.—Remark on examples of sense imitated in sound.

hand, the impression of smooth sounds resembles that of gentle motion. The following is an example of both:

> Two craggy rocks projecting from the main,
> The roaring wind's tempestuous rage restrain;
> Within, the waves in softer murmurs glide,
> And ships secure without the halsers ride.—*Odyssey*, iii. 118.

Another example of the latter:

> Soft is the strain when Zephyr gently blows,
> And the smooth stream in smoother numbers flows.
> *Essay on Crit.* 366.

Fifthly, Prolonged motion is expressed in an Alexandrine line. The first example shall be of slow motion prolonged:

> A needless Alexandrine ends the song;
> That like a wounded snake, drags its slow length along.
> *Ibid.* 356.

The next example is of forcible motion prolonged:

> The waves behind impel the waves before,
> Wide-rolling, foaming high, and tumbling to the shore.
> *Iliad*, xiii. 1004.

The last shall be of rapid motion prolonged:

> Not so when swift Camilla scours the plain,
> Flies o'er the unbending corn, and skims along the main.
> *Essay on Crit.* 373.

Again, speaking of a rock torn from the brow of a mountain:

> Still gath'ring force, it smokes, and urged amain,
> Whirls, leaps, and thunders down, impetuous to the plain.
> *Iliad*, xiii. 197.

Sixthly, A period consisting mostly of long syllables, that is, of syllables pronounced slow, produceth an emotion resembling faintly that which is produced by gravity and solemnity. Hence the beauty of the following verse:

> Olli sedato respondit corde Latinus.

It resembles equally an object that is insipid and uninteresting.

> Tædet quotidianarum harum formarum.
> *Terence*, *Eunuchus*, Act ii. Sc. 3.

Seventhly, A slow succession of ideas is a circumstance that belongs equally to settled melancholy, and to a period composed of polysyllables pronounced slow; and hence by similarity of emotions, the latter is imitative of the former:

> In those deep solitudes, and awful cells,
> Where heavenly pensive Contemplation dwells,
> And ever-musing Melancholy reigns.—*Pope*, *Elosia to Abelard.*

Eighthly, A long syllable made short, or a short syllable made long, raises, by the difficulty of pronouncing contrary to custom, a feeling similar to that of hard labor:

> When Ajax strives some rock's *vast* weight to throw,
> The line too labors, and the words move slow.
> *Essay on Crit.* 370.

Ninthly, Harsh or rough words pronounced with difficulty, excite a feeling similar to that which proceeds from the labor of thought to a dull writer:

> Just writes to make his barrenness appear,
> And strains from hard-bound brains eight lines a year.
> *Pope's Epistle to Dr. Arbuthnot*, I. 181.

455. I shall close with one example more, which of all makes the finest figure. In the first section mention is made of a climax in sound; and in the second, of a climax in sense. It belongs to the present subject to observe that when these coincide in the same passage, the concordance of sound and sense is delightful: the reader is conscious not only of pleasure from the two climaxes separately, but of an additional pleasure from their concordance, and from finding the sense so justly imitated by the sound. In this respect no periods are more perfect than those borrowed from Cicero in the first section.

The concord between sense and sound is no less agreeable in what may be termed an *anticlimax*, where the progress is from great to little; for this has the effect to make diminutive objects appear still more diminutive. Horace affords a striking example:

> Parturiunt montes, nascetur ridiculus mus.

The arrangement here is singularly artful: the first place is occupied by the verb, which is the capital word by its sense as well as sound; the close is reserved for the word that is the meanest in sense as well as in sound. And it must not be overlooked that the resembling sounds of the two last syllables give a ludicrous air to the whole.

I have had occasion to observe, that to complete the resemblance between sound and sense, artful pronunciation contributes not a little. Pronunciation, therefore, may be considered as a branch of the present subject; and with some observations upon it the section shall be concluded.

In order to give a just idea of pronunciation, it must be distinguished from singing. The latter is carried on by notes, requiring each of them a different aperture of the windpipe: the notes properly belonging to the former, are expressed by different apertures of the mouth, without varying the aperture of the windpipe. This, however, doth not hinder pronunciation to borrow from singing, as one sometimes is naturally led to do in expressing a vehement passion.

In reading, as in singing, there is a key-note: above this note the voice is frequently elevated, to make the sound correspond to the

---

454. Emotions raised by a succession of syllables.—Successive motion imitated. Slow motion. Swift motion. Laborious interrupted motion Rough or tumultuous motion Prolonged motion.—Gravity and solemnity.—Melancholy.—Feeling of hard labor.—Labor of thought imitated.

elevation of the subject: but the mind in an elevated state is disposed to action; therefore, in order to a rest, it must be brought down to the key-note. Hence the term *cadence.*

The only general rule that can be given for directing the pronunciation is, To sound the words in such a manner as to imitate the things they signify. In pronouncing words signifying what is elevated, the voice ought to be raised above its ordinary tone; and words signifying dejection of mind, ought to be pronounced in a low note. To imitate a stern and impetuous passion, the words ought to be pronounced rough and loud; a sweet and kindly passion, on the contrary, ought to be imitated by a soft and melodious tone of voice. In Dryden's ode of *Alexander's Feast*, the line *Fal'n, fal'n, fal'n, fal'n,* represents a gradual sinking of the mind; and therefore is pronounced with a falling voice by every one of taste, without instruction. In general, words that make the greatest figure ought to be marked with a peculiar emphasis. Another circumstance contributes to the resemblance between sense and sound, which is slow or quick pronunciation: for though the length or shortness of the syllables with relation to each other, be in prose ascertained in some measure, and in verse accurately; yet, taking a whole line or period together, it may be pronounced slow or fast. A period, accordingly, ought to be pronounced slow when it expresses what is solemn or deliberate; and ought to be pronounced quick when it expresses what is brisk, lively, or impetuous.

In this chapter I have mentioned none of the beauties of language but what arise from words taken in their proper sense. Beauties that depend on the metaphorical and figurative power of words, are reserved to be treated chapter xx.

[It seems desirable here to introduce some fine thoughts and illustrations from Hazlitt, upon topics treated in this chapter.—*Ed.*

456. Poetry, in its matter and form, is natural imagery or feeling combined with passion and fancy. In its mode of conveyance it combines the ordinary use of language with musical expression. There is a question of long standing—in what the essence of poetry consists; or what it is that determines why one set of ideas should be expressed in prose, another in verse. Milton has told us his idea of poetry in a single line:

> Thoughts that voluntary move
> Harmonious numbers.

As there are certain sounds that excite certain movements, and the song and dance go together, so there are, no doubt, certain thoughts that lead to certain tones of voice, or modulations of sound, and change "the words of Mercury into the songs of Apollo." There is a striking instance of this adaptation of the movement of

---

455. Coincidence of climax of sound and of sense in a passage.—Effect of anticlimax.—Pronunciation; distinguished from singing. General rule for pronunciation. Illustrations How it contributes to a resemblance between sound and sense.

sound and rhythm to the subject, in Spenser's description of the Satyrs accompanying Una to the cave of Sylvanus:

> So from the ground she fearless doth arise,
> And walketh forth without suspect of crime
> They, all as glad as birds of joyous prime,
> Thence lead her forth, about the dancing round,
> Shouting and singing all a shepherd's rhyme;
> And with green branches strewing all the ground,
> Do worship her as queen with olive garland crown'd.
> And all the way their merry pipes they sound,
> That all the woods and doubled echoes ring:
> And with their horned feet do wear the ground,
> Leaping like wanton kids in pleasant spring:
> So towards old Sylvanus they her bring,
> Who with the noise awaked, cometh out.
>
> *Faery Queen*, b. i. c. vi.

On the contrary, there is nothing either musical or natural in the ordinary construction of language. It is a thing altogether arbitrary and conventional. Neither in the sounds themselves, which are the voluntary signs of certain ideas, nor in their grammatical arrangements in common speech, is there any principle of natural imitation or correspondence to the individual ideas, or to the tone of feeling with which they are conveyed to others. The jerks, the breaks, the inequalities, and harshnesses of prose, are fatal to the flow of a poetical imagination, as a jolting road or stumbling horse disturbs the reverie of an absent man. But poetry makes these odds all even. It is the music of language answering to the music of the mind; untying, as it were, "the secret soul of harmony." Wherever any object takes such a hold of the mind, by which it seeks to prolong and repeat the emotion, to bring all other objects into accord with it, and to give the same movement of harmony, sustained and continuous, or gradually varied according to the occasion, to the sounds that express it—this is poetry. There is a deep connection between music and deep-rooted passion. In ordinary speech we arrive at a certain harmony by the modulations of the voice: in poetry the same thing is done systematically by a regular collocation of syllables.—Lect. i.]

SECTION IV.

Versification.

457. THE music of verse, though handled by every grammarian, merits more attention than it has been honored with. It is a subject intimately connected with human nature; and to explain it thoroughly, several nice and delicate feelings must be employed. But before entering upon it, we must see what verse is, or, in other

---

456. Poetry in its matter and form. In its mode of conveyance.—Milton's idea of poetry—The ordinary construction of language. Illustration of poetry.

words, by what mark it is distinguished from prose; a point not so easy as may at first be apprehended. It is true, that the construction of verse is governed by precise rules; whereas prose is more loose, and scarce subjected to any rules. But are the many who have no rules, left without means to make the distinction? and even with respect to the learned, must they apply the rule before they can with certainty pronounce whether the composition be prose or verse? This will hardly be maintained; and therefore instead of rules, the ear must be appealed to as the proper judge. But by what mark does the ear distinguish verse from prose? The proper and satisfactory answer is, That these make different impressions upon every one who hath an ear. This advances us one step in our inquiry.

["Poetry," remarks Sir Joshua Reynolds, "addresses itself to the same faculties and the same dispositions as painting, though by different means. The object of both is to accommodate itself to all the natural propensities and inclinations of the mind. The very existence of poetry depends on the license it assumes of deviating from actual nature, in order to gratify natural propensities by other means, which are found by experience full as capable of affording such gratification. It sets out with a language in the highest degree artificial, a construction of measured words, such as never is, and never was, used by man. Let this measure be what it may, whether hexameter or any other metre used in Latin or Greek—or rhyme, or blank verse, varied with pauses and accents, in modern languages, —they are all equally removed from nature, and equally a violation of common speech. When this artificial mode has been established as the vehicle of sentiment, there is another principle in the human mind to which the work must be referred, which still renders it more artificial, carries it still further from common nature, and deviates only to render it more perfect. That principle is the sense of congruity, coherence, and consistency, which is a real existing principle in man, and it must be gratified. Therefore, having once adopted a style and a measure not found in common discourse, it is required that the sentiments also should be in the same proportion elevated above common nature, from the necessity of there being an agreement of the parts among themselves, that one uniform whole may be produced.

To correspond, therefore, with this general system of deviation from nature, the manner in which poetry is offered to the ear, the tone in which it is recited, should be as far removed from the tone of conversation, as the words of which that poetry is composed, &c —*Works*, vol. ii. Discourse xiii.]

Taking it then for granted, that verse and prose make upon the

457. Verse, as distinguished from prose. The ear discriminates.—Remarks of Sir Joshua Reynolds.—How a musical impression is produced by language. The names given to a period producing such impression

ear different impressions, nothing remains but to explain this difference, and to assign its cause. To this end, I call to my aid an observation made above upon the sound of words, that they are more agreeable to the ear when composed of long and short syllables, than when all the syllables are of the same sort: a continued sound in the same tone, makes not a musical impression: the same note successively renewed by intervals is more agreeable, but still makes not a musical impression. To produce that impression, variety is necessary as well as number: the successive sounds or syllables must be some of them long, some of them short; and if also high and low, the music is the more perfect. The musical impression made by a period consisting of long and short syllables arranged in a certain order, is what the Greeks call *rhythmus*, the Latins *numerus*, and we *melody* or *measure*. Cicero justly observes, that in one continued sound there is no melody: "Numerus in continuatione nullus est."

458. It will probably occur, that melody, if it depend on long and short syllables combined in a sentence, may be found in prose as well as in verse; considering especially, that in both, particular words are accented or pronounced in a higher tone than the rest; and therefore that verse cannot be distinguished from prose by melody merely. The observation is just; and it follows that the distinction between them, since it depends not singly on melody, must arise from the difference of the melody, which is precisely the case; though that difference cannot with any accuracy be explained in words; all that can be said is, that verse is more musical than prose, and its melody more perfect. The difference between verse and prose resembles the difference in music, properly so called, between the song and the recitative; and the resemblance is not the less complete, that these differences, like the shades of colors, approximate sometimes so nearly as scarce to be discernible: the melody of a recitative approaches sometimes to that of a song; which, on the other hand, degenerates sometimes to that of a recitative. Nothing is more distinguishable from prose, than the bulk of Virgil's Hexameters: many of those composed by Horace are very little removed from prose: Sapphic verse has a very sensible melody: that, on the other hand, of an Iambic, is extremely faint.*

This more perfect melody of articulate sounds, is what distinguisheth verse from prose. Verse is subjected to certain inflexible laws; the number and variety of the component syllables being ascertained,

* Music, properly so called, is analyzed into melody and harmony. A succession of sounds so as to be agreeable to the ear constitutes melody: harmony arises from co-existing sounds. Verse therefore can only reach melody, and not harmony.

458. Verse not to be distinguished from prose by the melody alone; but from the difference of the melody. Compared to song and recitative. Verse, subjected to certain laws. Verse requires peculiar genius. The use and office of prose. Note on Washington Irving's prose.

and in some measure the order of succession. Such restraint makes it a matter of difficulty to compose in verse; a difficulty that is not to be surmounted but by a peculiar genius. Useful lessons conveyed to us in verse, are agreeable by the union of music with instruction: but are we for that reason to reject knowledge offered in a plainer dress? That would be ridiculous; for knowledge is of intrinsic merit, independent of the means of acquisition; and there are many, not less capable than willing to instruct us, who have no genius for verse. Hence the use of prose; which, for the reason now given, is not confined to precise rules. There belongs to it a certain melody of an inferior kind, which ought to be the aim of every writer; but for succeeding in it, practice is necessary more than genius. Nor do we rigidly insist for melodious prose: provided the work convey instruction, its chief end, we are little solicitous about its dress.*

459. Having ascertained the nature and limits of our subject, I proceed to the laws by which it is regulated. These would be endless, were verse of all different kinds to be taken under consideration. I propose therefore to confine the inquiry to Latin or Greek Hexameter, and to French and English Heroic verse; which perhaps may carry me farther than the reader will choose to follow. The observations I shall have occasion to make, will at any rate be sufficient for a specimen; and these, with proper variations, may easily be transferred to the composition of other sorts of verse.

Before I enter upon particulars, it must be premised in general, that

* [*Prose and Poetry:* A writer in the *N. A. Review*, speaking of the style of Washington Irving, remarks that "its attraction lies in the charm of finished elegance, which it never loses. The most harmonious and poetical words are carefully selected. Every period is measured and harmonized with nice precision. The length of the sentences is judiciously varied; and the *tout ensemble* produces on the ear an effect very little, if at all inferior to that of the finest versification. Indeed such prose, while it is from the nature of the topics substantially poetry, does not appear to us, when viewed merely as a form of language, to differ essentially from verse. The distinction between verse and prose evidently does not lie in *rhyme*, taking the word in its modern sense, or in any particular species of *rhythm*, as it was understood by the ancients. *Rhyme*, however pleasing to accustomed ears, is, we fear, but too evidently a remnant of the false taste of a barbarous age; and of *rhythm* there are a thousand varieties in the poetry of every cultivated language, which agree in nothing but that they are all harmonious arrangements of words. If then we mean by rhythm or verse merely the form of poetry, and not any particular measure or set of measures to which we are accustomed, it seems to imply nothing but such a disposition of words and sentences as shall strike the ear with a regular melodious flow; and elegant prose, like that of Mr. Irving for instance, comes clearly within the definition. Nor are we quite sure that this delicate species of rhythm ought to be regarded as inferior in beauty to the more artificial ones. The latter, which are obvious, and, as it were, coarse methods of arrangement, are perhaps natural to the ruder periods of language, and are absolutely necessary in poems intended for music; but for every other purpose, it would seem that the most perfect melody is that which is most completely unfettered, and in which the traces of art are best concealed. There is something more exquisitely sweet in the natural strains of the Æolian harp, as they swell and fall upon the ear, under the inspiration of a gentle breeze, on a fine moonlight evening, than in the measured flow of any artificial music."]

to verse of every kind, five things are of importance. 1st, The number of syllables that compose a verse line. 2d, The different lengths of syllables, *i. e.* the difference of time taken in pronouncing. 3d, The arrangement of these syllables combined in words. 4th, The pauses or stops in pronouncing. 5th, The pronouncing syllables in a high or low tone. The three first mentioned are obviously essential to verse: if any of them be wanting, there cannot be that higher degree of melody which distinguisheth verse from prose. To give a just notion of the fourth, it must be observed, that pauses are necessary for three different purposes: one to separate periods and members of the same period, according to the sense; another, to improve the melody of verse; and the last, to afford opportunity for drawing breath in reading. A pause of the first kind is variable, being long or short, frequent or less frequent, as the sense requires. A pause of the second kind, being determined by the melody, is in no degree arbitrary. The last sort is in a measure arbitrary, depending on the reader's command of breath. But as one cannot read with grace, unless, for drawing breath, opportunity be taken of a pause in the sense or in the melody, this pause ought never to be distinguished from the others; and for that reason shall be laid aside. With respect then to the pauses of sense and of melody, it may be affirmed without hesitation, that their coincidence in verse is a capital beauty; but as it cannot be expected, in a long work especially, that every line should be so perfect, we shall afterwards have occasion to see that the pause necessary for the sense must often, in some degree, be sacrificed to the verse-pause, and the latter sometimes to the former.

460. The pronouncing syllables in a high or low tone, contributes also to melody. In reading, whether verse or prose, a certain tone is assumed, which may be called *the key-note;* and in that tone the bulk of the words are sounded. Sometimes to humor the sense, and sometimes the melody, a particular syllable is sounded in a higher tone; and this is termed *accenting a syllable*, or gracing it with an accent. Opposed to the accent, is the cadence, which I have not mentioned as one of the requisites of verse, because it is entirely regulated by the sense, and hath no peculiar relation to verse. The cadence is a falling of the voice below the key-note at the close of every period; and so little is it essential to verse, that in correct reading the final syllable of every line is accented, that syllable only excepted which closes the period, where the sense requires a cadence. The reader may be satisfied of this by experiments; and for that purpose I recommend to him the *Rape of the Lock*, which, in point of versification, is the most complete performance in the English language.

Though the five requisites above mentioned enter the composition

---

459. Five things important to verse of every kind.—Pauses have three purposes. Pauses of sense and melody, when coincident, are beautiful.

of every species of verse, they are however governed by different rules, peculiar to each species. Upon quantity only, one general observation may be premised, because it is applicable to every species of verse, That syllables, with respect to the time taken in pronouncing, are long or short; two short syllables with respect to time, being precisely equal to a long one. These two lengths are essential to verse of all kinds; and to no verse, as far as I know, is a greater variety of time necessary in pronouncing syllables. The voice indeed is frequently made to rest longer than usual upon a word that bears an important signification; but this is done to humor the sense, and is not necessary for melody. A thing not more necessary for melody occurs with respect to accenting, similar to that now mentioned: A word signifying any thing humble, low, or dejected, is naturally in prose, as well as in verse, pronounced in a tone below the key-note.

461. We are now sufficiently prepared for particulars: beginning with Latin or Greek Hexameter, which are the same. What I have to observe upon this species of verse, will come under the four following heads: number, arrangement, pause, and accent; for as to quantity, what is observed above may suffice.

Hexameter lines, as to time, are all of the same length; being equivalent to the time taken in pronouncing twelve long syllables or twenty-four short. An Hexameter line may consist of seventeen syllables; and when regular and not Spondiac, it never has fewer than thirteen: whence it follows, that where the syllables are many, the plurality must be short; where few, the plurality must be long.

This line is susceptible of much variety as to the succession of long and short syllables. It is however subjected to laws that confine its variety within certain limits; and for ascertaining these limits, grammarians have invented a rule by Dactyles and Spondees, which they denominate *feet*. One at first view is led to think, that these feet are also intended to regulate the pronunciation, which is far from being the case; for were one to pronounce according to these feet, the melody of an Hexameter line would be destroyed, or at best be much inferior to what it is when properly pronounced. These feet must be confined to regulate the arrangement, for they serve no other purpose. They are withal so artificial and complex, that I am tempted to substitute in their stead other rules more simple and of more easy application: for example, the following. 1st, The line must always commence with a long syllable, and close with two long preceded by two short. 2d, More than two short can never be found together, nor fewer than two. And 3d, Two long syllables which have been preceded by two short, cannot also be followed by two short. These few rules fulfil all the conditions of

---

460. **The tones of pronunciation.—Accent.—Cadence.—Quantity.—When a low tone is used.**

an Hexameter line, with relation to order or arrangement. To these greater relish, as it regulates more affirmatively the construction of every part. That I may put this rule into words with perspicuity, I take a hint from the twelve long syllables that compose an Hexameter line, to divide it into twelve equal parts or portions, being each of them one long syllable or two short. A portion being thus defined, I proceed to the rule. The 1st, 3d, 5th, 7th, 9th, 11th, and 12th portions, must each of them be one long syllable; the 10th must always be two short syllables; the 2d, 4th, 7th, and 8th, may either be one long or two short. Or to express the thing still more curtly, The 2d, 4th, 6th, and 8th portions may be one long syllable or two short; the 10th must be two short syllables; all the rest must consist each of one long syllable. This fulfils all the conditions of an Hexameter line, and comprehends all the combinations of Dactyles and Spondees that this line admits.

462. Next in order comes the pause. At the end of every Hexameter line, every one must be sensible of a complete close, or full pause; the cause of which follows. The two long syllables preceded by two short, which always close an Hexameter line, are a fine preparation for a pause: for long syllables, or syllables pronounced slow, resembling a slow and languid motion, tending to rest, naturally incline the mind to rest, or to pause; and to this inclination the two preceding short syllables contribute, which, by contrast, make the slow pronunciation of the final syllables the more conspicuous. Besides this complete close or full pause at the end, others are also requisite for the sake of melody, of which I discover two clearly, and perhaps there may be more. The longest and most remarkable, succeeds the 5th portion; the other, which being shorter and more faint, may be called the *semi-pause*, succeeds the 8th portion. So striking is the pause first mentioned, as to be distinguished even by the rudest ear: the monkish rhymes are evidently built upon it; in which by an invariable rule, the final word always chimes with that which immediately precedes the said pause.

The difference of time in the pause and semi-pause, occasions another difference no less remarkable, that it is lawful to divide a word by a semi-pause, but never by a pause, the bad effect of which is sensibly felt in the following examples:

> Effusus labor, at‖que immitis rupta Tyranni

Again:

> Observans nido im‖plumes detraxit; at illa

Again:

> Loricam quam De‖moleo detraxerat ipse

---

461. Length of Hexameter lines; number of syllables.—Dactyles and Spondees.—More simple rules of arrangement.

The dividing a word by a semi-pause has not the same bad effect:

Jamque pedem referens ‖ casus e|vaserat omnes.

Again:

Qualis populea ‖ mœrens Philo|mela sub umbra

Again:

Ludere que vellem ‖ calamo per|misit agresti.

Lines, however, where words are left entire, without being divided even by a semi-pause, run by that means much the more sweetly:

Nec gemere aërea ‖ cessabit | turtur ab ulmo.

Again:

Quadrupedante putrem ‖ sonitu quatit | ungula campum.

Again:

Eurydicen toto ‖ referebant | flumine ripæ.

The reason of these observations will be evident upon the slightest reflection. Between things so intimately connected in reading aloud, as are sense and sound, every degree of discord is unpleasant: and for that reason it is a matter of importance to make the musical pauses coincide as much as possible with those of sense; which is requisite, more especially, with respect to the pause, a deviation from the rule being less remarkable in a semi-pause. Considering the matter as to melody solely, it is indifferent whether the pauses be at the end of words or in the middle; but when we carry the sense along, it is disagreeable to find a word split into two by a pause, as if there were really two words: and though the disagreeableness here be connected with the sense only, it is by an easy transition of perceptions transferred to the sound; by which means we conceive a line to be harsh and grating to the ear, when in reality it is only so to the understanding. (See chapter ii. part i. sec. 5.)

463. To the rule that fixes the pause after the fifth portion there is one exception, and no more: If the syllable succeeding the 5th portion be short, the pause is sometimes postponed to it.

Pupillis quos dura ‖ premit custodia matrum

Again:

In terras oppressa ‖ gravi sub religione

Again:

Et quorum pars magna ‖ fui; quis talia fando

This contributes to diversify the melody; and where the words are smooth and liquid, is not ungraceful; as in the following examples:

Formosam resonare ‖ doces Amaryllida sylvas

Again:

Agricolas, quibus ipsa ‖ procul discordibus armis

---

462. Pause; complete at the end of the line. Two other pauses.—The dividing of a word by a pause or semi-pause. Better not to divide a word.—Rule for musical pauses. The reason for it.

If this pause, placed as aforesaid after the short syllable, happen also to divide a word, the melody by these circumstances is totally annihilated. Witness the following line of Ennius, which is plain prose:

Romæ mœnia terru‖it impiger | Hannibal armis

Hitherto the arrangement of the long and short syllables of an Hexameter line and its different pauses, have been considered with respect to melody; but to have a just notion of Hexameter verse, these particulars must also be considered with respect to sense. There is not perhaps in any other sort of verse, such latitude in the long and short syllables; a circumstance that contributes greatly to that richness of melody which is remarkable in Hexameter verse, and which made Aristotle pronounce that an epic poem in any other verse would not succeed. (Poet. cap. 25.) One defect, however, must not be dissembled, that the same means which contribute to the richness of the melody, render it less fit than several other sorts for a narrative poem. There cannot be a more artful contrivance, as above observed, than to close an Hexameter line with two long syllables preceded by two short; but unhappily this construction proves a great embarrassment to the sense. Virgil, the chief of poets for versification, is forced often to end a line without any close in the sense, and as often to close the sense during the running of a line; though a close in the melody during the movement of the thought, or a close in the thought during the movement of the melody, cannot be agreeable.

464. The accent, to which we proceed, is no less essential than the other circumstances above handled. By a good ear it will be discerned that in every line there is one syllable distinguishable from the rest by a capital accent: that syllable, being the 7th portion, is invariably long.

Nec bene promeritis ‖ capitûr nec | tangitur ira.

Again:

Non sibi sed toto ‖ genitûm se | credere mundo.

Again:

Qualis spelunca ‖ subitô com|mota columba.

In these examples the accent is laid upon the last syllable of a word; which is favorable to the melody in the following respect, that the pause, which for the sake of reading distinctly must follow every word, gives opportunity to prolong the accent. And for that reason, a line thus accented has a more spirited air than when the accent is placed on any other syllable. Compare the foregoing lines with the following:

Alba neque Assyrio ‖ fucâtur | lana veneno.

Again:

Panditur interea ‖ domus ómnipo|tentis Olympi.

---

463. Exception to rule given for pause after the fifth portion.

Again:

Olli sedato ‖ respôndit | corde Latinus.

In lines where the pause comes after the short syllable succeeding the fifth portion, the accent is displaced and rendered less sensible: it seems to split into two, and to be laid partly on the 5th portion, and partly on the 7th, its usual place; as in

Nuda genu nodôque ‖ sinûs col|lecta fluentes

Again:

Formosam ransonâre ‖ docês Amar|yllida sylvas

Besides this capital accent, slighter accents are laid upon other portions; particularly upon the 4th, unless where it consists of two short syllables; upon the 9th, which is always a long syllable; and upon the 11th, where the line concludes with a monosyllable. Such conclusion, by the by, impairs the melody, and for that reason is not to be indulged, unless where it is expressive of the sense. The following lines are marked with all the accents:

Ludere quæ vêllem calamô permîsit agresti.

Again:

Et duræ quêrcus sudâbunt rôscida mella.

Again:

Parturiunt môntes, nascêtur rîdiculûs mus.

465. Reflecting upon the melody of Hexameter verse, we find that order or arrangement doth not constitute the whole of it; for when we compare different lines, equally regular as to the succession of long and short syllables, the melody is found in very different degrees of perfection; which is not occasioned by any particular combination of Dactyles and Spondees, or of long and short syllables, because we find lines where Dactyles prevail, and lines where Spondees prevail, equally melodious. Of the former take the following instance:

Æneadum genetrix hominum divumque voluptas.

Of the latter:

Molli paulatim flavescet campus arista.

What can be more different as to melody than the two following lines, which, however, as to the succession of long and short syllables, are constructed precisely in the same manner?

Spond. Dact. Spond. Spond. Dact. Spond.
Ad talos stola dimissa et circumdata palla.—*Hor.*

Spond. Dact. Spond. Spond. Dact. Spond.
Placatumque nitet diffuso lumine cœlum.—*Lucr.*

In the former, the pause falls in the middle of a word, which is a great blemish, and the accent is disturbed by a harsh elision of the

---

464. The capital accent. The slighter accents.

vowel *a* upon the particle *et*. In the latter, the pauses and the accent are all of them distinct and full: there is no elision; and the words are more liquid and sounding. In these particulars consists the beauty of an Hexameter line with respect to melody: and by neglecting these, many lines in the Satires and Epistles of Horace are less agreeable than plain prose; for they are neither the one nor the other in perfection. To draw melody from these lines, they must be pronounced without relation to the sense: it must not be regarded that words are divided by pauses, nor that harsh elisions are multiplied. To add to the account, prosaic low-sounding words are introduced; and, which is still worse, accents are laid on them. Of such faulty lines take the following instances:

> Candida rectaque sit, munda hactenus sit neque longa.
> Jupiter exclamat simul atque audirit; at in se
> Custodes, lectica, ciniflones, parasitæ
> Optimus, est modulator, ut Alfenus Vafer omni
> Nunc illud tantum quæram, meritone tibi sit.

466. Next in order comes English Heroic verse, which shall be examined under the whole five heads, of number, quantity, arrangement, pause, and accent. This verse is of two kinds; one named *rhyme* or *metre*, and one *blank verse*. In the former the lines are connected two and two by similarity of sound in the final syllables; and two lines so connected are termed a *couplet:* similarity of sound being avoided in the latter, couplets are banished. These two sorts must be handled separately, because there are many peculiarities in each. Beginning with rhyme or metre, the first article shall be discussed in a few words. Every line consists of ten syllables, five short and five long; from which there are but two exceptions, both of them rare. The first is where each line of a couplet is made eleven syllables, by an additional syllable at the end:

> There heroes' wits are kept in pond'rous vases,
> And beaus' in snuff-boxes and tweezer-cases.
>
> The piece, you think, is incorrect? Why, take it;
> I'm all submission; what you'd have it, make it.

This license is sufferable in a single couplet; but if frequent would give disgust.

The other exception concerns the second line of a couplet, which is sometimes stretched out to twelve syllables, termed an *Alexandrine line:*

> A needless Alexandrine ends the song,
> That, like a wounded snake, drags its slow length along.

It doth extremely well when employed to close a period with a certain pomp and solemnity, where the subject makes that tone proper.

---

465. Order or arrangement, not the whole of melody.

466. English heroic verse; two kinds.—Rhyme and blank verse distinguished. **Rhyme** number of syllables. Two exceptions.

467. With regard to quantity, it is unnecessary to mention a second time, that the quantities employed in verse are but two, the one double of the other; that every syllable is reducible to one or other of these standards; and that a syllable of the larger quantity is termed *long*, and of the lesser quantity *short*. It belongs more to the present article to examine what peculiarities there may be in the English language as to long and short syllables. Every language has syllables that may be pronounced long or short at pleasure; but the English above all abounds in syllables of that kind: in words of three or more syllables, the quantity for the most part is invariable: the exceptions are more frequent in dissyllables; but as to monosyllables, they may, without many exceptions, be pronounced either long or short; nor is the ear hurt by a liberty that is rendered familiar by custom. This shows that the melody of English verse must depend less upon quantity than upon other circumstances: in which it differs widely from Latin verse, where every syllable having but one sound, strikes the ear uniformly with its accustomed impression; and a reader must be delighted to find a number of such syllables disposed so artfully as to be highly melodious. Syllables variable in quantity cannot possess this power; for though custom may render familiar both a long and a short pronunciation of the same word, yet the mind, wavering between the two sounds, cannot be so much affected as where every syllable has one fixed sound. What I have further to say upon quantity, will come more properly under the following head or arrangement.

468. And with respect to arrangement, which may be brought within a narrow compass, the English Heroic line is commonly Iambic, the first syllable short, the second long, and so on alternately through the whole line. One exception there is, pretty frequent, of lines commencing with a Trochæus, *i. e.*, a long and a short syllable; but this affects not the order of the following syllables, which go on alternately as usual, one short and one long. The following couplet affords an example of each kind:

Sōme ĭn thĕ fīelds ŏf pūrĕst ēthĕr plāy,
ănd bāsk ănd whītĕn ĭn thĕ blāze ŏf dāy.

It is a great imperfection in English verse, that it excludes the bulk of polysyllables, which are the most sounding words in our language; for very few of them have such alternation of long and short syllables as to correspond to either of the arrangements mentioned. English verse accordingly is almost totally reduced to dissyllables and monosyllables: *magnanimity*, is a sounding word totally excluded: *impetuosity* is still a finer word, by the resemblance of the sound and sense; and yet a negative is put upon it, as well as upon numberless words of the same kind. Polysyllables

467. Quantity.—Peculiarities as to the pronunciation of long and short syllables.—Melody of English verse not dependent on quantity. Differs from Latin verse herein.

composed of syllables long and short alternately, make a good figure in verse: for example, *observance*, *opponent*, *ostensive*, *pindaric*, *productive*, *prolific*, and such others of three syllables. *Imitation*, *imperfection*, *misdemeanor*, *mitigation*, *moderation*, *observator*, *ornamental*, *regulator*, and others similar, of four syllables, beginning with two short syllables, the third long, and the fourth short, may find a place in a line commencing with a Trochæus. I know not if there be any of five syllables. One I know of six, viz., *misinterpretation:* but words so composed are not frequent in our language.

469. One would not imagine, without trial, how uncouth false quantity appears in verse; not less than a provincial tone or idiom. The article *the* is one of the few monosyllables that is invariably short: observe how harsh it makes a line where it must be pronounced long:

> This nȳmph tŏ thē dēstrūctiŏn ōf mănkīnd.

Again,

> Th' ădvēnt'rŏus bārŏn thē brīght lŏcks ădmīred.

Let it be pronounced short, and it reduces the melody almost to nothing: better so however than false quantity. In the following examples we perceive the same defect:

> And old impertinence ‖ expel by new
> With varying vanities ‖ from every part
> Love in these labyrinths ‖ his slaves detains
> New stratagems ‖ the radiant lock to gain
> Her eyes half languishing ‖ half drown'd in tears
> Roar'd from the handkerchief ‖ that caused his pain
> Passions like elements ‖ though born to fight.

The great variety of melody conspicuous in English verse, arises chiefly from the pauses and accents; which are of greater importance than is commonly thought. There is a degree of intricacy in this branch of our subject, and it will be difficult to give a distinct view of it; but it is too late to think of difficulties after we are engaged. The pause, which paves the way to the accent, offers itself first to our examination; and from a very short trial, the following facts will be verified. 1st, A line admits but one capital pause. 2d, In different lines, we find this pause after the fourth syllable, after the fifth, after the sixth, and after the seventh. These four places of the pause lay a solid foundation for dividing English Heroic lines into four kinds; and I warn the reader beforehand, that unless he attend to this distinction, he cannot have any just notion of the richness and variety of English versification. Each kind or order hath a melody peculiar to itself, readily distinguishable by a

---

468. Arrangement; commonly Iambic. One exception.—An imperfection in English verse with respect to polysyllables.

good ear; and I am not without hopes to make the cause of this peculiarity sufficiently evident. It must be observed, at the same time, that the pause cannot be made indifferently at any of the places mentioned; it is the sense that regulates the pause, as will be seen afterwards; and consequently, it is the sense that determines of what order every line must be: there can be but one capital musical pause in a line; and that pause ought to coincide, if possible, with a pause in the sense, in order that the sound may accord with the sense.

What is said shall be illustrated by examples of each sort or order. And first of the pause after the fourth syllable:

> Back through the paths ‖ of pleasing sense I ran.

Again,

> Profuse of bliss ‖ and pregnant with delight.

After the 5th:

> So when an angel ‖ by divine command,
> With rising tempests ‖ shakes a guilty land.

After the 6th:

> Speed the soft intercourse ‖ from soul to soul.

Again,

> Then from his closing eyes ‖ thy form shall part.

After the 7th:

> And taught the doubtful battle ‖ where to rage.

Again,

> And in the smooth description ‖ murmur still.

470. Besides the capital pause now mentioned, inferior pauses will be discovered by a nice ear. Of these there are commonly two in each line: one before the capital pause, and one after it. The former comes invariably after the first long syllable, whether the line begin with a long syllable or a short. The other in its variety imitates the capital pause: in some lines it comes after the 6th syllable, in some after the 7th, and in some after the 8th. Of these semi-pauses take the following examples:

1st and 8th:

> Led | through a sad ‖ variety | of woe.

1st and 7th:

> Still | on thy breast ‖ enamor'd | let me lie.

2d and 8th:

> From storms | a shelter ‖ and from heat | a shade.

2d and 6th:

> Let wealth | let honor ‖ wait | the wedded dame.

---

469 False quantity uncouth.—Variety of melody owing to pauses and accents.—How many capital pauses in a line?—Places of that pause?—How many kinds of English heroic lines?—What regulates the place of the pause? Examples.

2d and 7th:

Above | all pain ‖ all passion | and al pride.

Even from these few examples it appears, that the place of the last semi-pause, like that of the full pause, is directed in a good measure by the sense. Its proper place with respect to the melody is after the eighth syllable, so as to finish the line with an Iambus distinctly pronounced, which, by a long syllable after a short, is a preparation for rest: sometimes it comes after the 6th, and sometimes after the 7th syllable, in order to avoid a pause in the middle of a word, or between two words intimately connected; and so far melody is justly sacrificed to sense.

In discoursing of Hexameter verse, it was laid down as a rule, That a full pause ought never to divide a word: such license deviates too far from the coincidence that ought to be between the pauses of sense and of melody. The same rule must obtain in an English line; and we shall support reason by experiments:

A noble super‖fluity it craves
Abhor, a perpe‖tuity should stand

Are these lines distinguishable from prose? Scarcely, I think.

The same rule is not applicable to a semi-pause, which, being short and faint, is not sensibly disagreeable when it divides a word:

Relent|less walls ‖ whose darksome round contains
For her | white virgins ‖ hyme|neals sing
In these | deep solitudes ‖ and aw|ful cells.

It must however be acknowledged, that the melody here suffers in some degree: a word ought to be pronounced without any rest between its component syllables: a semi-pause that bends to this rule is scarce perceived.

471. The capital pause is so essential to the melody, that one cannot be too nice in the choice of its place, in order to have it clear and distinct. It cannot be in better company than with a pause in the sense; and if the sense require but a comma after the fourth. fifth, sixth, or seventh syllable, it is sufficient for the musical pause. But to make such coincidence essential, would cramp versification too much; and we have experience for our authority, that there may be a pause in the melody where the sense requires none. We must not however imagine, that a musical pause may come after any word indifferently: some words, like syllables of the same word, are so intimately connected, as not to bear a separation even by a pause. The separating, for example, a substantive from its article, would be harsh and unpleasant: witness the following line, which cannot be pronounced with a pause as marked,

If Delia smile, the ‖ flowers begin to spring;

---

470. Inferior pauses, their number.—Rule in regard to a full pause. Examples.

But ought to be pronounced in the following manner:

If Delia smile, ‖ the flowers begin to spring.

If then it be not a matter of indifference where to make the pause, there ought to be rules for determining what words may be separated by a pause, and what are incapable of separation. I shall endeavor to ascertain these rules; not chiefly for their utility, but in order to unfold some latent principles, that tend to regulate our taste even where we are scarce sensible of them; and to that end, the method that appears the most promising, is to run over the verbal relations, beginning with the most intimate. The first that presents itself is that of adjective and substantive, being the relation of subject and quality, the most intimate of all; and with respect to such intimate companions, the question is, whether they can bear to be separated by a pause. What occurs is, that a quality cannot exist independent of a subject; nor are they separate even in imagination, because they make parts of the same idea: and for that reason, with respect to melody as well as sense, it must be disagreeable to bestow upon the adjective a sort of independent existence, by interjecting a pause between it and its substantive. I cannot, therefore, approve the following lines, nor any of the sort; for to my taste they are harsh and unpleasant:

Of thousand bright ‖ inhabitants of air
The sprites of fiery ‖ termagants inflame
The rest, his many-color'd ‖ robe conceal'd
The same, his ancient ‖ personage to deck
Even here, where frozen ‖ Chastity retires
I sit, with sad ‖ civility, I read
Back to my native ‖ moderation slide
Or shall we ev'ry ‖ decency confound
Time was, a sober ‖ Englishman would knock
And place, on good ‖ security, his gold
Taste, that eternal ‖ wanderer, which flies
But ere the tenth ‖ revolving day was run
First let the just ‖ equivalent be paid
Go, threat thy earth-born ‖ myrmidons; but here
Haste to the fierce ‖ Achilles' tent, he cries
All but the ever-wakeful ‖ eyes of Jove
Your own resistless ‖ eloquence employ.

Considering this matter superficially, one might be apt to imagine that it must be the same, whether the adjective go first, which is the natural order, or the substantive, which is indulged by the laws of inversion. But we soon discover this to be a mistake: color, for example, cannot be conceived independent of the surface colored; but a tree may be conceived, as growing in a certain spot, as of a certain kind, and as spreading its extended branches all around, without ever thinking of its color. In a word, a subject may be considered with some of its qualities independent of others: though we cannot form an image of any single quality independent of the subject. Thus, then, though an adjective named first be inseparable from the substantive, the proposition does not reciprocate: an image can be formed of the substantive independent of the adjective; and for that reason, they may be separated by a pause, where the substantive takes the lead:

> For thee the fates ‖ severely kind ordain
> And cursed with hearts ‖ unknowing how to yield.

472. The verb and adverb are precisely in the same condition with the substantive and adjective. An adverb which modifies the action expressed by the verb, is not separable from the verb even in imagination; and therefore I must also give up the following lines:

> And which it much ‖ becomes you to forget
> 'Tis one thing madly ‖ to disperse my store.

But an action may be conceived with some of its modifications, leaving out others; precisely as a subject may be conceived with some of its qualities, leaving out others: and therefore, when by inversion the verb is first introduced, it has no bad effect to interject a pause between it and the adverb that follows. This may be done at the close of a line, where the pause is at least as full as that is which divides the line:

> While yet he spoke, the prince advancing drew
> Nigh to the lodge, &c.

473. The agent and its action come next, expressed in grammar by the active substantive and its verb. Between these, placed in their natural order, there is no difficulty of interjecting a pause: an active being is not always in motion; and therefore it is easily separable in idea from its action: when in a sentence the substantive takes the lead, we know not that action is to follow; and as rest must precede the commencement of motion, this interval is a proper opportunity for a pause.

But when by inversion the verb is placed first, is it lawful to separate it by a pause from the active substantive? I answer, No; because an action is not an idea separable from the agent, more than a quality from the subject to which it belongs. Two lines of the first rate for beauty, have always appeared to me exceptionable, upon account of the pause thus interjected between the verb and the consequent substantive; and I have now discovered a reason to support my taste:

> In these deep solitudes and awful cells,
> Where heavenly pensive ‖ Contemplation dwells,
> And ever musing ‖ Melancholy reigns.

---

471. Choice of place for the capital pause. Examples.—**Rules for determining what words may or may not be separated by a pause.**—Question respecting **adjective and substantive in their natural or inverted order.**

472. Respecting a pause between verb and adverb.

The point of the greatest delicacy regards the active verb and the passive substantive placed in their natural order. The best poets scruple not to separate by a pause an active verb from the thing upon which it is exerted. Such pauses in a long work may be indulged; but taken singly, they certainly are not agreeable; and I appeal to the following examples:

The peer now spreads ‖ the glitt'ring forsex wide
As ever sullied ‖ the fair face of light
Repair'd to search ‖ the gloomy cave of Spleen
Nothing, to make ‖ Philosophy thy friend
Should chance to make ‖ the well-dress'd rabble stare
Or cross to plunder ‖ provinces, the main
These madmen ever hurt ‖ the church or state
How shall we fill ‖ a library with wit
What better teach ‖ a foreigner the tongue
Sure, I if spare ‖ the minister, no rules
Of honor bind me, not to maul his tools.

On the other hand, when the passive substantive is by inversion first named, there is no difficulty of interjecting a pause between it and the verb, more than when the active substantive is first named. The same reason holds in both, that though a verb cannot be separated in idea from the substantive which governs it, and scarcely from the substantive it governs, yet a substantive may always be conceived independent of the verb: when the passive substantive is introduced before the verb, we know not that an action is to be exerted upon it; therefore we may rest till the action commences For the sake of illustration, take the following examples:

Shrines! where their vigils ‖ pale-eyed virgins keep
Soon as thy letters ‖ trembling I unclose
No happier task ‖ these faded eyes pursue.

474. What is said about the pause, leads to a general observation, That the natural order of placing the active substantive and its verb, is more friendly to a pause than the inverted order; but that in all the other connections, inversion affords a far better opportunity for a pause. And hence one great advantage of blank verse over rhyme; its privilege of inversion giving it a much greater choice of pauses than can be had in the natural order of arrangement.

We now proceed to the slighter connections, which shall be discussed in one general article. Words connected by conjunctions and prepositions admit freely a pause between them, which will be clear from the following instances:

Assume what sexes ‖ and what shape they please
The light militia ‖ of the lower sky

---

473. Pause between the agent and its action. When the verb is placed first.—The active verb and its objective substantive.

Connecting particles were invented to unite in a period two substantives, signifying things occasionally united in the thought, but which have no natural union: and between two things not only separable in idea, but really distinct, the mind, for the sake of melody, cheerfully admits by a pause a momentary disjunction of their occasional union.

475. One capital branch of the subject is still upon hand, to which I am directed by what is just now said. It concerns those parts of speech which singly represent no idea, and which become not significant till they be joined to other words. I mean conjunctions, prepositions, articles, and such like accessories, passing under the name of *particles.* Upon these the question occurs, Whether they can be separated by a pause from the words that make them significant? whether, for example, in the following lines, the separation of the accessory preposition from the principal substantive be according to rule?

> The goddess with ‖ a discontented air
> And heighten'd by ‖ the diamond's circling rays
> When victims at ‖ yon altar's foot we lay
> So take it in ‖ the very words of Creech
> An ensign of ‖ the delegates of Jove
> To ages o'er ‖ his native realm he reign'd
> While angels with ‖ their silver wings o'ershade.

Or the separation of the conjunction from the word that is connected by it with the antecedent word:

> Talthybius and ‖ Eurybates the good.

It will be obvious at the first glance, that the foregoing reasoning upon objects naturally connected, is not applicable to words which of themselves are mere ciphers; we must therefore have recourse to some other principle by solving the present question. These particles out of their place are totally insignificant: to give them a meaning, they must be joined to certain words; and the necessity of this junction, together with custom, forms an artificial connection that has a strong influence upon the mind: it cannot bear even a momentary separation, which destroys the sense, and is at the same time contradictory to practice. Another circumstance tends still more to make this separation disagreeable in lines of the first and third order, that it bars the accent, which will be explained afterwards in treating of the accent.

476. Hitherto upon that pause only which divides the line. We proceed to the pause that concludes the line; and the question is, Whether the same rules be applicable to both? This must be an-

---

474. Advantage of blank verse over rhyme as to pauses.—Words connected by conjunctions and prepositions.

475. Particles; whether separable by a pause from the words that make them significant.

swered by making a distinction. In the first line of a couplet, the concluding pause differs little, if at all, from the pause that divides the line; and for that reason the rules are applicable to both equally. The concluding pause of the couplet is in a different condition; it resembles greatly the concluding pause in an Hexameter line. Both of them, indeed, are so remarkable that they never can be graceful, unless where they accompany a pause in the sense. Herce it follows that a couplet ought always to be finished with some close in the sense; if not a point, at least a comma. The truth is, that this rule is seldom transgressed. In Pope's works, I find very few deviations from the rule. Take the following instances:

> Nothing is foreign: parts relate to whole;
> One all-extending, all-preserving soul
> Connects each being——

Another:

> To draw fresh colors from the vernal flow'rs,
> To steal from rainbows ere they drop in show'rs
> A brighter wash——

477. I add, with respect to pauses in general, that supposing the connection to be so slender as to admit a pause, it follows not that a pause may in every such case be admitted. There is one rule to which every other ought to bend, That the sense must never be wounded or obscured by the music; and upon that account I condemn the following lines:

> Ulysses, first ‖ in public cares, she found

And,

> Who rising, high ‖ th' imperial sceptre raised.

With respect to inversion, it appears, both from reason and experiments, that many words which cannot bear a separation in their natural order, admit a pause when inverted. And it may be added that when two words or two members of a sentence, in their natural order, can be separated by a pause, such separation can never be amiss in an inverted order. An inverted period, which deviates from the natural train of ideas, requires to be marked in some measure even by pauses in the sense, that the parts may be distinctly known. Take the following examples:

> As with cold lips ‖ I kiss'd the sacred veil
> With other beauties ‖ charm my partial eyes
> Full in my view ‖ set all the bright abode
> With words like these ‖ the troops Ulysses ruled
> Back to th' assembly roll ‖ the thronging train
> Not for their grief ‖ the Grecian host I blame.

---

476. The pause that concludes the line.—Distinction to be made in the first and second lines of a couplet. How a couplet should be finished.

477. One rule respecting pauses in general.—Remarks as to words in the inverted order. —What an inverted period requires.

The same where the separation is made at the close of the first line of the couplet:

> For spirits, freed from mortal laws, with ease
> Assume what sexes and what shapes they please.

The pause is tolerable even at the close of the couplet, for the reason just now suggested, that inverted members require some slight pause in the sense:

> 'Twas where the plane-tree spreads its shades around:
> The altars heaved; and from the crumbling ground
> A mighty dragon shot.

478. Abstracting at present from the peculiarity of melody arising from the different pauses, it cannot fail to be observed in general, that they introduce into our verse no slight degree of variety. A number of uniform lines having all the same pause, are extremely fatiguing; which is remarkable in French versification. This imperfection will be discerned by a fine ear even in the shortest succession, and becomes intolerable in a long poem. Pope excels in the variety of his melody; which, if different kinds can be compared, is indeed no less perfect than that of Virgil.

From what is last said, there ought to be one exception. Uniformity in the members of a thought demands equal uniformity in the verbal members which express that thought. When therefore resembling objects or things are expressed in a plurality of verse-lines, these lines in their structure ought to be as uniform as possible; and the pauses in particular ought all of them to have the same place. Take the following examples:

> By foreign hands ‖ thy dying eyes were closed;
> By foreign hands ‖ thy decent limbs composed;
> By foreign hands ‖ thy humble grave adorn'd.

Again:

> Bright as the sun ‖ her eyes the gazers strike;
> And, like the sun, ‖ they shine on all alike.

Speaking of Nature, or the God of Nature:

> Warms in the sun ‖ refreshes in the breeze,
> Glows in the stars ‖ and blossoms in the trees;
> Lives through all life ‖ extends through all extent,
> Spreads undivided ‖ operates unspent.

479. Pauses will detain us longer than was foreseen: for the subject is not yet exhausted. It is laid down above, that English Heroic verse admits no more but four capital pauses; and that the capital pause of every line is determined by the sense to be after the fourth, the fifth, the sixth, or the seventh syllable. That this doctrine holds true as far as melody alone is concerned, will be testified

---

478. Advantages to verse of the different pauses.—Fault of French versification.—In what Pope and Virgil excel.—Uniformity in the members of a thought requires what? Examples.

by every good ear. At the same time, I admit, that this rule may be varied where the sense or expression requires a variation, and that so far the melody may justly be sacrificed. Examples accordingly are not unfrequent, in Milton especially, of the capital pause being after the first, the second, or the third syllable. And that this license may be taken, even gracefully, when it adds vigor to the expression, will be clear from the following example. Pope, in his translation of Homer, describes a rock broke off from a mountain, and hurling to the plain, in the following words:

> From steep to steep the rolling ruin bounds;
> At every shock the crackling wood resounds;
> Still gathering force, it smokes; and urged amain,
> Whirls, leaps, and thunders down, impetuous to the plain:
> There stops. ‖ So Hector. Their whole force he proved,
> Resistless when he raged; and when he stopp'd, unmoved.

In the penult line, the proper place of the musical pause is at the end of the fifth syllable; but it enlivens the expression by its coincidence with that of the sense at the end of the second syllable: the stopping short of the usual pause in the melody, aids the impression that is made by the description of the stone's stopping short; and what is lost to the melody by this artifice, is more than compensated by the force that is added to the description. Milton makes a happy use of this license: witness the following examples from his *Paradise Lost:*

> ——— ———Thus with the year
> Seasons return, but not to me returns
> Day ‖ or the sweet approach of even or morn.

> Celestial voices to the midnight air
> Sole ‖ or responsive each to other's note.

> And over them triumphant Death his dart
> Shook ‖ but delay'd to strike.

> ————————And wild uproar
> Stood ruled ‖ stood vast infinitude confined.

> ——— ———And hard'ning in his strength
> Glories ‖ for never since created man
> Met such embodied force.

> From his slack hand the garland wreath'd for Eve
> Down dropp'd ‖ and all the faded roses shed.

> Of unessential night, receives him next,
> Wide gaping ‖ and with utter loss of being,
> Threatens him, &c.

> ——— ———For now the thought
> Both of lost happiness and lasting pain
> Torments him ‖ round he throws his baleful eyes, &c.

If we consider the foregoing passages with respect to melody singly, the pauses are undoubtedly out of their proper place; but

479. Rule for location of pauses may be varied when the sense or expression requires variation. Examples.

being united with those of the sense, they enforce the expression, and enliven it greatly; for, as has been more than once observed, the beauty of expression is communicated to the sound, which by a natural deception, makes even the melody appear more perfect than if the musical pauses were regular.

480. To explain the rules of accenting, two general observations must be premised. The first is, That accents have a double effect: they contribute to the melody, by giving it air and spirit: they contribute no less to the sense, by distinguishing important words from others.* These two effects never can be separated, without impairing the concord that ought to subsist between the thought and the melody: an accent, for example, placed on a low word, has the effect to burlesque it, by giving it an unnatural elevation; and the injury thus done to the sense does not rest there, for it seems also to injure the melody. Let us only reflect what a ridiculous figure a particle must make with an accent or emphasis upon it, a particle that of itself has no meaning, and that serves only, like cement, to unite words significant. The other general observation is, That a word of whatever number of syllables, is not accented upon more than one of them. The reason is, that the object is set in its best light by a single accent, so as to make more than one unnecessary for the sense; and if another be added, it must be for the sound merely; which would be a transgression of the foregoing rule, by separating a musical accent from that which is requisite for the sense.

481. Keeping in view the foregoing observations, the doctrine of accenting English Heroic verse is extremely simple. In the first place, accenting is confined to the long syllables; for a short syllable is not capable of an accent. In the next place, as the melody is enriched in proportion to the number of accents, every word that has a long syllable may be accented: unless the sense interpose which rejects the accenting a word that makes no figure by its signification. According to this rule, a line may admit five accents, a case by no means rare.

But supposing every long syllable to be accented, there is, in every line, one accent that makes a greater figure than the rest, being that which precedes the capital pause. It is distinguished into two kinds; one that is immediately before the pause, and one that is divided from the pause by a short syllable. The former belongs to lines of the first and third order; the latter to those of the second and fourth. Examples of the first kind:

Smooth flow the wâves ‖ the zephyrs gently play,
Belinda smîled ‖ and all the world was gay.

---

* An accent considered with respect to sense is termed *emphasis*.

---

480. Double effects of accent. Should not be separated.—The number of accented syllables in a word.

> He raised his azure wând ‖ and thus began.

Examples of the other kind:

> There lay three gârters ‖ half a pair of gloves,
> And all the trôphies ‖ of his former loves.
>
> Our humble prôvince ‖ is to tend the fair,
> Not a less pleâsing ‖ though less glorious care.
>
> And hew triumphant ârches ‖ to the ground.

These accents make different impressions on the mind, which will be the subject of a following speculation. In the mean time, it may be safely pronounced a capital defect in the composition of verse, to put a low word, incapable of an accent, in the place where this accent should be: this bars the accent altogether; than which I know no fault more subversive of the melody, if it be not the barring of a pause altogether. I may add affirmatively, that no single circumstance contributes more to the energy of verse, than to put an important word where the accent should be, a word that merits a peculiar emphasis. To show the bad effect of excluding the capital accent, I refer the reader to some instances given above (page 325), where particles are separated by a pause from the capital words that make them significant; and which particles ought, for the sake of melody, to be accented, were they capable of an accent. Add to these the following instances from the Essay on Criticism:

> Of leaving what ‖ is natural and fit — line 448.
> Not yet purged off, ‖ of spleen and sour disdained — l. 528.
> No pardon vile ‖ obscenity should find — l. 531.
> When love was all ‖ an easy monarch's care — l. 537.
> For 'tis but half ‖ a judge's task to know — l. 562.
> 'Tis not enough, ‖ taste, judgment, learning, join — l. 563.
> That only makes ‖ superior sense beloved — l. 578.
> Whose right it is, ‖ uncensured, to be dull — l. 590.
> 'Tis best, sometimes, ‖ your censure to restrain. — l. 597.

When this fault is at the end of a line that closes a couplet, it leaves not the slightest trace of melody:

> But of this frame, the bearings and the ties,
> The strong connections, nice dependencies.

In a line expressive of what is humble or dejected, it improves the resemblance between the sound and sense to exclude the capital accent. This, to my taste, is a beauty in the following lines:

> In thêse deep sôlitudes ‖ and awful cells
> The pôor inhâbitant ‖ behôlds in vain.

To conclude this article, the accents are not, like the syllables, confined to a certain number: some lines have no fewer than five, and there are lines that admit not above one. This variety, as we have seen, depends entirely on the different powers of the component words: particles, even where they are long by position, cannot be accented; and polysyllables, whatever space they occupy, admit but one accent. Polysyllables have another defect, that they generally exclude the full pause. It is shown above, that few polysyllables can find place in the construction of English verse: and here are reasons for excluding them, could they find place.

482. After what is said, will it be thought refining too much to suggest, that the different orders (Art. 470) are qualified for different purposes, and that a poet of genius will naturally be led to make a choice accordingly? I cannot think this altogether chimerical. As it appears to me, the first order is proper for a sentiment that is bold, lively, or impetuous; the third order is proper for what is grave, solemn, or lofty; the second for what is tender, delicate, or melancholy, and in general for all the sympathetic emotions; and the last for subjects of the same kind, when tempered with any degree of solemnity. I do not contend, that any one order is fitted for no other task than that assigned it; for at that rate, no sort of melody would be left for accompanying thoughts that have nothing peculiar in them. I only venture to suggest, and I do it with diffidence, that each of the orders is peculiarly adapted to certain subjects, and better qualified than the others for expressing them. The best way to judge is by experiment; and to avoid the imputation of a partial search, I shall confine my instances to a single poem, beginning with the

First order.

> On her white breast, a sparkling cross she wore,
> Which Jews might kiss, and infidels adore.
> Her lively looks a sprightly mind disclose,
> Quick as her eyes, and as unfix'd as those:
> Favors to none, to all she smiles extends;
> Oft she rejects, but never once offends.
> Bright as the sun, her eyes the gazers strike,
> And like the sun, they shine on all alike.
> Yet graceful ease, and sweetness void of pride,
> Might hide her faults, if belles had faults to hide;
> If to her share some female errors fall,
> Look on her face and you'll forget them all.—*Rape of the Lock.*

In accounting for the remarkable liveliness of this passage, it will be acknowledged by every one who has an ear, that the melody must come in for a share. The lines, all of them, are of the first order; a very unusual circumstance in the author of this poem, so eminent for variety in his versification. Who can doubt, that he has been led by delicacy of taste to employ the first order preferably to the others?

Second order.

> Our humble province is to tend the fair,
> Not a less pleasing, though less glorious care;

---

481. The doctrine of accenting English heroic verse.—The number of accents a line may admit, and on what syllables.—The accent that makes the greatest figure. Two kinds of this accent. Examples.—A capital defect in the composition of verse.—What gives energy to verse.—Bad effect of excluding the capital accent. One exception.—Accents allowable in a line.

To save the powder from too rude a gale,
Nor let th' imprison'd essences exhale;
To draw fresh colors from the vernal flowers;
To steal from rainbows, ere they drop their showers, &c.

Again:

Oh, thoughtless mortals! ever blind to fate,
Too soon dejected, and too soon elate.
Sudden, these honors shall be snatch'd away,
And cursed forever this victorious day.

Third order.

To fifty chosen sylphs, of special note,
We trust th' important charge, the petticoat.

Again:

Oh say what stranger cause yet unexplored,
Could make a gentle belle reject a lord?

A plurality of lines of the fourth order, would not have a good effect in succession; because, by a remarkable tendency to rest, their proper office is to close a period. The reader, therefore, must be satisfied with instances where this order is mixed with others.

Not louder shrieks to pitying Heaven are cast,
When husbands, or when lapdogs, breathe their last.

Again:

Steel could the works of mortal pride confound,
And hew triumphal arches to the ground.

Again:

She sees, and trembles at th' approaching ill,
Just in the jaws of ruin, and codille.

Again:

With earnest eyes, and round unthinking face,
He first the snuff-box open'd, then the case.

And this suggests another experiment, which is, to set the different orders more directly in opposition, by giving examples where they are mixed in the same passage.

First and second orders.

Sol through white curtains shot a tim'rous ray,
And ope'd those eyes that must eclipse the day.

Again:

Not youthful kings in battle seized alive,
Not scornful virgins who their charms survive.
Not ardent lovers robb'd of all their bliss,
Not ancient ladies when refused a kiss,
Not tyrants fierce that unrepenting die,
Not Cynthia when her mantua's pinn'd awry,
E'er felt such rage, resentment, and despair,
As thou, sad virgin! for thy ravish'd hair.

First and third.

Think what an equipage thou hast in air,
And view with scorn two pages and a chair.

Again:

Jove's thunder roars, heaven trembles all around,
Blue Neptune storms, the bellowing deeps resound,
Earth shakes her nodding towers, the ground gives way,
And the pale ghosts start at the flash of day!

Second and third.

> Sunk in Thalestris' arms, the nymph he found,
> Her eyes dejected, and her hair unbound.

Again:

> On her heaved bosom hung her drooping head,
> Which with a sigh she raised; and thus she said.

Musing on the foregoing subject, I begin to doubt whether all this while I have been in a reverie, and whether the scene before me, full of objects new and singular, be not mere fairy-land. Is there any truth in the appearance, or is it wholly a work of imagination? We cannot doubt of its reality, and we may with assurance pronounce that great is the merit of English Heroic verse; for though uniformity prevails in the arrangement, in the equality of the lines, and in the resemblance of the final sounds, variety is still more conspicuous in the pauses and in the accents, which are diversified in a surprising manner. Of the beauty that results from a due mixture of uniformity and variety (see chapter ix.), many instances have already occurred, but none more illustrious than English versification; however rude it may be in the simplicity of its arrangement, it is highly melodious by its pauses and accents, so as already to rival the most perfect species known in Greece or Rome; and it is no disagreeable prospect to find it susceptible of still greater refinement.

483. We proceed to *blank verse*, which has so many circumstances in common with rhyme, that its peculiarities may be brought within a narrow compass. With respect to form, it differs from rhyme in rejecting the jingle of similar sounds, which purifies it from a childish pleasure. But this improvement is a trifle compared with what follows. Our verse is extremely cramped by rhyme; and the peculiar advantage of blank verse is, that it is at liberty to attend the imagination in its boldest flights. Rhyme necessarily divides verse into couplets; each couplet makes a complete musical period, the parts of which are divided by pauses, and the whole summed up by a full close at the end: the melody begins anew with the next couplet, and in this manner a composition in rhyme proceeds couplet after couplet. I have often had occasion to mention the correspondence and concord that ought to subsist between sound and sense; from which it is a plain inference, that if a couplet be a complete period with regard to melody, it ought regularly to be the same with regard to sense. As it is extremely difficult to support such strictness of composition, licenses are indulged, as explained above; which, however, must be used with discretion, so as to preserve some degree of concord between the sense and the music: there ought never to be a full close in the sense, but at the end of a couplet; and there ought always to be some pause in the sense at the

---

482. To what sentiments the various orders of English verse are adapted. Examples.—The uniformity and the variety of English verse. The beauty of a due mixture of these

end of every couplet: the same period as to sense may be extended through several couplets; but each couplet ought to contain a distinct member, distinguished by a pause in the sense as well as in the sound; and the whole ought to be closed with a complete cadence.* Rules such as these, must confine rhyme within very narrow bounds: a thought of any extent cannot be reduced within its compass: the sense must be curtailed and broken into parts, to make it square with the curtness of the melody; and besides, short periods afford no latitude for inversion.

484. I have examined this point with the stricter accuracy, in order to give a just notion of blank verse, and to show that a slight difference in form may produce a great difference in substance. Blank verse has the same pauses and accents with rhyme, and a pause at the end of every line, like what concludes the first line of a couplet. In a word, the rules of melody in blank verse are the same that obtain with respect to the first line of a couplet; but being disengaged from rhyme, or from couplets, there is access to make every line run into another, precisely as to make the first line of a couplet run into the second. There must be a musical pause at the end of every line; but this pause is so slight as not to require a pause in the sense; and accordingly the sense may be carried on with or without pauses, till a period of the utmost extent be completed by a full close both in the sense and the sound: there is no restraint, other than that this full close be at the end of a line; and this restraint is necessary in order to preserve a coincidence between sense and sound, which ought to be aimed at in general, and is indispensable in the case of a full close, because it has a striking effect. Hence the fitness of blank verse for inversion, and consequently the lustre of its pauses and accents; for which, as observed above, there is greater scope in inversion than when words run in their natural order.

In the second section of this chapter it is shown that nothing contributes more than inversion to the force and elevation of language; the couplets of rhyme confine inversion within narrow limits; nor would the elevation of inversion, were there access for it in rhyme, readily accord with the humbler tone of that sort of verse. It is universally agreed that the loftiness of Milton's style supports admirably the sublimity of his subject; and it is not less certain that the loftiness of his style arises chiefly from inversion. Shakspeare deals little

* This rule is quite neglected in French versification. Even Boileau makes no difficulty to close one subject with the first line of a couplet, and to begin a new subject with the second. Such license, however sanctified by practice, is unpleasant by the discordance between the pauses of the sense and of the melody.

483. How blank verse differs from rhyme, and surpasses it.
484. The rules of melody in blank verse.—Fitness for inversion.—Milton and Shakspeare's style.

in inversion; but his blank verse being a sort of measured prose, is perfectly well adapted to the stage, where labored inversion is highly improper, because in dialogue it never can be natural.

485. Hitherto I have considered that superior power of expression which verse acquires by laying aside rhyme. But this is not the only ground for preferring blank verse: it has another preferable quality not less signal, and that is a more extensive and more complete melody. Its music is not, like that of rhyme, confined to a single couplet; but takes in a great compass, so as in some measure to rival music properly so called. The interval between its cadences may be long or short at pleasure; and, by that means, its melody, with respect both to richness and variety, is superior far to that of rhyme, and superior even to that of the Greek and Latin Hexameter. Of this observation no person can doubt who is acquainted with the *Paradise Lost;* in which work there are indeed many careless lines, but at every turn the richest melody as well as the sublimest sentiments are conspicuous. Take the following specimen:

> Now Morn her rosy steps in th' eastern clime
> Advancing, sow'd the earth with orient pearl;
> When Adam waked, so custom'd, for his sleep
> Was aëry light, from pure digestion bred
> And temp'rate vapors bland, which th' only sound
> Of leaves and fuming rills, Aurora's fan,
> Lightly dispersed, and the shrill matin song
> Of birds on every bough; so much the more
> His wonder was to find unwaken'd Eve,
> With tresses discomposed, and glowing cheek,
> As through unquiet rest; he on his side
> Leaning half-raised, with looks of cordial love
> Hung over her enamor'd, and beheld
> Beauty, which, whether waking or asleep,
> Shot forth peculiar graces; then with voice
> Mild, as when Zephyrus on Flora breathes,
> Her hand soft touching, whisper'd thus: Awake,
> My fairest, my espoused, my latest found,
> Heaven's last best gift, my ever-new delight,
> Awake; the morning shines, and the fresh field
> Calls us: we lose the prime, to mark how spring
> Our tended plants, how blows the citron grove,
> What drops the myrrh, and what the balmy reed,
> How nature paints her colors, and how the bee
> Sits on the bloom extracting liquid sweet.—Book V. l. 1.

Comparing Latin Hexameter with English Heroic rhyme, the former has obviously the advantage in the following particulars. It is greatly preferable as to arrangement, by the latitude it admits in placing the long and short syllables. Secondly, the length of an Hexameter line hath a majestic air: ours, by its shortness, is indeed more brisk and lively, but much less fitted for the sublime. And, thirdly, the long high-sounding words that Hexameter admits, add greatly to its majesty. To compensate these advantages, English rhyme possesses a greater number and greater variety both of pauses and of accents. These two sorts of verse stand indeed pretty much in opposition: in Hexameter, great variety of arrangement, none in the pauses nor accents; in English rhyme, great variety in the pauses and accents, very little in the arrangement.

486. In blank verse are united, in a good measure, the several properties of Latin Hexameter and English rhyme; and it possesses besides many signal properties of its own. It is not confined, like Hexameter, by a full close at the end of every line; nor, like rhyme, by a full close at the end of every couplet. Its construction, which admits the lines to run into each other, gives it a still greater majesty than arises from the length of an Hexameter line. By the same means it admits inversion even beyond the Latin or Greek Hexameter; for these suffer some confinement by the regular closes at the end of every line. In its music it is illustrious above all: the melody of Hexameter verse is circumscribed to a line; and of English rhyme to a couplet: the melody of blank verse is under no confinement, but enjoys the utmost privilege of which melody of verse is susceptible, which is to run hand in hand with the sense. In a word, blank verse is superior to Hexameter in many articles, and inferior to it in none, save in the freedom of arrangement, and in the use of long words.

487. In French Heroic verse, there are found, on the contrary, all the defects of Latin Hexameter and the English rhyme, without the beauties of either: subjected to the bondage of rhyme, and to the full close at the end of every couplet, it is also extremely fatiguing by uniformity in its pauses and accents: the line invariably is divided by the pause into two equal parts, and the accent is invariably placed before the pause:

> Jeune et vaillant hérôs ‖ dont la haute sagesse
> N'est point la fruit tardif ‖ d'une lente vieillesse.

Here every circumstance contributes to a tiresome uniformity: a constant return of the same pause and of the same accent, as well as an equal division of every line; which fatigue the ear without intermission or change. I cannot set this matter in a better light, than by presenting to the reader a French translation of the following passage of Milton:

> Two of far nobler shape, erect and tall,
> Godlike erect, with native honor clad,
> In naked majesty, seem'd lords of all,
> And worthy seem'd; for in their looks divine,
> The image of their glorious Maker, shone
> Truth, wisdom, sanctitude severe and pure;
> Severe, but in true filial freedom placed;
> Whence true authority in men; though both
> Not equal, as their sex not equal seem'd;
> For contemplation he and valor form'd,
> For softness she and sweet attractive grace;
> He for God only, she for God in him.

---

485. The melody of blank verse more extensive and complete than that of rhyme. Example.

486. Latin Hexameter compared with English heroic rhyme compared with blank verse. Peculiar advantages of the latter

Were the pauses of the sense and sound in this passage but a little better assorted, nothing in verse could be more melodious. In general, the great defect in Milton's versification, in other respects admirable, is the want of coincidence between the pauses of the sense and sound.

The translation is in the following words:

Ces lieux délicieux, ce paradis charmant,
Reçoit de deux objets son plus bel ornement;
Leur port majestueux, et leur démarche altière,
Semble leur mériter sur la nature entière
Ce droit de commander que Dieu leur a donné,
Sur leur auguste front de gloire couronné.
Du souverain du ciel brille la ressemblance;
Dans leurs simples regards éclate l'innocence,
L'adorable candeur, l'aimable vérité,
La raison, la sagesse, et la sevérité,
Qu'adoucit la prudence, et cet air de droiture
Du visage des rois respectable parure.
Ces deux objets divins n'ont pas les mêmes traits,
Ils paraissent formés, quoique tous deux parfaits;
L'un pour la majesté, la force, et la noblesse;
L'autre pour la douceur, la grâce, et la tendresse;
Celui-ci pour Dieu seul, l'autre pour l'homme encor.

Here the sense is fairly translated, the words are of equal power, and yet how inferior the melody!

488. Many attempts have been made to introduce Hexameter verse into the living languages, but without success. The English language, I am inclined to think, is not susceptible of this melody: and my reasons are these. First, the polysyllables in Latin and Greek are finely diversified by long and short syllables, a circumstance that qualifies them for the melody of Hexameter verse: ours are extremely ill qualified for that service, because they superabound in short syllables. Secondly, the bulk of our monosyllables are arbitrary with regard to length, which is an unlucky circumstance in Hexameter: for although custom, as observed above, may render familiar a long or a short pronunciation of the same word, yet the mind wavering between the two sounds, cannot be so much affected with either, as with a word that hath always the same sound; and for that reason, arbitrary sounds are ill fitted for a melody which is chiefly supported by quantity. In Latin and Greek Hexameter, invariable sounds direct and ascertain the melody. English Hexameter would be destitute of melody, unless by artful pronunciation; because of necessity the bulk of its sounds must be arbitrary. The pronunciation is easy in a simple movement of alternate long and short syllables; but would be perplexing and unpleasant in the diversified movement of Hexameter verse.

489. Rhyme makes so great a figure in modern poetry as to deserve a solemn trial. I have for that reason reserved it to be ex-

---

487. Defects of French heroic verse.—Defect in Milton's versification.

488. Attempts to introduce Hexameter verse into the living languages. The English language unsuited to it.

amined with deliberation; in order to discover, if I can, its peculiar beauties, and its degree of merit. The first view of this subject leads naturally to the following reflection: "That rhyme having no relation to sentiment, nor any effect upon the ear other than a mere jingle, ought to be banished all compositions of any dignity, as affording but a trifling and childish pleasure." It will also be observed, "That a jingle of words hath in some measure a ludicrous effect; witness the double rhymes of *Hudibras*, which contribute no small share to its drollery: that in a serious work this ludicrous effect would be equally remarkable, were it not obscured by the prevailing gravity of the subject: that having however a constant tendency to give a ludicrous air to the composition, more than ordinary fire is requisite to support the dignity of the sentiments against such an undermining antagonist."

These arguments are specious, and have, undoubtedly, some weight. Yet, on the other hand, it ought to be considered that in modern tongues rhyme has become universal among men as well as children; and that it cannot have such a currency without some foundation in human nature. In fact, it has been successfully employed by poets of genius, in their serious and grave compositions, as well as in those which are more light and airy. Here in weighing authority against argument, the scales seem to be upon a level; and therefore, to come at any thing decisive, we must pierce a little deeper.

Music has great power over the soul; and may successfully be employed to inflame or soothe passions, if not actually to raise them. A single sound, however sweet, is not music; but a single sound repeated after intervals, may have the effect to rouse attention, and to keep the hearer awake: and a variety of similar sounds, succeeding each other after regular intervals, must have a still stronger effect. This consideration is applicable to rhyme, which connects two verse-lines by making them close with two words similar in sound. And considering attentively the musical effect of a couplet, we find, that it rouses the mind, and produceth an emotion moderately gay without dignity or elevation: like the murmuring of a brook gliding through pebbles, it calms the mind when perturbed, and gently raises it when sunk. These effects are scarce perceived when the whole poem is in rhyme; but are extremely remarkable by contrast, in the couplets that close the several acts of our later tragedies: the tone of the mind is sensibly varied by them, from anguish, distress, or melancholy, to some degree of ease and alacrity. The speech of Alicia, at the close of the fourth act of *Jane Shore*, puts the matter beyond doubt: in a scene of deep distress, the rhymes which finish the act, produce a certain gayety and cheerfulness, far from according with the tone of the passion:

Alicia. Forever? Oh Forever!
Oh! who can bear to be a wretch forever!

My rival too! his last thoughts hung on her:
And, as he parted, left a blessing for her:
Shall she be bless'd, and I be cursed, forever!
No; since her fatal beauty was the cause
Of all my suff'rings, let her share my pains;
Let her, like me of every joy forlorn,
Devote the hour when such a wretch was born!
Like me to deserts and to darkness run,
Abhor the day, and curse the golden sun;
Cast every good and every hope behind;
Detest the works of nature, loathe mankind:
Like me with cries distracted fill the air,
Tear her poor bosom, and her frantic hair,
And prove the torments of the last despair.

490. Having described, the best way I can, the impression that rhyme makes on the mind; I proceed to examine whether there be any subjects to which rhyme is peculiarly adapted, and for what subjects it is improper. Grand and lofty subjects, which have a powerful influence, claim precedence in this inquiry. In the chapter of Grandeur and Sublimity it is established, that a grand or sublime object inspires a warm enthusiastic emotion disdaining strict regularity and order: which emotion is very different from that inspired by the moderately enlivening music of rhyme. Supposing then an elevated subject to be expressed in rhyme, what must be the effect? The intimate union of the music with the subject produces an intimate union of their emotions; one inspired by the subject, which tends to elevate and expand the mind; and one inspired by the music, which, confining the mind within the narrow limits of regular cadence and similar sound, tends to prevent all elevation above its own pitch. Emotions so little concordant cannot in union have a happy effect.

But it is scarce necessary to reason upon a case that never did, and probably never will happen, viz., an important subject clothed in rhyme, and yet supported in its utmost elevation. A happy thought or warm expression, may at times give a sudden bound upward; but it requires a genius greater than has hitherto existed, to support a poem of any length in a tone elevated much above that of the melody. Tasso and Ariosto ought not to be made exceptions, and still less Voltaire. And after all, where the poet has the dead weight of rhyme constantly to struggle with, how can we expect a uniform elevation in a high pitch; when such elevation, with all the support it can receive from language, requires the utmost effort of the human genius?

491. But now, admitting rhyme to be an unfit dress for grand and lofty images; it has one advantage, however, which is, to raise a low subject to its own degree of elevation. Addison (Spectator, No. 285) observes, "That rhyme, without any other assistance, throws the language off from prose, and very often makes an in-

---

489. Objections to rhyme. The answer.—The music of rhyme. Example.
490. Subjects to which rhyme is peculiarly adapted, and the reverse.

different phrase pass unregarded; but where the verse is not built upon rhyme, there, pomp of sound, and energy of expression are indispensably necessary to support the style, and keep it from falling into the flatness of prose." This effect of rhyme is remarkable in French verse; which, being simple, and little qualified for inversion, readily sinks down to prose where not artificially supported: rhyme is therefore indispensable in French tragedy, and may be proper even in French comedy. Voltaire assigns that very reason for adhering to rhyme in these compositions. He indeed candidly owns, that, even with the support of rhyme, the tragedies of his country are little better than conversation-pieces; which seems to infer, that the French language is weak, and an improper dress for any grand subject. Voltaire was sensible of the imperfection; and yet Voltaire attempted an epic poem in that language.

492. The cheering and enlivening power of rhyme, is still more remarkable in poems of short lines, where the rhymes return upon the ear in a quick succession; for which reason rhyme is perfectly well adapted to gay, light, and airy subjects. Witness the following:

> O the pleasing, pleasing anguish,
> When we love and when we languish!
>   Wishes rising,
>   Thoughts surprising,
>   Pleasure courting,
>   Charms transporting,
>   Fancy viewing,
>   Joys ensuing,
> O the pleasing, pleasing anguish!
>
> *Rosamond*, Act I. Sc. 2.

For that reason, such frequent rhymes are very improper for any severe or serious passion: the dissonance between the subject and the melody is very sensibly felt. Witness the following:

> Now under hanging mountains,
> Beside the fall of fountains,
> Or where Hebrus wanders,
> Rolling in meanders,
>   All alone,
>   Unheard, unknown,
>   He makes his moan,
>   And calls her ghost,
> Forever, ever, ever lost;
>   Now with furies surrounded,
>   Despairing, confounded,
>   He trembles, he glows,
>   Amidst Rodopé's snows.—*Pope*, Ode for Music, l. 97.

Rhyme is not less unfit for anguish or deep distress, than for subjects elevated and lofty; and for that reason has been long disused in the English and Italian tragedy. In a work where the subject is serious though not elevated, rhyme has not a good effect; because the airiness of the melody agrees not with the gravity of the

---

491. One advantage of rhyme.—Addison's remark.—Effect of rhyme in French verse.

subject: the *Essay on Man*, which treats a subject great and important, would make a better figure in blank verse. Sportive love, mirth, gayety, humor, and ridicule, are the province of rhyme. The boundaries assigned it by nature, were extended in barbarous and illiterate ages; and in its usurpations it has long been protected by custom; but taste in the fine arts, as well as in morals, improves daily, and makes a progress towards perfection, slow indeed but uniform; and there is no reason to doubt, that rhyme, in Britain, will in time be forced to abandon its unjust conquest, and to confine itself within its natural limits.

Having said what occurred upon rhyme, I close the section with a general observation, That the melody of verse so powerfully enchants the mind as to draw a veil over very gross faults and imperfections.

A LIST OF THE DIFFERENT FEET, AND OF THEIR NAMES.

1. Pyrrhichius, consists of two short syllables, examples: *Deus*, *given*, *cannot*, *hillock*, *running*.
2. Spondeus, consists of two long syllables: *omnes*, *possess*, *forewarn*, *mankind*, *sometime*.
3. Iambus, composed of a short and a long: *pios*, *intent*, *degree*, *appear*, *consent*, *repent*, *demand*, *report*, *suspect*, *affront*, *event*.
4. Trochæus, or Choreus, a long and short: *fervat*, *whereby*, *after*, *legal*, *measure*, *burden*, *holy*, *lofty*.
5. Tribrachys, three short: *melius*, *property*.
6. Molossus, three long: *delectant*.
7. Anapæstus, two short and a long: *animos*, *condescend*, *apprehend*, *overheard*, *acquiesce*, *immature*, *overcharge*, *serenade*, *opportune*.
8. Dactylus, a long and two short: *carmina*, *evident*, *excellence*, *estimate*, *wonderful*, *altitude*, *burdened*, *minister*, *tenement*.
9. Bacchius, a short and two long: *dolores*.
10. Hyppobacchius, or Antibacchius, two long and a short: *pelluntur*.
11. Creticus, or Amphimacer, a short syllable between two long: *insito*, *after noon*.
12. Amphibrachys, a long syllable between two short: *honore*, *consider*, *imprudent*, *procedure*, *attended*, *proposed*, *respondent*, *concurrence*, *apprentice*, *respective*, *revenue*.
13. Proceleusmaticus, four short syllables: *hominibus*, *necessary*.
14. Dispondeus, four long syllables: *infinitis*.
15. Diiambus, composed of two Iambi: *severitas*.
16. Ditrochæus, of two Trochæi: *permanere*, *procurator*.
17. Ionicus, two short syllables and two long: *properabant*.
18. Another foot passes under the same name, composed of two long syllables and two short: *calcaribus*, *possessory*.
19. Choriambus, two short syllables between two long: *nobilitas*.
20. Antispastus, two long syllables between two short: *Alexander*.

---

492. Power of rhyme in poems of short lines.—Frequent rhymes, where unsuitable Essay on Man – Subjects that form the province of rhyme.—List of Feet.

21. PÆON 1st, one long syllable and three short: *temporibus, ordinary, inventory, temperament.*
22. PÆON 2d, the second syllable long, and the other three short: *rapidity solemnity, minority, considered, imprudently, extravagant, respectfully, accordingly.*
23. PÆON 3d, the third syllable long and the other three short: *animatus, independent, condescendence, sacerdotal, reimbursement, manufacture.*
24. PÆON 4th, the last syllable long and the other three short: *celeritas.*
25. EPITRITUS 1st, the first syllable short and the other three long: *voluptates.*
26. EPITRITUS 2d, the second syllable short and the other three long: *pœnitentes.*
27. EPITRITUS 3d, the third syllable short, and the other three long: *discordias.*
28. EPITRITUS 4th, the last syllable short, and the other three long: *fortunatus.*
29. A word of five syllables composed of a Pyrrhichius and Dactylus: *ministerial.*
30. A word of five syllables composed of a Trochæus and Dactylus: *singularity.*
31. A word of five syllables composed of a Dactylus and Trochæus: *precipitation, examination.*
32. A word of five syllables, the second only long: *significancy.*
33. A word of six syllables composed of two Dactyles: *impetuosity.*
34. A word of six syllables composed of a Tribrachys and Dactylæ: *pusillanimity.*

N. B.—Every word may be considered as a prose foot, because every word is distinguished by a pause; and every foot in verse may be considered as a verse word, composed of syllables pronounced at once without a pause.

CHAPTER XIX.

COMPARISONS.

[HAZLITT has some observations on the subject of poetry that will serve as an introduction to the present chapter.—*Ed.*

493. Poetry is strictly *the language of the imagination;* and the imagination is that faculty which represents objects, not as they are in themselves, but as they are moulded by other thoughts and feelings, into an infinite variety of shapes and combinations of power. *This language is not the less true to nature because it is false in point of fact;* but so much the more true and natural, if it conveys the impression which the object under the influence of passion makes on the mind. Let an object, for instance, be presented to the senses in a state of agitation or fear, and the imagination will distort or magnify the object, and convert it into the likeness of whatever is most proper to encourage the fear. "Our eyes are made the fools of the other faculties." This is the universal law of the imagination.

We compare a man of gigantic stature to a tower, not that he is any thing like so large, but because the excess of his size beyond what we are accustomed to expect, or the usual size of things of the same class, produces by contrast a greater feeling of magnitude and of ponderous strength than another object of ten times the same dimensions. The intensity of the feeling makes up for the disproportion of the objects. Things are equal to the imagination which have the power of affecting the mind with an equal degree of terror, admiration, delight, or love.

Poetry is only the highest eloquence of passion, the most vivid form of expression that can be given to our conception of any thing, whether pleasurable or painful, mean or dignified, delightful or distressing. It is the perfect coincidence of the image and the words with the feeling we have, and of which we cannot get rid in any other way that gives an instant "satisfaction to the thought." This is equally the origin of wit and fancy, of comedy and tragedy, of the sublime and pathetic.—Lect. i.]

Comparisons, as observed above (chapter viii.), serve two purposes; when addressed to the understanding, their purpose is to instruct; when to the heart, their purpose is to please. Various means contribute to the latter: first, the suggesting some unusual resemblance or contrast; second, the setting an object in the strongest light; third, the associating an object with others, that are agreeable; fourth, the elevating an object; and fifth, the depressing it. And that comparisons may give pleasure by these various means, appears from what is said in the chapter above cited; and will be made still more evident by examples, which shall be given after premising some general observations.

Objects of different senses cannot be compared together; for such objects, being entirely separated from each other, have no circumstance in common to admit either resemblance or contrast. Objects of hearing may be compared together, as also of taste, of smell, and of touch: but the chief fund of comparison are objects of sight; because, in writing or speaking, things can only be compared in idea, and the ideas of sight are more distinct and lively than those of any other sense.

494. When a nation emerging out of barbarity begins to think of the fine arts, the beauties of language cannot long lie concealed; and when discovered, they are generally, by the force of novelty, carried beyond moderation. Thus, in the early poems of every nation, we find metaphors and similes founded on slight and distant resemblances, which, losing their grace with their novelty, wear gradually out of repute; and now, by the improvement of taste, none but correct metaphors and similes are admitted into any polite composition. To illustrate this observation a specimen shall be

---

493. Hazlitt's remarks on poetry.—Purposes answered by comparisons. By what means they give pleasure.—Objects that cannot be compared together.—The chief fund of comparisons.

given afterwards of such metaphors as I have been describing; with respect to similes, take the following specimen:

Behold, thou art fair, my love; thy hair is as a flock of goats that appear from Mount Gilead: thy teeth are like a flock of sheep from the washing, every one bearing twins: thy lips are like a thread of scarlet; thy neck like the tower of David built for an armory, whereon hang a thousand shields of mighty men; thy two breasts like two young roes that are twins, which feed among the lilies; thy eyes like the fish-pools in Heshbon, by the gate of Bath-rabbim; thy nose like the tower of Lebanon, looking towards Damascus.—*Song of Solomon.*

Thou art like snow on the heath; thy hair like the mist of Cromla, when it curls on the rocks, and shines to the beam of the west; thy breasts are like two smooth rocks seen from Branno of the streams, thy arms like two white pillars in the hall of the mighty Fingal.—*Fingal.*

495. It has no good effect to compare things by way of simile that are of the same kind; nor to compare by contrast things of different kinds. The reason is given in the chapter quoted above; and the reason shall be illustrated by examples. The first is a comparison built upon a resemblance so obvious as to make little or no impression.

This just rebuke inflamed the Lycian crew,
They join, they thicken, and the assault renew;
Unmoved th' embodied Greeks their fury dare,
And fix'd support the weight of all the war;
Nor could the Greeks repel the Lycian powers,
Nor the bold Lycians force the Grecian towers.
As on the confines of adjoining grounds,
Two stubborn swains with blows dispute their bounds;
They tug, they sweat; but neither gain, nor yield,
One foot, one inch, of the contended field;
Thus obstinate to death, they fight, they fall;
Nor these can keep, nor those can win the wall.—*Iliad*, xii. 505.

Another, from Milton, lies open to the same objection. Speaking of the fallen angels searching for mines of gold,

A numerous brigade hasten'd; as when bands
Of pioneers with spade and pick-axe arm'd,
Forerun the royal camp to trench a field
Or cast a rampart.

The next shall be of things contrasted that are of different kinds.

Queen. What, is my Richard both in shape and mind
Transform'd and weak? Hath Bolingbroke deposed
Thine intellect? Hath he been in thy heart!
The lion thrusteth forth his paw,
And wounds the earth, if nothing else, with rage
To be o'erpowored; and wilt thou, pupil-like,
Take thy correction mildly, kiss the rod,
And fawn on rage with base humility?
Richard II. Act V. Sc. 1.

This comparison has scarce any force; a man and a lion are of different species, and therefore are proper subjects for a simile; but there is no such resemblance between them in general, as to pro-

---

494. The early poems of every nation.
495. What things should not be compared by way of simile and contrast.

duce any strong effect by contrasting particular attributes or circumstances.

496. A third general observation is, That abstract terms can never be the subject of comparison, otherwise than by being personified. Shakspeare compares adversity to a toad, and slander to the bite of a crocodile; but in such comparisons these abstract terms must be imagined sensible beings.

To have a just notion of comparisons, they must be distinguished into two kinds; one common and familiar, as where a man is compared to a lion in courage, or to a horse in speed; the other more distant and refined, where two things that have in themselves no resemblance or opposition, are compared with respect to their effects. There is no resemblance between a flower-pot and a cheerful song; and yet they may be compared with respect to their effects, the emotions they produce being similar. There is as little resemblance between fraternal concord and precious ointment; and yet observe how successfully they are compared with respect to the impressions they make:

> Behold how good and how pleasant it is for brethren to dwell together in unity. It is like the precious ointment upon the head, that ran down upon Aaron's beard, and descended to the skirts of his garment.—*Psalm* 133.

For illustrating this sort of comparison, I add some more examples:

> Delightful is thy presence, O Fingal! it is like the sun on Cromla, when the hunter mourns his absence for a season, and sees him between the clouds.
>
> Did not Ossian hear a voice? or is it the sound of days that are no more? Often, like the evening sun, comes the memory of former times on my soul.
>
> His countenance is settled from war; and is calm as the evening beam, that from the cloud of the west looks on Crona's silent vale.
>
> Sorrow, like a cloud on the sun, shades the soul of Clessammor.
>
> The music was like the memory of joys that are past, pleasant and mournful to the soul.
>
> Pleasant are the words of the song, said Cuchullin, and lovely are the tales of other times. They are like the calm dew of the morning on the hill of roes, when the sun is faint on its side, and the lake is settled and blue in the vale.

These quotations are from the poems of Ossian, who abounds with comparisons of this delicate kind, and appears singularly happy in them.

497. I proceed to illustrate by particular instances the different means by which comparisons, whether of the one sort or the other, can afford pleasure; and, in the order above established, I begin with such instances as are agreeable, by suggesting some unusual resemblance or contrast:

> Sweet are the uses of adversity,
> Which, like the toad, ugly and venomous,
> Wears yet a precious jewel in his head.
>
> *As You Like It*, Act II. Sc. 1.

---

496. Abstract terms.—Two kinds of comparisons.—How a flower-pot and a cheerful song may be compared. Other examples.

Gardiner. Bolingbroke hath seized the wasteful king.
What pity is't that he had not so trimm'd
And dress'd his land, as we this garden dress,
And wound the bark, the skin of our fruit-trees;
Lest, being over proud with sap and blood,
With too much riches it confound itself.
Had he done so to great and growing men,
They might have lived to bear, and he to taste
Their fruits of duty. All superfluous branches
We lop away, that bearing boughs may live;
Had he done so, himself had borne the crown,
Which waste and idle hours have quite thrown down.
Richard II. Act II. Sc. 1

See, how the Morning opes her golden gates,
And takes her farewell of the glorious Sun;
How well resembles it the prime of youth,
Trimm'd like a younker prancing to his love!
Second Part Henry IV. Act II. Sc. 1.

Brutus. O Cassius, you are yoked with a lamb,
That carries anger as the flint bears fire;
Who much enforced, shows a hasty spark,
And straight is cold again. *Julius Cæsar*, Act IV. Sc. 3.

Thus they their doubtful consultations dark
Ended, rejoicing in their matchless chief;
As when from mountain-tops, the dusky clouds
Ascending, while the north-wind sleeps, o'erspread
Heaven's cheerful face, the low'ring element
Scowls o'er the darken'd landscape, snow and shower;
If chance the radiant sun with farewell sweet
Extends his evening beam, the fields revive,
The birds their notes renew, and bleating herds
Attest their joy, that hill and valley rings.
Paradise Lost, Book ii.

As the bright stars and milky way,
Show'd by the night are hid by day;
So we in that accomplish'd mind,
Help'd by the night, new graces find,
Which by the splendor of her view,
Dazzled before, we never knew. *Waller*.

The last exertion of courage compared to the blaze of a lamp before extinguishing, *Tasso Gierusalem*, Canto xix. st. xxii.

None of the foregoing similes, as they appear to me, tend to illustrate the principal subject; and therefore the pleasure they afford must arise from suggesting resemblances that are not obvious; I mean the chief pleasure; for undoubtedly a beautiful subject introduced to form the simile affords a separate pleasure, which is felt in the similes mentioned, particularly in that cited from Milton.

498. The next effect of a comparison in the order mentioned, is to place an object in a strong point of view; which effect is remarkable in the following similes:

As when two scales are charged with doubtful loads,
From side to side the trembling balance nods,
(Whilst some laborious matron, just and poor,
With nice exactness, weighs her woolly store),

---

497. Comparisons afford pleasure by suggestion.

Till poised aloft the resting beam suspends
Each equal weight: nor this nor that descends;
So stood the war, till Hector's matchless might,
With fates prevailing, turn'd the scale of fight,
Fierce as a whirlwind up the wall he flies,
And fires his host with loud repeated cries.—*Iliad*, b. xiii. 521.

Lucetta. I do not seek to quench your love's hot fire,
But qualify the fire's extreme rage,
Lest it should burn above the bounds of reason.
Julia. The more thou damm'st it up, the more it burns;
The current that with gentle murmur glides,
Thou know'st, being stopp'd, impatiently doth rage;
But when his fair course is not hindered,
He makes sweet music with th' enamell'd stones,
Giving a gentle kiss to every sedge
He overtaketh in his pilgrimage;
And so by many winding nooks he strays
With willing sport to the wild ocean.
Then let me go, and hinder not my course:
I'll be as patient as a gentle stream,
And make a pastime of each weary step,
Till the last step have brought me to my love;
And there I'll rest, as, after much turmoil,
A blessed soul doth in Elysium.
Two Gentlemen of Verona, Act II. Sc. 10

——————— She never told her love
But let concealment, like a worm i' the bud,
Feed on her damask cheek; she pined in thought
And with a green and yellow melancholy,
She sat like Patience on a monument,
Smiling at grief. *Twelfth-Night*, Act II. Sc. 6.

York. Then, as I said, the Duke, great Bolingbroke,
Mounted upon a hot and fiery steed,
Which his aspiring rider seem'd to know,
With slow but stately pace kept on his course;
While all tongues cried, God save thee, Bolingbroke.
Dutchess. Alas! poor Richard, where rides he the while?
York. As in a theatre, the eyes of men,
After a well-graced actor leaves the stage,
Are idly bent on him who enters next,
Thinking his prattle to be tedious:
Even so, or with much more contempt, men's eyes
Did scowl on Richard: no man cried, God save him!
No joyful tongue gave him his welcome home;
But dust was thrown upon his sacred head:
Which with such gentle sorrow he shook off,
His face still combating with tears and smiles,
The badges of his grief and patience;
That had not God, for some strong purpose, steel'd
The hearts of men, they must perforce have melted,
And barbarism itself have pitied him.
Richard II. Act V. Sc. 5.

Northumberland. How doth my son and brother?
Thou tremblest, and the whiteness in thy cheek
Is apter than thy tongue to tell thy errand.
Even such a man, so faint, so spiritless,
So dull, so dead in look, so woe-be-gone,
Drew Priam's curtain in the dead of night,
And would have told him, half his Troy was burn'd;
But Priam found the fire, ere he his tongue:
And I my Percy's death, ere thou report'st it.
Second Part Henry IV. Act I. Sc. 8.

Why, then I do but dream on sov'reignty,
Like one that stands upon a promontory,
And spies a far-off shore where he would tread,
Wishing his foot were equal with his eye,
And chides the sea that sunders him from thence,
Saying, he'll lave it dry to have his way:
So do I wish, the crown being so far off,
And so I chide the means that keep me from it,
And so (I say) I'll cut the causes off,
Flatt'ring my mind with things impossible.
Third Part Henry VI. Act III. Sc. 3.

——————— Out, out, brief candle!
Life's but a walking shadow, a poor player,
That struts and frets his hour upon the stage,
And then is heard no more. *Macbeth,* Act V. Sc. 5.

O thou Goddess,
Thou divine Nature! how thyself thou blazon'st
In these two princely boys! they are as gentle
As zeyhyrs blowing below the violet,
Not wagging his sweet head; and yet as rough,
(Their royal blood inchafed) as the rudest wind,
That by the top doth take the mountain pine,
And make him stoop to the vale. *Cymbeline,* Act IV. Sc. 4.

Why did not I pass away in secret, like the flower of the rock that lifts its fair head unseen, and strows its withered leaves on the blast?—*Fingal.*

There is a joy in grief when peace dwells with the sorrowful. But they are wasted with mourning, O daughter of Toscar, and their days are few. They fall away like the flower on which the sun looks in his strength, after the mildew has passed over it, and its head is heavy with the drops of night.—*Fingal.*

The sight obtained of the city of Jerusalem by the Christian army, compared to that of land discovered after a long voyage, Tasso's *Gierusalem,* canto iii. st. 4. The fury of Rinaldo subsiding when not opposed, to that of wind or water when it has a free passage, canto xx. st. 58.

499. As words convey but a faint and obscure notion of great numbers, a poet, to give a lively notion of the object he describes with regard to number, does well to compare it to what is familiar and commonly known. Thus Homer (book ii. l. 111) compares the Grecian army in point of number to a swarm of bees: in another passage (book ii. l. 551) he compares it to that profusion of leaves and flowers which appear in the spring, or of insects in a summer's evening: and Milton,

——————— As when the potent rod
Of Amram's son, in Egypt's evil day,
Waved round the coast, up call'd a pitchy cloud
Of locusts, warping on the eastern wind,
That o'er the realm of impious Pharao hung
Like night, and darken'd all the land of Nile:
So numberless were those bad angels seen,
Hovering on wing under the cope of hell,
Twixt upper, nether, and surrounding fires.—*Paradise Lost,* B. i

---

498 Second good effect of a comparison. Examples.

Such comparisons have, by some writers, been condemned for the lowness of the images introduced; but surely without reason; for, with regard to numbers, they put the principal subject in a strong light.

The foregoing comparisons operate by resemblance: others have the same effect by contrast.

> *York.* I am the last of noble Edward's sons,
> Of whom thy father, Prince of Wales, was first:
> In war, was never lion raged more fierce;
> In peace, was never gentle lamb more mild,
> Than was that young and princely gentleman.
> His face thou hast, for even so look'd he,
> Accomplish'd with the number of thy hours.
> But when he frown'd it was against the French,
> And not against his friend. His noble hand
> Did win what he did spend; and spent not that
> Which his triumphant father's hand had won.
> His hands were guilty of no kindred's blood,
> But bloody with the enemies of his kin.
> Oh, Richard! York is too far gone with grief,
> Or else he never would compare between.
>
> *Richard II.* Act II. Sc. 3.

500. Milton has a peculiar talent in embellishing the principal subject by associating it with others that are agreeable; which is the third end of a comparison. Similes of this kind have, besides a separate effect: they diversify the narration by new images that are not strictly necessary to the comparison: they are short episodes, which, without drawing us from the principal subject, afford great delight by their beauty and variety:

> He scarce had ceased, when the superior fiend
> Was moving toward the shore; his pond'rous shield
> Ethereal temper, massy, large, and round,
> Behind him cast; the broad circumference
> Hung on his shoulders like the moon, whose orb
> Through optic glass the Tuscan artist views
> At evening from the top of Fesolé,
> Or in Valdarno, to descry new lands,
> Rivers, or mountains, in her spotty globe.—*Milton*, b. i.

> ——— ———Thus far these, beyond
> Compare of mortal prowess, yet observed
> Their dread commander. He, above the rest
> In shape and gesture proudly eminent,
> Stood like a tower; his form had yet not lost
> All her original brightness, nor appear'd
> Less than archangel ruin'd and th' excess
> Of glory obscured: as when the sun new-risen
> Looks through the horizontal misty air
> Shorn of his beams; or from behind the moon
> In dim eclipse, disastrous twilight sheds
> On half the nations, and with fear of change
> Perplexes monarchs. *Milton*, b. i.

> As when a vulture on Imaus bred,
> Whose snowy ridge the roving Tartar bounds,

---

499. How the idea of a great number is best conveyed.

Dislodging from a region scarce of prey
To gorge the flesh of lambs, or yeanling kids,
On hills where flocks are fed, fly towards the springs
Of Ganges or Hydaspes, Indian streams,
But in his way lights on the barren plains
Of Sericana, where Chineses drive
With sails and wind their cany wagons light:
So on this windy sea of land, the fiend
Walk'd up and down alone, bent on his prey.—*Milton*, b. i.

——————Yet higher than their tops
The verdurous wall of Paradise up sprung:
Which to our general sire gave prospect large
Into this nether empire neighboring round.
And higher than that wall, a circling row
Of goodliest trees loaden with fairest fruit,
Blossoms and fruits at once of golden hue,
Appear'd, with gay enamell'd colors mix'd,
On which the sun more glad impress'd his beams
Than in fair evening cloud, or humid bow,
When God had shower'd the earth; so lovely seem'd
That landscape: and of pure now purer air
Meets his approach, and to the heart inspires
Vernal delight and joy, able to drive
All sadness but despair; now gentle gales
Fanning their odoriferous wings, dispense
Native perfumes, and whisper whence they stole
Those balmy spoils. As when to them who sail
Beyond the Cape of Hope, and now are past
Mozambic, off at sea north-east winds blow
Sabean odor from the spicy shore
Of Araby the blest; with such delay
Well pleased, they slack their course, and many a league,
Cheer'd with the grateful smell, old Ocean smiles.
Milton, b. iv.

With regard to similes of this kind, it will readily occur to the reader that when a resembling subject is once properly introduced in a simile, the mind is transitorily amused with the new object, and is not dissatisfied with the slight interruption. Thus, in fine weather, the momentary excursions of a traveller for agreeable prospects or elegant buildings, cheer his mind, relieve him from the languor of uniformity, and without much lengthening his journey, in reality, shorten it greatly in appearance.

501. Next of comparisons that aggrandize or elevate. These affect us more than any other sort: the reason of which may be gathered from the chapter of Grandeur and Sublimity; and, without reasoning, will be evident from the following instances:

As when a flame the winding valley fills,
And runs on crackling shrubs between the hills,
Then o'er the stubble, up the mountain flies,
Fires the high woods, and blazes to the skies,
This way and that, the spreading torrent roars;
So sweeps the hero through the wasted shores.
Around him wide, immense destruction pours,
And earth is deluged with the sanguine showers.
Iliad, xx. 569.

---

500. How Milton often embellishes the principal subject. The separate effect of such similes

Through blood, through death, Achilles still proceeds
O'er slaughter'd heroes, and o'er rolling steeds.
As when avenging flames with fury driven
On guilty towns exert the wrath of Heaven,
The pale inhabitants, some fall, some fly,
And the red vapors purple all the sky:
So raged Achilles; Death and dire dismay,
And toils, and terrors, fill'd the dreadful day.—*Iliad*, xxi. 605.

Methinks, King Richard and myself should meet
With no less terror than the elements
Of fire and water, when their thundering shock,
At meeting, tears the cloudy cheeks of heaven.
Richard II. Act III. Sc. 5.

As rusheth a foamy stream from the dark shady steep of Cromla, when thunder is rolling above, and dark brown night rests on the hill: so fierce, so vast, so terrible, rush forward the sons of Erin. The chief, like a whale of Ocean followed by all its billows, pours valor forth as a stream, rolling its might along the shore.—*Fingal*, b. i.

As roll a thousand waves to a rock, so Swaran's host came on; as meets a rock a thousand waves, so Inisfail met Swaran.—*Ibid.*

I beg peculiar attention to the following simile for a reason that shall be mentioned:

Thus breathing death, in terrible array,
The close compacted legions urged their way;
Fierce they drove on, impatient to destroy;
Troy charged the first, and Hector first of Troy.
As from some mountain's craggy forehead torn,
A rock's round fragment flies with fury borne,
(Which from the stubborn stone a torrent rends)
Precipitate the pond'rous mass descends;
From steep to steep the rolling ruin bounds;
At every shock the crackling wood resounds!
Still gath'ring force, it smokes; and, urged amain,
Whirls, leaps, and thunders down, impetuous to the plain·
There stops—So Hector. Their whole force he proved;
Resistless when he raged; and when he stopt, unmoved.
Iliad, xliii. 187.

The image of a falling rock is certainly not elevating (see chapter iv.), and yet undoubtedly the foregoing simile fires and swells the mind: it is grand, therefore, if not sublime. And the following simile will afford additional evidence that there is a real, though nice distinction between these two feelings:

So saying, a noble stroke he lifted high
Which hung not, but so swift with tempest fell
On the proud crest of Satan, that no sight,
Nor motion of swift thought, less could his shield
Such ruin intercept. Ten paces huge
He back recoil'd; the tenth on bended knee
His massy spear upstaid; as if on earth
Winds under ground or waters forcing way,
Sidelong had push'd a mountain from his seat
Half-sunk with all his pines. *Milton*, b. vi

502. A comparison by contrast may contribute to grandeur or

---

501. Comparisons that aggrandize.

elevation, no less than by resemblance; of which the following comparison of Lucan is a remarkable instance.

Victrix causa diis placuit, sed victa Catoni.

Considering that the heathen deities possessed a rank but one degree above that of mankind, I think it would not be easy, by a single expression, to exalt more one of the human species than is done in this comparison. I am sensible, at the same time, that such a comparison among Christians, who entertain more exalted notions of the Deity, would justly be reckoned extravagant and absurd.

The last article mentioned, is that of lessening or depressing a hated or disagreeable object; which is effectually done by resembling it to any thing low or despicable. Thus Milton, in his description of the rout of the rebel angels, happily expresses their terror and dismay in the following simile:

——————————As a herd
Of goats or timorous flock together throng'd,
Drove them before him thunderstruck, pursued
With terrors and with furies to the bounds
And crystal wall of heaven, which opening wide,
Roll'd inward, and a spacious gap disclosed
Into the wasteful deep: the monstrous sight
Struck them with horror backward, but far worse
Urged them behind; headlong themselves they threw
Down from the verge of heaven. *Milton*, b. vi.

In the same view, Homer, I think, may be justified in comparing the shouts of the Trojans in battle to the noise of cranes (beginning of book iii.), and to the bleating of a flock of sheep (book iv. l. 498): it is no objection that these are low images; for it was his intention to lessen the Trojans by opposing their noisy march to the silent and manly march of the Greeks. Addison (Guardian, No. 153), describing the figure that men make in the sight of a superior being, takes opportunity to mortify their pride by comparing them to a swarm of pismires.

A comparison that has none of the good effects mentioned in this discourse, but is built upon common and trifling circumstances, makes a mighty silly figure:

Non sum nescius, grandia consilia a multis plerumque causis, ceu magna navigia a plurimis remis, impelli. *Strada, de bello Belgico.*

503. By this time, I imagine the different purposes of comparison, and the various impressions it makes on the mind, are sufficiently illustrated by proper examples. This was an easy task. It is more difficult to lay down rules about the propriety or impropriety of comparisons; in what circumstances they may be introduced, and in what circumstances they are out of place. It is evident, that a comparison is not proper on every occasion: a man when cool and

---

502. Comparison by contrast for the purpose of elevation.—How a hated object is depressed. Milton's rout of the rebel angels. Instances from Homer and Addison.

sedate, is not disposed to poetical flights, nor to sacrifice truth and reality to imaginary beauties: far less is he so disposed when oppressed with care, or interested in some important transaction that engrosses him totally. On the other hand, a man, when elevated or animated by passion, is disposed to elevate or animate all his objects: he avoids familiar names, exalts objects by circumlocution and metaphor, and gives even life and voluntary action to inanimate beings. In this heat of mind, the highest poetical flights are indulged, and the boldest similes and metaphors relished.* But without soaring so high, the mind is frequently in a tone to relish chaste and moderate ornament; such as comparisons that set the principal object in a strong point of view, or that embellish and diversify the narration. In general, when by any animating passion, whether pleasant or painful, an impulse is given to the imagination; we are in that condition disposed to every sort of figurative expression, and in particular to comparisons. This in a great measure is evident from the comparisons already mentioned; and shall be further illustrated by other instances. Love, for example, in its infancy, rousing the imagination, prompts the heart to display itself in figurative language, and in similes:

> *Troilus.* Tell me, Apollo, for thy Daphne's love,
> What Cressid is, what Pandar, and what we?
> Her bed is, India; there she lies, a pearl:
> Between our Ilium, and where she resides,
> Let it be call'd the wild and wandering flood;
> Ourself the merchant; and the sailing Pandar
> Our doubtful hope, our convoy, and our bark.
>
> *Troilus and Cressida*, Act I. Sc. 1.

Again:

> Come, gentle Night; come, loving black-brow'd Night!
> Give me my Romeo; and when he shall die,
> Take him, and cut him out in little stars,
> And he will make the face of heaven so fine,
> That all the world shall be in love with Night,
> And pay no worship to the garish Sun.
>
> *Romeo and Juliet*, Act III. Sc. 4.

The dread of a misfortune, however imminent, involving always some doubt and uncertainty, agitates the mind, and excites the imagination:

> *Wolsey.* ——————Nay, then, farewell:
> I've touch'd the highest point of all my greatness,
> And from that full meridian of my glory
> I haste now to my setting. I shall fall,
> Like a bright exhalation in the evening,
> And no man see me more. *Henry VIII.* Act III. Sc. 4.

504. But it will be a better illustration of the present head, to

* It is accordingly observed by Longinus, in his Treatise on the Sublime, that the proper time for metaphor, is when the passions are so swelled as to hurry on like a torrent.

give examples where comparisons are improperly introduced. I have had already occasion to observe, that similes are not the language of a man in his ordinary state of mind, dispatching his daily and usual work. For that reason, the following speech of a gardener to his servants, is extremely improper:

> Go, bind thou up yon dangling apricots,
> Which, like unruly children, make their sire
> Stoop with oppression of their prodigal weight;
> Give some supportance to the bending twigs.
> Go thou; and like an executioner,
> Cut off the heads of two fast-growing sprays,
> That look too lofty in our commonwealth;
> All must be even in our government.
>
> *Richard II.* Act III. Sc. 7.

The fertility of Shakspeare's vein betrays him frequently into this error. There is the same impropriety in another simile of his:

> *Hero.* Good Margaret, run thee into the parlor;
> There shalt thou find my cousin Beatrice;
> Whisper her ear, and tell her, I and Ursula
> Walk in the orchard, and our whole discourse
> Is all of her: say that thou overheard'st us;
> And bid her steal into the pleached bower,
> Where honeysuckles, ripen'd by the sun,
> Forbid the sun to enter; like to favorites,
> Made proud by princes that advance their pride
> Against that power that bred it.
>
> *Much Ado about Nothing*, Act III. Sc. 1.

Rooted grief, deep anguish, terror, remorse, despair, and all the severe dispiriting passions, are declared enemies, perhaps not to figurative language in general, but undoubtedly to the pomp and solemnity of comparison. Upon that account, the simile pronounced by young Rutland, under a terror of death from an inveterate enemy, and praying mercy, is unnatural:

> So looks the pent-up lion o'er the wretch
> That trembles under his devouring paws,
> And so he walks insulting o'er his prey,
> And so he comes to rend his limbs asunder.
> Ah, gentle Clifford, kill me with thy sword,
> And not with such a cruel threat'ning look.
>
> *Third Part of Henry VI.* Act I. Sc. 5.

A man spent and dispirited after losing a battle, is not disposed to heighten or illustrate his discourse by similes:

> *York.* With this we charged again; but out, alas!
> We bodged again; as I have seen a swan
> With bootless labor swim against the tide,
> And spend her strength with over-matching waves.
> Ah! hark, the fatal followers do pursue;
> And I am faint and cannot fly their fury,
> The sands are number'd that make up my life;
> Here must I stay, and here my life must end.
>
> *Third Part Henry VI.* Act I. Sc. 6.

---

504. Examples where similes are improperly introduced. Relation to the dispiriting passions.

Far less is a man disposed to similes who is not only defeated in a pitched battle, but lies at the point of death mortally wounded:

> *Warwick.*——————My mangled body shows
> My blood, my want of strength; my sick heart shows
> That I must yield my body to the earth,
> And, by my fall, the conquest to my foe.
> Thus yields the cedar to the axe's edge,
> Whose arms gave shelter to the princely eagle;
> Under whose shade the ramping lion slept,
> Whose top branch over-peer'd Jove's spreading tree,
> And kept low shrubs from winter's powerful wind.
>
> *Third Part Henry VI.* Act V. Sc. 3.

Queen Katherine, deserted by the king, and in the deepest affliction on her divorce, could not be disposed to any sallies of imagination: and for that reason, the following simile, however beautiful in the mouth of a spectator, is scarce proper in her own:

> I am the most unhappy woman living,
> Shipwreck'd upon a kingdom, where no pity,
> No friends, no hope! no kindred weep for me!
> Almost no grave allow'd me! like the lily,
> That once was mistress of the field, and flourish'd,
> I'll hang my head and perish.
>
> *King Henry VIII.* Act III. Sc. 1.

Similes thus unseasonably introduced, are finely ridiculed in the *Rehearsal*:

> *Bayes.* Now here she must make a simile.
> *Smith.* Where's the necessity of that, Mr. Bayes?
> *Bayes.* Because she's surprised; that's a general rule; you must ever make a simile when you are surprised; 'tis a new way of writing.

505. A comparison is not always faultless even where it is properly introduced. I have endeavored above to give a general view of the different ends to which a comparison may contribute: a comparison, like other human productions, may fall short of its aim; of which defect instances are not rare even among good writers; and to complete the present subject, it will be necessary to make some observations upon such faulty comparisons. I begin with observing, that nothing can be more erroneous than to institute a comparison too faint: a distant resemblance or contrast fatigues the mind with its obscurity, instead of amusing it; and tends not to fulfil any one end of a comparison. The following similes seem to labor under this defect:

> Albus ut obscuro deterget nubila cœlo
> Sæpe Notus, neque parturit imbres
> Perpetuos: sic tu sapiens finire memento
> Tristitiam, vitæque labores. *Horat. Carm.* l. i. ode 7.

> *K. Rich.* Give me the crown.—Here, cousin, seize the crown,
> Here, on this side, my hand; on that side, thine.
> Now is this golden crown like a deep well,
> That owes two buckets, filling one another;
> The emptier ever dancing in the air,
> The other down, unseen and full of water:

---

505. Comparisons falling short of their aim.

That bucket down, and full of tears, am ,
Drinking my griefs, whilst you mount up on high.
Richard II. Act IV. Sc. 8.

K. John. Oh! cousin, thou art come to set mine eye;
The tackle of my heart is crack'd and burnt;
And all the shrouds wherewith my life should sail,
Are turned to one thread, one little hair;
My heart hath one poor string to stay it by,
Which holds but till thy news be uttered.
King John, Act V. Sc. 10.

York. My uncles both are slain in rescuing me:
And all my followers to the eager foe
Turn back, and fly like ships before the wind,
Or lambs pursued by hunger-starved wolves.
Third Part Henry VI. Act I. Sc. 6.

The latter of the two similes is good; the former, by its faintness of resemblance, has no effect but to load the narration with a useless image.

506. The next error I shall mention is a capital one. In an epic poem, or in a poem upon any elevated subject, a writer ought to avoid raising a simile on a low image, which never fails to bring down the principal subject. In general, it is a rule, That a grand object ought never to be resembled to one that is diminutive, however delicate the resemblance may be; for it is the peculiar character of a grand object to fix the attention, and swell the mind; in which state, to contract it to a minute object, is unpleasant. The resembling an object to one that is greater, has, on the contrary, a good effect, by raising or swelling the mind; for one passes with satisfaction from a small to a great object; but cannot be drawn down, without reluctance, from great to small. Hence the following similes are faulty:

Meanwhile the troops beneath Patroclus' care,
Invade the Trojans and commence the war.
As wasps, provoked by children in their play,
Pour from their mansions by the broad highway,
In swarms the guiltless traveller engage,
Whet all their stings, and call forth all their rage;
All rise in arms, and with a general cry
Assert their waxen domes, and buzzing progeny
Thus from the tents the fervent legion swarms,
So loud their clamor and so keen their arms.—*Iliad*, xvi. 312.

So burns the vengeful hornet (soul all o'er)
Repulsed in vain, and thirsty still of gore;
(Bold son of air and heat) on angry wings
Untamed, untired he turns, attacks and stings.
Fired with like ardor, fierce Atrides flew,
And sent his soul with every lance he threw.—*Iliad*, xvii. 642

507. An error, opposite to the former, is the introducing a resembling image, so elevated or great as to bear no proportion to the principal subject. Their remarkable disparity, seizing the mind, never fails to depress the principal subject by contrast, instead of

---

506. A simile on a low image.—The effect of resembling an object to one that is greater

raising it by resemblance: and if the disparity be very great, the simile degenerates into burlesque; nothing being more ridiculous than to force an object out of its proper rank in nature, by equalling it with one greatly superior or greatly inferior. This will be evident from the following comparisons:

> Fervet opus, redolentque thymo fragrantia mella.
> Ac veluti lentis Cyclopes fulmina massis
> Cum properant. alii taurinis follibus auras
> Accipiunt, redduntque: alii stridentia tingunt
> Æra lacu; gemit impositis incudibus Ætna;
> Illi inter sese magna vi brachia tollunt
> In numerum; versantque tenaci forcipe ferrum.
> Non aliter (si parva licet componere magnis)
> Cecropias innatus apes amor urget habendi,
> Munere quamque suo. Grandævis oppida curæ,
> Et munire favos, et Dædaia fingere tecta.
> At fessæ multâ referunt se nocte minores,
> Crura thymo plenæ: pascuntur et arbuta passim,
> Et glaucas salices, casiamque crocumque rubentem,
> Et pinguem tiliam, et ferrugineos hyacinthos,
> Omnibus una quies operum, labor omnibus unus.
>
> *Georgic*, iv. 169.

A writer of delicacy will avoid drawing his comparisons from any image that is nauseous, ugly, or remarkably disagreeable; for however strong the resemblance may be, more will be lost than gained by such comparison. Therefore I cannot help condemning, though with some reluctance, the following simile, or rather metaphor:

> O thou fond many! with what loud applause
> Didst thou beat heaven with blessing Bolingbroke,
> Before he was what thou wouldst have him be?
> And now being trimm'd up in thine own desires,
> Thou, beastly feeder, art so full of him,
> That thou provok'st thyself to cast him up:
> And so, thou common dog, did'st thou disgorge
> Thy glutton bosom of the royal Richard,
> And now thou wouldst eat thy dead vomit up,
> And howl'st to find it.
>
> *Second Part Henry IV.* Act I. Sc. 6.

508. The strongest objection that can lie against a comparison is, that it consists in words only, not in sense. Such false coin, or bastard wit, does extremely well in burlesque; but it is far below the dignity of the epic, or of any serious composition:

> The noble sister of Poplicola,
> The moon of Rome; chaste as the icicle
> That's curled by the frost from purest snow,
> And hangs on Dian's temple. *Coriolanus*, Act V. Sc. 3.

There is evidently no resemblance between an icicle and a woman, chaste or unchaste; but chastity is cold in a metaphorical sense, and an icicle is cold in a proper sense: and this verbal resemblance, in the hurry and glow of composing, has been thought

---

507. An image too elevated for the principal subject.—Disagreeable images.

a sufficient foundation for the simile. Such phantom similes are mere witticisms, which ought to have no quarter, except where purposely introduced to provoke laughter. Lucian, in his dissertation upon history, talking of a certain author, makes the following comparison, which is verbal merely:

> This author's descriptions are so cold that they surpass the Caspian snow and all the ice of the north.

Virgil has not escaped this puerility:

> ———— Galathæa thymo mihi dulcior Hyblæ.
> *Bucol.* vii. 37.

> ———— Ego Sardois videar tibi amarior herbis.
> *Ibid.* 41.

> Gallo, cujus amor tantum mihi crescit in horas,
> Quantum vere novo viridis se subjicit alnus. *Bucol.* x. 37.

Nor Tasso, in his Aminta:

> Picciola e' l' ape, e fa col picciol morso
> Pur gravi, e pur moleste le ferite;
> Ma, qual cosa é più picciola d' amore,
> Se in ogni breve spatio entra, e s' asconde
> In ogni breve spatio? hor, sotto a l' ombra
> De le palpebre, hor trá minuti rivi
> D'un biondo crine, hor dentro le pozzette
> Che forma un dolce riso in bella guancia;
> E pur fa tanto grandi, e si mortali,
> E cosi immedicabili le piaghe. Act II. Sc. 1.

Nor Boileau, the chastest of all writers, and that even in his Art of Poetry:

> Ainsi tel autrefois, qu'on vit avec Faret
> Charbonner de ses vers les murs d'un cabaret,
> S'en va mal à propos d'une voix insolente,
> Chanter du peuple Hébreu la fuite triomphante,
> Et poursuivant Moïse au travers des déserts,
> Court avec Pharaon se noyer dans les mers.—*Chant.* I. l. 21.

> Mais allons voir le Vrai, jusqu'en sa source même.
> Un dévot aux yeux creux, et d'abstinence blême,
> S'il n'a point le cœur juste, est affreux devant Dieu,
> L'Evangile au Chrétien ne dit, en aucun lieu,
> Sois dévot: elle dit, Sois doux, simple, équitable:
> Car d'un devot souvent au Chrétien véritable
> La distance est deux fois plus longue, à mon avis,
> Que du Pôle Antarctique au Détroit de Davis.
> *Boileau*, Satire xi.

> ———— But for their spirits and souls
> This word *rebellion* had froze them up
> As fish are in a pond. *Second Part Henry IV.* Act I. Sc. 3.

> *Queen.* The pretty vaulting sea refused to drown me;
> Knowing, that thou wouldst have me drown'd on shore;
> With tears as salt as sea, through thy unkindness.
> *Second Part Henry IV.* Act III. Sc. 6.

Here there is no manner of resemblance but in the word *drown*, for there is no real resemblance between being drowned at sea, and dying of grief at land. But perhaps this sort of tinsel wit may have a propriety in it, when used to express an affected, not a real passion, which was the Queen's case.

Pope has several similes of the same stamp. I shall transcribe one or two from the *Essay on Man*, the greatest and most instructive of all his performances:

> And hence one master passion in the breast,
> Like Aaron's serpent, swallows up the rest. *Epist.* ii. l. 181.

And again, talking of this same ruling or master passion:

> Nature its mother, Habit is its nurse;
> Wit, spirit, faculties, but make it worse;
> Reason itself but gives it edge and power;
> As heaven's bless'd beam turns vinegar more sour.—*Ibid.* l. 45.

Lord Bolingbroke, speaking of historians:

> Where their sincerity as to fact is doubtful, we strike out truth by the confrontation of different accounts; as we strike out sparks of fire by the collision of flints and steel.

Let us vary the phrase a very little, and there will not remain a shadow of resemblance. Thus:

> We discover truth by the confrontation of different accounts; as we strike out sparks of fire by the collision of flints and steel.

Racine makes Orestes say to Hermoine:

> Que les Scythes sont moins cruel qu' Hermoine.

Similes of this kind put one in mind of a ludicrous French song:

> Je croyois Janneton
> Aussi douce que belle:
> Je croyois Janneton
> Plus douce qu'un mouton;
> Hélas! Hélas!
> Elle est cent fois, mille fois, plus cruelle
> Que n'est le tigre aux bois.

Again:

> Hélas! l'amour m'a pris,
> Comme le chat fait la souris.

Where the subject is burlesque or ludicrous, such similes are far from being improper. Horace says pleasantly,

> Quanquam tu levior cortice.—L iii. ode 9.

And Shakspeare,

> In breaking oaths he's stronger than Hercules.

509. And this leads me to observe, that besides the foregoing comparisons, which are all serious, there is a species, the end and purpose of which is to excite gayety or mirth. Take the following examples:

---

508. Comparison in words only. Examples.

Falstaff, speaking to his page:

I do here walk before thee like a sow that hath overwhelmed all her litter but one.—*Second Part Henry VI.* Act I. Sc. 4.

I think he is not a pick-purse, nor a horse-stealer; but for his verity in love, I do think him as concave as a covered goblet, or a worm-eaten nut.
As You Like It, Act III. Sc. 10.

This sword a dagger had his page,
That was but little for his age;
And therefore waited on him so,
As dwarfs upon knights-errant do.—*Hudibras*, canto i.

Description of Hubibras's horse:

He was well stay'd, and in his gait
Preserved a grave majestic state.
At spur or switch no more he skipt,
Or mended pace than Spaniard whipt:
And yet so fiery, he would bound
As if he grieved to touch the ground:
That Cæsar's horse, who, as fame goes,
Had corns upon his feet and toes,
Was not by half so tender hooft,
Nor trod upon the ground so soft.
And as that beast would kneel and stoop,
(Some write) to take his rider up;
So Hudibras his ('tis well known)
Would often do to set him down.—Canto i.

The sun had long since in the lap
Of Thetis taken out his nap;
And, like a lobster boil'd, the morn
From black to red began to turn.—Part II. canto ii.

Books, like men their authors, have but one way of coming into the world, but there are ten thousand to go out of it, and return no more.
Tale of a Tub.

And in this the world may perceive the difference between the integrity of a generous author, and that of a common friend. The latter is observed to adhere close in prosperity; but, on the decline of fortune, to drop suddenly off: whereas the generous author, just on the contrary, finds his hero on the dunghill, from thence by gradual steps raises him to a throne, and then immediately withdraws, expecting not so much as thanks for his pains.
Tale of a Tub.

The most accomplished way of using books at present is, to serve them as some do lords, learn their *titles*, and then brag of their acquaintance.
Tale of a Tub

Clubs, diamonds, hearts, in wild disorder seen,
With throngs promiscuous strow the level green.
Thus when dispersed a routed army runs,
Of Asia's troops, and Afric's sable sons,
With like confusion, different nations fly.
Of various habit, and of various dye,
The pierced battalions disunited, fall
In heaps on heaps; one fate o'erwhelms them all.
Rape of the Lock, canto iii.

He does not consider that sincerity in love is as much out of fashion as sweet snuff; nobody takes it now.—*Careless Husband.*

---

509. Mirthful comparisons.

CHAPTER XX.

FIGURES.

THE endless variety of expressions brought under the head of tropes and figures by ancient critics and grammarians, makes it evident that they had no precise criterion for distinguishing tropes and figures from plain language. It was accordingly my opinion that little could be made of them in the way of rational criticism; till discovering, by a sort of accident, that many of them depend on principles formerly explained, I gladly embrace the opportunity to show the influence of these principles where it would be the least expected.

SECTION I.

Personification.

510. THE bestowing sensibility and voluntary motion upon things inanimate, is so bold a figure as to require, one should imagine, very peculiar circumstances for operating the delusion; and yet, in the language of poetry, we find variety of expressions, which, though commonly reduced to that figure, are used without ceremony, or any sort of preparation; as, for example, *thirsty* ground, *hungry* church-yard, *furious* dart, *angry* ocean. These epithets, in their proper meaning, are attributes of sensible beings: what is their meaning when applied to things inanimate? do they make us conceive the ground, the church-yard, the dart, the ocean, to be endued with animal functions? This is a curious inquiry; and whether so or not, it cannot be declined in handling the present subject.

The mind, agitated by certain passions, is prone to bestow sensibility upon things inanimate. This is an additional instance of the influence of passion upon our opinions and belief. (Chapter ii. part v.) I give examples. Antony, mourning over the body of Cæsar murdered in the senate-house, vents his passion in the following words:

> *Antony.* O pardon me, thou bleeding piece of earth,
> That I am meek and gentle with these butchers.
> Thou art the ruins of the noblest man
> That ever lived in the tide of time.—*Julius Cæsar*, Act III. Sc. 4.

Here Antony must have been impressed with a notion that the body of Cæsar was listening to him, without which the speech would be foolish and absurd. Nor will it appear strange, considering what is said in the chapter above cited, that passion should have such power over the mind of man. In another example of the same kind, the earth, as a common mother, is animated to give refuge against a father's unkindness:

> *Almeria.* O Earth, behold, I kneel upon thy bosom,
> And bend my flowing eyes to stream upon
> Thy face, imploring thee that thou wilt yield!
> Open thy bowels of compassion, take
> Into thy womb the last and most forlorn
> Of all thy race. Hear me, thou common parent:
> ——I have no parent else.——Be thou a mother,
> And step between me and the curse of him
> Who was—who was, but is no more a father;
> But brands my innocence with horrid crimes;
> And for the tender names of *child* and *daughter*,
> Now calls me *murderer* and *parricide*.
>
> *Mourning Bride*, Act IV. Sc. 7.

Plaintive passions are extremely solicitous for vent; and a soliloquy commonly answers the purpose; but when such passion becomes excessive, it cannot be gratified but by sympathy from others; and if denied that consolation in a natural way, it will convert even things inanimate into sympathizing beings. Thus Philoctetes complains to the rocks and promontories of the isle of Lemnos (Philoctetes of Sophocles, Act iv. Sc. 2); and Alcestes dying, invokes the sun, the light of day, the clouds, the earth, her husband's palace, &c. (Alcestes of Euripides, Act ii. Sc. 1.) Moschus, lamenting the death of Bion, conceives that the birds, the fountains, the trees, lament with him. The shepherd, who in Virgil bewails the death of Daphnis, expresseth himself thus:

> Daphni, tuum Pœnos etiam ingemuisse leones
> Interitum, montesque feri sylvæque loquuntur.—*Eclogue* v. 27

Again:

> Illum etiam lauri, illum etiam flevere myricæ.
> Pinifer illum etiam sola sub rupe jacentem
> Mænalus, et gelidi fleverunt saxa Lycæi.—*Eclogue* x. 13.

511. That such personification is derived from nature, will not admit the least remaining doubt, after finding it in poems of the darkest ages and remotest countries. No figure is more frequent in Ossian's works; for example:

> The battle is over, said the king, and I behold the blood of my friends. Sad is the heath of Lena, and mournful the oaks of Cromla.

Again:

> The sword of Gaul trembles at his side, and longs to glitter in his hand.

King Richard having got intelligence of Bolingbroke's invasion, says, upon landing in England from his Irish expedition, in a mixture of joy and resentment,

---

510. Boldness of the figure of personification. Expressions implying that figure, in common use. When we are disposed to use this figure.—Antony over the body of Cæsar.—Earth addressed as a mother.—Plaintive passions, how expressed. Illustrations.

——————I weep for joy
To stand upon my kingdom once again.
Dear earth, I do salute thee with my hand,
Though rebels wound thee with their horses' hoofs.
As a long-parted mother with her child
Plays fondly with her tears, and smiles in meeting;
So weeping, smiling, greet I thee, my earth,
And do thee favor with my royal hands.
Feed not thy sovereign's foe, my gentle earth,
Nor with thy sweets comfort his ravenous sense:
But let thy spiders that suck up thy venom,
And heavy-gaited toads lie in their way;
Doing annoyance to the treacherous feet,
Which with usurping steps do trample thee.
Yield stinging nettles to mine enemies;
And, when they from thy bosom pluck a flower,
Guard it, I pr'ythee, with a lurking adder;
Whose double tongue may with a mortal touch
Throw death upon thy sovereign's enemies.
Mock not my senseless conjuration, lords;
This earth shall have a feeling; and these stones
Prove armed soldiers, ere her native king
Shall falter under foul rebellious arms.

Richard II. Act III. Sc. 2.

After a long voyage it was customary among the ancients to salute the natal soil. A long voyage being of old a greater enterprise than at present, the safe return to one's country after much fatigue and danger, was a delightful circumstance; and it was natural to give the natal soil a temporary life, in order to sympathize with the traveller. See an example, *Agamemnon* of Eschylus, Act III. in the beginning. Regret for leaving a place one has been accustomed to, has the same effect (*Philoctetes* of Sophocles, at the close).

Terror produceth the same effect; it is communicated in thought to every thing around, even to things inanimate. Speaking of Polyphemus:

Clamorem immensum tollit, quo pontus et omnes
Intremuere undæ, penitusque exterrita tellus
Italiæ. *Æneid*, iii. 672.

————As when old Ocean roars,
And heaves huge surges to the *trembling* shores.

Iliad, ii. 249.

Go, view the settling sea. The stormy wind is laid; but the billows still tremble on the deep, and seem to fear the blast. *Fingal.*

Racine, in the tragedy of *Phedra*, describing the sea-monster that destroyed Hippolytus, conceives the sea itself to be struck with terror as well as the spectators:

Le flot qui l'apporta recule épouvanté.

A man also naturally communicates his joy to all objects around, animate or inanimate:

————As when to them who sail
Beyond the Cape of Hope, and now are past
Mozambic, off at sea northeast winds blow
Sabean odor from the spicy shore
Of Araby the blest; with such delay

Well pleased, they slack their course, and many a league,
Cheer'd with the grateful smell, old Ocean smiles.
Paradise Lost, b. iv.

512. I have been profuse of examples, to show what power many passions have to animate their objects. In all the foregoing examples, the personification, if I mistake not, is so complete as to afford conviction, momentary indeed, of life and intelligence. But it is evident, from numberless instances, that personification is not always so complete: it is a common figure in descriptive poetry, understood to be the language of the writer, and not of the persons he describes: in this case it seldom or never comes up to conviction, even momentary, of life and intelligence. I give the following examples:

First in *his* east the glorious lamp was seen
(Regent of day, and all th' horizon round
Invested with bright rays); jocund to run
His longitude through heaven's high road: the gray
Dawn and the Pleiades before *him* danced,
Shedding sweet influence. Less bright the moon,
But opposite, in levell'd west was set
His mirror, with full face borrowing *her* light
From *him*; for other light *she* needed none.
Paradise Lost, b. vii. l. 370.*

Night's candles are burnt out, and jocund day
Stands tiptoe on the misty mountain-tops.
Romeo and Juliet, Act III. Sc. 7

But look, the morn, in russet mantle clad,
Walks o'er the dew of yon high eastward hill.
Hamlet, Act I. Sc. 1.

It may, I presume, be taken for granted, that in the foregoing instances, the personification, either with the poet or his reader, amounts not to a conviction of intelligence: that the sun, the moon, the day, the morn, are not here understood to be sensible beings. What then is the nature of this personification? I think it must be referred to the imagination: the inanimate object is imagined to be a sensible being, but without any conviction, even for a moment, that it really is so. Ideas or fictions of imagination have power to raise emotions in the mind; and when any thing inanimate is, in imagination, supposed to be a sensible being, it makes by that means a greater figure than when an idea is formed of it according to truth. This sort of personification, however, is far inferior to the other in elevation. Thus personification is of two kinds. The first, being more noble, may be termed *passionate personification*; the other, more humble, *descriptive personification*; because seldom or never is personification in a description carried to conviction.

* The chastity of the English language, which in common usage distinguishes by genders no words but what signify beings male and female, gives thus a fine opportunity for the prosopopœia; a beauty unknown in other languages, where every word is masculine or feminine.

511 Proof of this figure being natural. Examples from *Ossian*; from *Richard II.*—Terror communicates itself. Examples. So does joy.

The imagination is so lively and active, that its images are raised with very little effort; and this justifies the frequent use of descriptive personification. This figure abounds in Milton's *Allegro* and *Penseroso.*

Abstract and general terms, as well as particular objects, are often necessary in poetry. Such terms, however, are not well adapted to poetry, because they suggest not any image: I can readily form an image of Alexander or Achilles in wrath; but I cannot form an image of wrath in the abstract, or of wrath independent of a person. Upon that account, in works addressed to the imagination, abstract terms are frequently personified; but such personification rests upon imagination merely, not upon conviction:

> Sed mihi vel Tellus optem prius ima dehiscat;
> Vel Pater omnipotens adigat me fulmine ad umbras,
> Pallentes umbras Erebi, noctemque profundam,
> Ante *pudor* quam te violo, aut tua jura resolvo.
> *Æneid*, iv. 24.

Thus, to explain the effects of slander, it is imagined to be a voluntary agent:

> ——— ———No, 'tis Slander;
> Whose edge is sharper than the sword; whose tongue
> Outvenoms all the worms of Nile; whose breath
> Rides on the posting winds, and doth belie
> All corners of the world, kings, queens, and states,
> Maids, matrons; nay, the secrets of the grave
> This viperous Slander enters.—*Cymbeline*, Act III. Sc. 4.

As also human passions; take the following example:

> ————For *Pleasure* and *Revenge*
> Have ears more deaf than adders, to the voice
> Of any true decision.—*Troilus and Cressida*, Act II. Sc. 4.

Virgil explains fame and its effects by a still greater variety of action (*Æneid*, iv. 173). And Shakspeare personifies death and its operations in a manner singularly fanciful:

> ————Within the hollow crown
> That rounds the mortal temples of a king,
> Keeps Death his court; and there the antic sits,
> Scoffing his state, and grinning at his pomp;
> Allowing him a breath, a little scene
> To monarchize, be fear'd, and kill with looks,
> Infusing him with self and vain conceit,
> As if this flesh, which walls about our life,
> Were brass impregnable; and humor'd thus,
> Comes at the last, and with a little pin
> Bores through his castle walls, and farewell king.
> *Richard II.* Act III. Sc. 1.

Not less successfully is life and action given even to sleep:

> *King Henry.* How many thousands of my poorest subjects
> Are at this hour asleep! O gentle *Sleep*,
> Nature's soft nurse, how have I frighted thee,
> That thou no more wilt weigh my eyelids down,
> And steep my senses in forgetfulness?
> Why rather Sleep, liest thou in smoky cribs,

Upon uneasy pallets stretching thee,
And hush'd with buzzing night-flies to thy slumber,
Than in the perfumed chambers of the great,
Under the canopies of costly state,
And lull'd with sounds of sweetest melody?
Oh thou dull god, why liest thou with the vile
In loathsome beds, and leav'st the kingly couch,
A watch-case to a common 'larum-bell?
Wilt thou upon the high and giddy mast
Seal up the ship-boy's eyes, and rock his brains
In cradle of the rude imperious surge,
And in the visitation of the winds,
Who take the ruffian billows by the top,
Curling their monstrous heads, and hanging them
With deafening clamors in the slippery shrouds,
That, with the hurly, death itself awakes,—
Canst thou, O partial Sleep, give thy repose
To the wet sea-boy in an hour so rude;
And in the calmest and the stillest night,
With all the appliances and means to boot,
Deny it to a king? Then, happy low! lie down;
Uneasy lies the head that wears a crown.
Second Part Henry IV. Act III. Sc. 1.

I shall add one example more, to show that descriptive personification may be used with propriety, even where the purpose of the discourse is instruction merely:

Oh! let the steps of youth be cautious,
How they advance into a dangerous world;
Our duty only can conduct us safe.
Our passions are seducers: but of all,
The strongest *Love*. He first approaches us
In childish play, wantoning in our walks:
If heedlessly we wander after him,
As he will pick out all the dancing-way,
We're lost, and hardly to return again.
We should take warning: he is painted blind,
To show us, if we fondly follow him,
The precipices we may fall into.
Therefore let *Virtue* take him by the hand:
Directed so, he leads to certain joy.—*Southern.*

513. Hitherto success has attended our steps: but whether we shall complete our progress with equal success, seems doubtful; for when we look back to the expressions mentioned in the beginning, *thirsty* ground, *furious* dart, and such like, it seems no less difficult than at first, to say whether there be in them any sort of personification. Such expressions evidently raise not the slightest conviction of sensibility: nor do I think they amount to descriptive personification; because, in them, we do not even figure the ground or the dart to be animated. If so, they cannot at all come under the present subject. To show which, I shall endeavor to trace the effect that such expressions have in the mind. Doth not the expression *angry ocean*, for example, tacitly compare the ocean in a storm to a

---

512. How passionate differs from descriptive personification.—Abstract and general terms not adapted to poetry How they may be advantageously used in poetry. Examples.

man in wrath? By this tacit comparison, the ocean is elevated above its rank in nature; and yet personification is excluded, because, by the very nature of comparison, the things compared are kept distinct, and the native appearance of each is preserved. It will be shown afterwards, that expressions of this kind belong to another figure, which I term *a figure of speech*, and which employs the seventh section of the present chapter.

Though thus in general we can distinguish descriptive personification from what is merely a figure of speech, it is, however, often difficult to say, with respect to some expressions, whether they are of one kind or of the other. Take the following instances:

The moon shines bright: in such a night as this,
When the sweet wind did gently *kiss* the trees,
And they did make no noise; in such a night,
Troilus methinks mounted the Trojan wall,
And sigh'd his soul toward the Grecian tents,
Where Cressid lay that night.
Merchant of Venice, Act V. Sc. 1.

——————I have seen
Th' *ambitious* ocean swell, and rage, and foam,
To be exalted with the threat'ning clouds.
Julius Cæsar, Act I. Sc. 6.

With respect to these and numberless other examples of the same kind, it must depend upon the reader, whether they be examples of personification, or of a figure of speech merely: a sprightly imagination will advance them to the former class; with a plain reader they will remain in the latter.

514. Having thus at large explained the present figure, its different kinds, and the principles upon which it is founded; what comes next in order, is, to show in what cases it may be introduced with propriety, when it is suitable, when unsuitable. I begin with observing, that *passionate personification* is not promoted by every passion indifferently. All dispiriting passions are averse to it; and remorse, in particular, is too serious and severe to be gratified with a phantom of the mind. I cannot therefore approve the following speech of Enobarbus, who had deserted his master Antony:

Be witness to me, O thou blessed moon,
When men revolted shall upon record
Bear hateful memory, poor Enobarbus did
Before thy face repent ————
Oh sovereign Mistress of true melancholy,
The poisonous damp of night dispunge upon me,
That life, a very rebel to my will,
May hang no longer on me.
Antony and Cleopatra, Act IV. Sc. 7.

If this can be justified, it must be upon the heathen system of theology, which converted into deities the sun, moon, and stars.

---

513. Certain expressions that do not quite amount to descriptive personification. What they are called.—Sometimes difficult to distinguish between descriptive personification and figures of speech.

Secondly, after a passionate personification is properly introduced it ought to be confined to its proper province, that of gratifying the passion without giving place to any sentiment or action but what answers that purpose for personification is at any rate a bold figure, and ought to be employed with great reserve. The passion of love, for example, in a plaintive tone, may give a momentary life to woods and rocks, in order to make them sensible of the lover's distress; but no passion will support a conviction so far-stretched, as that these woods and rocks should be living witnesses to report the distress to others. (*Pastor Fido*, Act III. Sc. 3.) No lover who is not crazed will utter such a sentiment; it is plainly the operation of the writer, indulging his inventive faculty without regard to nature. The same observation is applicable to the following passage:

In winter's tedious nights sit by the fire
With good old folks, and let them tell their tales
Of woeful ages, long ago betid:
And ere thou bid good night, to quit their grief,
Tell them the lamentable fall of me,
And send the hearers weeping to their beds.
For why? the senseless brands will sympathize
The heavy accent of thy moving tongue,
And in compassion weep the fire out.

Richard II. Act V. Sc. 2.

One must read this passage very seriously to avoid laughing. The following passage is quite extravagant; the different parts of the human body are too intimately connected with self to be personified by the power of any passion; and after converting such a part into a sensible being, it is still worse to make it to be conceived as rising in rebellion against self:

Cleopatra. Haste, bare my arm, and rouse the serpent's fury.
Coward flesh——————
Wouldst thou conspire with Cæsar to betray me,
As thou wert none of mine? I'll force thee to 't.

Dryden, All for Love, Act V.

515. Next comes *descriptive personification;* upon which I must observe, in general, that it ought to be cautiously used. A personage in a tragedy, agitated by a strong passion, deals in warm sentiments; and the reader, catching fire by sympathy, relisheth the boldest personifications; but a writer, even in the most lively description, taking a lower flight, ought to content himself with such easy personifications as agree with the tone of mind inspired by the description. Nor is even such easy personification always admitted; for in plain narrative the mind, serious and sedate, rejects personification altogether. Strada, in his history of the Belgic wars, has the following passage, which, by a strained elevation above the tone of the subject, deviates into burlesque:

Vix descenderat a prætoria navi Cæsar; cum fœda illico exorta in portu tem-

514. When a passionate personification is suitable; when not. What passions averse to it.—The proper province of a passionate personification.

pestas, classem impetu disjecit, prætoriam hausit; quasi non vecturam amplius Cæsarem, Cæsarisque fortunam.—*Dec.* I. l. 1.

Neither do I approve, in Shakspeare, the speech of King John, gravely exhorting the citizens of Angiers to a surrender; though a tragic writer has much greater latitude than an historian. Take the following specimen:

> The cannons have their bowels full of wrath
> And ready mounted are they to spit forth
> Their iron indignation 'gainst your walls.—Act II. Sc. 3.

Secondly, If extraordinary marks of respect to a person of low rank be ridiculous, no less so is the personification of a low subject. This rule chiefly regards descriptive personification; for a subject can hardly be low that is the cause of a violent passion; in that circumstance, at least, it must be of importance. But to assign any rule other than taste merely, for avoiding things below even descriptive personification, will, I am afraid, be a hard task. A poet of superior genius, possessing the power of inflaming the mind, may take liberties that would be too bold in others. Homer appears not extravagant in animating his darts and arrows; nor Thomson in animating the seasons, the winds, the rains, the dews; he even ventures to animate the diamond, and doth it with propriety:

> ———————That polish'd bright,
> And all its native lustre let abroad,
> Dares, as it sparkles on the fair one's breast,
> With vain ambition emulate her eyes.

But there are things familiar and base, to which personification can not descend. In a composed state of mind, to animate a lump of matter even in the most rapid flight of fancy, degenerates into burlesque:

> How now! What noise! that spirit's possess'd with haste,
> That wounds th' unresisting postern with these strokes.
> *Shakspeare*, *Measure for Measure*, Act IV. Sc. 6

> ———————Or from the shore
> The plovers when to scatter o'er the heath,
> And sing their wild notes to the list'ning *waste*.
> *Thomson*, *Spring*, l. 23.

Speaking of a man's hand cut off in battle:

> Te decisa suum, Laride, dextera quærit:
> Semianimesque micant digiti: ferrumque retractant.
> *Æneid*, x. 395.

The personification here of a hand is insufferable, especially in a plain narration; not to mention that such a trivial incident is too minutely described.

The same observation is applicable to *abstract terms*, which ought not to be animated unless they have some natural dignity. Thomson, in this article, is licentious; witness the following instances out of many:

> O vale of bliss! O softly swelling hills!
> On which *the power of cultivation* lies,
> And joys to see the wonders of his toil.—*Summer*, l. 1435.

> Then sated *Hunger* bids his brother *Thirst*
> Produce the mighty bowl;
> Nor wanting is the brown October, drawn
> Mature and perfect, from *his* dark retreat
> Of thirty years, and now *his honest front*
> Flames in the light refulgent.—*Autumn*, l. 516.

516. Thirdly, It is not sufficient to avoid improper subjects: some preparation is necessary in order to rouse the mind; for the imagination refuses its aid, till it be warmed at least, if not inflamed. Yet Thomson, without the least ceremony or preparation, introduceth each season as a sensible being:

> From brightening fields of ether fair disclosed,
> Child of the sun, refulgent *Summer* comes,
> In pride of youth, and felt through Nature's depth.
> He comes attended by the sultry hours,
> And ever fanning breezes, on his way;
> While from his ardent look, the turning Spring
> Averts her blushful face, and earth and skies
> All smiling to his hot dominion leaves.—*Summer*, l. 1.

> See *Winter* comes, to rule the varied year,
> Sullen and sad with all his rising train,
> *Vapors*, and *clouds*, and *storms*.—*Winter*, l. 1.

This has violently the air of writing mechanically without taste. It is not natural that the imagination of a writer should be so much heated at the very commencement; and, at any rate, he cannot expect such ductility in his readers. But if this practice can be justified by authority, Thomson has one of no mean note: Vida begins his first eclogue in the following words:

> Dicite, vos Musæ, et juvenum memorate querelas;
> Dicite; nam motas ipsas ad carmina cautes
> Et requiesse suos perhibent vaga flumina cursus.

Even Shakspeare is not always careful to prepare the mind for this bold figure. Take the following instance:

> ———————Upon these taxations,
> The clothiers all, not able to maintain
> The many to them 'longing, have put off
> The spinsters, carders, fullers, weavers; who,
> Unfit for other life, compell'd by hunger,
> And lack of other means, in desp'rate manner
> Daring th' event to th' teeth, are all in uproar,
> And *Danger* serves among them.—*Henry VIII.* Act I. Sc. 4.

Fourthly, Descriptive personification, still more than what is passionate, ought to be kept within the bounds of moderation. A reader warmed with a beautiful subject, can imagine, even without passion, the winds, for example, to be animated; but still the winds

---

515. How descriptive personification should be used. Degrees of it.—Personification of a low subject.—Things too familiar and base to be personified.

are the subject; and any action ascribed to them beyond or contrary to their usual operation, appearing unnatural, seldom fails to banish the illusion altogether: the reader's imagination, too far strained, refuses its aid; and the description becomes obscure, instead of being more lively and striking. In this view the following passage describing Cleopatra on shipboard, appears to me exceptionable:

> The barge she sat in, like a burnish'd throne,
> Burnt on the water: the poop was beaten gold,
> Purple the sails, and so perfumed, that
> The winds were love-sick with 'em.
>
> *Antony and Cleopatra*, Act II. Sc. 3.

The winds in their impetuous course have so much the appearance of fury, that it is easy to figure them wreaking their resentment against their enemies, by destroying houses, ships, &c.; but to figure them love-sick, has no resemblance to them in any circumstance. In another passage, where Cleopatra is also the subject, the personification of the air is carried beyond all bounds:

> ——————— The city cast
> Its people out upon her; and Antony
> Inthron'd i' th' market place, did sit alone,
> Whistling to th' air, which but for vacancy,
> Had gone to gaze on Cleopatra too,
> And made a gap in nature.
>
> *Antony and Cleopatra*, Act II. Sc. 3.

The following personification of the earth or soil is not less wild:

> She shall be dignified with this high honor,
> To bear mylady's train; lest the base earth
> Should from her vesture chance to steal a kiss;
> And of so great a favor growing proud,
> Disdain to root the summer-swelling flower,
> And make rough winter everlastingly.
>
> *Two Gentlemen of Verona*, Act II. Sc. 7.

Shakspeare, far from approving such intemperance of imagination, puts this speech in the mouth of a ranting lover. Neither can I relish what follows:

> Omnia quæ, Phœbo quondam meditante, beatus
> Audit Eurotas, jussitque ediscere lauros,
> Ille canit. *Virgil*, Buc. vi. 82.

The cheerfulness singly of a pastoral song, will scarce support personification in the lowest degree. But admitting, that a river gently flowing may be imagined a sensible being listening to a song, I cannot enter into the conceit of the river's ordering his laurels to learn the song: here all resemblance to any thing real is quite lost. This however is copied literally by one of our greatest poets; early indeed, before maturity of taste or judgment:

> Thames heard the numbers as he flow'd along,
> And bade his willows learn the moving song.
>
> *Pope's Pastorals*, Past. iv. l. 13.

This author, in riper years, is guilty of a much greater deviation from the rule. Dulness may be imagined a deity or idol, to be worshipped by bad writers; but then some sort of disguise is requisite, some bastard virtue must be bestowed, to make such worship in some degree excusable. Yet in the *Dunciad*, Dulness, without the least disguise, is made the object of worship. The mind rejects such a fiction as unnatural; for dulness is a defect, of which even the dullest mortal is ashamed:

> Then he: Great tamer of all human art!
> First in my care, and ever at my heart;
> Dulness! whose good old cause I yet defend,
> With whom my Muse began, with whom shall end,
> E'er since Sir Fopling's periwig was praise.
> To the last honors of the Bull and Bays!
> O thou! of bus'ness the directing soul!
> To this our head, like bias to the bowl,
> Which as more pond'rous, made its aim more true,
> Obliquely waddling to the mark in view:
> O! ever gracious to perplex'd mankind,
> Still spread a healing mist before the mind:
> And, lest we err by Wit's wild dancing light,
> Secure us kindly in our native night.
> Or, if to wit a coxcomb make pretence,
> Guard the sure barrier between that and sense;
> Or quite unravel all the reasoning thread,
> And hang some curious cobweb in its stead!
> As, forced from wind-guns, lead itself can fly,
> And pond'rous slugs cut swiftly through the sky;
> As clocks to weight their nimble motion owe,
> The wheels above urged by the load below:
> Me Emptiness and Dulness could inspire,
> And were my elasticity, and fire. **B. i. 163.**

517. Fifthly, The enthusiasm of passion may have the effect to prolong passionate personification; but descriptive personification cannot be dispatched in too few words: a circumstantiate description dissolves the charm, and makes the attempt to personify appear ridiculous. Homer succeeds in animating his darts and arrows; but such personification spun out in a French translation, is mere burlesque:

> Et la flèche en furie, avide de son sang,
> Part, vole à lui, l'atteint, et lui perce le flanc.

Horace says happily,

> Post equitem sedet atra Cura.

Observe how this thought degenerates by being divided, like the former, into a number of minute parts:

> Un fou rempli d'erreurs, que le trouble accompagne
> Et malade à la ville ainsi qu'à la campagne,
> En vain monte à cheval pour tromper son ennui,
> La Chagrin monte en croupe, et galope avec lui.

---

516. Preparation necessary.—Criticism on Th mson.—Limits to personification.—Faulty examples from Shakspeare and Pope.

A poet, in a short and lively expression, may animate his muse, his genius, and even his verse; but to animate his verse, and to address a whole epistle to it, as Boileau doth (*Epistle* x.), is insupportable.

The following passage is not less faulty:

> Her fate is whisper'd by the gentle breeze,
> And told in sighs to all the trembling trees;
> The trembling trees, in every plain and wood,
> Her fate remurmur to the silver flood;
> The silver flood, so lately calm, appears
> Swell'd with new passion, and o'erflows with tears
> The winds, and trees, and floods, her death deplore,
> Daphne, our grief! our glory! now no more.
>
> *Pope's Pastorals*, iv. 61.

Let grief or love have the power to animate the winds, the trees, the floods, provided the figure be dispatched in a single expression; even in that case, the figure seldom has a good effect; because grief or love of the pastoral kind, are causes rather too faint for so violent an effect as imagining the winds, trees, or floods, to be sensible beings. But when this figure is deliberately spread out, with great regularity and accuracy, through many lines, the reader, instead of relishing it, is struck with its ridiculous appearance.

SECTION II.

Apostrophe.

518. THIS figure and the former are derived from the same principle. If, to humor a plaintive passion, we can bestow a momentary sensibility upon an inanimate object, it is not more difficult to bestow a momentary presence upon a sensible being who is absent:

> Strike the harp in praise of Bragela, whom I left in the isle of mist, the spouse of my love. Dost thou raise thy fair face from the rock to find the sails of Cuchullin? The sea is rolling far distant, and its white foam shall deceive thee for my sails.—Retire, for it is night, my love, and the dark winds sigh in thy hair. Retire to the hall of my feasts, and think of the times that are past; for I will not return till the storm of war is gone. O Connal, speak of wars and arms, and send her from my mind; for lovely with her raven hair is the white-bosom'd daughter of Sorglan.—*Fingal*, b. i.

Speaking of Fingal absent:

> Happy are thy people, O Fingal; thine arm shall fight their battles. Thou art the first in their dangers; the wisest in the days of their peace; thou speakest, and thy thousands obey; and armies tremble at the sound of thy steel Happy are thy people, O Fingal.

This figure is sometimes joined with the former: things inanimate, to qualify them for listening to a passionate expostulation, are not only personified, but also conceived to be present:

---

517. Descriptive personification should be short. Examples.

Et si fata Deûm, si mems non læva fuisset,
Impulerat ferro Argolicas fœdare latebras;
Trojaque nunc stares, Priamique arx alta maneres.
Æneid, ii. 54.

Helena. ————Poor lord, is't I
That chase thee from thy country, and expose
Those tender limbs of thine to the event
Of non-sparing war? And is it I
That drive thee from the sportive court, where thou
Wast shot at with fair eyes, to be the mark
Of smoky muskets? *O you leaden messengers,*
That ride upon the violent speed of fire,
Fly with false aim; pierce the still moving air
That sings with piercing; do not touch my lord.
All's Well that End's Well, Act III. Sc. 4.

And let them lift ten thousand swords, said Nathos, with a smile; the sons of car-borne Usnoth will never tremble in danger. Why dost thou roll with all thy foam, thou roaring sea of Ullin? why do ye rustle on your dark wings, ye whistling tempests of the sky? Do ye think, ye storms, that ye keep Nathos on the coast? No; his soul detains him, children of the night! Althos, bring my father's arms, &c.—*Fingal.*

Whither hast thou fled, O wind, said the king of Morven! Dost thou rustle in the chambers of the south, and pursue the shower in other lands? Why comest not thou to my sails, to the blue face of my seas? The foe is in the land of Morven, and the king is absent.—*Fingal.*

Hast thou left thy blue course in heaven, golden-haired son of the sky! The west hath opened its gates; the bed of thy repose is there. The waves gather to behold thy beauty; they lift their trembling heads; they see thee lovely in thy sleep, but they shrink away with fear. Rest in thy shadowy cave, O Sun! and let thy return be in joy.—*Fingal.*

Daughter of Heaven, fair art thou! the silence of thy face is pleasant. Thou comest forth in loveliness; the stars attend thy blue steps in the east. The clouds rejoice in thy presence, O Moon! and brighten their dark-brown sides. —Who is like thee in heaven, daughter of the night! The stars are ashamed in thy presence, and turn aside their sparkling eyes. Whither dost thou retire from thy course, when the darkness of thy countenance grows? Hast thou thy hall like Ossian? Dwellest thou in the shadow of grief? Have thy sisters fallen from heaven? and are they who rejoiced with thee at night no more? Yes, they have fallen, fair light; and often dost thou retire to mourn.—But thou thyself shalt one night fail; and leave thy blue path in heaven. The stars will then lift their heads; they, who in thy presence were ashamed, will rejoice.—*Fingal.*

This figure, like all others, requires an agitation of mind. In plain narrative, as, for example, in giving the genealogy of a family, it has no good effect:

————Fauno Picus pater: isque parentem
Te, Saturne, refert; tu sanguinis ultimus auctor.—*Æneid*, vii. 48.

SECTION III.

Hyperbole.

519. In this figure, by which an object is magnified or diminished beyond truth, we have another effect of the foregoing principle. An

518. Define apostrophe. With what other figure is it often joined? The state of mind it requires.

object of an uncommon size, either very great of its kind or very little, strikes us with surprise; and this emotion produces a momentary conviction that the object is greater or less than it is in reality (see chapter viii.). The same effect, precisely, attends figurative grandeur or littleness; and hence the hyperbole, which expresses that momentary conviction. A writer, taking advantage of this natural delusion, warms his description greatly by the hyperbole; and the reader, even in his coolest moments, relishes the figure, being sensible that it is the operation of nature upon a glowing fancy.

It cannot have escaped observation, that a writer is commonly more successful in magnifying by an hyperbole than in diminishing. The reason is, that a minute object contracts the mind, and fetters the power of imagination; but that the mind, dilated and inflamed with a grand object, moulds objects for its gratification with great facility. Longinus, with respect to diminishing hyperbole, quotes the following ludicrous thought from a comic poet: "He was owner of a bit of ground no larger than a Lacedemonian letter." (Chapter xxxi. of his Treatise on the Sublime.) But, for the reason now given, the hyperbole has by far the greater force in magnifying objects; of which take the following examples:

For all the land which thou seest, to thee will I give it, and to thy seed forever. And I will make thy seed as the dust of the earth; so that if a man can number the dust of the earth, then shall thy seed also be numbered.—*Genesis*, xiii. 15, 16.

Illa vel intactæ segetis per summa volaret
Gramina: nec teneras cursu læsisset aristas.—*Æneid*, vii. 808

————Atque imo barathri ter gurgite vastos
Sorbet in abruptum fluctus, rursusque sub auras
Erigit alternos, et sidera verberat undâ.—*Ibid.* iii. 421.

————Horrificis juxta tonat Ætna ruinis,
Interdumque atram prorumpit ad æthera nubem,
Turbine fumantem piceo et candente favilla:
Attollitque globos flammarum, et sidera lambit.—*Ibid.* iii. 571.

Speaking of Polyphemus:

————Ipse arduus, altaque pulsat
Sidera. *Ibid.* iii. 619

————When he speaks,
The air, a charter'd libertine, is still.—*Henry V.* Act I. Sc. 1.

Now shield with shield, with helmet helmet closed,
To armor armor, lance to lance opposed.
Host against host with shadowy squadrons drew,
The sounding darts in iron tempests flew.
Victors and vanquish'd join promiscuous cries,
And shrilling shouts and dying groans arise:
With streaming blood the slippery fields are dyed,
And slaughter'd heroes swell the dreadful tide.—*Iliad*, iv. 508.

---

519. Define hyperbole. Why it is easier to magnify than to diminish by hyperbole The figure, natural.

520. Having examined the nature of this figure, and the principle on which it is erected, I proceed, as in the first section, to the rules by which it ought to be governed. And, in the first place, it is a capital fault to introduce an hyperbole in the description of any thing ordinary or familiar; for in such a case it is altogether unnatural, being destitute of surprise, its only foundation. Take the following instance, where the subject is extremely familiar, viz., swimming to gain the shore after a shipwreck:

I saw him beat the surges under him,
And ride upon their backs; he trode the water,
Whose enmity he flung aside, and breasted
The surge most swoln that met him: his bold head
'Bove the contentious waves he kept, and oar'd
Himself with his good arms, in lusty strokes,
To th' *shore*, that o'er his wave-borne basis bow'd,
As stooping to relieve him. *Tempest*, Act II. Sc. 1.

In the next place, it may be gathered from what is said, that an hyperbole can never suit the tone of any dispiriting passion: sorrow in particular will never prompt such a figure; for which reason the following hyperboles must be condemned as unnatural:

K. Rich. Aumerle, thou weep'st, my tender-hearted cousin!
We'll make foul weather with despised tears:
Our sighs, and they, shall lodge the summer-corn,
And make a dearth in this revolting land.—*Richard II.* Act III. Sc. 6.

Draw them to Tyber's bank, and weep your tears
Into the channel, till the lowest stream
Do kiss the most exalted shores of all.—*Julius Cæsar*, Act I. Sc. 1.

Thirdly, A writer, if he wish to succeed, ought always to have the reader in his eye: he ought in particular never to venture a bold thought or expression till the reader be warned and prepared. For that reason an hyperbole in the beginning of a work can never be in its place. Example:

Jam pauca aratro jugera regiæ
Moles relinquent. *Horat. Carm.* l. i. ode 15.

521. The nicest point of all is to ascertain the natural limits of an hyperbole, beyond which being overstrained, it hath a bad effect. Longinus, in the above-cited chapter, with great propriety of thought enters a caveat against an hyperbole of this kind: he compares it to a bow-string, which relaxes by overstraining, and produceth an effect directly opposite to what is intended. To ascertain any precise boundary would be difficult, if not impracticable. Mine shall be an humbler task, which is, to give a specimen of what I reckon overstrained hyperbole; and I shall be brief upon them, because examples are to be found everywhere: no fault is more common among writers of inferior rank, and instances are found even

---

520. Capital fault.—The passion that is unsuited to hyperbole.—When a bold thought or expression may be ventured.

among classical writers: witness the following hyperbole, too bold even for a Hotspur.

Hotspur talking of Mortimer:

> In single opposition hand to hand,
> He did confound the best part of an hour
> In changing hardiment with great Glendower.
> Three times they breathed, and three times did they drink,
> Upon agreement, of swift Severn's flood,
> Who then, affrighted with their bloody looks,
> Ran fearfully among the trembling reeds,
> And hid his crisp'd head in the hollow bank,
> Blood-stained with these valiant combatants.
>
> *First Part Henry IV.* Act I. Sc. 4.

Speaking of Henry V.:

> England ne'er had a king until his time:
> Virtue he had deserving to command;
> His brandish'd sword did blind men with his beams:
> His arms spread wider than a dragon's wings;
> His sparkling eyes, replete with awful fire,
> More dazzled, and drove back his enemies,
> Than mid-day sun fierce bent against their faces.
> What should I say? his deeds exceed all speech;
> He never lifted up his hand, but conquer'd.
>
> *First Part Henry VI.* Act I. Sc. 1.

Lastly, An hyperbole, after it is introduced with all advantages, ought to be comprehended within the fewest words possible: as it cannot be relished but in the hurry and swelling of the mind, a leisurely view dissolves the charm, and discovers the description to be extravagant at least, and perhaps also ridiculous. This fault is palpable in a sonnet which passeth for one of the most complete in the French language. Phillis, in a long and florid description, is made as far to outshine the sun as he outshines the stars:

> Le silence régnoit sur la terre et sur l'onde,
> L'air devenoit serein et l'Olympe vermeil,
> Et l'amoureux Zéphir affranchi du sommeil,
> Ressuscitoit les fleurs d'une haleine féconde,
> L'Aurore déployoit l'or de sa tresse blonde,
> Et semoit de rubis le chemin du soleil;
> Enfin ce Dieu venoit au plus grand appareil
> Qu'il soit jamais venu pour éclairer le monde.
>
> Quand la jeune Phillis au visage riant,
> Sortant de son palais plus clair que l'orient,
> Fit voir une lumière et plus vive et plus belle.
> Sacré flambeau du jour, n'en soyez point jaloux.
> Vous parûtes alors aussi peu devant elle,
> Que les feux de la nuit avoient fait devant vous.—*Malleville.*

There is in Chaucer a thought expressed in a single line, which gives more lustre to a young beauty than the whole of this much labored poem:

> Up rose the sun, and up rose Emelie.

---

521. The natural limits of hyperbole. In what words to be conveyed.

SECTION IV.

The Means or Instrument conceived to be the Agent.

522. When we survey a number of connected objects, that which makes the greatest figure employs chiefly our attention; and the emotion it raises, if lively, prompts us even to exceed nature in the conception we form of it. Take the following examples:

> For Neleus' son Alcides' *rage* had slain.
> A broken rock the *force* of Pirus threw.

In these instances, the rage of Hercules and the force of Pirus being the capital circumstances, are so far exalted as to be conceived the agents that produce the effects.

In the following instances, hunger being the chief circumstance in the description, is itself imagined to be the patient:

> Whose hunger has not tasted food these three days.—*Jane Shore.*

> ————————As when the force
> Of subterranean wind transports a hill.—*Paradise Lost.*

> ————————As when the potent rod
> Of Amram's son, in Egypt's evil day
> Waved round the coast, upcall'd a pitchy cloud
> Of locusts. *Paradise Lost.*

SECTION V.

A Figure which, among Related Objects, extends the Properties of one to another.

523. This figure is not dignified with a proper name, because it has been overlooked by writers. It merits, however, a place in this work; and must be distinguished from those formerly handled, as depending on a different principle. *Giddy brink. jovial wine, daring wound*, are examples of this figure. Here are adjectives that cannot be made to signify any quality of the substantives to which they are joined: a *brink*, for example, cannot be termed *giddy* in a sense, either proper or figurative, that can signify any of its qualities or attributes. When we examine attentively the expression, we discover that a *brink* is termed *giddy* from producing that effect in those who stand on it. In the same manner a wound is said to be

---

522. In surveying connected objects, what gains chief attention?—How the capital circumstances are sometimes exalted. Examples.

daring, not with respect to itself, but with respect to the boldness of the person who inflicts it; and wine is said to be *jovial*, as inspiring mirth and jollity. Thus the attributes of one subject are extended to another with which it is connected; and the expression of such a thought must be considered as a figure, because the attribute is not applicable to the subject in any proper sense.

How are we to account for this figure, which we see lies in the thought, and to what principle shall we refer it? Have poets a privilege to alter the nature of things, and at pleasure to bestow attributes upon a subject to which they do not belong? We have had often occasion to inculcate that the mind passeth easily and sweetly along a train of connected objects; and where the objects are intimately connected, that it is disposed to carry along the good and bad properties of one to another, especially when it is in any degree inflamed with these properties. (See chapter ii. part i. sec. 5.) From this principle is derived the figure under consideration. Language, invented for the communication of thought, would be imperfect if it were not expressive even of the slighter propensities and more delicate feelings: but language cannot remain so imperfect among a people who have received any polish; because language is regulated by internal feeling, and is gradually improved to express whatever passes in the mind. Thus, for example, when a sword in the hand of a coward is termed a *coward sword*, the expression is significative of an internal operation; for the mind, in passing from the agent to its instrument, is disposed to extend to the latter the properties of the former. Governed by the same principle, we say *listening* fear, by extending the attribute *listening* of the man who listens to the passion with which he is moved. In the expression *bold deed*, or *audax facinus*, we extend to the effect what properly belongs to the cause. But not to waste time by making a commentary upon every expression of this kind, the best way to give a complete view of the subject, is to exhibit a table of the different relations that may give occasion to this figure. And in viewing the table, it will be observed that the figure can never have any grace but where the relations are of the most intimate kind.

1. An attribute of the cause expressed as an attribute of the effect.

> Audax facinus.
>
> Of yonder fleet a *bold* discovery make.
>
> An impious mortal gave the *daring* wound.
>
> ——————— To my *adventurous* song,
> That with no middle flight intends to soar. *Paradise Lost.*

2. An attribute of the effect expressed as an attribute of the cause.

> Quos periisse ambos *misera* censebam in mari. *Plautus.*
>
> No wonder, fallen such a *pernicious* height. *Paradise Lost.*

3. An effect expressed as an attribute of the cause.

Jovial wine, Giddy brink, Drowsy night, Musing midnight, Painting height, Astonish'd thought, Mournful gloom.

Casting a dim *religious* light. *Milton, Comus.*

And the *merry* bells ring round,
And the *jocund* rebecks sound. *Milton, Allegro.*

4. An attribute of a subject bestowed upon one of its parts or members.

Longing arms.

It was the nightingale, and not the lark,
That pierced the *fearful* hollow of thine ear.
Romeo and Juliet, Act III. Sc. 7.

——————— Oh, lay by
Those most ungentle looks and angry weapons;
Unless you mean my griefs and killing fears
Should stretch me out at your relentless feet.
Fair Penitent, Act III.

——————— And ready now
To stoop with *wearied* wing and *willing* feet,
On the bare outside of this world.
Paradise Lost, b. iii.

5. A quality of the agent given to the instrument with which it operates.

Why peep your *coward* swords half out their shells!

6. An attribute of the agent given to the subject upon which it operates.

High-climbing hill. *Milton.*

7. A quality of one subject given to another.

Icci, *beatis* nunc Arabum invides
Gazis. *Horat. Carm.* l. i. ode 29.

When sapless age, and weak unable limbs,
Should bring thy father to his *drooping* chair. *Shakspeare.*

By art, the pilot through the boiling deep
And howling tempest, steers the *fearless* ship.
Iliad, xxiii. 385.

Then, nothing loth, th' enamor'd fair he led,
And sunk transported on the *conscious* bed.—*Odyssey*, viii. 337.

A *stupid* moment motionless she stood. *Summer*, l. 1336.

8. A circumstance connected with a subject, expressed as a quality of the subject.

Breezy summit.

'Tis ours the chance of *fighting* fields to try. *Iliad*, i. 301.

Oh! had I died before that *well-fought* wall. *Odyssey*, v. 395.

---

523. The expressions *giddy brink, jovial wine, daring wound,* explained. How this figure is to be accounted for. Table of the different relations that may give occasion to this figure.

524. From this table it appears that the adorning a cause with an attribute of the effect, is not so agreeable as the opposite expression. The progress from cause to effect is natural and easy: the opposite progress resembles retrograde motion (see chapter i.); and, therefore, *panting height*, *astonish'd thought*, are strained and uncouth expressions, which a writer of taste will avoid.

It is not less strained to apply to a subject in its present state, an epithet that may belong to it in some future state:

> *Submersasque* obrue puppes. — *Æneid*, i. 73
>
> And mighty *ruins* fall. — *Iliad*, v. 411.
>
> Impious sons their *mangled* fathers wound.

Another rule regards this figure, that the property of one subject ought not to be bestowed upon another with which that property is incongruous:

> *King Rich.* ——— How dare thy joints forget
> To pay their *awful* duty to our presence?
>
> *Richard II.* Act III. Sc. 6.

The connection between an awful superior and his submissive dependent is so intimate, that an attribute may readily be transferred from the one to the other; but awfulness cannot be so transferred, because it is inconsistent with submission.

SECTION VI.

Metaphor and Allegory.

525. A METAPHOR differs from a simile in form only, not in substance: in a simile, the two subjects are kept distinct in the expression, as well as in the thought; in a metaphor, the two subjects are kept distinct in the thought only, not in the expression. A hero resembles a lion, and, upon that resemblance, many similes have been raised by Homer and other poets. But instead of resembling a lion, let us take the aid of the imagination, and feign or figure the hero to be a lion: by that variation the simile is converted into a metaphor; which is carried on by describing all the qualities of a lion that resemble those of the hero. The fundamental pleasure here, that of resemblance, belongs to the thought. An additional pleasure arises from the expression: the poet, by figuring his hero to be a lion, goes on to describe the lion in appearance, but in reality the hero; and his description is peculiarly beautiful, by expressing the virtues and qualities of the hero in new terms, which, properly speaking, belong not to him but to the lion. This will better be understood by examples. A family connected with a

---

524 Inferences from the above table.

common parent, resembles a tree, the trunk and branches of which are connected with a common root: but let us suppose that a family is figured, not barely to be like a tree, but to be a tree; and then the simile will be converted into a metaphor, in the following manner:

> Edward's seven sons, whereof thyself art one,
> Were seven fair branches, springing from one root:
> Some of these branches by the dest'nies cut:
> But Thomas, my dear lord, my life, my Glo'ster,
> One flourishing branch of his most royal root,
> Is hack'd down, and his summer-leaves all faded,
> By Envy's hand and Murder's bloody axe.
> *Richard II.* Act I. Sc. 3.

Figuring human life to be a voyage at sea:

> There is a tide in the affairs of men,
> Which, taken at the flood, leads on to fortune
> Omitted, all the voyage of their life
> Is bound in shallows and in miseries.
> On such a full sea are we now afloat,
> And we must take the current while it serves,
> Or lose our ventures. *Julius Cæsar*, Act IV. Sc. 5.

Figuring glory and honor to be a garland of flowers:

> *Hotspur.* ——— ——— Would to heaven,
> Thy name in arms were now as great as mine!
> *Pr. Henry.* I'll make it greater, ere I part from thee,
> And all the budding honors on thy crest,
> I'll crop, to make a garland for my head.
> *First Part Henry IV.* Act V. Sc. 9.

Figuring a man who hath acquired great reputation and honor to be a tree full of fruit:

> ——— ——— ——— Oh, boys, this story
> The world may read in me: my body's mark'd
> With Roman swords; and my report was once
> First with the best of note. Cymbeline loved me;
> And when a soldier was the theme, my name
> Was not far off: then was I as a tree,
> Whose boughs did bend with fruit. But in one night,
> A storm or robbery, call it what you will,
> Shook down my mellow hangings, nay my leaves;
> And left me bare to weather. *Cymbeline*, Act III. Sc. 3.

Blessed be thy soul, thou king of shells, said Swaran of the dark-brown shield. In peace thou art the gale of spring; in war, the mountain-storm. Take now my hand in friendship, thou noble king of Morven. *Fingal.*

Thou dwellest in the soul of Melvina, son of mighty Ossian. My sighs arise with the beam of the east; my tears descend with the drops of night. I was a lovely tree in thy presence, Oscar, with all my branches round me; but thy death came like a blast from the desert, and laid my green head low: the spring returned with its showers, but no leaf of mine arose. *Ibid.*

526. I am aware that the term *metaphor* has been used in a more extensive sense than I give it; but I thought it of consequence, in a disquisition of some intricacy, to confine the term to its proper sense,

---

525. Illustrate the difference between metaphor and simile Examples.

and to separate from it things that are distinguished by different names. An allegory differs from a metaphor, and what I would choose to call *a figure of speech*, differs from both. I proceed to explain these differences. A metaphor is defined above to be an act of the imagination, figuring one thing to be another. An allegory requires no such operation, nor is one thing figured to be another: it consists in choosing a subject having properties or circumstances resembling those of the principal subject; and the former is described in such a manner as to represent the latter: the subject thus represented is kept out of view; we are left to discover it by reflection; and we are pleased with the discovery, because it is our own work. Quintilian (L. viii. cap. vi. sec. 2) gives the following instance of an allegory:

> O navis, referent in mare te novi
> Fluctus. O quid agis? fortiter occupa portum.
>
> *Horat.* lib. i. ode 14.

and explains it elegantly in the following words: "Totusque ille Horatii locus, quo navim pro republica, fluctuum tempestates pro bellis civilibus, portum pro pace, atque concordia dicit."

A finer or more correct allegory is not to be found than the following, in which a vineyard is made to represent God's own people, the Jews:

> Thou hast brought a vine out of Egypt; thou hast cast out the heathen, and planted it. Thou didst cause it to take deep root, and it filled the land. The hills were covered with its shadow, and the boughs thereof were like the goodly cedars. Why hast thou then broken down her hedges, so that all which pass do pluck her? The boar out of the wood doth waste it, and the wild beast doth devour it. Return, we beseech thee, O God of hosts; look down from heaven, and behold and visit this vine, and the vineyard thy right hand hath planted, and the branch thou madest strong for thyself. *Psalm* lxxx.

In a word, an allegory is in every respect similar to a hieroglyphical painting, excepting only that words are used instead of colors. Their effects are precisely the same: a hieroglyphic raises two images in the mind; one seen, which represents one not seen: an allegory does the same: the representative subject is described; and resemblance leads us to apply the description to the subject represented. In a figure of speech, there is no fiction of the imagination employed, as in a metaphor, nor a representative subject introduced, as in an allegory. This figure, as its name implies, regards the expression only, not the thought; and it may be defined, the using a word in a sense different from what is proper to it. Thus youth, or the beginning of life, is expressed figuratively by *morning of life:* morning is the beginning of the day; and in that view it is employed to signify the beginning of any other series, life especially, the progress of which is reckoned by days.

---

526. Metaphor and allegory distinguished. Examples.—To what an allegory is similar.—Distinguish metaphor and allegory from a figure of speech.

527. Figures of speech are reserved for a separate section; but metaphor and allegory are so much connected, that they must be handled together; the rules particularly for distinguishing the good from the bad, are common to both. We shall therefore proceed to these rules, after adding some examples to illustrate the nature of an allegory:

> *Queen.* Great lords, wise men ne'er sit and wail their loss
> But cheerly seek how to redress their harms.
> What though the mast be now thrown overboard
> The cable broke, the holding anchor lost,
> And half our sailors swallow'd in the flood;
> Yet lives our pilot still. Is 't meet that he
> Should leave the helm, and, like a fearful lad,
> With tearful eyes, add water to the sea,
> And give more strength to that which hath too much;
> While in his moan the ship splits on the rock,
> Which industry and courage might have saved?
> Ah, what a shame! ah, what a fault were this!
>
> *Third Part Henry VI.* Act V. Sc. 5

> *Oroonoko.* Ha! thou hast roused
> The lion in his den; he stalks abroad,
> And the wide forest trembles at his roar.
> I find the danger now. *Oroonoko*, Act III. Sc. 2.

My well-beloved hath a vineyard in a very fruitful hill. He fenced it, gathered out the stones thereof, planted it with the choicest vines, built a tower in the midst of it, and also made a wine-press therein: he looked that it should bring forth grapes, and it brought forth wild grapes. And now, O inhabitants of Jerusalem, and men of Judah, judge, I pray you, betwixt me and my vineyard. What could have been done more to my vineyard, that I have not done? Wherefore, when I looked that it should bring forth grapes, brought it forth wild grapes? And now go to; I will tell you what I will do to my vineyard: I will take away the hedge thereof, and it shall be eaten up; and break down the wall thereof, and it shall be trodden down. And I will lay it waste: it shall not be pruned nor digged, but there shall come up briers and thorns: I will also command the clouds that they rain no rain upon it. For the vineyard of the Lord of hosts is the house of Israel, and the men of Judah his pleasant plant. *Isaiah*, v. 1.

The rules that govern metaphors and allegories are of two kinds: the construction of these figures comes under the first kind; the propriety or impropriety of introduction comes under the other. I begin with rules of the first kind; some of which coincide with those already given for similes; some are peculiar to metaphors and allegories.

And, in the first place, it has been observed, that a simile cannot be agreeable where the resemblance is either too strong or too faint. This holds equally in metaphor and allegory; and the reason is the same in all. In the following instances, the resemblance is too faint to be agreeable:

> He cannot buckle his distemper'd cause
> Within the belt of rule. *Macbeth*, Act V. Sc. 2.

There is no resemblance between a distempered cause and any body that can be confined within a belt.

Again:

> Steep me in poverty to the very lips.—*Othello*, Act IV. Sc. 9.

Poverty here must be conceived a fluid, which it resembles not in any manner.

Speaking to Bolingbroke banished for six years:

> The sullen passage of thy weary steps
> Esteem a foil, wherein thou art to set
> The precious jewel of thy home-return.—*Richard II.* Act I. Sc. 6.

Again:

> Here's a letter, lady,
> And every word in it a gaping wound
> Issuing life-blood. *Merchant of Venice.* Act III. Sc. 3.

> Tantæ *molis* erat Romanam condere gentem.—*Æneid*, i. 37.

The following metaphor is strained beyond all endurance, Timurbec, known to us by the name of Tamerlane the Great, writes to Bajazet, emperor of the Ottomans, in the following terms:

> Where is the monarch who dares resist us? where is the potentate who doth not glory in being numbered among our attendants? As for thee, descended from a Turcoman sailor, since the vessel of thy unbounded ambition hath been wreck'd in the gulf of thy self-love, it would be proper, that thou shouldst take in the sails of thy temerity, and cast the anchor of repentance in the port of sincerity and justice, which is the port of safety; lest the tempest of our vengeance make thee perish in the sea of the punishment thou deservest.

Such strained figures, as observed above (chapter xix., Comparisons), are not unfrequent in the first dawn of refinement; the mind in a new enjoyment knows no bounds, and is generally carried to excess, till taste and experience discover the proper limits.

Secondly, Whatever resemblance subjects may have, it is wrong to put one for another, where they bear no mutual proportion; upon comparing a very high to a very low subject, the simile takes on an air of burlesque; and the same will be the effect where the one is imagined to be the other, as in a metaphor; or made to represent the other, as in an allegory.

Thirdly, These figures, a metaphor especially, ought not to be crowded with many minute circumstances; for in that case it is scarcely possible to avoid obscurity. A metaphor above all ought to be short: it is difficult for any time to support a lively image of a thing being what we know it is not; and for that reason, a metaphor drawn out to any length, instead of illustrating or enlivening the principal subject, becomes disagreeable by over-straining the mind. Here Cowley is extremely licentious; take the following instance:

> Great and wise conqueror, who where'er
> Thou com'st, doth fortify, and settle there!
> Who canst defend as well as get,
> And never hadst one quarter beat up yet;

---

527. Examples of Allegory.—Two kinds of rules of metaphor and allegory. 1st. As to degree of resemblance. 2d. As to proportion. 3d As to circumstances.

Now thou art in, thou ne'er wilt part
With one inch of my vanquish'd heart:
For since thou took'st it by assault from me,
'Tis garrison'd so strong with thoughts of thee,
It fears no beauteous enemy.

For the same reason, however agreeable long allegories may at first be by their novelty, they never afford any lasting pleasure; witness the *Fairy Queen*, which with great power of expression, variety of images, and melody of versification, is scarce ever read a second time.

528. In the fourth place, the comparison carried on in a simile, being in a metaphor sunk by imagining the principal subject to be that very thing which it only resembles; an opportunity is furnished to describe it in terms taken strictly or literally with respect to its imagined nature. This suggests another rule, that in constructing a metaphor, the writer ought to make use of such words only as are applicable literally to the imagined nature of his subject: figurative words ought carefully to be avoided; for such complicated figures, instead of setting the principal subject in a strong light, involve it in a cloud; and it is well if the reader, without rejecting by the lump, endeavor patiently to gather the plain meaning regardless of its figures:

A stubborn and unconquerable flame
Creeps in his veins, and drinks the streams of life.
Lady Jane Gray, Act I. Sc. 1.

Copied from Ovid,

Sorbent avidæ præcordia flammæ.—*Metamorph.* lib. ix. 172.

Let us analyze this expression. That a fever may be imagined a flame, I admit; though more than one step is necessary to come at the resemblance: a fever, by heating the body, resembles fire; and it is no stretch to imagine a fever to be a fire: again, by a figure of speech, flame may be put for fire, because they are commonly conjoined; and therefore a fever may be termed a flame. But now admitting a fever to be a flame, its effects ought to be explained in words that agree literally to a flame. This rule is not observed here; for a flame *drinks* figuratively only, not properly.

King Henry to his son, Prince Henry:

Thou hid'st a thousand daggers in thy thoughts,
Which thou hast whetted on thy stony heart
To stab at half an hour of my frail life.
Second Part Henry IV. Act IV. Sc. 11.

Such faulty metaphors are pleasantly ridiculed in the *Rehearsal:*

Physician. Sir, to conclude, the place you fill has more than amply exacted the talents of a wary pilot; and all these threatening storms, which like impregnate clouds, hover o'er our heads, will, when they once are grasped but by the eye of reason, melt into fruitful showers of blessings on the people.
Bayes. Pray mark that allegory. Is not that good?
Johnson. Yes, that grasping of a storm with the eye is admirable.
Act II. Sc. 1.

528. The sort of words to be employed in constructing a metaphor

529. Fifthly, The jumbling different metaphors in the same sentence, beginning with one metaphor and ending with another, commonly called a mixed metaphor, ought never to be indulged. Quintilian bears testimony against it in the bitterest terms; "Nam id quoque in primis est custodiendum, ut quo ex genere cœperis translationis, hoc desinas. Multi enim, cum initium a tempestate sumpserunt, incendio aut ruina finiunt: quæ est inconsequentia rerum fœdissima."—L. viii. cap. vi. sect. 2.

> *K. Henry.*———Will you again unknit
> This churlish knot of all abhorred war,
> And move in that obedient orb again,
> Where you did give a fair and natural light?
> *First Part Henry VI.* Act V. Sc. 1

> Whether 'tis nobler in the mind to suffer
> The stings and arrows of outrageous fortune,
> Or to take arms against a sea of troubles,
> And by opposing, end them. *Hamlet*, Act III. Sc. 2.

In the sixth place, It is unpleasant to join different metaphors in the same period, even where they are preserved distinct; for when the subject is imagined to be first one thing and then another, in the same period without interval, the mind is distracted by the rapid transition; and when the imagination is put on such hard duty, its images are too faint to produce any good effect:

> At regina gravi jamdudum saucia cura,
> Vulnus alit venis, et cæco carpitur igni. *Æneid*, iv. 1.

> ———Est mollis flamma medullas
> Interea, et tacitum vivit sub pectore vulnus. *Æneid*, iv. 66.

> Motum ex Metello consule civicum,
> Bellique causas, et vitia, et modos,
> Ludumque fortunæ, gravesque
> Principum amicitias, et arma
> Nondum expiatis uncta cruoribus,
> Periculosæ plenum opus aleæ,
> Tractas, et incedis per ignes
> Subpositos cineri doloso. *Horat. Carm.* l. ii. ode 1.

530. In the last place, It is still worse to jumble together metaphorical and natural expression, so as that the period must be understood in part metaphorically, in part literally; for the imagination cannot follow with sufficient ease changes so sudden and unprepared: a metaphor begun and not carried on hath no beauty; and instead of light there is nothing but obscurity and confusion. Instances of such incorrect composition are without number. I shall, for a specimen, select a few from different authors.

---

529. The jumbling of different metaphors in a sentence. The joining of different metaphors, though distinct, in the same period.

Speaking of Britain,

> This precious stone set in the sea,
> Which serves it in the office of a wall,
> Or as a moat defensive to a house
> Against the envy of less happier lands.
> *Richard II.* Act I. Sc. 1.

In the first line Britain is figured to be a precious stone: in the following lines, Britain, divested of her metaphorical dress, is presented to the reader in her natural appearance.

> These growing feathers, pluck'd from Cæsar's wing,
> Will make him fly an ordinary pitch,
> Who else would soar above the view of men,
> And keep us all in servile fearfulness.
> *Julius Cæsar*, Act I. Sc. 1.

The following is a miserable jumble of expressions, arising from an unsteady view of the subject, between its figurative and natural appearance:

> But now from gathering clouds destruction pours,
> Which ruins with mad rage our halcyon hours:
> Mists from black jealousies the tempest forms,
> Whilst late divisions reinforce the storm.
> *Dispensary*, canto iii.

> To thee, the world its present homage pays,
> The harvest early, but mature the praise.
> *Pope's Imitation of Horace*, b. ii.

Dryden, in his dedication of the translation of *Juvenal*, says,

> When thus, as I may say, before the use of the loadstone, or knowledge of the compass, I was sailing in a vast ocean, without other help than the pole star of the ancients, and the rules of the French stage among the moderns, &c.

[Upon this sentence Prof. Barron remarks: Every reader must feel the incoherence of the transition from the figurative expression in "the polar star of the ancients," to the literal phraseology, "the rules of the French stage among the moderns," and the inconsistency of pretending to navigate the ocean by the laws of the theatre.

The author of the *Rehearsal* has, with much poignancy, ridiculed such incongruous figures: "'Sir, to conclude, the place you fill has more than amply exacted the talents of a wary pilot; and all these threatening storms, which, like impregnate clouds, hang over our heads, will, when they are once grasped by the eye of reason, melt into fruitful showers of blessings on the people.' 'Pray mark that allegory. Is not that good?' says Mr. Bayes. 'Yes,' replies Mr. Johnson, 'that grasping of a storm by the eye is admirable.'"—*Barron's Lect.*]

This fault of jumbling the figure and plain expression into one confused mass, is not less common in allegory than in metaphor. Take the following examples:

> ———— Heu! quoties fidem,
> Mutatosque Deos flebit, et aspera
> Nigris æquora ventis

Emirabitur insolens,
Qui nunc te fruitur credulus aureâ:
Qui semper vacuam, semper amabilem
Sperat, nescius auræ
Fallacis. *Horat. Carm.* l. i. ode 1.

Pour moi sur cette mer, qu'ici bas nous courons,
Je songe à me pourvoir d'esquif et d'avirons,
A régler mes désirs, à prévenir l'orage,
Et sauver, s'il se peut, ma Raison du naufrage.
Boileau, Epître v.

["There is a time," observes Lord Bolingbroke, "when factions, by the vehemence of their fermentation, stun and disable one another." The author represents factions, first, as discordant fluids, the mixture of which produces violent fermentation; but he quickly relinquishes this view of them, and imputes to them operations and effects, consequent only on the supposition of their being solid bodies in motion: they maim and dismember one another by forcible collisions.

"Those whose minds are dull and heavy," according to Swift, "do not easily penetrate into the folds and intricacies of an affair, and therefore can only scum off what they find at the top." That the writer had a right to represent his affair, whatever it was, either as a bale of cloth or a fluid, nobody can deny. But the laws of common sense and perspicuity demanded of him to keep it either the one or the other, because it could not be both at the same time. It was absurd, therefore, after he had penetrated the folds of it, an operation competent only on the supposition of its being some pliable solid body, to speak of scumming off what floated on the surface, which could not be performed unless it was a fluid.—*Barron*, Lect. 17.]

531. A few words more upon allegory. Nothing gives greater pleasure than this figure, when the representative subject bears a strong analogy, in all its circumstances, to that which is represented: but the choice is seldom so lucky; the analogy being generally so faint and obscure, as to puzzle and not please. An allegory is still more difficult in painting than in poetry: the former can show no resemblance but what appears to the eye; the latter hath many other resources for showing the resemblance. And therefore, with respect to what the Abbé du Bos (*Reflections sur la Poésie*, vol. i. sect. 24) terms mixed allegorical compositions, these may do in poetry; because, in writing, the allegory can easily be distinguished from the historical part: no person, for example, mistakes Virgil's Fame for a real being. But such a mixture in a picture is intolerable; because in a picture the objects must appear all of the same kind, wholly real or wholly emblematical.

In an allegory, as well as in a metaphor, terms ought to be chosen

---

530. The jumbling of metaphorical and natural expression. Examples from Bolingbroke and Swift.

that properly and literally are applicable to the representative subject; nor ought any circumstance to be added that is not proper to the representative subject, however justly it may be applicable properly or figuratively to the principal. The following allegory is therefore faulty :

> Ferus et Cupido,
> Semper ardentes acuens sagittas
> Cote *cruenta*. *Horat.* l. ii. ode 8.

For though blood may suggest the cruelty of love, it is an improper or immaterial circumstance in the representative subject: water, not blood, is proper for a whetstone.

532. We proceed to the next head, which is, to examine in what circumstance these figures are proper, in what improper. This inquiry is not altogether superseded by what is said to be the same subject in the chapter of Comparisons; because upon trial it will be found that a short metaphor or allegory may be proper, where a simile, drawn out to a greater length, and in its nature more solemn, would scarce be relished.

And first, a metaphor, like a simile, is excluded from common conversation, and from the description of ordinary incidents.

Second, in expressing any severe passion that wholly occupies the mind, metaphor is improper. For which reason the following speech of Macbeth is faulty :

> Methought I heard a voice cry, Sleep no more!
> Macbeth doth murder sleep; the innocent sleep;
> Sleep that knits up the ravell'd sleeve of Care,
> The birth of each day's life, sore Labor's bath,
> Balm of hurt minds, great Nature's second course,
> Chief nourisher in Life's feast. Act II. Sc. 3.

The following example of deep despair, besides the highly figurative style, hath more the air of raving than of sense :

> *Calista.* It is the voice of thunder, or my father?
> Madness! Confusion! let the storm come on,
> Let the tumultuous roar drive all upon me,
> Dash my devoted bark; ye surges, break it;
> 'Tis for my ruin that the tempest rises,
> When I am lost, sunk to the bottom low,
> Peace shall return, and all be calm again.—*Fair Penitent*, Act IV.

The metaphor I next introduce is sweet and lively, but it suits not a fiery temper inflamed with passion: parables are not the language of wrath venting itself without restraint.

> *Chamont.* You took her up a little tender flower,
> Just sprouted on a bank, which the next frost
> Had nipp'd; and with a careful loving hand,
> Transplanted her into your own fair garden,
> Where the sun always shines: there long she flourish'd,

---

531. When allegory gives great pleasure.—More difficult in painting than **in poetry.**—Choice of terms in allegory —Circumstances.

532 When these figures are proper and when improper

Grew sweet to sense and lovely to the eye,
Till at the last a cruel spoiler came,
Cropt this fair rose, and rifled all its sweetness,
Then cast it like a loathsome weed away. *Orphan*, Act IV.

The following speech, full of imagery, is not natural in grief and dejection of mind:

Gonsalez. O my son! from the blind dotage
Of a father's fondness these ills arose.
For thee I've been ambitious, base, and bloody:
For thee I've plunged into the sea of sin;
Stemming the tide with only one weak hand,
While t'other bore the crown (to wreathe thy brow),
Whose weight has sunk me ere I reach'd the shore.
Mourning Bride, Act V. Sc. 6

533. There is an enchanting picture of deep distress in Macbeth (Act IV. Sc. 6), where Macduff is represented lamenting his wife and children, inhumanly murdered by the tyrant. Stung to the heart with the news, he questions the messenger over and over; not that he doubted the fact, but that his heart revolted against so cruel a misfortune. After struggling some time with his grief, he turns from his wife and children to their savage butcher; and then gives vent to his resentment, but still with manliness and dignity:

O, I could play the woman with mine eyes,
And braggart with my tongue. But, gentle Heaven!
Cut short all intermission; front to front
Bring thou this fiend of Scotland and myself;
Within my sword's length set him.—If he 'scape,
Then Heaven forgive him too.

The whole scene is a delicious picture of human nature. One expression only seems doubtful; in examining the messenger, Macduff expresses himself thus:

He hath no children—all my pretty ones!
Did you say all? what, all? Oh, hell-kite, all?
What! all my pretty little chickens and their dam,
At one fell swoop!

Metaphorical expression, I am sensible, may sometimes be used with grace, where a regular simile would be intolerable; but there are situations so severe and dispiriting, as not to admit even the slightest metaphor. It requires great delicacy of taste to determine with firmness, whether the present case be of that kind: I incline to think it is; and yet I would not willingly alter a single word of this admirable scene.

But metaphorical language is proper when a man struggles to bear with dignity or decency a misfortune however great; the struggle agitates and animates the mind:

Wolsey. Farewell, a long farewell, to all my greatness!
This is the state of man; to-day he puts forth

---

533. Picture of distress from *Macbeth*.—Instances where metaphorical expression is allowable.

The tender leaves of hope; to-morrow blossoms,
And bears his blushing honors thick upon him;
The third day comes a frost, a killing frost,
And when he thinks, good easy man, full surely
His greatness is a ripening, nips his root,
And then he falls as I do. *Henry VIII.* Act III Sc. 6.

SECTION VII.

Figure of Speech.

534. In the section immediately foregoing, a figure of speech is defined, "The using a word in a sense different from what is proper to it;" and the new or uncommon sense of the word is termed *the figurative sense.* The figurative sense must have a relation to that which is proper; and the more intimate the relation is, the figure is the more happy. How ornamental this figure is to language, will not be readily imagined by any one who hath not given peculiar attention; and therefore I shall endeavor to unfold its capital beauties and advantages. In the first place, a word used figuratively or in a new sense, suggests at the same time the sense it commonly bears; and thus it has the effect to present two objects; one signified by the figurative sense, which may be termed, *the principal object;* and one signified by the proper sense, which may be termed *accessory:* the principal makes a part of the thought; the accessory is merely ornamental. In this respect, a figure of speech is precisely similar to concordant sounds in music, which, without contributing to the melody, make it harmonious. I explain myself by examples. *Youth,* by a figure of speech, is termed *the morning of life.*—This expression signifies *youth,* the principal object, which enters into the thought; it suggests, at the same time, the proper sense of *morning,* and this accessory object, being in itself beautiful, and connected by resemblance to the principal object, is not a little ornamental. *Imperious ocean* is an example of a different kind, where an attribute is expressed figuratively: together with *stormy,* the figurative meaning of the epithet *imperious,* there is suggested its proper meaning, *viz.,* the stern authority of a despotic prince; and these two are strongly connected by resemblance.

535. In the next place, this figure possesses a signal power of aggrandizing an object, by the following means: Words which have no original beauty but what arises from their sound, acquire an adventitious beauty from their meaning: a word signifying any thing that is agreeable, becomes by that means agreeable; for the agreeableness of the object is communicated to its name. (See chapter ii. part i. sec. 5.) This acquired beauty, by the force of custom, ad-

---

584. The figurative sense. To what it must bear a close relation. Two objects presented Examples.—Youth, the morning of life.

heres to the word even when used figuratively; and the beauty received from the thing it properly signifies, is communicated to the thing which it is made to signify figuratively. Consider the fore going expression, *imperious ocean*, how much more elevated it is than *stormy ocean.*

Thirdly, This figure hath a happy effect by preventing the familiarity of proper names. The familiarity of a proper name is communicated to the thing it signifies by means of their intimate connection; and the thing is therefore brought down in our feeling. This bad effect is prevented by using a figurative word instead of one that is proper; as, for example, when we express the sky by terming it *the blue vault of heaven;* for though no work of art can compare with the sky in grandeur, the expression however is relished, because it prevents the object from being brought down by the familiarity of its proper name.

Lastly, By this figure language is enriched, and rendered more copious; in which respect, were there no other, a figure of speech is a happy invention. This property is finely touched by Vida:

> Quinetiam agricolas ea fandi nota voluptas
> Exercet, dum læta seges, dum trudere gemmas
> Incipiunt vites, sitientiaque ætheris imbrem
> Prata bibunt, ridentque satis surgentibus agri.
> Hanc vulgo speciem propriæ penuria vocis
> Intulit, indictisque urgens in rebus egestas.
> Quippe ubi se vera ostendebant nomina nusquam,
> Fas erat hinc atque hinc transferre simillima veris.
>
> *Poet.* lib. iii. l. 90.

The beauties I have mentioned belong to every figure of speech. Several other beauties, peculiar to one or other sort, I shall have occasion to remark afterwards.

536. Not only subjects, but qualities, actions, effects, may be expressed figuratively. Thus as to subject, *the gates of breath* for the lips, *the watery kingdom* for the ocean. As to qualities, *fierce* for stormy, in the expression *Fierce winter: Altus* for *profundus; Altus puteus, Altum mare: Breathing* for *perspiring; Breathing plants.* Again, as to actions, The sea *rages;* Time will *melt* her frozen thoughts; Time *kills* grief. An effect is put for the cause, as *lux* for the sun; and a cause for the effect, as *boum labores* for corn. The relation of resemblance is one plentiful source of figures of speech, and nothing is more common than to apply to one object the name of another that resembles it in any respect; height, size, and worldly greatness, resemble not each other; but the emotions they produce resemble each other, and, prompted by this resemblance, we naturally express worldly greatness by height or size: one feels a certain uneasiness in seeing a great depth; and hence depth is made to express any thing disagreeable by excess, as *depth*

---

535 By what means this figure aggrandizes an object How this figure has a happy effect. Its influence on language.

of grief, *depth* of despair. Again, height of place, and time long past, produce similar feelings, and hence the expression, *Ut altius repetam:* distance in past time, producing a strong feeling, is put for any strong feeling, *Nihil mihi antiquius nostra amicitia:* shortness with relation to space, for shortness with relation to time, *Brevis esse laboro, obscurus fio:* suffering a punishment resembles paying a debt; hence *pendere pœnas.* In the same manner, light may be put for glory, sunshine for prosperity, and weight for importance.

537. Many words, originally figurative, having by long and constant use lost their figurative power, are degraded to the inferior rank of proper terms. Thus the words that express the operations of the mind, have in all languages been originally figurative: the reason holds in all, that when these operations came first under consideration, there was no other way of describing them but by what they resembled: it was not practicable to give them proper names, as may be done to objects that can be ascertained by sight and touch. A *soft* nature, *jarring* tempers, *weight* of woe, *pompous* phrase, *beget* compassion, *assuage* grief, *break* a vow, *bend* the eye downward, *shower* down curses, *drowned* in tears, *wrapt* in joy, *warmed* with eloquence, *loaded* with spoils, and a thousand other expressions of the like nature, have lost their figurative sense. Some terms there are that cannot be said to be either altogether figurative or altogether proper: originally figurative, they are tending to simplicity, without having lost altogether their figurative power. Virgil's *Regina saucia cura,* is perhaps one of these expressions: with ordinary readers, *saucia* will be considered as expressing simply the effect of grief; but one of a lively imagination will exalt the phrase into a figure.

["There is," says Dr Mark Hopkins, "a natural correspondence between every state of the mind and some aspect, or movement, or voice of animate or inanimate nature. How extensive and minute this correspondence is, will perhaps be best seen if we observe *how that part of human language originates which is employed to express the affections of the mind.* It is a received doctrine among men learned in this department, that all words of this description had first a meaning purely physical, and that this meaning was afterwards transferred to express some affection of the mind analogous to the physical condition or act. Whether this is strictly and universally true or not, it certainly is true that the great mass of words of this description are thus formed; and if so, then it will follow, that for every mental state, act, or affection, which we can express in words, there must be some analogous state, act, or affection in the physical world. Who then can sufficiently admire that adjustment and correlation of parts by which mind and matter almost seem to be a part of one organization? * * * * * *

---

536. What, besides subjects, may be expressed figuratively. Examples.—When the name of one object may be applied to another.

"Perhaps one reason (for this correspondence) is to be found in what has already been referred to—the necessity of this for the formation of language. I would not limit the resources of God, but constituted as the human faculties now are, it would seem necessary, if they were to be fully developed, that words originally applicable to natural objects should be capable of being transferred so as to express the whole range of thought and emotion, and this would be impossible without the correspondence of which I have spoken. As it is, we speak of the light of knowledge, and the darkness of ignorance, and the sunshine of joy, and the night of grief, and the storms of passion, and the devious paths of error, and the pitfalls of vice; and we scarcely reflect that we are speaking in figures, or that the flowers of rhetoric, not less than the flowers of the field, have their origin in a material soil. Constituted as man now is, we do not see how he could have been furnished with the symbols of thought, the materials of language, in any other way."]

For epitomizing this subject, and at the same time for giving a clear view of it, I cannot think of a better method than to present to the reader a list of the several relations upon which figures of speech are commonly founded. This list I divide into two tables: one of subjects expressed figuratively, and one of attributes

FIRST TABLE.

Subjects expressed figuratively.

538. 1. A word proper to one subject employed figuratively to express a resembling subject.

There is no figure of speech so frequent as what is derived from the relation of resemblance. Youth, for example, is signified figuratively by the *morning* of life. The life of a man resembles a natural day in several particulars; the morning is the beginning of day, youth the beginning of life; the morning is cheerful, so is youth, &c. By another resemblance, a bold warrior is termed the *thunderbolt* of war; a multitude of troubles, a *sea* of troubles.

This figure, above all others, affords pleasure to the mind by a variety of beauties. Besides the beauties above mentioned, common to all sorts, it possesses in particular the beauty of a metaphor or of a simile: a figure of speech built upon resemblance, suggests always a comparison between the principal subject and the accessory; whereby every good effect of a metaphor or simile, may, in a very short and lively manner, be produced by this figure of speech.

2. A word proper to the effect employed figuratively to express the cause.

---

537. Words that have lost their figurative powe' Example.

Lux for the sun. *Shadow* for cloud. A helmet is signified by the expression *glittering terror*. A tree by *shadow* or *umbrage*. Hence the expression:

> Nec habet Pelion umbras. *Ovid.*
>
> Where the dun umbrage hangs. *Spring*, l. 1023.

A wound is made to signify an arrow:

> Vulnere non pedibus te consequar. *Ovid.*

There is a peculiar force and beauty in this figure: the word which signifies figuratively the principal subject, denotes it to be a cause by suggesting the effect.

3. A word proper to the cause, employed figuratively to express the effect.

Boumque labores, for corn. *Sorrow* or *grief*, for tears.

> Again, Ulysses veil'd his pensive head;
> Again, unmann'd, a shower of *sorrow* shed.
>
> Streaming *Grief* his faded cheek bedew'd.

Blindness for darkness:

> Cæcis erramus in undis. *Æneid*, iii. 200.

There is a peculiar energy in this figure, similar to that in the former: the figurative name denotes the subject to be an effect, by suggesting its cause.

4. Two things being intimately connected, the proper name of the one employed figuratively to signify the other.

Day for light. *Night* for darkness: and hence, A sudden night. *Winter* for a storm at sea:

> Interea magno misceri murmure pontum,
> Emissamque Hyemem sensit Neptunus.—*Æneid*, i. 128.

This last figure would be too bold for a British writer, as a storm at sea is not inseparably connected with winter in this climate.

5. A word proper to an attribute, employed figuratively to denote the subject.

Youth and *beauty* for those who are young and beautiful:

> Youth and beauty shall be laid in dust.

Majesty for the King:

> What art thou, that usurp'st this time of night,
> Together with that fair and warlike form,
> In which the *Majesty* of buried Denmark
> Did sometimes march? *Hamlet*, Act I. Sc. 1.
>
> ———Or have ye chosen this place
> After the toils of battle to repose
> Your wearied *virtue*. *Paradise Lost.*

Verdure for a green field.—*Summer*, l. 301

Speaking of cranes:

> The pigmy nations, wounds and death they bring,
> And all the *war* descends upon the wing.—*Iliad*, iii. 10.
>
> Cool *age* advances venerably wise.—*Iliad*, iii. 149.

The peculiar beauty of this figure arises from suggesting an attribute that embellishes the subject, or puts it in a stronger light.

6. A complex term employed figuratively to denote one of the component parts.

Funus for a dead body. *Burial* for a grave.

7. The name of one of the component parts instead of the complex term.

Tæda for a marriage. The *East* for a country situated east from us. *Jovis vestigia servat*, for imitating Jupiter in general.

8. A word signifying time or place, employed figuratively to denote what is connected with it.

Clime for a nation, or for a constitution of government; hence the expression *Merciful clime*. *Fleecy winter* for snow, *Seculum felix*.

9. A part for the whole.

The *Pole* for the earth. The *head* for the person:

> Triginta minas pro capite tuo dedi. *Plautus.*

Tergum for the man:

> Fugiens tergum. *Ovid.*

Vultus for the man:

> Jam fulgor armorum fugaces
> Terret equos, equitumque vultus. *Horat.*
>
> Quis desiderio sit pudor aut modus
> Tam chari *capitis?* *Horat.*
>
> Dumque virent *genua?* *Horat.*
>
> Thy growing virtues justified my cares,
> And promised comfort to my *silver hairs*.—*Iliad*, ix. 616.
>
> ————Forthwith from the pool he rears
> His mighty *stature*. *Paradise Lost.*
>
> The silent *heart* with grief assails. *Parnell.*

The peculiar beauty of this figure consists in marking that part which makes the greatest figure.

10. The name of the container, employed figuratively to signify what is contained.

Grove for the birds in it, Vocal *grove*. *Ships* for the seamen, Agonizing *ships*. *Mountains* for the sheep pasturing upon them, Bleating *mountains*. *Zacynthus*, *Ithaca*, &c., for the inhabitants *Ex mæstis domibus*, Livy.

11. The name of the sustainer, employed figuratively to signify what is sustained.

Altar for the sacrifice. *Field* for the battle fought upon it, Well fought *field*.

12. The name of the materials, employed figuratively to signify the things made of them.

Ferrum for *gladius*.

13. The names of the heathen deities, employed figuratively to signify what they patronize.

Jove for the air, *Mars* for war, *Venus* for beauty, *Cupid* for love, *Ceres* for corn, *Neptune* for the sea, *Vulcan* for fire.

The figure bestows great elevation upon the subject; and therefore ought to be confined to the higher strains of poetry.

SECOND TABLE.

Attributes expressed figuratively.

539. When two attributes are connected, the name of the one may be employed figuratively to express the other.

1. Purity and virginity are attributes of the same person: hence the expression, *Virgin* snow, for pure snow.

2. A word signifying properly an attribute of one subject, employed figuratively to express a resembling attribute of another subject.

Tottering state. *Imperious* ocean. *Angry* flood. *Raging* tempest. *Shallow* fears.

> My sure divinity shall bear the shield,
> And edge thy sword to *reap* the glorious field.
>
> *Odyssey*, xx. 61.

Black omen, for an omen that portends bad fortune.

> *Ater* odor. *Virgil.*

The peculiar beauty of this figure arises from suggesting a comparison.

3. A word proper to the subject, employed to express one of its attributes.

Mens for *intellectus*. *Mens* for a resolution:

> Istam, oro, exue mentem.

4. When two subjects have a resemblance by a common quality, the name of the one subject may be employed figuratively to denote that quality in the other.

Summer life for agreeable life.

---

538. The several relations on which figures of speech are founded.—First Table.—Subjects expressed figuratively.
539. Second table.—Attributes expressed figuratively.

5. The name of the instrument made to signify the power of employing it.

> ——— Melpomene, cui liquidam pater
> Vocem cum *cithera*, dedit.

540. The ample field of figurative expression displayed in these tables, affords great scope for reasoning. Several of the observations relating to metaphor, are applicable to figures of speech: these I shall slightly retouch, with some additions peculiarly adapted to the present subject.

In the first place, as the figure under consideration is built upon relation, we find from experience, and it must be obvious from reason, that the beauty of the figure depends on the intimacy of the relation between the figurative and proper sense of the word. A slight resemblance, in particular, will never make this figure agreeable; the expression, for example, *Drink down a secret*, for listening to a secret with attention, is harsh and uncouth, because there is scarce any resemblance between *listening* and *drinking*. The expression *weighty crack*, used by Ben Jonson for *loud crack*, is worse if possible: a loud sound has not the slightest resemblance to a piece of matter that is weighty. The following expression of Lucretius is not less faulty: "Et lepido quæ sunt *fucata* sonore" (i. 645.)

> ——— Sed magis
> Pugnas et exactos tyrannos
> Densum humeris *bibit* aure vulgus.
> *Horat. Carm.* l. ii. ode 13.

> Phemius! let acts of gods and heroes old,
> What ancient bards in hall and bower have told,
> Attemper'd to the lyre, your voice employ,
> Such the pleased *ear will drink* with silent joy.—*Odyssey*, i. 433.

> Strepitumque exterritus *hausit*. *Æneid*, vi. 559.

> ——— Write, my Queen,
> And with mine eyes I'll *drink* the words you send.
> *Cymbeline*, Act I. Sc. 2.

> As thus the effulgence tremulous I *drink*. *Summer*, l. 1684.

> Neque *audit* currus habenas. *Georg.* i. 514.

> O prince! (Lycaon's valiant son replied),
> As thine the steeds, be thine the task to guide.
> The horses, practised to their lord's command,
> Shall *hear* the rein, and answer to thy hand. *Iliad*, v. 288.

The following figures of speech seem altogether wild and extravagant, figurative and proper meaning having no connection whatever. *Moving* softness, Freshness *breathes*, *Breathing* prospect, *Flowing* spring, *Dewy* light, *Lucid* coolness, and many others of this false coin, may be found in Thomson's *Seasons*.

["Of all late writers of merit who have indulged in remote or unmeaning metaphors, Thomson, in his *Seasons*, is perhaps most exposed to reprehension. His desire to elevate and recommend a subject which had little in it to interest the understanding or the passions, and which depended almost entirely on the imagination, and the influence of picturesque description (the powers of which were in some measure untried and unknown), seems to have prompted him to call into his service every poetical embellishment of which he could with any propriety lay hold. He scruples not to personify on the most trivial occasions; but what is much more exceptionable, to these ideal personages he affixes many ideal attributes, which have little relation or resemblance to any thing that exists in nature. He enfeebles his diction by overloading it with epithets, and he obstructs the impression by the variety or tautology of his metaphors. What conception can arise, or what impulse can result, from the following combinations? 'Lone quiet,' 'pining grove,' 'pale dreary,' 'solid gloom,' and a thousand more of the same species? Such figures, however, abound chiefly in the first editions of the *Seasons;* many of them were afterwards improved or expunged. It is to be regretted, that the author or his friends had not been still more industrious to correct or suppress them. They are the chief blemishes of a poem, in other respects one of the most beautiful of its kind which any age has produced."—*Barron*, Lect. 17.]

Secondly, The proper sense of the word ought to bear some proportion to the figurative sense, and not soar much above it, nor sink much below it.

541. Thirdly, In a figure of speech, every circumstance ought to be avoided that agrees with the proper sense only, not the figurative sense; for it is the latter that expresses the thought, and the former serves for no other purpose but to make harmony:

> Zacynthus green with ever-shady groves,
> And Ithaca, presumptuous boast their loves;
> Obtruding on my choice a second lord,
> They press the Hymenean rite abhorr'd. *Odyssey*, xix. 152.

Zacynthus here standing figuratively for the inhabitants, the description of the island is quite out of place; it puzzles the reader, by making him doubt whether the word ought to be taken in its proper or figurative sense.

> ——— Write, my Queen,
> And with mine eyes I'll drink the words you send,
> Though ink be made of gall. *Cymbeline*, Act I. Sc. 2.

The disgust one has to drink ink in reality, is not to the purpose where the subject is drinking ink figuratively.

In the fourth place, To draw consequences from a figure of speech, as if the word were to be understood literally, is a gross absurdity, for it is confounding truth with fiction.

---

540. On what the beauty of figure of speech depends. Examples of too slight resemblance, and of no resemblance between the figurative and proper sense of the word.—Barron's criticism on Thomson.—The proportion of the proper to the figurative sense.

Be Moubray's sins so heavy in his bosom,
That they may break his foaming courser's back,
And throw the rider headlong in the lists,
A caitiff recreant to my cousin Hereford.

Richard II. Act I. Sc. 3.

Sin may be imagined heavy in a figurative sense; but weight in a proper sense belongs to the accessory only; and therefore to describe the effects of weight, is to desert the principal subject, and to convert the accessory into a principal:

Cromwell. How does your Grace?
Wolsey. Why, well,
Never so truly happy, my good Cromwell.
I know myself now, and I feel within me
A peace above all earthly dignities,
A still and quiet conscience. The king has cured me,
I humbly thank his Grace; and from these shoulders,
These ruined pillars, out of pity taken
A load would sink a navy, too much honor.

Henry VIII. Act III. Sc. 3.

Ulysses speaking of Hector:

I wonder now how yonder city stands,
When we have here the base and pillar by us.

Troilus and Cressida, Act IV. Sc. 9.

Othello. No; my heart is turn'd to stone: I strike it, and it hurts my hand.

Othello, Act IV. Sc. 5

Not less, even in this despicable now,
Than when my name fill'd Afric with affrights,
And froze your hearts beneath your torrid zone.

Don Sebastian, King of Portugal, Act I

How long a space, since first I loved, it is
To look into a glass I fear,
And am surprised with wonder when I miss
Gray hairs and wrinkles there. *Cowley*, vol. i. p. 86.

I chose the flourishing'st tree in all the park,
With freshest boughs and fairest head;
I cut my love into his gentle bark,
And in three days behold 'tis dead:
My very written flames so violent be,
They've burnt and wither'd up the tree.

Cowley, vol. i. p. 136.

Such a play of words is pleasant in a ludicrous poem.

Almeria. O Alphonso, Alphonso!
Devouring seas have wash'd thee from my sight,
No time shall rase thee from my memory
No, I will live to be thy monument:
The cruel ocean is no more thy tomb;
But in my heart thou art interr'd.

Mourning Bride, Act I. Sc. 1.

This would be very right, if there were any inconsistence in being interred in one place really, and in another place figuratively.

In me tota ruens Venus
Cyprum deseruit. *Horat. Carm.* l. i. ode 19.

---

541. **Circumstances to be avoided.—The drawing of consequences from a figure of speech Examples.**

542. From considering that a word used in a figurative sense suggests at the same time its proper meaning, we discover a fifth rule, That we ought not to employ a word in a figurative sense, the proper sense of which is inconsistent or incongruous with the subject; for every inconsistency, and even incongruity, though in the expression only and not real, is unpleasant:

> Interea genitor Tyberini ad fluminis undam
> Vulnera *siccabat* lymphis—————— *Æneid*, x. 833.
>
> Tres adeo incertos cæca caligine *soles*
> Erramus pelago, totidem sine sidere noctes. *Æneid*, iii. 203.

The foregoing rule may be extended to form a sixth, That no epithet ought to be given to the figurative sense of a word that agrees not also with its proper sense:

> ——————Dicat Opuntiæ
> Frater Megillæ, quo *beatus*
> Vulnere. *Horat. Carm.* lib. i. ode 27.
>
> Parcus deorum cultor, et infrequens,
> *Insanientis* dum sapientiæ
> Consultus erro. *Horat. Carm.* lib. i. ode 34.

543. Seventhly, The crowding into one period or thought different figures of speech, is not less faulty than crowding metaphors in that manner; the mind is distracted in the quick transition from one image to another, and is puzzled instead of being pleased:

> I am of ladies most deject and wretched,
> That suck'd the honey of his music-vows. *Hamlet.*
>
> My bleeding bosom sickens at the sound. *Odyssey*, i. 439.

Eighthly, If crowding figures be bad, it is still worse to graft one figure upon another: for instance,

> While his keen falchion drinks the warriors' lives. *Iliad*, xi. 211.

A falchion drinking the warrior's blood is a figure built upon resemblance, which is passable. But then in the expression, *lives* is again put for *blood;* and by thus grafting one figure upon another, the expression is rendered obscure and unpleasant.

544. Ninthly, Intricate and involved figures that can scarce be analyzed, or reduced to plain language, are least of all tolerable:

> Votis incendimus aras. *Æneid*, iii. 279.
>
> ———Onerantque canistris
> Dona laboratæ Cereris. *Æneid*, viii. 180.

Vulcan to the Cyclopes:

> Arma acri facienda viro: nunc viribus usus,
> Nunc manibus rapidis, omni nunc arte magistra:
> *Præcipitate* moras. *Æneid*, viii. 441.

---

542. What word should not be employed in a figurative sense.—What epithet should not be given to the figurative sense of a word.

543. The crowding of different figures of speech into one period or thought.—The grafting of one figure on another

Scribêris Vario fortis, et Hostium
Victor, Mæonii carminis *alite*. *Horat. Carm.* lib. i. ode 6.

Else shall our fates be number'd with the dead.—*Iliad*, v. 294.

Commutual death the fate of war confounds.
Iliad, viii. 85, and xi. 117

Rolling convulsive on the floor, is seen
The piteous object of a prostrate queen. *Ibid.* iv. 952.

The mingling tempest waves its gloom. *Autumn*, 337

A sober calm fleeces unbounded ether. *Ibid.* 738.

The distant waterfall swells in the breeze. *Winter*, 738.

545. In the tenth place, When a subject is introduced by its proper name, it is absurd to attribute to it the properties of a different subject to which the word is sometimes applied in a figurative sense:

Hear me, oh Neptune! thou whose arms are hurl'd
From shore to shore, and gird the solid world.—*Odyssey*, ix. 617.

Neptune is here introduced personally, and not figuratively, for the ocean: the description, therefore, which is only applicable to the latter, is altogether improper.

It is not sufficient that a figure of speech be regularly constructed, and be free from blemish: it requires taste to discern when it is proper, when improper; and taste, I suspect, is our only guide. One however may gather from reflection and experience, that ornaments and graces suit not any of the dispiriting passions, nor are proper for expressing any thing grave and important. In familiar conversation, they are in some measure ridiculous. Prospero, in the *Tempest*, speaking to his daughter Miranda, says,

The fringed curtains of thine eyes advance,
And say what thou seest 'yond.

No exception can be taken to the justness of the figure; and circumstances may be imagined to make it proper; but it is certainly not proper in familiar conversation.

In the last place, Though figures of speech have a charming effect when accurately constructed and properly introduced, they ought however to be scattered with a sparing hand; nothing is more luscious, and nothing consequently more satiating, than redundant ornaments of any kind.

---

544. Intricate and involved figures.
545. When a subject is introduced by its proper name, what is it absurd to attribute to it?—When a figure of speech is not to be used. To what extent to be used

CHAPTER XXI.

NARRATION AND DESCRIPTION.

546. The first rule is, That in history, the reflections ought to be chaste and solid; for while the mind is intent upon truth, it is little disposed to the operations of the imagination. Strada's Belgic history is full of poetical images, which discording with the subject, are unpleasant; and they have a still worse effect, by giving an air of fiction to a genuine history. Such flowers ought to be scattered with a sparing hand, even in epic poetry; and at no rate are they proper, till the reader be warmed, and by an enlivened imagination be prepared to relish them; in that state of mind they are agreeable; but while we are sedate and attentive to an historical chain of facts, we reject with disdain every fiction.

547. Second, Vida, following Horace, recommends a modest commencement of an epic poem; giving for a reason, that the writer ought to husband his fire. This reason has weight; but what is said above suggests a reason still more weighty: bold thoughts and figures are never relished till the mind be heated and thoroughly engaged, which is not the reader's case at the commencement. Homer introduces not a single simile in the first book of the Iliad, nor in the first book of the Odyssey. On the other hand, Shakspeare begins one of his plays with a sentiment too bold for the most heated imagination:

> *Bedford.* Hung be the heavens with black, yield day to night!
> Comets, importing change of times and states,
> Brandish your crystal tresses in the sky,
> And with them scourge the bad revolting stars,
> That have consented unto Henry's death!
> Henry the Fifth, too famous to live long!
> England ne'er lost a king of so much worth.
>
> *First Part Henry VI.*

A third reason ought to have no less influence than either of the former, That a man, who, upon his first appearance, strains to make a figure, is too ostentatious to be relished. Hence the first sentences of a work ought to be short, natural, and simple. Cicero, in his oration *pro Archia poeta*, errs against this rule: his reader is out of breath at the very first period; which seems never to end. Burnet begins the History of his Own Times with a period long and intricate.

548. A third rule or observation is, That where the subject is intended for entertainment solely, not for instruction, a thing ought to be described as it appears, not as it is in reality. In running, for

---

546. Rule for reflections in history.
547. How an epic poem should be commenced.

example, the impulse upon the ground is proportioned in some degree to the celerity of motion: though in appearance it is otherwise; for a person in swift motion seems to skim the ground, and scarcely to touch it. Virgil, with great taste, describes quick running according to appearance; and raises an image far more lively than by adhering scrupulously to truth:

> Hos super advenit Volsca de gente Camilla,
> Agmen agens equitum et florentes ære catervas,
> Bellatrix: non illa colo calathisve Minervæ
> Fœmineas assueta manus; sed prælia virgo
> Dura pati, cursuque pedum prævertere ventos.
> Illa vel intactæ segetis per summa volaret
> Gramina; nec teneras cursu læsisset aristas;
> Vel mare per medium, fluctu suspensa tumenti,
> Ferret iter; celeres nec tingeret æquore plantas.
> *Æneid*, vii. 803.

This example is copied by the author of *Telemachus:*

> Les Brutiens sont légères à la course comme les cerfs, et comme les daims. On croirait que l'herbe même la plus tendre n'est point foulée sous leurs pieds; a peine laissent-ils dans le sable quelques traces de leurs pas. *Liv.* x.

549. Fourth, In narration as well as in description, objects ought to be painted so accurately as to form in the mind of the reader distinct and lively images. Every useless circumstance ought indeed to be suppressed, because every such circumstance loads the narration; but if a circumstance be necessary, however slight, it cannot be described too minutely. The force of language consists in raising complete images (chap. ii. part i. sec. 7); which have the effect to transport the reader as by magic into the very place of the important action, and to convert him as it were into a spectator, beholding every thing that passes. The narrative in an epic poem ought to rival a picture in the liveliness and accuracy of its representations: no circumstance must be omitted that tends to make a complete image; because an imperfect image, as well as any other imperfect conception, is cold and uninteresting. I shall illustrate this rule by several examples, giving the first place to a beautiful passage from Virgil:

> Qualis *populeâ* mœrens Philomela sub umbrâ
> Amissos queritur fœtus, quos durus *arator*
> Observans nido *implumes* detraxit.—*Georg.* lib. iv. l. 511.

The poplar, ploughman, and unfledged young, though not essential in the description, tend to make a complete image, and upon that account are an embellishment.

Again:

> Hic viridem Æneas *frondenti ex ilice* metam
> Constituit, signum nautis.—*Æneid*, v 129.

Horace, addressing to Fortune:

---

548. Where the subject is intended for entertainment solely, how ought a thing to be described?

Te pauper ambit sollicita prece
Ruris colonus: te dominam æquoris,
Quicumque Bythinâ lacessit
Carpathium pelagus carinâ. *Carm.* lit. i ode 35.

Shakspeare says (Henry V. Act iv. sc. 4), "You may as well go about to turn the sun to ice by fanning in his face with a *peacock's* feather." The peacock's feather, not to mention the beauty of the object, completes the image: an accurate image cannot be formed of that fanciful operation, without conceiving a particular feather; and one is at a loss when this is neglected in the description. Again, "the rogues slighted me into the river with as little remorse, as they would have drowned a bitch's blind puppies, fifteen i' the litter." (*Merry Wives of Windsor*, Act iii. Sc. 15.)

Old Lady. You would not be a queen?
Anne. No, not for all the riches under heaven.
Old Lady. 'Tis strange: a threepence bow'd would hire me, old as I am, to queen it. *Henry VIII.* Act II. Sc. 5.

In the following passage, the action, with all its material circumstances, is represented so much to the life, that it would scarce appear more distinct to a real spectator; and it is the manner of description that contributes greatly to the sublimity of the passage:

He spake; and to confirm his words, out flew
Millions of flaming swords, drawn from the thigh
Of mighty cherubim; the sudden blaze
Far round illumined hell; highly they raged
Against the Highest, and fierce with grasped arms
Clash'd on their sounding shields the din of war,
Hurling defiance toward the vault of heaven. *Milton*, b. 1.

A passage I am to cite from Shakspeare, falls not much short of that now mentioned in particularity of description:

O you hard hearts! you cruel men of Rome!
Knew you not Pompey? Many a time and oft
Have you climb'd up to walls and battlements,
To towers and windows, yea, to chimney-tops,
Your infants in your arms: and there have sat
The live-long day with patient expectation
To see great Pompey pass the streets of Rome;
And when you saw his chariot but appear,
Have you not made an universal shout,
That Tyber trembled underneath his banks,
To hear the replication of your sounds,
Made in his concave shores?—*Julius Cæsar*, Act I. Sc. 1.

The following passage is scarce inferior to either of those mentioned:

Far before the rest the son of Ossian comes; bright in the smiles of youth, fair as the first beams of the sun. His long hair waves on his back: his dark brow is half beneath his helmet. The sword hangs loose on the hero's side; and his spear glitters as he moves. I fled from his terrible eye, King of high Temora.—*Fingal.*

The *Henriade* of Voltaire errs greatly against the foregoing rule:

every incident is touched in a summary way, without ever descending to circumstances. This manner is good in a general history, the purpose of which is to record important transactions; but in a fable it is cold and uninteresting; because it is impracticable to form distinct images of persons or things represented in a manner so superficial.

It is observed above, that every useless circumstance ought to be suppressed. The crowding such circumstances, is, on the one hand, no less to be avoided, than the conciseness for which Voltaire is blamed, on the other. In the *Æneid* (lib. iv. l. 632), Barce, the nurse of Sichæus, whom we never hear of before nor after, is introduced for a purpose not more important than to call Anna to her sister Dido: and that it might not be thought unjust in Dido, even in this trivial circumstance, to prefer her husband's nurse before her own, the poet takes care to inform his reader, that Dido's nurse was dead. To this I must oppose a beautiful passage in the same book, where, after Dido's last speech, the poet, without detaining his readers by describing the manner of her death, hastens to the lamentation of her attendants:

> Dixerat: atque illam media inter talia ferro
> Collapsam aspiciunt comites, ensemque cruore
> Spumantem, sparsasque manus. It clamor ad alta
> Atria, concussam bacchatur fama per urbem;
> Lamentis gemituque et fœmineo ululatu
> Tecta fremunt, resonat magnis plangoribus æther.
>
> *Lib.* iv. l. 663

550. As an appendix to the foregoing rule, I add the following observation, That to make a sudden and strong impression, some single circumstance happily selected, has more power than the most labored description. Macbeth, mentioning to his lady some voices he heard while he was murdering the king, says,

> There's one did laugh in 's sleep, and one cried Murder!
> They waked each other; and I stood and heard them:
> But they did say their prayers, and address them
> Again to sleep.
> *Lady.* There are two lodged together.
> *Macbeth.* One cried, God bless us! and Amen the other;
> As they had seen me with these hangman's hands.
> Listening their fear, I could not say Amen,
> When they did say, God bless us.
> *Lady.* Consider it not so deeply.
> *Macbeth.* But wherefore could not I pronounce Amen?
> I had most need of blessing, and Amen
> Stuck in my throat.
> *Lady.* These deeds must not be thought
> After these ways; so, it will make us mad.
> *Macbeth.* Methought I heard a voice cry, Sleep no more!
> Macbeth doth murder sleep, &c. Act II. Sc. 3.

---

549. In narration how objects should be painted.—In what consists the force of language?—A circumstance not to be omitted. Examples.—Circumstances that should be suppressed.

Describing Prince Henry:

I saw young Harry with his beaver on,
His cuisses on his thighs, gallantly arm'd,
Rise from the ground like feather'd Mercury;
And vaulted with such ease into his seat,
As if an angel dropp'd down from the clouds,
To turn and wind a fiery Pegasus,
And witch the world with noble horsemanship.
First Part Henry VI. Act IV. Sc. 2.

King Henry. Lord Cardinal, if thou think'st on Heaven's bliss,
Hold up thy hand, make signal of thy hope.
He dies, and makes no sign.—*Second Part Henry VI.* Act III. Sc. 10.

The same author, speaking ludicrously of an army debilitated with diseases, says,

Half of them dare not shake the snow from off their cassocks, lest they shake themselves to pieces.

I have seen the walls of Balclutha, but they were desolate.—The flame had resounded in the halls; and the voice of the people is heard no more. The stream of Clutha was removed from its place by the fall of the walls. The thistle shook there its lonely head; the moss whistled to the wind. The fox looked out from the windows; and the rank grass of the wall waved round his head. Desolate is the dwelling of Morna: silence is in the house of her fathers.
Fingal.

551. To draw a character is the master-stroke of description. In this Tacitus excels: his portraits are natural and lively, not a feature wanting or misplaced. Shakspeare, however, exceeds Tacitus in liveliness, some characteristical circumstance being generally invented or laid hold of, which paints more to the life than many words The following instance will explain my meaning, and at the same time prove my observation to be just:

Why should a man whose blood is warm within,
Sit like his grandsire cut in alabaster?
Sleep when he wakes, and creep into the jaundice,
By being peevish? I tell thee what, Antonio,
(I love thee, and it is my love that speaks),
There are a sort of men, whose visages
Do cream and mantle like a standing pond;
And do a wilful stillness entertain,
With purpose to be dress'd in an opinion
Of wisdom, gravity, profound conceit;
As who should say, I am Sir Oracle,
And when I ope my lips, let no dog bark!
O my Antonio, I do know of those,
That therefore only are reputed wise,
For saying nothing. *Merchant of Venice*, Act I. Sc. 2.

Again:

Gratiano speaks an infinite deal of nothing, more than any man in all Venice, his reasons are two grains of wheat hid in two bushels of chaff; you shall seek all day ere you find them, and when you have them they are not worth the search.—*Ibid.*

In the following passage a character is completed by a single stroke

---

550. Well-selected circumstances. Examples.

Shallow. O the mad days that I have spent; and to see how many of mine old acquaintance are dead.

Silence. We shall all follow, cousin.

Shallow. Certain, 'tis certain, very sure, very sure; Death (as the Psalmist saith), is certain to all: all shall die. How a good yoke of bullocks at Stamford fair?

Slender. Truly, cousin, I was not there.

Shallow. Death is certain. Is old *Double* of your town living yet?

Silence. Dead, sir.

Shallow. Dead! see, see; he drew a good bow: and dead. He shot a fine shoot. How a score of ewes now?

Silence. Thereafter as they be. A score of good ewes may be worth ten pounds.

Shallow. And is old *Double* dead?—*Second Part Henry IV.* Act III. Sc. 3.

Describing a jealous husband:

Neither press, coffer, chest, trunk, well, vault, but he hath an abstract for the remembrance of such places, and goes to them by his note. There is no hiding you in the house.—*Merry Wives of Windsor*, Act I. Sc. 3.

Congreve has an inimitable stroke of this kind in his comedy of *Love for Love:*

Ben Legend. Well, father, and how do all at home? how does brother Dick, and brother Val?

Sir Sampson. Dick: body o' me, Dick has been dead these two years. I writ you word when you were at Leghorn.

Ben. Mess, that's true; marry, I had forgot. Dick's dead, as you say.

Act III. Sc. 6.

Falstaff speaking of ancient Pistol:

He's no swaggerer, hostess: a tame cheater i' faith; you may stroke him as gently as a puppy-greyhound; he will not swagger with a Barbary hen, if her feathers turn back in any show of resistance.

Second Part Henry IV. Act II. Sc. 9.

Ossian, among his other excellencies, is eminently successful in drawing characters; and he never fails to delight his reader with the beautiful attitudes of his heroes. Take the following instance:

O Oscar! bend the strong in arm; but spare the feeble hand. Be thou a stream of many tides against the foes of thy people; but like the gale that moves the grass to those who ask thine aid.—So Tremor lived; such Trathal was; and such has Fingal been. My arm was the support of the injured; and the weak rested behind the lightning of my steel.

We heard the voice of joy on the coast, and we thought that the mighty Cathmore came. Cathmore the friend of strangers, the brother of red-haired Cairbar. But their souls were not the same; for the light of heaven was in the bosom of Cathmore. His towers rose on the banks of Atha: seven paths led to his halls: seven chiefs stood on these paths, and called the stranger to the feast. But Cathmore dwelt in the wood to avoid the voice of praise.

Dermid and Oscar were one; they reaped the battle together. Their friendship was strong as their steel: and death walked between them to the field. They rush on the foe like two rocks falling from the brow of Ardven. Their swords are stained with the blood of the valiant; warriors faint at their name. Who is equal to Oscar but Dermid? who to Dermid but Oscar?

Son of Comhal, replied the chief, the strength of Morni's arm has failed; I attempt to draw the sword of my youth, but it remains in its place; I throw the spear, but it falls short of the mark: and I feel the weight of my shield

---

53. The master-stroke of description? Who excel in it.

We decay like the grass of the mountain, and our strength returns no more. I have a son, O Fingal, his soul has delighted in the actions of Morni's youth; but his sword has not been fitted against the foe, neither has his fame begun. I come with him to battle, to direct his arm. His renown will be a sun to my soul in the dark hour of my departure. O that the name of Morni were forgot among the people! that the heroes would only say, "Behold the father of Gaul."

552. Some writers, through heat of imagination, fall into contradiction; some are guilty of downright absurdities; and some even rave like madmen. Against such capital errors one cannot be more effectually warned than by collecting instances; and the first shall be of a contradiction, the most venial of all. Virgil speaking of Neptune,

> Interea magno misceri murmure pontum,
> Emissamque hyemem sensit Neptunus, et imis
> Stagna refusa vadis: *graviter commotus*, et alto
> Prospiciens, summâ *placidum* caput extulit undâ.—*Æneid*, i. 128.

Again:

> When first young Maro, in his boundless mind,
> A work t' outlast *immortal* Rome design'd.
> *Essay on Criticism*, l. 130.

The following examples are of absurdities:

Alii pulsis e tormento catenis discerpti sectique, dimidiato corpore pugnabant sibi superstites, ac peremptæ partis ultores.—*Strada*, Dec. ii. l. 2.

> Il povér huomo, che non sen' era accorto,
> Andava combattendo, ed era morto.—*Berni.*

> He fled; but flying, left his life behind.—*Iliad*, xi. 433.

> Full through his neck the weighty falchion sped:
> Along the pavement roll'd the muttering head.
> *Odyssey*, xxii. 365.

The last article is of raving like one mad. Cleopatra speaking to the aspic:

> ——————— Welcome, thou kind deceiver,
> Thou best of thieves; who, with an easy key,
> Dost open life, and, unperceived by us,
> Even steal us from ourselves; discharging so
> Death's dreadful office, better than himself;
> Touching our limbs so gently into slumber,
> That Death stands by, deceived by his own image,
> And thinks himself but sleep.—*Dryden*, *All for Love*, Act V.

Reasons that are common and known to every one, ought to be taken for granted; to express them is childish, and interrupts the narration.

553. Having discussed what observations occurred upon the thoughts or things expressed, I proceed to what more peculiarly concern the language or verbal dress. The language proper for expressing passion being handled in a former chapter, several observations there made are applicable to the present subject; particularly, That as words are intimately connected with the ideas they represent

---

552 Some capital errors stated and exemplified.

the emotions raised by the sound and by the sense ought to be concordant. An elevated subject requires an elevated style; what is familiar ought to be familiarly expressed; a subject that is serious and important, ought to be clothed in plain nervous language: a description, on the other hand, addressed to the imagination, is susceptible of the highest ornaments that sounding words and figurative expression can bestow upon it.

I shall give a few examples of the foregoing rules. A poet of any genius is not apt to dress a high subject in low words; and yet blemishes of that kind are found even in classical works. Horace, observing that men are satisfied with themselves, but seldom with their condition, introduces Jupiter indulging to each his own choice:

> Jam faciam quod vultis; eris tu, qui modo miles,
> Mercator: tu, consultus modo, rusticus; hinc vos,
> Vos hinc mutatis discedite partibus: eia,
> Quid statis? nolint: atqui licet esse beatis.
> Quid causæ est, merito quin illis, *Jupiter ambas*
> *Iratas buccas inflet?* neque se fore posthac
> Tam facilem dicat, votis ut præbeat aurem?
>
> *Sat.* lib. i. *Sat.* i. l. 16

Jupiter in wrath puffing up both cheeks, is a low and even ludicrous expression, far from suitable to the gravity and importance of the subject: every one must feel the discordance. The following couplet, sinking far below the subject, is no less ludicrous:

> Not one looks backward, onward still he goes,
> Yet ne'er looks forward farther than his nose.
>
> *Essay on Man*, Ep. IV. 223.

554. On the other hand, to raise the expression above the tone of the subject, is a fault than which none is more common. Take the following instances:

> *Assuerus.* Ce mortel, qui montra tant de zèle pour moi, Vit-il encore?
> *Asaph.*——————Il voit l'astre qui vous éclare.—*Esther*, Act II. Sc. 3.

> No jocund health that Denmark drinks to-day,
> But the great cannon to the clouds shall tell;
> And the king's rowse the heavens shall bruit again,
> Respeaking earthly thunder. *Hamlet*, Act I. Sc. 2.

> ————————In the inner room
> I spy a winking lamp, that weakly strikes
> The ambient air, scarce kindling into light.
>
> *Southern*, *Fate of Capua*, Act III.

Montesquieu, in a didactic work, *L'esprit des Loix*, gives too great indulgence to imagination; the tone of his language swells frequently above his subject. I give an example:

M. le Comte de Boulainvilliers et M. l'Abbé Dubos ont fait chacun un systême, dont l'un semble être une conjuration contre le tiers-état, et l'autre une conjuration contre la noblesse. Lorsque le Soleil donna à Phaéton son char à conduire, il lui dit, Si vous montes trop haut, vous brûlerez la demeure

---

553. Suggestions as to the verbal dress of thought.—A high subject in low words.

céleste, si vous descendez trop bas, vous réduirez en cendres la terre: n'allez point trop à droite, vous tomberiez dans la constellation du serpent: n'allez point trop à gauche, vous iriez dans celle de l'autel: tenez-vous entre les deux.

L. xxx. ch. 10.

The following passage, intended, one would imagine, as a recipe to boil water, is altogether burlesque by the labored elevation of the diction:

A massy caldron of stupendous frame
They brought, and placed it o'er the rising flame:
Then heap the lighted wood; the flame divides
Beneath the vase, and climbs around the sides;
In its wide womb they pour the rushing stream;
The boiling water bubbles to the brim.—*Iliad*, xviii. 405.

In a passage at the beginning of the 4th book of Telemachus, one feels a sudden bound upward without preparation, which accords not with the subject:

Calypso, qui avoit été jusqu'à ce moment immobile et transportée de plaisir en écoutant les aventures de Télémaque, l'interrompit pour lui faire pendre quelque repôs. Il est tems, lui dit-elle, qui vous alliez goûter la douceur du sommeil après tant de travaux. Vous n'avez rien à craindre ici; tout vous est favorable. Abandonnez vous donc à la joie. Goutez la paix, et tous les autres dons des dieux dont vous allez être comblé. Demain, *quand l'Aurore avec ses doigts de roses entr'ouvrira les portes dorées de l'Orient, et que les Chevaux du Soleil sortons de l'onde amère repandront les flammes de jour, pour chasser devant eux toutes les étoiles du ciel*, nous reprendrons, mon cher Télémaque, l'histoire de vos malheurs.

This obviously is copied from a similar passage in the Æneid, which ought not to have been copied, because it lies open to the same censure; but the force of authority is great:

At regina gravi jamdudum saucia cura
Vulnus alit venis, et cæco carpitur igni.
Multa viri virtus animo, multusque recursat
Gentis honos: hærent infixi pectore vultus,
Verbaque; nec placidam membris dat cura quietem.
Postera Phœbea lustrabat lampade terras,
Humentemque Aurora polo dimoverat umbram;
Cum sic unanimem alloquitur male sana sororem.—Lib. iv. 1.

555. The language of Homer is suited to his subject, no less accurately than the actions and sentiments of his heroes are to their characters. Virgil, in that particular, falls short of perfection; his language is stately throughout; and though he descends at times to the simplest branches of cookery, roasting and boiling for example, yet he never relaxes a moment from the high tone (see *Æneid*, lib. i. 188–219). In adjusting his language to his subject, no writer equals Swift.

It is proper to be observed upon this head, that writers of inferior rank are continually upon the stretch to enliven and enforce their subject by exaggeration and superlatives. This unluckily has an effect contrary to what is intended; the reader, disgusted with language that swells above the subject, is led by contrast to think more meanly of the subject than it may possibly deserve. A man of

554. Expression above the tone of the subject. Examples

prudence, besides, will be no less careful to husband his strength in writing than in walking: a writer too liberal of superlatives, exhausts his whole stock upon ordinary incidents, and reserves no share to express, with greater energy, matters of importance.

Many writers of that kind abound so in epithets, as if poetry consisted entirely in high-sounding words. Take the following instance:

When black-brow'd Night her dusky mantle spread,
  And wrapp'd in solemn gloom the sable sky:
When soothing Sleep her opiate dews had shed,
  And seal'd in silken slumber every eye;
My wakeful thoughts admit no balmy rest,
  Nor the sweet bliss of soft oblivion share;
But watchful woe distracts my aching breast,
  My heart the subject of corroding care;
From haunts of men with wand'ring steps and slow
  I solitary steal, and soothe my pensive woe.

Here every substantive is faithfully attended by some tumid epithet; like young master, who cannot walk abroad without having a lac'd livery-man at his heels. Thus in reading without taste, an emphasis is laid on every word; and in singing without taste, every note is graced. Such redundancy of epithets, instead of pleasing, produces satiety and disgust.

556. The power of language to imitate thought, is not confined to the capital circumstances above mentioned; it reacheth even the slighter modifications. Slow action, for example, is imitated by words pronounced slow; labor or toil, by words harsh or rough in their sound. But this subject has been already handled (chapter xviii. sect. iii.)

In dialogue-writing, the condition of the speaker is chiefly to be regarded in framing the expression. The sentinel in *Hamlet*, interrogated with relation to the ghost, whether his watch had been quiet, answers with great propriety for a man in his station, "Not a mouse stirring."

I proceed to a second remark, no less important than the former. No person of reflection but must be sensible that an incident makes a stronger impression on an eye-witness, than when heard at second hand. Writers of genius, sensible that the eye is the best avenue to the heart, represent every thing as passing in our sight; and, from readers or hearers, transform us as it were into spectators: a skilful writer conceals himself, and presents his personages; in a word, every thing becomes dramatic as much as possible. Plutarch, *de gloria Atheniensium*, observes that Thucydides makes his reader a spectator, and inspires him with the same passions as if he were an eye-witness; and the same observation is applicable to our coun-

---

555. Remarks on the language of Homer, Virgil, Swift.—How inferior writers endeavor to enliven their subject.

556. The power of language to imitate thought, even in the slighter modifications.—Rule for dialogue-writing.—The eye being the best avenue to the heart, how writers of genius avail themselves of this principle.

tryman Swift. From this happy talent arises that energy of style which is peculiar to him: he cannot always avoid narration; but the pencil is his choice, by which he bestows life and coloring upon his object. Pope is richer in ornament, but possesseth not in the same degree the talent of drawing from the life. A translation of the sixth satire of Horace, begun by the former and finished by the latter, affords the fairest opportunity for a comparison. Pope obviously imitates the picturesque manner of his friend; yet every one of taste must be sensible, that the imitation, though fine, falls short of the original. In other instances, where Pope writes in his own style, the difference of manner is still more conspicuous.

557. Abstract or general terms have no good effect in any composition for amusement; because it is only of particular objects that images can be formed (see chapter iv.). Shakspeare's style in that respect is excellent: every article in his descriptions is particular, as in nature; and if accidentally a vague expression slip in, the blemish is discernible by the bluntness of its impression. Take the following example: Falstaff, excusing himself for running away at a robbery, says,

> I knew ye, as well as he that made ye. Why, hear ye, my masters; was it for me to kill the heir-apparent? should I turn upon the true prince? Why, thow knowest, I am as valiant as Hercules; but beware instinct, the lion will not touch the true prince: *instinct is a great matter*. I was a coward on instinct; I shall think the better of myself, and thee, during my life; I for a violent lion, and thou for a true prince. But, by the Lord, lads, I am glad you have the money. Hostess, clap to the doors, watch to-night, pray to-morrow. Gallants, lads, boys, hearts of gold, all the titles of fellowship come to you! What! shall we be merry? shall we have a play *extempore?*
>
> *First Part Henry IV.* Act II. Sc. 9.

The sentence I object to is, *instinct is a great matter*, which makes but a poor figure compared with the liveliness of the rest of the speech. It was one of Homer's advantages that he wrote before general terms were multiplied: the superior genius of Shakspeare displays itself in avoiding them after they were multiplied. Addison describes the family of Sir Roger de Coverly in the following words:

> You would take his valet-de-chambre for his brother, his butler is gray-headed, his groom is one of the gravest men that I have ever seen, and his coachman has the looks of a privy-counsellor.--*Spectator*, No. 106.

The description of the groom is less lively than that of the others; plainly because the expression being vague and general, tends not to form any image. "Dives opum variarum" (Georg. ii. 468) is an expression still more vague; and so are the following:

> ————————Mæcenas, *mearum*
> Grande decus, columenque *rerum.*—*Horat. Carm.* lib. ii. ode 17.

> ————————et fide Teïa
> Dices *laborantes in uno*
> Penelopen, vitreamque Circen.—*Iliad*, lib. i. ode 17.

---

557. On the use of abstract or general terms.—Shakspeare's style

——————Ridiculum acri
Fortius et melius magnas plerumque *secat res*.
Horat. Satir. lib. i. sat. 10.

558. In the fine arts it is a rule to put the capital objects in the strongest point of view; and even to present them oftener than once, where it can be done. In history-painting, the principal figure is placed in the front, and in the best light: an equestrian statue is placed in the centre of streets, that it may be seen from many places at once. In no composition is there greater opportunity for this rule than in writing:

——————Sequitur pulcherrimus Astur,
Astur equo fidens et versicoloribus armis.—*Æneid*, x. 130.

——————Full many a lady
I've eyed with best regard, and many a time
Th' harmony of their tongues hath into bondage
Brought my too diligent ear; for several virtues
Have I liked several women, never any
With so full soul, but some defect in her
Did quarrel with the noblest grace she own'd,
And put it to the foil. But you, O you,
So perfect, and so peerless, are created
Of every creature's best. *The Tempest*, Act III. Sc. 1.

Orlando.————Whate'er you are
That in this desert inaccessible,
Under the shade of melancholy boughs,
Lose and neglect the creeping hours of time:
If ever you have look'd on better days;
If ever been where bells have knoll'd to church;
If ever sat at any good man's feast;
If ever from your eyelids wiped a tear,
And know what 'tis to pity and be pitied;
Let gentleness my strong enforcement be,
In the which hope I blush and hide my sword.—*As You Like It.*

With thee conversing I forget all time;
All seasons and their change, all please alike.
Sweet is the breath of morn, her rising sweet,
With charm of earliest birds: pleasant the sun
When first on this delightful land he spreads
His orient beams on herb, tree, fruit, and flower,
Glist'ning with dew; fragrant the fertile earth
After soft showers; and sweet the coming on
Of grateful evening mild, the silent night
With this her solemn bird, and this fair moon,
And these the gems of heaven, her starry train.
But neither breath of morn, when she ascends
With charm of earliest birds, nor rising sun
On this delightful land, nor herb, fruit, flower,
Glist'ning with dew, nor fragrance after showers,
Nor grateful evening mild, nor silent night,
With this her solemn bird, nor walk by moon
Or glittering star-light, without thee is sweet.
Paradise Lost, b. iv. l. 634.

What mean ye, that ye use this proverb, The fathers have eaten sour grapes, and the children's teeth are set on edge? As I live, saith the Lord God, ye shall not have occasion to use this proverb in Israel. If a man keep my judgments to deal truly, he is just, he shall surely live, &c. *Ezekiel*, xviii.

---

558. Rule of the fine arts respecting capital objects.

559. The repetitions in Homer, which are frequent, have been the occasion of much criticism. Suppose we were at a loss about the reason, might not taste be sufficient to justify them? At the same time we are at no loss about the reason: they evidently make the narration dramatic, and have an air of truth, by making things appear as passing in our sight. But such repetitions are unpardonable in a didactic poem. In one of Hesiod's poems of that kind, a long passage occurs twice in the same chapter.

A concise comprehensive style is a great ornament in narration; and a superfluity of unnecessary words, no less than of circumstances, a great nuisance. A judicious selection of the striking circumstances clothed in a nervous style, is delightful. In this style, Tacitus excels all writers, ancient and modern; instances are numberless: take the following specimen:

> Crebra hinc prælia, et sæpius in modum latrocinii: per saltus, per paludes; ut cuique fors aut virtus; temere, proviso, ob iram, ob prædam, jussa, et aliquando ignaris ducibus.—*Annal*, lib. xii. sect. 39.

After Tacitus, Ossian in that respect justly merits the place of distinction. One cannot go wrong for examples in any part of the book; and at the first opening the following instance meets the eye:

> Nathos clothed his limbs in shining steel. The stride of the chief is lovely: the joy of his eye terrible. The wind rustles in his hair. Darthula is silent at his side: her look is fixed on the chief. Striving to hide the rising sigh, two tears swell in her eye.

I add one other instance, which, besides the property under consideration, raises delicately our most tender sympathy:

> Son of Fingal! dost thou not behold the darkness of Crothar's hall of shells? My soul was not dark at the feast, when my people lived. I rejoiced in the presence of strangers, when my son shone in the hall. But, Ossian, he is a beam that is departed, and left no streak of light behind. He is fallen, son of Fingal, in the battles of his father.——Rothmar, the chief of grassy Tromlo, heard that my eyes had failed; he heard that my arms were fixed in the hall, and the pride of his soul arose. He came towards Croma: my people fell before him. I took my arms in the hall, but what could sightless Crothar do? My steps were unequal; my grief was great. I wished for the days that were past; days! wherein I fought and won in the field of blood. My son returned from the chase; the fair-haired Fovar-gormo. He had not lifted his sword in battle, for his arm was young. But the soul of the youth was great; the fire of valor burnt in his eye. He saw the disordered steps of his father, and his sigh arose. King of Croma, he said, is it because thou hast no son? is it for the weakness of Fovar-gormo's arm that thy sighs arise; I begin, my father, to feel the strength of my arm; I have drawn the sword of my youth, and I have bent the bow. Let me meet this Rothmar, with the youths of Croma; let me meet him, O my father, for I feel my burning soul.
>
> And thou shalt meet him, I said, son of the sightless Crothar! But let others advance before thee, that I may hear the tread of thy feet at thy return: for my eyes behold thee not, fair-haired Fovar-gormo!——He went; he met the foe; he fell. The foe advances towards Croma He who slew my son is near, with all his pointed spears.

560. If a concise or nervous style be a beauty, tautology must be

---

559. Repetitions.—Concise style in narration.—Tacitus. Ossian.

a blemish; and yet writers, fettered by verse, are not sufficiently careful to avoid this slovenly practice: they may be pitied, but they cannot be justified. Take for a specimen the following instances from the best poet, for versification at least, that England has to boast of:

> High on his helm celestial lightnings play
> His beamy shield emits a living ray,
> Th' unweary blaze incessant streams supplies,
> Like the red star that fires th' autumnal skies.—*Iliad*, v. 5.
>
> Strength and omnipotence invest thy throne.—*Iliad*, viii. 576.
>
> So silent fountains, from a rock's tall head,
> In sable streams soft trickling waters shed.—*Iliad*, ix. 19.
>
> His clanging armor rung.—*Iliad*, xii. 94.
>
> Fear on their cheek, and horror in their eye.—*Iliad*, xv. 4.
>
> The blaze of armor flash'd against the day.—*Iliad*, xvii. 736.
>
> As when the piercing blasts of Boreas blow.—*Iliad*, xix. 380.
>
> And like the moon, the broad refulgent shield
> Blazed with long rays, and gleam'd athwart the field.
> *Iliad* xix. 402.
>
> No—could our swiftness o'er the winds prevail,
> Or beat the pinions of the western gale,
> All were in vain——— *Iliad*, xix. 460.
>
> The humid sweat from every pore descends.
> *Iliad*, xxiii. 829

Redundant epithets, such as *humid* in the last citation, are by Quintilian disallowed to orators; but indulged to poets, because his favorite poets, in a few instances, are reduced to such epithets for the sake of versification; for instance, *Prata canis albicant pruinis* of Horace, and *liquidos fontes* of Virgil.

As an apology for such careless expressions, it may well suffice, that Pope, in submitting to be a translator, acts below his genius In a translation, it is hard to require the same spirit or accuracy, that is cheerfully bestowed on an original work. And to support the reputation of that author, I shall give some instances from Virgil and Horace, more faulty by redundancy than any of those above mentioned:

> Sæpe etiam immensum cœlo venit agmen aquarum,
> Et Fœdam glomerant tempestatem imbribus atris
> Collectæ ex alto nubes; ruit arduus ether,
> Et pluviâ ingenti sata læta, boumque labores
> Diluit. *Georg.* i. 322.
>
> Postquam altum tenuere rates, nec jam amplius ullæ
> Apparent terræ; cœlum undique et undique pontus:
> Tum mihi cœruleus supra caput astitit imber,
> Noctem hyememque ferens; et inhorruit unda tenebris.
> *Æneid*, iii. 192.
>
> ——————Hinc tibi copia
> Manabit ad plenum benigno
> Ruris honorum opulenta cornu.
> *Horat. Carm.* lib. i. ode 17.

> Videre fessos vomerem inversum boves
> Collo trahentes languido. *Horat.* epod. ii. 63.

Here I can luckily apply Horace's rule against himself:

> Est brevitate opus, ut currat sententia, neu se
> Impediat verbis lassas onerantibus aures.
> *Satir.* lib. i. sat. x. 9.

561. I close this chapter with a curious inquiry. An object, however ugly to the sight, is far from being so when represented by colors or by words. What is the cause of this difference? With respect to painting, the cause is obvious: a good picture, whatever the subject be, is agreeable by the pleasure we take in imitation; and this pleasure overbalancing the disagreeableness of the subject, makes the picture upon the whole agreeable. With respect to the description of an ugly object, the cause follows. To connect individuals in the social state, no particular contributes more than language, by the power it possesses of an expeditious communication of thought and a lively representation of transactions. But nature hath not been satisfied to recommend language by its utility merely: independent of utility, it is made susceptible of many beauties, which are directly felt, without any intervening reflection (see chap. xviii.). And this unfolds the mystery; for the pleasure of language is so great, as in a lively description to overbalance the disagreeableness of the image raised by it (see chap. ii. part iv.). This, however, is no encouragement to choose a disagreeable subject; for the pleasure is incomparably greater where the subject and the description are both of them agreeable.

The following description is upon the whole agreeable, though the subject described is in itself dismal:

> Nine times the space that measures day and night
> To mortal men, he with his horrid crew
> Lay vanquish'd, rolling in the fiery gulf,
> Confounded though immortal! but his doom
> Reserved him to more wrath; for now the thought
> Both of lost happiness and lasting pain
> Torments him; round he throws his baleful eyes,
> That witness'd huge affliction and dismay,
> Mix'd with obdurate pride and steadfast hate;
> At once as far as angels ken he views
> The dismal situation, waste and wild;
> A dungeon horrible, on all sides round
> As one great furnace flamed: yet from those flames
> No light, but rather darkness visible
> Served only to discover sights of woe,
> Regions of sorrow, doleful shades, where peace
> And rest can never dwell, hope never comes
> That comes to all; but torture without end
> Still urges, and fiery deluge, fed
> With ever-burning sulphur unconsumed!
> Such place eternal justice hath prepared
> For those rebellious. *Paradise Lost*, book i. l. 50.

---

560. **Tautology—Redundant epithets**

An unmanly depression of spirits in time of danger is not an agreeable sight; and yet a fine description or representation of it will be relished:

K. Richard. What must the king do now? must he submit?
The king shall do it; must he be deposed?
The king shall be contented; must he lose
The name of king? i' God's name let it go:
I'll give my jewels for a set of beads;
My gorgeous palace for a hermitage;
My gay apparel, for an almsman's gown;
My figured goblets, for a dish of wood;
My sceptre, for a palmer's walking-staff;
My subjects, for a pair of carved saints;
And my large kingdom for a little grave;
A little, little grave;——an obscure grave.
Or, I'll be buried in the king's highway;
Some way of common tread, where subjects' feet
May hourly trample on their sovereign's head;
For on my heart they tread now, whilst I live;
And buried once, why not upon my head?
Richard II. Act III. Sc. 6.

Objects that strike terror in a spectator, have in poetry and painting a fine effect. The picture by raising a slight emotion of terror, agitates the mind; and in that condition every beauty makes a deep impression May not contrast heighten the pleasure, by opposing our present security to the danger of encountering the object represented?

——————The other shape,
If shape it might be call'd, that shape had none
Distinguishable in member, joint, or limb;
Or substance might be call'd that shadow seem'd,
For each seem'd either; black it stood as night,
Fierce as ten furies, terrible as hell,
And shook a dreadful dart. *Paradise Lost*, b. ii. l. 666.

——————Now storming fury rose,
And clamor such as heard in heaven till now
Was never; arms on armor clashing bray'd
Horrible discord, and the madding wheels
Of brazen chariots raged; dire was the noise
Of conflict; overhead the dismal hiss
Of fiery darts in flaming volleys flew,
And flying vaulted either host with fire.
So under fiery cope together rush'd
Both battles main, with ruinous assault
And inextinguishable rage; all heaven
Resounded; and had earth been then, all earth
Had to her centre shook. *Paradise Lost*, b. vi. l. 207.

Ghost.——————But that I am forbid
To tell the secrets of my prison-house,
I could a tale unfold, whose lightest word
Would harrow up thy soul, freeze thy young blood,
Make thy two eyes, like stars, start from their spheres,
Thy knotty and combined locks to part,
And each particular hair to stand on end,
Like quills upon the fretful porcupine:
But this eternal blazon must not be
To ears of flesh and blood. *Hamlet*, Act I. Sc. 8.

---

501. An ugly object represented in colors or words. Example.—Terrible objects

Gratiano. Poor Desdemona! I'm glad thy father's dead.
Thy match was mortal to him; and pure grief
Shore his old thread in twain. Did he live now,
This sight would make him do a desperate turn:
Yea, curse his better angel from his side,
And fall to reprobation. *Othello*, Act V. Sc. 8.

562. Objects of horror must be expected from the foregoing theory, for no description, however lively, is sufficient to overbalance the disgust raised even by the idea of such objects. Every thing horrible ought therefore to be avoided in a description. Nor is this a severe law: the poet will avoid such scenes for his own sake, as well as for that of his reader; and to vary his descriptions, nature affords plenty of objects that disgust us in some degree without raising horror. I am obliged therefore to condemn the picture of Sin in the second book of *Paradise Lost*, though a masterly performance: the original would be a horrid spectacle; and the horror is not much softened in the copy:

——— ——Pensive here I sat
Alone; but long I sat not, till my womb,
Pregnant by thee, and now excessive grown,
Prodigious motion felt and rueful throes.
At last this odious offspring whom thou seest,
Thine own begotten, breaking violent way,
Tore through my entrails, that with fear and pain
Distorted, all my nether shape thus grew
Transform'd; but he my inbred enemy
Forth issued, brandishing his fatal dart,
Made to destroy; I fled, and cried out Death,
Hell trembled at the hideous name, and sigh'd
From all her caves, and back resounded Death.
I fled; but he pursued (though more, it seems,
Inflamed with lust than rage), and swifter far,
Me overtook, his mother all dismay'd,
And in embraces forcible and foul
Ingend'ring with me, of that rape begot
These yelling monsters, that with ceaseless cry
Surround me, as thou saw'st, hourly conceived
And hourly born, with sorrow infinite
To me; for when they list, into the womb
That bred them they return, and howl and gnaw
My bowels, their repast; then bursting forth
Afresh with conscious terrors vex me round,
That rest or intermission none I find.
Before mine eyes in opposition sits
Grim Death, my son and foe, who sets them on,
And me his parent would full soon devour
For want of other prey, but that he knows,
His end with mine involved; and knows that I
Should prove a bitter morsel, and his bane,
Whenever that shall be. Book ii. l. 777.

Iago's character in the tragedy of *Othello*, is insufferably monstrous and satanical: not even Shakspeare's masterly hand can make the picture agreeable.

Though the objects introduced in the following scene is not

---

562. Objects of horror. Examples

altogether so horrible as Sin is in Milton's description; yet with every person of delicacy, disgust will be the prevailing emotion:

> ——Strophades Graio stant nomine dictæ
> Insulæ Ionio in magno: quas dira Celæno,
> Harpyiæque colunt aliæ: Phineia postquam
> Clausa domus, mensasque metu liquere priores.
> Tristius haud illis monstrum, nec sævior ulla
> Pestis et ira Deûm Stygiis sese extulit undis.
> Virginei volucrum vultus, fœdissima ventris
> Proluvies, uncæque manus, et pallida semper
> Ora fame, &c. *Æneid*, lib. iii. 210.

See also *Æneid*, lib. iii. 613.

CHAPTER XXII.

THE PHILOSOPHY OF STYLE.

[From the Westminster Review (1852), somewhat abridged and modified.

563. Dr. Latham, condemning the incessant drill in English Grammar, rightly observes that "gross vulgarity is a fault to be prevented; but the proper preventive is to be got from habit, not from rules." So it must be acknowledged that excellence in composition is more dependent upon practice and natural talent, than upon a mere acquaintance with rhetorical rules. He who daily reads and hears, with close attention, well-framed sentences, will naturally more or less be prompted to frame well his own sentences. Some practical advantage, however, cannot fail to be derived from a familiarity with the principles of style, and from an habitual endeavor to conform to them in one's own practice.

The maxims contained in works on rhetoric and composition, are not so well apprehended nor so much respected, as they would be if they had been arranged under some one grand principle from which they may fairly be deduced. We are told, for example, that "brevity is the soul of wit"—that every needless part of a sentence "interrupts the description and clogs the image"—that "long sentences fatigue the reader's attention"—that "to give the utmost force to a period, it ought, if possible, to be closed with the word that makes the greatest figure"—that "parentheses should be avoided"—that "Saxon words should be used in preference to those of Latin origin." We have certain styles condemned as verbose or involved Admitting these maxims to be just, they lose much of their intrinsic force and influence from their isolated position, and from the want of scientific deduction from some fundamental principle.

563. Dr. Latham's observation.—Excellence in composition dependent on what?—Fault in works on rhetoric.

FIRST DIVISION OF THE SUBJECT.

CAUSES OF FORCE IN LANGUAGE WHICH DEPEND UPON ECONOMY OF THE MENTAL ENERGIES.

564. In seeking for *the law which underlies these common maxims of rhetoric,* we may see shadowed forth in many of them *the importance of economizing the reader's or hearer's attention.* To present ideas in such a form that they may be apprehended with the least possible effort, is the aim of most of the rules above quoted. When we condemn writing that is wordy, or confused, or intricate; when we praise one style as easy, and condemn another as fatiguing, we consciously or unconsciously assume this as the proper aim or standard in writing or speaking. Regarding language as an apparatus of symbols for the conveyance of thought, it is proper to say, as with reference to any mechanical apparatus, that the more simple and the better arranged its parts, the greater will be the effect produced. In either case, whatever force is absorbed by the machine is deducted from the result. A reader or listener has at each moment but a limited *amount of mental power available.* To recognize and interpret the symbols presented to him requires part of this power: to arrange and combine the images suggested requires another part; and only that part which remains can be used for the realization of the thought conveyed. Hence the more time and attention it requires to receive and understand each sentence, the less time and attention can be given to the contained idea, and the less vividly will that idea be conceived.

That *language is in some measure a hindrance to thought* while one of the most valuable instruments of thought, is apparent when we notice the comparatively greater force with which some thoughts are conveyed by simple *signs and gestures.* To say "Leave the room" is less expressive than to point to the door. Placing a finger upon the lips is more forcible than whispering, "Do not speak." A beck of the hand is better than "Come here." No phrase can convey the idea of surprise so vividly as opening the eyes and raising the eyebrows. A shrug of the shoulders would lose much by translation into words.

565. Again, it may be remarked that when oral language is employed, the strongest effects are produced by *interjections*, which condense entire sentences into syllables; and, in other cases, where custom allows us to express thoughts by single words, as in *Beware, Fudge*, much force would be lost by expanding them into specific

---

564. The law which underlies the prominent maxims of rhetoric.—The aim of most of those maxims.—The demands upon the mental power of the reader or listener.—Language in some measure, a hindrance to thought.

verbal propositions. Hence, carrying out the metaphor that language is the vehicle of thought, there seems reason to think that in all cases the friction and inertia of the vehicle deduct from its efficiency; and that in composition the chief, if not the sole *thing to be done,* is to reduce this friction and inertia to the smallest possible amount. Let us then inquire whether *economy of the hearer's or reader's attention* is not the secret of effort, alike in the choice and collocation of words; in the best arrangement of clauses in a sentence, in the proper order of its principal and subordinate propositions; in the judicious use of simile, metaphor, and other figures of speech; and in even the rhythmical sequence of syllables.

I. THE CHOICE OF WORDS.

566. (1) *The superior forcibleness of Saxon English*, or rather non-Latin English, first claims our attention. The several special reasons assignable for this may all be reduced to the general reason—economy. The most important of them is *early association.* A child's vocabulary is almost wholly Saxon. He says, *I have*, not *I possess; I wish,* not *I desire:* he does not *reflect*, he *thinks;* he does not beg for *amusement*, but for *play;* he calls things *nice* or *nasty*, not *pleasant* or *disagreeable.* The synonyms which he learns in after years never become so closely, so organically connected with the ideas signified, as do these original words used in childhood; and hence the association remains less powerful. But in what does a powerful association between a word and an idea differ from a weak one? Simply in the greater rapidity and ease of comprehension, until, from its having been a conscious effort to realize their meanings, their meanings ultimately come without any effort at all; and if we consider that the same process must have gone on with the words of our mother tongue from childhood upward, we shall clearly see that the earliest-learnt and oftenest-used words, will, other things being equal, call up images with less loss of time and energy than their later-learned synonyms.

567. (2) The *comparative brevity of Saxon English* is another feature that brings it under the same generalization. If it be an advantage to express an idea in the smallest number of words, then will it be an advantage to express it in the smallest number of syllables. If circuitous phrases and needless expletives distract the attention and diminish the strength of the impression produced, then do surplus articulations do so. A certain effort, though commonly an inappreciable one, must be required to recognize every vowel and

---

565. Interjections. Single words.—The chief thing to be done in composition.—In what respects economy of attention is to be practised.

566. Superior forcibleness of Saxon English.—First reason.—In what a powerful association between a word and its idea differs from a weak one.

consonant. If, as we commonly find, the mind soon becomes fatigued when we listen to an indistinct or far-removed speaker, or when we read a badly-written manuscript; and if, as we cannot doubt, the fatigue is a cumulative result of the attention required to catch successive syllables, it obviously follows that attention is in such cases absorbed by each syllable. And if this be true when the syllables are difficult of recognition, it will also be true, though in a less degree, when the recognition of them is easy. Hence, the shortness of Saxon words becomes a reason for their greater force, as involving a saving of the articulations to be received.

568. (3) Again, that frequent cause of strength in Saxon and other primitive words—their *imitative character*—renders it a matter of economy to use them. Both those directly imitative, as *splash*, *bang*, *whiz*, *roar*, &c., and those analogically imitative, as *rough*, *smooth*, *keen*, *blunt*, *thin*, *hard*, *crag*, &c., by presenting to the perceptions symbols having direct resemblance to the things to be imagined, or some kinship to them, save part of the effort needed to call up the intended ideas, and leave more attention to the ideas themselves.

569. (4) *It contributes to economy* of the hearer's or reader's mental energy *to use specific rather than generic words.* That concrete terms produce more vivid impressions than abstract ones, and should, when possible, be used instead, is a current maxim of composition. As Dr. Campbell says, the more general the terms are, the picture is the fainter; the more special they are, the brighter. We should avoid such a sentence as,

———In proportion as the manners, customs, and amusements of a nation are cruel and barbarous, the regulations of their penal code will be severe.

And in place of it we should write:

———In proportion as men delight in battles, tourneys, bull-fights, and combats of gladiators, will they punish by hanging, beheading, burning, and the rack.

This superiority of specific expressions is clearly due to a saving of the effort required to translate words into thoughts. As we do not think in generals but in particulars; as, whenever any class of things is referred to, we represent it to ourselves by calling to mind individual members of it, it follows that when an abstract word is used, the hearer or reader has to choose, from among his stock of images, one or more by which he may figure to himself the genus mentioned. In doing this some delay must arise, some force be expended; and if, by employing a specific term, an appropriate image can be at once suggested, an economy is achieved, and a more vivid impression produced.

---

567. Brevity of Saxon English; how this contributes to effect.
568. Effect of the imitative character of primitive words.
569. Economy in using specific words.—Dr. Campbell's remark.—Why specific expressions economize effort.

II. COLLOCATION OF WORDS IN A SENTENCE

570. Turning now from the choice of words to their sequence, we shall find the same general principle hold good. We have, *a priori*, reason for believing that there is usually some one order of words in a sentence more effective than every other, and that this order is the one which presents the elements of the proposition in the succession in which they may be most readily put together. As, in a narrative, the events should be stated in such order that the mind may not have to go backwards and forwards in order rightly to connect them; as in a group of sentences, the arrangement adopted should be such that each of them may be understood as it comes, without waiting for subsequent ones; so in every sentence the sequence of words should be that which suggests the component parts of the thought conveyed, in the order most convenient for building up that thought. To enforce this truth, and to prepare the way for applications of it, we must (1) briefly inquire into *the mental process by which the meaning of a series of words is apprehended.*

We cannot more simply do this than by considering the *proper collocation of the substantive and adjective.* Is it better to place the adjective before the substantive, or the substantive before the adjective? Ought we to say with the French, *un cheval noir* (a horse black); or to say as we do, a black horse? Probably most persons of culture would decide that one is as good as the other. There is, however, a philosophical ground for deciding in favor of the English arrangement. If "a horse black" be the form used, immediately on the utterance of the word "horse" there arises, or tends to arise, in the mind a picture answering to that word; and as there has been nothing to indicate what *kind* of horse, any image of a horse suggests itself. Very likely, however, the image will be that of a brown horse, brown horses being equally or more familiar. The result is, that when the word "black" is added, a check is given to the process of thought. Either the picture of a brown horse already present in the imagination has to be suppressed, and the picture of a black one summoned in its place; or else, if the picture of a brown horse be yet unformed, the tendency to form it has to be stopped. Whichever be the case, a certain amount of hindrance results. But if, on the other hand, "a black horse" be the expression used, no such mistake can be made. The word "black," indicating an abstract quality, arouses no definite idea. It simply prepares the mind for conceiving of some object of that color; and the attention is kept suspended until that object is known. If then, by the precedence of the adjective, the idea is conveyed without the possibility of error, whereas the precedence of the substantive is liable to produce a misconception, it follows that the one gives the mind less trouble than the other, and is therefore more forcible. The right formation of a picture will always be facilitated by presenting its elements in the order in which they are wanted.

571. What is here said respecting the succession of the adjective and substantive, is obviously applicable, by change of terms, to the *adverb and verb.* And, without further explanation, it will be at once perceived, that in the use of prepositions and other particles, most languages spontaneously conform, with more or less completeness, to this law.

(2) On applying a like analysis to the *larger divisions of a sentence*, we find not only that the same principle holds good, but that there is great advantage in regarding it. In the arrangement of *predicate and subject*, for example, we are at once shown that as the predicate determines the aspect under which the subject is to be conceived, it should be placed first; and the striking effect produced by so placing it becomes comprehensible.

Take the often-quoted contrast between "Great is Diana of the Ephesians," and "Diana of the Ephesians is great." When the first arrangement is used, the utterance of the word "great" arouses those vague associations of an impressive nature with which it has been habitually connected; the imagination is prepared to clothe with high attributes whatever follows; and when the words "Diana of the Ephesians" are heard, all the appropriate imagery which can, on the instant, be summoned, is used in the formation of the picture: the mind being thus led directly, without error, to the intended impression. When, on the contrary, the reverse order is followed, the idea, "Diana of the Ephesians," is conceived in any ordinary way, with no special reference to greatness; and when the words "is great" are added, the conception has to be entirely remodelled; whence arises a manifest loss of mental energy, and a corresponding diminution of effect.

The following verse from Coleridge's "Ancient Mariner," though somewhat irregular in structure, well illustrates the same truth:

Alone, alone, all alone,
Alone on a wide, wide sea!
And never saint took pity on
My soul in agony.

Of course the principle equally applies when the predicate is a verb or a participle: and as effect is gained by placing first all words indicating quality, conduct, or condition of the subject, it follows that the copula should have precedence. It is true, that the general habit of our language resists this arrangement of predicate, copula, and subject: but we may readily find instances of the additional force gained by conforming to it. Thus, in the line from "Julius Cæsar,"

570. The order of words in a sentence which seems *a priori* to be more effective than another.—Process by which the meaning of a series of words is apprehended.—Collocation of substantive and adjective.—French and English arrangement. Why the latter is preferred.

> Then *burst* this mighty heart,

priority is given to a word embodying both predicate and copula.

In a passage contained in "The Battle of Flodden Field," the like order is systematically employed with great effect:

> The Border slogan rent the sky!
> *A Home! a Gordon!* was the cry;
> *Loud were* the clanging blows;
> *Advanced,—forced back,—now low, now high,*
> The pennon sunk and rose;
> As *bends* the bark's mast in the gale,
> When *rent are* rigging, shrouds, and sail,
> It waver'd 'mid the foes.

572. (3) Pursuing the principle yet further, it is obvious that for producing the greatest effect, not only should the main divisions of a sentence observe this order, but *the subdivisions of a sentence* should be similarly arranged. In nearly all cases *the predicate is accompanied by some limit or qualification called its complement:* commonly, also, *the circumstances of the subject, which form its complement,* have to be specified; and as these qualifications and circumstances must determine the mode in which the ideas they belong to shall be conceived, *precedence should be given to them.* Lord Kames notices the fact, that this order is preferable; though without giving the reason. He says, "When a circumstance is placed at the beginning of a period, or near the beginning, the transition from it to the principal subject is agreeable; is like ascending or going upward." A sentence arranged in illustration of this may be desirable. Perhaps the following will serve:

> ——Whatever it may be in theory, it is clear that in practice the French idea of liberty is—the right of every man to be master of the rest.

In this case, were the first two clauses up to the word "practice" inclusive, which qualify the subject, to be placed at the end instead of the beginning, much of the force would be lost; as thus:

> ——The French idea of liberty is—the right of every man to be master of the rest; in practice at least, if not in theory.

The effect of giving priority to the complement of the predicate, as well as the predicate itself, is finely displayed in the opening of "Hyperion:"

> *Deep in the shady sadness of a vale*
> *Far sunken from the healthy breath of morn,*
> *Far from the fiery noon and eve's one star,*
> *Sat* gray-haired Saturn, quiet as a stone.

Here it will be observed, not only that the predicate "sat" precedes the subject "Saturn," and that the three lines in italics constituting the complement of the predicate come before it, but that

---

571. Law for other parts of speech.—Arrangement of predicate and subject. Example: Great is Diana," &c. Other examples.

572. Subdivisions of a sentence.—Complement of the predicate.—Circumstances. Example from "Hyperion."

in the structure of that complement also, the same order is followed, each line being so arranged that *the qualifying words are placed before the words suggesting concrete images.*

573. (4) The right *succession of the principal and subordinate propositions in a sentence* will manifestly be regulated by the same law. Regard for economy of the recipient's attention, which, as we find, determines the best order for the subject, copula, predicate, and their complements, dictates that *the subordinate proposition shall precede the principal one when the sentence includes two.* Containing, as the subordinate proposition does, some qualifying or explanatory idea, its priority must clearly prevent misconception of the principal one; and must therefore save the mental effort needed to correct such misconception.

Example:—Those who go weekly to church, and there have doled out to them a quantum of belief which they have not energy to work out for themselves, are simply spiritual paupers.

The subordinate proposition, or rather the two subordinate propositions, contained between the first and second commas in this sentence, almost wholly determine the meaning of the principal proposition with which it ends; and the effect would be destroyed were they to be placed last instead of first.

(5) The general principle of right arrangement in sentences, which we have traced in its application to the leading divisions of them, equally determines *the normal order of the minor divisions of sentences.* The several clauses, of which the complements to the subject and predicate generally consist, may conform more or less completely to the law of easy apprehension. Of course, with these as with the larger members, *the succession should be from the abstract to the concrete.*

574. (6) Now, however, we must notice a further condition to be fulfilled in the proper combination of the elements of a sentence, but still a condition dictated by the same general principle with the other: the condition, namely, that *the words and expressions most nearly related in thought shall be brought the closest together.* Evidently the single words, the minor clauses, and the leading divisions of every proposition, severally qualify each other. The longer the time that elapses between the mention of any qualifying member and the member qualified, the longer must the mind be exerted in carrying forward the qualifying member ready for use. And the more numerous the qualifications to be simultaneously remembered and rightly applied, the greater will be the mental power expended and the smaller the effect produced. Hence, other things equal, force will be gained by so arranging the members of a sentence that these suspensions shall at any moment be the fewest in number,

---

573. Succession of the principal and subordinate propositions in the same sentence. Example.—Order of clauses

and shall also be of the shortest duration. The following is an *instance of defective combination :*

———A modern newspaper statement, though probably true, would be laughed at if quoted in a book as testimony; but the letter of a court-gossip is thought good historical evidence, if written some centuries ago.

A rearrangement of this, in accordance with the principle indicated above, will be found to increase the effect. Thus:

———Though probably true, a modern newspaper statement quoted in a book as testimony, would be laughed at; but the letter of a court-gossip, if written some centuries ago, is thought good historical evidence.

By making this change some of the suspensions are avoided, and others shortened; whilst there is less liability to produce premature conceptions. The passage quoted below from "Paradise Lost," affords a fine instance of sentences well arranged, alike in the priority of the subordinate members, in the avoidance of long and numerous suspensions, and in *the correspondence between the order of the clauses and the sequence of the phenomena described*, which, by the way, is a further prerequisite to easy comprehension, and therefore to effect:

As when a prowling wolf,
Whom hunger drives to seek new haunt for prey,
Watching where shepherds pen their flocks at eve
In hurdled cotes amid the field secure,
Leaps o'er the fence with ease into the fold:
Or as a thief bent to unhoard the cash
Of some rich burgher, whose substantial doors,
Cross-barr'd and bolted fast, fear no assault,
In at the window climbs, or o'er the tiles:
So clomb the first grand thief into God's fold;
So since into his church lewd hirelings climb.

575. (7) The habitual use of sentences in which all or most of the descriptive and limiting elements precede those described and limited, give rise to what is called *the inverted style ;* a title which is, however, by no means confined to this structure, but is often used where the order of the words is simply unusual. A more appropriate title would be *the direct style*, as contrasted with the other or *indirect style :* the peculiarity of the one being that it conveys each thought into the mind step by step, with little liability to error; and of the other, that it gets the right thought conceived by a series of approximations.

(8) *The superiority of the direct over the indirect form of sentence*, implied by the several conclusions that have been drawn, *must not, however, be affirmed without limitation.* Though up to a certain point it is well for all the qualifying clauses of a period to precede those qualified, yet, as carrying forward each qualifying clause costs some mental effort, it follows that when the number of them and the time they are carried become great, we reach a limit

---

574. Words to be brought most closely together.—Reason for juxtaposition.—Example of defective arrangement. Example of good arrangement.

beyond which more is lost than gained. Other things equal, *the arrangement should be such that no concrete image shall be suggested until the materials out of which it is to be made have been presented.* And yet, as lately pointed out, other things equal, *the fewer the materials to be held at once, and the shorter the distance they have to be borne, the better.* Hence, in some cases, it becomes a question whether most mental effort will be entailed by the many and long suspensions, or by the correction of successive misconceptions.

576. This question may sometimes be decided by considering the *capacity of the persons addressed.* A greater grasp of mind is required for the ready comprehension of thoughts expressed in the direct manner, when the sentences are in any wise intricate. To recollect a number of preliminaries stated in elucidation of a coming image, and to apply them all to the formation of it when suggested, demands a considerable power of concentration, and a tolerably vigorous imagination. To one possessing these, the direct method will mostly seem the best, whilst to one deficient in them it will seem the worst. Just as it may cost a strong man less effort to carry a hundred-weight from place to place at once, than by a stone at a time; so to an active mind it may be easier to bear along all the qualifications of an idea, and at once rightly form it when named, than to first imperfectly conceive such an idea, and then carry back to it one by one the details and limitations afterwards mentioned. Whilst, conversely, as for a boy the only possible mode of transferring a hundred-weight, is that of taking it in portions; so for a weak mind, the only possible mode of forming a compound perception may be that of building it up by carrying separately its several parts.

That *the indirect method*—the method of conveying the meaning by a series of approximations—*is best fitted for the uncultivated,* may indeed be inferred from their habitual use of it. The form of expression adopted by the savage, as in "Water, give me," is the simplest type of the approximative arrangement. In pleonasms, which are comparatively prevalent among the uneducated, the same essential structure is seen; as, for instance, in "The men, they were there." Again, the old possessive case, "The king, his crown," conforms to the like order of thought. Moreover, the fact that the indirect mode is called the *natural* one, implies that it is the one spontaneously employed by the common people—that is, the one easiest for undisciplined minds.

Before dismissing this branch of our subject, it should be remarked that even when addressing the most vigorous intellects, *the direct style is unfit for communicating thoughts of a complex or abstract*

---

575. Inverted style described. A more appropriate title for this style. The proper limitation to the direct style.—Rule where qualifying clauses are numerous.

character. So long as the mind has not much to do, it may be well to grasp all the preparatory clauses of a sentence, and to use them effectively; but if some subtilty in the argument absorb the attention—if every faculty be strained in endeavoring to catch the speaker's or writer's drift, it may happen that the mind, unable to carry on both processes at once, will break down, and allow all its ideas to lapse into confusion.

III. THE LAW OF EFFECT IN USING FIGURES OF SPEECH.

577. Turning now to consider Figures of Speech, we may equally discern the same law of effect. Underlying all the rules that may be given for the choice and right use of them, we shall find the same fundamental requirement—*economy of attention.* It is indeed chiefly because of their great ability to subserve this requirement, that figures of speech are employed. To bring the mind more easily to the desired conception, is in many cases solely, and in all cases mainly, their object.

(1) Let us begin with the figure called SYNECDOCHE. The advantage sometimes gained by putting a part for the whole is due to the more convenient, or more accurate, presentation of the idea thus secured. If, instead of saying "a fleet of ten ships," we say "a fleet of ten *sail*," the picture of a group of vessels at sea is more readily suggested; and is so because the sails constitute the most conspicuous part of vessels so circumstanced; whereas the word *ships* would more likely remind us of vessels in dock.

Again, to say "All *hands* to the pumps!" is better than to say "All *men* to the pumps!" as it suggests the men in the special attitude intended, and so saves effort. Bringing "*gray hairs* with sorrow to the grave," is another expression the effect of which has the same cause.

578. (2) The occasional increase of force produced by METONYMY may be similarly accounted for.

"The low morality of *the bar*" is a phrase both briefer and more significant than the literal one it stands for. A belief in the ultimate supremacy of intelligence over brute force, is conveyed in a more concrete, and therefore more realizable form, if we substitute *the pen* and *the sword* for the two abstract terms. To say "Beware of drinking!" is less effective than to say "Beware the bottle!" and is so, clearly because it calls up a less specific image.

(3) The SIMILE, though in many cases employed chiefly with a view to ornament, yet whenever it increases the force of a passage, does so by being an economy. Here is an instance:

---

576. Reference to the capacity of those addressed.—For whom the indirect method is best fitted. Title generally given to this method. For what thoughts the direct style is unfit.
577. Why chiefly figures of speech are employed.—Synecdoche. Example.
578. Metonymy. Example.—How simile increases the force of a passage. Example.

——The illusion that great men and great events came oftener in early times than now, is partly due to historical perspective. As in a range of equidistant columns, the furthest off look the closest, so the conspicuous objects of the past seem more thickly clustered the more remote they are.

To construct, by a process of literal explanation, the thought thus conveyed, would take many sentences; and the first elements of the picture would become faint whilst the imagination was busy in adding the others. But by the help of a comparison all effort is saved; the picture is instantly realized, and its full effect produced.

579. Of the *position of the Simile*,* it needs only to remark, that what has been said respecting the order of the adjective and substantive, predicate and subject, principal and subordinate propositions, &c., is applicable here. As whatever qualifies should precede whatever is qualified, *force will generally be gained by placing the simile upon the object to which it is applied*. That this arrangement is the best, may be seen in the following passage from the "Lady of the Lake:"

> As wreath of snow on mountain breast,
> Slides from the rock that gave it rest,
> Poor Ellen glided from her stay,
> And at the monarch's feet she lay.

Inverting these couplets will be found to diminish the effect considerably. There are cases, however, even where the simile is a simple one, in which it may with advantage be placed last; as in these lines from Alexander Smith's "Life's Drama."

> I see the future stretch
> All dark and barren as a rainy sea.

The reason for this seems to be, that so abstract an idea as that attaching to the word "future," does not present itself to the mind in any definite form, and hence the subsequent arrival at the simile entails no reconstruction of the thought.

Nor are such the only cases in which this order is the most forcible. As the advantage of putting the simile before the object depends on its being carried forward in the mind to assist in forming an image of the object, it must happen that if, from length or complexity, it cannot so be carried forward, the advantage is not gained The annexed sonnet, by Coleridge, is defective from this cause:

> As when a child on some long winter's night,
> Affrighted, clinging to its grandam's knees,
> With eager wondering and perturbed delight
> Listens strange tales of fearful dark decrees,
> Mutter'd to wretch by necromantic spell;

* Properly, the term "simile" is applicable only to the entire figure, inclusive of the two things compared and the comparison drawn between them. But as there exists no name for the illustrative member of the figure, there seems no alternative but to employ "simile" to express this also. The context will in each case show in which sense the word is used.

579. The position of the simile, and reason given. Example from Scott; from Smith from Coleridge.

Or of those hags who at the witching time
Of murky midnight, ride the air sublime,
And mingle foul embrace with fiends of hell;
Cold horror drinks its blood! Anon the tear
More gentle starts, to hear the beldame tell
Of pretty babes, that loved each other dear,
Murder'd by cruel uncle's mandate fell:
Ev'n such the shivering joys thy tones impart,
Ev'n so, thou, Siddons, meltest my sad heart.

Here, from the lapse of time and accumulation of circumstances, the first part of the comparison becomes more or less dim before its application is reached, and requires re-reading. Had the main idea been first mentioned, less effort would have been required to attain it, and to modify the conception of it in conformity with the comparison, and refer back to the recollection of its successive features for help in forming the final image.

580. (4) The superiority of the METAPHOR to the Simile is ascribed by Dr. Whately to the fact that "all men are more gratified at catching the resemblance for themselves than in having it pointed out to them." But after what has been said, the great economy it achieves will seem the more probable cause. If, drawing an analogy between mental and physical phenomena, we say,

——As, in passing through the crystal, beams of white light are decomposed into the colors of the rainbow; so in traversing the soul of the poet, the colorless rays of truth are transformed into brightly-tinted poetry;—

it is clear that in receiving the double set of words expressing the two portions of the comparison, and in carrying the one portion to the other, a considerable amount of attention is absorbed. Most of this is saved, however, by putting the comparison in a metaphorical form, thus:

——The white light of truth, in traversing the many-sided transparent soul of the poet, is refracted into iris-hued poetry.

How much is conveyed in a few words by the help of the Metaphor, and how vivid the effect consequently produced, may be abundantly exemplified. From a "Life Drama" may be quoted the phrase,

I spear'd him with a jest,

as a fine instance among the many which that poem contains.

A passage in the "Prometheus Unbound" of Shelley, displays the power of the Metaphor to great advantage:

Methought among the lawns together,
We wander'd underneath the young gray dawn,
And multitudes of dense white fleecy clouds
Were wandering in thick flocks along the mountains,
Shepherded by the slow unwilling wind.

---

580. Superiority of metaphor to simile; reasons given.—Example concerning Truth. Example from "Life Drama." Example from Shelley.—When metaphor should give place to simile

This last expression is remarkable for the distinctness with which it realizes the features of the scene; bringing the mind, as it were, at a bound to the desired conception.

But a limit is put to the advantageous use of the Metaphor, by the condition *it must be sufficiently simple to be understood from a hint.* Evidently, if there be any obscurity in the meaning or application of it, no economy of attention will be gained, but rather the reverse. Hence, *when the comparison is complex, it is usual to have recourse to the Simile.*

581. (5) There is, however, a species of figure sometimes classed under ALLEGORY, but which might perhaps be better called *Compound Metaphor*, that enables us to retain the brevity of the metaphorical form even where the analogy is intricate. This is done by indicating the application of the figure at the outset, and then leaving the mind to continue the parallel itself. Emerson has employed it with great effect in the first of his "Lectures on the Times:"

The main interest which any aspects of the times can have for us, is the great spirit which gazes through them, the light which they can shed on the wonderful questions, What we are? and whither do we tend? We do not wish to be deceived. Here we drift, like white sail across the wide ocean, now bright on the wave, now darkling in the trough of the sea: but from what port did we sail? who knows? or to what port are we bound? who knows? There is no one to tell us but such poor weather-tossed mariners as ourselves, whom we speak as we pass, or who have hoisted some signal, or floated to us some letter in a bottle from afar. But what know they more than we? They also found themselves on this wondrous sea. No: from the older sailors nothing. Over all their speaking-trumpets the gray sea and the loud winds answer—Not in us; not in Time.

582. (6) The division of the simile from the metaphor is by no means a definite one. Between the one extreme in which the two elements of the comparison are detailed at full length and the analogy pointed out, and the other extreme in which the comparison is implied instead of stated, come intermediate forms, in which the comparison is partly stated and partly implied. For instance:

———Astonished at the performances of the English plough, the Hindoos paint it, set it up and worship it; thus turning a tool into an idol: linguists do the same with language.

There is an evident advantage in leaving the reader or hearer to complete the figure. And generally those intermediate forms are good in proportion as they do this, provided the mode of completing it be obvious.

583. (7) Passing over much that may be said of like purport upon hyperbole, personification, apostrophe, &c., we close our remarks upon construction by a TYPICAL EXAMPLE.

The general principle that has been enunciated is, that the force of all verbal forms and arrangements is great in proportion as the

---

581. Advantage and nature of the compound metaphor. Example from Emerson.
582. Simile and metaphor not always distinct. Example.

time and mental effort they demand from the recipient is small. The special applications of this general principle have been several times illustrated; and it has been shown that the relative goodness of any two modes of expressing an idea may be determined by observing which requires the shortest process of thought for its comprehension. But though conformity in particular points has been exemplified, no cases of complete conformity have yet been quoted. It is, indeed, difficult to find them; for the English idiom scarcely permits the order which theory dictates. A few, however, occur in Ossian. Here is one:

> As autumn's dark storms pour from two echoing hills, so towards each other approached the heroes. As two dark streams from high rocks meet, and mix, and roar on the plain; loud, rough, and dark in battle meet Lochlin and Innisfail. * * * * As the troubled noise of the ocean when rolls the waves on high; as the last peal of the thunder of heaven;—such is the noise of the battle.

Except in the position of the verb in the first two similes, the theoretically best arrangement is fully carried out in each of these sentences. *The simile comes before the qualified image, the adjectives before the substantives, the predicate and copula before the subject, and their respective complements before them.* That the passage is more or less open to the charge of being bombastic proves nothing; or rather proves our case. For what is bombast but a force of expression too great for the magnitude of the ideas embodied? All that may rightly be inferred is, that only in very rare cases, and then only to produce a climax, should *all* the conditions of effective expression be fulfilled.

IV. CHOICE AND ARRANGEMENT OF THE MINOR IMAGES OUT OF WHICH PARTICULAR THOUGHTS ARE BUILT.

584. Passing on to a more complex application of the doctrine with which we set out, it must now be remarked, that not only in the structure of sentences and the use of figures of speech, may economy of the recipient's mental energy be assigned as the cause of force, but that *in the choice and arrangement of the minor images, out of which some large thought is to be built*, we may trace the same condition of effect.

To select from the sentiment, scene, or event described, those typical elements which carry many others along with them, and so by saying a few things but suggesting many, to abridge the description, *is the secret of producing a vivid impression.* Thus if we say, Real nobility is "not transferable;" besides the one idea expressed,

---

583. Force of verbal forms and arrangements is in proportion to what?—The relative goodness of two modes of expressing an idea, how determined. Example from Ossian Objection to this instance. Inference.

several are implied; and as these can be thought much sooner than they can be put in words, there is gain in omitting them. How the mind may be led to construct a complete picture by the presentation of a few parts, an extract from Tennyson's "Mariana" will well show:

> All day within the dreamy house,
> The door upon the hinges creak'd
> The fly sung i' the pane; the mouse
> Behind the mouldering wainscot shriek'd,
> Or from the crevice peer'd about.

The several circumstances here specified bring with them hosts of appropriate associations. Our attention is rarely drawn by the buzzing of a fly in the window, save when every thing is still. Whilst the inmates are moving about the house, mice usually keep silence; and it is only when extreme quietness reigns that they peep from their retreats. Hence, each of the facts mentioned, presupposing numerous others, calls up these with more or less distinctness, and revives the feeling of dull solitude with which they are connected in our experience. Were all these facts detailed instead of suggested, the attention would be so frittered away that little impression of dreariness would be produced. And here, without further explanation, it will be seen that, be the nature of the sentiment conveyed what it may, *this skilful selection of a few particulars which imply the rest, is the key to success.* In the choice of component ideas, as in the choice of expressions, THE AIM MUST BE TO CONVEY THE GREATEST QUANTITY OF THOUGHTS WITH THE SMALLEST QUANTITY OF WORDS.

V. SUPPLEMENTARY CAUSES OF FORCE IN EXPRESSION.

585. Before inquiring whether the law of effect, thus far traced, will account for the superiority of poetry to prose, it will be needful to notice some supplementary causes of force in expression that have not yet been mentioned. These are not, properly speaking, additional causes, but rather *secondary* ones, originating from those already specified—reflex manifestations of them.

In the first place, then, we may remark that *mental excitement spontaneously prompts the use of those forms of speech which have been pointed out as the most effective.* "Out with him!" "Away with him!" are the natural utterances of angry citizens at a disturbed meeting. A voyager, describing a terrible storm he had witnessed, would rise to some such climax as, "Crack went the ropes, and down went the mast." Astonishment may be heard expressed in the phrase, "Never was there such a sight!" All which sentences are, it will be observed, constructed after the direct type.

---

584. Selection of typical elements. Example from Tennyson. Remarks on it.

Again, every one will recognize the fact that *excited persons are given to figures of speech.* The vituperation of the vulgar abounds with them; often, indeed, consists of little else. "Beast," "brute," "gallows-rogue," "cut-throat villain,"—these and other like metaphors, or metaphorical epithets, at once call to mind a street quarrel.

586. Further, it may be remarked that extreme *brevity is one of the characteristics of passionate language.* The sentences are generally incomplete, the particles are omitted, and frequently important words are left to be gathered from the context. Great admiration does not vent itself in a precise proposition, as, "It is beautiful," but in a simple exclamation, "Beautiful!" He who, when reading a lawyer's letter, should say "Vile rascal!" would be thought angry; whilst "He is a vile rascal" would imply comparative coolness. Thus we see that, alike in the order of the words, in the frequent use of figures, and in extreme conciseness, the natural utterances of excitement conform to the theoretical conditions of forcible expression.

Here, then, the higher forms of speech acquire a secondary thought from *association.* Having, in actual life, habitually formed them in connection with vivid mental impressions; and having been accustomed to meet with them in the most powerful writing; they come to have in themselves a species of force. The emotions that have from time to time been produced by the strong thoughts wrapped up in these forms, are partially aroused by the forms themselves. They create a certain degree of animation; they induce a preparatory sympathy; and when the striking ideas looked for are reached, they are the more vividly realized.

VI. WHY POETRY IS ESPECIALLY IMPRESSIVE.

587. (1) The continuous use of those modes of expression that are alike forcible in themselves, and forcible from their associations, produces the peculiarly impressive species of composition which we call poetry. *Poetry,* we shall find, *habitually adopts those symbols of thought, and those methods of using them, which instinct and analysis agree in choosing as most effective, and becomes poetry by virtue of doing this.*

On turning back to the various specimens that have been quoted, it will be seen that *the direct or inverted form of sentence predominates* in them, and that *to a degree quite inadmissible in prose.* And not only in the frequency, but in what is termed the violence of the inversions will this distinction be remarked

---

585. How are the most effective forms of speech prompted. Example.—Kind of language used by excited persons. Example.

586. Characteristic of passionate language. Example.—Strength derived from association.

In the *abundant use of figures*, again, we may recognize the same truth. Metaphors, similes, hyperboles, and personifications, are the poet's colors, which he has liberty to employ almost without limit We characterize as "poetical" the prose which repeats these appli ances of language with any frequency; and condemn it as "overflorid" or "affected" long before they occur with the profusion allowed in verse.

Further, let it be remarked that in *brevity*—the other requisite of forcible expression which theory points out, and emotion spontaneously fulfils—poetical phraseology similarly differs from ordinary phraseology. Imperfect periods are frequent, elisions are perpetual, and many of the minor words which would be deemed essential in prose are dispensed with.

588. Thus *poetry, regarded as a vehicle of thought, is especially impressive because it obeys all the laws of effective speech, and partly because in so doing it imitates the natural utterances of excitement.* Whilst the matter embodied is idealized emotion, the vehicle is the idealized language of emotion. As the musical composer catches the cadences in which our feelings of joy and sympathy, grief and despair vent themselves, and out of these germs evolves melodies suggesting higher phases of these feelings; so the poet develops from the typical expressions in which men utter passion and sentiment, those choice forms of verbal combination in which concentrated passion and sentiment may be fitly presented.

(2) There is *one peculiarity of poetry conducing much to its effect*—the peculiarity which is indeed usually thought to be its characteristic one—still remaining to be considered: we mean *its rhythmical structure.* This, unexpected as it may be, will be found to come under the same generalization with the others. Like each of them, it is an idealization of the natural language of emotion, which is known to be more or less metrical if the emotion be not violent; and like each of them, it is an economy of the reader's or hearer's attention.

In the peculiar tone and manner we adopt in uttering versified language, may be discerned its relationship to the feelings; and *the pleasure which its measured movement gives* us is ascribable to the comparative ease with which words metrically arranged can be recognized. This last position will scarcely be at once admitted; but a little explanation will show its reasonableness. For if, as we have seen, there is an expenditure of mental energy in the mere act of listening to verbal articulations, or in that silent repetition of them which goes on in reading—if the perceptive faculties must be in active exercise to identify every syllable—then any mode of combining words so as to present a regular recurrence of certain traits

---

587. Characteristic of poetry.—What form of sentence predominates.—Use of figures Brevity.

which the *mind* can anticipate, will diminish that strain upon the attention required by the cold irregularity of prose.

589. In the same manner that the body, in receiving a series of varying concussions, must keep the muscles ready to meet the most violent of them, as not knowing when such may come; so the mind, in receiving unarranged articulations, must keep its perception active enough to recognize the least easily caught sounds. And as, if the concussions recur in a definite order, the body may husband its forces by adjusting the resistance needful for each concussion; so, if the syllables be rhythmically arranged, the mind may econonize its energies by anticipating the attention required for each syllable. Far fetched as this idea will perhaps be thought, a little introspection will countenance it.

That we *do* take advantage of the metrical language to adjust our perceptive faculties to the force of the expected articulations, is clear from the fact that we are balked by halting versification. Much as at the bottom of a flight of stairs, a step more or less than we counted upon gives us a shock, so, too, does a misplaced accent or a supernumerary syllable. In the one case we know that there is an erroneous pre-adjustment; and we can scarcely doubt that there is one in the other. But if we habitually pre-adjust our perceptions to the measured movement of verse, the physical analogy lately given renders it probable that by so doing we economize attention; and hence that metrical language is more effective than prose, simply because it enables us to do this.

Were there space, it might be worth while to inquire whether the pleasure we take in rhyme, and also that which we take in euphony, are not partly ascribable to the same general cause.

SECOND DIVISON OF THE SUBJECT.

CAUSES OF FORCE IN LANGUAGE WHICH DEPEND UPON ECONOMY OF MENTAL SENSIBILITIES.

590. A few paragraphs only can be devoted to a second division of our subject that here presents itself. To pursue in detail the laws of effect, as seen in the larger features of composition, would exceed both our limits and our purpose. But we may fitly indicate some further aspect of the general principle, and hint a few of its wider applications.

Thus far, then, we have considered only those causes of force in

---

588. Why poetry is especially impressive.—Poet compared with the musical composer.—Rhythmical structure, result of the law of economy.—Pleasure of the measured movement traced to what? Explanation of this.

589. Poetry more easily apprehended than prose. Illustrated by the body receiving varying concussions; by halting versification; descent of flight of stairs.

language which depend upon economy of the mental *energies:* we have now briefly to glance at those which depend upon economy of mental *sensibilities*. Indefensible though this division may be as a psychological one, it will yet serve roughly to indicate the remaining field of investigation. It will suggest, that besides considering the extent to which any faculty or group of faculties is tasked in receiving a form of words, and realizing its contained idea, we have to consider the state in which this faculty or group of faculties is left; and how the reception of subsequent sentences and images will be influenced by that state.

(1) Without going at length into so wide a topic as the exercise of faculties and its reactive effects, it will be sufficient here to call to mind that *every faculty (when in a state of normal activity) is most capable at the outset; and that the change in its condition, which ends in what we term exhaustion, begins simultaneously with its exercise.* This generalization, with which we are all familiar in our bodily experiences, and which our daily language recognizes as true of the mind as a whole, is equally true of each mental power, from the simplest of the senses to the most complex of the sentiments.

If we hold a flower to the nose for a long time, we become insensible to its scent. We say of a very brilliant flash of lightning that it blinds us; which means that our eyes have for a time lost their ability to appreciate light. After eating a quantity of honey, we are apt to think that our tea is without sugar. The phrase "a deafening roar" implies that men find a very loud sound temporarily incapacitates them for hearing faint ones. Now the truth which we at once recognize in these, its extreme manifestations, may be traced throughout; and it may be shown that alike in the reflective faculties, in the imagination, in the perceptions of the beautiful, the ludicrous, the sublime, in the sentiments, the instincts, in all the mental powers, however we may classify them—action exhausts; and that in proportion as the action is violent, the subsequent prostration is great.

591. (2) Equally, throughout the whole nature, may be traced the law that *exercised faculties are ever tending to resume their original state.* Not only after continued rest do they regain their full power; not only do brief cessations partially invigorate them; but even whilst they are in action, the resulting exhaustion is ever being neutralized. *The two processes of waste and repair go on together.* Hence, with faculties habitually exercised, as the senses in all, or the muscles in a laborer, it happens that, during moderate activity, the repair is so nearly equal to the waste, that the diminution of power is scarcely appreciable; and it is only when the activity has been long continued, or has been very violent, that the repair becomes so far in arrear of the waste as to produce a perceptible prostration. In all cases, however, when by the action of a faculty, waste has been

---

590. Second Division of the subject.—When each faculty is most vigorous.—Effect of exercise Flower held to the nose. Flash of lightning. Eating honey.

incurred, some lapse of time must take place before full efficiency can be re-acquired; and this time must be long in proportion as the waste has been great.

592. Keeping in mind these general truths, we shall be in a condition to understand certain causes of effect in composition now to be considered. Every perception received, and every conception realized, entailing some amount of waste—or, as Liebig would say, some changes of matter in the brain—and the efficiency of the faculties subject to this waste being thereby temporarily, though often but momentarily, diminished—the resulting partial inability must affect the acts of perception and conception that immediately succeed. And hence we may expect that the vividness with which images are realized will, in many cases, depend on the order of their presentation, even when one order is as convenient to the understanding as the other.

We shall find sundry facts which alike illustrate this and are explained by it. *Climax* is one of them. The marked effect obtained by placing last the most striking of any series of images, and the weakness—often the ludicrous weakness—produced by reversing this arrangement, depends on the general law indicated. As immediately after looking at the sun we cannot perceive the light of a fire, whilst by looking at the fire first and the sun afterwards we can perceive both; so after receiving a brilliant, or weighty, or terrible thought, we cannot appreciate a less brilliant, less weighty, or less terrible one, whilst, by reversing the order, we can appreciate each.

593. In *Antithesis*, again, we may recognize the same general truth. The opposition of two thoughts that are the reverse of each other in some prominent trait insures an impressive effect; and does this by giving a momentary relaxation to the faculties addressed. If, after a series of images of an ordinary character, appealing in a moderate degree to the sentiment of reverence, or approbation, or beauty, the mind has presented to it a very insignificant, a very unworthy, or a very ugly image—the faculty of reverence, or approbation, or beauty, as the case may be, having for the time nothing to do, tends to resume its full power; and will immediately afterwards appreciate a vast, admirable, or beautiful image better than it would otherwise do. Improbable as these momentary variations in susceptibility will seem to many, we cannot doubt their occurrence when we contemplate the analogous variations in the susceptibility of the senses. Referring once more to phenomena of vision, every one knows that a patch of black on a white ground looks blacker, and a patch of white on a black ground looks whiter than elsewhere. As the blackness and the whiteness must really be the same, the only

---

591. Tendency of exercised faculties.—Waste and repair illustrated.

592. The process of perception and conception attended with certain effects.—Climax explained.

593. Effect of antithesis explained.—Reference to phenomena of vision.

assignable cause for this is a difference in their action upon us, dependent on the different states of our faculties. It is simply a visual antithesis.

594. (3) But this extension of the general principle of economy—this further condition of effect in composition, that the power of the faculties must be continuously husbanded—includes much more than has yet been hinted. It implies not only that certain arrangements and certain juxtapositions of connected ideas are best; but that *some modes of dividing and presenting the subject will be more effective than others;* and that, too, irrespective of its local cohesion. It shows why *we must progress from the less interesting to the more interesting;* and why not only the composition as a whole, but each of its successive portions, should tend towards a climax. *At the same time it forbids long continuity of the same species of thought, or repeated production of the same effects.* It warns us against the error committed both by Pope in his poems and by Bacon in his essays—the error, namely, of constantly employing the most effective forms of expression; and it points out, that as the easiest posture by and by becomes fatiguing, and is with pleasure exchanged for one less easy; so *the most perfectly constructed sentences will soon weary, and relief will be given by using those of an inferior kind.*

595. Further, it involves that *not only should we avoid generally combining our words in one manner, however good, or working out our figures and illustrations in one way, however telling, but we should avoid any thing like uniform adherence, even to the wider conditions of effect.* We should not make every section of our subject progress in interest; we should not always rise to a climax. As we saw that, in single sentences, it is but rarely allowable to fulfil all the conditions of strength, so in the larger portions of composition we must not often conform entirely to the law indicated. We must subordinate the component effects to the total effect.

(4) In deciding how practically to carry out the principles of artistic composition, we may derive help by bearing in mind a fact already pointed out—*the fitness of certain verbal arrangements for certain kinds of thought.* The constant variety in the mode of presenting ideas which the theory demands, will in a great degree result from a skilful adaptation of the form to the matter. We saw how the direct or inverted sentence is spontaneously used by excited people; and how their language is also characterized by figures of speech and extreme brevity. Hence these may with advantage predominate in emotional passages, and may increase as the emotion rises.

596. On the other hand, for complex ideas the indirect sentence

---

594. Modes of dividing and presenting a subject. Tend to climax.—Continuity of same species of thought.—Error of Pope and Bacon.

595. Uniformity of a certain kind forbidden.—The fitness of certain verbal arrangements for certain kinds of thought

seems the best vehicle. In conversation, the excitement produced by the near approach to a desired conclusion will often show itself in a series of short, sharp sentences; whilst, in impressing a view already enunciated, we generally make our periods voluminous by piling thought upon thought. These natural modes of procedure may serve as guides in writing. Keen observation and skilful analysis would, in like manner, detect many other peculiarities of expression produced by other attitudes of mind; and by paying due attention to all such traits, a writer possessed of sufficient versatility might make some approach to a completely organized work.

(5) *This species of composition*, which the law of effect points out as the perfect one, is *the one which high genius tends naturally to produce.* As we found that the kinds of sentence which are theoretically best are those generally employed by superior minds, and by inferior minds when excitement has raised them; so we shall find that the ideal form for a poem, essay, or fiction, is that which the ideal writer would evolve spontaneously. One in whom the powers of expression fully responded to the state of mind would unconsciously use that variety in the mode of presenting his thoughts which Art demands.

597. This constant employment of one species of phraseology, which all have now to strive against, implies an undeveloped faculty of language. *To have a specific style is to be poor in speech.* If we glance back at the past, and remember that men had once only nouns and verbs to convey their ideas with, and that from then to now the growth has been towards a greater number of implements of thought, and consequently towards a greater complexity and variety in their combinations, we may infer that we are now, in our use of sentences, much what the primitive man was in his use of words, and that a continuance of the process that has hitherto gone on must produce increasing heterogeneity in our modes of expression. As now in a fine nature the play of the features, the tones of the voice and its cadences, vary in harmony with every thought uttered; so in one possessed of a fully developed power of speech, the mould in which each combination of words is cast will similarly vary with, and be appropriate to, the sentiment.

598. That *a perfectly endowed man must unconsciously write in all styles*, we may infer from considering how all styles originate. Why is Addison diffuse, Johnson pompous, Goldsmith simple? Why is one author abrupt, another rhythmical, another concise? Evidently in each case the habitual mode of utterance must depend upon the habitual balance of the nature. The predominant feelings have by use trained the intellect to represent them. But whilst long, though unconscious, discipline has made it do this efficiently,

---

596. The proper vehicle for complex ideas.—Varying structure of our sentences in conversation.—The kind of composition which genius tends to produce.

597. A specific style.—The adaptation to be aimed at.

it remains, from lack of practice, incapable of doing the same for the less powerful feelings; and when these are excited, the usual modes of expression undergo but a slight modification. Let the powers of speech be fully developed, however; let the ability of the intellect to convey the emotions be complete; and this fixity of style will disappear. *The perfect writer* will express himself as Junius, when in the Junius frame of mind; when he feels as Lamb felt, will use a like familiar speech; and will fall into the ruggedness of Carlyle, when in a Carlylean mood. Now he will be rhythmical, and now irregular; here his language will be plain, and there ornate; sometimes his sentences will be balanced, and at other times unsymmetrical; for a while there will be a considerable sameness, and then, again, great variety. From his mode of expression naturally responding to his state of feeling, there will flow from his pen a composition changing to the same degree that the aspects of his subject change. He will thus without effort conform to what we have seen to be the laws of effect. And whilst his work presents to the reader that variety needful to prevent continuous exertion of the same faculties, it will also answer to the description of all highly organized products, both of man and of nature; it will be not a series of like parts simply placed in juxtaposition, but one whole made up of unlike parts that are mutually dependent.

CHAPTER XXIII.

EPIC AND DRAMATIC COMPOSITION

599. TRAGEDY differs not from the epic in substance: in both the same ends are pursued, namely, instruction and amusement; and in both the same means is employed, namely, imitation of human actions. They differ only in the manner of imitating: epic poetry employs narration; tragedy represents its facts as passing in our sight: in the former, the poet introduces himself as an historian in the latter, he presents his actors, and never himself.*

* The dialogue in a dramatic composition distinguishes it so clearly from other compositions, that no writer has thought it necessary to search for any other distinguishing mark. But much useless labor has been bestowed to distinguish an epic poem by some peculiar mark. Bossuet defines it to be "A composition in verse, intended to form the manners by instructions disguised under the allegories of an important action;" which excludes every epic poem founded upon real facts, and perhaps includes several of Æsop's fables. Vol-

598. The endowed man will write in all styles. How shown.--How the perfect writer will express himself

This difference regarding form only, may be thought slight; but the effects it occasions are by no means so; for what we see makes a deeper impression than what we learn from others. A narrative poem is a story told by another: facts and incidents passing upon the stage, come under our own observation; and are besides much enlivened by action and gesture, expressive of many sentiments beyond the reach of words.

A dramatic composition has another property, independent altogether of action; which is, that it makes a deeper impression than narration: in the former, persons express their own sentiments; in the latter, sentiments are related at second hand. For that reason, Aristotle, the father of critics, lays it down as a rule, That in an epic poem, the author ought to take every opportunity of introducing his actors, and of confining the narrative part within the narrowest bounds. (*Poet.* chapter xxv. sec. vi.) Homer understood perfectly the advantage of this method; and his two poems abound in dialogue. Lucan runs to the opposite extreme, even so far as to stuff his *Pharsalia* with cold and languid reflections; the merit of which he assumes to himself, and deigns not to share with his actors. Nothing can be more injudiciously timed than a chain of such reflections, which suspend the battle of Pharsalia after the leaders had made their speeches, and the two armies are ready to engage (Lib. vii. from line 385 to line 460.)

600. Aristotle, regarding the fable only, divides tragedy into simple and complex; but it is of greater moment, with respect to dramatic as well as epic poetry, to found a distinction upon the different ends attained by such compositions. A poem, whether dramatic or epic, that has nothing in view but to move the passions and to exhibit pictures of virtue and vice, may be distinguished by the name of *pathetic;* but where a story is purposely contrived to illustrate some moral truth, by showing that disorderly passions naturally lead to external misfortunes, such composition may be denominated *moral.**

---

taire reckons verse so essential, as for that single reason to exclude the adventures of Telemachus. See his *Essay upon Epic Poetry*. Others, affected with substance more than with form, hesitate not to pronounce that poem to be epic. It is not a little diverting to see so many profound critics hunting for what is not: they take for granted, without the least foundation, that there must be some precise criterion to distinguish epic poetry from every other species of writing. Literary compositions run into each other precisely like colors: in their strong tints they are easily distinguished; but are susceptible of so much variety, and of so many different forms, that we never can say where one species ends and another begins. As to the general taste, there is little reason to doubt that a work where heroic actions are related in an elevated style, will, without further requisite, be deemed an epic poem.

* The same distinction is applicable to that sort of fable which is said to be the invention of Æsop. A moral, it is true, is by all critics considered as essential to such a fable. But nothing is more common than to be led blindly by authority; for of the numerous collections I have seen, the fables that

---

599. Tragedy and epic poetry compared. The dialogue of the former.—An epic poem defined.—Comparative effects of dramatic composition and of an epic poem.

Besides making a deeper impression than can be done by cool reasoning, a moral poem does not fall short of reasoning in affording conviction: the natural connection of vice with misery, and of virtue with happiness, may be illustrated by stating a fact as well as by urging an argument. Let us assume, for example, the following moral truths: that discord among the chiefs renders ineffectual all common measures; and that the consequences of a slightly-founded quarrel, fostered by pride and arrogance, are no less fatal than those of the grossest injury: these truths may be inculcated by the quarrel between Agamemnon and Achilles at the siege of Troy. If facts or circumstances be wanting, such as tend to rouse the turbulent passions, they must be invented: but no accidental nor unaccountable event ought to be admitted; for the necessary or probable connection between vice and misery is not learned from any events but what are naturally occasioned by the characters and passions of the persons represented, acting in such and such circumstances. A real event of which we see not the cause, may afford a lesson upon the presumption that what hath happened may again happen; but this cannot be inferred from a story that is known to be a fiction.

601. Many are the good effects of such compositions. A pathetic composition, whether epic or dramatic, tends to a habit of virtue, by exciting us to do what is right, and restraining us from what is wrong. (See chapter ii. part i. sec. 4.) Its frequent pictures of human woes produce, besides, two effects extremely salutary: they improve our sympathy, and fortify us to bear our own misfortunes. A moral composition obviously produces the same good effects, because by being moral it ceaseth not to be pathetic: it enjoys besides an excellence peculiar to itself; for it not only improves the heart, as above mentioned, but instructs the head by the moral it contains. I cannot imagine any entertainment more suited to a rational being than a work thus happily illustrating some moral truth; where a number of persons of different characters are engaged in an important action, some retarding, others promoting the great catastrophe; and where there is dignity of style as well as of matter. A work of that kind has our sympathy at command; and can put in motion the whole train of the social affections: our curiosity in some scenes is excited, in others gratified; and our delight is consummated at the close, upon finding, from the characters and situations exhibited at the commencement, that every inci-

clearly inculcate a moral, make a very small part. In many fables, indeed, proper pictures of virtue and vice are exhibited; but the bulk of these collections convey no instruction, nor afford any amusement beyond what a child receives in reading an ordinary story.

600. Aristotle's division of tragedy.—A better division of dramatic as well as of epic poetry. Illustration

dent down to the final catastrophe is natural, and that the whole in conjunction make a regular chain of causes and effects.

Considering that an epic and a dramatic poem are the same in substance, and have the same aim or end, one will readily imagine that subjects proper for the one must be equally proper for the other. But considering their difference as to form, there will be found reason to correct that conjecture at least in some degree. Many subjects may indeed be treated with equal advantage in either form; but the subjects are still more numerous for which they are not equally qualified; and there are subjects proper for the one, and not for the other. To give some slight notion of the difference, as there is no room here for enlarging upon every article, I observe, that dialogue is better qualified for expressing sentiments, and narrative for displaying facts. Heroism, magnanimity, undaunted courage, and other elevated virtues, figure best in action: tender passion, and the whole tribe of sympathetic affections figure best in sentiment. It clearly follows, that tender passions are more peculiarly the province of tragedy, grand and heroic actions of epic poetry.

602. In this chapter of Emotions and Passions* it is occasionally shown, that the subject best fitted for tragedy is where a man has himself been the cause of his misfortune; not so as to be deeply guilty, nor altogether innocent: the misfortune must be occasioned by a fault incident to human nature, and therefore in some degree venial. Such misfortunes call forth the social affections, and warmly interest the spectator. An accidental misfortune, if not extremely singular, doth not greatly move our pity: the person who suffers, being innocent, is freed from the greatest of all torments, that anguish of mind which is occasioned by remorse: an atrocious criminal, on the other hand, who brings misfortunes upon himself, excites little pity, for a different reason: his remorse, it is true, aggravates his distress, and swells the first emotions of pity; but these are immediately blunted by our hatred of him as a criminal. Misfortunes that are not innocent, nor highly criminal, partake the advantages of each extreme: they are attended with remorse to embitter the distress, which raises our pity to a height; and the slight indignation we have at a venial fault, detracts not sensibly from our pity. The happiest of all subjects accordingly for raising pity, is where a man of integrity falls into a great misfortune by doing an action that is innocent, but which, by some singular means, is conceived by him to be criminal: his remorse aggravates his distress; and our compassion, unrestrained by indignation, knows no bounds. Pity comes thus to be the ruling passion of a pathetic tragedy; and by proper

* [Consult Spalding's English Literature, pp. 251-4.]

601 Good effects of epic and dramatic compositions. Subjects suited to each

representation, may be raised to a height scarce exceeded by any thing felt in real life. A moral tragedy takes in a larger field; as it not only exercises our pity, but raises another passion, which, though selfish, deserves to be cherished equally with the social affection. The passion I have in view is fear or terror; for when a misfortune is the natural consequence of some wrong bias in the temper, every spectator who is conscious of such a bias in himself, takes the alarm, and dreads his falling into the same misfortune: and by the emotion of fear or terror, frequently reiterated in a variety of moral tragedies, the spectators are put upon their guard against the disorders of passion.

[There is no principle relative to human nature better established than this, that we can be deeply concerned for the fate of no man, whose character does not in some measure resemble our own, or concerning whose conduct we may not reasonably conclude that we might have acted the same part, had we been surrounded with the same circumstances and motives. This principle points out the most proper characters for tragedy. They should be possessed of high virtues, to interest the spectators in their happiness; but they should be exhibited as liable to errors and indiscretions, arising from the weakness of human nature, the violence of passion, or the intemperate pursuit of objects commendable and useful. The misfortunes of such persons properly painted, and artfully heightened, take hold of the mind with irresistible effect. They engage every sympathetic feeling of the soul, and they make us tremble, lest, by our indiscretion in similar indulgence of our passions, we should throw ourselves into similar distress.—*Barron*, Lect. 56.]

603. I had an early opportunity to unfold a curious doctrine, That fable operates on our passions, by representing its events as passing in our sight, and by deluding us into a conviction of reality. (Chapter ii. part i. sect. vii.) Hence, in epic and dramatic compositions, every circumstance ought to be employed that may promote the delusion; such as the borrowing from history some noted event, with the addition of circumstances that may answer the author's purpose; the principal facts are known to be true; and we are disposed to extend our belief to every circumstance. But in choosing a subject that makes a figure in history, greater precaution is necessary than where the whole is a fiction. In the latter case there is full scope for invention: the author is under no restraint other than that the characters and incidents be just copies of nature. But where the story is founded on truth, no circumstances must be added but such as connect naturally with what are known to be true; history may be supplied, but must not be contradicted: further, the subject chosen must be distant in time, or at least in place; for the familiarity of recent persons and events ought to be avoided. Fa-

---

602. The subject best fitted for tragedy.

miliarity ought more especially to be avoided in an epic poem, the peculiar character of which is dignity and elevation; modern manners make no figure in such a poem.*

After Voltaire, no writer, it is probable, will think of rearing an epic poem upon a recent event in the history of his own country. But an event of that kind is perhaps not altogether unqualified for tragedy; it was admitted in Greece, and Shakspeare has employed it successfully in several of his pieces. One advantage it possesses above fiction, that of more readily engaging our belief, which tends above any other circumstance to raise our sympathy. The scene of comedy is generally laid at home; familiarity is no objection; and we are peculiarly sensible of the ridicule of our own manners.

604. After a proper subject is chosen, the dividing it into parts requires some art. The conclusion of a book in an epic poem, or of an act in a play, cannot be altogether arbitrary; nor be intended for so slight a purpose as to make the parts of equal length. The supposed pause at the end of every book, and the real pause at the end of every act, ought always to coincide with some pause in the action. In this respect, a dramatic or epic poem ought to resemble a sentence or period in language, divided into members that are distinguished from each other by proper pauses; or it ought to resemble a piece of music, having a full close at the end, preceded by imperfect closes that contribute to the melody. Every act in a dramatic poem ought therefore to close with some incident that makes a pause in the action; for otherwise there can be no pretext for interrupting the representation; it would be absurd to break off in the very heat of action; against which every one would exclaim: the absurdity still remains where the action relents, if it be not actually suspended for some time. This rule is also applicable to an epic poem; though in it a deviation from the rule is less remarkable; because it is in the reader's power to hide the absurdity, by proceeding instantly to another book. The first book of *Paradise Lost* ends without any close, perfect or imperfect; it breaks off abruptly where Satan, seated on his throne, is prepared to harangue the convocated hosts of the fallen angels; and the second book begins with the speech. Milton seems to have copied the *Æneid*, of which the two first books are divided much in the same manner. Neither is there any proper pause at the end of the fifth book of the *Æneid*. There is no proper pause at the end of the seventh book

* I would not from this observation be thought to undervalue modern manners. The roughness and impetuosity of ancient manners, may be better fitted for an epic poem, without being better fitted for society. But without regard to that circumstance, it is the familiarity of modern manners that unqualifies them for the lofty subject. The dignity of our present manners will be better understood in future ages, when they are no longer familiar.

603. How fable operates upon our passions.—Circumstances that are to be employed.—Precaution requisite in choosing an historical subject.—An epic poem founded on recent events.—Subject for comedy.

of *Paradise Lost*, nor at the end of the eleventh. In the *Iliad* little attention is given to this rule.

This branch of the subject shall be closed with a general rule, That action being the fundamental part of every composition, whether epic or dramatic, the sentiments and tone of language ought to be subservient to the action, so as to appear natural, and proper for the occasion. The application of this rule to our modern plays, would reduce the bulk of them to a skeleton.

605. After carrying on together epic and dramatic compositions, I shall mention circumstances peculiar to each, beginning with the epic kind. In a theatrical entertainment, which employs both the eye and the ear, it would be a gross absurdity to introduce upon the stage superior beings in a visible shape. There is no place for such objection in a epic poem; and Boileau, with many other critics, declares strongly for that sort of machinery in an epic poem. But waving authority, which is apt to impose upon the judgment, let us draw what light we can from reason. I begin with a preliminary remark, That this matter is but indistinctly handled by critics; the poetical privilege of animating insensible objects for enlivening a description, is very different from what is termed *machinery*, where deities, angels, devils, or other supernatural powers, are introduced as real personages, mixing in the action, and contributing to the catastrophe; and yet these are constantly jumbled together in the reasoning. The former is founded on a natural principle (chapter xx. sect. i.); but can the latter claim the same authority? Far from it: nothing is more unnatural. Its effects, at the same time, are deplorable. First, it gives an air of fiction to the whole; and prevents that impression of reality which is requisite to interest our affections, and to move our passions (see chapter ii. part i. sect. vii.) This of itself is sufficient to explode machinery, whatever entertainment it may afford to readers of a fantastic taste or irregular imagination. And, next, were it possible, by disguising the fiction, to delude us into a notion of reality, which I think can hardly be, an insuperable objection would still remain, that the aim or end of an epic poem can never be attained in any perfection, where machinery is introduced; for an evident reason, that virtuous emotions cannot be raised successfully, but by the actions of those who are endued with passions and affections like our own, that is, by human actions; and as for moral instruction, it is clear that none can be drawn from beings who act not upon the same principles with us. A fable in Æsop's manner is no objection to this reasoning: his lions, bulls, and goats, are truly men in disguise; they act and feel in every respect as human beings; and the moral we draw is founded on that supposition. Homer, it is true, introduces the gods into his fable; but the religion of his country authorized that liberty; it

604. **The parts of a subject.—The close of an act in a dramatic poem. Also of a book in an Epic.—Paradise Lost.—The Æneid.—General rule for sentiments and tone of language.**

being an article in the Grecian creed, that the gods often interpose visibly and bodily in human affairs. I must, however, observe, that Homer's deities do no honor to his poems: fictions that transgress the bounds of nature, seldom have a good effect; they may inflame the imagination for a moment, but will not be relished by any person of a correct taste. They may be of some use to the lower rank of writers, but an author of genius has much finer materials of Nature's production, for elevating his subject, and making it interesting.

606. I have tried serious reasonings upon this subject; but ridicule, I suppose, will be found a more successful weapon, which Addison has applied in an elegant manner: "Whereas the time of a general peace is, in all appearance, drawing near; being informed that there are several ingenious persons who intend to show their talents on so happy an occasion, and being willing, as much as in me lies, to prevent that effusion of nonsense, which we have good cause to apprehend; I do hereby strictly require every person who shall write on this subject, to remember that he is a Christian, and not to sacrifice his catechism to his poetry. In order to it, I do expect of him, in the first place, to make his own poem, without depending upon Phœbus for any part of it, or calling out for aid upon any of the muses by name. I do likewise positively forbid the sending of Mercury with any particular message or dispatch relating to the peace; and shall by no means suffer Minerva to take upon her the shape of any plenipotentiary concerned in this great work. I do further declare, that I shall not allow the destinies to have had a hand in the deaths of the several thousands who have been slain in the late war; being of opinion that all such deaths may be well accounted for by the Christian system of powder and ball. I do therefore strictly forbid the fates to cut the thread of man's life upon any pretence whatsoever, unless it be for the sake of the rhyme. And whereas I have good reason to fear that Neptune will have a great deal of business on his hands in several poems which we may now suppose are upon the anvil, I do also prohibit his appearance, unless it be done in metaphor, simile, or any very short allusion; and that even here he may not be permitted to enter, but with great caution and circumspection. I desire that the same rule may be extended to his whole fraternity of heathen gods; it being my design to condemn every poem to the flames in which Jupiter thunders, or exercises any other act of authority which does not belong to him. In short, I expect that no pagan agent shall be introduced, or any fact related which a man cannot give credit to with a good conscience. Provided always, that nothing herein contained shall extend, or be construed to extend, to several of the female poets in this nation, who shall still be left in full possession of

605. The introduction upon the stage of superior beings in visible shape.—Effects of introducing such *machinery* in an epic poem.—Æsop's fables.—Homer's deities.

their gods and goddesses, in the same manner as if this paper had never been written." (Spectator, No. 523.)

The marvellous is indeed so much promoted by machinery, that it is not wonderful to find it embraced by the plurality of writers, and perhaps of readers. If indulged at all, it is generally indulged to excess. Homer introduceth his deities with no greater ceremony than as mortals; and Virgil has still less moderation: a pilot spent with watching cannot fall asleep and drop into the sea by natural means: one bed cannot receive the two lovers, Æneas and Dido, without the immediate interposition of superior powers. The ridiculous in such fictions, must appear even through the thickest veil of gravity and solemnity.

607. Angels and devils serve equally with heathen deities as materials for figurative language; perhaps better among Christians, because we believe in them, and not in heathen deities. But every one is sensible, as well as Boileau, that the invisible powers in our creed make a much worse figure as actors in a modern poem, than the invisible powers in the heathen creed did in ancient poems; the cause of which is not far to seek. The heathen deities, in the opinion of their votaries, were beings elevated one step only above mankind, subject to the same passions and directed by the same motives; therefore not altogether improper to mix with men in an important action. In our creed, superior beings are placed at such a mighty distance from us, and are of a nature so different, that with no propriety can we appear with them upon the same stage; man, a creature much inferior, loses all dignity in the comparison.

There can be no doubt, that an historical poem admits the embellishment of allegory, as well as of metaphor, simile, or other figure. Moral truth, in particular, is finely illustrated in the allegorical manner; it amuses the fancy to find abstract terms, by a sort of magic, metamorphosed into active beings; and it is highly pleasing to discover a general proposition in a pictured event. But allegorical beings should be confined within their own sphere, and never be admitted to mix in the principal action, nor to co-operate in retarding or advancing the catastrophe. This would have a still worse effect than invisible powers; and I am ready to assign the reason. The impression of real existence, essential to an epic poem, is inconsistent with that figurative existence which is essential to an allegory (see chapter xx. sect. vi.); and therefore no means can more effectually prevent the impression of reality, than to introduce allegorical beings co-operating with those whom we conceive to be really existing. The allegory of Sin and Death in the *Paradise Lost*, is, I presume, not generally relished, though it is not entirely of the same nature with what I have been condemning: in a work

---

606. Addison's ridicule of *machinery*.—Excess of it in Homer and Virgil.

607. The figure which angels and devils would make as actors in a modern poem, compared with the heathen deities in ancient poems.—Allegory in historical poems.

comprehending the achievements of superior beings, there is more room for fancy than where it is confined to human actions.

608. What is the true notion of an *episode?* or how is it to be distinguished from the principal action? Every incident that promotes or retards the catastrophe, must be part of the principal action. This clears the nature of an episode; which may be defined, "An incident connected with the principal action, but contributing neither to advance nor to retard it." The descent of Æneas into hell doth not advance nor retard the catastrophe, and therefore is an episode. The story of Nisus and Euryalus, producing an alteration in the affairs of the contending parties, is a part of the principal action. The family scene in the sixth book of the *Iliad* is of the same nature; for by Hector's retiring from the field of battle to visit his wife, the Grecians had opportunity to breathe, and even to turn upon the Trojans. The unavoidable effect of episode, according to this definition, must be, to break the unity of action; and therefore it ought never to be indulged unless to unbend the mind after the fatigue of a long narration. An episode, when such is its purpose, requires the following conditions: it ought to be well connected with the principal action; it ought to be lively and interesting; it ought to be short; and a time ought to be chosen when the principal action relents.*

In the following beautiful episode, which closes the second book of Fingal, all these conditions are united:

Comal was a son of Albion, the chief of a hundred hills. His deer drank of a thousand streams, and a thousand rocks replied to the voice of his dogs. His face was the mildness of youth; but his hand the death of heroes. One was his love, and fair was she! the daughter of mighty Conloch. She appeared like a sunbeam among women, and her hair was like the wing of the raven. Her soul was fixed on Comal, and she was his companion in the chase. Often met their eyes of love, and happy were their words in secret. But Gormal loved the maid, the chief of gloomy Ardven. He watched her lone steps on the heath, the foe of unhappy Comal.

One day tired of the chase, when the mist had concealed their friends, Comal and the daughter of Conloch met in the cave of Ronan. It was the wonted haunt of Comal. Its sides were hung with his arms: a hundred shields of thongs were there, a hundred helms of sounding steel. Rest here, said he, my love, Galvina, thou light of the cave of Ronan; a deer appears on Mora's brow; I go, but soon will return. I fear, said she, dark Gormal my foe: I will rest here; but soon return, my love.

He went to the deer of Mora. The daughter of Conloch, to try his love, clothed her white side with his armor, and strode from the cave of Ronan. Thinking her his foe, his heart beat high, and his color changed. He drew the bow; the arrow flew; Galvina fell in blood. He ran to the cave with hasty steps and called the daughter of Conloch. Where art thou, my love? but no answer.——He marked, at length, her heaving heart beating against the mortal arrow. O Conloch's daughter, is it thou! He sunk upon her breast.

The hunters found the hapless pair. Many and silent were his steps round the dark dwelling of his love. The fleet of the ocean came: he fought, and the

---

* Homer's description of the shield of Achilles is properly introduced at a time when the action relents, and the reader can bear an interruption. But the author of Telemachus describes the shield of that young hero in the heat of battle, a very improper time for an interruption.

strangers fell. He searched for death over the field; but who could kill the mighty Comal? Throwing away his shield, an arrow found his manly breast. He sleeps with his Galvina; their green tombs are seen by the mariner, when he bounds on the waves of the north.

609. Next, upon the *peculiarities of a dramatic poem.* And the first I shall mention is a double plot; one of which must resemble an episode in an epic poem; for it would distract the spectator instead of entertaining him, if he were forced to attend, at the same time, to two capital plots equally interesting. And even supposing it an under-plot like an episode, it seldom hath a good effect in tragedy, of which simplicity is a chief property; for an interesting subject that engages our affections, occupies our whole attention, and leaves no room for any separate concern. Variety is more tolerable in comedy, which pretends only to amuse, without totally occupying the mind. But even there, to make a double-plot agreeable, is no slight effort of art: the under-plot ought not to vary greatly in its tone from the principal; for discordant emotions are unpleasant when jumbled together; which, by the way, is an insuperable objection to tragi-comedy. Upon that account the *Provoked Husband* deserves censure: all the scenes that bring the family of the Wrongheads into action, being ludicrous and farcical, are in a very different tone from the principal scenes, displaying severe and bitter expostulations between Lord Townley and his lady. The same objection touches not the double-plot of the *Careless Husband;* the different subjects being sweetly connected, and having only so much variety as to resemble shades of colors harmoniously mixed. But this is not all. The under-plot ought to be connected with that which is principal, so much at least as to employ the same persons: the under-plot ought to occupy the intervals or pauses of the principal action; and both ought to be concluded together. This is the case of the *Merry Wives of Windsor.*

Violent action ought never to be represented on the stage. While the dialogue goes on, a thousand particulars concur to delude us into an impression of reality; genuine sentiments, passionate language, and persuasive gesture: the spectator once engaged, is willing to be deceived, loses sight of himself, and without scruple enjoys the spectacle as a reality. From this absent state he is roused by violent action: he awakes as from a pleasing dream, and, gathering his senses about him, finds all to be a fiction. Horace delivers the same rule, and founds it upon the same reason:

> Ne pueros coram populo Medea trucidet;
> Aut humana palam coquat exta nefarius Atreus;
> Aut in avem Progne vertatur, Cadmus in anguem:
> Quodcumque ostendis mihi sic, incredulus odi.

The French critics join with Horace in excluding blood from the

---

608. Episode, how designated from the principal action. Example.—Effect of an episode: when to be indulged; conditions.

stage; but, overlooking the most substantial objection, they urge only that it is barbarous and shocking to a polite audience.

610. A few words upon the *dialogue;* which ought to be so conducted as to be a true representation of nature. I talk not here of the sentiments, nor of the language; for these come under different heads: I talk of what properly belongs to dialogue-writing; where every single speech, short or long, ought to arise from what is said by the former speaker, and furnish matter for what comes after, till the end of the scene. In this view, all the speeches, from first to last, represent so many links of one continued chain. No author, ancient or modern, possesses the art of dialogue equal to Shakspeare. Dryden, in that particular, may justly be placed as his opposite: he frequently introduces three or four persons speaking upon the same subject, each throwing out his own notions separately, without regarding what is said by the rest: take for an example the first scene of *Aurenzebe.* Sometimes he makes a number club in relating an event, not to a stranger, supposed ignorant of it, but to one another, for the sake merely of speaking: of which notable sort of dialogue, we have a specimen in the first scene of the first part of the *Conquest of Granada.* In the second part of the same tragedy, scene second, the King, Abenamar, and Zulema, make their separate observations, like so many soliloquies, upon the fluctuating temper of the mob. A dialogue so uncouth, puts one in mind of two shepherds in a pastoral, excited by a prize to pronounce verses alternately, each in praise of his own mistress.

This manner of dialogue-writing, besides an unnatural air, has another bad effect: it stays the course of the action, because it is not productive of any consequence. In Congreve's comedies, the action is often suspended to make way for a play of wit.

No fault is more common among writers, than to prolong a speech after the impatience of the person to whom it is addressed ought to prompt him or her to break in. Consider only how the impatient actor is to behave in the mean time. To express his impatience in violent action without interrupting, would be unnatural; and yet to dissemble his impatience, by appearing cool where he ought to be highly inflamed, would be no less so.

Rhyme being unnatural and disgustful in dialogue, is happily banished from our theatre: the only wonder is that it ever found admittance, especially among a people accustomed to the more manly freedom of Shakspeare's dialogue. By banishing rhyme, we have gained so much as never once to dream of any further improvement. And yet, however suitable blank verse may be to elevated characters and warm passions, it must appear improper and affected in the mouths of the lower sort. Why then should it be a rule, That every scene in tragedy must be in blank verse? Shak-

---

609. **Double-plot in a dramatic poem; in a comedy.—Rules for the under-plot.—Violent action on the stage.**

speare, with great judgment, has followed a different rule; which is, to intermix prose with verse, and only to employ the latter where it is required by the importance or dignity of the subject. Familiar thoughts and ordinary facts ought to be expressed in plain language: to hear, for example, a footman deliver a simple message in blank verse, must appear ridiculous to every one who is not biased by custom. In short, that variety of characters and of situations, which is the life of a play, requires not only a suitable variety in the sentiments, but also in the diction.

[Upon the conduct of the dialogue, Lord Jeffrey thus contrasts the modern with the old English drama:

"On the modern stage, every scene is *visibly* studied and digested beforehand; and every thing from beginning to end, whether it be description, or argument, or vituperation, is very obviously and ostentatiously set forth in the most advantageous light, and with all the decorations of the most elaborate rhetoric. Now, for mere rhetoric and fine composition, this is very right; but for an imitation of nature, it is not quite so well. . . . . . .

"On the old English stage, however, the discussions always appear to be casual, and the argument quite artless and disorderly. The persons of the drama, in short, are made to speak like men and women who meet without preparation in real life. Their reasonings are perpetually broken by passion, or left imperfect for want of skill. They constantly wander from the point in hand, in the most un business-like manner in the world; and after hitting upon a topic that would afford to a judicious playwright room for a magnificent seesaw of pompous declamation, they have generally the awkwardness to let it slip, as if perfectly unconscious of its value; and uniformly leave the scene without exhausting the controversy, or stating half the plausible things for themselves that any ordinary advisers might have suggested—after a few weeks' reflection. As specimens of eloquent argumentation, we must admit the signal inferiority of our native favorites; but as true copies of nature—as vehicles of passion, and representations of character, we confess we are tempted to give them the preference. When a dramatist brings his chief characters on the stage, we readily admit that he must give them something to say, and that this something must be interesting and characteristic; but he should recollect also, that they are supposed to come there without having anticipated all they were to hear, or meditated on all they were to deliver; and that it cannot be characteristic therefore, because it must be glaringly unnatural, that they should proceed regularly through every possible view of the subject, and exhaust, in set order, the whole magazine of reflections that can be brought to bear upon their situation.

"It would not be fair, however, to leave this view of the matter, without observing, that this unsteadiness and irregularity of dialogue, which gives such an air of nature to our older plays, is frequently carried to a most blamable excess; and that, independent of their passion for verbal quibbles, there is an irregularity, and a capricious uncertainty in the taste and judgment of these good old writers, which excites at once our amusement and our compassion. If it be true that no other man has ever written so finely as Shakspeare has done in his happier passages, it is no less true that there is not a scribbler now alive who could possibly write worse than he has sometimes written,—who could, on occasion, devise more contemptible ideas, or misplace them so abominably, by the side of such incomparable excellence."—*Review of Ford.*]

CHAPTER XXIV.

THE THREE UNITIES.

611. MAN acts with deliberation, will, and choice: he aims at some end—glory, for example, or riches, or conquest, the procuring happiness to individuals, or to his country in general: he proposes means, and lays plans to attain the end purposed. Here are a number of facts or incidents leading to the end in view, the whole composing one chain by the relation of cause and effect. In running over a series of such facts or incidents, we cannot rest upon any one because they are presented to us as means only, leading to some end; but we rest with satisfaction upon the end or ultimate event; because there the purpose or aim of the chief person or persons is accomplished. This indicates the beginning, the middle, and the end, of what Aristotle calls *an entire action.* (*Poet.* cap. vi. See also cap. vii.) The story naturally begins with describing those circumstances which move the principal person to form a plan, in order to compass some desired event: the prosecution of that plan and the obstructions, carry the reader into the heat of action: the middle is properly where the action is the most involved; and the end is where the event is brought about, and the plan accomplished.

A plan thus happily accomplished after many obstructions, affords wonderful delight to the reader; to produce which, a principle mentioned above (chap. viii.) mainly contributes, the same that disposes the mind to complete every work commenced, and in general to carry every thing to a conclusion.

I have given the foregoing example of a plan crowned with success, because it affords the clearest conception of a beginning, a mid-

---

610. Rules for the dialogue. Shakspeare. Dryden. Congreve.—Rhyme.—Intermixture of blank verse and prose.—Lord Jeffrey's comparison of the modern and the old English drama.

dle, and an end, in which consists *unity* of action; and indeed stricter unity cannot be imagined than in that case. But an action may have unity, or a beginning, middle, and end, without so intimate a relation of parts; as where the catastrophe is different from what is intended or desired, which frequently happens in our best tragedies In the *Æneid*, the hero, after many obstructions, makes his plan effectual. The *Iliad* is formed upon a different model: it begins with the quarrel between Achilles and Agamemnon; goes on to describe the several effects produced by that cause; and ends in a reconciliation. Here is unity of action, no doubt, a beginning, a middle, and an end; but inferior to that of the *Æneid*, which will thus appear. The mind hath a propensity to go forward in the chain of history: it keeps always in view the expected event; and when the incidents or under parts are connected by their relation to the event, the mind runs sweetly and easily along them. This pleasure we have in the *Æneid*. It is not altogether so pleasant, as in the *Iliad*, to connect effects by their common cause; for such connection forces the mind to a continual retrospect: looking back is like walking backward.

Homer's plan is still more defective, upon another account, That the events described are but imperfectly connected with the wrath of Achilles, their cause: his wrath did not exert itself in action; and the misfortunes of his countrymen were but negatively the effects of his wrath, by depriving them of his assistance.

612. If unity of action be a capital beauty in a fable imitative of human affairs, a plurality of unconnected fables must be a capital deformity. For the sake of variety, we indulge an under-plot that is connected with the principal: but too unconnected events are extremely unpleasant, even where the same actors are engaged in both. Ariosto is quite licentious in that particular: he carries on at the same time a plurality of unconnected stories. His only excuse is, that his plan is perfectly well adjusted to his subject; for every thing in the *Orlando Furioso* is wild and extravagant.

Though to state facts in the order of time is natural, yet that order may be varied for the sake of conspicuous beauties. (See chapter i.) If, for example, a noted story, cold and simple in its first movements, be made the subject of an epic poem, the reader may be hurried into the heat of action, reserving the preliminaries for a conversation-piece, if thought necessary; and that method, at the same time, hath a peculiar beauty from being dramatic. (See chapter xxi.) But a privilege that deviates from nature ought to be sparingly indulged; and yet romance-writers make no difficulty of presenting to the reader, without the least preparation, unknown persons engaged in some arduous adventure equally unknown. In *Cassandra*, two personages, who afterwards are discovered to be heroes of the

---

611. Remarks on human action.—The beginning, middle, and end of a story.—A plan crowned with success, agreeable.—An action may have unity, though the catastrophe differ from what is intended. The Æneid. The Iliad

fable, start up completely armed upon the banks of the Euphrates, and engage in a single combat.*

A play analyzed, is a chain of connected facts, of which each scene makes a link. Each scene, accordingly, ought to produce some incident relative to the catastrophe or ultimate event, by advancing or retarding it. A scene that produceth no incident, and for that reason may be termed *barren*, ought not to be indulged, because it breaks the unity of action; a barren scene can never be entitled to a place, because the chain is complete without it.

Upon the whole, it appears that all the facts in an historical fable ought to have a mutual connection, by their common relation to the grand event or catastrophe. And this relation, in which the *unity* of action consists, is equally essential to epic and dramatic compositions.

613. How far the unities of time and of place are essential, is a question of greater intricacy. These unities were strictly observed in the Greek and Roman theatres; and they are inculcated by the French and English critics as essential to every dramatic composition. They are also acknowledged by our best poets, though in practice they make frequent deviation, which they pretend not to justify, against the practice of the Greeks and Romans, and against the solemn decision of their own countrymen. But in the course of this inquiry it will be made evident that in this article we are under no necessity to copy the ancients; and that our critics are guilty of a mistake in admitting no greater latitude of place and time than was admitted in Greece and Rome.†

All authors agree that *tragedy in Greece* was derived from the hymns in praise of Bacchus, which were sung in parts by a chorus. Thespis, to relieve the singers, and for the sake of variety, introduced one actor, whose province it was to explain historically the subject of the song, and who occasionally represented one or other personage. Æschylus, introducing a second actor, formed the dialogue,

---

* I am sensible that a commencement of this sort is much relished by readers disposed to the marvellous. Their curiosity is raised, and they are much tickled in its gratification. But curiosity is at an end with the first reading, because the personages are no longer unknown; and therefore at the second reading, a commencement so artificial loses its power, even over the vulgar. A writer of genius prefers lasting beauties.

† [By *unity of action* is meant that all the incidents of the poet shall point to one great catastrophe. By the *unities of time and place* is understood that the actual performance of the action may pass nearly during the time, and within the place of the representation. Without unity of action it is impossible to excite and agitate the passions; and without the unities of time and place it is impossible to preserve probability, and to persuade the spectators that the action is not imaginary. But with all these unities properly combined, the illusion will be complete, and the passions will be as effectually roused by the feigned events as if they were real.—*Barron*, Lect. 55.]

---

612. Capital deformity in a fable.—Order in which facts may be stated.—A play analyzed Rule for each scene. Unity of action defined.

by which the performance became dramatic; and the actors were multiplied when the subject represented made it necessary. But still the chorus, which gave a beginning to tragedy, was considered as an essential part. The first scene generally unfolds the preliminary circumstances that lead to the grand event; and this scene is by Aristotle termed the *prologue*. In the second scene, where the action properly begins, the chorus is introduced, which, as originally, continues upon the stage during the whole performance: the chorus frequently makes one in the dialogue; and when the dialogue happens to be suspended, the chorus, during the interval, is employed in singing. Sophocles adheres to this plan religiously, Euripides is not altogether so correct. In some of his pieces it becomes necessary to remove the chorus for a little time. But when that unusual step is risked, matters are so ordered as not to interrupt the representation: the chorus never leave the stage of their own accord, but at the command of some principal personage, who constantly waits their return.

Thus the Grecian drama is a continued representation without interruption; a circumstance that merits attention. A continued representation with a pause, affords not opportunity to vary the place of action, nor to prolong the time of the action beyond that of the representation. A real or feigned action that is brought to a conclusion after considerable intervals of time and frequent changes of place, cannot accurately be copied in a representation that admits no latitude in either. Hence it is that the unities of place and of time were, or ought to have been, strictly observed in the Greek tragedies; which is made necessary by the very constitution of their drama, for it is absurd to compose a tragedy that cannot be justly represented.

614. Modern critics, who for our drama pretend to establish rules founded on the practice of the Greeks, are guilty of an egregious blunder. The unities of place and of time were in Greece, as we see, a matter of necessity, not of choice; and I am now ready to show that if we submit to such fetters, it must be from choice, not necessity. This will be evident upon taking a view of the constitution of our drama, which differs widely from that of Greece; whether more or less perfect, is a different point, to be handled afterwards.* By dropping the chorus, opportunity is afforded to divide the representation by intervals of time, during which the stage is evacuated and the spectacle suspended. This qualifies our drama for subjects spread through a wide space both of time and of place: the time supposed to pass during the suspension of the representa-

* [For an interesting history of the mediæval and modern drama, see Shaw's English Literature, pp. 97-110.]

613. The unities of time and place; are they essential?—Grecian tragedy described. Inference.

tion is not measured by the time of the suspension: and any place may be supposed when the representation is renewed, with as much facility as when it commenced: by which means many subjects can be justly represented in our theatres that were excluded from those of ancient Greece. This doctrine may be illustrated by comparing a modern play to a set of historical pictures: let us suppose them five in number, and the resemblance will be complete. Each of the pictures resembles an act in one of our plays: there must necessarily be the strictest unity of place and of time in each picture; and the same necessity requires these two unities during each act of a play, because during an act there is no interruption in the spectacle. Now, when we view in succession a number of such historical pictures, let it be, for example, the history of Alexander by Le Brun, we have no difficulty to conceive that months or years have passed between the events exhibited in two different pictures, though the interruption is imperceptible in passing our eye from the one to the other; and we have as little difficulty to conceive a change of place, however great. In which view there is truly no difference between five acts of a modern play, and five such pictures. Where the representation is suspended, we can with the greatest facility suppose any length of time or any change of place: the spectator, it is true, may be conscious that the real time and place are not the same with what are employed in the representation; but this is a work of reflection; and by the same reflection he may also be conscious that Garrick is not King Lear, that the play-house is not Dover Cliffs, nor the noise he hears thunder and lightning. In a word, after an interruption of the representation, it is no more difficult for a spectator to imagine a new place, or a different time, than at the commencement of the play to imagine himself at Rome, or in a period of time two thousand years back. And indeed, it is abundantly ridiculous that a critic, who is willing to hold candle-light for sunshine, and some painted canvasses for a palace or a prison, should be so scrupulous about admitting any latitude of place or of time in the fable, beyond what is necessary in the representation.

615. There are, I acknowledge, some effects of great latitude in time that ought never to be indulged in a composition for the theatre: nothing can be more absurd than at the close to exhibit a full-grown person who appears a child at the beginning: the mind rejects, as contrary to all probability, such latitude of time as is requisite for a change so remarkable. The greatest change from place to place hath not altogether the same bad effect. In the bulk of human affairs place is not material; and the mind, when occupied with an interesting event, is little regardful of minute circumstances; these may be varied at will, because they scarce make any impression.

---

614. Blunder of modern critics.—How the English drama differs from the Grecian. Inference.—A modern play compared to a set of historical pictures.

But though I have taken arms to rescue modern poets from the despotism of modern critics, I would not be understood to justify liberty without any reserve. An unbounded license with relation to place and time, is faulty, for a reason that seems to have been overlooked, which is, that it seldom fails to break the unity of action. In the ordinary course of human affairs, single events, such as are fit to be represented on the stage, are confined to a narrow spot, and commonly employ no great extent of time: we accordingly seldom find strict unity of action in a dramatic composition, where any remarkable latitude is indulged in these particulars. I say further, that a composition which employs but one place, and requires not a greater length of time than is necessary for the representation, is so much the more perfect; because the confining an event within so narrow bounds, contributes to the unity of action; and also prevents that labor, however slight, which the mind must undergo in imagining frequent changes of place and many intervals of time. But still I must insist, that such limitation of place and time as was necessary in the Grecian drama, is no rule to us; and therefore, that though such limitation adds one beauty more to the composition, it is at best but a refinement, which may justly give place to a thousand beauties more substantial. And I may add, that it is extremely difficult, I was about to say impracticable, to contract within the Grecian limits, any fable so fruitful of incidents in number and variety, as to give full scope to the fluctuation of passion.

616. [It would be amusing to make a digest of the irrational laws which bad critics have framed for the government of poets. First in celebrity and in absurdity stand the dramatic unities of place and time. No human being has ever been able to find any thing that could, even by courtesy, be called an argument for these unities, except that they have been deduced from the general practice of the Greeks. It requires no very profound examination to discover that the Greek dramas, often admirable as compositions, are, as exhibitions of human character and of human life, far inferior to the English plays of the age of Elizabeth. Every scholar knows that the dramatic part of the Athenian tragedies was at first subordinate to the lyrical part. It would, therefore, be little less than a miracle if the laws of the Athenian stage had been found to suit plays in which there was no chorus. All the great master-pieces of the dramatic art have been composed in direct violation of the unities, and could never have been composed if the unities had not been violated. It is clear, for example, that such a character as that of Hamlet could never have been developed within the limits to which Alfieri confined himself. Yet such was the reverence of literary men during the last century for these unities, that Johnson, who, much to his honor, took the opposite side, was, as he says, "frighted at his own

---

615. Great latitude of time not admissible in a play

temerity;" and "afraid to stand against the authorities which might be produced against him."—*Macaulay*.

Lord JEFFREY, upon the same subject, has made the following observations: "When the moderns tie themselves down to write tragedies of the same length, and on the same simple plan, in other respects, with those of Sophocles and Æschylus, we shall not object to their adhering to the unities; for there can, in that case, be no sufficient inducement for violating them. But in the mean time, we hold that English dramatic poetry soars above *the unities*, just as the imagination does. The only pretence for insisting on them is, that we suppose the stage itself to be, actually and really, the very spot on which a given action is performed; and, if so, this space cannot be removed to another. But the supposition is manifestly quite contrary to truth and experience. The stage is considered merely as a place in which any given action *ad libitum* may be performed; and accordingly may be shifted, and is so in imagination, as often as the action requires it."—*British Essayists*, vol. vi. p. 320.

On this subject, consult also Sir Joshua Reynolds' Works, vol ii. 13th discourse.—*Ed.*]

X Begin study.

CHAPTER XXV.

GARDENING AND ARCHITECTURE.

617. THE books we have upon architecture and upon embellishing ground, abound in practical instruction, necessary for a mechanic; but in vain should we rummage them for rational principles to improve our taste. In a general system, it might be thought sufficient to have unfolded the principles that govern these and other fine arts, leaving the application to the reader; but as I would neglect no opportunity of showing the extensive influence of these principles, the purpose of the present chapter is to apply them to gardening and architecture; but without intending any regular plan of these favorite arts, which would be unsuitable not only to the nature of this work, but to the experience of its author.

Gardening was at first a useful art: in the garden of Alcinous, described by Homer, we find nothing done for pleasure merely But gardening is now improved into a fine art; and when we talk of a garden without any epithet, a pleasure-garden, by way of

---

616. Macaulay's remarks on the Grecian drama; upon the master-pieces of the modern drama.—Johnson.—Lord Jeffrey's remarks on the unities.

eminence, is understood. The garden of Alcinous, in modern language, was but a kitchen-garden. Architecture has run the same course: it continued many ages a useful art merely, without aspiring to be classed with the fine arts. Architecture, therefore, and gardening, being useful arts as well as fine arts, afford two different views. The reader, however, will not here expect rules for improving any work of art in point of utility; it being no part of my plan to treat of any useful art as such: but there is a beauty in utility; and in discoursing of beauty, that of utility must not be neglected. This leads us to consider gardens and buildings in different views: they may be destined for use solely, for beauty solely, or for both. Such variety of destination bestows upon these arts a great command of beauties, complex no less than various. Hence the difficulty of forming an accurate taste in gardening and architecture; and hence that difference and wavering of taste in these arts, greater than in any art that has but a single destination.

618. Architecture and gardening cannot otherwise entertain the mind, but by raising certain agreeable emotions or feelings; with which we must begin, as the true foundation of all the rules of criticism that govern these arts. Poetry, as to its power of raising emotions, possesses justly the first place among the fine arts; for scarce any one emotion of human nature is beyond its reach. Painting and sculpture are more circumscribed, having the command of no emotions but of what are raised by sight: they are peculiarly successful in expressing painful passions, which are displayed by external signs extremely legible. (See chapter xv.) Gardening, besides the emotions of beauty from regularity, order, proportion, color, and utility, can raise emotions of grandeur, of sweetness, of gayety, of melancholy, of wildness, and even of surprise or wonder.* In architecture, the beauties of regularity, order,

* [" It cannot be denied that the tasteful improvement of a country residence is both one of the most agreeable and the most natural recreations that can occupy a cultivated mind. With all the interest, and to many, all the excitement of the more seductive amusements of society, it has the incalculable advantage of fostering only the purest feelings, and (unlike many other occupations of business men) refining instead of hardening the heart.

" The great German poet, Goethe, says—

> Happy the man who hath escaped the town,
> Him did an angel bless when he was born.

" With us, country life is a leading object of nearly all men's desires. The wealthiest merchant looks upon his country-seat as the best ultimatum of his laborious days in the counting-house. The most indefatigable statesman dates, in his retirement, from his 'Ashland,' or his 'Lindenwold.' Webster has his 'Marshfield,' where his scientific agriculture is no less admirable than his profound eloquence in the Senate. Taylor's well-ordered plantation is not less significant of the man, than the battle of Buena Vista. Washington Irving's cottage, on the Hudson, is even more poetical than any chapter in his

617. Gardening as an art.—The garden of Alcinous. Gardening and buildings considered under two views

and proportion, are still more conspicuous than in gardening; but as to the beauty of color, architecture is far inferior. Grandeur can be expressed in a building, perhaps more successfully than in a garden; but as to the other emotions above mentioned, architecture hitherto has not been brought to the perfection of expressing them distinctly. To balance that defect, architecture can display the beauty of utility in the highest perfection.

Gardening indeed possesses one advantage, never to be equalled in the other art: in various scenes, it can raise successively all the different emotions above mentioned. But to produce that delicious effect, the garden must be extensive, so as to admit a slow succession; for a small garden, comprehended at one view, ought to be confined to one expression (see chapter viii.): it may be gay, it may be sweet, it may be gloomy; but an attempt to mix these would create a jumble of emotions not a little unpleasant. For the same reason, a building, even the most magnificent, is necessarily confined to one expression.

619. In gardening, as well as in architecture, simplicity ought to be a ruling principle. Profuse ornament hath no better effect than to confound the eye, and to prevent the object from making an impression as one entire whole. An artist destitute of genius for capital beauties, is naturally prompted to supply the defect by crowding his plan with slight embellishments: hence in a garden, triumphal arches, Chinese houses, temples, obelisks, cascades, fountains, without end; and in a building, pillars, vases, statues, and a profusion of carved work. Thus some women defective in taste, are apt to overcharge every part of their dress with ornament. Superfluity of decoration hath another bad effect; it gives the object a diminutive look: an island in a wide extended lake makes it appear larger; but an artificial lake, which is always little, appears still less by making an island on it.

In forming plans for embellishing a field, an artist without taste employs straight lines, circles, squares; because these look best upon paper. He perceives not, that to humor and adorn nature, is the perfection of his art; and that nature, neglecting regularity, distributes her objects in great variety with a bold hand. A large field

---

Sketch Book; and Cole, the greatest of our landscape painters, had his rural home under the very shadow of the Catskills.

"This is well. In the United States, nature and domestic life are better than society and the manners of towns. Hence all sensible men gladly escape, earlier or later, and partially or wholly, from the turmoil of the cities. Hence the dignity and value of country life is every day augmenting. And hence the enjoyment of landscape or ornamental gardening—which, when in pure taste, may properly be called *a more refined kind of nature*—is every day becoming more and more widely diffused."—*Downing's Rural Essays*, iii.]

---

618. How they entertain the mind.—Poetry, painting, sculpture, gardening, and architecture compared, as to power of raising emotions.

laid out with strict regularity, is stiff and artificial.* Nature, indeed, in organized bodies comprehended under one view, studies regularity, which, for the same reason, ought to be studied in architecture: but in large objects, which cannot otherwise be surveyed but in parts and by succession, regularity and uniformity would be useless properties, because they cannot be discovered by the eye.† Nature therefore, in her large works, neglects these properties; and in copying nature, the artist ought to neglect them.

620. Having thus far carried on a comparison between gardening and architecture, rules peculiar to each come next in order, beginning with gardening. The simplest plan of a garden, is that of a spot embellished with a number of natural objects, trees, walks, polished parterres, flowers, streams, &c. One more complex comprehends statues and buildings, that nature and art may be mutually ornamental. A third, approaching nearer perfection, is of objects assembled together in order to produce not only an emotion of beauty, but also some other particular emotion, grandeur, for example, gayety, or any other above mentioned. The completest plan of a garden is an improvement upon the third, requiring the several parts to be so arranged as to inspire all the different emotions that can be raised by gardening. In this plan, the arrangement is an important circumstance; for it has been shown, that some emotions figure best in conjunction, and that others ought always to appear in succession, and never in conjunction. It is mentioned (chapter viii.), that when the most opposite emotions, such as gloominess and gayety, stillness and activity, follow each other in succession, the pleasure, on the whole, will be the greatest; but that such emotions ought not to be united, because they produce an unpleasant mixture. (Chapter ii. part iv.) For this reason, a ruin affording a sort of melancholy pleasure, ought not to be seen from a flower-parterre which is gay and cheerful. But to pass from an exhilarating object to a ruin, has a fine effect; for each of the emotions is the more sensibly felt by being contrasted with the other. Similar emotions, on the other hand, such as gayety and sweetness, stillness and gloominess, motion and grandeur, ought to be raised together; for their effects upon the mind are greatly heightened by their conjunction.

621. Regularity is required in that part of a garden which is ad-

---

* In France and Italy, a garden is disposed like the human body, alleys, like legs and arms, answering each other; the great walk in the middle representing the trunk of the body. Thus an artist void of taste carries self along into every operation.

† A square field appears not such to the eye when viewed from any part of it; and the centre is the only place where a circular field preserves in appearance its regular figure.

---

619. Remarks of Mr. Downing.—A peculiar advantage of gardening.—Simplicity in gardening and architecture.—Embellishment of a field.
620. Plans for a garden

jacent to the dwelling-house; because an immediate accessory ought to partake the regularity of the principal object; but in proportion to the distance from the house considered as the centre, regularity ought less and less to be studied; for in an extensive plan, it hath a fine effect to lead the mind insensibly from regularity to a bold variety. Such arrangement tends to make an impression of grandeur; and grandeur ought to be studied as much as possible, even in a more confined plan, by avoiding a multiplicity of small parts. (See chapter iv.) A small garden, on the other hand, which admits not grandeur, ought to be strictly regular.

Milton, describing the garden of Eden, prefers justly grandeur before regularity:

> Flowers worthy of paradise, which not nice art
> In beds and curious knots, but Nature boon
> Pour'd forth profuse on hill, and dale, and plain;
> Both where the morning sun first warmly smote
> The open field, and where the unpierced shade
> Imbrown'd the noon-tide bowers. *Paradise Lost*, b. iv.

A hill covered with trees, appears more beautiful as well as more lofty than when naked. To distribute trees in a plain requires more art: near the dwelling-house they ought to be scattered so distant from each other, as not to break the unity of the field; and even at the greatest distance of distinct vision, they ought never to be so crowded as to hide any beautiful object.

In the manner of planting a wood or thicket, much art may be displayed. A common centre of walks, termed *a star*, from whence are seen remarkable objects, appears too artificial, and consequently too stiff and formal, to be agreeable: the crowding withal so many objects together, lessens the pleasure that would be felt in a slower succession.

622. By a judicious distribution of trees, other beauties may be produced. A landscape so rich as to engross the whole attention, and so limited as sweetly to be comprehended under a single view, has a much finer effect than the most extensive landscape that requires a wandering of the eye through successive scenes. This observation suggests a capital rule in laying out a field; which is, never at any one station to admit a larger prospect than can easily be taken in at once. A field so happily situated as to command a great extent of prospect, is a delightful subject for applying this rule: let the prospect be split into proper parts by means of trees, studying at the same time to introduce all the variety possible.

As gardening is not an inventive art, but an imitation of nature or rather nature itself ornamented, it follows necessarily that every thing unnatural ought to be rejected with disdain. Statues of wild beasts vomiting water, a common ornament in gardens, prevail in those of Versailles. Is that ornament in a good taste? A *jet d'eau*,

---

621. In what part of a garden regularity is most to be studied.—Arrangement of trees

being purely artificial, may, without disgust, be tortured into a thousand shapes; but a representation of what really exists in nature, admits not any unnatural circumstance. In the statues of Versailles the artist has displayed his vicious taste without the least color or disguise. A lifeless statue of an animal pouring out water, may be endured without much disgust; but here the lions and wolves are put in violent action, each has seized its prey, a deer or a lamb, in act to devour; and yet, as by hocus-pocus, the whole is converted into a different scene: the lion, forgetting his prey, pours out water plentifully; and the deer, forgetting its danger, performs the same work; a representation no less absurd than that in the opera, where Alexander the Great, after mounting the wall of a town besieged, turns his back to the enemy, and entertains his army with a song.*

623. In gardening, every lively exhibition of what is beautiful in nature has a fine effect; on the other hand, distant and faint imitations are displeasing to every one of taste. The cutting evergreens in the shape of animals is very ancient, as appears from the epistles of Pliny, who seems to be a great admirer of the conceit. The propensity to imitation gave birth to that practice, and has supported it wonderfully long, considering how faint and insipid the imitation is. But the vulgar, great and small, are entertained with the oddness and singularity of a resemblance, however distant, between a tree and an animal. An attempt in the gardens of Versailles to imitate a grove of trees by a group of *jets d'eau*, appears, for the same reason, no less childish.†

In designing a garden, every thing trivial or whimsical ought to be avoided. Is a labyrinth then to be justified? It is a mere con-

---

* Ulloa, a Spanish writer, describing the city of Lima, says that the great square is finely ornamented. "In the centre is a fountain, equally remarkable for its grandeur and capacity. Raised above the fountain is a bronze statue of Fame, and four small basins on the angles. The water issues from the trumpet of the statue, and from the mouths of eight lions surrounding it, which," in his opinion, "greatly heighten the beauty of the whole."

† ["The great mistake made by most novices is, that they study *gardens* too much, and *nature* too little. Now gardens, in general, are stiff and graceless, except just so far as nature, ever free and flowing, reasserts her rights in spite of man's want of taste, or helps him when he has endeavored to work in her own spirit. But the fields and woods are full of instruction, and in such features of our richest and most smiling and diversified country, must the best hints for the embellishment of rural homes always be derived. And yet it is not any portion of the woods and fields that we wish our finest pleasure-ground scenery to resemble. We rather wish to *select* from the finest sylvan features of nature, and to recompose the materials in a choicer manner, by rejecting any thing foreign to the spirit of elegance and refinement which should characterize the landscape of the most tasteful country residence—a landscape in which all that is graceful and beautiful in nature is preserved—all her most perfect forms and most harmonious lines, but with that added refinement which high keeping and continual care confer on natural beauty, without impairing its innate spirit of freedom, or the truth and freshness of its intrinsic character."—*Downing's Rural Essays*, iv.]

---

622. Capital rule as to prospect.—Things unnatural.- Versailles.

ceit, like that of composing verse in the shape of an axe or an egg: the walks and hedges may be agreeable; but in the form of a labyrinth they serve to no end but to puzzle: a riddle is a conceit not so mean, because the solution is proof of sagacity, which affords no aid in tracing a labyrinth.

The gardens of Versailles, executed with boundless expense by the best artists of that age, are a lasting monument of a taste the most depraved: the faults above mentioned, instead of being avoided, are chosen as beauties, and multiplied without end. Nature, it would seem, was deemed too vulgar to be imitated in the works of a magnificent monarch; and for that reason preference was given to things unnatural, which probably were mistaken for supernatural. I have often amused myself with a fanciful resemblance between these gardens and the Arabian tales: each of them is a performance intended for the amusement of a great king: in the sixteen gardens of Versailles there is no unity of design, more than in the thousand and one Arabian tales: and, lastly, they are equally unnatural; groves of *jets d'eau*, statues of animals conversing in the manner of Æsop, water issuing out of the mouths of wild beasts, give an impression of fairy-land and witchcraft, no less than diamond-palaces, invisible rings, spells, and incantations.

624. A straight road is the most agreeable, because it shortens the journey. But in an embellished field, a straight walk has an air of formality and confinement; and at any rate is less agreeable than a winding or waving walk; for in surveying the beauties of an ornamented field, we love to roam from place to place at freedom. Winding walks have another advantage; at every step they open new views. In short, the walks in a pleasure-ground ought not to have any appearance of a road; my intention is not to make a journey, but to feast my eye on the beauties of art and nature. This rule excludes not openings directing the eye to distant objects.

Avoid a straight avenue directed upon a dwelling-house: better far an oblique approach in a waving line, with single trees and other scattered objects interposed.

There are not many fountains in a good taste. Statues of animals vomiting water, which prevail everywhere, stand condemned as unnatural. In many Roman fountains, statues of fishes are employed to support a large basin of water. This unnatural conceit is not accountable, unless from the connection that water hath with the fish that swim in it; which by the way shows the influence of even the slighter relations. The best design for a fountain I have met with is what follows. In an artificial rock, rugged and abrupt, there is a cavity out of sight at the top: the water, conveyed to it by a pipe, pours or trickles down the broken parts of the rock, and is collected

---

623. Faint imitations of nature.—Mr. Downing's remarks.—Things trivial and whimsical.—Versailles.

624. Walks in a garden.—Fountains.

into a basin at the foot: it is so contrived as to make the water fall in sheets or in rills at pleasure.

625. Hitherto a garden has been treated as a work intended solely for pleasure, or, in other words, for giving impressions of intrinsic beauty. What comes next in order is the beauty of a garden destined for use, termed *relative beauty;* and this branch shall be dispatched in a few words. In gardening, luckily, relative beauty need never stand in opposition to intrinsic beauty: all the ground that can be requisite for use, makes but a small proportion of an ornamented field, and may be put in any corner without obstructing the disposition of the capital parts. At the same time, a kitchen-garden or an orchard is susceptible of intrinsic beauty; and may be so artfully disposed among the other parts, as by variety and contrast to contribute to the beauty of the whole.

In a hot country it is a capital object to have what may be termed a *summer-garden;* that is, a spot of ground disposed by art and by nature to exclude the sun, but to give free access to the air. In a cold country, the capital object should be a *winter-garden*, open to the sun, sheltered from wind, dry under foot, and taking on the appearance of summer by variety of evergreens.*

626. Gardening being in China brought to greater perfection than in any other known country, we shall close our present subject with a slight view of Chinese gardens, which are found entirely obsequious to the principles that govern every one of the fine arts. In general, it is an indispensable law there, never to deviate from nature: but in order to produce that degree of variety which is pleasing, every method consistent with nature is put in practice. Nature is strictly imitated in the banks of their artificial lakes and rivers; which sometimes are bare and gravelly, sometimes covered with wood quite to the brink of the water. To flat spots adorned with flowers and shrubs, are opposed others steep and rocky. We see meadows covered with cattle; rice-grounds that run into lakes; groves into which enter navigable creeks and rivulets: these gener-

* A correspondent, whose name I hitherto have concealed, that I might not be thought vain, and which I can no longer conceal (Mrs. Montagu), writes to me as follows: "In life we generally lay our account with prosperity, and seldom, very seldom, prepare for adversity. We carry that propensity even into the structure of our gardens: we cultivate the gay ornaments of summer, relishing no plants but what flourish by mild dews and gracious sunshine: we banish from our thoughts ghastly winter, when the benign influences of the sun, cheering us no more, are doubly regretted by yielding to the piercing north wind and nipping frost. Sage is the gardener, in the metaphorical as well as literal sense, who procures a friendly shelter to protect us from December storms, and cultivates the plants that adorn and enliven that dreary season. He is no philosopher who cannot retire into the Stoic's walk when the gardens of Epicurus are out of bloom: he is too much a philosopher who will rigidly proscribe the flowers and aromatics of summer, to sit constantly under the cypress-shade."

625. *Relative* beauty of a garden. Summer and winter gardens.

ally conduct to some interesting object, a magnificent building, terraces cut in a mountain, a cascade, a grotto, an artificial rock. Their artificial rivers are generally serpentine; sometimes narrow, noisy, and rapid; sometimes deep, broad, and slow: and to make the scene still more active, mills and other moving machines are often erected. In the lakes are interspersed islands; some barren, surrounded with rocks and shoals; others enriched with every thing that art and nature can furnish. Even in their cascades they avoid regularity, as forcing nature out of its course: the waters are seen bursting from the caverns and windings of the artificial rocks, here a roaring cataract, there many gentle falls; and the stream often impeded by trees and stones, that seem brought down by the violence of the current. Straight lines are sometimes indulged, in order to keep in view some interesting object at a distance.

Sensible of the influence of contrast, the Chinese artists deal in sudden transitions, and in opposing to each other forms, colors, and shades. The eye is conducted from limited to extensive views, and from lakes and rivers to plains, hills, and woods: to dark and gloomy colors, are opposed the more brilliant: the different masses of light and shade are disposed in such a manner, as to render the composition distinct in its parts, and striking on the whole. In plantations, the trees are artfully mixed, according to their shape and color; those of spreading branches with the pyramidal, and the light green with the deep green. They even introduce decayed trees, some erect, and some half out of the ground.* In order to heighten contrast much bolder strokes are risked: they sometimes introduce rough rocks, dark caverns, trees ill formed, and seemingly rent by tempests, or blasted by lightning; a building in ruins, or half consumed by fire. But to relieve the mind from the harshness of such objects, the sweetest and most beautiful scenes always succeed.

627. The Chinese study to give play to the imagination: they hide the termination of their lakes; and commonly interrupt the view of a cascade by trees, through which are seen obscurely the waters as they fall. The imagination once roused, is disposed to magnify every object.

Nothing is more studied in Chinese gardens than to raise wonder or surprise. In scenes calculated for that end, every thing appears like fairy-land; a torrent, for example, conveyed under ground dazzles a stranger by its uncommon sound to guess what it may be; and to multiply such uncommon sounds, the rocks and buildings are contrived with cavities and interstices. Sometimes one is led insensibly into a dark cavern, terminating unexpectedly in a land-

* Taste has suggested to Kent the same artifice. A decayed tree placed properly, contributes to contrast; and also in a pensive or sedate state of mind produces a sort of pity grounded on an imaginary personification.

626. Chinese gardens. Correspondence with nature. Sudden transitions.

scape enriched with all that nature affords the most delicious. At other times, beautiful walks insensibly conduct to a rough uncultivated field, where bushes, briers, and stones interrupt the passage: looking about for an outlet, some rich prospect unexpectedly opens to view. Another artifice is, to obscure some capital part by trees, or other interposed objects: our curiosity is raised to know what lies beyond; and after a few steps, we are greatly surprised with some scene totally different from what was expected.

628. These cursory observations upon gardening, shall be closed with some reflections that must touch every reader. Rough uncultivated ground, dismal to the eye, inspires peevishness and discontent: may not this be one cause of the harsh manners of savages? A field richly ornamented, containing beautiful objects of various kinds, displays in full lustre the goodness of the Deity, and the ample provision he has made for our happiness. Ought not the spectator to be filled with gratitude to his Maker, and with benevolence to his fellow-creatures? Other fine arts may be perverted to excite irregular, and even vicious emotions: but gardening, which inspires the purest and most refined pleasures, cannot fail to promote every good affection. The gayety and harmony of mind it produceth, inclining the spectator to communicate his satisfaction to others, and to make them happy as he is himself, tend naturally to establish in him a habit of humanity and benevolence.*

It is not easy to suppress a degree of enthusiasm when we reflect on the advantages of gardening with respect to virtuous education. In the beginning of life the deepest impressions are made; and it is a sad truth, that the young student, familiarized to the dirtiness and disorder of many colleges pent within narrow bounds in populous cities, is rendered in a measure insensible to the elegant beauties of art and nature. Is there no man of fortune sufficiently patriotic to think of reforming this evil? It seems to me far from an exaggeration, that good professors are not more essential to a college, than a spacious garden, sweetly ornamented, but without any thing glaring or fantastic, so as upon the whole to inspire our youth with a taste no less for simplicity than for elegance. In that respect, the university of Oxford may justly be deemed a model.

629. Having finished what occurred on gardening, I proceed to rules and observations that more peculiarly concern architecture. Architecture, being a useful as well as a fine art, leads us to distinguish buildings and parts of buildings into three kinds, namely, what

* The manufactures of silk, flax, and cotton, in their present advance towards perfection, may be held as inferior branches of the fine arts: because their productions in dress and in furniture inspire, like them, gay and kindly emotions favorable to morality.

---

627. The Chinese gardens give play to the imagination. Artifices for raising wonder and surprise.

628. Advantages of gardening.

are intended for utility solely, what for ornament solely, and what for both. Buildings intended for utility solely, such as detached offices, ought in every part to correspond precisely to that intention; the slightest deviation from the end in view will by every person of taste be thought a blemish. In general it is the perfection of every work of art, that it fulfils the purpose for which it is intended; and every other beauty, in opposition, is improper. But in things intended for ornament, such as pillars, obelisks, triumphal arches, beauty ought alone to be regarded. A heathen temple must be considered as merely ornamental; for being dedicated to some deity, and not intended for habitation, it is susceptible of any figure and any embellishment that fancy can suggest and beauty admit. The great difficulty of contrivance, respects buildings that are intended to be useful as well as ornamental. These ends, employing different and often opposite means, are seldom united in perfection; and the only practicable method in such buildings is, to favor ornament less or more according to the character of the building: in palaces and other edifices sufficiently extensive to admit a variety of useful contrivance, regularity justly takes the lead: but in dwelling-houses that are too small for variety of contrivance, utility ought to prevail, neglecting regularity as far as it stands in opposition to convenience.*

Intrinsic and relative beauty being founded on different principles, must be handled separately. I begin with relative beauty, as of the greater importance.

630. The proportions of a door are determined by the use to which it is destined. The door of a dwelling-house, which ought to correspond to the human size, is confined to seven or eight feet in height, and three or four in breadth. The proportions proper for the door of a barn or coach-house, are widely different. Another consideration enters. To study intrinsic beauty in a coach-house or barn, intended merely for use, is obviously improper. But a dwelling-house may admit ornaments; and the principal door of a palace demands all the grandeur that is consistent with the foregoing proportions dictated by utility: it ought to be elevated, and approached by steps; and it may be adorned with pillars supporting an architrave, or in any other beautiful manner. The door of a church ought to be wide, in order to afford an easy passage for a multitude: the width, at the same time, regulates the height, as will appear by and by. The size of windows ought to be proportioned

* A building must be large to produce any sensible emotion of regularity, proportion, or beauty: which is an additional reason for minding convenience only in a dwelling-house of small size.

629. Buildings and parts of buildings distinguished into three kinds.—Buildings intended for use solely.—Things intended for ornament.—Rule for buildings intended to be useful as well as ornamental.

"Downing": Gardening.

to that of the room they illuminate; for if the apertures be not sufficiently large to convey light to every corner, the room is unequally lighted, which is a great deformity. The steps of a stair ought to be accommodated to the human figure, without regarding any other proportion: they are accordingly the same in large and in small buildings, because both are inhabited by men of the same size.

Nothing can be more evident, than that the form of a dwelling-house ought to be suited to the climate; and yet no error is more common, than to copy in Britain the form of Italian houses; not forgetting even those parts that are purposely contrived for air, and for excluding the sun. I shall give one or two instances. A colonnade along the front of a building, hath a fine effect in Greece and Italy, by producing coolness and obscurity, agreeable properties in warm and luminous climates; but the cold climate of Britain is altogether averse to that ornament; and therefore a colonnade can never be proper in this country, unless for a portico, or to communicate with a detached building.

631. Having said what appeared necessary upon relative beauty, the next step is, to view architecture as one of the fine arts; which will lead us to the examination of such buildings, and parts of buildings, as are calculated solely to please the eye. In the works of Nature, rich and magnificent, variety prevails; and in works of Art that are contrived to imitate Nature, the great art is to hide every appearance of art; which is done by avoiding regularity, and indulging variety. But in works of art that are original, and not imitative, the timid hand is guided by rule and compass; and accordingly in architecture strict regularity and uniformity are studied, as far as consistent with utility.

Proportion is no less agreeable than regularity and uniformity; and therefore in buildings intended to please the eye, they are all equally essential.

Regularity and proportion are essential in buildings destined chiefly or solely to please the eye, because they produce intrinsic beauty. But a skilful artist will not confine his view to regularity and proportion; he will also study congruity, which is perceived when the form and ornaments of a structure are suited to the purpose for which it is intended.* The sense of congruity dictates the following rule, That every building have an expression corresponding to its destination: a palace ought to be sumptuous and grand; a private dwelling, neat and modest; a playhouse, gay and splendid; and a monument, gloomy and melancholy. A heathen temple has

* [On the subject of Proportion, consult Alison on Taste, pp. 295–323.]

630. Proportions of a door; of windows.—Form of a dwelling-house.
631. How far regularity and uniformity should be studied; how far, also, proportion.—Congruity; rule for it. Illustrations.

a double destination: it is considered chiefly as a house dedicated to some divinity; and in that respect it ought to be grand, elevated, and magnificent: it is considered also as a place of worship; and in that respect it ought to be somewhat dark or gloomy, because dimness produces that tone of mind which is suited to humility and devotion. A Christian church is not considered to be a house for the Deity, but merely a place of worship; it ought therefore to be decent and plain, without much ornament: a situation ought to be chosen low and retired; because the congregation during worship ought to be humble and disengaged from the world. Columns, besides their chief service of being supports, may contribute to that peculiar expression which the destination of a building requires: columns of different proportions serve to express loftiness, lightness, &c., as well as strength. Situation also may contribute to expression: conveniency regulates the situation of a private dwelling-house; but the situation of a palace ought to be lofty.*

632. And this leads to a question, Whether the situation, where there happens to be no choice, ought in any measure to regulate the form of the edifice? The connection between a large house and the neighboring fields, though not intimate, demands however some congruity. It would, for example, displease us to find an elegant building thrown away upon a wild uncultivated country: congruity requires a polished field for such a building; and besides the pleasure of congruity, the spectator is sensible of the pleasure of concordance from the similarity of the emotions produced by the two objects The old Gothic form of building seems well suited to the rough un-

* [On this as on every other subject connected with gardening and architecture, our lamented DOWNING has written with consummate taste and judgment and his "Rural Essays" should be carefully read, not only for the valuable information which they contain, but for the mental culture which they are fitted to impart. Many of them might with great advantage be read in connection with this chapter. The following extract is in point.—*Ed.*

"In this country, where so many are able to achieve a home for themselves, he who gives to the public a more beautiful and tasteful model of a habitation than his neighbors, is a benefactor to the cause of morality, good order, and the improvement of society where he lives. . . . . . We would encourage a taste for beautiful and *appropriate* architecture. The rock on which all novices split, and especially all men who are satisfied with a feeble imitation of some great example from other countries—this dangerous rock is *want of fitness or propriety*. Almost the first principle is, 'keep in mind PROPRIETY.' Do not build your houses like temples, churches, or cathedrals. Let them be, characteristically, dwelling-houses. And more than this, always let their individuality of purpose be fairly avowed; let the cottage be a cottage; the farm-house a farm-house; the villa a villa; and the mansion a mansion. Do not attempt to build a dwelling upon your farm after the fashion of the town-house of your friend, the city merchant; do not attempt to give the modest little cottage the ambitious air of the ornate villa. Be assured that there is, if you will search for it, a peculiar beauty that belongs to each of these classes of buildings that heightens and adorns it almost magically; while, if it borrows the ornaments of the other, it is only debased and falsified in character and expression. The most expensive and elaborate structure, overlaid with costly ornaments, will fail to give a ray of pleasure to the mind of real taste, if it is not appropriate to the purpose in view, or the means or position of its occupant."]

cultivated regions where it was invented: the only mistake was the transferring this form to the fine plains of France and Italy, better fitted for buildings in the Grecian taste; but by refining upon the Gothic form, every thing possible has been done to reconcile it to its new situation. The profuse variety of wild and grand objects about Inverary, demanded a house in the Gothic form; and every one must approve the taste of the proprietor, in adjusting so finely the appearance of his house to that of the country where it is placed.

633. Next of *ornaments*, which contribute to give buildings a peculiar expression. It has been doubted whether a building can regularly admit any ornament but what is useful, or at least has that appearance. But considering the different purposes of architecture, a fine as well as a useful art, there is no good reason why ornaments may not be added to please the eye without any relation to use. This liberty is allowed in poetry, painting, and gardening, and why not in architecture considered as a fine art? A private dwelling-house, it is true, and other edifices where use is the chief aim, admit not regularly any ornament but what has the appearance, at least, of use; but temples, triumphal arches, and other buildings intended chiefly or solely for show, admit every sort of ornament.

A thing intended merely as an ornament, may be of any figure and of any kind that fancy can suggest; if it please the spectator, the artist gains his end. Statues, vases, sculpture upon stone, whether basso or alto relievo, are beautiful ornaments relished in all civilized countries. The placing such ornaments so as to produce the best effect, is the only nicety. A statue in perfection is an enchanting work; and we naturally require that it should be seen in every direction, and at different distances; for which reason, statues employed as ornaments are proper to adorn the great staircase that leads to the principal door of a palace, or to occupy the void between pillars.

634. One at first view will naturally take it for granted, that in the ornaments under consideration beauty is indispensable. It goes a great way undoubtedly; but, upon trial, we find many things esteemed as highly ornamental that have little or no beauty. There are various circumstances, besides beauty, that tend to make an agreeable impression. For instance, the reverence we have for the ancients is a fruitful source of ornaments. Amalthea's horn has always been a favorite ornament, because of its connection with a lady who was honored with the care of Jupiter in his infancy. A fat old fellow and a goat are surely not graceful forms; and yet Selinus and his companions are everywhere fashionable ornaments. What else but our fondness for antiquity can make the horrid form of a sphinx so much as endurable? Original destination is another

---

632. Whether situation should regulate the form of the edifice.

633. Ornaments; whether any but what are useful may be admitted.—The form of any thing intended merely for ornament. The placing of such ornaments.—Statues.

circumstance that has influence to add dignity to things in themselves abundantly trivial. Triumphal arches, pyramids, obelisks, are beautiful forms; but the nobleness of their original destination has greatly enhanced the pleasure we take in them. Long robes appear noble, not singly for their flowing lines, but for their being the habit of magistrates. These examples may be thought sufficient for a specimen: a diligent inquiry into human nature will discover other influencing principles; and hence it is, that of all subjects, ornaments admit the greatest variety in point of taste.

635. And this leads to ornaments having relation to use. Ornaments of that kind are governed by a different principle, which is, that they ought to be of a form suited to their real or apparent destination. This rule is applicable as well to ornaments that make a component part of the subject, as to ornaments that are only accessory. An eagle's paw is an ornament improper for the foot of a chair or table: because it gives it the appearance of weakness, inconsistent with its destination of bearing weight. Blind windows are sometimes introduced to preserve the appearance of regularity: in which case the deceit ought carefully to be concealed: if visible, it marks the irregularity in the clearest manner, signifying, that real windows ought to have been there, could they have been made consistent with the internal structure. A pilaster is another example of the same sort of ornament; and the greatest error against its seeming destination of a support, is to sink it so far into the wall as to make it lose that seeming. A composition representing leaves and branches, with birds perching upon them, has been long in fashion for a candlestick; but none of these particulars is in any degree suited to that destination.

A large marble basin supported by fishes, is a conceit much relished in fountains. This is an example of accessory ornaments in a bad taste: for fishes here are unsuitable to their apparent destination. No less so are the supports of a coach, carved in the figure of Dolphins or Tritons; for what have these marine beings to do on dry land? and what support can they be to a coach?

636. With respect now to the parts of a column, a bare uniform cylinder without a capital appears naked; and without a base, appears too ticklishly placed to stand firm;* it ought therefore to have some finishing at the top and at the bottom. Hence the three chief parts of a column, the shaft, the base, and the capital. Nature

* A column without a base is disagreeable, because it seems in a tottering condition; yet a tree without a base is agreeable; and the reason is, that we know it to be firmly rooted. This observation shows how much taste is influenced by reflection.

---

634. Things ornamental that have little or no beauty.—Reverence for the ancients, a source of ornaments. Illustrations.

635. Ornaments for use. Rule for their form. Violations of good taste in this particular.

undoubtedly requires proportion among these parts, but it admits variety of proportion.

We find three orders of columns among the Greeks, the Doric, the Ionic, and the Corinthian, distinguished from each other by their destination as well as by their ornaments. It has been warmly disputed, whether any new order can be added to these; some hold the affirmative, and give for instances the Tuscan and Composite; others deny, and maintain that these properly are not distinct orders, but only the original orders with some slight variations. Among writers who do not agree upon any standard for distinguishing the different orders from each other, the dispute can never have an end. What occurs to me on this subject is what follows.

637. The only circumstances that can serve to distinguish one order from another, are the form of the column, and its destination. To make the first a distinguishing mark, without regard to the other, would multiply these orders without end; for a color is not more susceptible of different shades, than a column is of different forms. Destination is more limited, as it leads to distinguish columns into three kinds or orders: one plain and strong, for the purpose of supporting plain and massy buildings; one delicate and graceful, for supporting buildings of that character; and between these, one for supporting buildings of a middle character.

To illustrate this doctrine, I make the following observation. If we regard destination only, the Tuscan is of the same order with the Doric, and the Composite with the Corinthian; but if we regard form merely, they are of different orders.

638. The ornaments of these three orders ought to be so contrived as to make them look like what they are intended for. Plain and rustic ornaments would be not a little discordant with the elegance of the Corinthian order; and ornaments sweet and delicate no less so with the strength of the Doric. The Corinthian order has been the favorite of two thousand years, and yet I cannot force myself to relish its capital. The invention of this florid capital is ascribed to the sculptor Callimachus, who took a hint from the plant *Acanthus*, growing round a basket placed accidentally upon it; and in fact the capital under consideration represents pretty accurately a basket so ornamented. This object, or its imitation in stone, placed upon a pillar, may look well; but to make it the capital of a pillar intended to support a building, must give the pillar an appearance inconsistent with its destination.

639. With respect to buildings of every sort, one rule, dictated by utility, is, that they be firm and stable. Another rule, dictated by beauty, is, that they also appear so; for what appears tottering and in hazard of tumbling, produceth in the spectator the painful emo-

---

636. Chief parts of a column.—Three orders of columns.
637. Circumstances that distinguish one order from another.
638. The ornaments of the three orders.—The Corinthian order.

tion of fear, instead of the pleasant emotion of beauty; and, accordingly, it is the great care of the artist, that every part of his edifice appear to be well supported. Procopius, describing the church of St. Sophia, in Constantinople, one of the wonders of the world, mentions with applause a part of the fabric placed above the east front in form of a half-moon, so contrived as to inspire both fear and admiration; for though, says he, it is perfectly well supported, yet it is suspended in such a manner as if it were to tumble down the next moment. This conceit is a sort of false wit in architecture, which men were fond of in the infancy of the fine arts. A turret jutting out from an angle in the uppermost story of a Gothic tower, is a witticism of the same kind.

640. To succeed in allegorical or emblematical ornaments is no slight effort of genius; for it is extremely difficult to dispose them so in a building as to produce any good effect. The mixing them with realities, makes a miserable jumble of truth and fiction. (See chap. xx. sect. v.) But this is not all, nor the chief point; every emblem ought to be rejected that is not clearly expressive of its meaning; for if it be in any degree obscure, it puzzles, and doth not please.

The statue of Moses striking a rock from which water actually issues, is in a false taste; for it is mixing reality with representation. Moses himself may bring water out of the rock, but this miracle is too much for his statue. The same objection lies against the cascade where the statue of a water-god pours out of his urn real water.

641. It is observed above of gardening, that it contributes to rectitude of manners, by inspiring gayety and benevolence. I add another observation, That both gardening and architecture contribute to the same end, by inspiring a taste for neatness and elegance. In Scotland, the regularity and polish even of a turnpike-road has some influence of this kind upon the low people in the neighborhood. They become fond of regularity and neatness; which is displayed, first upon their yards and little inclosures, and next within-doors. A taste for regularity and neatness, thus acquired, is extended by degrees to dress, and even to behavior and manners.

[In concluding this chapter, another brief extract will be given from Downing's Rural Essays.—*Ed.*

"Two grand errors are the fertile causes of all the failures in the rural improvements of the United States at the present moment. The first error lies in supposing that good taste is a natural gift which springs heaven-born into perfect existence, needing no cultivation or improvement. The second is in supposing that taste alone is sufficient to the production of extensive or complete works in architecture or landscape-gardening.

"Now, although that delicacy of organization, usually called taste, is a natural gift, which can no more be acquired than hearing can

---

639. Rules for buildings of every sort.—The church of St. Sophia.
640. Allegorical or emblematic ornaments.

be by a deaf man, yet, in most persons, this sensibility to the Beautiful may be cultivated and ripened into good taste by *the study and comparison of beautiful productions in nature and art.*

"This is precisely what we wish to insist upon, to all persons about to commence rural establishments, who have not a cultivated or just taste; but only sensibility, or what they would call a natural taste. . . . . The study of the best productions in the fine arts is not more necessary to the success of the young painter and sculptor than that of buildings and grounds to the amateur or professional improver who desires to improve a country residence well and tastefully. In both cases comparison, discrimination, the use of the reasoning faculty, educate the natural delicacy of perception into taste, more or less just and perfect, and enable it not only to arrive at Beauty, but to select the most beautiful for the end in view.

"There are at the present moment, without going abroad, opportunities of cultivating a taste in landscape gardening, quite sufficient to enable any one of natural sensibility to the Beautiful, combined with good reasoning powers, to arrive at that point which may be considered good taste. . . . The study of books on taste is by no means to be neglected by the novice in rural embellishment; but the practical illustrations of different styles and principles, to be found in the best cottage and villa residences, are far more convincing and instructive to most minds, than lessons taught in any other mode whatever. . . . .

"We think, also, there can scarcely be a question that an examination of the best examples of taste in rural improvement at home, is far more instructive to an American, than an inspection of the finest country places in Europe; and this, chiefly, because a really successful example at home is based upon republican modes of life enjoyment and expenditure, which are almost the reverse of those of an aristocratic government. . . . No more should be attempted than can be done well, and in perfect harmony with our habits, mode of life, and domestic institutions."—*Rural Essays*, iii.]

CHAPTER XXVI.

STANDARD OF TASTE.

[The following chapter is taken from one of Dr. Blair's Lectures, being far superior to the one of Lord Kames, here omitted.]

642. It must be acknowledged, that no principle of the human mind is, in its operations, more fluctuating and capricious than

641. How gardening and architecture contribute to rectitude of manners.—Scotland. Two errors.—How taste may be improved.—Opportunities offered.

taste. Its variations have been so great and frequent, as to create a suspicion with some of its being merely arbitrary; grounded on no foundation, ascertainable by no standard, but wholly dependent on changing fancy; the consequence of which would be, that all studies or regular inquiries concerning the objects of taste were vain. In architecture, the Grecian models were long esteemed the most perfect. In succeeding ages, the Gothic architecture alone prevailed, and afterwards the Grecian taste revived in all its vigor, and engrossed the public admiration. In eloquence and poetry, the Asiatics at no time relished any thing but what was full of ornament, and splendid in a degree that we should denominate gaudy; whilst the Greeks admired only chaste and simple beauties, and despised the Asiatic ostentation. In our own country, how many writings that were greatly extolled two or three centuries ago, are now fallen into entire disrepute and oblivion! Without going back to remote instances, how very different is the taste of poetry which prevails in Great Britain now, from what prevailed there no longer ago than the reign of King Charles II., which the authors too of that time deemed an Augustan age: when nothing was in vogue but an affected brilliancy of wit; when the simple majesty of Milton was overlooked, and Paradise Lost almost entirely unknown; when Cowley's labored and unnatural conceits were admired as the very quintessence of genius; Waller's gay sprightliness was mistaken for the tender spirit of love poetry; and such writers as Suckling and Etheridge were held in esteem for dramatic composition?

The question is, what conclusion we are to form from such instances as these? Is there any thing that can be called a standard of taste, by appealing to which we may distinguish between a good and a bad taste? Or, is there in truth no such distinction? and are we to hold that, according to the proverb, there is no disputing of tastes; but that whatever pleases is right, for the reason that it does please? This is the question, and a very nice and subtle one it is, which we are now to discuss.

643. I begin by observing, that if there be no such thing as any standard of taste, this consequence must immediately follow, that all tastes are equally good; a position, which, though it may pass unnoticed in slight matters, and when we speak of the lesser differences among the tastes of men, yet when we apply it to the extremes, presently shows its absurdity. For is there any one who will seriously maintain that the taste of a Hottentot or a Laplander is as delicate and as correct as that of a Longinus or an Addison? or, that he can be charged with no defect or incapacity who thinks a common news-writer as excellent an historian as Tacitus? As it would be held downright extravagance to talk in this manner, we are led

642. Fluctuations of taste. Inference thence drawn by some.—Taste in architecture. In eloquence and poetry.—Questions suggested by fluctuations in taste.

unavoidably to this conclusion, that there is some foundation for the preference of one man's taste to that of another; or, that there is a good and a bad, a right and a wrong in taste, as in other things.

But to prevent mistakes on this subject, it is necessary to observe next, that the diversity of tastes which prevails among mankind, does not in every case infer corruption of taste, or oblige us to seek for some standard in order to determine who are in the right. The tastes of men may differ very considerably as to their object, and yet none of them be wrong. One man relishes poetry most; another takes pleasure in nothing but history: one prefers comedy; another, tragedy: one admires the simple; another, the ornamented style. The young are amused with gay and sprightly compositions. The elderly are more entertained with those of a graver cast. Some nations delight in bold pictures of manners, and strong representations of passion. Others incline to more correct and regular elegance both in description and sentiment. Though all differ, yet all pitch upon some one beauty which peculiarly suits their turn of mind; and therefore no one has a title to condemn the rest. It is not in matters of taste, as in questions of mere reason, where there is but one conclusion that can be true, and all the rest are erroneous. Truth, which is the object of reason, is one; beauty, which is the object of taste, is manifold. Taste, therefore, admits of latitude and diversity of objects, in sufficient consistency with goodness or justness of taste.

644. But then, to explain this matter thoroughly, I must observe farther that this admissible diversity of tastes can only have place where the objects of taste are different. Where it is with respect to the same object that men disagree, when one condemns that as ugly, which another admires as highly beautiful; then it is no longer diversity, but direct opposition of taste that takes place; and therefore one must be in the right, and another in the wrong, unless that absurd paradox were allowed to hold, that all tastes are equally good and true. One man prefers Virgil to Homer. Suppose that I, on the other hand, admire Homer more than Virgil. I have as yet no reason to say that our tastes are contradictory. The other person is more struck with the elegance and tenderness which are the characteristics of Virgil; I, with the simplicity and fire of Homer. As long as neither of us deny that both Homer and Virgil have great beauties, our difference falls within the compass of that diversity of tastes, which I have showed to be natural and allowable. But if the other man shall assert that Homer has no beauties whatever; that he holds him to be a dull and spiritless writer, and that he would as soon peruse any old legend of knight-errantry as the Iliad; then I exclaim, that my antagonist either is void of all taste, or that his

---

643. If there be no standard, what absurd consequence will follow?—Diversity of taste does not always infer corruption of taste.

taste is corrupted in a miserable degree; and I appeal to whatever I think the standard of taste, to show him that he is in the wrong.

645. What that standard is to which, in such opposition of tastes, we are obliged to have recourse, remains to be traced. A standard properly signifies that which is of such undoubted authority as to be the test of other things of the same kind. Thus a standard weight or measure, is that which is appointed by law to regulate all other measures and weights. Thus the court is said to be the standard of good breeding; and the scripture of theological truth.

When we say that nature is the standard of taste, we lay down a principle very true and just, as far as it can be applied. There is no doubt, that in all cases where an imitation is intended of some object that exists in nature, as in representing human characters or actions, conformity to nature affords a full and distinct criterion of what is truly beautiful. Reason hath in such cases full scope for exerting its authority, for approving or condemning, by comparing the copy with the original. But there are innumerable cases in which this rule cannot be at all applied; and conformity to nature, is an expression frequently used, without any distinct or determinate meaning. We must therefore search for somewhat that can be rendered more clear and precise, to be the standard of taste.

646. Taste, as I before explained it, is ultimately founded on an internal sense of beauty, which is natural to men, and which, in its application to particular objects, is capable of being guided and enlightened by reason. Now were there any one person who possessed in full perfection all the powers of human nature, whose internal senses were in every instance exquisite and just, and whose reason was unerring and sure, the determinations of such a person concerning beauty, would, beyond doubt, be a perfect standard for the taste of all others. Wherever their taste differed from his, it could be imputed only to some imperfection in their natural powers. But as there is no such living standard, no one person to whom all mankind will allow such submission to be due, what is there of sufficient authority to be the standard of the various and opposite tastes of men? Most certainly there is nothing but the taste, as far as it can be gathered, of human nature. That which men concur the most in admiring, must be held to be beautiful. His taste must be esteemed just and true, which coincides with the general sentiments of men. In this standard we must rest. To the sense of mankind the ultimate appeal must ever lie, in all works of taste. If any one should maintain that sugar was bitter and tobacco was sweet, no reasonings could avail to prove it. The taste of such a person would infallibly be held to be diseased, merely because it differed so widely

---

644. Where an admissible diversity of tastes can have place.—Homer and Virgil cited for illustration.

645. Standard defined. Is it sufficient to say that nature is the standard of taste?

from the taste of the species to which he belongs. In like manner, with regard to the objects of sentiment or internal taste, the common feelings of men carry the same authority, and have a title to regulate the taste of every individual.

647. But have we then, it will be said, no other criterion of what is beautiful, than the approbation of the majority? Must we collect the voices of others, before we form any judgment for ourselves, of what deserves applause in eloquence or poetry? By no means; there are principles of reason and sound judgment which can be applied to matters of taste, as well as to the subjects of science and philosophy. He who admires or censures any work of genius, is always ready, if his taste be in any degree improved, to assign some reasons for his decision. He appeals to principles, and points out the grounds on which he proceeds. Taste is a sort of compound power, in which the light of the understanding always mingles, more or less, with the feelings of sentiment.

But though reason can carry us a certain length in judging concerning works of taste, it is not to be forgotten that the ultimate conclusions to which our reasonings lead, refer at last to sense and perception. We may speculate and argue concerning propriety of conduct in a tragedy, or an epic poem. Just reasonings on the subject will correct the caprice of unenlightened taste, and establish principles for judging of what deserves praise. But, at the same time, these reasonings appeal always in the last resort to feeling. The foundation upon which they rest, is what has been found from experience to please mankind universally. Upon this ground we prefer a simple and natural, to an artificial and affected style; a regular and well-connected story, to loose and scattered narratives; catastrophe which is tender and pathetic, to one which leaves us unmoved. It is from consulting our own imagination and heart, and from attending to the feelings of others, that any principles are formed which acquire authority in matters of taste.

648. When we refer to the concurring sentiments of men as the ultimate taste of what is to be accounted beautiful in the arts, this is to be always understood of men placed in such situations as are favorable to the proper exertions of taste. Every one must perceive, that among rude and uncivilized nations, and during the ages of ignorance and darkness, any loose notions that are entertained concerning such subjects, carry no authority. In those states of society, taste has no materials on which to operate. It is either totally suppressed, or appears in its lower and most imperfect form. We refer to the sentiments of mankind in polished and flourishing nations; when arts are cultivated and manners refined; when works

---

646. The foundation of taste. No living standard of taste. The taste of human nature the standard. How ascertained.

647. Have we no criterion but the approbation of the majority? Principles to be applied.—Is the ultimate appeal made to reason or to feeling?

of genius are subjected to free discussion, and taste is improved by science and philosophy.

Even among nations, at such a period of society, I admit that accidental causes may occasionally warp the proper operations of taste; sometimes the taste of religion, sometimes the form of government, may for a while pervert; a licentious court may introduce a taste for false ornaments, and dissolute writings. The usage of one admired genius may procure approbation for his faults, and even render them fashionable. Sometimes envy may have power to bear down, for a little, productions of great merit; while popular humor, or party spirit, may, at other times, exalt to a high, though short-lived reputation, what little deserved it. But though such casual circumstances give the appearance of caprice to the judgments ot taste, that appearance is easily corrected. In the course of time, the genuine taste of human nature never fails to disclose itself and to gain the ascendant over any fantastic and corrupted modes of taste which may chance to have been introduced. These may have currency for a while, and mislead superficial judges; but being subjected to examination, by degrees they pass away; while that alone remains which is founded on sound reason, and the native feelings of men.

649. I by no means pretend that there is any standard of taste, to which, in every particular instance, we can resort for clear and immediate determination. Where, indeed, is such a standard to be found for deciding any of those great controversies in reason and philosophy, which perpetually divide mankind? In the present case, there was plainly no occasion for any such strict and absolute provision to be made. In order to judge of what is morally good or evil, of what man ought, or ought not in duty to do, it was fit that the means of clear and precise determination should be afforded us. But to ascertain in every case with the utmost exactness what is beautiful or elegant, was not at all necessary to the happiness of man. And therefore some diversity in feeling was here allowed to take place; and room was left for discussion and debate, concerning the degree of approbation to which any work of genius is entitled.

650. The conclusion, which it is sufficient for us to rest upon, is, that taste is far from being an arbitrary principle, which is subject to the fancy of every individual, and which admits of no criterion for determining whether it be false or true. Its foundation is the same in all human minds. It is built upon sentiments and perceptions which belong to our nature, and which, in general, operate with the same uniformity as our other intellectual principles. When these

---

648. To the sentiments of what class of men do we appeal in matters of taste?—Accidental causes affecting the correctness of taste.

649. No standard of taste for every particular instance. In what other matters is there none?

sentiments are perverted by ignorance and prejudice, they are capable of being rectified by reason. Their sound and natural state is ultimately determined by comparing them with the general taste of mankind. Let men declaim as much as they please concerning the caprice and the uncertainty of taste, it is found, by experience, that there are beauties, which, if they be displayed in a proper light, have power to command lasting and general admiration. In every composition, what interests the imagination, and touches the heart, pleases all ages and all nations. There is a certain string to which, when properly struck, the human heart is so made as to answer.

Hence the universal testimony which the most improved nations of the earth have conspired, throughout a long tract of ages, to give to some few works of genius; such as the Iliad of Homer, and the Æneid of Virgil. Hence the authority which such works have acquired, as standards in some degree of poetical composition; since from them we are enabled to collect what the sense of mankind is concerning those beauties which give them the highest pleasure, and which therefore poetry ought to exhibit. Authority or prejudice may, in one age or country, give a temporary reputation to an indifferent poet or a bad artist; but when foreigners, or when posterity examine his works, his faults are discerned, and the genuine taste of human nature appears. "Opinionum commenta delet dies; naturæ judicia confirmat." Time overthrows the illusions of opinion, but establishes the decisions of nature.

---

650. The conclusion arrived at.—What taste is built upon.—Works of genius that have been universally approved.

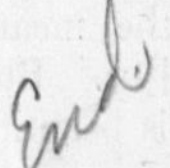

MATHEMATICS.

DAVIES'S COMPLETE SERIES.

ARITHMETIC.

Davies' Primary Arithmetic.
Davies' Intellectual Arithmetic.
Davies' Elements of Written Arithmetic.
Davies' Practical Arithmetic.
Davies' University Arithmetic.

TWO-BOOK SERIES.

First Book in Arithmetic, Primary and Mental.
Complete Arithmetic.

ALGEBRA.

Davies' New Elementary Algebra.
Davies' University Algebra.
Davies' New Bourdon's Algebra.

GEOMETRY.

Davies' Elementary Geometry and Trigonometry.
Davies' Legendre's Geometry.
Davies' Analytical Geometry and Calculus.
Davies' Descriptive Geometry.
Davies' New Calculus.

MENSURATION.

Davies' Practical Mathematics and Mensuration.
Davies' Elements of Surveying.
Davies' Shades, Shadows, and Perspective.

MATHEMATICAL SCIENCE.

Davies' Grammar of Arithmetic.
Davies' Outlines of Mathematical Science.
Davies' Nature and Utility of Mathematics.
Davies' Metric System.
Davies & Peck's Dictionary of Mathematics.

BARNES'S NEW MATHEMATICS.

In this series JOSEPH FICKLIN, Ph. D., Professor of Mathematics and Astronomy in the University of Missouri, has combined all the best and latest results of practical and experimental teaching of arithmetic with the assistance of many distinguished mathematical authors.

Barnes's Elementary Arithmetic.

Barnes's National Arithmetic.

These two works constitute a *complete arithmetical course in two books.*

They meet the demand for text-books that will help students to acquire the greatest amount of useful and practical knowledge of Arithmetic by the smallest expenditure of *time, labor,* and *money.* Nearly every topic in Written Arithmetic is introduced, and its principles illustrated, by exercises in *Oral* Arithmetic. The free use of Equations ; the concise method of combining and treating Properties of Numbers ; the treatment of Multiplication and Division of Fractions in *two* cases, and then reduced to *one;* Cancellation by the use of the vertical line, especially in Fractions, Interest, and Proportion ; the brief, simple, and greatly superior method of working Partial Payments by the "Time Table" and Cancellation ; the substitution of formulas to a great extent for rules ; the full and practical treatment of the Metric System, &c., indicate their completeness. A *variety* of methods and processes for the *same topic,* which deprive the pupil of the great benefit of doing a part of the *thinking* and *labor* for himself, have been discarded. The statement of principles, definitions, rules, &c., is brief and simple. The illustrations and methods are explicit, direct, and practical. The great number and variety of Examples embody the actual business of the day. The very large amount of matter condensed in so small a compass has been accomplished by economizing every line of space, by rejecting superfluous matter and obsolete terms, and by avoiding the *repetition* of analyses, explanations, and operations in the advanced topics which have been used in the more elementary parts of these books.

AUXILIARIES.

For use in district schools, and for supplying a text-book in advanced work for classes having finished the course as given in the ordinary Practical Arithmetics, the National Arithmetic has been divided and bound separately, as follows : —

Barnes's Practical Arithmetic.

Barnes's Advanced Arithmetic.

In many schools there are classes that for various reasons never reach beyond Percentage. It is just such cases where *Barnes's Practical Arithmetic* will answer a good purpose, at a *price to the pupil* much less than to buy the complete book. On the other hand, classes having finished the ordinary Practical Arithmetic can proceed with the higher course by using *Barnes's Advanced Arithmetic.*

For primary schools requiring simply a table book, and the earliest rudiments forcibly presented through object-teaching and copious illustrations, we have prepared

Barnes's First Lessons in Arithmetic,

which begins with the most elementary notions of numbers, and proceeds, by simple steps, to develop all the fundamental principles of Arithmetic.

Barnes's Elements of Algebra.

This work, as its title indicates, is elementary in its character and suitable for use (1) in such public schools as give instruction in the Elements of Algebra ; (2) in institutions of learning whose courses of study do not include Higher Algebra ; (3) in schools whose object is to prepare students for entrance into our colleges and universities. This book will also meet the wants of students of Physics who require some knowledge of

DRAWING.

BARNES'S POPULAR DRAWING SERIES.

Based upon the experience of the most successful teachers of drawing in the United States.

The Primary Course, consisting of a manual, ten cards, and three primary drawing books, A, B, and C.

Intermediate Course. Four numbers and a manual.

Advanced Course. Four numbers and a manual.

Instrumental Course. Four numbers and a manual.

The Intermediate, Advanced, and Instrumental Courses are furnished either in book or card form at the same prices. The books contain the usual blanks, with the unusual advantage of opening from the pupil, — placing the copy directly in front and above the blank, thus occupying but little desk-room. The cards are in the end more economical than the books, if used in connection with the patent blank folios that accompany this series.

The cards are arranged to be bound (or tied) in the folios and removed at pleasure. The pupil at the end of each number has a complete book, containing only his own work, while the copies are preserved and inserted in another folio ready for use in the next class.

Patent Blank Folios. No. 1. Adapted to Intermediate Course. No. 2. Adapted to Advanced and Instrumental Courses.

ADVANTAGES OF THIS SERIES.

The Plan and Arrangement. — The examples are so arranged that teachers and pupils can see, at a glance, how they are to be treated and where they are to be copied. In this system, copying and designing do not receive all the attention. The plan is broader in its aims, dealing with drawing as a branch of common-school instruction, and giving it a wide educational value.

Correct Methods. — In this system the pupil is led to rely upon himself, and not upon delusive mechanical aids, as printed guide-marks, &c.

One of the principal objects of any good course in freehand drawing is to educate the eye to estimate location, form, and size. A system which weakens the motive or removes the necessity of *thinking* is false in theory and ruinous in practice. The object should be to educate, not cram; to develop the intelligence, not teach tricks.

Artistic Effect. — The beauty of the examples is not destroyed by crowding the pages with useless and badly printed text. The Manuals contain all necessary instruction.

Stages of Development. — Many of the examples are accompanied by diagrams, showing the different stages of development.

Lithographed Examples. — The examples are printed in imitation of pencil drawing (not in hard, black lines) that the pupil's work may resemble them.

One Term's Work. — Each book contains what can be accomplished in an average term, and no more. Thus a pupil *finishes* one book before beginning another.

Quality — not Quantity. — Success in drawing depends upon the amount of *thought* exercised by the pupil, and *not* upon the large number of examples drawn.

Designing. — Elementary design is more skilfully taught in this system than by any other. In addition to the instruction given in the books, the pupil will find printed on the insides of the covers a variety of beautiful patterns.

Enlargement and Reduction. — The practice of enlarging and reducing from copies is not commenced until the pupil is well advanced in the course and therefore better able to cope with this difficult feature in drawing.

Natural Forms. — This is the only course that gives at convenient intervals easy and progressive exercises in the drawing of natural forms.

Economy. — By the patent binding described above, the copies need not be thrown aside when a book is filled out, but are preserved in perfect condition for future use. The blank books, only, will have to be purchased after the first introduction, thus effecting a saving of more than half in the usual cost of drawing-books.

Manuals for Teachers. — The Manuals accompanying this series contain practical instructions for conducting drawing in the class-room, with *definite* directions for drawing *each* of the examples in the books, instructions for designing, model and object drawing, drawing from natural forms, &c.

DRAWING — *Continued.*

Chapman's American Drawing-Book.

The standard American text-book and authority in all branches of art. A compilation of art principles. A manual for the amateur, and basis of study for the professional artist. Adapted for schools and private instruction.

CONTENTS. — "Any one who can Learn to Write can Learn to Draw." — Primary Instruction in Drawing. — Rudiments of Drawing the Human Head. — Rudiments in Drawing the Human Figure. — Rudiments of Drawing. — The Elements of Geometry. — Perspective. — Of Studying and Sketching from Nature. — Of Painting. — Etching and Engraving. — Of Modelling. — Of Composition. — Advice to the American Art-Student.

The work is of course magnificently illustrated with all the original designs.

Chapman's Elementary Drawing-Book.

A progressive course of practical exercises, or a text-book for the training of the eye and hand. It contains the elements from the larger work, and a copy should be in the hands of every pupil; while a copy of the "American Drawing-Book," named above, should be at hand for reference by the class.

Clark's Elements of Drawing.

A complete course in this graceful art, from the first rudiments of outline to the finished sketches of landscape and scenery.

Allen's Map-Drawing and Scale.

This method introduces a new era in map-drawing, for the following reasons: 1. It is a system. This is its greatest merit. — 2. It is easily understood and taught. — 3. The eye is trained to exact measurement by the use of a scale. — 4. By no special effort of the memory, distance and comparative size are fixed in the mind. — 5. It discards useless construction of lines. — 6. It can be taught by any teacher, even though there may have been no previous practice in map-drawing. — 7. Any pupil old enough to study geography can learn by this system, in a short time, to draw accurate maps. — 8. The system is not the result of theory, but comes directly from the school-room. It has been thoroughly and successfully tested there, with all grades of pupils. — 9. It is economical, as it requires no mapping plates. It gives the pupil the ability of rapidly drawing accurate maps.

FINE ARTS.

Hamerton's Art Essays (Atlas Series): —

No. 1. The Practical Work of Painting.
With portrait of Rubens. 8vo. Paper covers.

No. 2. Modern Schools of Art.
Including American, English, and Continental Painting. 8vo. Paper covers.

Huntington's Manual of the Fine Arts.

A careful manual of instruction in the history of art, up to the present time.

Boyd's Kames' Elements of Criticism.

The best edition of the best work on art and literary criticism ever produced in English.

Benedict's Tour Through Europe.

A valuable companion for any one wishing to visit the galleries and sights of the continent of Europe, as well as a charming book of travels.

Dwight's Mythology.

A knowledge of mythology is necessary to an appreciation of ancient art.

Walker's World's Fair.

The industrial and artistic display at the Centennial Exhibition.

DR. STEELE'S ONE-TERM SERIES, IN ALL THE SCIENCES.

Steele's 14-Weeks Course in Chemistry.
Steele's 14-Weeks Course in Astronomy.
Steele's 14-Weeks Course in Physics.
Steele's 14-Weeks Course in Geology.
Steele's 14-Weeks Course in Physiology.
Steele's 14-Weeks Course in Zoölogy.
Steele's 14-Weeks Course in Botany.

Our text-books in these studies are, as a general thing, dull and **uninteresting.** They contain from 400 to 600 pages of dry facts and unconnected details. They abound in that which the student cannot learn, much less remember. The pupil commences the study, is confused by the fine print and coarse print, and neither knowing exactly what to learn nor what to hasten over, is crowded through the single term generally assigned to each branch, and frequently comes to the close without a definite and exact idea of a single scientific principle.

Steele's "Fourteen-Weeks Courses" contain only that which every well-informed person should know, while all that which concerns only the professional scientist is omitted. The language is clear, simple, and interesting, and the illustrations bring the subject within the range of home life and daily experience. They give such of the general principles and the prominent facts as a pupil can make familiar as household words within a single term. The type is large and open; there is no fine print to annoy; the cuts are copies of genuine experiments or natural phenomena, and are of fine execution.

In fine, by a system of condensation peculiarly his own, the author reduces each branch to the limits of a single term of study, while sacrificing nothing that is essential, and nothing that is usually retained from the study of the larger manuals in common use. Thus the student has rare opportunity to *economize his time*, or rather to employ that which he has to the best advantage.

A notable feature is the author's charming "style," fortified by an enthusiasm over his subject in which the student will not fail to partake. Believing that Natural Science is full of fascination, he has moulded it into a form that attracts the attention and kindles the enthusiasm of the pupil.

The recent editions contain the author's "Practical Questions" on a plan never before attempted in scientific text-books. These are questions as to the nature and cause of common phenomena, and are not directly answered in the text, the design being to test and promote an intelligent use of the student's knowledge of the foregoing principles.

Steele's Key to all His Works.

This work is mainly composed of answers to the Practical Questions, and solutions of the problems, in the author's celebrated "Fourteen-Weeks Courses" in the several sciences, with many hints to teachers, minor tables, &c. Should be on every teacher's desk.

Prof. J. Dorman Steele is an indefatigable student, as well as author, and his books have reached a fabulous circulation. It is safe to say of his books that they have accomplished more tangible and better results in the class-room than any other ever offered to American schools, and have been translated into more languages for foreign schools. They are even produced in raised type for the blind.

PHONOGRAPHY.

Eames's Light-Line Short-Hand.

This book presents a practical phonetic system, without shading. It is prepared to meet the requirements of business, corresponding, and verbatim reporting. It is especially adapted to the use of schools and colleges. It gives a vocabulary of more than 4,500 words and phrases. The illustrations are very numerous, and both in variety and quantity are unprecedented. There are 58 pages of engraved short-hand matter for practice-copies. The book is highly endorsed, and the system is the best and shortest known.

COMPOSITION AND RHETORIC.

Brookfield's First Book in Composition.

Making the cultivation of this important art feasible for the smallest child. By a new method, to induce and stimulate thought.

Boyd's Composition and Rhetoric.

This work furnishes all the aid that is needful or can be desired in the various departments and styles of composition, both in prose and verse.

Day's Art of Rhetoric.

Noted for exactness of definition, clear limitation, and philosophical development of subject; the large share of attention given to invention, as a branch of rhetoric, and the unequalled analysis of style.

Bardeen's Sentence-Making.

Bardeen's Shorter Rhetoric.

Bardeen's Complete Rhetoric.

The plan of this treatise is wholly novel, and is its most characteristic feature.

The author begins with **Sentence-Making,** which is to rhetoric what carpentry or masonry is to architecture, — not properly a part of it, but to be absolutely mastered, so that the architect's ideas may be carried out with promptness and precision.

This "handicraft," so to speak, having been acquired, the student is ready to apply it according to the rules of the art. Where first? He is required to converse almost constantly, and he has already learned that it is sometimes difficult to converse well. Let him see that the rules of rhetoric apply primarily to the every-day talk in which he is engaged, and rhetoric becomes a real thing. Accordingly, the author follows with a full and familiar treatment of **Conversation.**

As all must talk, so nearly all must write letters of one kind or another; and the second part of the book is devoted to **Letter-Writing**. In itself this subject is treated with incisive directness and practical force, business letters receiving special attention.

With the **Essay** arises a new necessity, — of formal invention. The author clearly shows that a distinct part of what is often called "inspiration" in writing comes from hard labor under fixed rules here laid down; that this labor is indispensable even to respectable writing, and that without this labor no production is worthy to be called an essay.

The **Oration** introduces a new feature, — the oral delivery to an audience, with all the principles of articulation, emphasis, gesture, and other principles usually referred to elocution as a distinct subject. The discussion of extempore speaking is remarkably terse and helpful.

Finally comes the **Poem**, more briefly treated, with the most important directions as to Rhythm and Rhyme.

Here we have then six distinct parts, — Sentence-Making, Conversation, Letter-Writing, the Essay, the Oration, and the Poem.

When all this is taken into consideration, the book seems small instead of large, and we must wonder how so much was got into so little space.

Landmarks of history.